Test Questions for Physical Education Activities

Rosemary McGee, PhD
University of North Carolina
at Greensboro

Andrea Farrow, EdD
Delta State University

Human Kinetics Publishers, Inc.
Champaign, Illinois

Library of Congress-Cataloging-in-Publication Data

McGee, Rosemary, 1926-
   Test questions for physical education activities.

   Bibliography: p.
   Includes index.
   1. Physical education and training—Examinations,
questions, etc.   2. Sports—Examinations, questions,
etc.   I. Farrow, Andrea.   II. Title.
GV362.5.M33   1987   613.7'076   86-21093
ISBN 0-87322-088-9

Senior Editor: Gwen Steigelman, PhD
Production Director: Ernie Noa
Assistant Production Director: Lezli Harris
Copy Editors: Laura Larson and Kathy Kane
Assistant Editor: Julie Anderson
Proofreader: Jennifer Merrill
Typesetter: Yvonne Winsor and Theresa Bear
Text Design: Keith Blomberg
Text Layout: Denise Peters, Nancy Lopeman, Floyd Brewer, Craig Ronto
Cover Design: Jack Davis
Printed By: Braun-Brumfield

Appreciation is extended to the International Gymnastics Federation (FIG) for
permission to use illustrations from the *Code of Points, Artistic Gymnastic for
Men* (1985) and *Code of Points, Artistic Gymnastic for Women* (1985). Diagrams in questions number 84, 88, 92, 97, 98, 101, 155, 156, 160, 191, 227,
263, 300, 301, 312, and 313 (pp. 146-168) are provided with the approval of
the International Gymnastics Federation.

Appreciation is also extended to the United States Gymnastics Federation
(USGF) for permission to reprint Diagram 28 (p. 165) from the *USGF Gymnas-
tic Safety Manual* (p. 116) by G.S. George (Ed.) 1985, Indianapolis, IN: USGF
Publications, 1099 N. Meridian St., Suite 380, Indianapolis, IN 46204.

ISBN: 0-87322-088-9

Printed in the United States of America

10 9 8 7 6 5 4 3 2 1

Human Kinetics Publishers, Inc.
Box 5076, Champaign, IL 61820

1-800-DIAL-HKP
1-800-334-3665 (in Illinois)

Acknowledgments

In addition to the consultants for each activity area, whose contributions are especially noteworthy and greatly appreciated, students at Delta State University and the University of North Carolina at Greensboro, on whom many of the questions were tested in activity and measurement classes, are credited with a significant role in the development of these question collections.

Assistance for proofing, secretarial support, and helpful comments that stretched our minds is credited to Jane Weare, Gail Hennis, Julia Moore, Evelyn Pearce, Sally Chandler, and Joanne Lunt. Sally Robinson and DeDe Owens are recognized for their contributions to the substantial professional growth of the authors.

Contents

Preface

Cognitive measurement should go hand in hand with psychomotor measurement in physical education, sport, and fitness. Knowledge tests, however, are not as plentiful as skills tests and other psychomotor measures and so teachers usually develop their own tests. This practice is desirable because it helps to ensure that the test reflects the unit of instruction. Frequently, an instructor could be assisted in preparing a good test if a collection of test questions were available as a resource. This volume contains just such a collection of knowledge test questions for 15 different physical education activities.

Physical education teachers who want to give good tests often have neither the time nor the skills to make good knowledge tests. Having available a group of test questions to get the process underway may make the difference. From our experience in teaching test construction and item writing, and from making tests for our own classes, the initial trauma can be greatly relieved if some questions are available to get the process started.

Collections of test questions are available in other fields such as biology and psychology. These collections usually parallel a certain textbook and are provided as a resource for the teacher using that text. The test questions presented in this book, however, concide with no particular text. Instead, they were drawn from many sources and are intended to cover the content of a physical education activity.

Several steps were undertaken to reduce an initial list of over 40 activities to the 15 included in this collection of knowledge test questions. Activities covered in physical education instructional handbooks and workbooks were noted, as well as activities included in the series by such publishers as Brown and Saunders. The survey available from the American Alliance for Health, Physical Education, Recreation, and Dance (AAHPERD) of activities taught most prevalently in public schools and colleges was consulted. And, because a commitment to covering a variety of activities was important, consideration was also given to whether the activity was taught widely at both the secondary and college levels.

Ideas for test questions were gleaned from many sources including our personal collections of activity tests, tests provided by colleagues and former students, and sample questions located in activity books. Many items were written by the authors using instructional books as resources. These were edited and organized into content areas and additional questions were written to fill in content areas which were not adequately covered.

An objective test format was chosen because of the great range of content that can be covered. In addition, the ease of scoring leads to rapid feedback to the students and to the potential for a careful analysis of the test questions. The multiple choice format was chosen because the multiple-choice item is versatile enough to test for content along the full range of the cognitive taxonomy. We wanted to demonstrate that virtue.

Consultants were identified for each activity. Their role was to check on the clarity and accuracy of each question, to verify the answer key, to confer about the overall content covered by the questions, and to be sure the questions reflected current strategy, terminology, and rules of the activity. The suggestions and revisions made by the expert consultants add credibility to the individual questions and to the overall balance of questions for each activity. The following consultants reviewed the questions for the activities indicated:

Badminton	Andrea Farrow
Basketball	Lynne C. Agee
Bowling	Joan Hensley
Field Hockey	Jo Ann Messick
Golf	Mary Beth McGirr
Gymnastics	Robert M. Dailey
Racquetball	Edward T. Turner
Recreational Dance	Julia Hobby
Soccer	Andreas Koth
Softball	Sandra K. Johnson
Swimming and Diving	Lynne P. Gaskin
Tennis	Andrea Farrow
Track and Field	Le Roy T. Walker
Volleyball	Samye Johnson
Weight Training	George White

''Test Development and Analysis'' covers some of the important issues to be considered when developing tests, such as content coverage and format, and when evaluating a knowledge test once it is given, such as validity, reliability, item analysis, and revision. In addition, some specific points are provided about using these particular test questions. An understanding of the material in this first section of the book should help the professional become a better evaluator of the knowledge aspects of his or her activity program.

The discussion on test development and analysis is followed by 15 sections containing questions for each of the physical education activities. Each activity section is organized into three parts: (a) introductory comments and a mini index for the questions in the activity, (b) between 250 and 400 test questions, and (c) a list of helpful references. Some questions have accompanying diagrams to help clarify and test content that could not be covered without their use. They are numbered consecutively within each activity.

This volume was inspired by the desire to improve knowledge testing in physical education and sport activities and to enhance the professional competence of teachers in the process. It is hoped also that it will make knowledge test construction easier and less time consuming for the teacher.

Rosemary McGee
Andrea Farrow

Test Development and Analysis

The primary purpose of this book is to help teachers create quality knowledge tests for physical education activity classes. Between 250 and 400 questions are presented for each of 15 activities. The teacher should consider the content of a particular unit of instruction, then select test questions to cover that content. The questions can be used for short quizzes on one content area, such as rules and scoring, or can be selected to measure the attainment of objectives in a curriculum guide, or to measure competencies for testing programs. Regardless of their use, these test questions should be viewed as initial collections to which the teacher should continually make additions, deletions, and revisions. In this way, the teacher will have an up-to-date, ready resource for constructing and revising knowledge tests.

Organization of Physical Education Activity Questions

Each physical education activity is divided into content areas depending upon the nature of the activity. For example, questions are divided into areas such as techniques, strategy, rules and scoring, terminology, history, equipment, safety, and etiquette. A brief introduction at the beginning of each chapter explains the specific organizational pattern for that activity. Questions are grouped by topic in each content area. For example, a question on trapping from the Technique area of the Soccer activity reads:

Trapping

Where should the ball make contact on an instep trap?
- a. top of ankle
- *b. all of shoelace area
- c. inside of the foot at the arch
- d. top of toes

Trapping identifies the specific topic within the Technique area and helps the instructor select appropriate questions. The asterisk (*) next to answer "b" indicates the suggested answer to the question and generally is the answer to use. The answer should be keyed, however, to coincide with the way the content was taught. Because of different philosophies about technique and strategy or perhaps to match the skill level of the students being tested, the instructor may want to change the suggested key.

Within each activity area diagrams are used to help test for information that would be too wordy to explain in a multiple-choice question. The diagrams are numbered consecutively throughout each activity. Diagrams enhance test questions by providing convenience to the test maker and clarity to the test taker.

The emphasis in each activity is on technique questions because the greatest percentage of instructional time is usually spent in this area. However, special attention is given also to the specific needs of a particular activity. For example, in gymnastics, a significant number of questions involve spotting and safety. The content subcategories are covered sufficiently to encompass most of the concepts the teacher might wish to test. The teacher should develop specific questions to cover content unique to specialized programs.

The amount of knowledge required to answer the test questions varies. Most questions are designed for beginning participants in the activity. Some questions, however, are suitable for intermediate and advanced participants. Generally, the questions are written to test the knowledge of players, but questions pertinent for a knowledgeable spectator are also included. Not every participant can be a highly skilled player, but most students can learn to be appreciative spectators if they understand the content of an activity.

Wherever possible, questions were written so that right-handed or left-handed dominance would make no difference in the answer. Where this could not be avoided, however, questions were written for right-handed players. The instructor may (a) alert the students to the fact that the questions are designed for right-handed players so the left-handed players will know they are to make the appropriate adjustments in their thinking, (b) re-key the questions involved when scoring the papers for left-handed players, or (c) prepare a parallel form of the test designed specifically for left-handed players. Either of the latter two choices is more acceptable than the first. The left-handed student should not be penalized in test-taking performance because of hand dominance.

Gender terms used in questions should fit the composition of the class. If a class is made up totally of males, for example, masculine pronouns should be used. In coed classes, *he* or *she*, *his*, or *her* should be used. It would be preferable to avoid these terms, however, by using such words as *player(s)*, *student(s)*, or *you* in the question.

Question Format

There are two reasons for selecting an objective rather than an essay format for questioning. In the limited amount of time available for testing, all the content covered during instruction cannot be tested; it must be sampled. Because students can answer objective questions more quickly than essay items, many more questions can be included on an objective test, thus giving the test a broader sampling of the content taught. A second reason for using the objective testing format is accuracy and ease of scoring. Scoring is clerical for objective tests, and answer sheets can be used to further expedite the process.

The multiple-choice question format, preferred by most test construction experts, was selected for several reasons. Guessing the correct answer is less likely than in true-false or alternate response questions. Consequently, some of the chance element is reduced, and the problem of trying to control student guessing is minimized. Another advantage (Safrit, 1981) of multiple-choice items over true-false items is that the correct answer does not have to be totally true, but it must be the best answer of those given. This gives the question writer a greater range of content with which to work. One of the criticisms of objective testing is that the questions tend to measure only the lowest level of learning in the cognitive domain—remembering. Multiple-choice items are unique among objective question formats in that questions can be written to measure all levels of learning on a cognitive domain taxonomy. Another advantage of the multiple-choice format is that the incorrect choices made by students provide information about misunderstandings or misinformation students have that can be subsequently clarified.

Revision of Questions

Revision may be needed in the stems, choices, or answers in some questions. A question may contain a concept that the teacher wants to use, but the question may not agree with the way the content was taught, or it might use terminology different from what was used in class. These questions should be revised to fit the specific teaching situation. The questions in this collection have been designed for use with seventh grade through collegiate age classes. The language level is not appropriate in each question for all age groups, but question topics are suitable for each age group. In selecting the items, the instructor may want to revise the vocabulary to match the level of the group being tested.

Questions and answers on rules and scoring may need periodic updating as rules change. Answers given for questions in the rules sections are usually taken from 1985-86 or 1986-87 national rule books. Rules change yearly in some activities, less frequently in others. Junior or senior high school play may differ from collegiate rules. Men's rules may differ from women's. If a school uses local rules in playing a sport, changes in the questions or answers may be necessary. The question usually specifies the rule being used. This is not true in all cases, however, so questions or answers may need to be adjusted accordingly.

Test Layout

The best layout for a test is one that uses space efficiently and is easy to read. All parts of a question should be on the same page so students will not miss the question because they did not see part of it. For emphasis, negatives such as never, not or none should be underlined or written in all capitals so these words are not overlooked, causing the student to miss the question because of a reading error. Correct answers should not follow any pattern of choices. Diagrams, if used, should be placed in close proximity to the question and should be clearly presented. If an answer sheet is used, directions for recording answers on it should be explained and perhaps illustrated.

The number of questions included on a test should be determined partially by the purpose of giving the test. Students should be able to answer all the questions in the allotted time, but too many questions can cause boredom or fatigue. Generally, a test of 35 to 60 questions will serve most purposes.

Scoring

Scoring is more efficient in terms of time and accuracy when answer sheets are used (Marshall & Hales, 1972). Another advantage of using answer sheets is that test booklets can be reused. Answer sheets usually take one of two formats. One lists the possible answers by each question number, and the other provides a blank space by each question number.

Answer Format 1	Answer Format 2
1. a b c d	1. _____
2. a b c d	2. _____

In the first format, the student marks through the correct answer. This answer sheet format is designed to be used with an overlay key with the correct answers punched or cut out. The key is then placed over each answer sheet and the responses are marked incorrect where no mark appears. The overlay key has the additional advantage of marking what the correct choice should have been. This is helpful when tests are returned to students for follow-up. In the second answer sheet format, the student writes the letter or number of the correct response in the space provided. A strip key works well with this type of answer sheet. A blank answer sheet is marked with the correct answers and then cut or folded so it can be placed next to the answers on the student's answer sheet. The student's responses are compared with the strip key, and questions answered incorrectly are marked.

A standard answer sheet should be designed that will be appropriate for all the knowledge tests the teacher plans to administer. Constructing an answer sheet that is unique to each test is unnecessary and a waste of time.

Some schools may use electronic optical scanning machines for scoring tests. In this case, commercially prepared answer sheets are needed. These machines are helpful when preparing test results for each student and when processing the performance of a total group on the test. Scanners are more expensive but they save time and usually are programmed to provide an analysis of the responses made by the group to each question on the test.

Content Validity

Content validity is the agreement between the test and the unit of instruction. The instructor should have some assurance that the test is a valid instrument for measuring students' knowledge of course content. Content validity is built into a test as it is being developed. For a test to have content validity, the questions must match the course objectives, course content, and course outline. The number of questions included from each content area should reflect the importance of the objective or the time spent in class on that topic. Content areas for sports, for example, might include techniques, rules and scoring, strategy, and safety, whereas content areas for dance might include formations, steps, calls, and dances.

Content validity also involves determining the level of knowledge expected from the students. The instructor may want the students simply to recall information, such as knowing how many innings there are in a softball game, or to think at a higher level, such as analyzing a game situation to determine which strategy would be best.

The Educational Testing Service (Cooperative Test Division, n.d.; Diederich, 1973) has developed a three-level taxonomy for the cognitive domain to be used especially by classroom teachers.

Remembering	Understanding	Thinking
• Recall of facts, rules, procedures	• Classification	• Analysis
• Routine manipulation	• Application	• Generalization
• Reproduction	• Translation	• Evaluation

An example question for each of the three levels illustrates the use of the taxonomy:

Remembering (Softball)
When does a foul tip become an out?
a. when it occurs on the third strike
b. when it goes above the batter's head
c. when it occurs on the second strike
d. when it occurs on the first strike

Understanding (Golf)
Which club would be used if the shot requires a high loft with a minimal amount of run?
a. pitching wedge
b. 7 iron
c. 5 iron
d. 4 iron

Thinking (Basketball)
A player has just been called for a third foul and the game is still in the first half. What would be the best thing to do?
a. leave the player in
b. switch to a different defense
c. take the player out until the 2nd half
d. take the player out for 30 seconds to cool down

Most tests should include a number of questions from each level. Often beginning level tests contain more questions at the remembering level, and intermediate to advanced tests have more questions at the higher levels.

The development of a table of specifications will help ensure that a test has content validity. A two-way table is recommended. One direction lists the content areas to be covered and the other direction, the levels of knowledge expected. Categories in both content and cognitive levels are weighted to indicate the number of questions in each category appropriate for the test being prepared. The table of specifications for a 50-item test on beginning basketball might look like Table 1.

Table 1
Specifications for a 50-Question Test
for Beginning Basketball

Content areas	Cognitive taxonomy levels		
	Remembering	Understanding	Thinking
Technique–40%	20%	10%	10%
20 questions	10 questions	5 questions	5 questions
Rules & scoring–20%	16%	4%	
10 questions	8 questions	2 questions	
Strategy–20%	6%	10%	4%
10 questions	3 questions	5 questions	2 questions
Safety–10%	10%		
5 questions	5 questions		
Terminology–10%	10%		
5 questions	5 questions		
Total–100%	62%	24%	14%
50 questions	31 questions	12 questions	7 questions

In Table 1, the first column lists the content areas to be covered, the percentage of the test that should be devoted to each content area and the number of questions needed in each area to build a 50-question test. The remaining three columns list the percentage of the total test that should be devoted to each cognitive level in each content area and the number of questions needed in each. For example, in the Technique category, 20% of 50 questions equals 10 questions that should be included at the remembering level. The last row indicates the total percentage of questions and total number of questions for the test and for each knowledge level. Thus, the table of specifications provides a picture of the test regarding both content balance and cognitive levels.

After determining a table of specifications, the instructor selects and/or writes appropriate test questions until the number of questions coincides with the specifications of the test in both content and cognitive levels. This procedure ensures content validity of the test.

Reliability

Reliability refers to the consistency of a test. The reliability of an objective knowledge test is influenced primarily by two factors: test length and test difficulty. Test length (Verducci, 1980) has the greatest effect. As the length of the test increases, the reliability increases. Increasing the number of questions reduces the influence of such chance factors as luck and guessing. It also allows for a broader sample of the student's knowledge, thus increasing the consistency of the test and determining more real differences in the amount of knowledge of each individual taking the test.

Test difficulty also affects the reliability of a test. Generally, the closer the average test score is to half the length of the test, and the broader the range of scores, the more reliable a test will be (Verducci, 1980). A test that is too easy or too hard not only reduces the possibility that the average test score will approximate 50% of the items but also reduces the range of test scores. Constructing a challenging test in order to achieve better reliability does not mean, however, that nearly all of the students would be assigned low or failing grades. The scaling of scores can be adjusted upward for grading purposes.

The Kuder-Richardson Formula 21 is recommended for estimating the reliability of knowledge tests. This reliability coefficient can be computed either by using the computer program for the K-R formula which appears in the Appendix or by hand. The number of items on the test, the mean of the scores made on the test, and the standard deviation of the test scores are needed to compute the formula. The mean can be determined by summing the scores made on the test and dividing by the total number of test scores. An efficient way to find the standard deviation (σ) is to use the following formula:

$$\sigma = \sqrt{\frac{\Sigma X^2 - \frac{(\Sigma X)^2}{N}}{N}}$$

where ΣX^2 = sum of squared scores, (ΣX) = sum of scores, and N = number of scores. For five students taking a test with scores of 2, 4, 7, 8, and 10, the standard deviation would be:

X	X^2
2	4
4	16
7	49
8	64
10	100
$\Sigma X = 31$	$\Sigma X^2 = 233$

$$\sigma = \sqrt{\frac{233 - \frac{(31)^2}{5}}{5}} = \sqrt{\frac{233 - 192.2}{5}}$$

$$= \sqrt{\frac{40.8}{5}} = \sqrt{8.16} = 2.86$$

When computing by hand, the Kuder-Richardson Formula 21 is:

$$r_{KR_{21}} = \frac{n}{n-1}\left(1 - \frac{M(n-M)}{n\sigma^2}\right)$$

where n = number of test items, M = mean of the test scores, and σ = the standard deviation of the test scores. For example, for a 50-question test with a mean of 25 and a standard deviation of 6;

$$r_{KR_{21}} = \frac{50}{50-1}\left(1 - \frac{25(50-25)}{50(6)^2}\right)$$

$$= 1.02\left(1 - \frac{25(25)}{50(36)}\right) = 1.02\left(1 - \frac{625}{1800}\right)$$

$$= 1.02\,(1 - .327) = 1.02\,(.653) = .666$$

A reliability coefficient of .80 or above is desirable but rarely attained because this formula is very conservative and estimates the lower limit of what the real reliability of the test may be. A reliability estimate between .60 and .80 is generally considered adequate for teacher-made tests. The test needs to be fairly difficult to achieve this degree of reliability. Teachers, however, tend to make tests too easy to meet this reliability standard.

Item Analysis

Item analysis, another approach to validity, indicates the difficulty of each question and how well each question discriminates between high and low achiever on the test. After students have taken a test, their performance on each test question is analyzed. Used in combination, item analysis and content validity enable the teacher to have confidence in the knowledge tests administered to students. The difficulty of a question, or difficulty rating, is the proportion of students who answer the question correctly. Additionally, an item is said to have an acceptable index of discrimination when the students who do well on the total test do well on a particular question, and the students who do poorly on the total test do poorly on the same question.

The Educational Testing Service (Barrow & McGee, 1979; Cooperative Test Division, n.d.) has developed an effective item analysis method that requires little time and computation. The steps for using it follow:

1. After scoring the test papers, put the papers in rank order.
2. Take the top 10 papers; these are the "high" group. Take the bottom 10 papers; these are the "low" group. Put the rest of the papers aside; they will not be used in the item analysis.
3. Prepare an *item analysis data sheet:*

Question number	High	Low	H + L	H − L
1.	8	4	12	4
2.				
.				
.				
.				

4. Spread out the high papers so the number of correct answers can be counted. Record this for each item under the High column.
5. Spread out the low papers and record the number of correct answers in these 10 papers under the Low column.
6. Add the High column to the Low column (H + L) to get the difficulty rating for each question. The Educational Testing Service (ETS) suggests that questions with a difficulty rating between 7 and 17 are acceptable. If the number is less than 7, the question is probably too hard. If it is more than 17, it is probably too easy.
7. Subtract the Low column from the High column (H − L) to get the index of discrimination for each question. A negative number is possible. ETS suggests that an index of discrimination of 3 or more is acceptable. If lower than 3, the question may need to be revised or discarded. If the number is negative, the question definitely needs to be revised or thrown out.

Alternate Method for Calculating Item Analysis

An alternate method of calculating the difficulty rating and index of discrimination using the ETS method is to count the number of *wrong* answers. This may be easier because there should be fewer wrong answers to count. In addition, the second, third, and so on columns of an answer sheet are difficult to tally when the answer sheets are spread out as described earlier. After the "high" and "low" groups are selected, these steps should be followed:

1. Prepare the item analysis data sheet as recommended previously and change the last column from "H − L" to "L − H".
2. Tally the wrong answers from *each* paper in

the High group and then *each* paper in the Low group.

3. Add the High to the Low column (H + L) to get the difficulty rating for each question. A score between 4 and 13 is acceptable. If the number is more than 13, the question is probably too hard. If it is less than 4, it is probably too easy.

4. Subtract the High column from the Low column (L − H) to get the index of discrimination. A negative number is possible. ETS suggests that an index of discrimination of 3 or more is acceptable. If lower than 3, the question may need to be revised or discarded. If the number is negative, the question definitely needs to be revised or thrown out.

The item analysis is incomplete without two final steps. First, questions that did not meet the difficulty and discrimination standards should be eliminated from the test and the papers regraded. This will help raise the test scores to an acceptable range, although some scaling upward may still be necessary. Second, questions that need to be revised or discarded before using the test again should be identified.

Although item analysis provides a means of identifying problem questions and weaknesses within questions, it only estimates question effectiveness when used with small classes. Results will vary from one class to another, consequently the teacher with small classes should have less confidence in the analysis results and should examine questions closely before deciding to keep, revise, or discard them. In addition, sometimes test questions that the item analysis indicates are too easy or too difficult are desirable because they measure important learning outcomes. At times, it also may be important for motivational reasons to leave questions on a test that are too easy.

The results of item analysis can help to improve instruction by building better tests. Questions are identified that need to be changed or discarded before the test is reused. Concepts or materials tested may be too hard or too easy for the students, indicating that changes are needed in the amount of time spent on particular topics, in the method of presentation, or in curriculum offerings. Some information may not have been learned and needs to be covered again before students can move to the next instructional activity. Item analysis can also provide a guide for class discussion as a follow-up to most tests.

Competence and confidence in constructing and analyzing knowledge tests *is* possible for teachers who wish to develop these professional skills. The results of knowledge tests often receive considerable weight when determining unit grades. Therefore, the teacher must be able to administer tests that are technically sound.

References

Barrow, H.M., & McGee, R. (1979). *A practical approach to measurement in physical education* (3rd ed.). Philadelphia: Lea & Febiger.

Diederich, P.B. (1973). *Short-cut statistics for teacher-made tests*. Princeton, NJ: Educational Testing Service.

Making your own test (n.d.). Princeton, NJ: Educational Testing Service, Cooperative Test Division.

Marshall, J.C., & Hales, L.W. (1972). *Essentials of testing*. Reading, MA: Addison Wesley.

Safrit, M.J. (1981). *Evaluation in physical education*. Englewood Cliffs, NJ: Prentice-Hall.

Verducci, F.M. (1980). *Measurement concepts in physical education*. St. Louis, MO: C.V. Mosby.

Badminton

Andrea Farrow, Consultant

This collection of test questions on badminton is divided into seven content areas:

- **History**
- **Etiquette**
- **Equipment**
- **Terminology**
- **Rules and Scoring**
- **Technique**
- **Strategy**

Some terminology may seem confusing, especially that describing the body and racket positions in the Technique section. Such directions as *opposite of, diagonal to,* and so forth may be confusing if the instructor used other descriptions. Some questions may need to be revised to make terminology consistent with that used in class.

Many of the questions assume the player is right-handed. If these questions are used, it should be noted in the test directions, or a key should be made for left-handed players.

Badminton

History	1 to 16
Etiquette	17 to 25
Equipment	26 to 35
Terminology	36 to 49
Rules and Scoring	50 to 98
Technique	99 to 204
Strategy	205 to 270

History

Organizations

1. What is the national governing organization of badminton in the United States?
    - a. American Badminton Association
    - b. National Badminton Association
    - *c. United States Badminton Association
    - d. National Badminton Rules Committee

2. What is the name of the organization that governs the sport internationally?
    - a. International Badminton Association
    - b. World Badminton Association
    - *c. International Badminton Federation
    - d. Olympic Badminton Federation

Origin

3. In what country was the modern game of badminton developed?
    - a. United States
    - *b. England
    - c. Denmark
    - d. Japan

Andrea Farrow is a professor of health, physical education and recreation, and behavioral sciences at Delta State University, Cleveland, Mississippi. She was a tournament player and coach for many years, played in competition from the local to national levels, and has coached college teams at the Mississippi University for Women and Northwestern Louisiana State University.

4. From what game is the modern game of badminton thought to have developed?
   a. squash
   b. tennis
   *c. poona
   d. featherball

5. Which term has *not* been a previous name for badminton?
   a. poona
   b. battledore
   *c. feather tennis
   d. shuttlecock

6. Who introduced the game in England?
   a. The Duke of Wellington
   b. The Prince of Badminton
   *c. The Duke of Beaufort
   d. King George III

Competition

7. What is the international cup competition for men called?
   a. The Davis Cup
   b. The Uber Cup
   c. The Wightman Cup
   *d. The Thomas Cup

8. In what year was the first international cup competition for men held?
   a. 1861
   b. 1901
   *c. 1948
   d. 1970

9. What is the international cup competition for women called?
   a. The Davis Cup
   *b. The Uber Cup
   c. The Wightman Cup
   d. The Thomas Cup

10. In what year was the first international cup competition for women held?
    a. 1875
    b. 1914
    c. 1945
    *d. 1956

11. How often are the international cup competitions for men and women held?
    a. every year
    b. every 2 years
    *c. every 3 years
    d. every 4 years

12. What is the oldest and most famous badminton tournament?
    a. The United States Open
    b. The Southeastern Asia Games
    c. The Olympic Badminton Tournament
    *d. The All-England Championships

Popularity

13. In what part of the world is badminton the most popular?
    a. Southern Europe
    b. South America
    c. The Middle East
    *d. Southeast Asia

Court

14. When the first great championships were played, what was the shape of the court?
    a. more like the present tennis court
    b. smaller than the present court
    c. circular in shape
    *d. hourglass shaped

15. How has the court size changed since the beginning of the game?
    *a. It is about one quarter the original size.
    b. It is about 2 times the original size.
    c. It is longer and narrower than the original.
    d. It is the same length but narrower.

Players

16. How many players were on a team when the game was played in India in the early 1900s?
    a. 2
    b. 3
    *c. up to 5
    d. up to 10

Etiquette

Games

17. Which practice is *not* good sportsmanship?
    a. congratulating an opponent on good shots
    b. stopping the service when an opponent is unready
    *c. asking that points be replayed when shots are close to lines
    d. asking if the opponent is ready

18. Who should call violations and out-of-bounds shots?
    *a. A player calls violations and lines on his or her side of the court.
    b. A player calls the violations and lines on the opponent's side of the court.
    c. A player calls the opponent's violations and helps call lines on the opponent's side of the court.
    d. A match should have an official to call all violations and lines.

19. How should a shuttle be recovered that has fallen into the alley of an adjacent court where play is in progress?
    a. Reach in quickly with the racket and pull the shuttle out.
    b. Run onto the court quickly and pick it up.
    *c. Wait until the point is finished and ask for its return.
    d. Get a new bird.

20. If a player *cannot* decide if a shot is in or out, what is the preferred practice?
    a. Ask the opponent.
    b. Ask the spectators.
    c. Call it out.
    *d. Call it good.

21. When should the score be called out loud?
    a. at the end of the game
    b. at the end of each point
    c. when the score changes
    *d. before each serve

22. How should the shuttle be returned to the serving side when the point is over?
    a. pushed under the net to the other court
    b. pushed under the net to the server
    c. hit over the net to the other court
    *d. hit over the net to the server

23. During a point, a shuttle from another court lands in the playing area and interferes with play. What should the player who has been interfered with do?
    a. Call a let and return the shuttle to the other court.
    b. Call a let and allow the player from the other court to retrieve the shuttle.
    *c. Call a let and return the shuttle to the server on the other court.
    d. Continue play and allow the player from the other court to retrieve the shuttle at the end of the point.

Dress

24. What kind of clothing is preferred for tournament play?
    a. dark colored clothing
    b. any clothing that is not bright colored
    c. dark colored shorts and white shirts
    *d. all white clothing

Warm-Up

25. What procedure should be followed during the warm-up?
    *a. Hit the shuttle to the opponent so he or she can warm up also.
    b. Hit power shots to intimidate the opponent.
    c. Hit the shuttle away from the opponent to tire him or her out.
    d. Hit the shuttle to the four corners of the court.

Equipment

Racket

26. What type of racket is most likely to warp if not kept in a press?
    a. wooden frame and nylon strings
    *b. wooden frame and gut strings
    c. metal frame and nylon strings
    d. metal frame and gut strings

27. What kind of grip is on good rackets?
    a. plastic
    b. nylon
    *c. leather
    d. composition

28. Of what type of material are the best rackets made?
    a. wooden heads and shafts
    b. wooden heads and metal shafts
    c. metal heads and wooden shafts
    *d. metal heads and shafts

Strings

29. What type of string lasts longest?
    a. cat gut
    b. sheep gut
    *c. nylon
    d. polyester

30. What type of string has the greatest resiliency?
    *a. gut
    b. polyester
    c. dacron
    d. nylon

31. What are the different colored strings sometimes put at the top and bottom of the strings?
    a. extra strength strings for added power
    b. regular strings for added color
    c. special strings to keep the racket from
    warping
    *d. trim strings used in spinning the
    racket

Net

32. What is the correct height of the badminton
net at the middle of the court?
    a. 3 feet
    *b. 5 feet
    c. 7 feet
    d. 8 feet

33. How should a badminton net look when it is
set up properly?
    a. The heavier taped edge is at the bot-
    tom of the net.
    *b. The difference in the height of the net
    at the posts and in the middle is 1 inch.
    c. The difference in the height of the net
    at the posts and in the middle should
    not exceed 6 inches.
    d. The net posts should sit on the singles
    sidelines.

Shuttlecock

34. What is the difference in an indoor and out-
door shuttlecock?
    a. band of color around the base
    b. material of the feathers
    *c. weight of the shuttle
    d. color of the shuttle

35. What is the difference in practice shuttles and
official tournament shuttles?
    a. band of color around the base
    *b. material of the feathers
    c. weight of the shuttle
    d. color of the shuttle

Terminology

Down

36. What is *down*?
    a. The team with the fewest points is
    down.
    *b. One player on the serving side has lost
    his or her serve.
    c. Both players on the serving team have
    lost their terms of service.
    d. The team on the defensive is down.

Let

37. A point must be replayed. What is this called?
    a. fault
    *b. let
    c. down
    d. replay

Offense

38. What does it mean when a team is on the
offensive?
    a. The team is serving.
    b. The team has the higher score.
    c. The team is the more skilled.
    *d. The team has hit the shuttle down-
    ward.

Fault

39. Which term indicates a violation of the rules?
    *a. fault
    b. feint
    c. let
    d. replay

Setting

40. What is *setting*?
    a. hitting the shuttle on the racket frame
    b. determining the player who serves first
    c. winning the serve from an opponent
    *d. extending a tied game

Rally

41. Players hit the shuttle back and forth to each
other. What is this called?
    a. playing a point
    *b. rallying
    c. pinging
    d. hitting

Second Service

42. What is meant by *second service*?
    a. A player has missed the first serve and
    serves again.
    b. A player is the second server in a
    game.
    *c. One player in a doubles game has lost
    his or her serve.
    d. A serve hits the top of the net and is
    re-served.

Inning

43. What is the period called during which a
player or team holds the serve?
    a. one hand
    b. in side
    *c. inning
    d. game

Love-All

44. What is the score at the beginning of a game?
    a. no score
    b. 0-0
    c. love
    *d. love-all

No Shot

45. What is it called when a player carries or slings the shuttle off the racket?
    a. fault
    *b. no shot
    c. let
    d. carry

Smash

46. What is the shot called that travels downward with great force?
    a. slam
    b. drive
    c. drop
    *d. smash

Drop Shot

47. Which stroke should barely clear the net and immediately fall into the opponent's court?
    *a. drop
    b. drive
    c. smash
    d. dink

Clear

48. Which stroke is hit high to the back of the opponent's court?
    a. lob
    b. drive
    *c. clear
    d. smash

Drive

49. What stroke sends the shuttle skimming low over the net in a more or less parallel line with the floor?
    a. drop
    b. smash
    c. clear
    *d. drive

Rules and Scoring

Court

50. How can the singles playing court best be described?
    *a. long and narrow
    b. long and wide
    c. short and narrow
    d. short and wide

51. How can the singles serving court best be described?
    *a. long and narrow
    b. long and wide
    c. short and narrow
    d. short and wide

52. How can the doubles playing court best be described?
    a. long and narrow
    *b. long and wide
    c. short and narrow
    d. short and wide

53. How can the doubles serving court best be described?
    a. long and narrow
    b. long and wide
    c. short and narrow
    *d. short and wide

54. What is the purpose of the line parallel to the backline and about 2½ feet closer to the net?
    a. out line for singles play
    b. out line for singles serve
    c. out line for doubles play
    *d. out line for doubles serve

Spin for Serve

55. How should players decide who should serve first in a match?
    a. Players rally or ping and the winner serves first.
    b. Players toss a coin and the winner serves first.
    *c. Players spin a racket and the winner may serve, receive, or choose the side of the court.
    d. Players spin a racket, and the winner may serve or receive.

56. How many points does the server get for winning a rally?
    *a. 1
    b. 2
    c. 3
    d. 5

57. How many points must be won by one player to complete a game of women's singles?
    a. 6
    *b. 11
    c. 15
    d. 21

58. How many points must be won by one player to complete a game of men's singles?
    a. 11
    *b. 15
    c. 21
    d. 15 or 21, as decided before the match

59. How many points must be won by one team to complete a game of women's doubles?
    a. 11
    *b. 15
    c. 21
    d. 15 or 21, as decided before the match

60. How many points must be won by one team to complete a game of men's doubles?
    a. 11
    *b. 15
    c. 21
    d. 15 or 21, as decided before the match

61. How many points must be won by one team to complete a game of mixed doubles?
    *a. 15
    b. 11 or 15, as decided before the match
    c. 21
    d. 15 or 21, as decided before the match

62. A game reaches the point at which it may be set. What is the procedure?
    a. The server may set the game.
    *b. The receiver may set the game.
    c. Either player may set the game.
    d. The game must be set.

63. In women's singles, if the game is tied at 9-9, for how many points may it be set?
    a. 1
    b. 2
    *c. 3
    d. It may not be set at 9-9.

64. In men's singles, if the game is tied at 13-13, for how many points may it be set?
    a. 1
    b. 3
    *c. 5
    d. It may not be set at 13-13.

65. In women's singles, when can the game be set for three points?
    *a. at 9-9
    b. at 10-10
    c. at 13-13
    d. at 14-14

66. In men's singles, when can the game be set for three points?
    a. at 13-13
    *b. at 14-14
    c. at 19-19
    d. at 20-20

67. In doubles, if the game is tied at 13-13, for how many points may it be set?
    a. 2
    b. 3
    *c. 5
    d. It may not be set at 13-13.

68. A game reaches the first tied score at which it can be set and is set. What may happen if it is tied again at the next score?
    a. It may be reset by the server.
    b. It may be reset by the receiver.
    c. It may be reset if both players agree to reset.
    *d. It may not be reset.

69. When is a match completed?
    a. when a player has won a game
    *b. when a player has won two out of three games
    c. when a player has won three out of five games
    d. when a player has won a set

Change Courts

70. When do players change sides of the net in doubles?
    a. after every eight points are played
    b. after every game is played
    *c. after the first and second games and after one team has eight points in the third game
    d. after one team has won eight points

Serving

71. Who serves the second game in a match?
    a. the player who received first in the first game
    b. the player who served first in the first game
    *c. the player who won the first game
    d. the player who lost the first game

72. Which is not a service fault?
    a. Racket face is above the hand when contact is made.
    *b. Server completely misses the shuttle.
    c. Server feints as if to hit the shuttle but does not strike it.
    d. Racket face is above the waist when contact is made.

73. How many points may a player serve consecutively?
    a. A player serves one and then the opponent serves one.
    b. A player serves five and then the opponent serves five.
    *c. A player serves as long as he or she is making points.
    d. A player serves as long as he or she is making points unless the game is set, then serves alternate.

74. The score is 5-4 in a singles game. From which court should the next point be served?
    a. the right court
    *b. the left court
    c. the other court from where the last point was served
    d. impossible to determine from the information given

75. The score is 8-3 in a singles game between Players A and B. A has three points. Who is serving?
    a. A is serving.
    *b. B is serving.
    c. Either could be serving; it depends on who served first in the game.
    d. Either could be serving; it depends on who won the last point.

76. In singles, what determines from which court a serve should be made?
    a. the total number of points that have been played
    *b. the server's score
    c. the server always serves from the right court first
    d. the court from which the previous point was served

77. In singles, Player A serves the shuttle over the net to Player B. It lands in the area between the net and short service line. What is the ruling?
    a. point for Player A
    b. second service for Player A
    c. point for Player B
    *d. Player B serves.

78. In singles, Player A's serve to Player B skims the top of the net and lands in the correct service court. What is the decision?
    *a. point for Player A
    b. second service for Player A
    c. point for Player B
    d. Player B serves.

79. In singles, Player A serves to Player B from the right service court. The shuttle lands in the service court directly across the net. What is the ruling?
    a. point for Player A
    b. second service for Player A
    c. point for Player B
    *d. Player B serves.

80. In singles, Player A is serving to Player B. Player A swings at the shuttle and misses it completely. What is the ruling?
    *a. Player A may serve again without penalty.
    b. Player A takes a second serve.
    c. Point is awarded to Player B.
    d. Player B serves.

81. The score is 12-10 in a doubles match between Teams A and B. Team A is serving. It is second service. From which court should the serve be played?
    a. the right court
    b. the left court
    *c. the court opposite from where the last serve was played
    d. impossible to determine from the information given

82. In doubles, when do players change courts to serve or receive?
    a. Serving team changes courts after losing first service.
    b. Receiving team changes courts when serving team wins a point.
    *c. Serving team changes courts after winning a point.
    d. Serving team changes courts each time they begin an inning.

83. At the beginning of a doubles game, the first player to serve on Team A loses his or her serve. After Team B has had its term of service, who serves?
    a. the player on Team A who has *not* yet served
    *b. the player on Team A who began serving the game
    c. the player on Team A who is in the left service court
    d. the player on Team A who received the last service from Team B

84. In the first rally of a doubles game, the server serves a fault. What is the procedure?
    a. The server serves the second serve.
    b. The server's partner serves.
    *c. The opponent in the right service court serves.
    d. The opponent in the left service court serves.

85. In doubles, from where is the first service in an inning made?
    *a. from the right service court
    b. diagonally across from where the last service was made
    c. from the right service court if the server's score is an even number and from the left if it is an odd number
    d. from the right service court if the server's score is an odd number and from the left if it is an even number

86. During a doubles game, A is serving to C. C's partner returns the serve. What is the situation?
    a. Play continues.
    *b. A point is awarded to the serving team.
    c. A point is awarded to the receiving team.
    d. A let is called and the serve is replayed.

87. In doubles, when does only one player on the team get a term of service?
    a. The team that serves first in a game only gets one service term throughout the game.
    *b. The team that serves first in a game only gets one service term at the beginning of the game.
    c. Only the player in the right service court gets a term of service throughout the game.
    d. When the game is set only one player on a team gets a term of service.

88. In doubles, when should a player be in the service court in which he or she began the game?
    a. when his or her term of service begins
    b. when he or she is receiving the service
    *c. when his or her team's score is an even number
    d. when the total number of points scored in the match is even

89. For the serve in doubles, when may players on the serving team change service courts?
    *a. after winning a rally
    b. after losing a rally
    c. after losing the serve to the opponents
    d. never

Receiving
90. For the serve in doubles, when may players on the receiving team change service courts?
    a. after losing a rally
    b. after the serving team loses first service
    c. after winning the rally that gives them the service
    *d. never

Playing
91. Which is a fault when playing a net shot?
    a. The racket follows through over the net.
    b. The shuttle contacts the frame of the racket.
    c. The player steps outside the court to contact the shuttle.
    *d. The racket touches the net on the return shot.

92. What happens when the shuttle touches the net during play?
    a. A let is called.
    b. The point is replayed.
    *c. Play is continued.
    d. The point is ended.

93. What may touch the net without a fault being called?
    a. a racket
    b. a player's clothing
    c. a player's body
    *d. a shuttle

94. In a singles game, Player A serves a shuttle that would have gone out-of-bounds if Player B had not returned it. What should Player A do?
    a. Play the point over.
    b. Give Player B the serve.
    *c. Continue the point.
    d. Claim a point.

95. During play a shuttle hits the backline and bounces out of the court. What is the decision?
    *a. The shot is good because the lines are part of the court.
    b. The shot is out because the lines are *not* part of the court.
    c. The shot is out because it bounced out.
    d. The point is replayed because it hit a line and bounced.

96. Player A hits a shot on the frame of his or her racket while rallying with Player B. What is the situation?
    a. Point is awarded to Player A.
    b. Point is awarded to Player B.
    *c. Play continues.
    d. Player B wins the rally.

97. During a rally with Player B, Player A, the server, hits a shot that contacts his or her racket twice before going over the net. What is the situation?
    a. point awarded to Player A
    b. point awarded to Player B
    c. Play continues.
    *d. Player B wins the rally.

98. What happens when any unusual occurrence interferes with play?
    a. Play continues.
    b. The server wins the point.
    c. The receiver wins the point.
    *d. A let is called.

Technique

99. When badminton is properly played, which ability is *least* important?
    a. power
    b. quickness
    c. finesse
    *d. strength

100. What portion of the body provides most of the power in badminton strokes?
    a. shoulder
    *b. wrist
    c. arm
    d. trunk

101. What does good wrist action add to a stroke?
    a. control
    b. placement
    *c. power
    d. quickness

102. How can the proper forehand grip best be described?
    a. It is the grip that feels the most natural.
    b. It is tight and tense.
    c. It is the same as gripping a hammer.
    *d. It is firm but relaxed.

103. How should the feet be placed in the ready position?

    *a. Net _____   b. Net _____

    c. Net _____   d. Net _____

104. How should the body weight be distributed during the ready position?
    a. Most of the weight should be on the back foot.
    b. Most of the weight should be on the front foot.
    c. The weight should be on the heels of both feet.
    *d. The weight should be on the balls of both feet.

105. How far apart should the feet be in the ready position?
    a. about 6 inches
    *b. about shoulder width
    c. slightly more than shoulder width
    d. about 3 feet

106. How can a player best position him- or herself for shots requiring quick movements to the left or right?
    a. Take a couple of small sliding steps in that direction.
    b. Reach as far as possible, keeping the feet stationary.
    *c. Pivot and take running steps in that direction.
    d. Run quickly in that direction.

107. How can a player best position him- or herself for shots in the back of the court?
    a. turn and run
    *b. pivot and slide
    c. run backward
    d. skip backward

108. How high are the most effective badminton shots contacted?
    *a. above the player's head
    b. above the top of the net
    c. level with the top of the net
    d. below the player's waist

109. Why is it desirable to hit overhead shots at the peak of a player's reach?
    a. The shuttle is traveling faster and thus rebounds off the racket at the greatest speed.
    b. The wrist can be snapped most efficiently at this point and gives the shuttle the greatest velocity.
    *c. The lever arm is longest at this point and provides maximum force behind the shot.
    d. The bird is closest to the net at this point and has less distance to travel back to the net.

110. How is the weight distributed in the back-swing of forehand overhead strokes?
    *a. The weight is on the back foot.
    b. The weight is on the front foot.
    c. The weight is evenly distributed over both feet.
    d. The weight shifts from the front to back foot.

111. Why is weight transference important in badminton strokes?
    *a. It provides maximum power for the stroke.
    b. It helps the placement of the shuttle.
    c. It ensures proper footwork.
    d. It helps the player relax.

112. During the follow-through, why should a player allow the racket to continue in a natural path in the direction of the shot?
    a. to reduce fatigue
    b. to ensure proper weight transfer
    c. to allow the arm to extend fully
    *d. to get better control of the placement

113. Which combination of strokes requires the same execution until just before the shuttle is contacted?
    a. clear, service, net shots
    b. smash, clear, drive
    c. drop shot, drive, smash
    *d. drop shot, smash, clear

Forehand
114. What is the advantage in using the handshake grip for a forehand?
    a. It is the most comfortable way to hold the racket.
    *b. It allows the player to have the most wrist snap.
    c. It allows the player to hold the racket tightly.
    d. It allows the player to shift grips rapidly.

115. Which grip is used for a forehand by most good players?
    *a. Eastern grip
    b. Western grip
    c. Continental grip
    d. Hammer grip

116. Which statement best describes the Eastern grip?
    *a. The top bevel of the handle comes in the middle of the V made by the thumb and index finger.
    b. The thumb exerts the most pressure in maintaining the grip.
    c. The racket face is parallel to the ground when the player grasps the racket.
    d. The forefinger extends up the handle of the racket.

Backhand
117. How should a player grip the racket to hit a backhand?
    a. The grip is the same as it is on the forehand.
    b. The V is on the right, top bevel of the racket.
    c. The grip is the same as a person grips a hammer.
    *d. The V is on the left, top bevel of the racket.

118. What part of the hand gives the racket support in hitting a backhand?
    a. the index finger
    b. the little finger
    c. the palm
    *d. the ball of the thumb

Clear
119. From what point should the swing of the racket head begin for the overhead clear? [Refer to Diagram 1.]
    *a.

Diagram 1

120. How high should the shuttle be contacted on the overhead clear? [Refer to Diagram 2.]
    *c.

D

C

B

A

Diagram 2

121. If the player in the diagram were hitting a clear, which point would be the best for contacting the shuttle? [Refer to Diagram 3.]
    *b.

A B C D

Diagram 3

122. Which diagram shows the correct stance for the forehand clear?

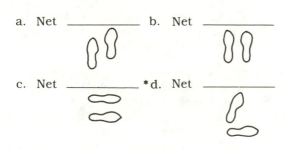

a. Net _____ b. Net _____

c. Net _____ *d. Net _____

123. For a forehand clear, what is the position of the arm at contact?
    a. The elbow is slightly bent and the wrist cocked.
    b. The elbow is bent at a right angle as the wrist uncocks.
    c. The arm is extended and the wrist cocked.
    *d. The arm and hand are extended as the wrist uncocks.

124. For a forehand clear, what is the position of the shoulders in the backswing?
    a. parallel with the net
    *b. at a right angle to the net
    c. diagonal with the right shoulder toward the net
    d. diagonal with the left shoulder toward the net

125. For a forehand clear, how is the player's weight distributed on the forward swing?
    a. shifts from the back to front foot as the swing begins
    b. stays equally on both feet throughout the swing
    *c. shifts from the back to front foot just before contact
    d. shifts from the back to front foot just after contact

126. For a forehand clear, what is the position of the racket head at the end of the follow-through?
    a. beside the right knee
    *b. beside the left thigh
    c. in front of the body at shin level
    d. in front of the body at waist level

127. A clear is going too high and *not* deep enough. What might the player do to correct the problem?
    a. Use more wrist action.
    *b. Hit the shot more in front of his or her body.
    c. Take a bigger backswing and follow through.
    d. Reach more upward on the follow-through.

128. A clear is going far enough but is too flat. What might the player do to correct the problem?
    a. Use more wrist action.
    b. Hit the shot more in front of his or her body.
    *c. Reach more upward on the follow-through.
    d. Take a bigger backswing and follow through.

129. What is the difference in hitting an attacking and a defensive clear?
  a. A defensive clear is hit with more wrist action.
  b. An attacking clear is hit with more follow-through.
  c. A defensive clear is contacted at a higher point.
  *d. An attacking clear is hit with a lower follow-through.

Drop Shot

130. What is the greatest difference in hitting the overhead clear and overhead drop shot?
  a. amount of backswing
  *b. speed of the wrist snap
  c. amount of follow-through
  d. point of contact

131. The flight pattern of what stroke is shown in the diagram? [Refer to Diagram 4.]
  a. smash
  b. short serve
  *c. drop shot
  d. drive

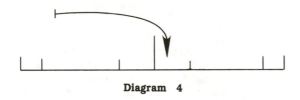

Diagram 4

132. From what point should the swing of the racket head begin for the overhead drop shot? [Refer to Diagram 1, Question 119.]
  *a.

133. How high should the shuttle be contacted on the drop shot? [Refer to Diagram 2, Question 120.]
  *c.

134. If the player in the diagram were hitting a drop shot, which point would be the best for contacting the shuttle? [Refer to Diagram 3, Question 121.]
  *b.

135. Which diagram below shows the correct stance for an overhead drop shot?

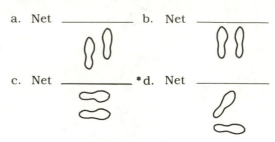

136. When hitting an overhead drop shot, where should the shuttle be contacted?
  a. behind the right shoulder
  b. to the side of the right shoulder
  *c. slightly in front of the right shoulder
  d. directly overhead

137. In hitting an overhead drop shot, what is the position of the shoulders in the backswing?
  a. facing the net
  *b. at a right angle to the net
  c. diagonal with the right shoulder forward
  d. diagonal with the left shoulder forward

138. In hitting an overhead drop shot, where is the player's weight on the forward swing?
  a. It stays equally distributed over both feet.
  b. It is primarily over the back foot.
  c. It shifts from the back to front foot as the swing begins.
  *d. It shifts from the back to front foot as contact is made.

139. For an overhead drop shot, what is the position of the racket head at the end of the follow-through?
  a. stops at contact
  b. above and slightly in front of the head
  *c. in front of the player waist high
  d. beside the player's left knee

140. A player wants to hit an overhead drop shot with less arc in its flight. What might he or she change about the stroke?
  *a. Change the angle of the racket face at contact.
  b. Contact the shuttle slightly back of the right shoulder.
  c. Swing the racket head easier.
  d. Let the shuttle fall lower before contacting it.

141. A player is hitting a drop shot too deep into the opponent's court. How can he or she get it to land closer to the net?
     a. Hit it later.
     b. Hit it after it has dropped lower.
     c. Take less backswing.
     *d. Uncock the wrist more slowly.

Smash

142. What is the biggest difference in hitting a clear and a smash?
     a. amount of wrist snap
     *b. angle of the racket face
     c. amount of backswing
     d. speed of the forward swing

143. Which shot is contacted at the greatest distance in front of the body of the player?
     a. clear
     b. overhead drop shot
     *c. smash
     d. backhand clear

144. From what point should the swing of the racket head begin for the smash? [Refer to Diagram 1, Question 119.]
     *a.

145. How high should the shuttle be contacted on the smash? [Refer to Diagram 2, Question 120.]
     *c.

146. If the player in the diagram were hitting a smash, which point would be the best for contacting the shuttle? [Refer to Diagram 3, Question 121.]
     *c.

147. What is different about the grip on the smash?
     a. It is firmer throughout the stroke.
     b. It is more relaxed throughout the stroke.
     *c. It is firmer at contact.
     d. It is more relaxed at contact.

148. Which diagram below shows the correct stance for the smash?

     a. Net _____   b. Net _____

     c. Net _____   *d. Net _____

149. In hitting a smash, what is the position of the arm at contact?
     a. slightly bent
     b. bent at a right angle
     *c. fully extended
     d. hyperextended

150. In hitting a smash, where does the follow-through end?
     a. in front of the player at waist height
     b. in front of the player at shin height
     *c. to the left of the player at knee height
     d. to the right of the player at knee height

151. A player's smash lacks velocity. What might be the problem?
     *a. The wrist is *not* cocked in the backswing.
     b. The shuttle is being hit too early.
     c. The shuttle is being hit too late.
     d. The direction of the follow-through is too high.

152. A player is hitting a smash too flat. What is the most probable cause?
     a. The backswing is too short.
     b. The follow-through is too short.
     c. The shuttle is hit too early.
     *d. The shuttle is hit too late.

Drive

153. From what point should the swing of the racket head begin for the drive? [Refer to Diagram 1, Question 119.]
     *b.

154. How high should the shuttle be contacted on the drive? [Refer to Diagram 2, Question 120.]
     *a.

155. If the player in the diagram were hitting a drive, which point would be the best for contacting the shuttle? [Refer to Diagram 3, Question 121.]
     *b.

156. What is the position of the racket head at the beginning of the backswing of a forehand drive?
     a. behind the right shoulder
     b. to the side of the right shoulder
     c. behind the head
     *d. between the shoulder blades

157. What is the position of the elbow at the beginning of the backswing of a forehand drive?
   a. level with the top of the player's head
   b. slightly above the level of the player's shoulders
   c. level with the top of the player's shoulders
   *d. between the player's shoulders and waist

158. Which stance illustrated below is preferred for hitting a forehand drive?

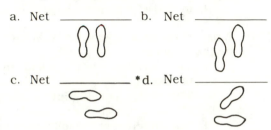

159. What is the wrist action in hitting a forehand drive?
   *a. rapidly uncocked and rotated inward
   b. rapidly uncocked and rotated outward
   c. little or no wrist action
   d. rapidly uncocked but not rotated

160. Where is the racket head at the end of the follow-through in a forehand drive?
   a. in front of the player about waist high
   b. to the player's right side about knee high
   *c. to the player's left side about shoulder high
   d. to the player's left side about knee high

Underhand Clear

161. Where should the racket head be in hitting underhand strokes?
   a. below the shoulders
   b. below the waist
   *c. below the hand
   d. below the knees

162. Which stance illustrated below is best for hitting an underhand clear?

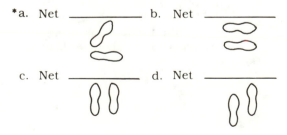

163. What is the position of the wrist in the backswing of the underhand clear?
   a. cocked and above the level of the hand
   *b. cocked and below the level of the hand
   c. extended and above the level of the hand
   d. extended and below the level of the hand

164. What is the starting position of the racket when hitting an underhand clear?
   *a. behind the player's body at about waist level
   b. behind the player's body at about shoulder level
   c. to the right of the player's body at about waist level
   d. to the right of the player's body at about shoulder level

165. When hitting an underhand clear, where is the contact point?
   a. to the side of the player at about knee level
   b. to the side of the player at about chest level
   *c. ahead of the player's body at about knee level
   d. ahead of the player's body at about chest level

166. What is the path of the follow-through for an underhand clear?
   a. up and out
   b. approximately a circle perpendicular to the floor
   c. up and over the player's left shoulder
   *d. in the direction of the intended flight

Net Shots

167. Why is the grip changed when hitting net shots?
   a. for more deception
   *b. for more touch
   c. for more power
   d. for more reach

168. When should the shuttle be contacted when hitting net shots?
   a. when it reaches a point level with the top of the net
   b. when it reaches a point halfway down the net
   c. when it reaches a point below the bottom of the net
   *d. when it can first be reached by the player

169. What is the court position for playing the net?
    a. as close to the net as possible
    *b. an arm and racket length away from the net
    c. one step toward the net from the center of the court
    d. inside the short service line

170. Which are the most difficult net shots to return?
    a. those falling perpendicular to the floor
    *b. those falling diagonally to the floor
    c. those hit crosscourt from midcourt
    d. those hit crosscourt from side to side

171. What is the most important factor in hitting effective net shots?
    *a. Meet the shuttle as high as possible.
    b. Keep the wrist relaxed.
    c. Hold the racket tightly.
    d. Use little backswing.

Around-the-Head

172. What shots may be hit as around-the-head shots?
    a. clear, smash, and drop shots
    b. clear, half-smash, and drive shots
    c. smash, half-smash, and drop shots
    *d. clear, half-smash, and drop shots

173. Where is the contact point for an around-the-head shot?
    a. over the right shoulder
    b. slightly in front of the head
    *c. over the left shoulder
    d. slightly in back of the head

174. What is the position of the player's shoulder in the backswing of the around-the-head shot?
    *a. facing the net
    b. at a right angle to the net
    c. diagonal to the net with the right shoulder forward
    d. diagonal to the net with the left shoulder forward

175. Where is the racket head at the end of the follow-through in the around-the-head shot?
    a. out from the right shoulder
    *b. out from the right knee
    c. out from the left knee
    d. out in front of the knees

176. What is the most important reason for using the around-the-head shot instead of a backhand shot?
    a. It can be hit with more power.
    *b. It requires less movement from the center of the court.
    c. It is more deceptive.
    d. It can be controlled better.

Backhand Clear

177. Why is the thumb placed on the back of the racket grip when hitting a backhand clear?
    *a. for added leverage
    b. for added force
    c. for added wrist action
    d. for added control

178. A player is hitting a backhand clear. At the end of the backswing, what is the position of the elbow?
    a. pointing at the net
    b. pointing diagonally above the net
    *c. pointing at the oncoming shuttle
    d. pointing at the ceiling

179. What is the most important part of the swing in a backhand clear?
    a. the transfer of weight
    b. the rotation of the body
    c. the placement of the feet
    *d. the timing of the wrist snap

180. What is the position of the shoulders in the backswing of backhand clear?
    a. facing the net
    b. at a right angle to the net
    *c. diagonal to the net toward the left net post
    d. diagonal to the net toward the right net post

181. What is the action of the wrist in hitting a backhand clear?
    a. Uncock the wrist and rotate it quickly inward.
    *b. Uncock the wrist and rotate it quickly outward.
    c. Uncock the wrist and rotate it smoothly inward.
    d. Uncock the wrist and rotate it smoothly outward.

182. Where should the backhand be contacted for the most effective shot? [Refer to Diagram 5.]
    *a.

A

B

C

D

Diagram 5

Backhand Drive

183. What part of the body leads the swing in hitting a backhand drive?
    a. the hand
    b. the wrist
    *c. the elbow
    d. the shoulder

Serve

184. How should a player hold the shuttle to serve?
    a. Pinch the feathers with the thumb and first two fingers.
    b. Cup the feathers with the thumb and index finger.
    *c. Pinch the base of the shuttle with the thumb and index finger.
    d. Cup the base with the thumb and index finger.

185. Where should the shuttle be positioned as the player prepares to serve?
    *a. The player's left arm should be extended shoulder high toward the net.
    b. The player's left arm should be extended downward with the shuttle knee high.
    c. The player's left elbow should be next to the waist with the shuttle waist high.
    d. The player's left elbow should be next to the waist with the shuttle thigh high.

186. Which diagram below shows the correct foot placement for serving the basic singles serve?

    a. Net _____   b. Net _____

    c. Net _____   d. Net _____

187. What is the position of the player's wrist and racket in the backswing on a basic singles serve?
    a. The wrist is cocked with the racket head above the wrist.
    *b. The wrist is cocked with the racket head below the wrist.
    c. The wrist is extended with the racket head above the wrist.
    d. The wrist is extended with the racket head below the wrist.

188. How should the shuttle be contacted in hitting the singles serve?
    *a. The shuttle falls to meet the racket at about thigh level.
    b. The shuttle falls to meet the racket just below knee level.
    c. The shuttle is tossed up and meets the racket at waist level.
    d. The shuttle is held and the racket comes up to meet it.

189. In hitting a high singles serve, where does the follow-through end?
    a. over the player's right shoulder
    *b. over the player's left shoulder
    c. by the player's left hip
    d. over the player's head

190. What is the primary difference between hitting a low and high singles serve?
    a. amount of backswing
    b. transfer of weight
    *c. amount of wrist snap
    d. contact point

191. Where is a player's weight centered in the follow-through on a long singles serve?
    a. equally over both feet
    b. primarily over the back foot
    c. mostly over the front foot with some over the back foot
    *d. over the front foot

192. What is the difference in hitting the singles and doubles serves?
    a. less backswing, weight transfer, and wrist action in the doubles serves
    *b. less backswing, follow-through, and weight transfer in the doubles serves
    c. less weight transfer and wrist action in the doubles serves
    d. less wrist action and higher contact point in the doubles serves

193. What is the difference in the stance in hitting a singles and doubles serve?
    a. The stance is narrower in a singles serve.
    *b. The stance is narrower in a doubles serve.
    c. The player stands facing more toward the sideline in a doubles serve.
    d. The player's weight is more over the back foot in a doubles serve.

194. What is the action of the wrist in hitting a short doubles serve?
    *a. cocked in the backswing and remains cocked throughout the swing
    b. cocked in the backswing and gently uncocked at contact
    c. extended in the backswing and gently rotated at contact
    d. extended in the backswing and remains extended throughout the swing

195. At what height should a short doubles serve be contacted?
    a. knee high
    b. thigh high
    *c. hip high
    d. waist high

196. A player's short serve is too high when crossing the net. How can this best be corrected?
    *a. Swing more horizontally.
    b. Swing easier.
    c. Use less wrist action.
    d. Take less backswing.

197. How can the path of the swing in a short doubles serve be described?
    *a. almost parallel with the floor, slightly low to high
    b. almost parallel with the floor, slightly high to low
    c. semicircular, down and up
    d. diagonal to the floor, low to high

198. Where should the follow-through end in a doubles short serve?
    a. over the player's right shoulder
    b. over the player's left shoulder
    c. over the player's head
    *d. out in the direction of the hit

199. How is the racket gripped in hitting a backhand serve?
    a. with an Eastern grip
    *b. with the ball of the thumb on the back bevel of the racket
    c. with the hand more toward the butt of the racket
    d. with more firmness

200. How should a player stand to hit a backhand serve?

201. How is the shuttle held in hitting a backhand serve?
    a. to the left side of the body with the base pointing at the floor
    b. to the left side of the body with the base pointing at the racket face
    *c. in front of the body with the base pointing at the racket face
    d. in front of the body with the base pointing at the floor

202. What is the position of the racket head in the backswing of a backhand serve?
    *a. in front of the player's body below the waist and wrist
    b. in front of the player's body below the chest and wrist
    c. to the left of the player's body below the waist and wrist
    d. to the left of the player's body below the chest and wrist

Receiving Serve

203. Where is the best height for a player to make contact in returning a serve?
    a. below the waist
    b. above the waist
    c. above the top of the net
    *d. above the head

204. A player is getting ready to return a serve. In the ready position, what is the best position for the head of the racket?
    a. in front of the player about knee high
    b. in front of the player about waist high
    c. to the side of the player about knee high
    *d. in front of the player just above the head

Strategy

205. Which shots can be used effectively from anywhere on the court?
    a. clears and smashes
    b. drops and smashes
    *c. clears and drops
    d. drives and drops

206. In the course of the game, which shot is probably hit most frequently by the winner?
    a. drop
    b. drive
    *c. clear
    d. smash

207. What is the most important shot in badminton for a player to be able to hit?
    a. clear
    *b. serve
    c. drop
    d. smash

208. To what area of the court should a player generally try to avoid hitting a shot?
    a. the front
    *b. the middle
    c. the right
    d. the left

209. What shot should only be used by a player when he or she is in the front three quarters of the court?
    a. clear
    b. overhead drop shot
    c. underhand clear
    *d. smash

210. Which shots can be hit effectively from the backhand side?
    a. clear, smash, and drop
    b. drop, smash, and drive
    *c. clear, drop, and drive
    d. clear, smash, and drive

211. What should a player do after hitting a shot?
    a. Stand and watch to see if it goes in.
    *b. Return to the center of the court.
    c. Rush the net.
    d. Go to where the opponent will probably hit the return.

212. How can the drop shot best be used?
    a. to win points
    *b. to put the opponent on the defensive
    c. to force the opponent to touch the net
    d. to keep the opponent in the front part of the court

213. How can the clear best be used?
    a. to win points
    b. to tire the opponent
    *c. to get the opponent to hit a weak shot
    d. to put the opponent on the defensive

214. What is the most effective shot for scoring when the shuttle is hit to the middle of the court?
    *a. smash
    b. drop
    c. clear
    d. drive

215. What shot generally should be used to return a short, high serve?
    a. drive
    *b. smash
    c. drop
    d. clear

Singles

216. In singles, where should the shuttle be hit most frequently?
    a. directly at the opponent
    *b. away from the opponent
    c. to the front of the court
    d. to the right side of the court

217. In singles, to what area of the court should a player try to hit shots to set up a winning shot?
    a. the front of the court
    b. the sides of the court
    c. the middle of the court
    *d. the back of the court

218. In singles, a player wishes to put his or her opponent on the defensive. What shot should be used?
    a. clear
    b. high, deep serve
    *c. drop
    d. driven serve

219. Which is the best strategy in playing singles?
    a. hit the shuttle upward whenever possible
    b. hit all clears to the center of the opponent's court
    *c. hit a high, deep clear when in doubt as to what to hit
    d. smash any shot the opponent hits upward

220. Shots aimed to which corner of the court will most probably draw the weakest return from the opponent in singles?
    a. front and right
    b. front and left
    c. back and right
    *d. back and left

221. What percentage of shots should a player try to hit to the opponent's backhand in singles?
    a. less than 10%
    b. 10 to 25%
    *c. 50 to 75%
    d. 90 to 100%

222. What is the most frequently used effective pattern of play in singles?
    *a. clear, drop, clear, drop
    b. drop, smash, drop, smash
    c. clear, smash, clear, smash
    d. clear, smash, drop, drive

223. What shot should be used to return an effective long singles serve?
    a. smash down the line
    *b. overhead drop shot down the line
    c. forehand clear crosscourt
    d. smash down the middle

224. Which is the best strategy for playing singles?
    a. Hit mostly smashes.
    b. Hit the shuttle high and hard.
    c. Hit the shuttle down the center.
    *d. Hit clears to the opponent's backhand.

225. What serve is considered the basic serve for singles play?
    a. low to the front of the service court
    b. low to the front and near the sideline of the service court
    *c. high to the back of the service court
    d. driven to the back and near the center line of the service court

226. Why is the long service used in singles play?
    *a. because the receiver is more likely to hit a weak return from deep in the court
    b. because it gives the server time to get ready for the return
    c. because a change-of-pace serve is needed to keep an opponent guessing
    d. because the receiver is limited to the clear in choice of returns

227. Which square in the diagram shows the correct location of the home base position for a singles player? [Refer to Diagram 6.]
    *b.

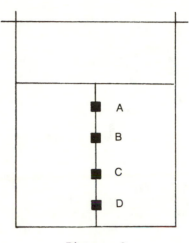

Diagram 6

228. In singles, what would be the most desirable return for a player to make from the back of the court if the opponent is moving to the net?
    a. drive
    b. drop
    *c. clear
    d. smash

229. When receiving a serve in the right court in singles, where should the player stand? [Refer to Diagram 7.]
    *b.

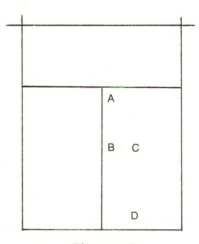

Diagram 7

230. When receiving a serve in the left court in singles, where should the player stand? [Refer to Diagram 8.]
    *c.

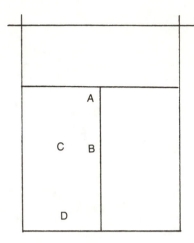

Diagram 8

231. When serving in the right court in singles, where should the player stand? [Refer to Diagram 7, Question 229.]
    *b.

232. When serving in the left court in singles, where should the player stand? [Refer to Diagram 8, Question 230.]
    *b.

233. Why should a player use a short serve in singles?
    a. because it puts the receiver on the defensive
    b. because the return is more likely to be set up for a smash
    c. because the receiver is limited to fewer choices of returns
    *d. because a change-of-pace serve is needed to keep an opponent guessing

234. The diagram shows different court positions. Players A and B are playing singles. Player A, standing at f, clears to 7. What is the best return for Player B to make? [Refer to Diagram 9.]
    *a. drop to b
    b. smash to c
    c. clear to i
    d. clear to h

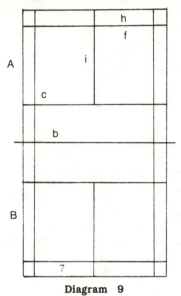

Diagram 9

235. The diagram shows different court positions. Players A and B are playing singles. Player A is serving from the left court. The serve is hit to 9. What is the best return for Player B to make? [Refer to Diagram 10.]
    a. smash to d
    *b. smash to c
    c. drop to e
    d. clear to f

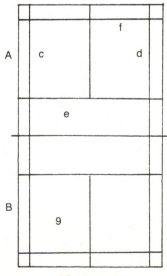

Diagram 10

Doubles

236. In men's and women's doubles, which system of doubles play is most frequently used by tournament players?
    a. parallel
    b. up-and-back
    c. diagonal
    *d. combination

237. What is the basic serve used in doubles?
    a. high and deep to the sidelines
    b. high and deep to the backhand side of the service court
    *c. short and low to the center line
    d. short and low to the sidelines

238. South is receiving the serve in the right-hand court at C. What is North's best service choice? [Refer to Diagram 11.]
    a. short serve to 1
    b. short serve to 2
    *c. driven serve to 3
    d. high serve to 4

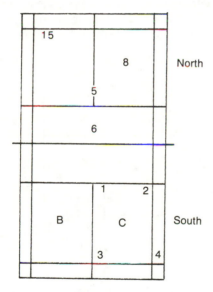

Diagram 11

Doubles-Parallel

239. In playing a parallel system of doubles, where should the server stand when serving from the right court? [Refer to Diagram 12.]
    *a.

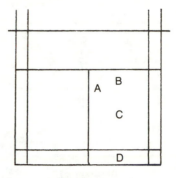

Diagram 12

240. In playing a parallel system of doubles, where should the server stand when serving from the left court? [Refer to Diagram 13.]
    *c.

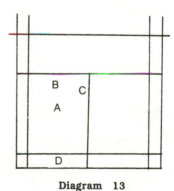

Diagram 13

241. In playing a parallel system of doubles, where should the server's partner stand when the serve is being made from the right court? [Refer to Diagram 14.]
    *d.

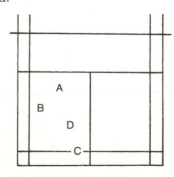

Diagram 14

242. A team is playing the parallel system of doubles. Which dotted line in the diagram shows how the court is divided? [Refer to Diagram 15.]
    *b.

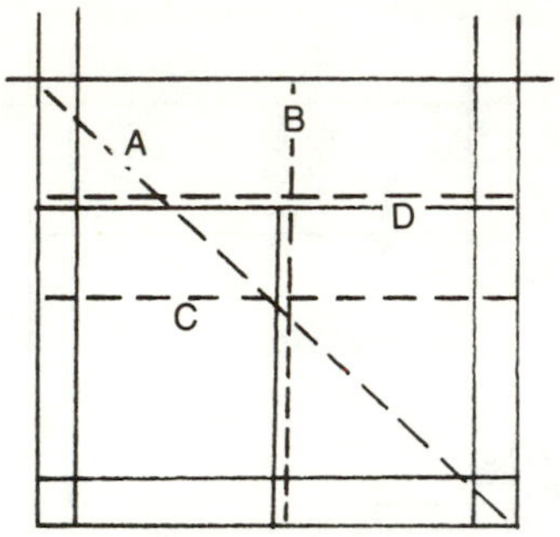

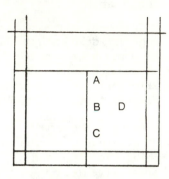

Diagram 15

243. In women's doubles, the serving team is playing a parallel system. Where is the best place to aim most serves?
    a. deep to the opponent's forehand
    *b. deep to the opponent's backhand
    c. short to the center line
    d. short to the side line

244. South is playing a parallel system of doubles at B and C. North hits a clear to 3. What is South's best return? [Refer to Diagram 11, Question 238.]
    a. B smashes to 8
    *b. B drops to 6
    c. C clears to 15
    d. C smashes to 5

245. In playing the parallel positions, who should hit the shots down the middle of the court?
    a. the player who hit the previous shot
    b. the player who did *not* hit the previous shot
    c. the best player
    *d. the player whose forehand is to the middle

Doubles-Up-and-Back

246. The team is using the up-and-back system of doubles. Where should the back player stand when serving from the right-hand court? [Refer to Diagram 16.]
    *b.

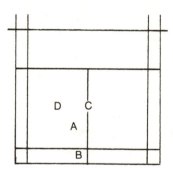

Diagram 16

247. The team is playing an up-and-back system of doubles. The up player is serving from the right-hand court. Where should the partner of the server stand? [Refer to Diagram 17.]
    *c.

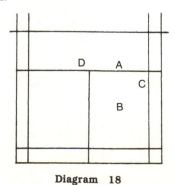

Diagram 17

248. The team is playing an up-and-back system of doubles. The back player is serving from the left-hand court. Where should the partner of the server stand? [Refer to Diagram 18.]
    *d.

Diagram 18

249. A team is playing the up-and-back system of doubles. Which dotted line in the diagram shows how the court is divided? [Refer to Diagram 19.]

 *d.

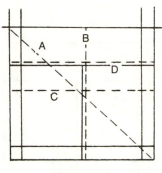

Diagram 19

250. The receiving team is playing an up-and-back system of doubles. The up player is receiving the serve in the right-hand court. What position should he or she take? [Refer to Diagram 20.]

 *a.

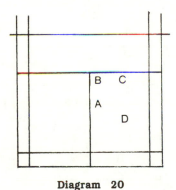

Diagram 20

251. The receiving team is playing an up-and-back system of doubles. The back player is receiving the serve in the left-hand court. What position should the up player take? [Refer to Diagram 21.]

 *c.

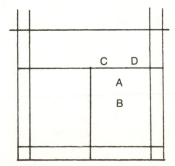

Diagram 21

252. The serving team is playing an up-and-back system of doubles. Where is the best place to aim most serves?
 a. deep to the opponent's forehand
 b. deep to the opponent's backhand
 *c. short to the center line
 d. short to the sideline

253. North is playing an up-and-back system of doubles. South receives a clear at X. What is South's best return? [Refer to Diagram 22.]
 a. clear to 11
 b. smash to 4
 c. clear to 14
 *d. smash to 7

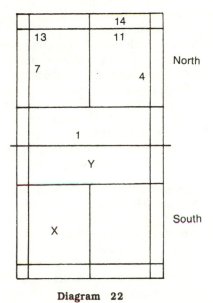

Diagram 22

254. North is playing an up-and-back system of doubles. South receives a drop shot at Y. What is South's best return? [Refer to Diagram 22, Question 253.]
 a. net shot to 1
 *b. attacking clear to 14
 c. defensive clear to 13
 d. drive to 4

255. Where is the best area to aim most shots if the opposing team is playing an up-and-back system of doubles?
 a. deep to the back of the court
 b. short to the front of the court
 *c. midcourt to the sidelines
 d. deep to the sidelines

256. When a team is playing an up-and-back system of doubles, what shot should it use more often than it would in other situations?
    a. clear
    b. smash
    c. drop
    *d. drive

257. If a team is playing an up-and-back system of doubles, what is its basic strategy?
    *a. hit the shuttle downward as often as possible
    b. hit the shuttle to the back of the court mostly
    c. hit the shuttle hit and deep as often as possible
    d. hit the shuttle using a variety of shots

Doubles-Combination

258. A team is playing the combination system of doubles. The team is put on the defensive. What positions should these players take?
    a. stay in the same place
    *b. parallel
    c. up and back with player in the right court going up
    d. up and back with player in the left court going up

259. A team is playing the combination system of doubles. The opposing team hits a short clear to the center of the court. What positions should these players take?
    a. stay in the same place
    b. parallel
    *c. up and back with player in the right court going up
    d. up and back with player in the left court going up

260. The serving team is playing a combination system of doubles. Where is the best place to aim most serves?
    a. deep to the opponent's forehand
    b. deep to the opponent's backhand
    *c. short to the center line
    d. short to the side line

261. The serving team is playing a combination system of doubles. Where should the server stand when serving from the right-hand court? [Refer to Diagram 23.]
    *b.

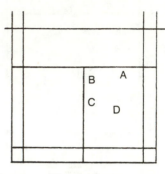

Diagram 23

262. The serving team is playing a combination system of doubles. Where should the server's partner stand when the service is from the right-hand court? [Refer to Diagram 24.]
    *c.

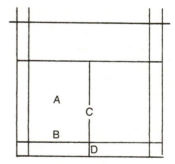

Diagram 24

263. The receiving team is playing a combination system of doubles. Where should the receiver's partner stand when the serve is to the left-hand court? [Refer to Diagram 25.]
    *b.

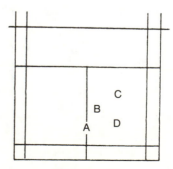

Diagram 25

264. Which best describes a team using a combination system of doubles?
    a. The team plays up and back when serving and parallel when receiving.
    b. The team plays parallel when serving and up and back when receiving.
    *c. The team plays up and back when on offense and parallel when on defense.
    d. The team hits a great variety of shots.

265. Players A and B are playing a combination system of doubles. They are in a defensive position. Player A hits a smash. What positions should they take now?
    a. stay as they are
    b. move to side by side
    c. move to up and back with A moving up
    *d. move to up and back with B moving up

266. Players A and B are playing a combination system of doubles. They are in a defensive position. Player A hits a drop shot. What positions should they take now?
    a. stay as they are
    b. move to up and back with A moving up
    *c. move to up and back with B moving up
    d. move to side by side

267. Players A and B are playing a combination system of doubles. They are in an offensive position. Player A hits a clear. What positions should they take now?
    a. stay as they are
    *b. move to side by side
    c. move to up and back with A moving up
    d. move to up and back with B moving up

268. Players A and B are playing a combination system of doubles. A serves a short, low serve from the right-hand court. What positions should they take?
    *a. up and back with A going up
    b. up and back with B going up
    c. side by side with A on the right side
    d. side by side with B on the right side

269. Players A and B are playing a combination system of doubles. A serves a high, deep serve from the right-hand court. What positions should they take?
    a. up and back with A going up
    b. up and back with B going up
    *c. side by side with A on the right side
    d. side by side with B on the right side

Mixed Doubles

270. In mixed doubles, which system of doubles play is most frequently used?
    a. parallel
    *b. up and back
    c. diagonal
    d. combination

Suggested Readings

Bloss, M.V. (1980). *Badminton* (4th ed.). Dubuque, IA: William C. Brown.

Friedrich, J., & Rutledge, A. (1969). *Beginning badminton*. Belmont, CA: Wadsworth.

Hashman, J., & Jones, C.M. (1977). *Beginning badminton*. New York: Arco.

National Association of Girls' and Women's Sports. (1984). *Badminton/squash/racquetball guide: May 1984-May 1986*. Reston, VA: AAHPERD.

Pelton, B.C. (1971). *Badminton*. Englewood Cliffs, NJ: Prentice-Hall.

Poole, J. (1982). *Badminton* (3rd ed.). Glenview, IL: Scott Foresman.

Basketball

Lynne C. Agee, Consultant

This collection of test questions on basketball is divided into four content areas:

- General Knowledge
- Techniques
- Strategy
- Rules

Some of the questions or the answer key may need to be revised to match the level of skill, the intellectual maturity of the players, or the intent of the teacher. Questions should reflect the unit as taught, including the teacher's philosophy about the proper execution of skills and strategy of the game.

The instructor can make appropriate selections from a sizeable pool of questions, adding to, revising, and updating the collection as changes in techniques and rules occur.

General Knowledge

History	1 to 13
Safety and Conditioning	14 to 27
Equipment and Facilities	28 to 31
Miscellaneous	32 to 33

History

1. Who won the gold medal in men's basketball in the 1984 Olympics?
   - a. China
   - *b. United States
   - c. Russia
   - d. Yugoslavia

2. Who created the game of basketball?
   - a. John Wooden
   - *b. James Naismith
   - c. Wilt Chamberlain
   - d. Bob Cousy

3. What was the original type of basket used for basketball?
   - *a. peach basket
   - b. sewing basket
   - c. fish basket
   - d. trash basket

4. In which city was the game of basketball developed?
   - a. Milwaukee, Wisconsin
   - b. Boston, Massachusetts
   - *c. Springfield, Massachusetts
   - d. Baltimore, Maryland

5. In what country did basketball originate?
   - a. England
   - *b. United States
   - c. Russia
   - d. Canada

6. In what year was basketball created?
   - a. 1869
   - b. 1874
   - *c. 1891
   - d. 1899

7. Which of the college men's postseason basketball tournaments are the oldest?
   - a. NCAA and NBA
   - b. NCAA and ABA
   - *c. NCAA and NIT
   - d. NIT and NAIA

Lynne C. Agee is Women's Basketball Coach at the University of North Carolina at Greensboro, Greensboro, North Carolina.

8. What was the primary reason for the invention of basketball?
   - *a. to provide an indoor activity for the winter
   - b. to provide a sport less strenuous than football
   - c. to provide a sport for women
   - d. to provide a fitness activity

9. Who is the all-time leading scorer in NBA history?
   - a. John Havlicek
   - b. Bill Russell
   - *c. Wilt Chamberlain
   - d. Kareem Abdul-Jabbar

10. Which coach has won the most NCAA men's championships?
    - a. Dean Smith
    - b. Al McGuire
    - c. Adolph Rupp
    - *d. John Wooden

11. Approximately when did the game for girls and women change from six to five players?
    - *a. late 1960s
    - b. early 1970s
    - c. late 1970s
    - d. early 1980's

12. When did women's basketball first appear as an official Olympic sport?
    - a. 1972
    - *b. 1976
    - c. 1980
    - d. 1984

13. Which organization affiliated with Kodak to establish all-American women collegiate basketball players?
    - *a. Women's Basketball Coaches Association
    - b. Women's Professional Basketball League
    - c. National Association of Intercollegiate Athletics
    - d. National Basketball Association

Safety and Conditioning

Safety

14. Which is the safest way to catch a hard pass?
    - a. Absorb the shock with both hands held stiffly.
    - b. Bat the ball to the floor to avoid injury.
    - c. Relax the hands and absorb the shock with the fingers.
    - *d. "Give" with the ball and catch it with relaxed hands.

15. In which situation would a coach be most likely to remove a player from the game?
    - a. when the player misses a few shots
    - *b. when the player is injured
    - c. when the player seems fatigued
    - d. when the player is out of position

16. What provides the best prevention against injury in basketball?
    - a. philosophy of the coach
    - b. qualifications of the trainer
    - *c. conditioning program
    - d. lack of physical contact

17. What is a good way to make sure the feet are in good shape?
    - a. Wear heavy shoes.
    - *b. Wear two pairs of socks.
    - c. Wear shoes that are slightly large.
    - d. Wear socks that are loose.

Conditioning

18. For what factor of physical fitness should the rebounder specifically condition?
    - a. agility
    - b. flexibility
    - c. endurance
    - *d. strength

19. Which aspect of physical conditioning does quick stops, jumping, and sprinting develop?
    - a. endurance
    - b. flexibility
    - *c. agility
    - d. power

20. What is the most common injury to players early in the season?
    - *a. blisters
    - b. shin splints
    - c. sprains
    - d. strains

21. Which is the best conditioning technique during the basketball season?
    - a. weight training
    - *b. short explosive runs
    - c. long distance runs
    - d. diet control

22. What conditioning technique is most beneficial during the off-season and preseason?
    - *a. weight training
    - b. short explosive runs
    - c. long distance runs
    - d. diet control

23. Which form of circulorespiratory conditioning gives the best results for in-season training?
    a. sustained, long distance running
    *b. fast, short, repetitive running
    c. sustained, repetitive running
    d. sit-ups

24. Which form of muscular conditioning gives the best results for basketball?
    a. isometric exercises
    *b. isotonic exercises
    c. isokinetic exercises
    d. endurance running

25. Which exercise or drill tends to improve quickness and speed?
    a. running laps
    b. lay-up drill
    c. squat jumps
    *d. line drills

26. Prior to the game, everyone on the team must prepare physically for the competitive event. What is the best method to use?
    *a. game-like drills
    b. vigorous calisthenics
    c. running at top speed around the gym 10 times
    d. running sprints back and forth on the court

27. Basketball players need the ability to adapt and function when sustained demands are imposed on their bodies. What is this ability called?
    a. strength
    b. power
    c. agility
    *d. endurance

Equipment and Facilities

Equipment

28. How does sitting on a basketball affect its performance?
    a. makes it softer and thus easier to catch
    *b. makes it less round and thus changes its flight
    c. makes it smoother and thus easier to shoot
    d. has no effect on the ball's performance

29. What is the reason for girls and women playing with a ball that is 1 inch smaller in diameter than the regular sized ball?
    a. more turnovers
    b. increase range for shooting
    *c. better ball control
    d. more steals

30. What is the most practical reason for wearing rubber-soled shoes while playing basketball?
    a. to keep feet and socks clean
    *b. to aid in stopping and starting quickly
    c. to prevent the toes from being stepped on during play
    d. to provide a soft cushion for the feet

Facilities

31. The backboards and rims in your opponent's gymnasium are stiffer than the baskets in your gymnasium. How should you position yourself on your opponent's court when rebounding as compared to your position on your home court?
    a. closer to the sideline
    b. closer to the midline
    c. closer to the basket
    *d. farther from the basket

Miscellaneous

Tournament

32. Eight teams are playing in a tournament. How many games will the champions play?
    a. two
    *b. three
    c. four
    d. five

Behavior

33. The official calls traveling on a player. What should the player do?
    a. Put the ball on the floor and walk away from it.
    *b. Toss the ball to the official.
    c. Throw the ball to the nearest opponent.
    d. Let the ball roll down the court.

Techniques

Shooting

Free Throw

34. Which shot provides one of the easiest scoring opportunities in the game?
    - a. lay-up
    - b. set shot
    - *c. free throw
    - d. jump shot

35. What type of spin is on a well-executed foul shot?
    - *a. backspin
    - b. forward spin
    - c. side spin
    - d. no spin

36. What is the most important element to develop in shooting foul shots?
    - *a. concentration
    - b. consistency
    - c. confidence
    - d. control

37. What should a player do before shooting a free throw?
    - a. Check the score clock to see what the score is.
    - b. See that teammates are properly placed on the lane.
    - c. Check to see where the player is who is assigned to guard him or her.
    - *d. Relax and concentrate on the shot.

Lay-Up

38. What is the best shot for a player to use when close to the basket and driving the lane on a fast break?
    - *a. lay-up
    - b. set shot
    - c. fall-away shot
    - d. jump shot

39. Which is the easiest shot when *not* being guarded?
    - a. jump shot
    - b. set shot
    - *c. lay-up
    - d. hook shot

40. Which movement would be most efficient when shooting a lay-up from the right side of the basket?
    - *a. Take off from the left foot, shoot with right hand.
    - b. Take off from right foot, shoot with right hand.
    - c. Take off from left foot, shoot with both hands.
    - d. Stand on both feet, shoot with right hand.

41. What is the point of aim when shooting a right-hand lay-up?
    - a. the middle of the backboard about 3 inches above the rim
    - b. slightly to the right of the basket
    - c. the middle of the backboard about 2 inches left of center
    - *d. slightly above and to the right of the basket

42. Which shot is most likely taken on the run?
    - a. hook shot
    - *b. lay-up
    - c. jump shot
    - d. two-hand overhead shot

43. You are shooting from the left side of the basket. With which hand should you shoot and from which leg should you leave the floor?
    - *a. left hand, right leg
    - b. left hand, left leg
    - c. right hand, right leg
    - d. right hand, left leg

44. Why is it difficult for players to shoot a lay-up from the left side of the goal?
    - *a. Most players are right-handed.
    - b. Most players are left-handed.
    - c. Most of the playing action is on the right side of the goal.
    - d. The point of aim is more difficult to judge on the left side.

45. What is the main purpose of the knee lift, long last stride, and backward lean in a driving lay-up?
    *a. to transfer forward momentum to upward momentum
    b. to transfer speed of the body to force on the ball
    c. to transfer dribbling force to shooting force
    d. to transfer running momentum to shooting momentum

Set Shot

46. What is the key to accuracy in making the one-hand set shot?
    *a. keeping the elbow close to the body
    b. extending the shooting arm quickly
    c. directing the ball with the fingers and wrist
    d. supporting the ball with the nonshooting hand

47. What is the main advantage of the two-hand set shot over the one-hand set shot?
    a. ensures better balance
    *b. provides weaker player with greater shooting range
    c. enables quicker release
    d. provides better ball protection

Jump Shot

48. When should a player shoot when performing a jump shot?
    a. jump and shoot at the same time
    b. jump and shoot on the way down
    *c. jump, then shoot at the top of the jump
    d. jump and shoot as soon as the feet leave the floor

49. Which body part is essential to keep in line with the basket when shooting a jump shot?
    *a. shoulders
    b. hips
    c. legs
    d. arms

50. A player is getting a jump shot blocked consistently. What adjustment should be made when releasing the shot?
    *a. shoot sooner
    b. wait until more time is available
    c. fake the opposing player
    d. force the shot

51. Which shot is the most difficult to guard?
    a. lay-up
    b. one-hand set shot
    *c. jump shot
    d. set shot

Hook Shot

52. From which position would a right-handed player execute a hook shot?
    a. with the back to the basket
    *b. with the left shoulder to the basket
    c. with the right shoulder to the basket
    d. with the chest toward the basket

Tip-In

53. What play on the ball is most efficient for executing a tip-in?
    a. batting
    b. slapping
    *c. pushing
    d. knocking

Banked

54. From which position on the floor, indicated in the diagram, should the shot be banked off the backboard? [Refer to Diagram 1.]
    *d.

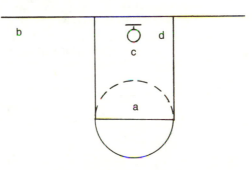

Diagram 1

Arc

55. What is the major difference between shooting with a high arc and with a low arc?
    *a. The high arc requires more strength but has greater accuracy.
    b. The high arc requires less strength but has greater accuracy.
    c. The high arc requires more strength but has less accuracy.
    d. The high arc requires less strength but has less accuracy.

56. What is the purpose of arching shots toward the basket?
    a. so the ball will go a longer distance
    b. so the players will have time to get into rebounding positions
    *c. so the ball will be dropping into the basket
    d. so there will be less chance of a guard blocking the shot

57. Which factor determines the actual trajectory of a shot?
    a. velocity
    *b. angle of release
    c. direction
    d. spin

Aim

58. What is the essential fundamental for taking any shot?
    a. height off the floor
    *b. aim of the shot
    c. timing of the shot
    d. follow-through

59. At what area above the rim should a player aim the shot when shooting from the position indicated in the diagram? [Refer to Diagram 2.]
    *a. at the backboard, toward the shooting side
    b. at the backboard, directly over the basket
    c. at the backboard, 2 feet above and over the center of the basket
    d. at the backboard, 2 feet above and directly over the rim of the basket

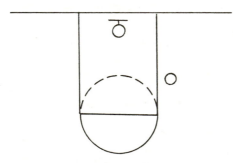

Diagram 2

Percentage

60. What is a good percentage shot?
    a. one taken outside the lane area
    *b. one taken close to the basket
    c. one taken from the corner
    d. one taken from 20 feet

61. Which shot is the lowest percentage shot?
    a. free throw
    *b. an open jump shot from the corner
    c. lay-up
    d. jump shot from the top of the key

Rim

62. From which position on the court would a shot most likely hit the rim or be an air ball?
    a. from a position under the basket
    b. from directly in front of the basket
    *c. from the side of the basket
    d. from a position diagonally away from the basket

Touch

63. Which factor does *not* contribute to the softness of the shot?
    a. arc of the ball
    b. spin on the ball
    c. follow-through
    *d. length of the shot

Passing

General

64. What is the most significant factor to stress when executing a pass?
    *a. stepping into the pass
    b. handling the ball with the fingers
    c. keeping the elbows in
    d. using a wrist snap upon release

65. Which practice is *not* a general rule for successful passing?
    a. hitting the receiver at about waist level
    b. reducing the speed of the pass to a player moving toward you
    *c. lobbing the pass to closely guarded players
    d. passing ahead of a moving player

Bounce Pass

66. An opponent has arms up on defense. The offensive player may use what type of pass most effectively?
    a. two-hand overhead pass
    b. chest pass
    c. lob pass
    *d. bounce pass

67. Which pass is used most to penetrate a zone defense?
    a. chest pass
    b. lob pass
    *c. bounce pass
    d. baseball pass

68. What is the most essential factor in the execution of an accurate bounce pass?
    a. lowering the release point
    b. rotating the wrists inward
    *c. having correct point of contact on the floor
    d. initiating the pass with a stride

69. When should a bounce pass be used?
    * a. when a short pass is needed in the key area
    b. when the opponent is close to the receiver
    c. when the opponent is close to the passer
    d. when a fast pass is necessary

70. Where should a bounce pass contact the floor?
    a. halfway between the passer and receiver
    b. closer to the passer than the receiver
    * c. closer to the receiver than the passer
    d. about a foot from the receiver

One-Hand Overhead

71. Which pass is most often used as a long pass?
    a. two-hand chest pass
    b. two-hand overhead pass
    c. one-hand jump pass
    * d. one-hand overhead pass

Two-Hand Overhead

72. Which pass is effective for attacking a zone defense?
    a. bounce pass
    b. chest pass
    * c. two-hand overhead pass
    d. one-hand overhead pass

Crosscourt Pass

73. Which pass is *not* a high percentage pass to complete?
    a. short, quick pass
    * b. crosscourt pass
    c. two-hand chest pass
    d. two-hand bounce pass

Chest Pass

74. What action should be evident in the follow-through of the chest pass?
    a. The wrists are fully flexed.
    * b. The palms of the hands are facing downward.
    c. The thumbs are pointing upward.
    d. The knees are bent.

75. Which pass gives the best control and therefore is the most accurate?
    * a. chest pass
    b. one-hand overhead
    c. hook pass
    d. crosscourt pass

Hook Pass

76. Which pass could be used most effectively to clear the ball from a congested area?
    a. two-hand chest pass
    b. one-hand pass
    c. bounce pass
    * d. hook pass

77. When would a hook pass most likely be used?
    a. when the passer is not closely guarded
    * b. when the passer is closely guarded
    c. when the ball is held in one hand
    d. when the passer jumps into the air

Intercept

78. Which pass is the hardest to intercept?
    a. lob pass
    b. chest pass
    * c. short pass
    d. long pass

Turnover

79. What is an example of a turnover?
    a. the defensive team getting the ball after its opponent scores
    b. a defensive player getting a rebound
    * c. a defensive player intercepting a pass
    d. a player missing a foul shot

Pass Receiver

80. Who would be the best pass receiver?
    * a. an open teammate moving to the ball
    b. a teammate moving toward the ball
    c. a teammate moving away from the ball but toward the basket
    d. a teammate moving between the opponent and the ball

Error

81. What is the most common error in receiving a pass?
    a. standing too far from the passer
    * b. standing still to wait for the pass
    c. failing to square up to receive the pass
    d. moving too fast to control the pass

When to Pass

82. When should a pass be made to a teammate?
    * a. when the teammate is looking at the passer
    b. when the teammate is running toward the basket
    c. when the teammate and the opponents least expect the pass
    d. when the teammate has gotten away from the opponent

Dribbling

General Dribble

83. Which part of the body is *least* important in dribbling?
    - a. the wrist
    - b. the fingers
    - c. the forearm
    - *d. the palm

84. A player immediately dribbles the ball after catching a pass. Is this good or bad technique and why?
    - *a. Bad; it wastes a dribble and eliminates the drive as an option.
    - b. Bad; it slows the game and makes it hard for teammates to time their moves.
    - c. Good; it gives time to look over the defense to decide on the best play.
    - d. Good; the player can evade an opponent while teammates move into positions to receive a pass.

85. Which factor is essential when dribbling?
    - a. Keep the eyes on the ball.
    - b. Go as fast as possible.
    - *c. Maintain control.
    - d. Bounce the ball waist high.

Poor Dribble

86. What is the best defense against a guard who dribbles poorly with the left hand?
    - *a. Overplay the right-hand dribble and force him or her to the left.
    - b. Overplay the left-hand dribble and force him or her to the right.
    - c. Play directly in front and force him or her to either side.
    - d. Play directly in front and force him or her to the right.

Speed Dribble

87. Where should the ball be in relation to the body when using a speed dribble?
    - *a. in front
    - b. slightly toward the dribbling-hand side
    - c. in front and slightly toward the non-dribbling hand side
    - d. to the side when closely guarded

Focus

88. Where should a player's eyes be focused when dribbling?
    - a. downward in order to control the ball
    - b. downward in order to see the feet of a defensive player
    - *c. forward in order to pass to a teammate
    - d. forward in order to alternate hands quickly

Error

89. Which technique is *not* an error in dribbling technique?
    - a. slapping the ball with the palm
    - b. watching the ball
    - c. using a high vertical bounce
    - *d. pushing the ball with firm forearm

Use

90. When is the best time for the offensive player to use a dribble?
    - a. when a pass is not possible
    - b. when the defensive player has committed him- or herself
    - *c. when the path to the goal is clear
    - d. when the defensive player is guarding loosely

Reverse

91. Which dribble is most advanced?
    - a. change-of-pace dribble
    - b. crossover dribble
    - c. speed dribble
    - *d. reverse dribble

92. Which dribble should be used to change directions when closely guarded?
    - a. crossover
    - *b. reverse
    - c. control
    - d. backward

Footwork

General Footwork

93. What is the basic footwork used in playing defense?
    - a. hopping step
    - *b. sliding step
    - c. crossover step
    - d. backward step

94. Which ability does *not* refer to good footwork?
    - a. starting and stopping quickly
    - *b. jumping and landing on two feet
    - c. using various faking techniques
    - d. changing direction and pivoting

95. What is the best weight location for stopping and changing directions?
    - *a. The weight is low and back.
    - b. The weight is high and forward.
    - c. The weight is toward the right side.
    - d. The weight is toward the left side.

Agility

96. Which ability is needed most to dodge an opponent?
    a. ability to dribble with either hand
    b. ability to run faster than opponent
    *c. ability to change directions quickly
    d. ability to jump high in relation to own height

Parallel Stop

97. Why would a parallel stop be more advantageous than a stride stop?
    a. The player can stop faster.
    *b. The player can use either foot as the pivot foot.
    c. The player can have better balance.
    d. The player can use only the right foot as the pivot foot.

Defense

98. What is the key to moving the feet on defense?
    a. using a sliding step
    b. balancing the weight with the feet at shoulder width
    c. shifting the weight to the heels
    *d. having the weight on the balls of the feet

Drive Right

99. What should a guard do when the dribbler drives to the guard's right?
    a. Step sideways with the right foot.
    b. Slide sideways with the left foot.
    *c. Step backward with the right foot.
    d. Step forward with the left foot.

Adjustment

100. An offensive player cuts to the right. What foot adjustment should the defensive player make? [Refer to Diagram 3.]
    *b.

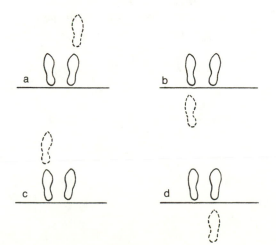

Diagram 3

Pivot

101. What is the main purpose of the pivot?
    a. to turn into a position to rebound
    b. to position the ball in readiness to shoot
    *c. to move the ball away from a defensive opponent
    d. to get into position to pass the ball

102. Which statement concerning the pivot is *untrue*?
    a. It is a method of evading an opponent.
    b. It is an offensive maneuver.
    c. It is a defensive maneuver.
    *d. It is executed by lifting both feet from the floor.

103. What is a good offensive maneuver when catching a pass before taking a shot or driving toward the basket?
    *a. turn and face the basket
    b. fake to the right and left
    c. jab and go
    d. rocker step

Movement

104. Why is movement without the ball important?
    *a. frees the player to get the ball
    b. worries the defense
    c. makes the game faster
    d. makes the player harder to defend

Jumping

Position

105. How should a player stand when preparing for a jump ball?
    a. facing opponent, arms down at sides
    b. facing opponent, one arm raised
    *c. side to opponent, arms down at sides
    d. side to opponent, one arm raised

Blocking

106. When does the defender jump to block a shot?
    *a. slightly after the shooter leaves the floor
    b. slightly before the shooter leaves the floor
    c. at the same time the shooter leaves the floor
    d. at the same time the shooter releases the ball

Rebounding

107. What is the key to successful rebounding?
    a. jumping
    b. arm and hand position
    c. not fouling
    *d. positioning

108. To what does boxing out refer?
    a. offensive rebounding
    *b. defensive rebounding
    c. defensive double-teaming
    d. defensive zone pattern

109. What is the defensive player's main concern when blocking out?
    *a. the movements of the opponents
    b. the flight of the ball
    c. the location in the lane
    d. the time remaining on the clock

110. What should be the utmost thought in a player's mind when getting an offensive rebound close to the basket?
    a. passing to an open teammate
    *b. taking the shot
    c. dribbling away from the goal
    d. tipping the ball in the basket

111. Which factor should a player be aware of when rebounding?
    a. The force with which the ball is thrown.
    b. The force with which the ball hits the backboard.
    c. The angle at which the ball is released.
    *d. The angle at which the ball rebounds from the backboard.

112. What is a basic prerequisite for an effective fast break?
    a. must have good dribblers and ball handlers
    *b. must have good defensive rebounders
    c. must have two quick guards
    d. must have at least one tall player

Faking

113. What technique should a player with the ball use to open passing lanes, get free for a shot, or drive toward the basket?
    a. jab step
    b. reverse cut
    *c. fake
    d. pivot

114. In a man-to-man situation, how can a defensive player best avoid a faking move by the opponent?
    a. Stay between the opponent and the basket.
    b. Look directly into the opponent's eyes.
    *c. Focus on the opponent's waist.
    d. Tap the opponent constantly to check position.

115. Which is the most serious mistake a defensive player makes in responding to a fake?
    a. shifting the weight too late
    *b. shifting too far in the direction of the fake
    c. ignoring the fake
    d. watching the eyes

Cutting

116. Cutting requires a player to be adept at all of these skills *except* one. Which skill is the exception?
    *a. jumping
    b. stopping
    c. faking
    d. changing direction quickly

117. Why is the cut one of the best offensive techniques?
    *a. The cut is the hardest move to defend against.
    b. The majority of players can cut easily.
    c. The pass to the cutting player must be too well timed to be effective.
    d. Guards often stand so close together that a cut will not work.

118. Which statement concerning an offensive cut is usually true?
    *a. taken into a space
    b. taken around a player
    c. taken toward the sideline
    d. taken away from the basket

119. Which diagram shows the most efficient path to take when making a cut toward the basket off the high post player? [Refer to Diagram 4.]
    *d.

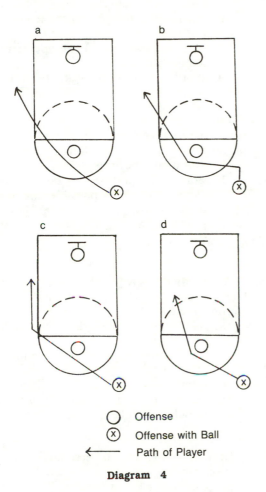

○   Offense

ⓧ   Offense with Ball

←   Path of Player

Diagram 4

120. What is the action of the player without the ball who moves into an open lane to receive a pass?
    a. faking
    b. feinting
    c. driving
    *d. cutting

Out-of-Bounds

121. A player has the ball awarded out-of-bounds at the end line. What should the player do?
    *a. Signal for a set play.
    b. Put the ball in play as soon as possible.
    c. Wait 4 seconds before passing the ball.
    d. Execute a bounce pass.

Setting Pick

122. What should you do after you set a pick?
    *a. Roll toward the goal, keeping the defensive player at your back.
    b. Roll away from the goal, keeping the defensive player at your back.
    c. Keep the defensive player from moving.
    d. Wait to receive the pass.

Give-and-Go

123. Which statement best describes a give-and-go?
    a. setting a screen against a teammate's guard and roll
    *b. passing to a teammate followed by a cut and a return pass
    c. moving into an open space hoping to receive the ball
    d. moving in one direction followed by a quick move in another direction

Guarding

General

124. What is the correct position to guard an opponent?
    a. Face opponent rather than the ball.
    b. Keep feet close together for better stability.
    c. Keep center of gravity high for quick changes of direction.
    *d. Stay between the opponent and the basket.

125. Which defensive positioning is recommended for man-to-man play near the goal?
    *a. ball-you-man triangle
    b. ball-you-basket straight line
    c. ball-you-man straight line
    d. ball-you-teammate triangle

Overplaying

126. What technique have you used if you force the player to dribble with the weaker hand?
    *a. overplaying
    b. ball-you-man triangle
    c. boxing out
    d. squaring up

Point Guard

127. What is the most important skill for the point guard to have?
    a. passing
    *b. dribbling
    c. shooting
    d. guarding

Position

128. When should the defensive player *not* guard the offensive player closely?
    a. when the defense is pressing the offense
    b. when the offensive player is shooting
    c. when the offensive player is driving for the basket
    *d. when the offensive player has the ball out of the scoring zone

129. A forward has the ball, following a dribble. How far away would the forward like to be guarded?
    *a. One foot or less; the opponent will be more likely to foul.
    b. One foot or less; the opponent will be easier to fake.
    c. Two to 3 feet; the opponent will be less likely to intercept.
    d. Two to 3 feet; the opponent will be less likely to foul.

130. Which position is best for a defensive player to maintain?
    a. guarding as close to the opponent as possible
    *b. staying between the opponent and the basket
    c. playing the opponent slightly to the right
    d. playing the opponent slightly to the left

Fast Break

131. Where should a lone defensive player take position in a two-on-one fast break situation?
    a. toward the sideline to force the two players into the middle of the court
    *b. far enough away to make the open player look guarded
    c. at half court and wait for a teammate to help out
    d. as close as possible to the dribbler until the ball is passed

Getting Back

132. The offensive player has beaten the defensive player. What is the most effective way for the defensive player to get back into position?
    a. Run straight forward and pick up the offensive player.
    *b. Run on a diagonal and pick up the offensive player.
    c. Chase the offensive player from behind, trying to knock the ball away.
    d. Yell ''switch'' and hope a teammate picks up the player.

Distract

133. What is the most acceptable way to distract an opponent?
    a. wave a hand in the face so the opponent cannot see the basket clearly
    b. talk to keep the opponent from concentrating
    *c. be in the path when the opponent is ready to move
    d. shout as the opponent attempts to shoot

Long Shot

134. How should the defensive player guard a player who might shoot a long shot?
    a. Jump into the air with both hands up.
    b. Hold both hands out to the side.
    c. Move as close as possible and wave both hands.
    *d. Hold one hand up and one hand out to the side.

Stealing

135. Which method of stealing the ball from a dribbler is most likely to be successful without committing a foul?
    a. Reach with both hands as the dribbler passes by.
    b. Tap the ball with a downward motion of one hand.
    c. Punch at the ball with one hand.
    *d. Move one hand in an upward motion to deflect the ball.

Switching

136. Who should call a switch between two defensive players?
    a. the player being picked
    *b. the player who is guarding the player who sets the pick
    c. the coach of the team on defense
    d. the closest defensive player who is not involved in the play

Strategy

General

Purpose

137. What is the main objective of basketball?
     a. to shoot more times than the opponent
     b. to make more foul shots than the opponent
     *c. to score more points than the opponent
     d. to commit fewer fouls than the opponent

Force Action

138. Which team is most likely to force the action the last few seconds of the game?
     a. the defense, if ahead
     *b. the offense, if tied
     c. the defense, if tied
     d. the offense, if ahead

Foul Trouble

139. A player has just been called for a third foul, and the game is still in the first half. What would be the best thing to do?
     a. leave the player in
     b. switch to a different defense
     *c. take the player out until the second half
     d. take the player out for 30 seconds to cool down

Jump Ball

140. Where should player X try to tap the ball in this jump situation? [Refer to Diagram 5.]
     *d.

Point Guard

141. Which duty is *not* one of the main roles of the point guard?
     *a. rebounding
     b. dribbling
     c. setting up offense
     d. setting up defense

142. What is the major role of the point guard?
     a. to rebound
     b. to score
     c. to dribble through any type of press
     *d. to set up the offense

Defense

143. What are 2-1-2, 1-3-1, 3-2, and man-to-man?
     a. offenses
     *b. defenses
     c. fast break plays
     d. advanced plays

144. What is the greatest asset of a good defensive player?
     *a. great desire
     b. great speed
     c. good coaching
     d. exceptional height

145. What is the main advantage of a good defensive over a good offensive team?
     a. A good defensive team doesn't need to score much.
     *b. A good defensive team will hold up game after game.
     c. A good defensive team will have greater dedication.
     d. A good defensive team will break up the timing of the offense.

146. Sometimes combination defenses must be used to combat certain offenses. Which defense is *not* a combination?
     a. triangle and two defense
     b. diamond and one defense
     *c. 1-2-2 defense
     d. match-up zone defense

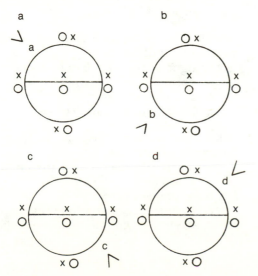

Diagram 5

Guarding Areas

147. Which diagram shows the area where the defense should concentrate guarding efforts? [Refer to Diagram 6.]
    *d.

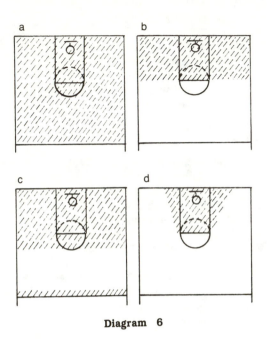

a   b

c   d

Diagram 6

Communicate

148. Which factor is most important in defense?
    a. ability to switch
    b. ability to cover the entire shooting area
    *c. ability to communicate with each other
    d. ability to intercept passes

Changing Defense

149. What is the most important factor in deciding to switch to a different defense?
    a. condition of the players
    b. size of the team
    *c. maneuvers of the offense
    d. experience of the team

Hot Streak

150. The opposing team gets in a hot streak and scores three or four baskets in succession. What is the best plan of action to take?
    a. Try to make up the points by hurrying the offense.
    b. Continue playing calmly making up the points gradually.
    *c. Call a time-out when your team gets the ball.
    d. Try pressing defensively to keep the opponents from scoring as easily.

Trapping

151. What is trapping?
    *a. double-teaming the player with the ball
    b. playing a pick and roll
    c. using a split-the-post pattern
    d. breaking a man-to-man press

152. What is a defensive maneuver in which two defenders attempt to stop an offensive dribbler from making a successful pass?
    a. screen
    *b. trap
    c. switch
    d. press

Terminology

153. Which phrase does *not* identify a type of defense?
    a. 2-1-2
    b. man-to-man
    c. 3-2
    *d. give-and-go

Helpside

154. What is the meaning of *helpside*?
    a. The dribbler uses the weak hand.
    *b. the opposite side of the floor from where the ball is
    c. a player who is shorter and weaker than you
    d. more players on the other side of the court

Man-to-Man

155. What advantage does the man-to-man style of defense have over the zone defense?
    *a. more effective against long set shots
    b. involves less movement on part of the guards
    c. results in more open style of play
    d. results in fewer fouls and more interceptions

156. Which defense should a team use against a poor ball-handling team?
    *a. tight or pressing man-to-man defense
    b. normal man-to-man defense
    c. 2-3 zone
    d. loose man-to-man defense

157. What is the main purpose of a sagging man-to-man defense?
    a. to force the opposition into committing mistakes
    *b. to prevent easy scores
    c. to guard against strong set shooters
    d. to slow down the opponent's offense

158. What is the major strength of a man-to-man defense?
     a. It increases fast breaks.
     b. It is effective against screens.
     c. It tires out opponents by spreading their offense.
     *d. It matches opponents with ability, speed, or size.

159. Which diagram shows a man-to-man defense? [Refer to Diagram 7.]
     *a.

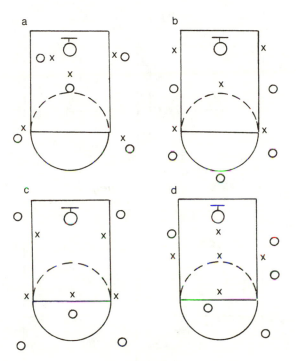

Diagram 7

160. What is the main purpose of the full-court, man-to-man press?
     *a. to cause the other team to commit violations
     b. to cause the other team to become fatigued
     c. to cause the other team to commit more fouls
     d. to cause the other team to become rattled

Zone

161. What is the basic purpose of a zone defense?
     *a. to prevent the offensive team from scoring easy shots
     b. to prevent the offensive team from using the fast break
     c. to prevent the defensive team from tiring easily
     d. to prevent the defensive team from committing many fouls

162. What is the main *disadvantage* of a zone defense?
     *a. too hard to stop a good outside shooting team
     b. too slow to get set up
     c. too hard to catch up when behind in the score
     d. too hard to penetrate

163. What is the main point that distinguishes a zone defense from a man-to-man defense?
     a. The man-to-man defense is more difficult to learn.
     b. The zone defense is more effective against slow players.
     c. The man-to-man defense requires running with an opponent.
     *d. The zone defense requires a player to guard an area.

Box-and-One

164. A team has one outstanding shooter. Which defense would be most effective?
     *a. box-and-one
     b. man-to-man
     c. 3-2
     d. give-and-go

2-3 Zone

165. What is the best defense to play against a team with obvious superior height and talent?
     a. man-to-man
     b. half-court zone trap
     *c. 2-3 zone
     d. It doesn't matter.

166. The main concern in playing a particular team is to keep its two players who are excellent shooters from the corners. What zone defense would be most effective?
     a. 1-3-1 zone
     *b. 2-3 zone
     c. 1-2-2 zone
     d. 2-1-2 shifting zone

167. Which diagram illustrates a 2-3 zone defense? [Refer to Diagram 8.]
    *a.

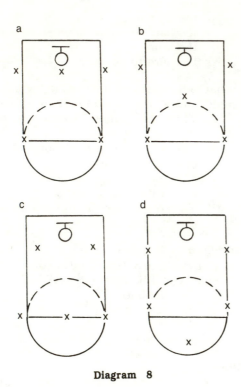

Diagram 8

Zone Press

168. Which diagram shows a 1-2-1-1 full-court zone press? [Refer to Diagram 9.]
    *d.

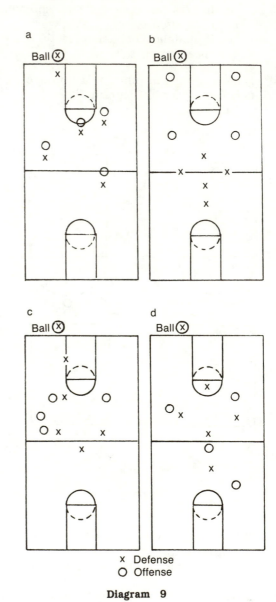

x Defense
O Offense

Diagram 9

169. What is the most effective way to break a zone press?
    a. Dribble through the zone press.
  *b. Pass to keep the zone press moving.
    c. Wait for the defense to make the first move.
    d. Throw a long pass to the other end of the court.

2-1-2 Zone

170. A 2-1-2 zone defense is used to combat what type of attack?
     *a. 2-1-2 offensive set
     b. 3-2 offensive set
     c. 1-3-1 offensive set
     d. 1-2-2 offensive set

171. Which diagram shows a 2-1-2 zone defense? [Refer to Diagram 10.]
     *b.

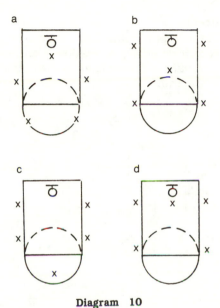

Diagram   10

1-3-1 Zone

172. What is the major weakness of the 1-3-1 zone defense?
     a. stopping the alley-oop
     *b. cutting off baseline shots
     c. stopping a big opponent
     d. stopping a drive down the middle

3-2 Zone

173. Which diagram shows the shaded areas that are most vulnerable when using a 3-2 defense? [Refer to Diagram 11.]
     *a.

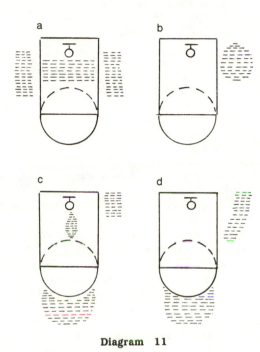

Diagram   11

1-2-2 Zone

174. Which diagram shows a 1-2-2 defense? [Refer to Diagram 12.]
     *c.

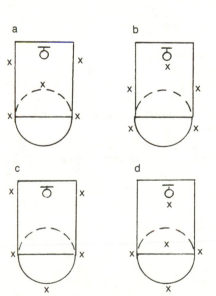

Diagram   12

Out-of-Bounds

175. What defense should be used when the opponents have the ball out-of-bounds underneath their own goal?
    *a. 2-3 zone
    b. man-to-man
    c. full-court press
    d. half-court trap

Rebounding

176. What type of zone defense provides the strongest rebounding formation?
    a. 1-3-1
    b. 1-1-2-1
    *c. 2-1-2
    d. 3-2

177. Which team has the advantage on a rebound and why?
    a. Offensive team; they are moving toward the basket.
    b. Offensive team; they know from where the shot will be taken.
    *c. Defensive team; they are between the opponents and the basket.
    d. Defensive team; they expect the shot to be missed.

178. You know from past experience that the team you are about to play scores many of its baskets on second shots because of good offensive rebounding. What zone defense would aid your team the most in defensive rebounding strength?
    a. 1-3-1 zone
    *b. 2-3 zone
    c. 1-2-2 zone
    d. 3-2 zone

End of Game

179. Team A is behind by four points with 1 minute remaining in the game. Team B has the ball in its own backcourt. What would be the best strategy for Team A to use to get the ball?
    a. Play a 2-1-2 zone defense.
    *b. Go into a pressing man-to-man defense.
    c. Play a sinking man-to-man defense.
    d. Wait for the offense to make an error.

180. There are only 20 seconds left in the game. The defensive team is two points ahead. The opposing team has the ball. What should the defensive team do?
    a. Immediately foul the player with the ball.
    *b. Avoid fouling any member of the opposing team.
    c. Immediately foul only the poorest shooter on the opposing team.
    d. Spread out and let the opposing team attempt a shot.

Fast Break

181. The offensive team has a 3-on-2 fast break. Which defensive formation is the most appropriate to defend against the break? [Refer to Diagram 13.]
    *a.

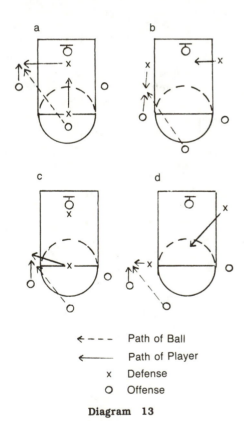

    ← - - -   Path of Ball
    ←——   Path of Player
    x   Defense
    o   Offense

Diagram 13

Offense

182. Which team skill is most characteristic of a good offensive basketball team?
    a. a team that can score on a fast break
    b. a team that is patient on offense and waits for openings to occur
    c. a team that has centers who can make high percentage shots
    *d. a team that has balanced scoring

183. What is the first thing a team should do when it has the ball on offense?
    a. Drive for the basket to score.
    b. Set up a play and score.
    c. Pass to the pivot player and let him or her shoot.
    *d. Determine what type of defense the opponent is using.

184. What is the primary goal of players on offense?
    a. dribble
    b. rebound
    *c. score
    d. pass

185. What is the most important phase of offensive basketball a coach must develop in the team?
    a. jagging movements
    *b. finding open player
    c. options
    d. floor balance

Free-Lance
186. What is free-lance play?
    a. a defensive maneuver to change guarding responsibilities
    b. a defensive move to gain an advantage over the offense
    c. a method of performing certain shots
    *d. an offense that is unstructured

Selecting
187. What is the biggest factor determining a team's offensive strategy?
    a. height of the offensive team
    b. height of the opponent
    *c. defense of the opponent
    d. offense of the opponent

188. What is the most important point for the coach to consider when determining the offensive style for the team?
    a. Choose the offense that the coach knows best.
    *b. Choose the offense that is best suited to the personnel.
    c. Choose the offense that the players know the most about.
    d. Choose the offense that is the most complex.

Outlet Area
189. Where is the designated outlet area?
    a. the midcourt jump circle
    *b. the foul line extended out to the sidelines
    c. directly under the offensive basket
    d. anywhere a player is open

Assist
190. What has occurred when a player is credited with an assist?
    a. The player replaces a teammate in the lineup.
    *b. The player makes a pass that leads directly to a basket.
    c. The player helps a teammate on defense.
    d. The player rebounds a missed shot and scores a basket.

Point Guard
191. While bringing the ball downcourt, the point guard sees that the defense has gone man-to-man. What should the point guard do?
    a. Keep playing and ignore the change in defense.
    *b. Yell to teammates that the defense has changed.
    c. Tell the coach what has happened.
    d. Get the referee's attention to call a time-out.

192. Why is penetration of the point guard a desirable offensive strategy?
    a. to spread the defense
    *b. to draw the defense
    c. to deceive the defense
    d. to force a change in defense

Beating Press
193. Which method of beating a full-court zone press is the most consistent?
    a. making crosscourt lob passes
    b. making the best dribbler take it through the middle
    *c. using short, quick passes
    d. doing none of the above

Sagging Defense
194. The defense is sagging. Which is the best action for the offensive player to take when passing?
    a. stay in position and pass quickly
    b. fake and pass quickly
    *c. dribble toward the defender and pass around this player
    d. dribble to the side of the defender and pass

Overload

195. Which diagram shows the players in situations where the offense will most likely beat the defense? [Refer to Diagram 14.]

    *d.

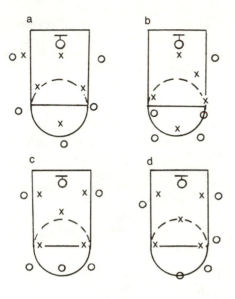

    x   Defense
    O   Offense

Diagram 14

Double-Team

196. The defense has set up a weak double-team situation. What is the most desirable response of the offensive player?

    a. fake and draw a foul
    b. hold the ball for 5 seconds
    *c. step through the double team
    d. bounce the ball off the defender's leg

Breaking Zone

197. What is the best pass to move the ball around a zone defense?

    a. chest pass
    *b. overhead pass
    c. baseball pass
    d. bounce pass

Offensive Set

198. The opposing team sets up in a 1-3-1 defense. What offensive set should the team use?

    a. man-to-man
    *b. 2-3
    c. 3-2
    d. 1-2-1

199. Which statement is especially true about the 3-2 offensive set?

    a. The point must be able to analyze the opponent's defense.
    b. The posts are the short and quick players.
    c. The posts set up the offense most of the time.
    *d. The wing players are good perimeter shooters.

200. Which diagram shows the best offensive set to use against a 2-1-2 zone? [Refer to Diagram 15.]

    *b.

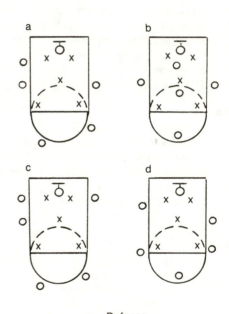

    x   Defense
    O   Offense

Diagram 15

Screen

201. In which case would a screen be *inappropriate*?

    *a. to block a player's view of the basket
    b. to prevent a defensive player from guarding an offensive player
    c. to give a forward an unguarded shot at the goal
    d. to give a player a chance to receive a pass unguarded

202. A screen is *not* used for which purpose?
    *a. guarding an opponent with the ball who has slipped past a teammate
    b. providing a teammate with the ball the opportunity to shoot
    c. freeing a teammate without the ball for a pass
    d. going behind a teammate to receive a pass

Drive

203. A blue player has a one-on-one situation driving in against a red player under the basket. Which shot could be used most effectively to score?
    a. hook shot
    b. jump shot
    c. set shot
    *d. lay-up

204. Player O_4 has to come out to the wing position in order to receive a pass from O_2. What is the *poorest* option for O_4? [Refer to Diagram 16.]
    a. pass to O_1 cutting
    b. pass to O_2 cutting
    *c. pass to O_3 stationary
    d. pass to O_5 stationary

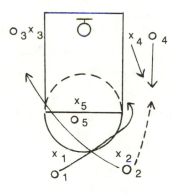

x	Defense
○	Offense
←	Path of Player
←---	Path of Ball

Diagram 16

Backdoor Cut

205. When is a backdoor cut generally used?
    *a. when overplayed in a man-to-man defense
    b. against a 2-3 zone defense
    c. when facing a sagging man-to-man defense
    d. against any defense

Fast Break

206. What is the best way for a team to attack a defense?
    a. overloading three offensive players onto one side of the court
    b. moving the ball around the perimeter quickly with short, crisp passes
    *c. fast breaking before the defense has time to become organized
    d. splitting patterns in which offensive players cut in or across the zone defense

207. What play by the offensive team would move them rapidly from the back court to the front court in an attempt to gain an offensive advantage?
    *a. fast break
    b. give-and-go
    c. bounce pass
    d. full-court press

208. A team begins to fast break while one of its forwards rebounds the ball. What should the forward do after rebounding the ball?
    a. Hold the ball to see who is free.
    b. Dribble the ball to a guard.
    c. Dribble the ball all the way downcourt.
    *d. Make an outlet pass.

209. Who is the key person in a successful fast break?
    *a. the rebounder who clears the ball out
    b. the person who makes the shot
    c. the person who takes the ball downcourt
    d. the person who passes the ball to the shooter

210. You are in the middle of the court with the ball and leading a 3-on-2 fast break. What is the best thing to do after you make a pass to either side?
    a. Continue down the middle of the lane for a rebound.
    b. Stop where you are.
    c. Move to the opposite side of the floor to give your teammate room.
    *d. Move to the corner of the foul lane on the side to which you passed.

Out-of-Bounds

211. A blue guard, throwing the ball in from out-of-bounds near the defensive basket, throws a long, high pass to a blue forward waiting near the center line. Is this usually good strategy? Why or why not?
    a. Yes, it is the quickest way to get the ball upcourt.
    b. Yes, the opposing players have less chance to intercept.
    c. No, a long pass is harder to catch.
    *d. No, a long pass is more easily intercepted.

Rebounding

212. An offensive player rebounds the ball near the basket. What is the best option?
    a. Dribble away from the basket.
    b. Pass to a teammate.
    *c. Shoot.
    d. Set up a screen.

End of Game

213. There are 15 seconds left in the first half. What is the best strategy for the team with possession of the ball?
    a. Shoot quickly so there may be a chance for another shot.
    b. Try to draw a foul.
    c. Keep the ball away from the other team until halftime.
    *d. Hold the ball for one shot.

Rules

Note. Four sets of rules are currently in use: federation rules for high school competition, Men's Collegiate NCAA rules, Women's Collegiate NCAA rules, and International Rules. The key to some of the rules questions may need to be changed to fit the set of rules being taught. The key also may need to be changed to coincide with any rule changes.

General

Purpose

214. What is the purpose of the rules?
    *a. to control the game
    b. to provide fair play
    c. to give offensive players a chance to score
    d. to build breaks into the game

Game Ball

215. Who is responsible for providing the official game ball?
    a. referee
    *b. home team
    c. visiting team
    d. the conference

Starting Second Half

216. How does the second half of a men's college basketball game begin?
    a. with a jump ball
    b. with the team ahead receiving the ball
    c. with the team behind receiving the ball
    *d. with the direction of the ball possession arrow determining which team gets the ball

Forfeit

217. In which situation is the game forfeited?
    a. A team commits five team fouls.
    b. A team is 10 minutes late to start the game.
    c. One team fails to be ready within 30 seconds after a time-out.
    *d. A team refuses to play after being instructed to do so.

Coaching Box

218. What is the main purpose of the coaching box?
     a. to help players on the court identify the coach on the sideline
     b. to restrict the mobility of the coach
     c. to give officials easier access to coaches
     *d. to clear area around the scorer's table

Officials

Scorer

219. To whom does a substitute report before entering the game?
     *a. scorer
     b. referee
     c. timer
     d. umpire

220. Whose responsibility is it to notify the officials when a player should be disqualified?
     a. the official timer
     *b. the official scorer
     c. the assistant scorer
     d. the assistant timer

Timer

221. When does the timer stop the clock?
     a. when the official gives the hand signal
     b. when the scorer's buzz alerts the official of a substitution
     *c. when the official's whistle blows
     d. when two opposing players collide attempting to get a loose ball

Dimensions

Free Throw Shot

222. What is the distance of the free throw shot?
     a. 10 feet
     *b. 15 feet
     c. 18 feet
     d. 20 feet

Height of Goal

223. How high above the floor is the goal?
     a. 8 feet
     b. 8½ feet
     *c. 10 feet
     d. 12 feet

Width of Lane

224. How wide is the free throw lane?
     a. 10 feet
     *b. 12 feet
     c. 14 feet
     d. 15 feet

Diameter of Basket

225. What is the diameter of the basket?
     a. 15 inches
     b. 16 inches
     c. 17 inches
     *d. 18 inches

Time Designations

Dead Ball

226. The ball is temporarily out of play. What is this called?
     *a. dead ball
     b. jump ball
     c. time-out
     d. delay of game

Shooting Clock

227. What is the main purpose of the 30-second/45-second clock?
     *a. to discourage stalling
     b. to speed up defensive play
     c. to conform with international rules
     d. to develop high-caliber players

Clock

228. When does the clock *not* stop during the game?
     a. when a player shoots a free throw
     *b. when a goal has been made
     c. when a player commits a foul
     d. when a substitute enters the game

Held Ball

229. A player has stopped the dribble. How long can the same player hold the ball when closely guarded?
     a. 3 seconds
     *b. 5 seconds
     c. 10 seconds
     d. indefinitely

Lane

230. How many seconds may a defensive player stay in the lane?
     a. 3 seconds
     b. 5 seconds
     c. 10 seconds
     *d. no time limit

Half Court

231. A team must get the ball across the half-court line in how many seconds?
     *a. 10 seconds
     b. 8 seconds
     c. 5 seconds
     d. 3 seconds

Tie Game

232. Time expires with the score tied. What happens?
    a. The game ends.
    *b. The game goes into overtime.
    c. The first team that scores wins.
    d. The game is replayed.

Inbounds

233. How much time does a player have to pass the ball inbounds?
    a. 3 seconds
    *b. 5 seconds
    c. 10 seconds
    d. an indefinite amount of time

Time-Out

234. How many time-outs can each team have during a regulation game?
    a. three
    b. four
    *c. five
    d. six

235. How many additional time-outs are allowed each team during an overtime period?
    *a. one
    b. two
    c. three
    d. four

Substitution

Entry

236. When may a substitute enter the game?
    a. when the ball is in play
    b. during the first period only
    c. whenever requested by the coach
    *d. when the ball is dead

Procedure

237. What procedure should a player follow when entering the game as a substitute?
    *a. report to scorer, enter the game when the official signals
    b. report to scorer, enter the game on the first dead ball
    c. report to scorer, enter the game as soon as his or her team gets the ball
    d. report to scorer, enter the game as soon as a teammate comes out

Illegal Entry

238. A substitute enters the game before summoned by the official. What happens?
    *a. The game is stopped and a technical foul is assessed.
    b. The game is stopped to allow the player to enter.
    c. The game continues and the player goes back to the bench.
    d. The game continues and a teammate goes to the bench.

Player Numbers

239. What is considered a legal number on a player's jersey?
    *a. Legal numbers must be two digits from 0 to 5.
    b. Legal numbers must be two digits over 5.
    c. Legal numbers must be single digits.
    d. Legal numbers must not include zeros.

Out-of-Bounds

Clock

240. When does the clock begin on an out-of-bounds play?
    a. when the ball is handed to the player to throw it in bounds
    *b. when the ball is touched by a player on the court
    c. when the ball crosses the boundary line
    d. when the player throwing the ball in releases it

Location

241. From what location on the floor is the ball put into play after a field goal?
    *a. from anywhere along the end line
    b. from a specific spot on the end line
    c. from anywhere on the sideline
    d. from a specific spot on the sideline

Throw-In

242. A player making a throw-in from under the basket hits the back of the backboard and the ball rebounds into the court. Who gains possession of the ball?
    a. Ball is awarded to opponents out-of-bounds at the sideline.
    *b. Ball continues in play.
    c. Ball is awarded to opponents out-of-bounds at the end line.
    d. Ball is awarded to the same player and the end line play is repeated.

243. A player from the red team is going out of bounds with the ball. In an attempt to save it, the player throws the ball back in and it hits a blue player. The ball then rebounds out-of-bounds. Whose ball is it?
    a. jump ball
    b. official's decision
    *c. red team
    d. blue team

Jump Ball

Number of Taps
244. How many times may a player tap the ball on a jump ball?
    a. once
    *b. twice
    c. three times
    d. any number of times

Ruling
245. In which jump ball situation is a violation called on the jumper?
    a. An opposing player touches the ball first, then the jumper's teammate controls it.
    *b. A teammate enters the circle before the tap.
    c. The opposing jumper controls the ball following a bounce.
    d. The opposing jumper taps the ball twice, and a teammate gains control.

Double Foul
246. When is a jump ball always taken in the center circle?
    a. on a tie ball
    b. after a double violation
    *c. to begin an overtime
    d. after two opposing players hit the ball out-of-bounds

Violations

General
247. Which play is legal?
    *a. An offensive player fumbles the ball and proceeds to dribble it.
    b. A defensive player kicks the ball in an attempt to block a pass.
    c. An offensive player steps over the sideline when passing the ball inbounds.
    d. A player involved in a jump ball situation taps the ball and then catches it.

248. Which action is a violation of the rules?
    a. lifting the pivot foot when shooting
    b. jumping to catch the ball, landing on both feet, then taking one step
    c. using either foot as a pivot foot after catching the ball while standing still
    *d. pivoting on the forward foot after a two-step stop

Kicking
249. Which way of advancing the ball is *illegal*?
    a. throwing
    b. rolling
    *c. kicking
    d. batting

Penalty
250. What is the penalty for a violation?
    a. one free throw
    b. two free throws
    c. jump ball
    *d. opponent's ball out-of-bounds

Backcourt
251. You dribble the ball past the half-court line and get trapped. You then throw the ball to another player on the other side of the half-court line. What happens?
    a. Nothing happens.
    b. A traveling violation is called.
    c. A charging foul is called.
    *d. A backcourt violation is called.

Traveling
252. A player makes a two-step stop after receiving a pass. What is the player permitted to do?
    a. pivot in any direction on the front foot
    *b. pivot in any direction on the back foot
    c. pivot in any direction on either foot
    d. pivot in any direction on both feet

253. How many steps can a player take without traveling?
    a. 1
    b. 1½
    *c. 2
    d. 2½

254. Which player has traveled with the ball?
     a. Player A fumbles the ball attempting to receive a pass, catches the ball after it bounces, fakes, and dribbles around an opponent.
     b. Player B catches the ball with the right foot on the floor, steps on the left foot, and uses it as the pivot foot.
   *c. Player C uses a two-step stop while receiving a pass, and then uses the forward foot as the pivot foot.
     d. Player D jumps to catch a rebound, lands on both feet simultaneously, and takes a second step with the right foot.

3-Second
255. What is a 3-second violation?
     a. An offensive player is guarded closely for 3 seconds.
     b. A team is 3 seconds late coming out of the huddle.
   *c. An offensive player stays inside the free throw lane more than 3 seconds without the ball.
     d. A defensive player stays inside the free throw lane for 3 seconds.

256. The blue team has possession of the ball in its front court. Which situation illustrates a 3-second lane violation?
     a. A blue forward stays under the basket for 3 seconds. Not receiving a pass, the player steps out of the lane and then back into it.
     b. A blue forward runs into the lane, receives a pass, and begins to drive for the basket.
   *c. A blue forward moves into the lane to wait for a pass. This player receives the ball after 4 seconds and shoots immediately.
     d. The red players stand in the lane and will not let the blue players get close to the basket.

Fouls

General
257. Which action is *not* a foul?
     a. accidentally tripping an opponent
     b. holding an opponent who is trying to move into the lane
   *c. remaining too long in the lane
     d. pulling an opponent off balance while trying to tie the ball

258. Which action is a foul?
     a. hitting the ball out-of-bounds
     b. holding the ball more than 5 seconds when guarded closely
     c. using two steps to stop after completing a dribble
   *d. holding both arms out to the sides to guard a player

Number of Foul Shots
259. What is the maximum number of foul shots for a single foul?
     a. one
   *b. two
     c. three
     d. four

260. Two free throw shots are awarded for all but one of these situations. Which one?
     a. A player is fouled while shooting and misses the shot.
   *b. A player is fouled while shooting and makes the shot.
     c. A player commits an intentional foul.
     d. A player commits an unsportsmanlike foul.

Disqualify
261. How many fouls disqualify a player from the game?
     a. one technical foul
     b. two disqualifying fouls
     c. four personal fouls
   *d. five personal fouls

Player Control
262. What happens after a player-control foul?
     a. The player fouled shoots one free throw.
     b. The player fouled shoots two free throws.
   *c. The player who fouled loses possession of the ball.
     d. There is a jump ball between the two players involved.

Double Foul
263. Player A and Player B are on opposing teams and foul simultaneously. What is the ruling?
     a. Player A shoots a free throw.
   *b. Ball is awarded to team indicated by alternating possession arrow.
     c. Player A and Player B shoot free throws.
     d. There is a jump ball between any two opposing players.

Charging

264. Player A is cutting for the basket and runs into Player B who has established a guarding position. What is the official's decision?
    a. blocking on Player A
    b. blocking on Player B
    c. charging on Player B
    *d. charging on Player A

265. Charging should be called on which of these players?
    a. a forward who pushes the guard out of the way
    *b. a forward who falls into the guard after shooting
    c. a guard who runs into the path of an opponent
    d. a player who bumps into an opponent while trying to catch a pass

Bonus

266. What is the bonus situation?
    *a. Make the first free throw, shoot a second.
    b. Get two tries to make one free throw.
    c. Get two free throws.
    d. Shoot a free throw, then take the ball out on the sideline.

267. On which team foul does the opposition go into the bonus situation?
    a. fourth
    b. fifth
    c. sixth
    *d. seventh

Shooting

Dunk

268. What call is made by the official after a player dunks the ball?
    a. violation
    b. technical foul
    *c. basket is good
    d. goaltending

Goaltending

269. What is goaltending?
    a. touching the net when the ball is in the air
    b. giving up the ball without getting a shot
    c. touching the backboard while the ball is in flight
    *d. affecting the downward flight of the ball

270. An offensive player shoots the ball and the defensive player blocks the shot. What must occur for the ruling to be defensive goaltending?
    a. The defensive player has blocked the shot after the ball has left the offensive player's hands.
    b. The defensive player has touched the ball during its upward flight toward the basket.
    c. The defensive player has blocked the ball out-of-bounds after it has left the offensive player's hands.
    *d. The defensive player has touched the ball during its downward flight to the basket.

Foul While Shooting

271. A foul is committed against a player who is able to make the goal in spite of the foul. Does the shot count?
    a. No, a free throw is awarded.
    b. No, a jump ball is called.
    *c. Yes, a free throw is awarded.
    d. Yes, the other team takes the ball out-of-bounds.

Free Throw

272. Team B is shooting a free throw. A member of Team B steps into the lane too soon. What is the ruling?
    a. No basket; the ball is given to the opponents at the end line.
    b. If the free throw is missed, the ball continues in play.
    *c. No basket; the ball is given to the opponents at the sideline.
    d. If the free throw is missed, it is repeated.

273. A player shoots a free throw, which hits the backboard and rebounds to a member of the opposing team. What should the official call?
    a. No call; play continues.
    b. Violation on shooting team; ball is awarded at end line.
    *c. Violation on shooting team; ball is awarded at sideline.
    d. Foul is called on shooter.

274. Which lineup shows the correct positions of the players for a free throw? [Refer to Diagram 17.]

    *a.

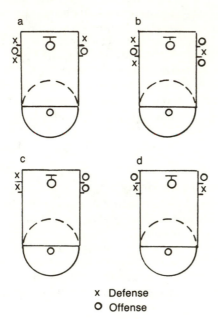

    x Defense
    o Offense

Diagram 17

Lay-Up

275. You are shooting a lay-up. How many steps are allowed after you stop dribbling?

    a. 0
    b. 1
    c. 1½
    *d. 2

Shot at End of Game

276. A basket is shot and made at the end of the game. When does it count?

    *a. when the ball has left the shooter's hand before the buzzer
    b. when the shooter has already started motion to shoot
    c. when the ball is being tapped after the buzzer
    d. when a personal foul is committed after the buzzer and a basket scores

Rim

277. Why are players allowed to grasp the rim?

    a. to reduce the number of broken backboards
    b. to allow a follow-through on the dunk
    c. to minimize goaltending
    *d. to prevent injuries

Game Statistics

278. What was the team's score at the half and at the end of the game? [Refer to Diagram 18.]

    *a. 44-79
    b. 25-45
    c. 16-75
    d. 50-90

STAT SHEET

Tot. Foul	No.	Name	S.A.	S.M.	%	Off. Reb.	Def. Reb.	Def. Steal	Jump Ball	Ball Control Errors I	II	F.T.A.	F.T.M.
I/I	32	Bailey	⊤⊤⊤/III	⊤⊤⊤/I	75	I/	I/I	I/II		b/		I/	I/
I/	22	Woodson	⊤⊤⊤/II	IIII/	33	II/II	IIII/IIII	I/		/dd		II/I	I/
II/II	10	Moon	⊤⊤⊤/I/III	III/	33	II/I	III/III		w/w	/d		I/III	I/II
/I	34	Sliker	⊤⊤⊤/IIII	IIII/III	50	/I	I/	IIII/II		a/b		II/	I/
/III	41	Lotz	⊤⊤⊤/III	II/II	50	I/I	I/III		/w	/c	/a	II/II	II/II
II/	14	Delk	II/⊤⊤⊤	I/⊤⊤⊤	50	/I	I/II	/II	/L	d/d			/II	/I
I/	42	Lynch	I/⊤⊤⊤	/IIII	33	/II	I/III	I/I		/a		/II	/I
Team Totals			75	34	45	14	28	14	3w 1L	10	1	16	11

Key to ball control errors:

I. a. Traveling
    b. Taken away
    c. Fumble
    d. Bad pass

II. a. Off. foul on dribbler

Diagram 18

279. Which player had the most outstanding offensive game in the first half? [Refer to Diagram 18, Question 278.]
    *a. Bailey
    b. Moon
    c. Woodson
    d. Lotz

280. Which statement about the stat chart is correct? [Refer to Diagram 18, Question 278.]
    a. There were no held balls.
    b. There was only one offensive foul.
    *c. The team got one third of the rebounds at their basket.
    d. All of the above statements are correct.

281. Which player proved to be the most aggressive on the team? [Refer to Diagram 18, Question 278.]
    a. Bailey
    *b. Woodson
    c. Sliker
    d. Moon

Suggested Readings

Barnes, M. J. (1972). *Women's basketball*. Boston: Allyn & Bacon.

Bonham, A., & Paye, B. (1984). *Secrets of winning fast break basketball*. West Nyack, NY: Parker.

Harris, D. (1971). *Multiple defenses for winning basketball*. West Nyack, NY: Parker.

National Federation of State High School Associations (1986-87). *Basketball rules book*. Kansas City, MO: Author.

NCAA Men's Basketball Rules (1987). Mission, KS: National Collegiate Athletic Association.

NCAA Women's Basketball Rules (1987). Mission, KS: National Collegiate Athletic Association.

Samaras, B. (1984). *A treasury of winning basketball tips*. West Nyack, NY: Parker.

Smith, D. (1982). *Basketball: Multiple offense and defense*. Englewood Cliffs, NJ: Prentice-Hall.

Warren, W. E. (1983). *Coaching and motivation*. Englewood Cliffs, NJ: Prentice-Hall.

Acknowledgments

Colleagues and students who contributed suggestions and ideas for the Basketball test questions are: L. Agee, B. Anderson, P. Andrews, M. Bodie, N. Boetel, K. Brown, S. Crank, S. Davis, D. Dilday, D. Groff, E. Holcomb, S. Hudson, B. Jaynes, S. Jones, M. J. Lentz, S. Linder, S. McCutcheon, C. Morgan, D. Packard, H. Pearce, C. Peters, J. Reynolds, S. Rudy, M. Saintsing, R. Scott, J. Shelton, B. Smith, L. Tamblyn, S. Tarlton, K. Thomas, B. J. Thompson, M. Tolley, T. Watson, T. Whiteley, R. Wiggs, M. Wilhelm, B. Winfrey, and L. Wood.

Bowling

Joan Hensley, Consultant

This collection of test questions on bowling is divided into six content areas:

- History
- Etiquette
- Terminology
- Rules and Scoring
- Technique
- Strategy

Questions in the Techniques and Strategy areas relate to bowling either a straight ball or a hook ball because these are the throws recommended by most bowling experts. The Strategy area deals primarily with spot bowling because this is the aim method most experts recommend.

Many of the questions assume that the bowler is right-handed. If these questions are used, this should be noted in the test directions or questions and answers should be revised to accommodate left-handed bowlers.

Bowling

History	1 to 13
Etiquette	14 to 19
Terminology	20 to 50
Rules and Scoring	51 to 105
Technique	106 to 171
Strategy	172 to 253

History

Origin

1. Where was the earliest game similar to the modern game of bowling played?
   - a. Greece
   - *b. Egypt
   - c. England
   - d. China

2. When was the earliest known game of bowling developed?
   - *a. 5200 B.C.
   - b. 52 B.C.
   - c. 1820
   - d. 1901

3. When was bowling introduced into Europe?
   - a. 5200 B.C.
   - *b. 52 B.C.
   - c. 1820
   - d. 1901

4. What was the name of bowling when it was introduced into Europe?
   - a. nine pins
   - b. 10 pins
   - *c. boccie
   - d. kegels

5. Who authored the first famous book on bowling?
   - *a. Pehle
   - b. Martin Luther
   - c. Billy Sixty
   - d. Dick Weber

6. As early as the fourth century, what was the significance of a bowler knocking down all the pins?
   - a. It was a requirement for knighthood.
   - b. It was a way of settling a dispute.
   - *c. It indicated a clean and pure life.
   - d. It determined a village's leader.

Joan Hensley has been an outstanding league and tournament bowler for many years.

7. Who established the nine pin game in Germany?
    a. Pehle
    *b. Martin Luther
    c. Kaiser Wilhelm
    d. Rasputen

8. What was the early game of bowling called in England?
    a. boccie
    b. kegler
    c. lawn bowling
    *d. skittles

9. Why did the Connecticut state legislature prohibit nine pin bowling in the mid-1800s?
    a. Commoners were spending too much time bowling.
    b. It violated religious beliefs.
    c. It was not an American game.
    *d. Gamblers had taken over the sport.

10. When was bowling brought to the United States?
    a. 1620
    b. 1776
    *c. 1820
    d. 1840

11. When were the first rules for 10 pin bowling formed in the U.S.?
    a. 1820
    b. 1840
    *c. 1895
    d. 1901

Organization

12. What is the name of the organization that makes rules for bowling in the United States?
    *a. American Bowling Congress
    b. American Bowling Association
    c. National Bowling Federation
    d. North American Bowling Institute

13. What is the name of the women's bowling organization?
    a. Women's Bowling Congress
    b. Women's American Bowling Association
    c. National Bowling Congress for Women
    *d. Women's International Bowling Congress

Etiquette

14. Which is *not* proper behavior in bowling?
    *a. lofting the ball
    b. observing the foul line
    c. limiting body movements to one's own lane
    d. a little "needling" between turns

15. Which statement describes proper ball use?
    *a. Use your own ball each time.
    b. Use the ball at the end of the rack each time.
    c. Use the ball nearest the ball return each time.
    d. Use the ball most convenient to you each time.

16. Who should bowl first when two adjacent bowlers are ready at the same time?
    *a. The bowler on the right always rolls first.
    b. The bowler on the left always rolls first.
    c. The bowler rolling his or her first ball bowls before the bowler rolling his or her second ball.
    d. The bowler rolling his or her second ball bowls before the bowler rolling his or her first ball.

17. Where should you stand between rolling your first and second ball?
    a. at the ball return
    b. at the end of the approach
    *c. off the approach
    d. behind the foul line

18. Where should refreshments be kept?
    a. at the scoring table
    b. on the bench
    c. in the bowling area
    *d. out of the bowling area

19. When should you put on your bowling shoes?
    a. before you enter the bowling alley
    b. before you enter the bowling area
    *c. before you walk on the lanes
    d. before you roll your first frame

Terminology

Anchor Man

20. Who is the *anchor man* on a team?
    a. the player with the highest average
    b. the player with the lowest average
    c. the first player in the lineup
    *d. the last player in the lineup

Baby Split

21. Which pins are standing in a *baby split*?
    *a. 3 and 10
    b. 5 and 10
    c. 2 and 5
    c. 3 and 7

Backup

22. What is a *backup*?
    a. a substitute player on a team
    b. a second ball
    c. a ball that curves right to left for a right-handed player
    *d. a ball that curves left to right for a right-handed player

Bedposts

23. Which pins are standing in a *bedposts*?
    a. 3 and 10
    b. 2 and 7
    *c. 7 and 10
    d. 6 and 7

Blind

24. What is *blind*?
    a. bowling without looking at the pins
    b. bowling by looking at the diamonds
    c. bowling with a handicap
    *d. bowling one player short on a team

Brooklyn Hit

25. What is a *Brooklyn hit*?
    *a. hit in the pocket on the wrong side of the head pin
    b. hit in the pocket on the correct side of the head pin
    c. heavy hit on the head pin
    d. light hit on the head pin

Channel

26. What is the *channel*?
    a. the lane
    b. the middle of the lane
    c. the path for a strike ball
    *d. the gutter

Creeper

27. What is a *creeper*?
    a. a slow bowler
    b. a slow falling pin
    *c. a very slow rolling ball
    d. a slightly curving roll of a ball

Curve

28. What is a *curve*?
    *a. a ball that curves the same direction as a hook, but more than a hook
    b. a ball that curves the same direction as a hook, but less than a hook
    c. a ball that curves the opposite direction from a hook
    d. a ball that curves only in the last few feet before making contact with the pins

Dead Ball

29. What is a *dead ball*?
    a. a ball rolled into the gutter
    *b. a poorly rolled ball with little action
    c. an old ball that has lost its firmness
    d. a ball that does not curve

Double

30. What is a *double*?
    a. hitting two pins at the same time
    b. hitting a pin that hits a second pin
    *c. making two strikes in succession
    d. making two spares in succession

Fast Lane

31. When is a lane considered to be "fast"?
    a. when the bowler can slide further than usual on the approach
    b. when the ball return sends the ball back quickly
    c. when a hook curves more than usual
    *d. when a hook curves less than usual

Frame

32. What is the part of the scoresheet called where the score is recorded for each player's turn?
    a. box
    *b. frame
    c. line
    d. sheet

Gutterball

33. What is a ball called that goes off the lane before it reaches the pins?
    a. dead ball
    b. leave
    *c. gutterball
    d. miss

Head Pin

34. Which pin is the *head pin*?
    *a. 1
    b. 3
    c. 5
    d. 10

King Pin

35. Which pin is the *king pin*?
    a. 1
    b. 3
    *c. 5
    d. 10

Leave

36. What is a *leave*?
    a. a ball that goes off the lane before reaching the pins
    b. the pins standing after both balls are rolled in a frame
    *c. the pins standing after one ball is rolled in a frame
    d. a ball that rolls through without touching any pins in a split

Line

37. When has a player bowled a *line*?
    a. when he or she has bowled three games
    b. when he or she has bowled two strikes in a row
    c. when he or she has bowled two spares in a row
    *d. when he or she has bowled a game of 10 frames

Mark

38. What is a *mark*?
    a. the spot left on the lane by a lofted ball
    b. the spot on the lane used by spot bowlers for aiming
    c. a frame in which there is no strike or spare
    *d. a frame in which there is a strike or spare

Open Frame

39. What is an *open frame*?
    a. a frame the player still has left to bowl
    *b. a frame without a strike or spare
    c. a frame in which no pins were knocked down
    d. a frame in which a spare was missed

Pocket

40. Where is the *pocket* for a right-handed bowler?
    a. area defined by the 1 and 2 pins
    *b. area defined by the 1 and 3 pins
    c. area defined by the 4 and 6 pins
    d. area defined by the 7 and 10 pins

Scratch Bowler

41. What is a *scratch bowler*?
    a. one that lofts the ball down the lanes
    b. one that frequently goes over the foul line
    *c. one that has no handicap
    d. one that bowls in a league

Sleeper

42. What is a *sleeper*?
    a. a slow rolling ball
    b. a slow player
    c. a 7-10 split
    *d. a pin hidden behind another pin

Spare

43. What is a *spare*?
    a. knocking down all the pins with the first ball
    *b. knocking down all the pins with the first and second ball
    c. leaving one or more pins standing after the second ball
    d. leaving pins standing on both sides of the lane after the first ball

Strike

44. What is a *strike*?
    *a. knocking down all the pins with the first ball
    b. knocking down all the pins with the first and second ball
    c. leaving one or more pins standing after the second ball
    d. leaving pins standing on both sides of the lane after the first ball

Split

45. With the first ball, the head pin is knocked down, and two or more pins are left standing with adjacent pins knocked down in front and between. What is this called?
    a. spare
    b. strike
    *c. split
    d. mark

Strike Out

46. What is a *strike out*?
    a. making three strikes in a row
    *b. making three strikes in the tenth and final frame
    c. missing three strikes in a row
    d. missing three strikes in a game

Turkey

47. What is a *turkey*?
    a. a missed spare
    b. a second ball that misses all the pins left standing
    c. two strikes in a row
    *d. three stikes in a row

2 Pin

48. In the diagram, which is the 2 pin? [Refer to Diagram 1.]
    a. B
    b. C
    *c. H
    d. I

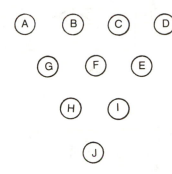

Diagram 1

4 Pin

49. In the diagram, which is the 4 pin? [Refer to Diagram 1, Question 48.]
    a. A
    b. D
    c. E
    *d. G

10 Pin

50. In the diagram, which is the 10 pin? [Refer to Diagram 1, Question 48.]
    a. A
    *b. D
    c. F
    d. J

Rules and Scoring

51. How many frames are in a game?
    a. 1
    b. 5
    *c. 10
    d. 30

52. Unless you roll a strike, how many balls do you roll in a frame?
    a. 1
    *b. 2
    c. 10
    d. 20

Scoring

53. How is a strike scored?
    a. 10 pins
    b. 10 pins plus pins knocked down on next ball
    *c. 10 pins plus pins knocked down on next two balls
    d. 10 pins plus pins knocked down in the next two frames

54. How is a spare scored?
    a. 10 pins
    *b. 10 pins plus pins knocked down on next ball
    c. 10 pins plus pins knocked down on next two balls
    d. 10 pins plus pins knocked down in the next frame

55. Which symbol indicates a miss? [Refer to Diagram 2.]
    *c.

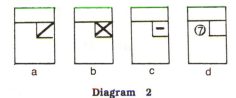

Diagram 2

56. Which symbol indicates a strike? [Refer to Diagram 2, Question 55.]
    *b.

57. Which symbol indicates a spare? [Refer to Diagram 2, Question 55.]
    *a.

58. Which symbol indicates a split? [Refer to Diagram 2, Question 55.]
    *d.

59. In which frame was a foul committed? [Refer to Diagram 3.]
    *b.

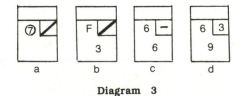

Diagram 3

60. In which frame was a split converted? [Refer to Diagram 3, Question 59.]
    *a.

61. In which frame did the bowler miss all the pins with his or her second ball? [Refer to Diagram 3, Question 59.]
    *c.

62. In which frame did the bowler knock down some of the pins with his or her second ball? [Refer to Diagram 3, Question 59.]
    *d.

63. What is the score in the first frame? [Refer to Diagram 4.]
    a. 28
    *b. 20
    c. 17
    d. 10

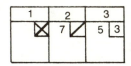

Diagram 4

64. What is the score in the first frame? [Refer to Diagram 5.]
    a. 7
    b. 10
    *c. 19
    d. 20

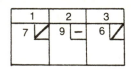

Diagram 5

65. What is the score in the first frame? [Refer to Diagram 6.]
    a. 10
    b. 20
    *c. 30
    d. 49

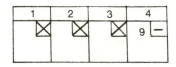

Diagram 6

66. What is the score in the tenth frame? [Refer to Diagram 7.]
    a. 175
    *b. 165
    c. 155
    d. 145

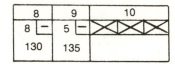

Diagram 7

67. What is the score in the ninth frame? [Refer to Diagram 8.]
    a. 140
    b. 150
    *c. 156
    d. 175

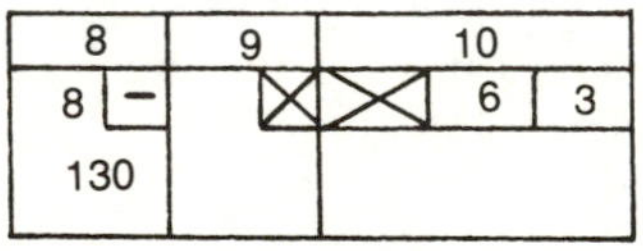

Diagram 8

68. What is the score in the tenth frame? [Refer to Diagram 8, Question 67.]
    a. 156
    b. 166
    c. 160
    *d. 175

69. What is the score in the ninth frame? [Refer to Diagram 9.]
    *a. 137
    b. 140
    c. 149
    d. 150

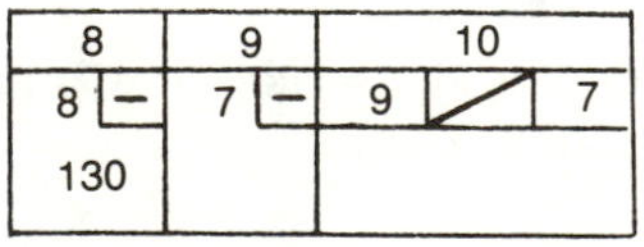

Diagram 9

70. What is the score in the tenth frame? [Refer to Diagram 9, Question 69.]
    a. 146
    b. 149
    c. 150
    *d. 154

71. What is the score in this frame? [Refer to Diagram 10.]
    a. 0
    b. 8
    *c. 9
    d. 10

Diagram 10

72. What is the score in this frame? [Refer to Diagram 11.]
    a. 2
    b. 7
    *c. 9
    d. 10

Diagram 11

Ball
73. What is the maximum amount a bowling ball can weigh?
    a. 10 pounds
    b. 15 pounds
    *c. 16 pounds
    d. 22 pounds

Pin Count
74. A bowler's first ball goes into the gutter, rebounds out, and knocks down three pins. What happens?
    a. The bowler rolls the second ball.
    b. The bowler resets the pins and rolls another first ball.
    *c. The bowler resets the pins and rolls his or her second ball.
    d. The bowler's score is three, and the pins are reset for the next bowler.

75. A bowler's second ball goes into the gutter, rebounds out, and knocks down the four pins standing. What happens?
    a. The bowler's score is a spare.
    *b. The bowler's score is six.
    c. The pins are reset and the bowler re-bowls that frame.
    d. The four pins that were standing are reset, and the bowler gets another second ball.

76. A bowler's first ball knocks down two pins and causes the four pin to bounce off the lane, but it remains standing. What happens?
    *a. Two is scored for the first ball.
    b. Three is scored for the first ball, and the four pin is removed.
    c. Three is scored for the first ball, and the four pin is left standing.
    d. The pins are reset, and the bowler rolls his or her first ball again.

77. A bowler's first ball knocks down nine pins. His or her second ball causes the remaining pin to bounce off the wall, but it remains standing. What happens?
    a. A spare is scored.
    *b. A miss is scored.
    c. The pins are reset, and the frame is replayed.
    d. The pins are reset with the one pin standing, and the second ball is replayed.

78. A bowler's first ball knocks down seven pins and displaces another. The automatic pin setter knocks over the displaced pin. What happens?
    a. The score for the first ball is 8, and the second ball is rolled.
    b. The score for the first ball is 8, the pin is removed, and the second ball is rolled.
    *c. The score for the first ball is 7, the pin is reset, and the second ball is rolled.
    d. The pins are reset, and the bowler rolls his or her first ball again.

Foul

79. Which situation is *not* a foul?
    a. The bowler's foot touches the foul line on the approach.
    b. The bowler's foot goes over the foul line, touching the lane on the pin side of the foul line.
    c. The bowler's hand touches the lane on the pin side of the foul line after the ball is released.
    *d. The bowler's hand follows through over the foul line after the ball is released.

80. A bowler slides over the foul line on his or her first ball. The ball knocks down eight pins. What happens?
    a. The pins are reset and the bowler rolls his or her first ball.
    *b. The pins are reset and the bowler rolls his or her second ball.
    c. Eight is scored for the first ball, and the second ball is rolled.
    d. Zero is scored for the first ball, and the second ball is rolled.

81. You are bowling on an end lane. You roll your first ball and must touch the wall beyond the foul line with your hand to maintain your balance. The ball knocks down nine pins. What happens?
    a. Nine is scored for the first ball, and the second ball is rolled.
    b. Zero is scored for the first ball, and the second ball is rolled.
    c. The pins are reset, and the first ball is replayed.
    *d. The pins are reset, and the second ball is rolled.

82. On your first ball you foul. On your next ball you knock down all 10 pins. What happens?
    *a. It is scored as a spare.
    b. It is scored as a strike.
    c. It is scored as 10 pins.
    d. It is scored as a strike-out.

83. A bowler knocks down seven pins on the first ball. On the second ball, he or she knocks down two pins but commits a foul. What happens?
    *a. The score for the frame is 7.
    b. The score for the frame is 9.
    c. The pins are reset and the frame replayed.
    d. The three pins are reset for the second ball, and the second ball is replayed.

84. On the first ball, a bowler knocks down five pins but fouls. On the second ball, he or she knocks down four pins but fouls. What happens?
    a. The score for the frame is 4.
    b. The score for the frame is 5.
    *c. The score for the frame is 0.
    d. The frame is replayed.

Dead Ball

85. You roll your first ball. Before it hits the pins, you realize that a pin is missing from the setup. The ball knocks down five pins. What happens?
    a. The score for the first ball is 5.
    b. The score for the first ball is 6.
    *c. The pins are reset, and you roll your first ball again.
    d. You may accept the score of 6 or reset the pins to roll your first ball again.

86. You roll your first ball. Before it reaches the pins, a human pinsetter accidently knocks down one of the pins. The ball knocks down six pins. What happens?
    a. The score for the first ball is 6.
    b. The score for the first ball is 7.
    *c. The pins are reset, and you roll your first ball again.
    d. You may accept the score of 7 or reset the pins to roll your first ball again.

87. You are bowling your first ball. As you make your approach the bowler on the next lane hits your arm with his or her hand. Your ball goes into the gutter. What is the ruling?
    a. The score for the first ball is 0.
    b. The pins are reset, and you roll your first ball again.
    *c. You must declare interference before the ball reaches the pins in order to reset the pins for another first ball attempt.
    d. You may accept the score or reset the pins and roll your first ball again.

Handicapping

88. When is a bowler considered a scratch bowler in league play?
    a. when he or she has an average of 150 or more
    *b. when he or she has an average of 180 or more
    c. when he or she has an average of 200 or more
    d. when he or she has an average of 225 or more

89. How are handicaps generally determined for beginning bowlers?
    a. 150 − bowler's average
    b. 180 − bowler's average
    c. 75% of the difference between 150 and the bowler's average
    *d. 90% of the difference between 180 and the bowler's average

90. How are handicaps generally determined for intermediate and advanced bowlers?
    a. 180 − bowler's average
    b. 200 − bowler's average
    *c. 75% of the difference between 180 and the bowler's average
    d. 90% of the difference between 200 and the bowler's average

91. A beginning bowler's average is 100. What is his or her handicap?
    a. 38
    b. 50
    *c. 72
    d. 80

92. An advanced bowler's average is 160. What is his or her handicap?
    *a. 15
    b. 20
    c. 36
    d. 40

League Play

93. How many players bowl for each team in league competition?
    a. three
    *b. four
    c. five
    d. six

94. Team A's handicap is 100 pins. Team B's handicap is 150 pins. Which team has the best overall bowlers? How much better than its opponents must it bowl to win?
    *a. Team A is the best and must knock down 51 more pins than its opponents to win.
    b. Team B is the best and must knock down 51 more pins than its opponents to win.
    c. Team A is the best and must knock down 1 more pin than its opponents to win.
    d. Team B is the best and must knock down 1 more pin than its opponents to win.

95. Team A's handicap is 100 pins. Team B's handicap is 150 pins. Which team is given marks at the beginning of the game? How many marks is it given?
    a. Team A; 5
    b. Team A; 10
    *c. Team B; 5
    d. Team B; 15

96. When a team is given marks at the beginning of a game in league play, how many pins represent one mark?
    a. 1
    b. 5
    *c. 10
    d. 20

97. A league team is bowling with only three players. How is the team handicap figured?
    a. It is the total of the three bowlers' handicaps.
    b. It is the total of the three bowlers' handicaps plus the lowest handicap of the other team members.
    c. It is the total of the three bowlers' handicaps plus the highest handicap of the other team members.
    *d. It is the total of the three bowlers' handicaps plus the handicap of the team member who did not show up.

98. In league play, a team starts a game with three players. The fourth player comes when the teams have already bowled five frames. What is the procedure?
    a. The bowler may begin on the sixth frame.
    b. The bowler quickly bowls the first five frames to catch up.
    *c. The bowler may begin on the next game.
    d. The bowler may not bowl in this match.

Tournaments

99. In ABC championships, what qualifications must a bowler have to participate in the Classic Division?
    a. be a professional bowler with at least a 180 average
    *b. be a professional bowler with at least a 190 average
    c. be an amateur bowler with at least a 180 average
    d. be an amateur bowler with at least a 190 average

100. In ABC team championships, how many men are on a team?
    a. three
    b. four
    *c. five
    d. six

101. In ABC Booster Division championships, what must team members average?
    a. 150 or more
    b. 150 or less
    c. 170 or more
    *d. 170 or less

102. For ABC and WIBC championships, in what events must "all events" competitors participate?
    a. singles and team
    b. singles and doubles
    *c. singles, doubles, and team
    d. doubles and team

103. In WIBC championships, what must a bowler average to compete in the Open Division?
    a. 145 or less
    b. 146 to 170
    c. 170 or less
    *d. over 170

104. In WIBC championships, what must a bowler average to compete in Division I?
    a. 145 or less
    *b. 146 to 170
    c. 170 or less
    d. over 170

105. In WIBC championships, what must a bowler average to compete in Division II?
    *a. 145 or less
    b. 146 to 170
    c. 170 or less
    d. over 170

Technique

Ball Selection

106. What weight ball do most men use?
    a. 10 pounds
    b. 12 pounds
    c. 14 pounds
    *d. 16 pounds

107. If a bowler is having trouble with control, what would be the best change to try?
    a. use a heavier ball
    *b. use a lighter ball
    c. use a shorter backswing
    d. use a longer backswing

108. How should your thumb fit into the hole on the ball?
    a. very tight fit
    b. slightly tight fit
    *c. slightly loose fit
    d. very loose fit

109. You put your thumb into the thumbhole and lay your hand across the ball. Where should the finger holes be in relation to your middle two fingers?
    *a. The knuckles should be directly over the inside edge of the finger holes.
    b. The knuckles should be directly over the center of the finger holes.
    c. The knuckles should be directly over the outside edge of the finger holes.
    d. The knuckles should be slightly past the outside edge of the finger holes.

110. When you put your thumb and fingers into the holes, how much space should there be between your palm and the ball?
    a. none
    *b. enough for a pencil to fit snugly
    c. enough for your index finger to fit into the space
    d. about one-half inch at the greatest distance

111. What weight ball should a player use?
    a. the lightest one he or she can control
    *b. the heaviest one he or she can control
    c. the lightest one he or she can throw hard
    d. the heaviest one he or she can throw hard

112. How can you tell if you can handle the weight of a ball without losing control of it?
    a. It is not too heavy if you can swing it back and forth without dropping it in the backswing.
    b. It is not too heavy if you can swing it back and forth without dropping it in the forward swing.
    *c. It is not too heavy if you can swing it back and forth without dropping your shoulder.
    d. It is not too heavy if you can swing it back and forth and hold it firmly with your fingers.

Address

113. How should a bowler stand in the address?
    *a. body erect with knees slightly bent and weight on the balls of the feet
    b. body slightly bent forward with knees slightly bent and weight on the balls of the feet
    c. body erect with knees straight and weight on the outside of the feet
    d. body slightly bent forward with knees straight and weight on the heels

114. A bowler is using a four-step approach. How far should he or she stand from the foul line in the starting position?
    a. four steps
    *b. four and one half steps
    c. five steps
    d. five and one half steps

115. What should be the position of a bowler's feet in the starting position?
    a. toes straight ahead with right foot forward one-half foot length
    *b. toes straight ahead with left foot forward one-half foot length
    c. toes slightly outward with feet next to each other
    d. toes slightly outward with right foot forward one-half foot length

116. In the starting position, where should the right hand be?
    *a. waist high and in line with the right hip
    b. waist high and in line with the center of the bowler's body
    c. hip high and slightly outside a line with the right hip
    d. hip high and slightly inside a line with the right hip

117. In the starting position, where should the left hand be?
    *a. on the left side of the ball with little fingers of both hands touching
    b. under the ball with little fingers of both hands overlapping
    c. back of the ball with little fingers about 2 inches apart
    d. slightly to the top of the ball on the left side with the little fingers about 2 inches apart

118. In the starting position, what is the position of the hand, wrist, and forearm?
    a. wrist cocked forming 45° angle between back of hand and back of forearm
    b. wrist cocked forming slight angle between back of hand and back of forearm
    c. wrist cocked forming 45° angle between palm and inside of forearm
    *d. wrist straight forming straight line from hand to forearm

119. In the starting position, what is the position of the right elbow?
    a. about 6 inches away from bowler's side at the waist
    b. about 6 inches away from the bowler's waist and slightly forward from the side of his or her body
    *c. snugly against bowler's side at the waist
    d. snugly against bowler's waist slightly forward from the side of his or her body

120. A bowler holds the ball higher than usual in the address position. What will this cause?
    *a. increase in the ball speed
    b. decrease in the ball speed
    c. increase in the hooking action of the ball
    d. decrease in the hooking action of the ball

Approach

121. For beginners, how many steps are recommended in the approach?
    a. two
    b. three
    *c. four
    d. five

122. Which phrase best describes the first step taken in the four-step approach?
    *a. a short step with the right foot
    b. a short step with the left foot
    c. a long step with the right foot
    d. a long step with the left foot

123. When should the pushaway begin?
    a. just before the first step
    *b. with the first step
    c. at the end of the first step
    d. with the second step

124. What is the position of the arms at the end of the pushaway?
    a. both arms slightly bent
    b. right arm slightly bent, left arm extended
    c. left arm slightly bent, right arm extended
    *d. both arms extended

125. When should your left hand leave the ball?
    a. at the beginning of the pushaway
    *b. at the end of the pushaway
    c. at the beginning of your first step
    d. at the beginning of your second step

126. How high should the ball be at the end of the back swing?
    a. hip high
    *b. waist high
    c. chest high
    d. shoulder high

127. Which statement best describes the swing of the ball?
    *a. Allow the ball to swing in a pendulum motion.
    b. Push the ball backward and let it swing forward.
    c. Allow the ball to swing backward and pull it forward.
    d. Push the ball backward and pull it forward.

128. When should the bowler slide?
    a. with the forward swing of the ball
    b. with the release of the ball
    *c. as the forward swing is completed
    d. after the ball is released

129. What is the position of the wrist throughout the swing?
    a. loose
    b. relaxed
    c. tense
    *d. firm

130. When you throw your first few balls, you realize the lane is fast. What should you do?
    a. Start your approach a half step closer to the foul line.
    b. Start your approach a half step further from the foul line.
    *c. Move slightly to the right to begin your approach.
    d. Move slightly to your left to begin your approach.

131. You are throwing a hook ball. The ball is consistently hooking more than usual. What should you do?
    a. Start your approach a half step closer to the foul line.
    b. Start your approach a half step further from the foul line.
    c. Move slightly to the right to begin your approach.
    *d. Move slightly to your left to begin your approach.

132. A bowler increases the length of his or her pushaway. What will this cause?
    *a. increase in the ball speed
    b. decrease in the ball speed
    c. increase in the hooking action of the ball
    d. decrease in the hooking action of the ball

133. A bowler slows down his or her approach. What will this cause?
    a. increase in the ball speed
    *b. decrease in the ball speed
    c. increase in the hooking action of the ball
    d. decrease in the hooking action of the ball

134. A bowler shortens his or her approach. What will this cause?
    a. increase in the ball speed
    *b. decrease in the ball speed
    c. increase in the hooking action of the ball
    d. decrease in the hooking action of the ball

Release

135. Where should your left foot be in relation to your right on your final step?
    *a. next to it and then sliding forward
    b. a half step in front of it and then sliding forward
    c. one step in front of it and then sliding forward
    d. a half step behind it and then sliding forward

136. In what direction should the foot slide in the final step of the approach?
    a. straight toward the pocket
    *b. straight forward
    c. slightly to the right
    d. slightly to the left

137. In what position should your left knee be as you complete your slide?
    a. straight
    b. slightly bent
    *c. bent at a 45° angle
    d. bent at a 90° angle

138. In what position should a bowler's shoulders be as the ball is released?
    a. diagonal to the foul line with the right shoulder forward
    b. diagonal to the foul line with the left shoulder forward
    *c. square to the foul line
    d. at a right angle to the foul line

139. Where should the ball be when it is released?
    a. even with the left foot and in line with the right shoulder
    b. even with the left foot and slightly to the side of the right shoulder
    *c. in front of the left foot and in line with the right shoulder
    d. in front of the left foot and slightly to the side of the right shoulder

140. What is the position of the thumb when the bowler releases a straight ball?
    a. 1 o'clock
    b. 9 o'clock
    c. 10 o'clock
    *d. 12 o'clock

141. What is the position of the thumb when the bowler releases a hook ball?
    a. 1 o'clock
    b. 9 o'clock
    *c. 10 o'clock
    d. 12 o'clock

142. What is the position of the thumb when the bowler releases a curve ball?
    a. 1 o'clock
    *b. 9 o'clock
    c. 10 o'clock
    d. 12 o'clock

143. What is the position of the thumb when the bowler releases a backup ball?
    *a. 1 o'clock
    b. 9 o'clock
    c. 10 o'clock
    d. 12 o'clock

144. What is the position of the ring finger when the bowler releases a straight ball?
    a. 3 o'clock
    b. 4 o'clock
    *c. 6 o'clock
    d. 7 o'clock

145. What is the position of the ring finger when the bowler releases a hook ball?
    a. 3 o'clock
    *b. 4 o'clock
    c. 6 o'clock
    d. 7 o'clock

146. Where should the bowler's hand be in relation to the foul line when the ball is released?
    a. 15 to 18 inches behind the foul line
    b. 2 to 3 inches behind the foul line
    c. 2 to 3 inches beyond the foul line
    *d. 15 to 18 inches beyond the foul line

147. What is the position of the ring finger when the bowler releases a curve ball?
    *a. 3 o'clock
    b. 4 o'clock
    c. 6 o'clock
    d. 7 o'clock

148. What is the position of the ring finger when the bowler releases a backup ball?
    a. 3 o'clock
    b. 4 o'clock
    c. 6 o'clock
    *d. 7 o'clock

Follow-Through

149. Where should your hand point on the follow-through?
    a. toward the 7 pin
    b. toward the 10 pin
    *c. straight down the alley
    d. toward the floor in front of you

150. How high should your hand come in the follow-through?
    a. knee high
    b. waist high
    c. chest high
    *d. ear high

151. What should you watch as you release the ball?
    a. the pocket
    b. the head pin
    c. the pins
    *d. the appropriate diamond

Delivery

152. Which ball will cause the most pins to fall?
    a. extremely fast ball
    b. fast ball
    *c. moderately paced ball
    d. slow ball

153. Which type of ball is most easily controlled?
    a. backup
    b. curve
    c. hook
    *d. straight

154. Which type of ball has a clockwise spin?
    *a. backup
    b. curve
    c. hook
    d. straight

155. Which type of ball generally has the best combination of control and action?
    a. backup
    b. curve
    *c. hook
    d. straight

156. If you throw a hook ball with great speed, what will happen?
    a. increases side spin on ball
    b. increases forward spin on ball
    *c. decreases side spin on ball
    d. decreases forward spin on ball

157. The diagram shows the ring around a bowler's ball formed by the dust and oil on the lanes. What kind of ball is this bowler rolling? [Refer to Diagram 12.]
    a. curve
    *b. full roller
    c. semiroller
    d. spinner

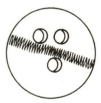

Diagram 12

158. You are bowling a hook ball. You move your hand more counterclockwise in holding the ball. What will this cause?
    *a. more hook
    b. less hook
    c. more control
    d. less control

159. Which will decrease the amount of hook?
    *a. increasing the speed of the ball
    b. increasing the amount of dressing on the lanes
    c. bending the wrist slightly forward
    d. lifting the ball more

160. How does a bowler increase the amount of lift he or she is getting on the ball?
    a. by leaving the thumb in the thumbhole longer
    b. by removing the thumb from the thumbhole sooner
    *c. by applying more pressure with the fingers
    d. by applying less pressure with the fingers

161. Which type of grip will cause the ball to hook most?
    a. convention grip
    b. palm grip
    c. fingertip grip
    *d. semifingertip grip

Errors

162. You are dropping the ball too soon. Which is the most probable cause of this happening?
    *a. Your weight is on your back foot in your stance.
    b. Your weight is too far forward in your stance.
    c. The ball is too light.
    d. You are holding the ball too loosely.

163. Your backswing and forward swing seem to be rushed in order to get the ball to the right place for the delivery. What is the most probable cause of this happening?
    a. Your backswing is too long.
    *b. Your pushaway is up and above your head.
    c. The ball is too heavy.
    d. Your first step is too long.

164. You find that you are *not* walking straight in your approach. What should you check to try to correct this?
    a. if your feet are in the correct position at the beginning of your approach
    b. if you are holding the ball out in front of your right shoulder at the beginning of your approach
    *c. if your shoulders are square with your stance at the beginning of your approach
    d. if the ball is too heavy

165. A bowler is running on his or her approach. Which will help correct this?
    a. Push away sooner.
    b. Take a longer first step.
    *c. Take longer strides after the first step.
    d. Lean forward more in the stance.

166. What will *not* cause a bowler to consistently send the ball into the right gutter?
    a. dropping the ball too soon
    b. leaning back on the release
    c. ill-fitting ball
    *d. throwing the ball across the body

167. What will cause a bowler to send the ball consistently into the left gutter?
    a. dropping the ball too soon
    b. leaning back on the release
    c. ill-fitting ball
    *d. throwing the ball across the body

168. What will cause a bowler to throw the ball under his or her body and, consequently, to the left?
    a. body twisting to the left on the delivery
    b. wrap around swing
    c. drifting to the left in the approach
    *d. side of foot parallel to the foul line

169. What is the most probable cause of the ball being rolled without any power?
    a. Ball is too heavy.
    b. Ball is too light.
    *c. Backswing is too short.
    d. Bowler does not have sufficient strength.

170. You are consistently fouling. What would be the best change to make?
    *a. Take a shorter first step.
    b. Slow down your approach.
    c. Take fewer steps.
    d. Release the ball sooner.

171. You consistently loft the ball on the release. What is the most probable cause of this happening?
    a. Your fingers and thumb are releasing the ball at the same time.
    b. You are releasing the ball too late.
    *c. Your knees are not bent enough on your slide.
    d. You are trying to throw the ball too hard.

Strategy

Strikes

172. Where should the bowler try to roll the ball to make a strike?
    a. straight at the 1 pin
    b. between the 1 and 2 pins
    *c. between the 1 and 3 pins
    d. at the 5 pin

173. From where should most straight-ball bowlers begin their approach for the first ball?
    *a. right foot on the board with the right-most dot
    b. right foot on the board with the second dot from the right
    c. right foot on the board with the center dot
    d. right foot on the board with the second dot from the left

174. Which diamond on the lane should most straight-ball bowlers use for spot bowling on the first ball?
    a. rightmost
    *b. second diamond from the right
    c. third diamond from the right
    d. center diamond

175. From where should most hook-ball bowlers begin their approach for the first ball?
    a. right foot on the board with the right-most dot
    b. right foot on the board with the second dot from the right
    *c. right foot on the board with the center dot
    d. right foot on the board with the second dot from the left

176. Which diamond on the lane should most hook-ball bowlers use for spot bowling on the first ball?
    a. rightmost
    *b. second diamond from the right
    c. third diamond from the right
    d. center diamond

177. Your first ball rolled over your "spot" and hit the right side of the pocket instead of the center. What should you do to get the ball to hit the center of the pocket?
    *a. move to the right one board to begin your approach
    b. move to the left one board to begin your approach
    c. move your aim at the diamonds one board to the right
    d. move your aim at the diamonds one board to the left

178. Your first ball rolled over your "spot" and hit the head pin straight on. What should you do to get the ball to hit the center of the pocket?
    a. move to the right one board to begin your approach
    *b. move to the left one board to begin your approach
    c. move your aim at the diamonds one board to the right
    d. move your aim at the diamonds one board to the left

Spares

179. To what does the rule, "throw the best angle while using the most alley," refer?
    a. making strikes
    *b. making spares
    c. throwing a hook ball
    d. lengthening the approach

180. In picking up spares using the 3-6-9 method, which pin is generally the key pin?
    a. 3 pin
    b. 3, 6, or 9 pin
    c. the middle pin
    *d. the pin nearest the bowler

181. A hook-ball bowler is using the 3-6-9 method for picking up spares. If the 2 pin is the key pin, what stance position does the bowler take?
    *a. three boards to the right of his or her strike position
    b. six boards to the right of his or her strike position
    c. nine boards to the right of his or her strike position
    d. three boards to the right of his or her 10 pin position

182. A hook-ball bowler is using the 3-6-9 method for picking up spares. If the 7 pin is the key pin, what stance position does the bowler take?
    a. three boards to the right of his or her strike position
    b. six boards to the right of his or her strike position
    *c. nine boards to the right of his or her strike position
    d. three boards to the right of his or her 10 pin position

183. A hook-ball bowler is using the 3-6-9 method for picking up spares. If the 4 pin is the key pin, what stance position does the bowler take?
    a. three boards to the right of his or her strike position
    *b. six boards to the right of his or her strike position
    c. nine boards to the right of his or her 10 pin position
    d. three boards to the right of his or her 10 pin position

184. A hook-ball bowler is using the 3-6-9 method for picking up spares. If the 6 pin is the key pin, what stance position does the bowler take?
    a. three boards to the right of his or her strike position
    b. six boards to the right of his or her strike position
    *c. three boards to the right of his or her 10 pin position
    d. six boards to the right of his or her 10 pin position

185. A hook-ball bowler is using the 3-6-9 method for picking up spares. If the 3 pin is the key pin, what stance position does the bowler take?
    a. three boards to the right of his or her strike position
    b. six boards to the right of his or her strike position
    c. three boards to the right of his or her 10 pin position
    *d. six boards to the right of his or her 10 pin position

186. A hook-ball bowler is using the 3-6-9 method for picking up spares. If the 10 pin is the key pin, what stance position does the bowler take?
    *a. outside of left foot on first dot on left side of approach
    b. outside of left foot on first board on left side of approach
    c. outside of left foot on center dot of the approach
    d. outside of left foot on nineteenth board from the right

187. On all perimeter spares, what direction should the bowler's toes point?
    a. straight down the alley
    b. toward the second diamond from the right
    c. toward the second diamond from the left
    *d. toward the third diamond from the right

188. On all perimeter spares, which diamond should a spot bowler be using?
    a. outermost right diamond
    b. second diamond from the right
    *c. third diamond from the right
    d. center diamond

Strike Ball Spares

189. On all strike ball spares, which diamond should a spot bowler be using?
    a. outermost right diamond
    *b. second diamond from the right
    c. third diamond from the right
    d. center diamond

190. What spares can you pick up by rolling the strike ball?
    a. 5 pin
    b. 5-8 spare
    c. 1-2-9 spare
    *d. all of the above

5 Pin Spare

191. In spot bowling, from where should most straight-ball bowlers begin their approach to pick up the 5 pin spare?
    a. right foot on the board with the right-most dot
    *b. right foot on the board with the second dot from the right
    c. right foot on the board with the center dot
    d. right foot on the board with the second dot from the left

192. In spot bowling, which diamond on the lane should most straight ball bowlers use to pick up the 5 pin spare?
    a. rightmost
    *b. second diamond from the right
    c. third diamond from the right
    d. center diamond

193. In spot bowling, from where should most hook-ball bowlers begin their approach to pick up the 5 pin spare?
    a. right foot on the board with the right-most dot
    b. right foot on the board with the second dot from the right
    *c. right foot on the board with the center dot
    d. right foot on the board with the second dot from the left

194. In spot bowling, which diamond on the lane should most hook-ball bowlers use to pick up the 5 pin spare?
    a. rightmost
    *b. second diamond from the right
    c. third diamond from the right
    d. center diamond

5-8 Pin Spare

195. What other spare can be picked up using the same position and aim as the 5-8 spare?
    *a. 5 pin
    b. 2 pin
    c. 7 pin
    d. 4 pin

1-2-9 Spare

196. In spot bowling, from where should most straight-ball bowlers begin their approach to pick up the 1-2-9 spare?
    a. right foot on the board with the right-most dot
    *b. right foot on the board with the second dot from the right
    c. right foot on the board with the center dot
    d. right foot on the board with the second dot from the left

197. In spot bowling, which diamond on the lane should most straight-ball bowlers use to pick up the 1-2-9 spare?
    a. rightmost
    *b. second diamond from the right
    c. third diamond from the right
    d. center diamond

198. In spot bowling, from where should most hook-ball bowlers begin their approach for picking up the 1-2-9 spare?
    a. right foot on the board with the right-most dot
    b. right foot on the board with the second dot from the right
    *c. right foot on the board with the center dot
    d. right foot on the board with the second dot from the left

199. In spot bowling, which diamond on the lane should most hook-ball bowlers use to pick up the 1-2-9 spare?
    a. rightmost
    *b. second diamond from the right
    c. third diamond from the right
    d. center diamond

8 Pin Spare

200. In spot bowling, from where should most straight-ball bowlers begin their approach to make the 8 pin spare?
    *a. one board to the right from their strike position
    b. one board to the left from their strike position
    c. one dot to the right from their strike position
    d. one dot to the left from their strike position

201. In spot bowling, which diamond on the lane should most straight-ball bowlers use to pick up the 8 pin spare?
    a. rightmost
    *b. second diamond from the right
    c. third diamond from the right
    d. center diamond

202. In spot bowling, from where should most hook-ball bowlers begin their approach to make the 8 pin spare?
    *a. one board to the right from their strike position
    b. one board to the left from their strike position
    c. one dot to the right from their strike position
    d. one dot to the left from their strike position

203. In spot bowling, which diamond on the lane should most hook-ball bowlers use to pick up the 8 pin spare?
    a. rightmost
    *b. second diamond from the right
    c. third diamond from the right
    d. center diamond

2 Pin Spare

204. In spot bowling, from where should most straight-ball bowlers begin their approach to make the 2 pin spare?
    a. one board to the right from their strike position
    b. one board to the left from their strike position
    *c. two boards to the right from their strike position
    d. two boards to the left from their strike position

205. In spot bowling, which diamond on the lane should most straight-ball bowlers use to pick up the 2 pin spare?
    a. rightmost
    *b. second diamond from the right
    c. third diamond from the right
    d. center diamond

206. In spot bowling, from where should most hook-ball bowlers begin their approach to make the 2 pin spare?
    a. one board to the right from their strike position
    b. one board to the left from their strike position
    *c. two boards to the right from their strike position
    d. two boards to the left from their strike position

207. In spot bowling, which diamond on the lane should most hook-ball bowlers use to pick up the 2 pin spare?
    a. rightmost
    *b. second diamond from the right
    c. third diamond from the right
    d. center diamond

208. What other spares can be converted by using the same position and aim as the 2 pin spare?
    *a. 2-8 spare
    b. 1-2-5 spare
    c. 1-2-9 spare
    d. all of the above

1-2-4-7 Spare

209. In spot bowling, from where should most straight-ball bowlers begin their approach to make the 1-2-4-7 spare?
    a. one board to the right from their strike position
    b. one board to the left from their strike position
    *c. two boards to the right from their strike position
    d. two boards to the left from their strike position

210. In spot bowling, which diamond on the lane should most straight-ball bowlers use to pick up the 1-2-4-7 spare?
    a. rightmost
    *b. second diamond from the right
    c. third diamond from the right
    d. center diamond

211. In spot bowling, from where should most hook-ball bowlers begin their approach to make the 1-2-4-7 spare?
    a. one board to the right from their strike position
    b. one board to the left from their strike position
    *c. two boards to the right from their strike position
    d. two boards to the left from their strike position

212. In spot bowling, which diamond on the lane should most hook-ball bowlers use to pick up the 1-2-4-7 spare?
    a. rightmost
    *b. second diamond from the right
    c. third diamond from the right
    d. center diamond

7 Pin Spare

213. In spot bowling, from where should most straight-ball bowlers begin their approach to make the 7 pin spare?
    a. two boards to the right from their strike position
    b. two boards to the left from their strike position
    *c. with their right foot on the fifth board from the right edge of the lane
    d. with their right foot on the eighth board from the right edge of the lane

214. In spot bowling, which diamond on the lane should most straight-ball bowlers use to pick up the 7 pin spare?
    a. rightmost
    b. second diamond from the right
    *c. third diamond from the right
    d. center diamond

215. In spot bowling, from where should most hook-ball bowlers begin their approach to make the 7 pin spare?
    a. two boards to the right from their strike position
    b. two boards to the left from their strike position
    c. with their right foot on the fifth board from the right edge of the lane
    *d. with their right foot on the eighth board from the right edge of the lane

216. In spot bowling, which diamond on the lane should most hook-ball bowlers use to pick up the 7 pin spare?
    a. rightmost
    b. second diamond from the right
    *c. third diamond from the right
    d. center diamond

4 Pin Spare

217. In spot bowling, from where should most straight-ball bowlers begin their approach to make the 4 pin spare?
    a. two boards to the right from their strike position
    b. two boards to the left from their strike position
    c. one board to the right from their 7-pin-spare position
    *d. one board to the left from their 7-pin-spare position

218. In spot bowling, which diamond on the lane should most straight-ball bowlers use to pick up the 4 pin spare?
    a. rightmost
    b. second diamond from the right
    *c. third diamond from the right
    d. center diamond

219. In spot bowling, from where should most hook-ball bowlers begin their approach to make the 4 pin spare?
    a. two boards to the right from their strike position
    b. two boards to the left from their strike position
    c. one board to the right from their 7-pin-spare position
    *d. one board to the left from their 7-pin-spare position

220. In spot bowling, which diamond on the lane should most hook-ball bowlers use to pick up the 4 pin spare?
    a. rightmost
    b. second diamond from the right
    *c. third diamond from the right
    d. center diamond

221. What other spares can be picked up by using the same position and aim as the 4 pin spare?
    a. 4-7-8
    b. 2-4-7
    c. 7-8
    *d. all of the above

7-8 Spare

222. In spot bowling, from where should most straight-ball bowlers begin their approach to make the 7-8 spare?
    a. two boards to the right from their strike position
    b. two boards to the left from their strike position
    c. one board to the right from their 7-pin-spare position
    *d. one board to the left from their 7-pin-spare position

223. In spot bowling, which diamond on the lane should most straight-ball bowlers use to pick up the 7-8 spare?
     a. rightmost
     b. second diamond from the right
     *c. third diamond from the right
     d. center diamond

224. In spot bowling, from where should most hook-ball bowlers begin their approach to make the 7-8 spare?
     a. two boards to the right from their strike position
     b. two boards to the left from their strike position
     c. one board to the right from their 7-pin-spare position
     *d. one board to the left from their 7-pin-spare position

225. In spot bowling, which diamond on the lane should most hook-ball bowlers use to pick up the 7-8 spare?
     a. rightmost
     b. second diamond from the right
     *c. third diamond from the right
     d. center diamond

10 Pin Spare

226. In spot bowling, from where should most straight-ball bowlers begin their approach to make the 10 pin spare?
     a. two boards to the right from their strike position
     b. two boards to the left from their strike position
     c. with their left foot on the first board from the left edge of the lane
     *d. with their left foot on the fifth board from the left edge of the lane

227. In spot bowling, which diamond on the lane should most straight-ball bowlers use to pick up the 10 pin spare?
     a. rightmost
     b. second diamond from the right
     *c. third diamond from the right
     d. center diamond

228. In spot bowling, from where should most hook-ball bowlers begin their approach to make the 10 pin spare?
     a. two boards to the right from their strike position
     b. two boards to the left from their strike position
     *c. with their left foot on the first board from the left edge of the lane
     d. with their left foot on the fifth board from the left edge of the lane

229. In spot bowling, which diamond on the lane should most hook-ball bowlers use to pick up the 10 pin spare?
     a. rightmost
     b. second diamond from the right
     *c. third diamond from the right
     d. center diamond

6 Pin Spare

230. In spot bowling, from where should most straight-ball bowlers begin their approach to make the 6 pin spare?
     a. two boards to the right from their strike position
     b. two boards to the left from their strike position
     *c. one board to the right from their 10-pin-spare position
     d. one board to the left from their 10-pin-spare position

231. In spot bowling, which diamond on the lane should most straight-ball bowlers use to pick up the 6 pin spare?
     a. rightmost
     b. second diamond from the right
     *c. third diamond from the right
     d. center diamond

232. In spot bowling, from where should most hook-ball bowlers begin their approach to make the 6 pin spare?
     a. two boards to the right from their strike position
     b. two boards to the left from their strike position
     *c. one board to the right from their 10-pin-spare position
     d. one board to the left from their 10-pin-spare position

233. In spot bowling, which diamond on the lane should most hook-ball bowlers use to pick up the 6 pin spare?
     a. rightmost
     b. second diamond from the right
     *c. third diamond from the right
     d. center diamond

234. What other spares can be picked up by using the same position and aim as the 6 pin spare?
     a. 6-10 spare
     b. 9-10 spare
     c. 3-6-10 spare
     *d. all of the above

9-10 Spare

235. In spot bowling, from where should most straight-ball bowlers begin their approach to make the 9-10 spare?
    a. two boards to the right from their strike position
    b. two boards to the left from their strike position
    *c. one board to the right from their 10-pin-spare position
    d. one board to the left from their 10-pin-spare position

236. In spot bowling, which diamond on the lane should most straight ball bowlers use to pick up the 9-10 spare?
    a. rightmost
    b. second diamond from the right
    *c. third diamond from the right
    d. center diamond

237. In spot bowling, from where should most hook-ball bowlers begin their approach to make the 9-10 spare?
    a. two boards to the right from their strike position
    b. two boards to the left from their strike position
    *c. one board to the right from their 10-pin-spare position
    d. one board to the left from their 10-pin-spare position

238. In spot bowling, which diamond on the lane should most hook-ball bowlers use to pick up the 9-10 spare?
    a. rightmost
    b. second diamond from the right
    *c. third diamond from the right
    d. center diamond

Splits

239. You are consistently hitting the head pin too high, causing splits. What would be the best change to make to try to correct this?
    a. Aim more to the right.
    b. Throw the ball harder.
    c. Move to the right for your stance.
    *d. Increase the angle of your throw.

240. What generally causes the 5-10 and 5-7 splits?
    a. throwing the ball too easy
    b. throwing the ball too hard
    *c. hitting the head pin too light
    d. hitting the head pin too high

"Impossible" Splits

241. You have a 7-10 split. How should you play it?
    *a. From the right side of the lane, aim for the 7.
    b. From the center of the lane, aim for the 7.
    c. From the center of the lane, aim for the 10.
    d. From the left side of the lane, aim for the 10.

242. You have a 7-10, 4-6, or 7-9 split. How should you play it?
    *a. From the right of the lane, aim for the pin on the left.
    b. From the right of the lane, aim for the pin on the right.
    c. From the center of the lane, aim for the pin on the left.
    d. From the left of the lane, aim for the pin on the right.

243. You are trying to convert an 8-10 split. How should you play it?
    a. From the right side of the alley, aim for the center of the 8 pin.
    *b. From the right side of the alley, aim for the left side of the 8 pin.
    c. From the left side of the alley, aim for the right side of the 10 pin.
    d. From the right of the alley, aim for the center of the 10 pin.

244. You are trying to convert a 4-7-10 split. How should you play it?
    a. From the right of the alley, aim for the center of the 4 pin.
    *b. From the right of the alley, aim for the center of the 7 pin.
    c. From the right of the alley, aim for the right side of the 4 pin.
    d. From the left side of the alley, aim for the 10 pin.

Baby Splits

245. In spot bowling, from where should most straight-ball bowlers begin their approach to make the 2-7 split?
    a. two boards to the right from their strike position
    b. two boards to the left from their strike position
    c. one board to the right from their 7-pin-spare position
    *d. one board to the left from their 7-pin-spare position

246. In spot bowling, which diamond on the lane should most straight-ball bowlers use to pick up the 2-7 split?
    a. rightmost
    b. second diamond from the right
    *c. third diamond from the right
    d. center diamond

247. In spot bowling, from where should most hook-ball bowlers begin their approach to make the 2-7 split?
    a. two boards to the right from their strike position
    b. two boards to the left from their strike position
    c. one board to the right from their 7-pin-spare position
    *d. one board to the left from their 7-pin-spare position

248. In spot bowling, which diamond on the lane should most hook-ball bowlers use to pick up the 2-7 split?
    a. rightmost
    b. second diamond from the right
    *c. third diamond from the right
    d. center diamond

249. In spot bowling, from where should most straight-ball bowlers begin their approach to make the 3-10 split?
    a. two boards to the right from their strike position
    b. two boards to the left from their strike position
    *c. one board to the right from their 10-pin-spare position
    d. one board to the left from their 10-pin-spare position

250. In spot bowling, which diamond on the lane should most straight-ball bowlers use to pick up the 3-10 split?
    a. rightmost
    b. second diamond from the right
    *c. third diamond from the right
    d. center diamond

251. In spot bowling, from where should most hook-ball bowlers begin their approach to make the 3-10 split?
    a. two boards to the right from their strike position
    b. two boards to the left from their strike position
    *c. one board to the right from their 10-pin-spare position
    d. one board to the left from their 10-pin-spare position

252. In spot bowling, which diamond on the lane should most hook-ball bowlers use to pick up the 3-10 split?
    a. right most
    b. second diamond from the right
    *c. third diamond from the right
    d. center diamond

Exact Splits

253. You have a 4-5 split. How should you play it?
    a. Aim for the center of the 4 pin.
    b. Aim for the center of the 5 pin.
    c. Aim for the left side of the 4 pin.
    *d. Aim for the center of the space between them.

Suggested Readings

Barsanti, R.A. (1974). *Bowling*. Boston: Allyn & Bacon.

Kenny, J. (1982). *Strike through bowling*. Champaign, IL: Leisure Press.

Mackey, R.T. (1980). *Bowling* (3rd ed.). Palo Alto, CA: Mayfield.

Martin, J.L., & Tandy, R.E. *Bowling* (4th ed.). Dubuque, IA: William C. Brown.

NAGWS Bowling/golf guide: January 1983–January 1985. (1983). Reston, VA: AAHPERD.

Ritger, D., & Soutar, J. *Bowlers Guide*. Greendale, WI: American Bowling Congress and Women's International Bowling Congress.

Schunk, C. (1976). *Bowling* (2nd ed.). Philadelphia: W.B. Saunders.

Showers, N. (1980). *Bowling* (3rd ed.). Glenview, IL: Scott Foresman.

Field Hockey

Jo Ann Messick, Consultant

This collection of test questions on field hockey is divided into four content areas:

- **General Knowledge**
- **Techniques**
- **Strategy**
- **Rules**

Some questions and answers in these categories may be revised, reflecting changes in technique and strategy as the students' level of skill progresses. Teachers should select questions and answers that will accurately assess knowledge based on each group's level of skill. In addition, some questions may need to be revised if used to test individual age groups or coeducational groups.

General Knowledge

History	1 to 12
Etiquette	13 to 14
Safety and Conditioning	15 to 20
Equipment and Facilities	21 to 28

History

Origin

1. The ancient game of hockey goes back to which nationality?
   - *a. Greek
   - b. Roman
   - c. Turkish
   - d. Danish

Location

2. Which country was the home of the first field hockey club for women?
   - a. France
   - b. Ireland
   - c. Germany
   - *d. England

Country

3. Which country has dominated Olympic men's field hockey?
   - a. United States
   - b. Holland
   - c. England
   - *d. India

Date

4. What was the first year that a women's field hockey team from the United States competed internationally?
   - *a. 1920
   - b. 1928
   - c. 1935
   - d. 1946

5. When was women's field hockey first played in the United States?
   - a. 1882
   - *b. 1901
   - c. 1913
   - d. 1926

6. When did Henry Greer bring men's field hockey to the United States?
   - a. 1921
   - *b. 1928
   - c. 1936
   - d. 1960

Jo Ann Messick is an umpire, selector, and coach in the Deep South Field Hockey Association, Greensboro, North Carolina.

7. Men's field hockey has been an Olympic sport since 1908. What year did the United States first enter a men's field hockey team in the Olympics?
   a. 1908
   *b. 1932
   c. 1964
   d. 1985

8. When did women's field hockey become an Olympic sport?
   a. 1908
   b. 1948
   c. 1968
   *d. 1980

Name

9. Who was Constance Applebee?
   a. the founder of the United States Field Hockey Association
   b. the author of women's field hockey rules
   *c. the person who brought field hockey to America
   d. the first American member of the International Federation of Women's Hockey Associations

Organization

10. What is the governing body for women's field hockey competition in the United States?
    a. NASPE
    *b. USFHA
    c. AAHPERD
    d. AAUFH

11. What is the major purpose of the USFHA?
    a. to raise money for the national teams
    b. to publish rulebooks and develop guidelines for competition
    c. to select Olympic and national teams
    *d. to provide knowledge of the game and opportunities to play

12. When did the USFHA celebrate its golden anniversary?
    a. 1959
    *b. 1972
    c. 1980
    d. 1984

Etiquette

13. What is one unwritten rule that should be followed before and after a game?
    a. wear a warm-up jacket to keep from getting chilled
    *b. shake hands with your opponent
    c. get into a team huddle to say a cheer
    d. examine your stick to make sure it is in good condition

14. A player commits a foul that is *not* seen by the official. What should the player do?
    a. Continue playing the ball.
    b. Tell the official when the half ends.
    c. Deliberately send the ball to the opponent.
    *d. Raise his or her hand and call the foul.

Safety and Conditioning

Injury

15. What is the best way to keep from getting injured in a hockey game?
    a. Dodge the ball if it is coming too fast.
    b. Play conservatively with as little body contact as possible.
    *c. Keep moving and be alert for any situation.
    d. Wear shin guards and good hockey shoes.

16. Why are shin guards worn?
    a. to enhance the beauty of the uniform
    b. to hold up the player's socks
    *c. to protect the shins from injury
    d. to satisfy the game regulations

17. Why is it usually unwise to hit a ball without first stopping and controlling it?
    a. It is likely that the player will miss and lose the ball to an opponent.
    *b. There is a good chance that the ball will be undercut and result in dangerous hitting.
    c. The ball can be hit harder and more accurately if it is first controlled.
    d. The time it takes to control the ball may be used to decide what to do next.

Medical

18. What should each player have before starting a field hockey conditioning program?
    a. a hockey stick
    b. hockey shoes
    c. shin guards
    *d. a medical examination

Rules

19. What two rules were made with the safety of the players in mind?
    *a. sticks and dangerous hitting
    b. advancing and dangerous hitting
    c. sticks and being 5 yards away on free hits
    d. obstruction and advancing

Conditioning

20. What is the best conditioning exercise for hockey?
    - a. leg stretching
    - b. windmills
    - *c. running
    - d. sit-ups

Equipment and Facilities

Stick

21. Which term does *not* identify a part of the stick?
    - a. handle
    - b. toe
    - *c. arm
    - d. heel

22. How is a field hockey stick measured to fit a player?
    - a. according to the distance between a player's waist and the ground
    - b. according to the width of the handle and a player's hand size
    - *c. according to the distance between a player's hip and the ground
    - d. according to its weight compared to the player's own weight

23. The weight of the stick should be determined by which factor?
    - a. the height of the player
    - b. the position of the player
    - *c. the player's own preference
    - d. the length of the stick

24. A player's stick has just broken. What should the player do?
    - a. Play without a stick.
    - b. Use the goalie's stick.
    - *c. Run to the sideline to get another stick.
    - d. Call time-out.

25. What should a player do with the stick after a game?
    - a. Throw the stick over the goal cage.
    - b. Wash the head of the stick with warm water.
    - c. Prop the stick against a wall.
    - *d. Wipe the stick clean and store it flat.

26. The foot of your stick is starting to fray. What should you do?
    - a. apply beeswax to the frayed edges
    - b. discard the stick because it is dangerous
    - *c. smooth the frayed edges with sandpaper
    - d. wrap the frayed edges with adhesive tape

Dress

27. How should the home team be dressed?
    - *a. neatly, uniformly, and comfortably in order to play and represent the team well
    - b. neatly, in kilts because this is the traditional uniform
    - c. uniformly with white socks and shirts
    - d. uniformly with dark socks and shirts

Field

28. What are the standard dimensions of a hockey field?
    - a. length 90 yards, width 60 yards
    - b. length 110 yards, width 50 yards
    - *c. length 100 yards, width 60 yards
    - d. length 90 yards, width 40 yards

Techniques

Footwork	**29 to 31**
Stickwork	**32 to 39**
Player Characteristics	**40 to 46**
Goalkeeper	**47 to 51**
Dribble	**52 to 61**
Pass	**62 to 101**
Fielding	**102 to 109**
Dodge	**110 to 118**
Tackle	**119 to 129**

Footwork

29. Why should a player use small, quick steps?
    - a. to prevent an offsides penalty
    - *b. to be ready to change directions
    - c. to maintain balance
    - d. to increase endurance

30. What kind of strides are recommended when dribbling on a breakaway?
    - a. slow, long strides
    - b. slow, short strides
    - *c. quick, long strides
    - d. quick, short strides

31. What should you do to prevent your teammate's pass from being intercepted?
    - a. Tell your teammate when to pass.
    - b. Stay close to your teammate at all times.
    - c. Be aware of your opponent's position.
    - *d. Move to meet the ball.

Stickwork

32. "Asking for the ball" is done by which means?
    a. facing the teammate from whom you wish the pass
    b. raising your stick approximately waist high
    c. calling out the name of the teammate from whom you wish the pass
    *d. running into an open space with your stick leading just off the ground

33. What is the primary advantage of a short backswing?
    *a. Less time is required to hit the ball.
    b. More spin is imparted to the ball.
    c. Greater angle is obtained in shooting.
    d. More momentum is transferred to the ball.

34. The ball is coming on a diagonal from the right and behind the player. How should the stick be positioned to deflect the ball forward?
    a. straight ahead
    b. reversed
    *c. angled toward the player
    d. angled toward the ball

35. What should you do to avoid losing the ball?
    a. Keep your hands together.
    b. Keep moving at all times.
    c. Keep your eyes on the ball.
    *d. Keep the ball close to your stick.

36. How can you control the ball while running as fast as possible?
    a. Take small strides.
    b. Hit the ball hard.
    c. Keep your eyes on the ball.
    *d. Keep the ball out in front.

37. What is the probable cause if a player continually "tops" the ball?
    *a. The player straightens up at contact.
    b. The player uses too much follow-through.
    c. The player stands too close to the ball.
    d. The player uses a stick that is too long.

Reverse Sticks

38. What is *reverse sticks*?
    a. the use of the round side of the stick
    b. the use of the stick with its toe pointing upward
    *c. the use of the stick with its toe pointing downward
    d. the use of the stick so that the round side of the toe points upward

39. In which instances could reverse sticks be used?
    1. A player executes a pull-to-the-right dodge.
    2. A player quickly stops the ball on the non-stick side.
    3. A right wing reaches ahead to keep the ball from going out over the sideline.
    4. A left inner executes a back pass.
    5. A right link drives flat across the top of the circle.
    *a. 1, 2, 4
    b. 1, 3
    c. 2, 4, 5
    d. 3, 4

Player Characteristics

40. What is the major advantage of developing fundamental skills before playing an actual game?
    a. The game will look good to spectators.
    b. Team success will be maximized at the beginning.
    *c. The play will be more controlled.
    d. Skills will compensate for lack of conditioning.

41. What unique aspect of field hockey requires a player to be quick, flexible, and agile?
    a. there are no timeouts
    b. all skills must be executed with a stick
    *c. only the flat side of the stick may be used
    d. success in the game depends on years of practice

42. Which skills are needed by all defensive players?
    a. mark, tackle back, and obstruct
    b. undercut, field, and dodge
    c. cover, bully, and score
    *d. tackle back, cover, and mark

43. What skill is needed most by defensive backs?
    *a. quick, strong drive
    b. high, long scoop
    c. quick flick
    d. short, quick dribble

44. What is one of the most important skills for a left wing to master?
    *a. to get the feet around on a strong drive flat across the circle
    b. to do a reverse sticks drive across the field
    c. to use a pull-to-the-right dodge
    d. to use a strong left-hand lunge

45 Which player will use the reverse sticks most extensively?
    *a. the left wing
    b. the right wing
    c. the left back
    d. the center back

46. Which asset is it most important for a skilled wing to possess?
    a. long, hard drive
    *b. speed
    c. determination
    d. good stickwork

Goalkeeper

47. Which positions for the goalkeeper, shown in the diagram, are correct in relation to the ball? [Refer to Diagram 1.]
    a. 1, 2
    b. 1, 3, 4
    *c. 1, 2, 4
    d. 1, 2, 3

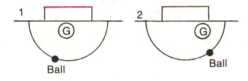
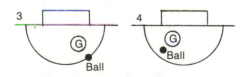

Diagram 1

48. What is the best position for the goalie when a corner is taken?
    a. stand to the outside of the cage nearest the corner hit
    *b. stand to the inside of the cage nearest the corner hit
    c. stand in the middle of the cage
    d. stand to the inside of the cage farthest from the corner hit

49. Where should the goalie position when trying to prevent a goal?
    a. Stand inside the cage to protect all angles.
    b. Stand on the line to keep the ball from entering the cage.
    *c. Stand in front of the cage in line with the ball.
    d. Never come out of the cage to block a shot.

50. What is the most important skill that a beginning goalkeeper must master?
    a. to clear the ball down the end line
    *b. to stop the ball before attempting to clear it
    c. to hand stop an aerial ball
    d. to use the stick to clear slow rolling balls

51. What is the most difficult part of being the goalie?
    a. getting used to the kickers
    b. using both the stick and feet to clear the ball
    c. wearing the pads
    *d. overcoming fear of the ball

Dribble

52. Which skill is described as a series of short taps?
    a. push pass
    b. lunge
    *c. dribble
    d. tackle

53. What is the best way to dribble?
    a. Keep the ball directly in front of your left foot and lightly tap the ball with the stick.
    *b. Keep the ball in front of your feet and lightly tap the ball.
    c. Keep the ball slightly to the right of your right foot and strongly tap the ball with the stick.
    d. Keep the ball slightly to the left of your left foot and strongly tap the ball with the stick.

54. What is the most important technique to remember when dribbling?
    a. to hold the stick at a 45° angle to the ground
    b. to form a straight line from the elbow to the back of the stick
    *c. to keep the ball in front of the feet
    d. to grip the stick so that the back of the left hand faces the direction of the dribble

55. How is the grip on the hockey stick described when dribbling?
    a. The hands are close together.
    b. The fingers are slightly spread.
    c. The V between the thumb and the index finger of the left hand is pointing to the face of the stick.
    *d. The back of the left hand and fingers of the right hand are facing forward.

56. How do the hands work in dribbling?
    a. Push with left hand, pull with right.
    b. Push with both hands.
    *c. Push with right hand, pull with left.
    d. Push with one hand only on the stick.

57. What is the position of the arms when dribbling?
    *a. left arm flexed and right arm extended halfway down the stick
    b. right arm flexed and left arm extended halfway down the stick
    c. left arm flexed and right arm flexed halfway down the stick
    d. right arm extended and left arm extended halfway down the stick

58. What is the most effective stick position when dribbling?
    a. the top of the stick slanted closer to the player than the bottom of the stick
    *b. the top of the stick slanted farther away from the player than the bottom of the stick
    c. the top and bottom of the stick positioned in line with each other
    d. None of the above statements describes the correct stick position for dribbling.

59. Where should the stick be held when dribbling?
    *a. in front and to the right of the body
    b. in front and to the left of the body
    c. in the middle of the body
    d. behind and to the right of the body

60. When should a loose dribble be used?
    a. only when trying to beat an opponent
    *b. only when the opponent has been dodged and the player is trying to maintain the advantage
    c. only when wanting to get the ball in the correct position to drive
    d. only when practicing

61. When is the best time to use a loose dribble?
    a. when the player is in the defensive half of the field
    b. when the player is in the offensive half of the field
    *c. when the player is ahead of the other teammates and opponents
    d. when the player is behind the other teammates and needs to catch up

Pass

General

62. What is the most important concept to remember when moving the ball downfield?
    *a. Look for open spaces.
    b. Pass to your right.
    c. Look at your opponent.
    d. Protect the ball.

63. Which passing technique is *least* effective?
    *a. The player with the ball must be ready to stop, look, and then pass.
    b. The player receiving the pass should determine the direction of the pass.
    c. The ball should be passed well ahead of the player receiving it.
    d. The game play should be shifted often by passes to the opposite side of the field.

64. What is the surest way to beat an opponent?
    a. to dodge on the nonstick side
    *b. to pass the ball
    c. to scoop the ball
    d. to dodge to the left

65. When is the best moment to make a pass?
    *a. as the opponent makes an attempt to tackle
    b. as the teammate has completed a cut
    c. immediately after dodging the opponent
    d. as the defense begins marking the space

66. When is passing between teammates best?
    a. Pass and then cut into the space.
    b. Pass after the teammate has cut into the space.
    *c. Pass to the space where the teammate is cutting.
    d. Pass as the teammate is cutting.

67. What should you remember when passing to a moving teammate?
    *a. Hit the ball ahead of the teammate.
    b. Run along beside the teammate.
    c. Stay behind the teammate.
    d. Send the ball diagonally to the teammate.

68. What is the best way to avoid a tackle?
    a. Speed up.
    b. Sidestep quickly.
    *c. Pass to a teammate.
    d. Dribble around opponent.

69. After tackling successfully, a player should pass the ball to a teammate. Why?
    a. The player probably doesn't have control of the ball.
    b. A teammate will be waiting for the ball.
    *c. Any tackled opponent will likely tackle back.
    d. The player needs to change the direction of the ball.

70. Which pass is *not* used in field hockey?
    a. flat
    b. diagonal
    c. through
    *d. under

Drive

71. What is an effective method for aiming a drive?
    a. Point the right shoulder in the desired direction.
    *b. Point the left shoulder in the desired direction.
    c. Point the stick in the desired direction.
    d. Stand square to the desired direction.

72. What is the most influential factor in executing a good drive?
    *a. placing both hands together on the stick
    b. continuing to move forward after contacting the ball
    c. shortening the backswing
    d. placing the left foot forward at contact

73. The force of the hit depends most on which factor?
    a. the speed of the downswing
    b. the hardness of the ball
    c. the player's approach speed
    *d. the shift of body weight to the forward foot

74. What is the most important action that imparts speed on a driven ball?
    a. running prior to striking the ball
    b. taking a long backswing
    *c. firmly snapping the wrists
    d. contracting the muscles in the forearms

75. What is the most important factor in executing a good, solid drive?
    a. position of the hands on the stick
    *b. position of the feet in relation to the ball
    c. position of the stick on the backswing
    d. position of the ball in relation to the stick

76. Which foot positioning in the diagram is correct when performing a forward drive? [Refer to Diagram 2.]
    *b.

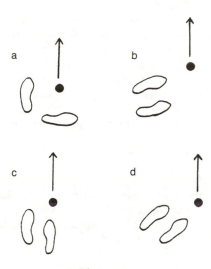

Diagram 2

77. What is the position of the feet when driving?
    a. The feet are even, weight evenly balanced.
    *b. The left foot is ahead, weight over the left foot.
    c. The right foot is ahead, weight over the right foot.
    d. The left foot is ahead, weight over the right foot.

78. In which skill should the hands be together on the stick?
    a. dribble
    *b. drive
    c. flick
    d. push pass

79. Which technique requires a backswing?
    a. scoop
    *b. drive
    c. flick
    d. push

80. Which move is *not* a preparatory action for a drive?
    a. sliding the hands together
    b. stepping forward with the left foot
    c. rotating the trunk to the right
    *d. rotating the hips to the left

81. Which skill is used to get the ball up the field quickly on a breakaway?
    a. push pass
    b. scoop
    *c. drive
    d. flick

82. Which factor is most influential in performing the drive to the right?
    *a. getting the feet around to perform the drive to the right
    b. changing the grip to perform a reverse drive
    c. pulling the ball back to perform a drive to the right
    d. stopping the ball to perform a drive to the right

83. A player consistently undercuts the ball when attempting a long drive. What should be recommended to eliminate this hazard?
    a. Keep the hands together and the head down.
    b. Try not to chop at the ball.
    *c. Step into your drive and follow through close to the ground.
    d. Move the ball in front of the left foot and away from the body.

84. What is the most influential factor in the successful penalty corner?
    a. short, quick backswing by the forward on the circle
    *b. smooth, strong hit by the forward taking the corner hit
    c. controlled stop by the forward on the circle
    d. hands together on the hit out and the shot

Push Pass

85. Which pass is the most accurate?
    *a. push
    b. scoop
    c. drive
    d. flick

86. Why it is advantageous to use a push pass when marked closely by your opponent?
    a. It results in increased power.
    *b. It can be performed without much preliminary action.
    c. It is easy to send the ball a long distance.
    d. It is not necessary to transfer the body weight.

87. What is the major difference between a push pass and a drive?
    *a. The push pass has no backswing.
    b. The push pass is more accurate.
    c. The push pass requires more strength.
    d. The push pass takes longer to perform.

88. In which instances should a push pass be used?
    1. to pass the ball from inner to inner across the goal cage
    2. to clear the ball from the center of the striking circle
    3. to send the ball from the sweeper to the forward on the 50-yard line
    4. to send the ball from the left wing to the right inner
    5. to execute a nonstick dodge
       a. 2, 3, 5
       *b. 1, 5
       c. 1, 4
       d. 1, 2, 5

Scoop

89. Which technique uses a lifting motion?
    a. drive
    *b. scoop
    c. flick
    d. push pass

90. Which statement is true of a high scoop pass?
    a. The left foot is ahead of the right, with the ball in front of the right foot.
    *b. The right foot is ahead of the left, with the ball in front of the left foot.
    c. The left hand pushes down to increase leverage.
    d. The force of the pass is increased with greater muscle tension.

91. How should the stick be held to execute a scoop?
    a. The hands are together at the top of the stick.
    *b. The bottom hand is halfway down the stick.
    c. Both hands are moved 5 inches down the stick.
    d. The hands are in the opposite position from normal.

92. Which action is *least* effective in performing the scoop?
    a. placing the right hand halfway down the stick
    b. lifting the ball on the curve of the stick
    *c. pushing down with the left hand
    d. raising the body as the ball is lifted

Through Pass

93. Which diagram shows the procedure involved in executing a through pass from Player X1 to Player X2? The broken line indicates the path of the ball, and the solid line indicates the path of Player X2, when necessary, to receive the ball. (Refer to Diagram 3.)

   *b.

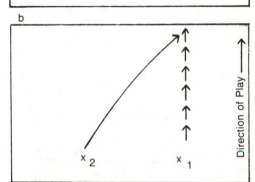

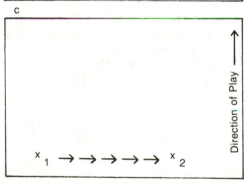

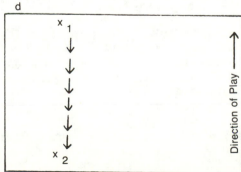

Diagram 3

Diagonal Pass

94. Which pass is the easiest for a quick defensive player to intercept?
   a. push pass
   b. flat pass
   *c. diagonal pass
   d. through pass

Flat Pass

95. Where is contact made with the ball when sending a flat pass to the left?
   a. in front of the right foot
   *b. in front of the left foot
   c. to the right of the right foot
   d. to the right of the left foot

Drop Pass

96. What should the passer do after drop passing to the right?
   a. Stand still to screen out the opponent.
   b. Sprint ahead to receive a pass.
   c. Move to the right to receive a pass on the stick side.
   *d. Move to the left to avoid obstruction.

Flick

97. Which skill is described as a quick, strong pass in the air, primarily used for scoring?
   *a. flick
   b. scoop
   c. push-in
   d. drive

98. Why is the flick a hard stroke to intercept?
   a. The stroke is fast and hard.
   b. The stroke is directed to the defender's nonstick side.
   *c. The ball travels off the ground.
   d. The ball bounces along the ground.

99. Why is the flick more difficult to receive than the push pass?
   a. It requires a greater backswing.
   b. It is often a surprise move.
   *c. It has increased spin and added force.
   d. Its pathway cannot be estimated.

100. What is the main difference between a flick and a scoop?
   a. the distance the ball travels
   b. the position of the hands on the stick
   c. the position of the feet
   *d. the height of the ball in the air

101. What is one reason for a flick *not* traveling high enough through the air?
    a. The player is not stepping forward with the right foot.
    *b. The player is not lowering the right hip and shoulder.
    c. The player is not extending the left arm on the follow-through.
    d. The player is keeping the ball on the stick too long.

Fielding

102. Which technique is correct when stopping a ball with the stick?
    a. Hold the stick perpendicular to the ground.
    b. Angle the stick slightly forward as the ball approaches.
    *c. Angle the stick slightly forward and trap the ball.
    d. Angle the stick slightly backward and give with the ball.

103. What should be the first concern when fielding a ball?
    *a. Move in line with the path of the ball.
    b. Place the stick on the ground.
    c. Decide how to angle the face of the stick.
    d. Judge the speed with which the ball is traveling.

104. How should force be absorbed when fielding the ball?
    *a. by relaxing the hands
    b. by taking a step backward
    c. by keeping the arms close to the body
    d. by stopping the ball behind and to the side of the body

105. Timing will be the best under which condition when fielding the ball?
    a. waiting directly in line with the ball
    *b. running forward to meet the ball
    c. waiting off to the right of the ball
    d. backing up in line with the ball

106. What is the key factor in receiving a hockey ball on your stick?
    a. keep your body facing the goal
    b. stay ahead of the ball
    *c. give with the ball
    d. run with your left arm straight

107. In which direction should the feet point when receiving a pass from behind right? [Refer to Diagram 4.]
    *c.

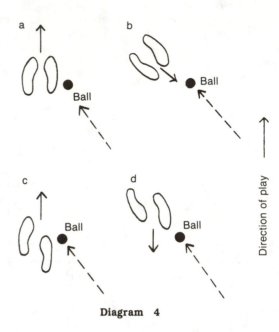

Diagram 4

108. What can you do to be ready to field the ball?
    a. face the player with the ball
    *b. keep your stick low to the ground
    c. move quickly down the field
    d. keep both hands on your stick

109. How should you field a bouncing ball?
    a. wait for the ball with the stick on the ground
    b. move to the ball with the stick off the ground to catch a high bounce
    *c. move to the ball with stick held low ready to raise it for a high bounce
    d. back up with the stick held low ready to raise it for a high bounce

Dodge

General

110. A player wants to keep possession of the ball and evade an opponent who is attacking from straight on. What skill might the player use most effectively?
    *a. dodge
    b. dribble
    c. pass
    d. drive

111. Approximately how close should a player be to another player before making a dodge?
     a. 1 foot
     *b. 3 feet
     c. 7 feet
     d. 10 feet

112. What is the most important thing to remember when executing a dodge?
     *a. Keep the stick on the ball for control.
     b. Slow down for accuracy.
     *c. Retain full speed for deception.
     d. Make the dodge big in order to clear the opponent.
     [Answer a = beginner; c = advanced]

113. What are the three dodges used to maneuver around a defensive player?
     *a. pull-to-the-left, triangular, scoop
     b. scoop, square, pull-to-the-left
     c. triangular, scoop, straightaway
     d. pull-to-the-left, circular, straightaway

114. Which technique is often used prior to dodging?
     a. flick
     b. drive
     c. jab
     *d. feint

Nonstick Side Dodge

115. Which diagram shows the pattern of the nonstick side dodge? The broken line is the path of the ball, and the solid line is the path of the player executing the dodge. [Refer to Diagram 5.]
     *a.

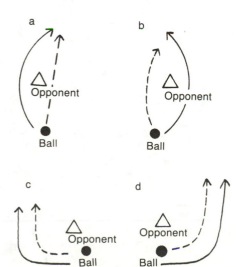

Diagram 5

116. The most effective dodge a right wing can execute is the nonstick side dodge. This is true for all but one reason. What is the exception?
     a. The pull-to-the-left dodge brings the ball in toward other defenders.
     b. It is easy for the right wing to accelerate around the opponent and pick up the ball.
     c. It is harder to defend the ball on the left side of the body.
     *d. It is one of the most difficult dodges to master.

Pull-to-the-Left Dodge

117. The effectiveness of the pull-to-the-left dodge depends most on which technique?
     a. the ability to dribble at full speed with the ball under close control
     b. the ability to slow down as you approach your opponent
     c. the ability to pull the ball to the left at the last moment
     *d. the ability to quickly sidestep to the left and then accelerate forward

118. Which technique involves a pull to the left as a part of the skill?
     a. circular tackle
     *b. staircase dodge
     c. dodge to the nonstick side
     d. straight tackle

Tackle

General

119. What does the term *tackling* mean?
     a. taking the opponent out by tripping
     b. taking the opponent out by falling into him or her
     *c. taking the ball away from an opponent
     d. taking the ball down the field

120. When is the most effective time to tackle an opponent?
     a. at the same time the opponent contacts the ball
     b. just after the opponent contacts the ball
     c. just before the opponent contacts the ball
     *d. when the ball is farthest from the opponent's stick

121. When is the left-hand lunge most effective in tackling an opponent who is dribbling down the field?
     a. just before the opponent taps the ball
     *b. just after the opponent taps the ball
     c. as the opponent taps the ball
     d. when the opponent overruns the ball

122. Which skill is *not* a tackle?
     *a. jab
     b. circular
     c. left-hand lunge
     d. straight

123. Which statement about tackles is *not* correct?
     a. The straight tackle is used by both offensive and defensive players.
     *b. The left-hand lunge is used mainly by the left link and the left back.
     c. The circular tackle is used to tackle back on the nonstick side.
     d. The circular tackle is the most difficult tackle.

124. How should you avoid contacting an opponent while tackling?
     a. stay as far away as possible
     *b. play the ball and not the person
     c. use only your left hand
     d. keep your eyes on your opponent

Left-Hand Lunge

125. Where should the player position in relation to the opponent when executing a left-hand lunge?
     a. directly in front of the opponent
     b. to the opponent's left and slightly ahead
     c. even with the opponent's left shoulder
     *d. to the opponent's right and slightly ahead

126. What is the most common fault in executing the left-hand lunge?
     *a. being too far behind the opponent
     b. being too far ahead of the opponent
     c. being too close to the opponent
     d. being too far from the opponent

127. You are on the right side of your opponent and coming from behind. What is the most appropriate tackle to use?
     *a. left-hand lunge
     b. circular tackle
     c. jab
     d. right-hand lunge

Straight Tackle

128. Why is it advantageous to have the left foot forward when completing a straight tackle?
     *a. It helps to bring the left shoulder and hip forward to continue the forward momentum.
     b. It keeps the body weight evenly distributed, so it is possible to move backward quickly.
     c. It makes it easier to finish the play with a flick.
     d. It makes it easier to use reverse sticks to pass across to a teammate.

129. What is the most effective technique in executing a straight tackle?
     a. move the feet, stay low, and jab at the ball
     b. stay low and use both hands on the stick
     c. move the feet and lunge toward the ball
     *d. move the feet, stay low, and keep both hands on the stick

Strategy

Playing Areas and Positions	**130 to 142**
Offense	**143 to 184**
Defense	**185 to 207**

Playing Areas and Positions

Interchange

130. What do the right inner and the right wing do when they take each other's positions?
     a. switch
     b. trade
     *c. interchange
     d. change

131. The right inner makes a through pass that is intended for the left inner. Which action should take place?
     a. The right inner should hang back to make room for the left inner who is cutting to get the ball.
     b. The right inner should go after the ball and then tap it over to the left inner's position.
     *c. The left inner should cut to get the ball and the right inner should move into the vacated left inner position.
     d. The center forward should run on a diagonal to the left to make room for the left inner who is cutting for the ball.

132. When does an interchange occur?
    a. when the wing receives the ball on a push-in
    *b. when two teammates switch positions
    c. when a player changes the stick from one hand to the other
    d. when the ball changes from an offensive player to a defensive player

System Play

133. What is the basic working concept in the system formation?
    a. partners
    *b. the triangle
    c. the diagonal pass
    d. the long pass

134. Which players are responsible for both offense and defense?
    a. uppers
    *b. links
    c. backs
    d. forwards

135. How can confusion on the field best be avoided?
    *a. by having only two players on the ball at a time
    b. by playing only the balls that come to you
    c. by avoiding tackles
    d. by waiting for a pass before trying for the ball

136. Which player is the last defensive player in front of the goalie?
    a. center half
    b. left link
    c. right back
    *d. sweeper

137. What is player X_1's position? [Refer to Diagram 6.].
    a. right inner
    b. left inner
    *c. left back
    d. right back

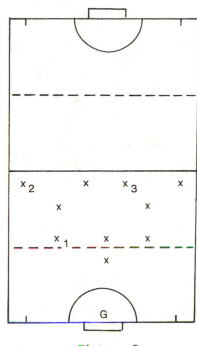

Diagram 6

138. What is the position and function of Player X_2? [Refer to Diagram 6, Question 137.]
    *a. left wing, brings ball down left side of the field
    b. left inner, backs up the left fullback on defense
    c. right wing, backs up right inner on offense
    d. right wing, brings ball down right side of the field

139. What position is Player X_3 playing in the diagram? [Refer to Diagram 6, Question 137.]
    a. left inner
    b. left sweeper
    c. right wing
    *d. right inner

140. Which positions make up the front line?
    a. left wing, left inner, right inner, right wing, right link
    b. left inner, right wing, right inner, center halfback, left wing
    *c. right inner, right wing, left wing, left inner
    d. left wing, right inner, right halfback, left inner, center forward

141. What are the positions of the backs when the ball is on the right side of the field at their offensive 25-yard line?
    a. The right back is up and the left back is diagonally back.
    b. The left back is up and the right back is diagonally back.
    *c. All the backs are up.
    d. All the backs are back.

142. What should be characteristic of the player taking a short corner?
    a. The player should have the best flick on the team.
    *b. The player should have a hard, smooth, and accurate drive.
    c. The player should be the quickest player on the team.
    d. The player should be the weakest player on the forward line.

Offense

General

143. What is the major advantage of spreading the offense?
    a. It forces players to play their positions.
    b. It avoids confusion.
    c. It decreases possibility of injury.
    *d. It creates spaces in the defense.

144. How can an offensive player create space?
    *a. move away from the ball
    b. move away from spaces
    c. cut to the goal
    d. position between the defense and the ball

145. What should you do as soon as you have made a successful tackle?
    a. dribble three times and pass
    *b. look to pass the ball
    c. drive the ball as hard as you can
    d. dribble to the sideline

Passing

146. Why it is good for the offense to pass from one side of the field to the other?
    a. It allows a few passes to cover a long distance.
    b. It causes the goalie to pay attention.
    c. It makes the opponent anticipate through passes.
    *d. It forces the defense to change positions.

147. What is the best combination of passes for the attack to use?
    a. diagonal and flat
    *b. flat and through
    c. diagonal and direct
    d. through and direct

Clearing

148. Play seems to be clustered in the middle of the field. Where would be the best place for the center half to hit the ball?
    a. directly to the center forward
    *b. out to either of the wings
    c. back to the sweeper
    d. up the field as hard as possible to uncluster play

Centering

149. Player X in the diagram is attempting to center a pass. Where should it be aimed? [Refer to Diagram 7.]
    a. a
    b. b
    *c. c
    d. d

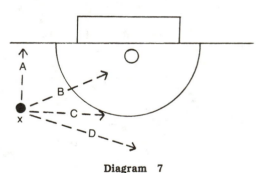

Diagram 7

Drive

150. The right wing has the ball 3 feet from the offensive end line. What is the best strategy?
    *a. drive the ball to the top of the striking circle
    b. give a short push pass to the right inner
    c. hit the ball to the right halfback
    d. turn and dribble the ball into scoring position

Pass

151. An offensive player is covered by a defensive player. The only open offensive player is 5 yards away. What pass would be the best to use?
    a. flick
    b. drive
    c. scoop
    *d. push pass

152. What is the best pass to make when the defense is marking closely?
     a. a through pass
   *b. a flat pass
     c. a diagonal pass
     d. a scoop pass

153. The left inner has the ball. The right back moves in to tackle. Where should the left inner pass the ball?
     a. to the right wing
     b. to the center back
   *c. to the left wing
     d. to the right inner

154. What is the best play for the right inner (RI)? [Refer to Diagram 8.]
     a. diagonal pass to the left inner
     b. through pass to the right wing
     c. flick over the left back's stick
   *d. pass back to the right link

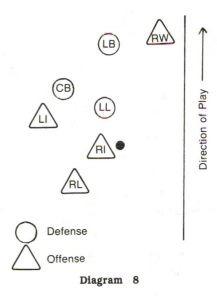

Diagram 8

Push Pass

155. Why is the push pass a good technique for the attack to use in the striking circle?
     a. It is a very accurate way to hit the angles.
     b. It is not likely to be called dangerous hitting.
   *c. It is not easily defended because it has no backswing.
     d. It may be effective in lofting the ball off the ground.

Side-In

156. What would be the *least* effective method of receiving a side-in from the right sideline?
   *a. The left wing should cut over to receive the ball.
     b. The right wing should cut through, down the sideline.
     c. The right back should cut upfield then cut back.
     d. The right inner should cut straight toward the ball.

157. Which player is used most frequently to take the side-in?
     a. the right link
   *b. the left back
     c. the center back
     d. the left wing

158. Where and by whom should the ball be directed when a side-in is taken in the defensive end of the field?
     a. downfield by the wing
   *b. downfield by the back
     c. across field by the wing
     d. across field by the back

159. Team A has been awarded a side-in. Which strategy would *not* be effective?
     a. team A's wing cuts up the sideline
     b. team B's forwards position 5 yards from the player taking the side-in
   *c. team A's inner cuts behind team B's forwards
     d. team A's link takes the side-in

160. Where is the *least* effective place to send a ball on a side-in on the right side of the field?
   *a. diagonally forward to a waiting teammate
     b. flat to a cutting teammate
     c. back to a waiting teammate
     d. through to a cutting teammate

161. The diagram shows that a member of team
A is about to take a side-in. The arrow indicates the direction team A is moving. What
would be the best strategy? [Refer to Diagram
9.]
  a. Push the ball straight ahead and follow
   it.
 *b. Push the ball to teammate A1.
  c. Push the ball to teammate A2.
  d. Push the ball to teammate A3.

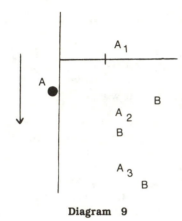

Diagram 9

Interception

162. The left back has intercepted the ball near the
top of the striking circle. How should the
player start the attack?
 *a. Dribble the ball out of the circle and
   drive it to an unmarked forward.
  b. Drive it across the circle to the unmarked right wing.
  c. Drive it up the middle of the field to a
   forward.
  d. Drive it diagonally to the left wing.

Shot on Goal

163. Where is the most effective place for a shot
on goal?
 *a. goalie's upper right-hand corner of the
   goal
  b. goalie's upper left-hand corner of the
   goal
  c. goalie's lower left-hand corner of the
   goal
  d. goalie's lower right-hand corner of the
   goal

164. The left inner, at the top of the circle, receives
a flat hit from the wing. What is the best
strategy?
  a. Pass back to the left wing.
  b. Pass across to the right inner.
  c. Dribble a little closer to the goal and
   shoot.
 *d. Drive immediately.

Scoring

165. A forward is driving for the goal cage. Which
location is most advantageous for scoring?
 *a. from the top center of the striking
   circle
  b. from an angle to the left of the goal
   cage
  c. from a position as close to the goal as
   possible
  d. from the end line on line with the
   goalie

166. What should an offensive player do after
taking a shot on goal?
  a. Move back to receive the deflection off
   the goalie pads.
  b. Stand in a stationary position to
   receive the deflection.
  c. Move out to the sides of the goal to
   receive a ball sent toward the sideline.
 *d. Follow the ball, rushing the goalie's
   pads to send the ball immediately back
   into the goal.

167. Which move is *not* considered good game
strategy?
  a. passing crossfield to confuse the
   defense
  b. maneuvering down the center of the
   field to save time
  c. spacing the players across the entire
   field to avoid bunching
 *d. working the ball in close to the cage to
   get a better shot

168. What is the best shot to take on goal when
under pressure?
  a. flick
  b. drive
  c. scoop
 *d. push

169. What is the best offensive strategy on a
breakaway when the forward is facing a goalkeeper one-on-one?
  a. to dribble the ball in toward the goal
   cage and drive at the goalkeeper when
   as close as possible
  b. to dribble the ball in toward the goal
   cage and push the ball past the goalkeeper
 *c. to drive the ball from the top of the
   circle while the goalkeeper is moving
  d. to flick the ball from the top of the circle while the goalkeeper is moving

Rushing

170. What procedure should an attacking player follow when rushing the goalie?
    a. Watch the ball when it is hit until it hits the goalie's pads.
    *b. Watch the pads after the ball is initially hit.
    c. Watch the goalie to determine which way to move.
    d. Watch the other forwards to see which angles they cover.

171. Who is responsible for rushing the goal after a corner hit?
    *a. the forward line players
    b. the two wings
    c. the right and left inners
    d. the links

172. What is the best strategy for the forwards when rushing the goalkeeper after a shot?
    a. to have all forwards get "on the pads" of the goalkeeper
    b. to have three forwards get "on the pads" of the goalkeeper, but send one forward back to the top of the circle
    *c. to have the inners get "on the pads" of the goalkeeper and set the two wings diagonally back from the edges of the goal cage
    d. to have all forwards hang back slightly from the goalkeeper and wait for a deflection

Striking Circle

173. Where is the one area in the striking circle that is often left unmarked during intense circle play?
    *a. the top of the circle
    b. the left wing area
    c. the area in front of the goal cage
    d. the right link area

Penalty Corner

174. Which player normally takes the initial hit on a penalty corner?
    a. inner
    *b. wing
    c. link
    d. sweeper

175. A player receives the ball from a penalty corner hit. What is the best strategy?
    *a. stop the ball and drive it for goal
    b. stop the ball and pass it back to the wing
    c. control the ball and dribble it closer to the goal
    d. drop pass the ball to the defensive back

176. Where should the right wing direct the penalty corner hit?
    a. to the right inner for a quick score
    *b. to the forward with the strongest, quickest drive
    c. across the circle so any rushing forward might score
    d. across the end line to confuse the defense

177. Where should the wing hit or push the ball on a corner hit?
    a. to the edge of the circle
    *b. to the stick side of the receiver
    c. to the feet of the receiver
    d. to the nonstick side of the receiver

178. The receiver should wait for the ball to arrive on which situation?
    a. side-in
    b. defense hit
    c. free hit
    *d. corner hit

Long Hit

179. Where may the offense position on a long hit?
    a. outside the circle
    b. anywhere within the circle
    *c. anywhere on the field
    d. on sides with the last defensive player

Free Hit

180. What is the best strategy on a free hit?
    a. to take the hit quickly and send it as far as possible upfield toward the attacking goal
    *b. to take the hit quickly and send it to a cutting teammate
    c. to take the hit slowly to give your teammates plenty of time to set up
    d. to take the hit quickly and pass it to a space where you think a teammate might cut

181. What should an attack player do on a free hit?
    a. sprint downfield to receive a pass
    b. cut behind the defense to receive the hit
    *c. cut in front of the defense to receive the hit
    d. move after the ball has been contacted

182. Who should take free hits near the attacking end line and why?
     - a. the wings so the halfbacks are not pulled out of position
     - *b. the wings so the hit can be taken more quickly
     - c. the center back so the link and forwards can be ahead and ready to shoot for goal
     - d. the forward line player closest to the ball so that the defense is confused

183. Where is the best place to send the ball on a defense hit when the opposing team has had time to encircle the hitter?
     - a. up the middle of the field to a waiting center forward
     - b. on a diagonal to the inner
     - c. flat across the circle to the other wing
     - *d. flat to a link on the same side of the circle

184. Where is the best place to direct a free hit?
     - a. directly to the closest teammate
     - *b. to a forward cutting to an open space
     - c. upfield along the sideline
     - d. across the field to uncluster play

Defense

General

185. When do forwards become the first line of defense?
     - a. when penalty corners are taken by the opposition
     - b. when long hits are taken by the opposition
     - *c. at the moment the ball is lost to the opposing defensive player
     - d. when the defense has trouble getting the ball out of the opponent's circle

Tackle

186. What should a forward do after losing the ball?
     - a. Cut toward the center of the field to make a space.
     - b. Rush ahead to be ready for a pass from the defense.
     - *c. Tackle back immediately to try to regain the ball.
     - d. Hang back and try to intercept a pass from the opponent.

Marking

187. What is the primary purpose of defensive marking?
     - a. to position yourself so that you are between your opponent and the goal
     - b. to position yourself so that you may intercept a pass
     - *c. to prevent the opponents from receiving a pass
     - d. to prevent the attack from penetrating the circle

188. What player does the right back mark when using the 4-2-3-1 system?
     - *a. the left wing
     - b. the right wing
     - c. the left inner
     - d. the left link

189. The opposing team has an inner who is highly skilled. What would be the best defensive strategy?
     - a. Play person-to-person.
     - b. Play zone.
     - *c. Have the center half mark the player beyond the 50-yard line.
     - d. Have a forward drop back and mark the player.

190. How should defensive players defend when the ball is in the circle?
     - *a. Mark each forward stick-to-stick.
     - b. Mark opposing forwards who are nearest the goal cage.
     - c. Mark a specific area.
     - d. Mark within 5 feet of each forward.

Goalkeeper

191. What is the best way for a goalkeeper to intercept and clear a hard driven shot on goal?
     - a. to take the time to stop the ball with the stick and kick it down the end line
     - *b. to take the time to stop the ball with the pads and clear it toward the sideline
     - c. to kick the ball out of the circle quickly before the forward has time to rush the goalkeeper
     - d. to take the time to stop the ball with the pads and drive it out of the circle

192. Which area shown in the diagram is the most vulnerable for the goalie to stop the ball? [Refer to Diagram 10.]
    *a. a
    b. b
    c. c
    d. d

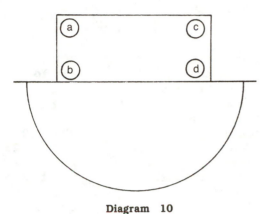

Diagram 10

193. The goalkeeper stops a shot on goal. Where should the ball be cleared?
    a. to the front
    *b. to the side
    c. to the wing
    d. to the sweeper

194. How should a ball in front of the goal be cleared?
    a. across the cage to the open area
    b. straight out in front of the cage
    *c. to the side the ball is on
    d. to the goalie for protection

195. The red center forward has driven the ball from the top of the circle toward the goal. There are many players concentrated around the goal cage. Both the goalkeeper and the sweeper can intercept the ball. What play should be made?
    a. The sweeper should intercept the ball and drive it to the right side of the field, parallel to the end line.
    b. The goalkeeper should intercept the ball and kick it back up the center of the circle beyond the red center forward.
    c. The sweeper should intercept the ball and drive it to the left side of the field, parallel to the end line.
    *d. The goalkeeper should intercept the ball and kick it to the side of the field, parallel to the end line.

196. The red left wing is dribbling the ball on a breakaway. The only blue defensive players between the red wing and the goal are the sweeper and the goalkeeper. What should the sweeper do?
    *a. Make a move toward the wing but continue to back up until another defensive player arrives.
    b. Sprint toward the wing and make the tackle before the wing gets any closer to the circle.
    c. Retreat and make the tackle in the circle.
    d. Remain in position and wait for the wing to come close enough to tackle.

197. What is the best strategy for a goalkeeper to use when facing a forward, one-on-one, on a breakaway?
    a. Stay within 5 yards of the goal cage to stop the shot.
    b. Come out 10 yards from the goal cage and wait for help to come.
    c. Rush as soon as the forward comes within 5 yards of the goal cage.
    *d. Rush as soon as the forward comes within 10 yards of the goal cage.

Defensive Back

198. The right back takes the ball away from an opposing forward in the circle. What should the right back do?
    a. Push the ball to the center back who is free.
    *b. Dribble out of the circle and drive the ball to a cutting forward.
    c. Drive the ball straight up the field.
    d. Drive the ball to the sweeper.

199. The ball is brought down the field by the right wing. The left back moves up to cover. What is the best position for the right back?
    *a. Drop back and angle off to the goal.
    b. Play parallel to the left back.
    c. Move up to cover the right wing.
    d. Move directly behind the left back in case the ball gets through.

Sweeper

200. Where should the sweeper *not* direct the ball when clearing the ball from the circle?
    a. straight to a teammate
    b. diagonally to the strong side offense
    *c. across the face of the goal
    d. flat to a teammate toward the sideline

201. A sweeper has just intercepted a pass at the 25-yard line. What would be the best strategy?
    a. Dribble up the field.
    b. Drive the ball to the center forward.
    c. Push pass to a link.
    *d. Clear to the wing.

Left Link

202. The left link misses the tackle against the right wing at the 50-yard line. The covering left back picks up the right wing. What should the left link do?
    a. Run alongside the right wing and jab at the ball.
    b. Sprint back in order to double-team the right wing.
    *c. Circle back in order to back up the left back.
    d. Sprint to the top of the striking circle to help the goalie.

Halfback

203. The right wing dodges the left back at the 50-yard line. Which recovery action should *not* be taken by the left back?
    a. Sprint back and attempt a circular tackle.
    b. Circle back and support the left link.
    *c. Sprint back and execute a left-hand lunge.
    d. Sprint back and execute a straight tackle.

Corners

204. Which type of defensive strategy is best on a penalty corner?
    a. zone
    *b. stick-to-stick
    c. 2-3 wave
    d. 3-2 wave

205. What is the most necessary characteristic of the defensive team on a penalty corner hit?
    a. agility
    b. strength
    c. endurance
    *d. speed

206. What is the most influential factor in the successful defensive short corner?
    *a. ability of the defense to tackle the opponent quickly
    b. ability of the defense to play a zone defense in the circle
    c. ability of the goalie to stop the ball
    d. ability of the defense to stop play by committing an infraction

207. What is the surest way for the defense to defend against a goal on a short corner?
    a. Hang back and help the goalie stop shots.
    b. Rush the player taking the shot.
    *c. Mark the offensive players stick-to-stick.
    d. Shift to the side where the ball is.

Rules

Game	208 to 213
Officiating	214 to 217
Field Dimensions	218
Stick	219
Substitution	220
Bully	221 to 223
Time	224 to 225
Score	226 to 229
Penalty Corner	230 to 235
Long Hit	236 to 237
Side-In	238 to 240
Free Hit	241 to 248
16-Yard Hit	249 to 251
Penalty Stroke	252 to 257
Dangerous Hitting	258 to 259
Sticks	260
Obstruction	261 to 263
Offsides	264 to 266
Advancing	267
Out-of-Bounds	268 to 269
Pass-Back	270

Game

208. What is the length of an official game?
    a. four 15-minute quarters
    *b. two 35-minute halves
    c. two 20-minute halves
    d. four 10-minute quarters

Number of Players

209. How many players are on a hockey team?
    a. 6 players
    b. 8 players
    c. 10 players
    *d. 11 players

210. How many players on a team are eligible to score?
    a. 3
    b. 5
    c. 8
    *d. 11

211. Which situation is *not* a violation in hockey?
    a. The goalie, positioned outside the circle, kicks the ball.
    b. A player hits a moving ball on a free hit.
    *c. A team has only 10 players on the field due to injury.
    d. A defensive player crosses the end line before the ball has been hit initially off a short corner.

Starting the Game

212. How does a field hockey game begin?
    a. with a face-off
    b. with a bully
    *c. with a pass-back
    d. with a toss-up

213. What option does the captain who wins the coin toss have?
    a. chooses which end of the field to attack
    b. chooses which end of the field to defend
    c. chooses to have possession of the ball
    *d. chooses either the end of the field to attack or to have possession of the ball

Officiating

214. What is the major function of an official?
    a. to help the game run smoothly
    b. to prevent accidents
    *c. to enforce the rules
    d. to limit play on the ball

215. What should the players do when the official blows the whistle?
    a. Quickly take the free hit.
    b. Set up for a penalty corner.
    *c. Look for the official's signal.
    d. Look at the coach for instructions.

216. Why does the umpire sometimes *not* stop the game when a foul occurs?
    a. The umpire must not have seen the foul.
    b. The umpire does not feel that the foul has affected the game play.
    c. The umpire is not in a position to call the foul fairly.
    *d. The umpire waits to see which team gains the advantage.

217. A foul has been committed but the whistle has not been blown. What should the players do?
    a. Call time-out to question the official.
    b. Stop play immediately until a whistle is blown.
    c. Ask the coach to question the official.
    *d. Continue playing until the whistle is blown.

Field Dimensions

218. What is the distance of the striking circle at Point A in the diagram? [Refer to Diagram 11.]
    a. 25 yards
    *b. 16 yards
    c. 12 yards
    d. 10 yards

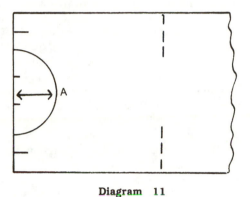

Diagram 11

Stick

219. A blue defensive player hits the ball with the rounded side of the stick causing the ball to go out over the sideline. What is the result of this action?
    *a. Hitting with the rounded side of the stick results in a free hit for the opponents.
    b. Hitting with the rounded side of the stick is legal.
    c. Hitting the ball over the sideline results in a side-in for the blue team.
    d. Hitting the ball over the sideline results in a side-in for the red team.

Substitution

220. When may substitutions be made?
    a. on a penalty corner
    b. during a time-out called by the coach
    *c. during any stoppage of play except a penalty corner or penalty stroke
    d. during a penalty stroke

Bully

221. How many times must the flat surface of the two sticks touch on a bully?
    a. one time
    b. two times
    *c. three times
    d. four times

222. A player is injured. Neither team has possession when the official calls time-out. How will play be resumed?
    a. a bully at the center line
    b. a free hit for the team whose player was injured
    *c. a bully on the spot where the injury occurred
    d. a free hit for the team that was nearest the ball when the injury occurred

223. The red center forward flicks the ball toward the goal. The goalkeeper reacts quickly and moves into the pathway of the ball. The ball is stopped, and it becomes lodged in the goalie's pads. The goalkeeper is unable to shake it loose. What is the ruling?
    a. The red team is awarded a penalty flick.
    b. The red team is awarded a penalty corner.
    *c. Neither team is awarded an advantage and a bully is taken on the spot.
    d. The red team is awarded a long corner because the foul was unintentional.

Time

224. When is the clock stopped?
    a. when a player knocks another player down
    b. when a foul occurs
    c. when a goal is scored
    *d. when a player is injured

225. When and by whom may time-out be called?
    a. by a coach when a player is injured
    b. by a team captain on the field
    c. by an official if, in the opinion of the official, both teams need a time-out
    *d. by an official for an injury

Score

226. How many points are awarded for a field goal?
    *a. 1 point
    b. 2 points
    c. 3 points
    d. 4 points

227. When is a goal scored?
    a. when the ball is hit from outside the circle and into the cage
    b. when the ball is hit over the end line above the cage
    *c. when the ball is hit from inside the circle and into the cage
    d. when the ball is hit partially over the goal line but kicked back out

228. A player on the blue team makes a shot on goal from outside the striking circle. The ball glances off a red player's stick and rebounds into the goal. What is the official ruling?
    a. A goal is not scored because the ball rebounded off a red player's stick.
    *b. A goal is not scored because the blue team shot from outside the circle.
    c. A goal is scored because a shot on goal may be taken from anywhere on the field.
    d. A goal is scored because the ball glanced off a stick within the striking circle.

229. What is the official call if a defensive player in the circle hits the ball over the end line between the goal posts?
    a. defensive hit out
    *b. goal scored for opponents
    c. corner hit
    d. offensive free hit

Penalty Corner

230. Where must the forwards position initially on a penalty corner?
    a. inside the circle
    *b. outside the circle
    c. on the end line
    d. on the sideline

231. When may movement occur on a penalty corner?
    a. when the goalie says, "Go"
    b. when the player taking the corner is ready
    *c. when the ball is struck by the player taking the initial hit
    d. when the official blows the whistle

232. When is the offense awarded a penalty corner?
    a. when the defense hits the ball over the sideline
    b. when the goalie stops the ball and it rolls over the end line
    *c. when the defense intentionally sends the ball over the end line
    d. when the defense unintentionally sends the ball over the end line

233. What is the penalty for undercutting the ball?
    a. a free hit if the foul is made by the defense in the circle
    b. a penalty bully if the foul is made by the defense outside the striking circle
    c. a penalty bully if the foul occurs inside the striking circle by the offense
    *d. a penalty corner if the foul occurs inside the striking circle by the defense

234. The ball glances off the rounded side of the blue center back's stick within the striking circle. The blue sweeper collects the ball and sends it out of the circle to a teammate. What is the official ruling?
     a. The play is stopped and the red team is awarded a long hit because the foul was unintentional.
     *b. The play is stopped and the red team is awarded a penalty corner because the foul occurred within the striking circle.
     c. The play continues and no call is made because it is legal for the ball to unintentionally hit the rounded side of the stick.
     d. The play is stopped and the red team is awarded a free hit to be taken on the spot where the foul occurred.

235. A defensive player in the circle moves between the ball and an attacking forward. What is the official's decision?
     *a. penalty corner
     b. free hit
     c. penalty stroke
     d. long hit

Long Hit

236. Which situation results in a long hit?
     a. Defense commits dangerous sticks within the circle.
     b. Defense intentionally hits the ball out over the end line.
     c. Defense commits obstruction within the circle.
     *d. Defense unintentionally deflects the ball out over the end line.

237. Where must the defense position on a long hit?
     a. behind the end line
     b. anywhere within the circle
     *c. anywhere on the field
     d. on-side with the last offensive player

Side-In

238. When is a side-in awarded?
     *a. when the ball goes over the sideline
     b. when the ball rolls along the sideline
     c. when a player accidentally kicks the ball out-of-bounds
     d. when the goalie kicks the ball over the end line

239. The blue link takes the side-in before all the red players are 5 yards away. The blue wing receives the ball. What is the result?
     a. The red team is awarded a side-in.
     b. The side-in is repeated by the blue link.
     c. No call is made; it is a hold-whistle situation.
     *d. No call is made; it is up to the red players to be 5 yards away.

240. The right wing deflects the ball over the sideline unintentionally. What shall be awarded by the official?
     a. bully on the spot
     b. defense hit
     c. free hit
     *d. side-in for the opponent

Free Hit

241. How far away must the opposing players be on a free hit?
     a. 10 yards
     b. 6 yards
     *c. 5 yards
     d. 5 feet

242. The blue team puts the ball in play with a side-in. While trying to play the ball, the red halfback obstructs the blue wing receiving the ball. What does the official call?
     a. The blue team is awarded a free hit.
     b. The blue team is awarded another side-in.
     *c. The blue team is awarded a free hit if the red team gets the ball.
     d. A bully is taken on the spot.

243. The ball glances off the foot of a blue player. Another blue teammate collects the ball and sends it upfield only to be intercepted by a red player. What is the official ruling?
     a. No call is made because the red player intercepted the ball.
     b. No call is made because the blue halfback did not play the ball.
     c. A red free hit is awarded immediately because the blue player kicked the ball.
     *d. A red free hit is awarded as soon as the blue teammate collects the ball.

244. An unintentional foul is committed by the defense outside the striking circle. What is the official's decision?
     a. penalty corner
     b. side-in
     *c. free hit
     d. long hit

245. Which action is a violation by the player taking a free hit?
     a. pushing the ball to a teammate
     b. stopping the ball before taking the free hit
     *c. contacting the ball twice before a teammate contacts the ball
     d. repeating the hit if missed

246. Which situation calls for a free hit?
     *a. The attack fouls in the circle.
     b. The defense fouls in the circle.
     c. Two players foul simultaneously.
     d. The player taking a corner hit misses the ball.

247. The red right inner deflects the initial corner hit into the goal cage. What is the ruling?
     *a. The blue team is awarded a free hit.
     b. The blue team is awarded a 16-yard hit opposite the spot where the ball crossed the goal line.
     c. The goal is scored.
     d. The penalty corner is repeated.

248. When is the defense awarded a free hit?
     a. when the defense fouls in the circle
     *b. when the player taking a corner hit remains offside
     c. when two players foul simultaneously in the circle
     d. when the attack sends the ball over the end line

16-Yard Hit

249. Which situation does *not* result in a 16-yard hit?
     a. the attack fouls inside the striking circle
     b. the ball is hit over the end line by the attack
     *c. the ball is unintentionally hit over the end line by the defense
     d. an attack player kicks the ball into the goal

250. A center back, taking an offensive free hit just outside the circle, scoops the ball over the heads of the opponents and into the goal. What is the result?
     a. legal play—goal
     b. legal play—16-yard hit
     *c. illegal play—free hit
     d. dangerous hitting—defense hit

251. The red right wing drives for goal. The shot is wide to the left of the goal cage and rolls out-of-bounds over the end line. What is the ruling?
     *a. The blue team is awarded a 16-yard hit opposite the spot where the ball crossed the end line.
     b. The blue team is awarded a free hit anywhere along the 16-yard line.
     c. The blue team is awarded a free hit to be taken opposite the spot where the ball crossed the end line.
     d. The blue team is awarded a hit-in to be taken on the spot where the ball crossed the end line.

Penalty Stroke

252. The goalie has fallen on the ball during circle play. What is the official's call?
     a. penalty corner
     b. long hit
     *c. penalty stroke
     d. defense hit

253. Where must all players be, except the goalie and the striker, during a penalty stroke?
     a. over the end line
     b. around the striking circle
     *c. beyond the 25-yard line
     d. at least 5 yards away

254. What stroke may *not* be used for a penalty stroke?
     a. flick
     *b. drive
     c. scoop
     d. push pass

255. When is a penalty stroke awarded?
     a. when the ball becomes lodged in the goalkeeper's pads
     b. when the defense unintentionally deflects the ball into the opponent's goal
     *c. when the goalkeeper raises the stick above shoulder height to stop a probable goal
     d. when a defensive player obstructs a player with the ball in the circle

256. Which procedure is *not* correct on a penalty stroke?
    a. Both the goalkeeper and the striker must indicate their readiness before the umpire blows the whistle.
    b. The defending team is awarded a 16-yard hit if the striker fails to score.
    *c. Any defensive player may be substituted for the goalkeeper on a penalty stroke.
    d. The game is restarted with a push-back at the center of the field if the goal is scored.

257. Which situation is a *violation* of the penalty stroke rule?
    a. The striker begins the stroke on a designated mark 7 yards in front of the center of the goal.
    b. The striker takes one stride forward in performing the stroke.
    c. The goalkeeper catches the ball.
    *d. The striker begins the stroke before the umpire blows the whistle.

Dangerous Hitting

258. What is dangerous hitting?
    a. a ball that leaves the ground
    b. a stick that is raised above shoulder height
    *c. an aerial ball that causes evasive action by the players
    d. a goal that is scored above the height of the goalie's pads

259. A dangerous hit outside the circle is penalized by which procedure?
    a. bully on the spot
    b. side-in directly across from the violation
    c. a penalty stroke
    *d. free hit at the site of the violation

Sticks

260. When will sticks probably be called?
    *a. when a player brings the stick above the shoulder on the follow-through in the striking circle
    b. when a player hacks at the opponent's stick
    c. when the player places the stick between the opponent and the ball
    d. when the player gets the stick tangled in the opponent's feet

Obstruction

261. What foul occurs when a player cuts between the opponent and the ball?
    a. advancing
    *b. obstruction
    c. sticks
    d. blocking

262. Which foul occurs commonly when attempting a circular tackle?
    a. advancing
    *b. obstruction
    c. offsides
    d. wrong side of stick

263. The red right link is loosely dribbling the ball down field. A blue defensive player runs between the red right link and the ball. The blue player intercepts the ball. What is the result of this action?
    a. no foul, play continues
    b. offside, free hit
    c. advancing, free hit
    *d. obstruction, free hit

Offsides

264. When is Player A offside?
    a. when Player A has possession of the ball and there are less than two opponents between Player A and the goal
    b. when Player A is ahead of another teammate with the ball and in the offensive half of the field
    c. when Player A has possession of the ball and three opponents are between Player A and the goal
    *d. when Player A is ahead of the teammate with the ball and less than two opponents are between Player A and the goal

265. What is the best positioning for the forward line to avoid offsides on a breakaway?
    a. The wings should position ahead of the inners.
    *b. All forward line players should position even with the player with the ball.
    c. All forward line players should position approximately 15 yards behind the player with the ball.
    d. All forward line players should position even with the sweeper.

266. The red inner is dribbling the ball on a break-away. The red wing sprints downfield to join the inner in the breakaway. Having passed all the blue players, only the goalkeeper remains between the red forwards and the goal cage. As they enter the circle, the goalkeeper rush-es the inner. The wing cuts behind the goalkeeper, receives the through pass, shoots, and scores. What is the official ruling?
    a. The goal is scored and play is resumed with a bully on the 50-yard line.
    *b. The goal is not scored because the wing was offsides; play is resumed with a free hit.
    c. The goal is scored and play is resumed with a pass-back at the center of the field.
    d. The goal is not scored; the red team is awarded a long corner.

Advancing

267. What is advancing?
    *a. propelling the ball forward with any part of the body
    b. getting the body between the ball and a close opponent
    c. dribbling downfield
    d. fouling in the striking circle

Out-Of-Bounds

268. The wing's feet are out-of-bounds while drib-bling up the field. What should the official do?
    a. stop play; free hit for opponents
    *b. nothing; legal play
    c. stop play; push-in for opponents
    d. stop play; on-side bully

269. Which position of the feet is not permitted?
    *a. The goalkeeper must have both feet be-hind the end line on a penalty stroke.
    b. The player taking the shot on goal may have one or both feet outside the strik-ing circle.
    c. The player taking the initial corner hit may straddle the end line.
    d. The player taking the side-in may straddle the sideline.

Pass-Back

270. Which procedure is a *violation* in starting or restarting the game with a pass-back?
    a. After a goal, the game is restarted with a pass-back at the center of the field.
    b. The opposing players are 5 yards away from the ball on a pass-back.
    *c. The player taking the pass-back plays the ball before it is contacted by another player.
    d. The ball moves only a few inches on the pass-back.

Acknowledgments

Colleagues and students who contributed sugges-tions and ideas for the Field Hockey test questions are: B. Belt, K. Bishop, J. Blandford, J. Bretz, B. Buckner, C. Chlad, L. Clark, V. Gompf, E. Groves, H. Hamm, C. Harner, T. Holley, K. Jacobs, S. Jewett, D. Kaatz, A. Laughinghouse, J. Mangus, M. Marcher, E. McLaughlin, J.A. Messick, M. Parker, M. Rock-wood, R. Smith, C. Tamsberg, C. Tucker, L. Tucker, J.A. Waugh, and C. Wilhelmy.

Suggested Readings

Gros, V. (1978). *Coaching manual.* Colorado Springs, CO: United States Field Hockey As-sociation.

Gros, V. (1979). *Inside field hockey.* Chicago: Con-temporary Books.

Hockey Rules Board. (1986). *Rules of the game of hockey with guidance for players and umpires and advice to umpires.* Woking, England: Ban-tingford.

National Federation of State High School Associa-tions. *1985-86 National Federation edition field hockey rules.* Kansas City, MO: National Federa-tion Publications.

Golf

Mary Beth McGirr, Consultant

This collection of test questions on golf is divided into ten content areas:

- General Knowledge
- Terminology
- Full Swing
- Short Game
- Putting
- Errors and Corrections
- Special Situations
- Course Management
- Etiquette
- Rules

These questions cover materials appropriate for beginning and intermediate units with a few more advanced questions. Several questions are written especially for right handed players; however, in most cases hand dominance will not be a factor in answering the question.

Note also that the rules covered are those more frequently used by persons developing their game and do not include the highly technical and less often encountered situations in which rulings are necessary.

General Knowledge

History	1 to 8
Course	9
Equipment	10 to 36
Safety	37 to 41

History

1. In what country was golf most likely first played?
    - a. Holland
    - *b. Scotland
    - c. England
    - d. United States

2. Which country has the greatest golf heritage?
    - a. England
    - *b. Scotland
    - c. Holland
    - d. Greenland

3. Which golf club is the most famous?
    - a. Pinehurst Country Club
    - b. Prestwick Golf Club
    - c. Augusta National Golf Club
    - *d. The Royal and Ancient Golf Club of St. Andrews

4. What was the composition of the first golf balls?
    - a. stones covered with hard clay
    - b. unknown filling covered with sheep skin
    - c. stones covered with moss
    - *d. feathers covered with leather

5. From what materials were the first golf clubs made?
    - a. fiberglass rods
    - *b. bent limbs
    - c. metal pipes
    - d. bamboo poles

Mary Beth McGirr is an LPGA Teaching Professional—Class A at The Farm, Randleman, North Carolina.

6. Which organization is the governing body of golf in the United States?
   a. PGA
   *b. USGA
   c. LPGA
   d. AGA

7. Which competition are the international team matches between the women amateurs of the United States and Great Britain?
   a. Ryder Cup
   *b. Curtis Cup
   c. Walker Cup
   d. Stanley Cup

8. Which competition are the international team matches between the men amateurs of the United States and Great Britain?
   *a. Walker Cup
   b. Stanley Cup
   c. Wightman Cup
   d. Ryder Cup

Course

9. How many holes make up an official golf course?
   a. 9
   *b. 18
   c. 27
   d. 36

Equipment

Clubs

10. What is the makeup of a traditional, full set of golf clubs?
    a. three woods, ten irons, and a putter
    b. three woods, nine irons, and a putter
    c. four woods, ten irons, and a putter
    *d. four woods, nine irons, and a putter

11. What would be the best club selection for a beginner or starter set?
    a. 1, 3, 5, and 9 irons; a driver; and a putter
    b. 3, 4, 7, and 9 irons; a 2 iron; and a putter
    c. 2, 4, 6, and 9 irons; a driver; and a putter
    *d. 5, 7, and 9 irons; a 3 wood; a 5 wood; and a putter

12. Which clubs should every player carry?
    a. driver, 2 wood, 5 iron, putter
    b. 3 wood, 6 iron, 7 iron, 9 iron
    *c. 3 wood, 5 iron, 9 iron, putter
    d. driver, 3 iron, wedge, putter

13. What does the actual length of the club determine?
    a. the trajectory of the ball
    *b. the golfer's distance from the ball
    c. the amount of flex in the club shaft
    d. the club's relation to the ground

14. What is a general rule to remember about clubs?
    *a. as loft increases, club number increases
    b. as loft increases, shaft length increases
    c. as loft decreases, club number increases
    d. as loft decreases, shaft length decreases

15. Which part of the club is used to hold it?
    a. the head
    *b. the grip
    c. the handle
    d. the sole

16. In what two ways will the clubs in a matching set of golf clubs differ?
    a. length and flexibility
    b. weight and flexibility
    c. weight and clubface loft
    *d. length and clubface loft

17. What is the purpose of the scoring lines on the face of the golf club?
    a. distance
    *b. spin
    c. height
    d. loft

18. What is the name of the part of the club nearest the shaft?
    *a. heel
    b. link
    c. top
    d. sclaff

19. What part of the club is labeled *a* in the diagram? [Refer to Diagram 1.]
    a. clubface
    b. heel
    c. toe
    *d. sole

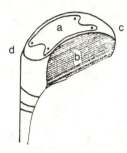

Diagram 1

20. Which part of the club is labeled *b* in the diagram? [Refer to Diagram 1, Question 19.]
    *a. clubface
    b. toe
    c. neck
    d. sole

Irons

21. For what distances are the 2, 3, and 4 irons used?
    a. distances near the green
    b. short distance shots
    c. middle distance shots
    *d. long distance shots

22. Which club should yield the greatest accuracy?
    a. 2 iron
    b. 5 iron
    *c. 9 iron
    d. 5 wood

23. Which irons are designed for distance?
    *a. 2 and 3 irons
    b. 4, 5, and 6 irons
    c. 7, 8, and 9 irons
    d. Only the woods are built for distance.

24. Which clubs will produce the highest trajectory?
    *a. 7, 8, and 9 irons
    b. 2 and 3 irons
    c. 5, 6, and 7 irons
    d. 4, 5, and 6 irons

25. Which club has the most loft?
    *a. 9 iron
    b. 7 iron
    c. 3 wood
    d. 3 iron

26. What is the general distance and trajectory for a 7 iron in relation to the 3, 5, and 9 irons? [Refer to Diagram 2.]
    a. a
    *b. b
    c. c
    d. d

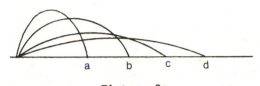

Diagram 2

Woods

27. How does a fairway wood differ from the driver?
    *a. It is shorter, more lofted, and heavier.
    b. It is longer, more lofted, and heavier.
    c. It is shorter, less lofted, and heavier.
    d. It is longer, more lofted, and lighter.

28. Which club is considered the most powerful?
    a. 4 wood
    b. 9 iron
    c. 6 iron
    *d. 1 wood

29. How does the driver compare to other woods?
    a. shortest shaft and greatest loft angle
    b. longest shaft and greatest loft angle
    c. shortest shaft and least loft angle
    *d. longest shaft and least loft angle

Putter

30. Blade, mallet, and two-way are terms associated with which club?
    *a. putter
    b. sand wedge
    c. 1 iron
    d. 2 wood

31. Which club is essential for all golfers?
    a. 9 iron
    b. 5 iron
    *c putter
    d. driver

Wedge

32. Which club is especially designed for bunker shots?
    *a. sand wedge
    b. pitching wedge
    c. utility club
    d. two-way putter

33. Which club can be distinguished from other clubs by its flange?
    *a. sand wedge
    b. 9 iron
    c. 5 wood
    d. putter

Ball

34. Why is the smaller ball, permitted for play in England, desirable?
    a. because of economic factors related to manufacturing it
    *b. because of extremely windy conditions on the British Isles
    c. because it contributes to greater accuracy
    d. because of its worldwide use

Ball Marker

35. Where is a ball marker primarily used?
    a. in the rough
    b. on the fairway
    *c. on the green
    d. in a bunker

Glove

36. Why do golfers wear a golf glove?
    a. to prevent blisters
    *b. to enhance the grip
    c. to abide by the rules
    d. to keep the hand warmer

Safety

Teeing Off

37. You are in the second foursome teeing off on the 420-yard first hole. When is it appropriate for you to tee off?
    a. when the tournament official tells you
    b. when the first foursome is on the green
    *c. when the first foursome has moved out of your range
    d. when the first foursome has completed the hole

Fore

38. Which procedure should players follow?
    *a. Yell "fore" if there is danger of hitting a player ahead.
    b. Wave players on while you are still on the green.
    c. Take practice swings in the direction of the hole.
    d. Record scores while standing on the green.

Away

39. Why does the player farthest from the hole play first?
    a. It is a rule of the game.
    b. It is a convenience.
    *c. It is the safest order of play.
    d. It speeds up the game.

Storm

40. What is the wisest precaution to take if an electrical storm comes up while you are playing?
    a. Hide under an isolated tree.
    *b. Lie flat at the foot of a hill or in a depression.
    c. Seek shelter in a golf cart.
    d. Lie flat in the fairway, protecting your clubs.

Sunstroke

41. What first aid treatment should be administered to a golfer suffering from sunstroke?
    *a. lay the victim on his or her back in the shade, head slightly elevated
    b. lay the victim on his or her stomach and administer back pressure-arm life artificial respiration
    c. lay the victim on his or her back in the shade, feet elevated
    d. give the victim cold water to drink

Terminology

Techniques	**42 to 45**
Shots	**46 to 52**
Playing Procedures	**53 to 57**
Scoring	**58 to 66**
Equipment	**67**
Course	**68 to 73**

Techniques

Address

42. What is the phrase for taking a stance and grounding the club before starting the backswing?
    a. lining up the ball
  *b. addressing the ball
    c. approaching the ball
    d. teeing up the ball

Waggle

43. How would you identify a waggle?
    a. forward press of the swing
  *b. preliminary movements with the clubhead
    c. the crosscut mowing of the grass on the green
    d. the cover on the wood club

Open Stance

44. The left foot is drawn back from the imaginary target line. Which type of stance is this?
    a. square
    b. parallel
  *c. open
    d. closed

Bite

45. What does the term *bite* refer to in a golf context?
    a. rub of the green
    b. lie of the ball
  *c. backspin on the ball
    d. wind on the course

Shots

Slice

46. What is a shot called that curves to the right for a right-handed player?
    a. push, due to an open clubface
  *b. slice, due to an open clubface
    c. hook, due to a closed clubface
    d. pull, due to a closed clubface

47. What is a slice?
    a. a ball that starts out to the right but ends up curving to the left of the target line
  *b. a ball that starts out to the left but ends up curving to the right of the target line
    c. a ball that goes at a straight angle to the left of the target line
    d. a ball that goes at a straight angle to the right of the target line

48. Which diagram shows a slice? [Refer to Diagram 3.]
  *a.

Diagram 3

Push

49. Which statement best describes a push?
    a. a straight shot to the left of the target
    b. a shot played from the rough
  *c. a straight shot to the right of the target
    d. a shot played from the apron of the green

Pull

50. Which statement best describes a pull?
  *a. a shot that travels to the left of the intended line
    b. a shot that travels to the right of the intended line
    c. a shot that curves to the left
    d. a shot that goes over the green

Explosion Shot

51. What is an explosion shot?
    a. a shot in which the ground is hit before contacting the ball
    b. a shot played to the putting surface
  *c. a shot played from the bunker
    d. a shot that travels straight and then curves sharply to the left

Whiff

52. What golf term refers to a swing in which the player misses the ball entirely?
    a. bisque
    b. stymie
    c. waggle
  *d. whiff

Playing Procedures

Honor
53. To what does the term *honor* refer?
    a. the winner in stroke play
    b. the number of holes a player is ahead in match play
    c. the person who scores a hole-in-one
    *d. the privilege of teeing off first

Mulligan
54. What is a Mulligan?
    a. a brand of golf balls
    *b. an illegal practice of taking a second tee shot on the first tee
    c. an illegal practice of awarding "gimme" putts
    d. a local rule

Provisional Ball
55. What is a provisional ball?
    a. an old ball used as a substitute of a good one in a hazardous situation
    b. a practice shot from the first tee
    *c. a second ball hit from the tee to save time in case the first ball is out-of-bounds
    d. a new ball used to replace a lost ball

Fore
56. Which term is used in golf to give a warning?
    a. Move!
    b. Look!
    *c. Fore!
    d. Watch out!

57. What does the call "Fore" mean?
    a. You have just scored a hole-in-one.
    b. You are taking a penalty stroke.
    *c. You are warning a player ahead of an oncoming ball.
    d. You are signaling for a faster group to play through.

Scoring

Par
58. What is the name of the regulation score for each hole?
    a. bogey
    b. ace
    c. birdie
    *d. par

Birdie, Eagle, Bogey
59. Which statement is true about scoring?
    a. Birdie is 1 over par, eagle is 2 under par.
    b. Bogey is 1 under par, birdie is 2 under par.
    c. Eagle is 1 under par, birdie is 2 under par, and ace is 1 over par.
    *d. Birdie is 1 under par, eagle is 2 under par, and bogey is 1 over par.

Double Bogey
60. Your score on a par 4 hole was 6 strokes. What is the term for this score?
    a. bogey
    b. birdie
    *c. double bogey
    d. eagle

Birdie
61. If a bogey on a hole is 4, what would a birdie be?
    a. 1
    *b. 2
    c. 3
    d. 5

Triple Bogey
62. On a par 3 hole, a player drives the ball out-of-bounds off the tee. The player tees up another ball, lands it on the green, and then 3 putts. What is the player's score on this hole?
    a. double bogey
    *b. triple bogey
    c. par
    d. eagle

Net Score
63. Which term refers to the total score minus the player's handicap?
    *a. net score
    b. gross score
    c. Nassau score
    d. lowest score

Match Play

64. What is match play?
    *a. competition where the winner is determined by the number of holes won at the end of the round
    b. competition where the winner is determined by the total number of strokes at the end of the round
    c. competition where the winner is determined by both the total number of holes won and the total number of strokes taken
    d. competition where the winner is determined by the number of birdies made during the round

Dormie

65. What does *dormie* mean?
    *a. You are up by as many holes as remain to be played.
    b. You are up more holes than remain to be played.
    c. You are down as many holes as remain to be played.
    d. Your opponent's ball is between you and the cup.

Down

66. What is the meaning of *down* in the context of golf?
    *a. the number of holes or strokes a player is behind
    b. two strokes under the designated par
    c. slant of the fairway
    d. angle of the clubface

Equipment

Hood

67. To which aspect of the game is the term *hooded* related?
    a. the course
    b. the rules
    *c. the clubs
    d. the etiquette of the game

Course

Fairway

68. What is the name of the closely mown grass area from the tee to the green?
    a. rough
    *b. fairway
    c. field
    d. course

Dogleg

69. What is the name of a fairway that curves either to the left or right?
    a. hook
    *b. dogleg
    c. slice
    d. dormie

Casual Water

70. What is an example of casual water on the golf course?
    *a. a rain puddle
    b. a pond
    c. a lateral water hazard
    d. a water fountain

Lateral Water Hazard

71. What is a lateral water hazard?
    a. water that runs across the fairway
    *b. water that is parallel to the fairway
    c. a pond anywhere in the fairway
    d. It is similar to casual water.

Bunker

72. What is an example of a hazard in the fairway?
    a. dogleg
    b. rough
    c. divot
    *d. bunker

Apron

73. What is the term for the grassy fringe surrounding the putting area?
    a. flange
    b. green
    *c. apron
    d. rough

Full Swing

Full Swing	**74 to 82**
Grip	**83 to 89**
Routine Approach/Setup	**90 to 98**
Backswing	**99 to 102**
Downswing/Forward Swing	**103 to 105**
Impact	**106 to 108**
Follow-Through	**109 to 110**
Spin	**111**
Irons	**112 to 114**
Middle Irons	**115 to 117**
Long Irons	**118**
Woods	**119 to 123**

Full Swing

74. The golf swing, thought of as a whole movement, includes all of these characteristics but one. What is the exception?
    a. a definite sequential flow of body parts
    b. a constant arc
    *c. an uneven pattern
    d. a plane for the hands and arms to follow

75. What part of the body forms the axis around which the club is swung?
    a. head
    b. shoulders
    c. hips
    *d. spine

76. Which word best describes the movement of the body during a full golf swing?
    *a. coil
    b. sway
    c. lunge
    d. thrust

77. What is the most important factor influencing a person's score?
    *a. a consistent swing under a variety of circumstances
    b. the ability to adjust to hazards
    c. the ability to remain relaxed and confident
    d. complete concentration on each shot

78. What are the crucial factors in determining the total distance the ball will travel?
    *a. the length of the club shaft and angle of the clubface
    b. strength of the player and angle of the clubface
    c. the weight of the clubhead and length of the club shaft
    d. the strength of the player and weight of the clubhead

79. In which situation will a well-hit golf ball go the longest distance?
    a. when it is hit high and straight
    b. when it is hit high and with a little slice
    *c. when it is hit high and with a little hook
    d. when it is hit high and as hard as possible

80. What effect does uncocking the wrists have on the golf swing?
    *a. increases the power of the total swing
    b. gives an acceleration of right-hand action
    c. decreases the power of the total swing
    d. gives a deceleration of right-hand action

81. What is the result if a golfer tenses the muscles of the hands, wrists, and forearms?
    *a. prevents the natural cocking of the wrists
    b. ensures a more powerful stroke
    c. helps the player get a feel for the swing
    d. ensures a grooved swing

82. What is the purpose of the forward press?
    *a. to initiate the swing
    b. to shift the weight
    c. to provide a longer arc in the swing
    d. to move the hands behind the line of the club

Grip

83. What is the primary purpose of the grip?
    a. to keep the club from flying out of the hands
    b. to increase the speed of the clubhead at impact
    *c. to make the connection between the club and the player
    d. to aid in keeping the left arm straight and the right elbow tucked

84. Which factor is considered the foundation of a good golf swing?
    a. shoulder strength
    *b. grip
    c. hip rotation
    d. stance

85. Which grip places the little finger of the right hand on top of the left index finger?
    a. natural grip
    *b. overlapping grip
    c. interlocking grip
    d. reverse overlapping grip

86. Which grip is used by the majority of golfers?
    a. the natural or 10-finger grip
    b. the interlocking grip
    c. the reverse overlapping grip
    *d. the overlapping grip

87. Why is one of the grips called the overlapping grip?
    *a. The little finger of one hand goes over the index finger of the other hand.
    b. The little finger interlocks with the index finger of the other hand.
    c. One hand lies over the other hand with its lifeline covering the thumb of the other hand.
    d. The thumb and forefinger of one hand go over the little finger of the other hand.

88. In golfing terms, what does it mean to strengthen your grip?
    a. squeeze the club more firmly
    b. exercise your forearm muscles
    *c. rotate your left hand over the top of the club slightly
    d. slightly rotate your left hand under the club

89. Which factor is used to choose the best grip for a golfer?
    *a. size of hands
    b. length of club
    c. type of shot to be made
    d. size of the grip on the club

Routine Approach and Setup

Setup

90. Which aspect of the swing is the most important?
    a. the backswing
    b. the downswing
    *c. the routine setup
    d. the follow-through

91. How should you start your setup routine?
    a. by establishing a square stance
    *b. by imagining a straight line from the target to the ball
    c. by placing feet parallel to the target line
    d. by flexing the knees slightly

Address

92. How should the body weight be distributed during the address position?
    a. concentrated on the outside of the left foot
    *b. concentrated on the inside of both feet
    c. concentrated on the outside of the right foot
    d. concentrated on the outside of both feet

93. What is the correct lie of the clubhead when addressing the ball?
    a. toe slightly off the ground
    b. heel slightly off the ground
    c. entire clubhead just slightly off the ground
    *d. sole of the club flat on the ground

94. Which body position is *not* a part of a correct address position?
    a. extended arms holding the club
    b. straight back, leaning forward
    c. bending at hips
    *d. straight legs, shoulder width apart

95. Which statement gives the most correct description of the right elbow at the address position?
    a. perfectly straight
    b. higher than the left elbow
    c. hyperextended
    *d. relaxed

Stance

96. In which stance is the right foot placed slightly forward and the left foot slightly back of it with the left toe turned slightly left?
    *a. open
    b. square
    c. square, slightly closed
    d. closed

97. Which diagram shows an open stance? [Refer to Diagram 4.]
    *d.

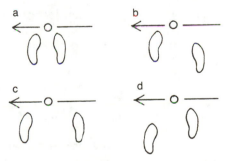

Diagram 4

98. Which stance is recommended for most novice golfers?
    *a. square stance
    b. closed stance
    c. the stance that allows the widest base
    d. open stance

Backswing

99. What is the primary function of the backswing?
    - a. to get the clubhead in motion
    - *b. to position the club to hit the ball
    - c. to establish the arc of the swing
    - d. to ensure a rhythmical swing

100. Which statement most accurately describes the shift of weight during the backswing?
    - a. left instep to right instep to right heel
    - b. left instep to right instep
    - *c. left and right insteps to center of right foot
    - d. left and right insteps to center of right foot to right heel

101. Which statement best describes the beginning part of the backswing?
    - *a. Swing the clubhead back low to the ground.
    - b. Move the head to follow the club takeaway.
    - c. Pull from the right side.
    - d. Dip the left shoulder below the chin.

102. Which statement best describes the top of the backswing?
    - *a. The right elbow points to the right hip.
    - b. The grip changes position.
    - c. The back faces to the left of the target.
    - d. The club points to the left of the target.

Downswing and Forward Swing

Forward Swing

103. Which action should happen at the beginning of the forward swing?
    - *a. The left heel lowers as weight shifts forward.
    - b. The left hip spins to the left.
    - c. The right arm begins downward motion.
    - d. The right shoulder lowers.

104. What is the most efficient sequential movement of the body on the forward swing?
    - *a. knees, hips, shoulders
    - b. shoulders, hips, hands
    - c. hands, shoulders, hips
    - d. knees, hands, shoulders

Downswing

105. At what point in the downswing should the uncocking action of the wrists occur?
    - a. at the top of your backswing
    - b. during the follow-through
    - c. at the very beginning of your downswing
    - *d. when your hands have reached hip level on the downswing

Impact

106. How is it best to ensure solid contact?
    - *a. a smooth rhythm
    - b. a well-arced swing
    - c. brute strength
    - d. a well-grooved swing

107. What action must occur to get the ball to go straight?
    - *a. square up the clubface at impact
    - b. slide the hips around as the first movement of the downswing
    - c. tuck the right elbow in
    - d. hold back the shoulders

108. Which factor is the most important in determining the distance the ball will travel?
    - a. angle at which the club contacts the ball
    - b. arc at which the backswing is executed
    - *c. speed of clubhead through the impact zone
    - d. degree of force used to hit the ball

Follow-Through

109. Which statement most accurately describes the follow-through?
    - a. Hands finish high, above and slightly to the right of the head.
    - b. Weight is transferred from the right to the left side.
    - c. Weight is equally balanced on both feet.
    - *d. Hips and right knee point toward the target.

110. Which aspect of the swing following impact is most important?
    - a. power from hips, back, and arms
    - b. tension of muscles
    - c. rotation of arms
    - *d. balance

Spin

111. How does topspin affect the ball when it lands?
     * a. It increases forward roll.
     b. It has no effect.
     c. It decreases the amount of roll.
     d. It makes the ball bounce sideward.

Irons

Address

112. Which diagram represents the correct position of an iron at address? Why? [Refer to Diagram 5.]
     * a. A, because the clubhead is balanced to hit the ball at the center of the clubface.
     b. B, because the ball will be lifted faster with the widest part of the clubface.
     c. C, because the ball will be hit with the heaviest part of the clubface.
     d. A, B, or C could be used as correct positions according to the situation.

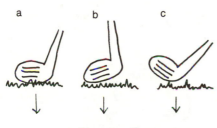

Diagram 5

113. Where, in relation to the feet, should most iron shots be played, in general?
     a. off the front of the left foot
     b. off the front of the right foot
     c. back from the center of the stance
     * d. forward from the center of the stance

Impact

114. Which statement best describes the downswing with an iron at impact?
     * a. The ball is contacted first and then the turf.
     b. The ball is hit on the upswing to ensure loft.
     c. The turf is contacted first, then the ball for loft.
     d. The clubhead hits through the ball, never contacting the turf.

Middle Irons

Address

115. What is the best position for the ball in relation to the feet when hitting a middle iron shot?
     a. even with the right foot
     b. even with the left foot
     * c. centered or slightly forward in the stance
     d. between the center line and the right foot

Stance

116. How will a stance wider than the width of the player's shoulders affect a 5-iron shot?
     a. allows the player to put more into the stroke
     b. ensures balance during the stroke
     c. ensures more accurate drives
     * d. inhibits correct body action

Backswing

117. Which diagram shows the best form at the top of the backswing for a middle iron? [Refer to Diagram 6.]
     * a.

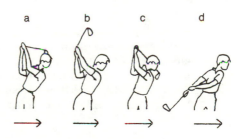

Diagram 6

Long Irons

118. Which iron is considered the most difficult to hit well?
     * a. 1 iron
     b. 3 iron
     c. 5 iron
     d. 9 iron

Woods

119. Which adjustment is *not* appropriate for a wood shot?
     a. Play the ball off the forward foot when driving from the tee.
     b. Use a wider and square stance.
     c. Play fairway shots closer to the center of the stance.
     *d. Use a partial swing for the distance desired.

Stance

120. Where should the ball be placed in relation to the stance when driving from the tee?
     a. off the right heel
     *b. off the left heel
     c. slightly to the right of center
     d. in the center of the stance

Address

121. Where should the hands be located in relation to the ball when addressing the ball with a driver?
     a. hands even with the ball
     *b. hands slightly behind the ball
     c. hands slightly in front of the ball
     d. hands in front of the ball

Tee

122. Why is the driver only used with a tee?
     *a. because of the amount of loft on the clubface
     b. because of the distance it creates
     c. because of the length of the shaft
     d. because of the difficulty of hitting with it

Fairway

123. Where, in relation to the stance, should the 5 wood be played?
     a. toward the center of the stance
     b. as far forward as when hitting a drive
     *c. toward the front of center of the stance
     d. toward the back of the stance

Short Game

Approach Shots	124 to 130
Chip Shots	131 to 133
Pitch-and-Run Shots	134 to 136
Bunker Shots	137 to 143
Comparison of Iron to Wood Shots	144
Spin	145

Approach Shots

124. When is an approach shot used?
     a. when the player is ready to start a new hole
     *b. when the player is within a short distance of the green
     c. when the player is on the green
     d. when the player is approaching a trap

125. Which factor need *not* be considered when making an approach shot?
     *a. location of partner's ball on the green
     b. condition of the course
     c. contour of the green
     d. lie of the ball

Address

126. Where should the ball be placed in relation to the feet for a 7-iron shot? [Refer to Diagram 7.]
     *b.

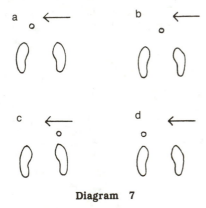

Diagram 7

127. What is the weight distribution when addressing the ball for a short iron shot?
     *a. favors left foot rather than right
     b. favors right foot rather than left
     c. distributed evenly over both feet
     d. distributed over heels of both feet

Technique

128. You are playing a short iron shot. Which practice is *not* recommended?
     a. Use a shortened swing for desired distance.
     *b. Hit the ball with an ascending swing.
     c. Keep arms and body close to the ball.
     d. Use a square to open stance.

129. Which is the best suggestion for executing short approach shots?
    a. Use a 9 iron or wedge, always try to pitch the ball, hit the ball with backspin.
  *b. Grip down on the club, choose a middle or short iron to suit the situation, take a narrow stance.
    c. Take a divot after striking the ball, use only the wedge, take an open stance.
    d. Use a 5 iron or wedge depending on the shot desired, hit down on the ball, grip down on the leather.

Stance

130. You are making a 9-iron approach shot to the green and will need approximately a half swing. How should you adjust your stance?
  *a. narrow and open
    b. narrow and closed
    c. wide and open
    d. wide and closed

Chip Shots

131. Which shot is used when the ball is close to the green with a clear approach?
  *a. chip
    b. putt
    c. bunker
    d. pitch-and-run

132. What is the key to good chipping?
  *a. Get the ball on the green and let it run to the cup.
    b. Select a club with little loft and land the ball close to the cup.
    c. Grip the club near the top for better control.
    d. Close the clubface throughout the shot.

Address

133. What is the correct position of the ball in relation to the body for a chip shot?
    a. on a line slightly left of center
  *b. centered or slightly right of center
    c. on a line with the left toe
    d. on a line with the right toe

Pitch-and-Run Shots

134. What is the basic difference between the pitch shot and the pitch-and-run shot?
  *a. the amount of roll and time the ball is in the air
    b. the club selection
    c. the length of the swing
    d. the stance and ball placement

135. What determines the distance of the pitch-and-run shot?
    a. length of the follow-through
    b. snap of the wrists
  *c. length of the backswing
    d. the amount of turf taken

136. Which statement describes a 5-iron pitch-and-run shot?
    a. The distance the ball rolls equals about half the distance of flight.
    b. The distance the ball rolls equals about the distance of flight.
  *c. The distance the ball rolls equals about twice the distance of flight.
    d. The distance the ball rolls equals about three times the distance of flight.

Bunker Shots

137. What adjustment should be made for playing a ball out of a bunker?
    a. Use a low trajectory club.
    b. Use a slightly closed stance.
  *c. Use a slightly open clubface.
    d. Hold back on the follow-through.

138. What is most important when playing the ball out of a bunker?
    a. keeping the head down
  *b. hitting the sand behind the ball
    c. getting a deep stance
    d. trying not to follow through

139. What procedure is recommended for exploding a ball out of the bunker?
    a. Sole the club at address and swing smoothly.
  *b. Work the feet into the sand to establish a solid stance for balance.
    c. Concentrate the eyes at the point on the ball that the club should contact.
    d. Remove all twigs, cigarette butts, and stones so the swing is not impaired.

140. What type of swing is most effective for the explosion shot out of the bunker?
    a. an upright swing
  *b. an outside-in swing
    c. an inside-out swing
    d. a flat swing

141. Which statement is associated with an explosion shot?
    a. The club must contact the ball directly.
    *b. The compression of the club against the sand provides the lifting action.
    c. The use of a 7 iron provides the high trajectory.
    d. The use of a fast swing provides added power.

142. You are in a bunker near the green approximately 50 feet from the hole. The trap is fairly shallow with a slightly overhanging lip, and your ball is 2 feet from the lip. The sand is hard and packed from a recent rain. Between your ball and the green is a thick fringe. What is the best shot?
    a. Blast out of the trap.
    b. Putt out of the trap.
    c. Declare casual water and drop the ball.
    *d. Chip out of the trap.

Fairway Bunker

143. You have driven into a fairway bunker and are 120 yards from the green. What should you do?
    a. Use a 5 iron to hit a long explosion shot.
    *b. Play the ball in its normal position and be sure to hit the ball first.
    c. Close the face of the club and take it back slightly to the outside.
    d. Aim to the right of the target to avoid a fading shot.

Comparison of Iron to Wood Shots

144. What three things are identical for both wood and short iron shots?
    *a. rhythm of swing, target line, grip
    b. arc of swing, grip, head position
    c. target line, position of grip on club, stance
    d. head position, stance, arc of swing

Spin

145. Which club imparts the most backspin on the ball?
    *a. pitching wedge
    b. 7 iron
    c. 5 iron
    d. 3 iron

Putting

These questions on putting cover the techniques related to style, reading the green, and so forth. The rules about putting are in the Rules category.

Theory	**146 to 147**
Technique	**148 to 151**
Grip	**152 to 153**
Reading the Green	**154 to 161**
Order of Putting	**162 to 163**

Theory

146. Which skill in golf is the most individualized?
    a. pitching
    *b. putting
    c. chipping
    d. driving

147. What is the most important aspect of putting?
    a. reading the greens correctly
    *b. developing a consistent feel for distance and direction
    c. drawing a mental line from the hole to the ball
    d. striving for good balance with the head over the ball

Technique

148. Which technique is prevalent among all good putters?
    a. Stand with feet close together.
    b. Flex left wrist at contact with the ball.
    c. Use the same grip as with other strokes.
    *d. Have eyes directly over the target line.

149. What are the best suggestions for improving your putting?
    a. Practice, take more time to study each putt, take several practice swings before each putt.
    *b. Increase your practice, work on a smooth, effective stroke, know that you can become skillful in putting.
    c. Change to a different putter, copy the form of a professional, and take more time studying each putt.
    d. On long putts, do not putt past the hole, point your left elbow toward the hole, and keep your head down.

150. Which type of putt has a long, smooth stroke with backswing and follow-through of equal length?
    a. tap putt
    b. punch putt
    c. wrist putt
    *d. stroke putt

151. What should golfers do to improve their putting if they are punching the ball?
    a. Grip the club more tightly.
    *b. Follow through toward the target.
    c. Use a rigid arm movement.
    d. Stroke harder.

Grip

152. Which putting grip is most commonly used by professional golfers?
    a. the overlap
    b. the interlock
    *c. the reverse overlap
    d. the 10-finger

153. Which putting grip is most appropriate for the novice golfer?
    a. the interlocking grip
    *b. the grip most comfortable to the player
    c. the baseball grip
    d. the overlapping grip

Reading the Green

154. What should a player do first when preparing to putt?
    a. Draw a mental line from the hole to the ball.
    b. Address the ball.
    *c. Notice the contour factors that might influence the line of the putt.
    d. Make routine movements with the feet striving for comfort and balance.

155. What is the most important factor to consider when making a short putt?
    a. width of stance
    *b. direction
    c. slope of the green
    d. distance

156. The position of the ball on the green is such that the putt will be against the grain of the grass. What adjustment should be made?
    *a. Putt with more force, using a firmer stroke.
    b. Putt to the left side of the hole.
    c. Putt with less force, using a lighter stroke.
    d. Putt to the right side of the hole.

157. Which way will the ball roll when putting downhill with the hole located on your right?
    *a. break from left to right
    b. straight
    c. not be affected by the hill
    d. break from right to left

158. Which factor has the greatest influence on a sidehill putt?
    *a. speed
    b. aim
    c. gravitational pull of the slope
    d. stance

159. What determines the direction to hit the ball on the green?
    a. the straightest line to the hole
    b. the distance to the hole
    c. the type of grass on the green
    *d. the slope of the green

160. Where should the golfer aim the putt if the break on the green slopes from left to right?
    *a. to the left of the cup
    b. to the right of the cup
    c. straight at the cup
    d. short of the cup

161. When lining up a putt, the golfer sees that the green slopes away and slightly to the left. Where is the best place to aim?
    a. Aim directly at the hole and hit the ball harder than usual to overcome the effect of gravity.
    b. Aim to the left of the hole and let gravity operate.
    c. Aim at the hole but follow through to the left.
    *d. Aim to the right of the hole and let gravity operate.

Order of Putting

162. Players A and B are both on the green. Player A is "away," but Player B's ball is directly between A's ball and the cup. What is the correct procedure?
    *a. Player B should mark his or her ball, remove it, and then Player A should putt.
    b. Player B should putt first because his or her ball lies on the line of direction for A.
    c. Player B must putt first according to the rule because his or her ball is the closer one.
    d. Player A must ask B if he or she will observe the rule of etiquette and putt first.

Marking

163. You are waiting for your turn to putt. Where should you place a small marker when you lift your ball from the putting green?
    a. where the ball lay
    b. to the left or right of where the ball lay
    *c. directly behind where the ball lay
    d. in front of where the ball lay

Errors and Corrections

Slicing

164. Which type of shot is caused by swinging from the outside in with an open clubface?
    a. hook
    b. push
    c. pull
    *d. slice

165. What factor can cause a slice?
    a. a closed stance
    *b. an outside-in swing path
    c. an inside-out swing path
    d. a "strong" grip

166. The left hand is placed far to the left on the grip when swinging the club. What action will result?
    *a. The ball will probably slice.
    b. The ball will probably hook.
    c. The ball will travel on the correct line.
    d. The ball will be topped.

167. A golfer changes the grip so that the left hand is moved more on top of the golf club and the right hand is turned under the club slightly. What is the most likely reason for this change?
    *a. to straighten out a slice
    b. to purposely slice the ball
    c. to purposely hit the ball higher
    d. to straighten out a hook

168. Your golf ball repeatedly slices. What aspect of your swing should you check first?
    *a. Check your alignment.
    b. Make certain that you keep your eye on the ball.
    c. Check your grip.
    d. Check your weight distribution.

Hooking

169. What is a *hook* and what causes it?
    a. a ball curving to the left of the intended line of flight due to a push
    b. a ball curving to the right of the intended line of flight due to a pull
    *c. a ball curving to the left of the intended line of flight due to counterclockwise spin
    d. a ball curving to the right of the intended line of flight due to clockwise spin

170. Which stance would most likely result in a hook?
    a. a square stance
    *b. a closed stance
    c. an open stance
    d. a wide stance

171. What spin causes the flight of the ball to curve to the left for a right-handed player?
    a. clockwise spin
    *b. counterclockwise spin
    c. topspin
    d. backspin

Pulling and Pushing

Pushing

172. What is the result when the ball is struck with an inside-out swing with an open clubface?
    *a. push
    b. pull
    c. hook
    d. slice

173. What is the best suggestion for curing the fault of consistently hitting the ball on a straight line to the right of the target?
    a. Check your stance, aim, and try to hit from inside out.
    *b. Check your alignment, go back to practicing the short shots, and work up to the long shots.
    c. Take an open stance and aim for the left of the target, thereby allowing for the error.
    d. Try to pivot more on your backswing and keep your head down.

Pull Hook

174. Your right hand is placed on the club so that the palm faces upward. In which direction will the ball travel?
    * *a. to the left of the target
    b. to the right of the target
    c. straight toward the target
    d. straight, then to the right of the target

Topping Ball

175. You have topped your tee shot. Where did you contact the ball?
    a. below its center
    b. to the left of its center
    c. to the right of its center
    * *d. above its center

176. What is the best suggestion for curing the error of topping the ball?
    a. Keep your left arm straight and your right elbow in to your side.
    b. Hold your head down until the end of the follow-through and swing from the inside out.
    c. Try to get under the ball and swing your right shoulder under your chin.
    * *d. Watch the clubhead strike the ball and try to sweep the grass after striking the ball.

177. Ralph lifts his head and takes his eye off the ball before contact is made. What will likely occur?
    a. hook the ball
    * *b. top the shot
    c. take a deep divot
    d. slice the ball

178. What is the usual result if you lift your shoulders and hips rather than rotate them on the backswing?
    a. a hook or pull shot
    b. a slice or shank shot
    c. a missed or skied shot
    * *d. a topped or sculled shot

179. A golfer lifts his or her head and shoulders during the backswing. What is likely to happen?
    a. hits behind the ball
    * *b. tops the ball
    c. slices the ball
    d. pulls the shot

Hitting Behind Ball

180. A golfer dips his or her left shoulder on the downswing. What will be the most likely result?
    * *a. hit behind the ball
    b. top the ball
    c. slice the ball
    d. push the shot

Bunker

181. What is the most common error in bunker play?
    * *a. failing to follow through
    b. hitting the ball with the clubface
    c. taking too much backswing
    d. taking too little backswing

Divot

182. Which action is *not* an error in golf?
    a. lifting the head
    b. swaying back and forth
    c. bending the elbows
    * *d. taking a divot

Special Situations

Uneven Lies	**183 to 189**
Intentional Slice	**190**
Intentional Hook	**191**
Rough	**192 to 193**
Punch Shot	**194**
Inclement Weather	**195 to 200**

Uneven Lies

Uphill

183. How would the stance probably be adjusted when playing a ball that is on an uphill lie?
    a. Adjust the stance to play the ball more off the right foot.
    * *b. Adjust the stance to play the ball more off the left foot.
    c. Adjust the stance to play the ball from beyond the right foot.
    d. Adjust the stance to play the ball from outside the left foot.

184. What adjustment is needed to hit the ball from an uphill lie?
    a. Aim an inch or two behind the ball.
    b. Use a reverse overlap grip.
    c. Select a club with more loft.
    * *d. Play the ball left of center.

185. Which diagram shows the correct stance for an uphill lie? [Refer to Diagram 8.]
*c.

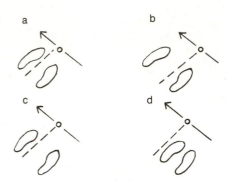

Diagram 8

186. What is the correct position of the ball in relation to the body on an uphill wood shot?
   a. on a line midway between the left and right feet
   b. on a line closer to the right heel than usual
   *c. on a line closer to the left heel than usual
   d. on a line that best suits the individual player

Downhill
187. What are the essential things to remember when hitting from a downhill lie?
   1. closed stance, with weight carried on right side
   2. open stance, with weight carried on left side
   3. ball played farther back than usual
   4. ball played farther forward than usual
      a. 1 and 3
      b. 1 and 4
      *c. 2 and 3
      d. 2 and 4

Sidehill
188. What adjustment needs to be made to hit a ball on a sidehill lie with the ball above the feet?
   *a. The swing should take a flatter plane.
   b. The aim should be adjusted to avoid a fade.
   c. The ball should be played toward the middle of the stance.
   d. The golfer should use a longer backswing.

189. The golfer has a sidehill lie with the ball below the feet. Which shot is likely to happen?
   *a. a slice
   b. a hook
   c. a high ball
   d. a pull

Intentional Slice
190. What adjustment is made to hit a deliberate slice?
   a. Use an inside-out swing path.
   *b. Use an outside-in swing path.
   c. Alter the grip.
   d. Alter the weight distribution.

Intentional Hook
191. What adjustment is made to hit a deliberate hook?
   *a. Use an inside-out swing path.
   b. Use an outside-in swing path.
   c. Alter the grip.
   d. Alter the weight distribution.

Rough
192. Kathy lies 1 in heavy rough on a par 4 hole. She is 160 yards from the green. On the driving range, she can hit her 5 wood 160 yards. What should she do?
   a. hit her 3 wood and go for the green
   *b. hit an iron to the fairway short of the green
   c. hit her 5 wood and go for the green
   d. hit her 5 wood to the fairway short of the green

193. You are lying 3 yards behind a tall, branchy tree just off the fairway. What is the best shot to make?
   a. Hit the ball through the branches in the direction of the green.
   b. Loft the ball over the tree.
   *c. Hit a low shot underneath the branches in the direction of the green.
   d. Move your ball to a better location.

Punch Shot
194. Which statement characterizes the punch shot?
   a. Play the ball more toward the left foot.
   b. Hit down in a chopping motion and do not follow through.
   c. Concentrate on a high follow-through.
   *d. Set the hands ahead of the ball at address and play the ball back in your stance.

Inclement Weather

195. What is the basic strategy to remember when playing in inclement weather?
    *a. Be prepared to play conservatively.
    b. Keep the ball low to the ground.
    c. Hit the ball harder to compensate for the adverse weather conditions.
    d. Play your regular game.

Wind

196. What is the *worst* adjustment for a tee shot into the wind?
    *a. Swing faster and harder for added power.
    b. Tee the ball higher.
    c. Use a longer club.
    d. Try to hit the ball in a low trajectory.

197. How should you adjust your game when playing against the wind?
    a. Try to swing harder than usual and use more club.
    b. Try to swing easier with the usual club.
    *c. Try to swing a little slower than usual and use more club.
    d. Try to swing a little slower than usual and use the same club, but hit it lower by adjusting your swing.

198. The wind is blowing in the opposite direction to your tee shot. What should you do?
    *a. Tee the ball lower.
    b. Tee the ball higher.
    c. Use the wind to get greater distance.
    d. Swing harder.

199. You are teeing off with the wind behind you. What should you do?
    a. Tee the ball lower and use a more lofted club.
    b. Tee the ball lower and use a less lofted club.
    *c. Tee the ball higher and use a more lofted club.
    d. Tee the ball higher and use a less lofted club.

Rain

200. What should be done differently when playing golf in the rain or on wet fairways?
    *a. One less club than normal should be used because the ball tends to fly farther.
    b. The ball should be aimed to the left of the target to counteract a fading shot into the green.
    c. One less club than normal should be used because of wind usually associated with rain.
    d. The ball should be aimed to the right of the target to counteract a fading shot to the green.

Course Management

General Strategy	**201 to 202**
Club Selection	**203 to 209**

General Strategy

201. What kinds of information should help the golfer select the proper club for a particular shot?
    a. distance to go and whether or not winter rules are in use
    b. loft necessary, uphill or downhill lie, and location of hazards around the green
    *c. lie of the ball, hazards involved, and individual ability
    d. individual ability and presence or absence of bunkers

202. You are playing a match and find yourself in the woods on the right side of the fairway 120 yards from the green. Your ball is in the position shown in the diagram. Your opponent lies 2 and is 50 feet from the pin. You also lie 2. What should you do? [Refer to Diagram 9.]
    *a. Go for the green aiming to the right side of the tree as you face it.
    b. Play safe aiming left of the tree and then playing a punch shot onto the fairway.
    c. Go for the green aiming left of the tree and slicing the ball.
    d. Concede the hole to your opponent.

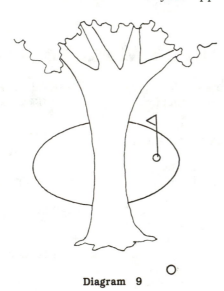

Diagram 9

Club Selection

203. The ball is lying on the closely mown fringe, as shown in the diagram, just barely off the green. How would you play the shot? [Refer to Diagram 10.]
    a. Use the 5 iron to pitch and run.
    *b. Putt onto the green.
    c. Chip the ball to the middle of the green.
    d. Tap the ball with the 9 iron.

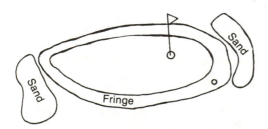

Diagram 10

204. Which clubs are most appropriate for approach shots over a bunker?
    a. 3 and 5 irons
    *b. 7 and 9 irons
    c. 3 and 7 irons
    d. 5 and 9 irons

205. Which club is used for a pitch shot?
    a. driver
    b. 4 iron
    c. 7 iron
    *d. wedge

206. Which club would be used if the shot requires a high loft with a minimal amount of run?
    *a. pitching wedge
    b. 7 iron
    c. 5 iron
    d. 4 iron

207. Your ball lies 35 yards from the green. The green is surrounded by bunkers. Which club would you use?
    a. Use a half swing with a 5 iron so the ball will not go too far.
    b. Use a very short swing with a 3 iron to roll the ball onto the green.
    c. Use a 7 iron so the ball will land just short of the green and roll to the cup.
    *d. Use a pitching wedge so the ball will be lofted high into the air, land on the green, and roll very little.

208. You are 40 yards from the green in the fairway with low hanging limbs between you and the green. The limbs are about 12 feet above the ground. What is the best club and type of shot for you to play in this situation?
    a. pitching wedge, trying to land the ball on the green near the hole
    b. 9 iron, trying to land the ball on the front of the green and let it run up
    c. 2 iron, using a three-quarter swing to keep the ball low and get plenty of speed on it
    *d. 5 iron, using a half swing to run the ball low up to the green

209. On a narrow fairway, par 5, lined with dense woods on each side, you might decide to tee off with a 3 or 4 wood rather than a driver. What is the most likely reason for doing so?
     a. to get distance at the expense of height
     b. to get loft or height on the ball at the expense of distance
     *c. to get accuracy at the expense of distance
     d. to get distance at the expense of accuracy

Etiquette

Honor

210. What general policy determines who should tee off first on each hole?
     *a. the one with the least number of strokes on the preceding hole
     b. the one with the most strokes on the preceding hole
     c. the one with the fewest total strokes at that point
     d. the one with the highest score at that point

211. Which player has the honor on the next tee when the hole just completed was tied?
     *a. the player winning the preceding hole
     b. the player with the higher total score
     c. the player with the lower total score
     d. the player with the lower handicap

212. Players teed off in the following order for Hole 5: Don, Tom, Jim, Joe. The scores for the hole are Joe—4, Tom—4, Jim—5, Don—5. In what order should they tee off for Hole 6?
     a. Don, Tom, Jim, Joe
     *b. Tom, Joe, Don, Jim
     c. Tom, Don, Joe, Jim
     d. Don, Jim, Tom, Joe

213. On the 16th hole, Player A had a birdie, Player B had a double bogey, Player C had an eagle, and Player D was even for that hole. Who has the honor on the 17th hole?
     a. Player A
     b. Player B
     *c. Player C
     d. Player D

Playing Through

214. While putting, someone in your threesome notices that you are holding up a twosome playing behind you. What is the proper thing to do?
     a. Stop putting and signal the twosome to play through.
     *b. Finish putting and let the twosome tee off before you on the next hole.
     c. Finish putting, tee off on the next hole, and then signal the twosome to play through.
     d. Continue playing and invite the twosome to join your group.

215. What would be the acceptable procedure when coming upon a foursome looking for a lost ball?
     a. Play through.
     *b. Wait until motioned through.
     c. Help them find the ball.
     d. Call to them.

Lost Ball

216. A golfer has lost his or her golf ball. What is considered the correct behavior by the members of the group?
     *a. Assist in searching for the ball.
     b. Offer him or her one of your own golf balls.
     c. Continue to play your own ball.
     d. Wait patiently until the golfer finds the ball.

217. What is the accepted procedure if you think you have lost your golf ball?
     a. Look until you find it and then continue play.
     b. Immediately wave the group following to play through.
     *c. Wave the group following to play through if you are having trouble finding the ball.
     d. Play a provisional ball without looking for the original ball.

Bag and Club Placement

218. Where should the golf bag be placed when a person is going to putt?
    a. on the edge of the green, close to the ball so the bag is easily accessible
    b. off the green, close to the ball so the bag is easily accessible
    *c. off the green, close to the next tee
    d. near the partner's bag

219. Which procedure should *not* be followed while playing golf?
    a. Let faster groups play through.
    b. Play without delay.
    *c. Rest your clubs on the green while putting.
    d. Replace and press down divots.

Bunker

220. A player has just hit out of a bunker. What should happen next?
    a. Leave the bunker by the route entered.
    b. Smooth out the hole made by the shot.
    c. Leave the bunker by the shortest route.
    *d. Smooth out all holes left by the club, golf ball, and feet.

Remaining Quiet

221. What should playing companions do while a player is teeing off?
    *a. Stand by quietly watching the shot.
    b. Record the scores from the previous hole.
    c. Take practice swings.
    d. Clean their golf balls at the ball washer.

222. Which procedure is assumed behavior on a golf course?
    a. Help your opponent select clubs.
    *b. Remain quiet while others are hitting.
    c. Share your ball-cleaning towel.
    d. Stand behind the hitter.

Recording Score

223. Where should you stand while recording the score for the hole just played?
    a. on the edge of the green just played
    b. on the way to the next tee
    c. on the next tee
    *d. on the next tee, before teeing off

Putting

224. Which procedure is an example of *poor* etiquette?
    a. replacing divots
    b. smoothing the sand as you leave a trap
    c. using a repair tool to fix a ball mark
    *d. standing between the sun and a person putting

Fore

225. What is the best thing to do when your golf ball is traveling toward a person?
    a. Call for medical help.
    *b. Yell "fore."
    c. Hide behind a tree.
    d. Administer first aid.

Teeing Off

226. Where should you stand while others are teeing off?
    a. off the tee area
    b. off the tee area, two club lengths
    c. off the tee area, two club lengths behind the tee
    *d. off the tee area, perpendicular to the tee markers

Divot

227. What typically should be done with a divot?
    a. Leave it.
    *b. Replace it.
    c. Lift it.
    d. Tramp it down.

Wrong Fairway

228. What should you do if the ball comes to rest in the wrong fairway?
    a. Hurry and play the ball immediately.
    b. Lift the ball and drop it in the correct fairway.
    c. Tee off again and take a one-stroke penalty.
    *d. Play the ball when it is safe to do so and without interfering with the other players.

Rules

Note: Questions on Etiquette are covered in a separate category. Questions on Honor are included in the Etiquette category.

Number of Clubs

229. What is the maximum number of clubs a golfer may carry without penalty?
    a. 10
  *b. 14
    c. 17
    d. There is no limit to the number of clubs a golfer may carry.

Match Play

230. Joe beat Harry "3 and 2" in an 18-hole match play competition. What does this mean?
    a. that Joe won 3 holes, Harry won 2 holes, and the rest of the holes were halved
    b. that Joe scored 3 under par whereas Harry scored only 2 under par
  *c. that Joe had won 3 more holes than Harry after having played 16 holes
    d. that Joe was 3 holes ahead after 9 holes and 2 holes ahead after 18 holes

231. Beth and Jim played 18 holes of golf. Beth's score was the lowest; however, Jim won the greater number of holes. Who won the match if the two of them were playing match play?
    a. Beth
  *b. Jim
    c. One cannot tell from the information given.
    d. It was a tie.

232. On which hole did the match end if Player A defeated Player B by the score of "6 and 4"?
    a. on the 12th hole
    b. on the 13th hole
  *c. on the 14th hole
    d. on the 18th hole

Stroke Play

233. In which type of play is the golfer who uses the least number of strokes over the designated course declared the winner?
    a. match play
    b. even play
  *c. stroke play
    d. casual play

Strokes Taken

234. A player swings at the ball and misses it. What happens next?
    a. The player replays the shot keeping his or her eye on the ball.
    b. The player moves the ball back two club lengths from the original lie and replays the shot.
  *c. The player adds a stroke to the score and takes another swing at the ball where it lies.
    d. The player lets the opponent take the next shot before trying to strike the ball again.

235. Steve is playing a 420-yard par 4 hole. He hits his first shot out-of-bounds and plays a provisional ball that he hits into the lake. He drops a ball beside the lake and shoots on up the fairway, landing in a bunker. He blasts his way out onto the green. On his first putt, he hits his opponent's ball. His next putt goes into the cup. How many strokes did it take him to complete the hole?
    a. 8
    b. 9
  *c. 10
    d. 11

Teeing Area

236. From where on the teeing area may the ball be legally hit?
   a. only within the tee markers
   b. anywhere in front of the markers
   c. anywhere within and one club length behind the tee markers
   *d. anywhere within and two club lengths behind the tee markers

Use of Tee

237. When is it permissible to use a tee?
   *a. only on the teeing area for each hole
   b. at all times when playing winter rules
   c. when using one of the wood clubs
   d. when hitting a ball that is in the rough

Ball Falling Off Tee

238. You accidentally knock your ball off the tee during your preswing routine. Which rule applies in this case?
   a. You must add one penalty stroke to your score for this hole.
   b. You must count the accidental hit as one stroke and play the ball as it lies.
   c. You may play the ball as it lies adding no penalty.
   *d. You may tee the ball up again and continue with no penalty.

Loose Impediments

239. You slice the ball off the tee. You discover it behind a clump of weeds, among some cans. What can you do?
   a. Play the ball from where it lies.
   b. Use your clubhead to knock down the weeds to improve your lie.
   c. Drop the ball away from the weeds and trash without penalty.
   *d. Use your hands to remove trash from around the ball and play it out of the weeds.

240. Which objects on the course *cannot* be removed or pressed down without penalty?
   a. stones and gravel
   b. misplaced divots
   *c. small plants and live tree limbs
   d. cigarette stubs

241. Which action may be taken legally?
   a. pressing down irregularities of the ground to improve your lie
   *b. removing loose natural impediments such as leaves, stones, or twigs
   c. moving your ball while preparing to putt
   d. pulling up weeds growing around your ball

Out-of-Bounds Stake

242. Which obstacle are you *not* allowed to move your ball away from if it interferes with your swing or stance?
   a. a sprinkler head
   *b. an out-of-bounds stake or fence
   c. a water pipe
   d. a protective screen

Dropping Ball

243. What is the correct way to drop the ball?
   a. Stand in front of the hazard closest to the tee and drop the ball from your hand relaxed by your side.
   *b. Stand erect, hold the ball at shoulder height and arm's length, and drop it.
   c. Face the green, stand erect, and drop the ball over your shoulder.
   d. Face the tee with eyes closed and drop the ball in front of you at arm's length away from the body.

Cleaning Ball

244. Where on the course may a player pick up the ball to clean it?
   a. in the fairway
   b. in the rough
   *c. on the green
   d. in the bunker

Ball at Rest Moved

245. Your ball moves after you have addressed it on the fairway. What should you do?
   a. It doesn't matter if it was an accident.
   b. Add one stroke to your score only if it was touched by your club.
   c. Pick up the ball and drop it no nearer to the hole.
   *d. Add one stroke to your score.

Accidental Hit

246. What should Jane do if she accidentally hits her golf ball while taking a practice swing on the fairway?
    *a. Play the ball from where it landed counting the practice swing as a stroke.
    b. Play the ball from where it landed with no penalty.
    c. Replace the ball with one-stroke penalty.
    d. Replace the ball with no penalty.

Out-of-Bounds

247. What happens when the ball is hit out-of-bounds?
    a. Play it as it lies with no penalty.
    b. Drop a ball on the fairway and play it from there with no penalty.
    *c. Take the ball back to the place from where it was hit and play it again with a one-stroke penalty.
    d. Drop a ball and take one penalty stroke.

248. Bill thinks his tee shot is out-of-bounds. What should he do?
    *a. Play a provisional ball from the tee in case the original ball is in fact out-of-bounds.
    b. Play another ball at the point the first ball went out; no penalty.
    c. Use his Mulligan.
    d. Play another ball at the point the first ball went out; one-stroke penalty.

249. In which situation would the player return to the tee with the understanding that the next shot is the third stroke?
    *a. first shot goes out-of-bounds
    b. unplayable lie from the second shot
    c. tee shot rolls into a lateral water hazard
    d. ball lost after second shot

Lost Ball

250. How long is a player allowed to search for a lost ball?
    a. a reasonable amount of time but no longer than 15 minutes
    *b. 5 minutes
    c. 8-10 minutes
    d. There is no time limit.

251. What is the penalty for a ball lost or out-of-bounds?
    a. loss of distance and no stroke penalty
    b. loss of distance and the ball dropped
    *c. loss of distance and one-stroke penalty
    d. loss of distance and two-stroke penalty

Provisional Ball

252. When may you play a provisional ball?
    *a. when you think your ball may be lost
    b. when you are not satisfied with your initial tee shot
    c. after you have looked for your first ball and cannot locate it
    d. when your first ball lands in a hazard

253. What is the procedure when a provisional ball has been hit and then the original ball is found playable?
    a. Play the original ball at the better location.
    b. Play the provisional ball and pick up the original ball.
    *c. Play the original ball and pick up the provisional ball.
    d. Play the ball closest to the hole.

Obstructions

254. You add one stroke in all these situations except one. Which is the exception?
    a. when you swing and miss on the tee
    b. when the ball moves as the club is drawn back
    *c. when the ball is moved from an immovable obstruction
    d. when you land in a water hazard

255. A player may move the ball one club length, no closer to the hole, without penalty in all but one situation. Which condition is the exception?
    a. ball lies under an immovable bench
    *b. ball settles in a divot in the fairway
    c. ball lies next to a staked tree
    d. ball rolls under a greenskeeping machine

Casual Water

256. What is the proper procedure to follow when a ball lands in casual water?
    a. Remove ball from the water, drop it no closer to the hole, and add a stroke.
    b. Remove the ball, place it in front of the water, and add a stroke.
    *c. Remove the ball, drop it at your nearest point of relief, no closer to the hole, and do not add a stroke.
    d. Play the ball from where it lands.

257. Your tee shot lands in casual water. What is the most important rule to remember when taking the appropriate relief?
    a. Face the green and drop the ball over your shoulder.
    b. Keep the ball within two club lengths of the water.
    *c. Do not drop the ball closer to the green.
    d. Do not move the ball with anything but the club.

258. When may a player take a drop without incurring a penalty?
    a. when too close to a tree to hit the ball
    b. when in a divot
    *c. when in casual water
    d. when in a hazard

Hole by Burrowing Animal

259. Your tee shot bounces into a hole made by a burrowing animal. Your procedure would be similar to which situation?
    a. when the ball is behind a tree
    b. when the ball is out-of-bounds
    *c. when the ball is in casual water
    d. when the ball is in a bunker

260. When may a player lift the ball without penalty and drop it no closer to the hole?
    a. out of a hazard
    *b. out of a hole made by a burrowing animal
    c. out of a divot hole
    d. out of a tree stump

Hazards

261. What is your penalty for dropping the ball out of a hazard such as a ditch or lake?
    a. no penalty
    *b. one stroke
    c. two strokes
    d. loss of the hole

262. What is the ruling if Susie's club touches the sand on her downswing as she is hitting her ball out of the bunker?
    a. two-stroke penalty
    *b. no penalty
    c. one-stroke penalty
    d. replay the shot with a one-stroke penalty

263. Which parts of a golf course are considered hazards?
    *a. greenside bunkers
    b. out-of-bounds stakes
    c. maintenance vehicles along the fairway
    d. casual water and doglegs

Water Hazard

264. You hit your ball into a lateral water hazard. What should you do?
    a. Drop and play another ball immediately; two-stroke penalty.
    b. Drop ball out on side it entered; two-stroke penalty.
    *c. Drop ball on either side; one-stroke penalty.
    d. Drop ball behind hazard; one-stroke penalty.

Flagstick

265. You are putting from the fringe and your ball hits the flagstick. What is your penalty?
    a. one stroke
    b. two strokes
    c. loss of hole
    *d. no penalty

Putting

266. In what case may a putting green *not* be touched?
    a. to clean the ball
    b. to repair ball marks
    c. to remove loose debris
    *d. to improve the line of putt

267. If both players are putting, what is the procedure if your ball strikes another player's ball on the green?
    a. You must take a one-stroke penalty and return the displaced ball to its original position.
    *b. You must take a two-stroke penalty and return the displaced ball to its original position.
    c. You may play your ball without penalty and must return the displaced ball to its original position.
    d. You must take a two-stroke penalty, and the displaced ball remains in its new position.

268. Which procedure is *not* permitted on the green?
    a. repairing ball marks
    *b. testing the surface by rolling another ball
    c. removing loose impediments
    d. cleaning your ball

269. You lift your ball from the putting green. Where must you place a small ball marker?
    a. where the ball lay
    b. to the left or right of where the ball lay
    *c. directly behind where the ball lay
    d. in front of where the ball lay

270. What should you do if your ball lands on a putting green other than the hole being played?
    *a. You should remove the ball from the green, drop it no closer to the hole, and continue play; no penalty.
    b. You should putt off the green and continue play.
    c. You should hit a provisional ball and add a one-stroke penalty.
    d. You should hit a provisional ball; no penalty.

271. Bill lies 3 on the green and John lies 3 about 20 yards off the green. John chips up and hits Bill's ball, which rolls into the cup. What is each player's score at this point?
    *a. Bill 3, John 4
    b. Bill 3, John 5
    c. Bill 4, John 4
    d. Bill 4, John 5

Winter Rules

272. What is the major difference between the regular rules and the "winter rules" of golf?
    a. In winter rules, the ball must be played from where it lies.
    b. In regular rules, the ball may be moved to a better lie.
    c. In regular rules, you may play a second ball if the first ball is lost.
    *d. In winter rules, the ball may be moved to a better lie.

Tournament Format

273. What is the format of most professional golf tournaments?
    a. 54 holes of match play
    *b. 72 holes of stroke play
    c. 72 holes of match play
    d. 90 holes of stroke play

Scoring

274. What is the main method for determining par for a hole or a course?
    a. general terrain and number of hazards
    b. decision of an established USGA committee
    *c. yardage of a hole or course
    d. average score of the club pro

275. How is par determined on each hole?
    a. by the difficulty of the hole
    *b. by the length of the hole
    c. by professional golfers' rating of each hole
    d. by the United States Golf Association

276. How is a handicap determined?
    a. It is the same as par for the course.
    b. It is based on a player's average score.
    *c. It is based on a percentage of the differential between course par and the player's average score.
    d. It is based on a percentage of average scores made by the people who play that particular course regularly.

277. You have completed 18 holes of golf with a score of 97. What is your net score if you had a handicap of 14?
    *a. 83
    b. 90
    c. 97
    d. 111

278. The player with which handicap is the most proficient golfer?
    a. 25
    b. 30
    c. 16
    *d. 12

279. Which score is the total score minus the handicap?
    *a. net score
    b. gross score
    c. Nassau score
    d. lowest score

280. On which hole did Dana have a birdie? [Refer to Diagram 11.]
    *a. 5
    b. 1
    c. 3
    d. 7

Handicap	7	4	1	5	2	3	9	8	6	
Yards	495	345	378	150	510	361	130	341	325	3135
Par	5	4	4	3	5	4	3	4	4	36
Holes	1	2	3	4	5	6	7	8	9	Tot.
Dana	7	4	5	4	4	4	3	5	4	
John	5	3	5	1	4	6	3	4	4	

Won +	We									
Lost −										
Halve 0	They									

Date _____	Scorer _____	Attest _____

Diagram 11

281. On which hole did John have an eagle? [Refer to Diagram 11, Question 280.]
    a. 1
    b. 2
    c. 3
    *d. 4

282. Who won the match if John and Dana were playing match play? [Refer to Diagram 11, Question 280.]
    *a. John won.
    b. Dana won.
    c. They tied the match.
    d. It isn't possible to tell from the scorecard.

283. Who won the match and what were the scores if John and Dana were playing stroke play and Dana's handicap was 9 and John's was 4? [Refer to Diagram 11, Question 280.]
    a. Dana, score 39
    b. John, score 30
    *c. John, score 35
    d. Dana, score 31

284. Which hole was the most difficult? [Refer to Diagram 11, Question 280.]
    a. 1
    *b. 3
    c. 5
    d. 7

Acknowledgments

Colleagues and students who contributed suggestions and ideas for the Golf section test questions are: S. Anastas, L. Dillard, H.B. Duntz, A. Farrow, N. Ferebee, D. Hooker, C. Hughes, D. Hull, K. Ley, F. Malizola, N. Matthews, F. O'Meara, D. Owens, L. Powell, P. Stortstrom, M. Whitesell, E. Williford, B. Wolfe, D. Workman, and C. Yoos.

Suggested Readings

Bunker, L.K., & Owens, D.D. (1984). *Golf: Better practice for better play.* Champaign, IL: Leisure Press.

Davies, P. (1980). *Davies' dictionary of golfing terms.* New York: Simon and Schuster.

Nance, V.L., & Davis, E.C. (1985). *Golf* (5th ed.). Dubuque, IA: Wm. C. Brown.

Toski, B., & Flick, J. (1984). *How to become a complete golfer* (2nd ed.). Norwalk, CT: Golf Digest.

United States Golf Association. (1986). *The rules of golf.* New York: Author.

Vroom, J. (1983). *So you want to be a golfer!* (rev. ed.). San Jose, CA: Vroom Enterprises.

Gymnastics

Robert M. Dailey, Consultant

The questions assembled in this gymnastics collection are appropriate to Olympic gymnastics. If questions are required for rhythmical gymnastics or educational gymnastics, some revisions in content and answers will be necessary. Test questions are included that should be suitable for both the participant and the observer of gymnastics. Six competitive events for men and four competitive events for women are covered. Questions in the vaulting and floor exercise categories are appropriate for both men and women.

Questions are organized in the following categories:

- General knowledge
- Floor exercise
- Vaulting
- Balance beam
- Uneven bars
- Horizontal bar
- Parallel bars
- Pommel horse
- Still rings

The general knowledge category contains questions that either cut across all events or are not related specifically to any one event. Included are test questions on individual moves, terminology, history, safety, spotting, warm-up, physical attributes, mechanical principles, and judging.

Each competitive event has questions that fall into various subheadings: recognition of moves, progression of moves, execution of moves, combination of moves, spotting, and judging. Questions in these subheadings cover many general concepts and specific skills. The questions are not, however, all inclusive.

Robert M. Dailey is coordinator of health, physical education, athletics, and driver education at Pitt County Schools in Greenville, North Carolina.

General Knowledge

Moves and Technique

Recognition of Moves

1. What type of quality does the body have in gymnastics?
    a. stiff
    *b. linear
    c. limp
    d. circular

Progression of Moves

2. What two women's events, when one is followed by the other, may be taught together to improve the quality of instruction?
    *a. from floor exercise to beam
    b. from beam to uneven bars
    c. from floor exercise to vaults
    d. from beam to floor exercise

3. What would be the best source to learn about proper progression of moves?
    a. Code of Points
    *b. USGF Gymnastics Safety Manual
    c. USA Gymnastics Manual
    d. a textbook on gymnastics

4. Which concept is most essential to sound progression of moves?
    a. The gymnast should strive to achieve ever more difficult moves.
    b. The gymnast should become competent on one event before devoting time to other events.
    *c. The gymnast's skills should be excellent before going to the next level.
    d. The gymnast's coach should be the only person to determine when the next level is appropriate.

Execution of Moves

5. What is a common factor in all dismounts?
    a. All are done with fully extended legs upon landing.
    b. All are done with the arms out to the sides.
    c. All are done with the head down.
    *d. All are done with a slight knee bend to a stretched body position upon landing.

6. What must one do when landing from an aerial movement?
    a. Use arms to aid in balance.
    *b. Plié to absorb shock.
    c. Remain erect with no body lean.
    d. Focus out rather than down.

7. How can amplitude of movement best be established?
    *a. by emphasizing focus and projection
    b. by emphasizing strength to perform movements
    c. by emphasizing body control throughout movements
    d. by emphasizing security in one's capabilities

Terminology

Amplitude

8. Which term means the fullest extent to which a movement can be performed?
    a. connections
    b. difficulty
    c. bridge
    *d. amplitude

Connections

9. Which term is used to describe the movements that link individual parts of a routine?
    a. lay-out
    *b. connections
    c. bridges
    d. body tension

FIG

10. What is the FIG?
    *a. International Gymnastics Federation
    b. Finnish Independent Gymnastics Association
    c. First International Gymnastics League
    d. Foreign Independent Gymnastics Club

Flic-Flac

11. What is a flic-flac?
    a. forward aerial cartwheel
    b. double back salto
    *c. back handspring
    d. back walkover

USGF

12. What is the USGF?
    a. International Gymnastics Federation
    b. United Sovereign Federation of Gymnasts
    c. United Society for Gymnastic Followers
    *d. United States Gymnastics Federation

History

13. Who is the father of Swedish gymnastics?
    a. Sargent
    *b. Ling
    c. Wood
    d. Dio Lewis

14. What characterized gymnastics in early Roman civilizations?
    a. apparatus and weight work
    b. comic court jester acrobatics
    c. flowing, spontaneous dance
    *d. rigid, systematic exercises

15. Which group of names includes founders of modern gymnastic systems?
    a. Cozens, Stumpf, Dunaway
    b. Lawther, Oxindine, Singer
    *c. Guts Muths, Jahn, Ling
    d. Wundt, Weber, Fechner

16. What is the name of the American organization for gymnastics that began in 1950?
    a. American Gymnastics
    b. National Gymnastic Congress
    c. Rounders
    *d. Turners

17. Which country was a major contributor in the development of modern rhythmical gymnastics?
    *a. Germany
    b. Japan
    c. Russia
    d. United States

18. What was the German gymnastic society that promoted gymnastics in the United States?
    a. Denvarkane
    b. Jahsen
    *c. Turnvereine
    d. Sargent

19. Which phrase would best describe Dio Lewis's school of gymnastics?
    a. thorough examinations and detailed measurements of the body
    b. marching exercises performed in definite unison
    *c. light rhythmical exercises using rings, wands, and wooden dumbbells
    d. heavy weight exercises done to music

20. What is one characteristic of the Danish gymnastic system introduced by Neils Bukh?
    a. rigid
    b. precise
    c. definite
    *d. rhythmical

21. Who invented the horizontal bar, parallel bars, and the side horse?
    a. Johann Guts Muths
    b. Dudley Sargent
    c. Dio Lewis
    *d. Friedrich Jahn

22. Who published the first book on gymnastics?
    a. Dio Lewis
    b. Ling
    *c. Guts Muths
    d. Jahn

23. Who is credited with helping to introduce gymnastics in America?
    *a. Sargent
    b. Hitchcock
    c. Dio Lewis
    d. Ling

24. Which gymnast achieved five perfect scores at the 1976 Montreal Olympics?
    a. Olga Korbut
    b. Cathy Rigby Mason
    *c. Nadia Comaneci
    d. Lynn Rogers

Safety, Spotting, and Warm-Up

Safety

25. What is the most essential factor when participating in gymnastics?
    a. precision
    b. confidence
    c. power
    *d. safety

26. What is an overall concept applicable to the area of safety in gymnastics?
    a. The spotter must be present for the execution of any skill.
    b. The spotter must be familiar with the movements to be spotted.
    c. The performer must know the spotting for the skill being performed.
    *d. The performer must feel confident in his or her ability and knowledge of a skill before attempting to execute the skill.

27. Which factor is *not* an important safety consideration when preparing for participation in a gymnastics meet?
    a. Chalk the hands.
    b. Check the equipment.
    c. Check the location of the mats.
    *d. Talk to the judge about safety tips.

28. What can be used on a gymnast's hands to improve his or her grip?
    a. resin
    b. sand
    *c. chalk
    d. tar

29. When is a gymnast's body in the most danger?
    a. when off the floor
    b. when on the apparatus
    c. when spotting
    *d. when inverted

30. What is an important reason for a gymnast to wear a pair of handgrips?
    a. to slide easier on the apparatus
    b. to hold chalk
    c. to set up apparatus
    *d. to prevent tearing

31. In what area of the body is the gymnast most likely to be injured?
    a. neck
    b. spine
    c. ribs
    *d. joints

32. What is the safest way to move gymnastics equipment?
    a. Slide it across the floor.
    *b. Use transporters.
    c. Have several people carry the equipment.
    d. Place it on a mat and then pull the mat.

33. What is the composition of the chalk used on the gymnast's hands to help the grip?
    a. sodium
    b. rosin
    c. carbonate of potassium
    *d. carbonate of magnesium

34. What is probably the most common injury in gymnastics?
    *a. a "rip" of the hand
    b. an ankle sprain
    c. a strain or muscle pull
    d. a broken wrist

Spotting
35. What is the main purpose of spotting?
    a. to enable the performer to do moves that would otherwise be beyond his or her ability
    b. to give confidence to the beginner
    c. to prevent injury when the performer is tired
    *d. to provide for the participants' safety

36. What is the spotter's greatest concern?
    a. injury to self
    *b. injury to performer
    c. execution of the stunt
    d. safety of the equipment

37. What is the most important asset of a spotter?
    a. friendliness
    b. strength
    *c. alertness
    d. size

38. What must a spotter be able to do?
    a. Catch the performer.
    b. Perform the move being attempted.
    *c. Anticipate faulty movement before it happens.
    d. Talk to the performer.

39. Which responsibility is *not* the role of the spotter?
    a. to provide for safety of performer
    b. to help the performer get the feel of the move
    c. to build confidence in performer
    *d. to assist those who are too weak to perform the move

Warm-Up
40. What is the effect of warm-up?
    a. eliminates the chance of injury
    *b. reduces the chance of injury
    c. increases the chance of injury
    d. has little effect on the chance of injury

41. What would be the best method of warm-up before participating in a gymnastic activity?
    a. ballistic-type stretches
    b. no stretching
    *c. static stretching
    d. jumping jacks

Physical Attributes

Flexibility
42. What is the most efficient type of flexibility exercise?
    a. ballistic stretching
    b. static stretching
    c. a combination of ballistic and static stretching
    *d. contraction-relaxation stretching

43. What is an example of a flexibility exercise?
    a. pull-ups
    *b. splits
    c. push-ups
    d. dips

44. When is the most effective and efficient time to develop flexibility?
    a. at least a half hour before the workout
    b. directly before the workout
    c. between exercises in the workout
    *d. after the workout

Balance

45. Which movement is *not* considered an exercise for balance?
    *a. squat thrust
    b. front scale
    c. arabesque
    d. handstand

46. Which position shown in the diagram requires the greatest degree of balance for the average gymnast? [Refer to Diagram 1.]
    *a.

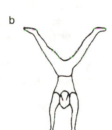

Diagram 1

Mechanical Principles

Center of Gravity

47. Where should your center of gravity be for you to most likely be able to maintain your balance?
    *a. close to the base
    b. slightly in front of the base
    c. far away from the base
    d. slightly behind the base

48. A balance is performed best when the center of gravity is in which position?
    a. outside the base of support
    b. below the base of support
    *c. within the base of support
    d. above the base of support

49. Where is a woman's center of gravity usually located?
    a. chest
    *b. hips
    c. knees
    d. waist

50. What is the usual difference between the center of gravity for men and women?
    *a. lower for women
    b. lower for men
    c. It depends on the body structure.
    d. It varies with the body position.

51. Where is the center of gravity located for the position shown in the diagram? [Refer to Diagram 2.]
    *c.

Diagram 2

52. Where is the center of gravity located for the position shown in the diagram? [Refer to Diagram 3.]
    *b.

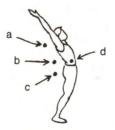

Diagram 3

Axis

53. Which movement rotates around the medial axis?
    *a. cartwheel
    b. back handspring
    c. forward somersault
    d. pirouette

54. Which movement rotates around the transverse axis?
    a. cartwheel
    b. side aerial
    *c. back handspring
    d. pirouette

55. Which movement rotates around the longitudinal axis?
    a. back handspring
    b. forward sumi
    c. side aerial
    *d. handstand half turn

56. A gymnast wishes to decrease torque. Which position shown in the diagram would be most conducive? [Refer to Diagram 4.]
    *d.

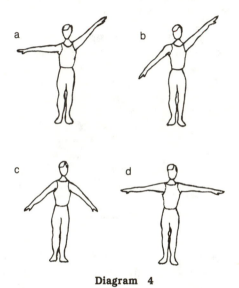

a   b

c   d

Diagram 4

Weightlessness
57. At what point in any swinging movement does the performer assume weightlessness?
    *a. just prior to downswing
    b. just prior to upswing
    c. just after upswing begins
    d. just after downswing begins

Judging

Procedures
58. In how many events do male and female gymnasts compete?
    a. male, 4; female, 4
    b. male, 6; female, 6
    c. male, 5; female, 5
    *d. male, 6; female, 4

59. What are the international competitive events for women?
    a. horizontal bar, floor exercise, unevens, vaulting
    b. parallel bars, balance beam, horizontal bar, unevens
    c. balance beam, floor exercise, still rings, parallel bars
    *d. vaulting, unevens, balance beam, floor exercise

60. What is the classification of the most difficult gymnastic moves?
    a. A
    b. B
    c. C
    *d. D

61. What must be done in competition immediately prior to mounting the apparatus?
    a. Test the apparatus.
    *b. Salute the judge.
    c. Rearrange the mats.
    d. Mentally practice the routine.

62. How much time does a male gymnast have to remount an apparatus after a fall?
    a. 15 seconds
    b. 20 seconds
    *c. 30 seconds
    d. 60 seconds

Evaluation
63. What does judging gymnastics events involve?
    *a. subjective ratings made by judges
    b. objective ratings made by judges
    c. only joint decisions made by judges
    d. consultations with the superior judge

64. Which factor is *not* considered when judging a competitive routine?
    a. difficulty and technical execution
    b. originality and composition
    *c. experience of competitor
    d. general impression

65. Which element is *not* a major factor in the evaluation of an exercise?
    a. difficulty
    b. execution and virtuosity
    *c. originality
    d. combination

66. Which factor does *not* identify combination in a routine?
    a. change in direction
    b. change in tempo and rhythm
    *c. optimal extension and posture
    d. a dismount that corresponds to the difficulty level of the exercise

67. What area is given the greatest weighting in judging optional routines in gymnastics?
    *a. execution of the exercise
    b. value of the difficult elements
    c. value of the general composition
    d. general impression of the exercise

68. What factors are considered when determining bonus points in men's gymnastics?
    a. difficulty, combination, execution
    b. combination, courage, construction
    c. difficulty, execution, originality
    *d. courage, originality, virtuosity

69. What is the highest score possible in men's gymnastics without bonus points?
    *a. 9.4
    b. 9.6
    c. 9.8
    d. 10.0

70. Which factor has the most weighting in judging events?
    a. difficulty
    b. combination
    *c. execution
    d. bonus

71. What does the *D* in *ODV* represent?
    a. difficulty
    *b. additional difficulty
    c. direction
    d. overall discipline

72. What is another term for value parts?
    a. combinations
    b. originality
    *c. difficulties
    d. virtuosities

Scoring

73. What is the highest score possible on any event?
    a. 9.4
    b. 9.8
    *c. 10.0
    d. 10.2

74. How does the evaluation of difficulty compare in men's and women's gymnastics?
    a. The difficulty is the same for both.
    *b. The difficulty for men is higher.
    c. The difficulty for women is higher.
    d. The difficulty comparison cannot be determined without knowing the exercise.

75. Which two scores are thrown out when judging gymnastic routines?
    a. two lowest
    b. two middle
    *c. highest and lowest
    d. two highest

76. Four judges arrive at the score of 9.20, 9.30, 9.30, and 9.20. Which score represents the final score?
    a. 9.20
    *b. 9.25
    c. 9.30
    d. 9.35

77. Which fault would result in the greatest deduction?
    a. interruption in exercise
    b. technical error
    c. incorrect posture after the exercise
    *d. falling from the apparatus

78. After falling from the apparatus, the gymnast remounts and completes the routine. What is the deduction?
    a. 0.30
    b. 0.40
    *c. 0.50
    d. 0.60

79. A routine that contains no mount or dismount results in what maximum deduction?
    a. 0.20
    b. 0.30
    c. 0.40
    *d. 0.60

80. An infraction of the time prescription for a balance beam or floor exercise routine results in what deductions (under time or over time)?
    *a. 0.20
    b. 0.30
    c. 0.40
    d. 0.50

81. What is the Code of Points?
    a. book on proper conduct in competition
    *b. standards for judging artistic gymnastics competition
    c. almanac of gymnastics championships
    d. Olympic scores for artistic gymnastics

Floor Exercise

Recognition of Moves

82. Which floor position has the greatest stability?
    a. arabesque
    b. relevé
    *c. lunge
    d. headstand

83. Which ballet movements are sometimes used in floor exercise?
    *a. arabesque, pirouette
    b. contraction, Swedish fall
    c. grapevine, polka
    d. time step, Wideman push up

84. Which move in the diagram is most dependent on strength? [Refer to Diagram 5.]
    *a.

Flitfis

85. How is a flitfis described in floor exercise?
    a. any double salto
    b. any triple salto
    c. any single salto with a twist
    *d. any double salto with a twist

Plié

86. What is a plié?
    a. hop
    b. kick
    c. step
    *d. knee bend

Headstand

87. Which gymnastic move uses a tripod?
    *a. headstand
    b. handstand
    c. forward roll
    d. backward roll

Handspring

88. Each series of illustrations shows a front handspring. Which performer is doing the most technically correct front handspring? [Refer to Diagram 6.]
    *a.

Diagram 5

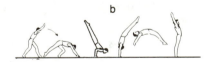
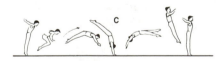
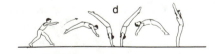

Diagram 6

Back Handspring

89. Which diagram shows the correct position to begin execution of the backward handspring? [Refer to Diagram 7.]

    *b.

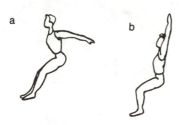
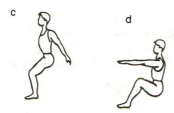

Diagram 7

90. Which phrase in this descriptive statement is *incorrect*?

    When coming out of a straddle forward roll, the performer should reach forward with the body from the hips, place the hands close to the crotch, shoulders far out in front of the body, head tucked close to the chest, arms straight and in line with the shoulders.
    a. reach forward with the body from the hips
    b. place the hands close to the crotch
    c. shoulders far out in front of the body
    *d. head tucked close to the chest

Back Bend

91. Which diagram shows the best form for a back bend? [Refer to Diagram 8.]
    a. A is best because the tumbler has the lowest center of gravity and the widest base of support, thus being the most stable.
    b. B is best because the tumbler has the most flexion of the upper and lower back.
    *c. C is best because the tumbler has equal flexion of the upper and lower back.
    d. No one is best because the best form is the form that feels best for the tumbler.

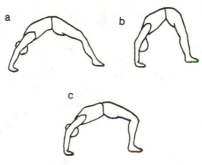

Diagram 8

Cartwheel

92. Which move is shown in the diagram? [Refer to Diagram 9.]
    a. front walkover
    *b. cartwheel
    c. handstand
    d. aerial cartwheel

Diagram 9

93. Which movements are variations of the cartwheel?
    1. dive cartwheel
    2. straddle cartwheel
    3. switch kick cartwheel
    4. one-arm cartwheel
       a. 1, 2
       *b. 1, 4
       c. 1, 2, 3
       d. 1, 2, 3, 4

Stag Leap

94. Which diagram illustrates a stag leap? [Refer to Diagram 10.]
       *b.

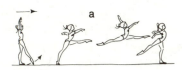

Diagram 10

Tinsica

95. What would a combination of a cartwheel and a front walkover be called?
       a.   round-off
       b.   handspring
       c.   two-foot limber
       *d. tinsica

Front Walkover

96. Which stunt is illustrated in the diagram? [Refer to Diagram 11.]
       *a.   front walkover
       b.   back walkover
       c.   front handspring
       d.   back handspring

Diagram 11

Back Walkover

97. Each series of illustrations shows a back walkover being performed. Which series shows the best back walkover? [Refer to Diagram 12.]
       *d.

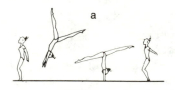

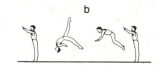

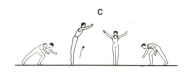

Diagram 12

Valdez

98. Which move is shown in the diagram? [Refer to Diagram 13.]
   - a. back walkover
   - *b. valdez
   - c. back tinsica
   - d. back handspring

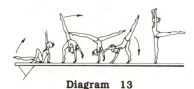

Diagram 13

Kip

99. Which phrase describes the kip?
   - a. handspring backward
   - *b. closing and opening action and reaction for thrust
   - c. movement in tuck
   - d. static balance position

Flic-Flac

100. Which phrase describes flic-flac?
   - a. straddled support lever
   - b. body in scale
   - *c. back handspring
   - d. elongated circular swing

Pike

101. Which position is illustrated in the diagram? [Refer to Diagram 14.]
   - a. layout
   - b. tuck
   - *c. pike
   - d. gainer

Diagram 14

Progression of Moves

102. The beginning tumbler must be able to execute which lead-up move well before attempting the dive forward roll?
   - a. backward roll
   - b. wrestler's bridge
   - c. shoulder roll
   - *d. forward roll

103. What lead-up moves should be learned prior to attempting the headstand?
   - a. cartwheel and one-hand cartwheel
   - b. forward roll, backward roll, cartwheel
   - *c. squat head balance, squat hand balance, forward roll
   - d. back extension and snapdown

104. Which order of moves reflects the best progression?
   - a. forward roll, backward straddle roll, backward roll, backward extension roll
   - b. backward roll, forward roll, backward extension roll, backward straddle roll
   - *c. forward roll, backward roll, backward straddle roll, backward extension roll
   - d. backward roll, backward straddle roll, backward extension roll, forward roll

105. How would this handstand progression be evaluated: handstand, handstand forward roll, handstand-limber-press handstand?
   - a. very advanced
   - b. reversed in order
   - *c. very sound
   - d. confused in the order

106. Which of these cartwheel moves should be changed in the learning progression: cartwheel, one-arm cartwheel, aerial cartwheel, front aerial walkover, and dive cartwheel?
   - a. Switch one-arm cartwheel and aerial cartwheel.
   - *b. Insert dive cartwheel after the one-arm cartwheel.
   - c. Switch front aerial walkover and aerial cartwheel.
   - d. Insert aerial cartwheel after cartwheel.

107. Is this progression for salto moves acceptable: back salto tuck position, back salto pike position, back layout salto, back full twisting salto?
   - *a. yes
   - b. no
   - c. It depends on the skill level of the performer.
   - d. It depends on the teaching strategy of the coach.

108. A gymnast is having trouble with a hand-stand. What exercise might help?
    a. crab walk
    b. duck waddle
    c. elephant walk
    *d. wall push-ups

109. Which move is a lead-up to the standing backward roll?
    a. back extension
    *b. backward roll from a squat
    c. cartwheel
    d. headstand

110. A limber is a lead-up to which move?
    *a. walkover
    b. headstand
    c. handstand
    d. cartwheel

111. What is the best progression to precede the learning of a limber?
    a. Master a handstand first.
    *b. Practice back arches first.
    c. Learn a walkover.
    d. Precede a limber with a run.

112. For proper progression, which move would be taught after a gymnast learns a cartwheel?
    a. back handspring
    b. front handspring
    *c. round-off
    d. front somersault

Execution of Moves

Twisting Back Somersault

113. When is the twisting action initiated in a full twisting back somersault in floor exercise?
    *a. at the 6 o'clock position as the feet are leaving the floor
    b. at the 8 o'clock position just after the feet leave the floor
    c. at the 10 o'clock position as the body is rising
    d. at the 12 o'clock position as the body is inverted

Forward Roll

114. Where should the head be placed in a forward roll?
    a. facedown on the mat
    b. outside the hands
    c. with the forehead on the mat
    *d. with chin tucked to chest and head on mat

115. Where should the hands be placed at the beginning of a forward roll?
    a. where they are most comfortable
    *b. in front of the feet
    c. between the feet
    d. to the sides of the feet

116. How should the tumbler land in the diving forward roll?
    *a. body vertical, extended, and in an inverted position
    b. body in a tucked position
    c. body piked and in an inverted position
    d. body tucked and then stretched

Forward Straddle Roll

117. What is the most important cue to remember when executing a forward straddle roll?
    a. Keep legs straight, toes pointed.
    b. Focus out in front of the body.
    c. Keep arms straight and close together on recovery.
    *d. Place hands close to the crotch to enable hips to be elevated.

Shoulder Roll

118. You are executing a right shoulder roll. Where must your weight be placed next as you roll over on your left shoulder?
    *a. left knee
    b. right knee
    c. back
    d. right arm

Headstand

119. Which two factors are most crucial to executing a headstand?
    a. flexibility and strength
    *b. strength and balance
    c. balance and agility
    d. agility and strength

120. Why is the weight placed on the forehead rather than the top of the head in the headstand?
    a. keeps head up for balance
    *b. places the hips in the center of the base
    c. keeps more weight on the head for greater leverage
    d. keeps more weight on the hands for greater leverage

121. What contributes most to produce good balance in a headstand?
    a. the toes pointed
    *b. a broad base of support
    c. the elbows bent at a 90° angle
    d. the head in the same line with the hands

122. What is a common fault when performing a headstand?
    a. balancing on the hairline
    b. placing the hands and head in a triangular position
    *c. balancing on the top of the head
    d. kicking up too fast

123. Which diagram shows the best base of support for the headstand? The darkened areas are touching the floor. [Refer to Diagram 15.]
    *b.

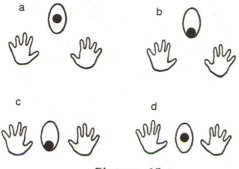

Diagram 15

Handstand

124. The performer, trying to execute a handstand, continually overbalances and lands on his or her back. What would be the best analysis of the fault?
    a. insufficient arm strength
    *b. center of gravity not over base of support
    c. roll-out is incomplete
    d. legs not straight, toes not pointed

125. Which sequence describes best the correct order of execution of the handstand roll-out from the handstand?
    a. Pull the chin under, flex the arms, move the center of gravity off the supporting base, flex the hips, and roll out.
    b. Flex the arms, pull the chin under, flex the hips, move the center of gravity off the supporting base, and roll out.
    *c. Move the center of gravity off the supporting base, flex the arms, flex the hips, pull the chin under, and roll out.
    d. Move the center of gravity off the supporting base, flex the hips, pull the chin under, flex the arms, and roll out.

126. Which part of the body is the fulcrum for the snapdown when performing a handstand to a snapdown?
    a. shoulders
    *b. hips
    c. thighs
    d. knees

Forward Handspring

127. Which factor is the most important to remember in the execution of a forward handspring?
    *a. A strong push is made from the shoulders.
    b. The arms remain flexed throughout the move.
    c. The legs whip from the hips.
    d. The focus is out and the body is arched.

Backward Roll

128. When is the most crucial point of the backward roll?
    a. when assuming the squat position
    b. when bringing the hands over the shoulders, palms up, fingers pointing backward
    c. when regaining balance
    *d. when the back of the head and the hands are simultaneously touching the mat

129. In which position should the knees be kept during execution of the backward roll in a tuck position?
    a. pike position
    b. jackknife position
    *c. close to the chest
    d. arch position

130. Of what use are the hands in the first-contact movement of the standing back roll?
    a. bracing the body
    b. balancing
    c. springing off the mat
    *d. breaking the fall

131. What is the most important part of the backward extension?
    a. keeping the legs straight
    b. keeping the chin tucked
    *c. extending the arms and legs at the same time
    d. putting the hands close to the head

Cartwheel

132. What is the proper rhythm of a cartwheel?
    a. hand, foot, hand, foot
    *b. hand, hand, foot, foot
    c. foot, foot, hand, hand
    d. foot, hand, foot, hand

133. When should the hands contact the mat while doing the cartwheel to the right side?
    a. at the same time
    *b. right hand first, then left hand
    c. left hand first, then right hand
    d. at no point in the stunt

Split

134. How should the hips be positioned when performing a split?
    a. facing the side
    *b. perpendicular to the lead foot
    c. rolled over on the mat
    d. halfway facing the side and halfway facing the lead foot

Combination of Moves

135. What is the recommended sequence for floor exercise?
    a. Start with harder and progress to easier skills.
    b. Start off fast and progress to a slower tempo.
    *c. Start with easy and progress to more difficult skills.
    d. Start off slow and progress to a faster tempo.

136. Which of the moves listed is the most appropriate combination from a forward walkover in a floor exercise routine?
    a. arabesque
    *b. split
    c. forward roll
    d. tour jeté

137. Which factor should *not* be a component of a floor exercise routine?
    *a. balances held for 3 to 5 seconds
    b. variations in level
    c. variations in tempo
    d. tumbling and acrobatic skills

138. Which sequence describes the most continuous flow of movements?
    a. forward roll, backward roll, back straddle roll, back walkover
    *b. forward roll, forward straddle roll, headstand forward roll to a stand
    c. forward roll to a stand, two foot limber, cartwheel, forward roll to a stand
    d. forward roll, forward straddle roll, backward roll to a back extension

139. Which of these four routine passes is the *poorest* in continuity?
    a. headstand, roll-out, forward roll to straddle, straddle to forward roll
    b. handstand, limber, front walkover, front walkover
    c. front handspring, front roll, turn, back roll, back extension
    *d. round-off, front roll to straddle, straddle to front roll

Spotting

Backward Roll

140. The beginner is having difficulty "getting over" on the backward roll. Where would the spotter assist the performer? [Refer to Diagram 16.]
    a. D and B
    *b. E and I
    c. G and J
    d. K and F

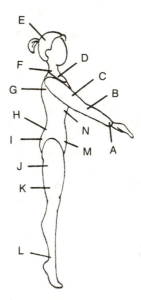

Diagram 16

141. The protection of which part of the body is of most concern when spotting a backward roll?
    *a. head
    b. eyes
    c. chin
    d. arms

142. The gymnast is beginning to learn the back handspring. What should be the location of the spotting? [Refer to Diagram 16, Question 140.]
    a. C and G
    b. D and H
    c. J and F
    *d. K and H

Front Handspring

143. The gymnast has learned to execute a front handspring except for the correct angle in lift-off. Where would you provide assistance? [Refer to Diagram 16, Question 140.]
    a. F and K
    *b. A and H
    c. L and I
    d. G and D

Cartwheel

144. Where does the spotter stand for a person doing a cartwheel?
    *a. behind the performer
    b. in front of the performer
    c. to the side of the performer
    d. very close to the performer

Limber

145. Where should the hands be placed when spotting a front limber?
    1. middle of the back
    2. shoulder
    3. low back
    4. back of the neck
    a. 3
    b. 1, 2
    *c. 2, 3
    d. 1, 4

Judging

146. What component is *not* involved in judging floor exercise?
    *a. use of apparatus
    b. tumbling skills
    c. dance movements
    d. balances

147. Which move in floor exercise is rated as a "B" move for women?
    a. stretched jump with arch
    *b. body wave sideward to scale sideward
    c. jump to handstand
    d. jump with 1/1 (360°) turn

148. Which move in floor exercise is rated as a "C" move for men?
    a. American straddled flank circle, one time
    *b. salto forward stretched to stand
    c. salto backward piked to stand
    d. handspring backward to stand

149. What are the time limits of competitive floor exercise routines for men and women?
    a. 30 to 60 seconds for women, 45 to 60 seconds for men
    b. 45 to 75 seconds for women, 45 to 75 seconds for men
    *c. 60 to 90 seconds for women, 50 to 70 seconds for men
    d. 60 to 120 seconds for women, 60 to 100 seconds for men

150. What is the acceptable musical accompaniment for a woman's floor exercise routine?
    a. piano
    *b. any single instrument
    c. semiclassical
    d. orchestra with singing

151. What is the regulation size of the mat on which the floor exercise event is performed?
    a. 10 meters by 10 meters
    *b. 12 meters by 12 meters
    c. 12 meters by 15 meters
    d. 15 meters by 15 meters

152. What is the deduction if the gymnast leaves the designated floor exercise area?
    a. maximum of 0.5 for the routine
    b. maximum of 0.4 for the routine
    c. 0.2 for each time
    *d. 0.1 for each time

153. What factor distinguishes floor exercise for men and women?
    a. Men's routines are longer.
    b. Men's routines have more hesitations.
    c. Women use small apparatus.
    *d. Women use musical accompaniment.

154. What characteristic is *not* desirable in floor exercise routines?
    a. use of the total mat area
    b. use of moves showing strength
    *c. use of balance moves that predominate
    d. use of creative moves

Vaulting

Recognition of Moves

155. When does the second flight begin in a vault? [Refer to Diagram 17.]
    *b.

Diagram 17

156. Which move is illustrated in the diagram? [Refer to Diagram 18.]
    a. handspring
    b. cartwheel on, 1-1/4 turn (540°) off
    c. handspring on, tucked 1-1/2 salto forward off
    *d. round-off, flic-flac on; piked 1-1/2 salto backward off

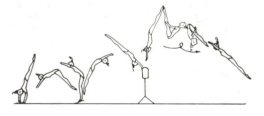

Diagram 18

Straddle

157. Which diagram shows the proper hand position for the straddle vault? [Refer to Diagram 19.]
    *a.

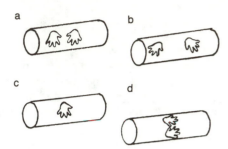

Diagram 19

Tsukahara

158. Which phrase best describes the Tsukahara vault?
    *a. a round-off backward salto
    b. a handspring front somersault
    c. a handspring full twist
    d. a cartwheel full twist

Yamashita

159. What does a Yamashita vault involve?
    *a. a handspring with a deep pike immediately off the horse
    b. a handspring with a half twist
    c. a round-off
    d. a cartwheel

Hecht Vault

160. Which vault is shown in the diagram? [Refer to Diagram 20.]
    a. stoop
    *b. Hecht vault
    c. handspring
    d. Yamashita

Diagram 20

Progression of Moves

161. Which vault would be the first in a progression of beginning vaults?
    a. straddle
    b. stoop
    c. handspring
    *d. squat

162. What beginning progression is recommended for all vaulters?
    *a. Vaulters should begin with the horse positioned sideways.
    b. Vaulters should first be proficient in all other events.
    c. Vaulters should start with the handspring vault.
    d. Vaulters should learn the squat vault before the stoop vault.

Execution of Moves

163. The ideal handspring vault should consist of which takeoff, preflight, after-flight, and landing positions? [Refer to Diagram 21.]
    *a. A, E, G, K
    b. B, F, H, M
    c. C, F, G, M
    d. B, E, H, L

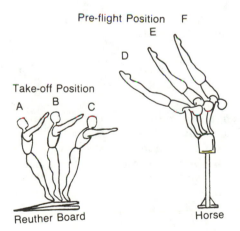

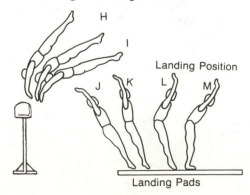

Diagram 21

164. Which statement best describes the correct head position for upright vaults?
    a. The head is down with the chin toward the chest.
    *b. The head is held in a neutral position.
    c. The head is back with the chin pointing upward.
    d. The head position has no effect on an upright vault.

165. Which statement about the approach in vaulting movements is true?
    a. resemble a slow, easy jog
    *b. be done with a sprinting action
    c. have a long, easy stride
    d. be characterized by swinging hips

166. What is the usual takeoff and landing combination from the springboard onto apparatus?
    *a. 2-foot takeoff, landing on two feet
    b. 1-foot takeoff, landing on the same foot
    c. 1-foot takeoff, landing on two feet
    d. 1-foot takeoff, landing on the non-takeoff foot

Takeoff

167. Which diagram shows the correct placement of the feet on the reuther board? [Refer to Diagram 22.]
    *d.

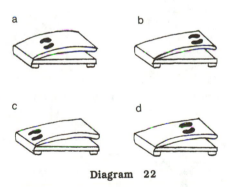

Diagram 22

168. Where should the reuther board be placed?
    a. a full body length from the horse
    b. 3 feet from the horse
    c. according to the gymnast's weight
    *d. according to the type of vault

Preflight

169. Which statement is true about the center of gravity in the preflight phase of vaulting?
    a. It should be close to the horse.
    *b. It should rise with the body rotating around it.
    c. It should remain as low as possible.
    d. It should delay the ascent phase.

Contact

170. Where should the weight be taken when arriving on the horse?
    a. fingertips
    *b. entire hand
    c. upper arm
    d. forearm

Landing

171. What is the best way to land after doing a vault on the horse?
    a. the legs straight and the body upright
    b. the knees bent and the arms extended backward
    c. the legs straight and the waist bent
    *d. the knees bent and then extended

172. The vaulter leaves the horse in after-flight "G" and lands in "M" position. Why? [Refer to Diagram 21, Question 163.]
    a. looked for the landing pad
    *b. flexed the hips while in flight
    c. take-off speed was too slow
    d. stayed in a layout position too long

173. The vaulter lifts off the reuther board in "C" position and contacts the horse in "D" position with little momentum and a flexed body position. What will be the most probable after-flight and landing positions? [Refer to Diagram 21, Question 163.].
    *a. I and J
    b. H and K
    c. I and M
    d. H and L

Squat Vault

174. What is the most common reason for hitting the horse with the knees when attempting a squat vault?
    a. bringing knees to chest too late
    b. having a poor hurdle
    c. landing flat-footed on the board
    *d. improper takeoff

175. What is a common error made when performing a squat vault?
    a. lifting the hips too high
    b. straightening the arms too soon
    *c. leaving the hands on the horse too long
    d. dropping the head too soon

Giant Cartwheel

176. Which statement is correct when attempting a giant cartwheel over the horse?
    *a. The one-quarter turn occurs so that the lead hand touches the horse as the legs swing to a vertical position.
    b. The one-quarter turn occurs after the legs have swung up to a vertical position.
    c. The one-quarter turn occurs during flight from the horse.
    d. The one-half turn occurs after the legs have swung up to a vertical position.

Spotting

177. What procedure would the spotter follow when the performer is attempting the straddle vault on the horse?
    a. Stand to one side of the horse and grasp the arm.
    b. Stand to one side of the horse and grasp the shoulder.
    c. Stand in front of the horse and grasp the legs.
    *d. Stand in front of the horse and grasp the arm and upper torso.

Judging

178. How many categories of vaults are there for women gymnasts?
    a. two
    b. three
    *c. four
    d. five

179. What is the requirement for a legal vault performed by women gymnasts?
    *a. Both hands must touch the horse.
    b. One hand must touch the horse.
    c. No hands must touch the horse.
    d. Either hands or feet must touch the horse.

180. How many forward steps is the vaulter allowed after landing without penalty?
    *a. none
    b. one
    c. two
    d. any number

181. Which statement is true of vaulting requirements?
    *a. two attempts allowed
    b. continuous difficulty
    c. show of strength
    d. predominantly swings

182. What is the maximum approach length allowed for men's Olympic vaulting?
    a. 10 meters
    b. 15 meters
    c. 20 meters
    *d. 25 meters

183. Which factor is *not* one of the five factors considered when judging a vault?
    *a. combination
    b. landing position
    c. second flight
    d. preflight

184. What is true about the base score for the Tsukahara tucked vault and the Kasamatsu tucked vault?
    a. The Tsukahara tucked vault base score is higher.
    *b. The Tsukahara tucked vault base score is lower.
    c. The base score for both vaults is the same.
    d. The Tsukahara is not a vault.

185. What is the main difference in the use of equipment for men and women vaulters?
    a. The men position the horse higher.
    b. The men use a longer run.
    *c. The horse is placed lengthwise for the men and sideways for the women.
    d. The men use the pommels for vaults while the women do not.

186. What is the deduction for receiving aid during the landing from a vault?
    a. 0.20 points
    b. 0.25 points
    c. 0.30 points
    *d. 0.50 points

187. What are the requirements for the run phase of the vault?
    a. It must not be longer than 20 meters.
    *b. The run can be individually determined.
    c. The run must be moderately slow.
    d. The maximum distance differs for men and women.

188. In which instance will a vault receive a *void* score?
    *a. The vaulter fails to complete the vault.
    b. The vaulter has bent arms in a basket vault.
    c. The vaulter does not attain sufficient height.
    d. The vaulter takes two steps when landing.

Balance Beam

Recognition of Moves

189. Which list of moves would be most closely associated with the balance beam?
    a. full turn, Tsukahara, pirouette, handspring
    b. arch jump, forward roll, salto, swivel hips
    *c. barani, half turn, tuck jump, back sommie
    d. gainer, giant cartwheel, front layout, knee spin

190. The straddle, squat, and wolf are names for which type of movements on the beam?
    *a. mounts
    b. dismounts
    c. turns
    d. balances

191. Which diagram shows a cat leap? [Refer to Diagram 23.]
    *c.

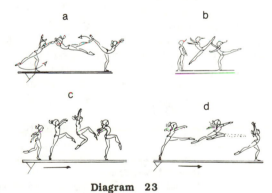

a   b

c   d

Diagram 23

192. What move is shown in the diagram? [Refer to Diagram 24.]
    a. forward drop
    b. front lying
    c. English balance
    *d. Swedish fall

Diagram 24

Progression of Moves

193. What is the most appropriate progression from a backward roll on the beam?
    a. lunge
    b. stand to pivot turn
    *c. knee scale
    d. swing through to V seat

194. What is the most important safety factor to remember in balance beam performance?
    a. Mounts and dismounts should not be made near the legs or supports of the beam.
    b. Matting should be of double thickness at the ends of the beam.
    c. Two spotters should be present for new movements made on the beam.
    *d. Movements should be learned and perfected on the floor before taking them to the beam.

Execution of Moves

195. Which quality is most important on the beam?
    a. strength
    b. endurance
    *c. balance
    d. flexibility

196. Which technique is *incorrect* for the straddle mount on the balance beam?
    *a. head down
    b. arms straight
    c. shoulders forward
    d. legs straight

197. Where does the performer look while performing a running or walking exercise on the beam?
    a. at the middle of the beam
    b. at the feet
    *c. at the end of the beam
    d. at a line on the floor

198. Which group of muscles helps the most with standing balance on the beam?
    *a. abdominal muscles
    b. arm muscles
    c. leg muscles
    d. shoulder muscles

Backward Shoulder Roll

199. How does the grip on the balance beam change for a shoulder roll backwards?
    a. a mixed to an over grip
    *b. an under to an over grip
    c. an over to an under grip
    d. an under to a mixed grip

200. What is the most important factor to remember in the execution of a back shoulder roll on the beam?
    a. hands gripping under the beam
    b. elbows held close together
    *c. center of gravity maintained over the beam
    d. focus down, head arched

201. Why are the elbows squeezed together in a back shoulder roll on the beam?
    *a. to increase stability
    b. to hold the head in place
    c. to increase leverage
    d. to shorten radius of rotation

Backward Roll

202. Where are the hands placed in a backward roll on the beam?
    a. one on either side of the beam beside the head
    *b. one on either side of the beam behind the head
    c. one on top of the beam and one under the beam near the head
    d. both on the underside of the beam behind the back

Forward Roll

203. Why is the forward roll more difficult to perfect on the balance beam than on the floor?
    a. There is a smaller base of support.
    *b. The center of gravity is higher.
    c. More flexibility is required.
    d. More strength is required.

Cartwheel

204. Which element is *not* an important consideration in the execution of a cartwheel on the beam?
    a. inertia
    b. center of gravity
    c. equal and opposite reaction
    *d. increased acceleration

Combination of Moves

205. Which phrase best characterizes work on the balance beam?
    a. beautiful static poses
    b. a test of static balance
    *c. floor exercise in a different medium
    d. variety in locomotion

206. Moves performed on the floor can be applied most appropriately to which piece of apparatus?
    a. uneven bars
    *b. balance beam
    c. still rings
    d. side horse

207. Which statement best represents the concept behind the balance beam area of gymnastics?
    a. emphasizes form in balance, inversions, and springs
    b. concentrates on strength, uniformity, and quickness
    *c. is preceded by floor work and emphasizes balance and precision in movement
    d. emphasizes design and allows freedom for individual experimentation

208. What is considered desirable tempo on the balance beam?
    a. lively and energetic
    b. gentle and subdued
    c. moderate and controlled
    *d. variety and mood changes

209. Which move can be used as a dismount from the beam?
    a. V sit
    b. forward roll
    *c. back salto
    d. scale

210. Which of these elements is the most important in a balance beam routine?
    a. strength
    b. posture
    c. elevation
    *d. continuity

211. A routine done on the balance beam should include all of these factors except one. What is the exception?
    a. poses
    b. tumbling
    c. dance
    *d. music

212. Which element should be minimized in balance beam routines?
    a. jumps and turns
    b. changes of level
    c. changes of tempo
    *d. static positions

213. What characterizes a well-done competitive balance beam performance?
    a. a definite, set rhythm
    b. a predominance of sustained positions
    c. a predominance of strength moves
    *d. a combination of tumbling, dance, and poses

Spotting

214. What is the primary duty when spotting a gymnast on the balance beam?
    a. to grasp the performer's hand
    *b. to be ready to assist if balance is lost
    c. to wait to be called on before helping
    d. to remain at least a foot away from the beam

215. Where is the spotter for the back walkover on the balance beam?
    *a. to the side and supporting the back
    b. to the front and assisting the first leg through the vertical position
    c. to the back and supporting the head
    d. to the back and assisting the front leg placement

Judging

216. What is the general degree of difficulty of lying, kneeling, and sitting balances performed on the beam?
    a. high because joints are bent and movement, unless very controlled, appears jerky
    b. high because the lower center of gravity makes balance more difficult
    c. low because the base of support is wide and this makes balance easier
    *d. low because the lower center of gravity makes balancing easier

217. What is the regulation width of a balance beam?
    *a. 3-9/10 inches
    b. 4-1/2 inches
    c. 5-1/8 inches
    d. 5-1/2 inches

218. How much time does the gymnast have to fall, remount, and resume her routine on the balance beam?
    a. 5 seconds
    b. 8 seconds
    *c. 10 seconds
    d. 15 seconds

219. What is the length of an optional balance beam routine?
    a. between 1:00 and 1:30 minutes
    *b. between 1:10 and 1:30 minutes
    c. between 1:10 and 1:45 minutes
    d. between 1:20 and 1:45 minutes

220. How many static elements are permitted in a balance beam routine?
    a. two
    *b. three
    c. four
    d. five

221. Which element is *not* one of the three designated for balance beam competition?
    *a. gymnastic strength elements
    b. acrobatic elements
    c. acrobatic strength elements
    d. gymnastic elements

222. Which move would be classified as a gymnastic element in beam competition?
    *a. leap
    b. round-off
    c. walkover
    d. head kip

Uneven Bars

Recognition of Moves

223. Which move is *inappropriate* on the uneven bars?
    a. glide kip
    b. front hip circle
    *c. arabesque
    d. forward roll

224. What is the name of the grip on the uneven bars where the hands are pronated?
    *a. forward
    b. reverse
    c. dislocation
    d. combined

225. Which move is *not* an example of a dismount from the uneven bars?
    a. a front somersault
    b. a hecht
    c. a flyaway
    *d. a squat

226. "Cast off to rear" describes what type of move on the uneven bars?
    a. turning movement
    b. mount
    *c. dismount movement
    d. balance movement

227. Which move on the uneven bars is shown in the diagram? [Refer to Diagram 25.]
    a. rear lying hang, short kip-up on HB
    b. stoop through over HB with flight to support on LB
    c. pike sole circle forward to handstand
    *d. free hip circle forward on LB with flight to eagle hang on HB

Diagram   25

Progression of Moves

228. What safety suggestion is related to progression of skills on the uneven bars?
    *a. The gymnast should learn the basic skills in each family of skills.
    b. The gymnast should learn all the circling skills before progressing to other families of skills.
    c. The gymnast should be proficient in floor exercise before progressing to uneven bars.
    d. The gymnast should learn all the kipping skills first.

229. What is the suggested prerequisite to the kip catch on the uneven bars?
    a. cast to handstand from support
    *b. glide kip to straight arm support
    c. back hip pull over to front support position
    d. backward hip circle

Execution of Moves

Mount
230. What is an important point to remember when executing a back pull-over mount onto the uneven parallel bars?
    a. throw head forward
    b. keep legs bent
    *c. drive hips upward and back over bar
    d. use underhand grip

Grip
231. Which grip is *not* used on the uneven bars?
    a. forward grip
    *b. backward grip
    c. mixed grip
    d. reverse grip

Undergrip
232. The undergrip is used for which two moves on the uneven bars?
    a. dislocate, skin the cat
    b. back hip circle, back hip pullover
    *c. forward seat circle, mill circle
    d. eagle, straight arm hang

Back Hip Circle
233. Why is it important to keep the legs straight when executing a back hip circle on the unevens?
    *a. longer radius slows the movement
    b. longer radius speeds up the movement
    c. shorter radius slows the movement
    d. shorter radius speeds up the movement

234. What is the most important action to remember when performing a back hip circle on the uneven bars?
    a. Bend the knees to shorten the level.
    *b. Keep the hips as close to the bar as possible.
    c. Keep the arms straight.
    d. Keep the head tucked.

Front Hip Circle
235. Which part of the body should contact the low bar when attempting the front hip circle mount?
    a. waist
    *b. upper thighs
    c. abdomen
    d. under arms

Straddle Mount
236. What is the correct hand position when attempting a straddle mount to the high bar?
    *a. Both hands must first grasp the low bar.
    b. Both hands must first grasp the high bar.
    c. One hand should first grasp the low bar, and the other hand must grasp the high bar.
    d. The hand position varies with the performer.

Strength
237. What body part is the major source of strength when working on the uneven parallel bars?
    a. hands
    b. hips
    c. legs
    *d. arms

Combination of Moves

238. Which phrase characterizes moves on the uneven parallel bars?
    *a. predominantly swings
    b. continuous difficulty
    c. show of strength
    d. stops during routine

239. Which muscle groups need to be especially strong for a gymnast to perform well on the uneven bars?
    *a. arm and abdominal muscles
    b. shoulder and leg muscles
    c. back and abdominal muscles
    d. leg and back muscles

240. A front hip circle on uneven parallel bars usually precedes which stunt?
    a. a back hip circle
    *b. a handstand
    c. a reverse pirouette
    d. a flyaway

241. What is an appropriate connection following a back hip circle on the low bar?
    *a. single-leg shoot through
    b. cast-off
    c. swan balance
    d. straddle seat

242. Which move is done from the low bar to the high bar?
    a. penny drop
    *b. pullover
    c. V sit
    d. cast wrap

243. Which move is done from the high bar to the low bar?
    a. handstand
    b. pullover
    c. back pullaway
    *d. cast wrap

244. What would be the most likely move after a shoot over the low bar from a long hang on the high bar?
    *a. a back hip pullover to high bar
    b. squat stand on low bar
    c. arabesque on low bar
    d. back pullaway

245. What would be the most continuous move following from a handstand to a straddle sole circle on the unevens?
    a. back hip pullover to high bar
    *b. straddle sole circle underswing dismount
    c. back stride circle
    d. hip circle backward

246. The cast before a hip circle demonstrates which principle?
    a. The acceleration of a body is proportional to the force causing it.
    b. A body in motion tends to remain in motion until acted upon by another force.
    c. For every action there is an equal and opposite reaction.
    *d. Momentum has been developed when inertia has been overcome and the body is moving at a given speed.

Spotting

Back Hip Circle
247. Where should the back hip circle be spotted?
    a. behind the high bar
    b. in front of the gymnast
    c. to the back of the gymnast
    *d. between the bars and on side of the gymnast

Forward Hip Circle
248. Where does the spotter place the hands when spotting for a forward hip circle?
    a. at the waist and legs
    b. at the wrist and hips
    c. at the wrist and legs
    *d. at the back and legs

Straddle
249. What is the role of the spotter when a person is attempting a handstand straddle to a straddle sole circle on the low bar?
    a. to support the small of the back
    b. to support the shoulders
    c. to support the wrists
    *d. to support the wrist and shoulder

Safety
250. Why is spotting above the bar *dangerous* for the uneven bars?
    a. It may hamper the performer.
    b. It may injure the performer.
    c. It may hamper the spotter.
    *d. It may injure the spotter.

251. How is the proper distance between the bars determined?
    a. by standing in between the bars with one arm on the high bar and one on the low bar
    b. by checking to see if the legs hit the high bar when performing a back hip circle on the low bar
    *c. by hanging on the high bar, swinging toward the low bar, and seeing if the low bar is at hip level
    d. by measuring the performer's height

252. What procedure is *not* considered a safety measure when using uneven parallel bars?
    a. to use chalk to prevent palms of hands from being ripped
    *b. to use a vaulting board to get maximum height
    c. to adjust the bars according to the gymnast's size
    d. to surround the bars with mats to cover areas for mounts and dismounts

253. What is the best rule to follow in spotting moves on the uneven parallel bars?
     a. Spotters should stand at the front of the unevens.
     *b. Spotters should know the exact movements to be executed by the performer.
     c. Spotting should generally be just above the wrist and above the elbow.
     d. Two spotters should assist in learning new movements.

Judging

254. How many movements are usually in an optional routine on the uneven bars?
     a. 6 to 9
     *b. 10 to 18
     c. 18 to 24
     d. 24 to 30

255. Which mount has the lowest difficulty rating on the uneven bars?
     *a. jump with half turn to hang on high bar
     b. jump with 1/1 to hang on high bar
     c. with half turn, kip to support on high bar
     d. jump with extended body to handstand on low bar

256. How many stops are usually permitted for momentary positions of balance and/or a brief period of preparation prior to a difficult movement in competition on the uneven bars?
     *a. none
     b. one
     c. two
     d. three

257. What is the penalty if a performer's routine lasts more than 2 minutes during competition on the uneven bars?
     a. disqualified from the competition
     b. penalized points
     *c. No penalty; there is no time limit.
     d. No penalty; 2 minutes is within the time limit.

258. How many elements must be present in a routine on the uneven bars?
     a. at least 8
     *b. at least 10
     c. at least 12
     d. at least 15

259. What penalty is imposed for using uncharacteristic bar elements in an uneven bars routine?
     a. 0.10 points
     *b. 0.20 points
     c. 0.25 points
     d. 0.30 points

260. How much interruption time is permitted during a fall onto or from the uneven bars?
     a. 15 seconds
     b. 20 seconds
     *c. 30 seconds
     d. 45 seconds

Horizontal Bar

Recognition of Moves	**261 to 263**
Progression of Moves	**264 to 265**
Execution of Moves	**266 to 268**
Combination of Moves	**269 to 270**
Spotting	**271**
Judging	**272 to 273**

Recognition of Moves

261. What are 360° circles done on the high bar called?
     *a. giants
     b. swings
     c. circles
     d. revolutions

262. Which phrase describes a forward giant?
     *a. elongated circular swing
     b. movement in tuck
     c. body in scale
     d. inverted stretch

263. Which move on the horizontal bar is illustrated in the diagram? [Refer to Diagram 26.]
     *a. free hip circle rearways backward to handstand
     b. free hip circle forward to handstand
     c. giant swing backward
     d. Stalder circle backward to handstand

Diagram 26

Progression of Moves

264. Is this progression of moves for the horizontal bar sound: half turn, back uprise, giant swing forward, and kip?
    a. yes
    *b. No, work on the kip should follow the half turn.
    c. No, work on the giant swing forward should precede practice on the back uprise.
    d. No, proficiency on the kip should come before work on the half turn.

265. Which progression is recommended for work on the horizontal bar?
    a. hop turn, giant swing forward, half turn, elgrip giant swing
    b. elgrip giant swing, giant swing forward, hop turn, half turn
    c. hop turn, half turn, elgrip giant swing, giant swing forward
    *d. half turn, hop turn, giant swing forward, elgrip giant swing

Execution of Moves

Giants

266. For which move is a good swing on the horizontal bar used to the most advantage?
    a. Stalder circle
    *b. Russian giant
    c. reverse giant
    d. regular giant

267. How is the forward or reverse giant on the horizontal bar best performed?
    a. Body is straight, arms slightly bent.
    b. Body is straight, legs straight.
    *c. Body is slightly piked, arms straight.
    d. Body is deeply arched, arms straight.

268. Which element is most important when performing a German giant?
    *a. swing
    b. grip strength
    c. shoulder flexibility
    d. eye spotting technique

Combination of Moves

269. Which phrase is characteristic of movements on the high bar?
    a. clockwise movements
    b. pendular swings
    *c. circular swings
    d. show of flexibility

270. What is characteristic of work on the horizontal bar?
    a. holds
    b. strength moves
    *c. continuous swinging moves
    d. balances

Spotting

271. Where should the spotter be in relation to the performer when back giant circle moves are being developed?
    *a. standing at side
    b. standing in front
    c. standing in back
    d. standing underneath the performer

Judging

272. What is the deduction for each hold in a horizontal bar routine?
    a. 0.05
    b. 0.10
    c. 0.15
    *d. 0.20

273. Which element is *not* permitted in horizontal bar moves?
    a. virtuosity parts
    b. connecting parts
    *c. hold parts
    d. value parts

Parallel Bars

Recognition of Moves	**274 to 277**
Progression of Moves	**278 to 280**
Execution of Moves	**281 to 286**
Combination of Moves	**287 to 288**
Spotting	**289 to 290**
Judging	**291 to 297**

Recognition of Moves

274. Which move would be suitable for a mount on the parallel bars?
    a. handstand pirouette
    b. double back salto
    c. squat
    *d. glide kip

275. Which move performed on the parallel bars is considered the most advanced?
    *a. Stutz to a handstand
    b. Stutz to an upper arm hang
    c. Stutz to an under bar cast
    d. Stutz to a layout forward roll

276. Which move on the parallel bars is illustrated in the diagram? [Refer to Diagram 27.]
  a. slide kip rearward to upper arm hang
  b. back uprise to support
  c. Stemme backward to handstand pivot
  *d. Stemme forward to support

Diagram 27

277. Which support is shown in the diagram? [Refer to Diagram 28.]
  a. straight-arm cross support
  *b. inverted hang support
  c. straight long hanging support
  d. underarm support

Diagram 28

Progression of Moves

278. Which move on the parallel bars should be learned first among the ones listed?
  *a. back uprise
  b. giant roll forward and backward
  c. peach basket
  d. swinging pirouette forward and backward

279. Which move on the parallel bars is the most difficult?
  *a. handstand
  b. straddle travel
  c. walking across bar
  d. shoulder stand

280. Which sequence of skill mastery shows the best progression?
  a. back uprise, glide kip, kip, peach basket
  b. peach basket, kip, glide kip, back uprise
  *c. back uprise, kip, glide kip, peach basket
  d. kip, glide kip, back uprise, peach basket

Execution of Moves

281. In which position should the performer keep the head in a swing on the parallel bars?
  a. chin to chest
  *b. normal anatomical position
  c. head held back
  d. so the eyes watch the bar

282. What probably causes most falls from the parallel bars?
  a. incorrect hand position
  b. poor head position
  c. lack of balance
  *d. lack of arm strength

283. Which combined elements are necessary for the height achieved in performing a straight-arm peach basket on the parallel bars?
  a. the swing and the arms
  *b. the swing and the legs
  c. the hand and arm release, regrasp
  d. the arm pull once over the bars

284. Which elements are the most important ones when performing a stiff-stiff on the parallel bars?
  a. straight arms and straight body
  b. straight arms and straddle legs
  c. straight legs and straight body
  *d. straight arms and straight legs

285. The performer is executing a back hip circle. Where does the hand change occur to decrease rotational speed so the body can be stopped in a support position?
  a. prior to the bottom of the downswing
  b. prior to the completion of the upswing
  *c. just after the upswing begins
  d. just at the point between downswing and upswing

286. Which are the most important factors in performing a Diamidov?
  *a. speed of swing, timing of rotation, balance
  b. speed of swing, strength, balance
  c. timing of swing, aerial speed, strength
  d. timing of rotation, strength, balance

Combination of Moves

287. Which piece of apparatus is *not* used by women in gymnastics competition?
  a. vaulting horse
  b. balance beam
  *c. parallel bars
  d. floor exercise mats

288. What condition is *not* considered detracting if it is seen in a parallel bar routine?
    a. strength used to attain position
    b. spotter near the performer
    c. majority of the routine above the bar
    *d. combination of movements

Spotting

289. A beginning student is learning how to swing in a front support position on the bars. Where would you spot the performer? [Refer to Diagram 29.]
    *a. N and J
    b. A and D
    c. C and D
    d. A and B

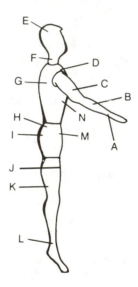

Diagram 29

290. A gymnast needs strong assistance while performing the glide kip on the bars. How would you assist the performer? [Refer to Diagram 29, Question 289.]
    a. C and F
    b. D and G
    *c. H and J
    d. F and H

Judging

291. What must the performer do to receive the highest credit in performing a double-leg cut catch on the bars?
    a. Work straight-arm dropping to a cast.
    *b. Work straight-arm to straight body support.
    c. Work straight-arm to L position.
    d. Work straight-arm and straight body.

292. Which routine on the parallel bars could receive the most points if performed perfectly?
    a. L support press, handstand, double rear pirouette
    b. L support press, handstand, double forward pirouette
    c. V support press, handstand, double forward pirouette
    *d. V support press, handstand, double rear pirouette

293. How long must handstands be held in men's Olympic parallel bar routines?
    a. 1 second
    *b. 2 seconds
    c. 3 seconds
    d. 4 seconds

294. What is the maximum number of second hold parts that can be allowed in a parallel bar routine?
    a. 0
    b. 1
    c. 2
    *d. 3

295. What special requirement is imposed upon routines in parallel bar competition?
    *a. The routine must contain one swinging C part.
    b. The routine must contain two swinging C parts.
    c. The routine must contain one regrasp movement.
    d. The routine must contain four second hold parts.

296. What is the deduction if more than three pronounced hold parts are performed in the parallel bars routine?
    a. 0.05
    *b. 0.10
    c. 0.15
    d. 0.20

297. How many steps with the hands is the gymnast allowed on the parallel bars?
    *a. 0
    b. 1
    c. 2
    d. 3

Pommel Horse

Recognition of Moves

298. Which event calls for movements that must be continuous?
    a. still rings
    *b. pommel horse
    c. floor exercise
    d. parallel bars

299. On which piece of apparatus are single leg circles executed?
    a. horizontal bar
    *b. pommel horse
    c. uneven parallel bars
    d. balance beam

300. What move does the diagram illustrate? [Refer to Diagram 30.]
    *a. double leg circle
    b. direct Stockli
    c. travels
    d. double Suisse

Diagram 30

301. What move on the pommel horse is shown in the diagram? [Refer to Diagram 31.]
    *a. scissors forward
    b. scissors backward
    c. simple Suisse
    d. scissors backward with a half turn

Diagram 31

Progression of Moves

302. Which mount to the pommel horse should be learned first?
    a. Swiss mount
    b. single leg cut mount
    *c. front support mount
    d. circle mount

303. What move should a gymnast learn before attempting a forward scissors?
    *a. single leg circle
    b. Magyar spindle
    c. double leg circles
    d. Stockli

Execution of Moves

304. What factor is considered when double leg circles are performed with good execution?
    a. Legs are flexed.
    b. Feet are flexed.
    *c. Legs and hips are extended.
    d. Legs are flexed and hips are extended.

Combination of Moves

305. Which phrase is most characteristic of work on the pommel horse?
    a. clockwise movements
    *b. circular swings
    c. pendular swings
    d. exclusively swings

306. What move should predominate on the pommel horse?
    a. forward leg circles
    *b. double leg circles
    c. backward scissors
    d. forward scissors

Judging

307. Which pommel horse move receives the most credit if done properly?
    a. simple Swiss followed by Kehre out
    b. flank start to Moore followed by Tromlet
    c. front German with half turn to cross stand
    *d. Moore start to Czech followed by Tromlet

308. What is one of the special requirements of pommel competition?
    a. There must be at least one strength part of at least B value.
    b. At least one exercise part must be a hold part.
    *c. At least one exercise part must be executed on one pommel.
    d. At least one scissors must be used in connections.

309. What is the deduction if one part of the pommel horse is not used?
    a. 0.1
    b. 0.2
    *c. 0.3
    d. 0.5

Still Rings

Recognition of Moves

310. Which statement best describes a skin-the-cat movement on the still rings?
    a. swinging the legs forward to an inverted hang and holding the position
    b. making one complete swing through the rings and releasing
    *c. extending rearward from a piked inverted hang and returning to the starting position
    d. straddling the legs outside the rings at the front end of the swing and releasing as the legs contact the arms

311. Which ring move takes the least strength?
    a. inverted cross
    b. planche
    c. Maltese cross
    *d. Olympic cross

312. Which move is illustrated in the diagram? [Refer to Diagram 32.]
    a. felge upward to support
    b. stemme forward to support
    c. stemme backward to support
    *d. giant swing forward

Diagram 32

313. Which move is illustrated in the diagram? [Refer to Diagram 33.]
    a. giant swing backward
    *b. back kip to support
    c. kip to support
    d. felge backward, bent body, to support

Diagram 33

314. With which gymnastic event is the term *bail* associated?
    a. horizontal bar
    b. parallel bars
    c. pommel horse
    *d. still rings

Progression of Moves

315. Which skill is the essential first step in learning to perform on the still rings?
    *a. basic swing
    b. mount
    c. dismount
    d. regular bail

316. Which is the best move for a novice gymnast to use as a dismount?
    *a. double-leg straddle cut off
    b. back salto
    c. double back salto
    d. double twisting back salto in layout position

317. Proficiency should come first on which of the skills listed in a progression of skills on the still rings?
    a. forward uprise
    b. backward uprise
    *c. piked inlocate
    d. shoot to shoulder stand from basic swing

Execution of Moves

318. What is the proper position of the rings during performance?
    *a. stationary
    b. swinging
    c. uneven
    d. near the floor

319. What is the beginning position for a still ring exercise?
    a. swinging
    b. arms extended downward
    *c. hanging
    d. arms extended to the sides

Reverse Giant
320. Which factors are most important in performing a straight-arm reverse giant on the rings?
    a. strength and balance
    *b. strength and swing
    c. swing and balance
    d. height and balance

Muscle-Up
321. A gymnast doing a muscle-up on the rings should be using what type of grip?
    a. regular
    *b. false
    c. mixed
    d. irregular

Crow's Nest
322. The crow's nest movement on the still rings requires what type of position?
    a. inverted piked position
    b. one-handed position upside down
    *c. backbend position with the stomach facing the mat
    d. handstand position with the elbows above the rings

Combination of Moves

323. With which move on the rings can a kip be used?
    a. back uprise
    b. front uprise
    *c. back hip circle
    d. back lever

Spotting

324. A gymnast is learning the inlocate on the rings. Where should the spotter assist the performer? [Refer to Diagram 34.]
    a. D and H
    b. E and K
    *c. J and M
    d. F and H

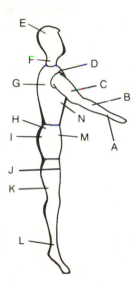

Diagram 34

325. What safety measure is recommended as a proper coaching technique when working on bails?
    a. resin
    *b. dowel hand grips
    c. low rings
    d. overhead spotting belt

Judging

326. Which combination of moves could receive the most credit if performed perfectly?
    a. cross, planche, handstand, back kip
    b. handstand, back kip, planche, cross
    *c. back kip, cross, planche, handstand
    d. planche, cross, back kip, handstand

327. A cross is a Class C move on what apparatus?
   a. parallel bars
   b. vaulting horse
   c. uneven parallel bars
   *d. still rings

328. What characterizes composition requirements for the rings?
   a. clockwise movement
   b. must show flexibility
   *c. two handstands
   d. simultaneous grip release

329. What must be true of the rings during strength parts?
   a. They must be within 2 feet of each other.
   *b. They must be still.
   c. They must be lowered.
   d. They must be held with an inverted grip.

330. What is the deduction is there is no handstand executed with swing during the routine on the still rings?
   a. 0.1
   b. 0.2
   *c. 0.3
   d. 0.4

Acknowledgments

Colleagues and students who contributed suggestions and ideas for the Gymnastics test questions are: J. Barbour, W. Cook, R. Dailey, K. Davidson, P. Davis, T. Forkner, Sa. Gordon, Su. Gordon, C. Green, M. Little, G. McGinty, C. Porter, R. Roll, N. Smith, T. Stricklin, D. Tagalos, R. Travers, and J. Wilson.

Suggested Readings

Brown, J., & Wardell, D. (1980). *Teaching and coaching gymnastics for men and women.* New York: John Wiley and Sons.

Cooper, P., & Trnka, M. (1982). *Teaching gymnastics skills to men and women.* Minneapolis, MN: Burgess.

George, G.S. (Ed.). (1985). *USGF Gymnastic Safety manual.* Indianapolis, IN: USGF Publications.

International Gymnastics Federation (FIG). (1985). *Code of points, artistic gymnastic for men.* Lucerne, Switzerland: FIG.

International Gymnastics Federation (FIG). (1985). *Code of points, artistic gymnastic for women.* Lucerne, Switzerland: FIG.

Schembri, G. (1983). *Introductory gymnastics: A guide for coaches and teachers.* Moorabbin, Australia: Australia Gymnastics Federation.

Racquetball

Edward T. Turner, Consultant

This collection of racquetball test questions is divided into six content areas:

- **History**
- **Equipment**
- **Terminology**
- **Techniques**
- **Strategy**
- **Rules and Scoring**

Some confusion may be evident in the terminology used, especially in describing techniques and areas of the court. Such wording as *opposite end, diagonal to, middle of,* and so forth may be confusing if the instuctor used other descriptions. Some revision of items may be necessary to make the terminology consistent with that used in class.

Assume the player is right-handed unless otherwise stated. This should be noted in the test directions or a key should be made for left-handed players.

Racquetball

History	1 to 7
Equipment	8 to 25
Terminology	26 to 53
Techniques	54 to 159
Strategy	160 to 214
Rules and Scoring	215 to 262

History

Personalities

1. Who was the founder of racquetball?
   a. Abner Doubleday
   b. Bud Muehleisen
   c. James Naismith
   *d. Joe Sobek

2. Who is credited with promoting racquetball and making it known nationwide?
   a. Larry Liles
   *b. Bud Muehleisen
   c. Joe Sobek
   d. Randy Stafford

3. Who is "Dr. Bud"?
   a. founder of racquetball
   *b. promoter of racquetball
   c. current national racquetball champion
   d. greatest racquetball player of all time

Dates

4. When was racquetball founded?
   a. about 1500
   b. about 1850
   *c. about 1950
   d. about 1975

5. When did the racquetball boom begin in the United States?
   a. about 1900
   b. about 1950
   *c. about 1970
   d. about 1980

Edward T. Turner is a professor of health, physical education, and leisure services at Appalachian State University, Boone, North Carolina. He is a racquetball teacher and coach and the author of numerous articles and a book on racquetball.

Organizations

6. What was the first organization formed to promote and organize racquetball?
    *a. International Racquetball Association
    b. American Racquetball Association
    c. United States Racquetball Organization
    d. Professional Racquetball Association

7. What is the official governing body of amateur racquetball today?
    a. International Racquetball Association
    *b. American Amateur Racquetball Association
    c. National Racquetball Club
    d. United States Racquetball Association

Equipment

Clothing

8. What is the best type of clothing to wear in order to try to keep cool?
    a. acrylic
    *b. cotton
    c. nylon
    d. polyester

9. Why should players avoid wearing dark colored clothes?
    a. Dark colored clothes are hotter than white clothes.
    b. Dark colored clothes do not absorb as much perspiration.
    c. Dark colored clothes absorb more heat.
    *d. Dark colored clothes sometimes make the ball more difficult to see.

Racquets

10. What is the smallest grip size recommended?
    a. 3 in.
    *b. 3-5/16 in.
    c. 4 in.
    d. 4-1/2 in.

11. Generally, what grip sizes are recommended for women?
    a. 3 to 4 in.
    b. 3 to 3-5/16 in.
    *c. 3-11/16 to 3-15/16 in.
    d. 3-1/2 to 4-1/4 in.

12. Generally what grip sizes are recommended for men?
    *a. 3-15/16 to 4-1/8 in.
    b. 3-1/8 to 4-1/2 in.
    c. 4 to 4-11/16 in.
    d. 4-1/2 to 5 in.

13. Why do players use smaller grips for playing racquetball than for playing tennis?
    a. for more confort
    *b. for more wrist action
    c. for more control
    d. for more touch

14. You want to see if you are using the correct grip size. Grip the racquet. If the size is correct, which finger or fingers should touch the base of your thumb?
    a. index
    b. index and middle
    *c. middle and fourth
    d. fourth

15. A player uses much wrist action with a fast stroke. Generally, what weight racquet should this player use?
    *a. light
    b. medium
    c. heavy
    d. appropriate weight depends on other factors

16. A player has a slow, controlled stroke. Generally, what weight racquet should this player use?
    a. light
    b. medium
    *c. heavy
    d. appropriate weight depends on other factors

17. Which statement about racquet selection is *true*?
    a. Players with controlled games should use heavier racquets.
    b. Players with wristy games should use heavier racquets.
    c. Women should use lighter racquets than men.
    *d. There is no reason for women to use lighter racquets than men use.

18. Generally, why do players buy stiff racquets?
    *a. to increase their power
    b. to increase their control
    c. to increase their wrist action
    d. to decrease their wrist action

19. You feel your racquet is too stiff. What can you do to make it seem more flexible?
    a. Choke up on the grip.
    b. Grip it more loosely.
    *c. String it with less tension.
    d. Build up the grip.

Balls

20. How can you determine whether or not balls are of acceptable quality?
    a. They bounce 24 inches high when dropped from waist level.
    b. They are made by a well-known manufacturer.
    c. They are marked ''IRA Approved.''
    *d. They are marked ''AARA Approved.''

21. What is the advantage of using pressureless balls?
    a. bounce higher
    b. bounce truer
    c. create less shock in hitting
    *d. last longer

Gloves

22. What is the most frequent problem caused by wearing a glove?
    a. causes blisters
    b. causes a player to loose his or her grip
    *c. causes a player to have less feel of the racket
    d. causes a player's hand to sweat more

Eyeguards

23. Who should wear eyeguards?
    a. professional players
    b. beginners
    c. young players
    *d. all players

Thongs

24. Who should use a thong when playing?
    a. professional players
    b. beginners
    c. hard hitters
    *d. all players

25. Which phrase best describes how the thong should be worn?
    a. looped around the wrist
    b. loosely looped around the wrist
    *c. securely looped around the wrist
    d. tightly looped around the wrist

Terminology

Ace

26. A legal serve is completely missed by the receiver. What is this called?
    *a. an ace
    b. a winner
    c. a fault serve
    d. a hinder

Apex

27. What is the *apex*?
    a. the height the ball travels before hitting the wall
    b. the height the ball reaches before hitting the floor
    *c. the highest point the ball reaches after the first bounce from the floor
    d. the highest point the ball reaches after it hits the front wall

Avoidable Hinder

28. A player intentionally interferes with an opponent's shot. What is this called?
    a. intentional interference
    b. interference
    *c. avoidable hinder
    d. hinder

Back-Into-Back Wall Shot

29. When is a ball a back-into-back wall shot?
    a. when the ball hits the back court and the back wall
    *b. when the ball hits the back wall and then the front wall on the fly
    c. when the ball hits the front wall and then the back wall on the fly
    d. when the ball hits the back wall on two successive plays

Back Wall Shot

30. When is a ball a back wall shot?
    a. when a ball rebounds off the back wall
    *b. when a ball is hit toward the front wall after rebounding off the back wall
    c. when a ball is hit toward the back wall
    d. when a ball rebounds only off the back wall

Block

31. A player moves his or her body in front of the opponent, preventing the opponent from hitting the ball. What is this called?
    *a. block
    b. hinder
    c. cutthroat
    d. screen

Bye

32. A player is *not* scheduled to play a match in the first round of a tournament. What is this called?
    a. pass
    *b. bye
    c. seeded
    d. luck of the draw

Ceiling Serve

33. When does a ceiling serve occur?
    a. when the ball hits the ceiling before hitting the front wall
    *b. when the ball hits the ceiling after hitting the front wall
    c. when the receiver hits the return of serve into the ceiling before it hits a wall
    d. when the receiver hits the return of serve into the ceiling before it hits the front wall

Center Court Position

34. Where is the center court position?
    a. center of the service zone
    b. center of the court in front of the service zone
    c. center of the court behind the service zone
    *d. center of the court 2 to 4 feet behind the service zone

Crosscourt Shot

35. A shot is hit diagonally toward the front wall from one side of the court, then rebounds from the front wall and lands in the opposite back corner. What is this shot called?
    *a. crosscourt shot
    b. crack ball
    c. crotch ball
    d. defensive shot

Crotch Ball

36. A ball strikes the junction of two playing surfaces. What is this shot called?
    a. crosscourt shot
    b. crack ball
    *c. crotch ball
    d. defensive shot

Crowding

37. What is *crowding*?
    a. playing too close to the ball
    *b. playing too close to an opponent
    c. playing the ball on the fly
    d. playing a position to block out the opponent

Cutthroat

38. What is a game with three players called?
    a. singles
    b. doubles
    c. triples
    *d. cutthroat

Defensive Shot

39. A shot is hit for the purpose of continuing the rally. What is this shot called?
    a. lob shot
    b. crosscourt shot
    *c. defensive shot
    d. float shot

Die

40. A ball loses momentum or slows down after striking a wall. What is this called?
    a. dead ball
    *b. dying
    c. flat rollout
    d. skip ball

Flat Rollout

41. A kill shot strikes the front wall so low that it rebounds without a bounce. What is this shot called?
    a. drive shot
    b. fly shot
    c. crotch shot
    *d. flat rollout

Garbage Serve

42. Which serve is sometimes called a *garbage serve*?
    a. lob serve
    *b. low lob serve
    c. low drive serve
    d. high Z serve

Half Volley

43. A ball is hit immediately after it strikes the floor. What is this called?
    a. flat rollout
    b. crack ball
    c. crotch ball
    *d. half volley

Unavoidable Hinder

44. A player unintentionally interferes with an opponent during play. What is this called?
    *a. unavoidable hinder
    b. interference
    c. blocking
    d. crowding

Plum

45. What is a *plum*?
    a. a great shot
    *b. an easy setup for a kill shot
    c. a serve untouched by the opponent
    d. an easy win in a match

Rally

46. Players hit the ball back and forth from the serve until the point is over. What is this called?
    a. a point
    b. a volley
    *c. a rally
    d. a donut

Rekill

47. A player hits an opponent's kill attempt for a kill shot of his or her own. What is this called?
    a. winner
    b. overkill
    *c. rekill
    d. dead ball

Screening

48. A ball passes so close to a player that it obstructs the opponent's view and ability to return the ball. What is this called?
    a. crowding
    *b. screening
    c. blocking
    d. interfering

Shoot

49. A player attempts to hit a kill shot. What is this called?
    *a. shooting
    b. slamming
    c. smashing
    d. killing

Shooter

50. A player depends heavily on the kill shot. What is this player called?
    a. a donut
    b. a pumpkin
    c. a power player
    *d. a shooter

Thong

51. What is a *thong*?
    a. a player who fails to score in a game
    b. an easy setup
    c. a shot that ends a rally
    *d. a nylon strap attached to the butt of the racquet

Volley Shot

52. A player hits a ball after it hits the front wall and before it hits the floor. What is this shot called?
    a. overhead shot
    b. lob shot
    *c. volley shot
    d. kill shot

Wallpaper Shot

53. A ball hugs the side wall as it travels to the rear of the court. What is this shot called?
    a. pass shot
    b. pinch shot
    *c. wallpaper shot
    d. crotch shot

Techniques

54. What should you concentrate on when hitting a shot?
    a. your opponent's position
    b. the place you want to hit the ball
    *c. the ball
    d. your stroke

55. A ball contacts the front wall while traveling in a downward path. How will it rebound?
    a. straight out
    b. almost straight out
    c. upward
    *d. downward

56. A ball contacts the front wall while traveling in an upward path. How will it rebound?
    a. straight out
    b. almost straight out
    *c. upward
    d. downward

57. Generally, what is true about the direction a ball rebounds?
    a. It rebounds parallel to the floor.
    b. It rebounds back the same direction it came from.
    c. It rebounds at a 45° angle to the direction it came from.
    *d. It rebounds at a 90° angle to the direction it came from.

58. What will *not* affect the angle at which a ball rebounds from a surface?
    a. velocity of the ball
    b. spin on the ball
    *c. accuracy of the shot
    d. gravity

59. When will a ball rebound shallow and slowly off the back wall?
    a. when it was hit softly
    b. when it was hit hard
    *c. when it hit the floor before hitting the back wall
    d. when it hits the back wall without hitting the floor

60. When will a ball rebound off the back wall with a sudden jump out into the center court area?
    a. when it was hit softly
    b. when it was hit hard
    c. when it hit the floor before hitting the back wall
    *d. when it hits the back wall without hitting the floor

61. What is the most important factor in determining the spin of a returned ball?
    a. the wall it hit
    b. the stiffness of the racquet
    *c. the racquet angle at ball contact
    d. the speed of the ball

62. You need two quick steps to get to a shot. How should you begin your move toward the ball?
    a. by taking a slide step
    b. by stepping out with the foot nearest the ball
    *c. by crossing over with the foot farthest from the ball
    d. by pushing off with your dominant foot

63. In the ready position, what should be the position of the feet?

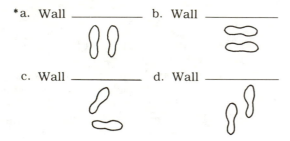

*a. Wall _____   b. Wall _____

c. Wall _____   d. Wall _____

Forehand

64. A player is holding the racquet so that the head is perpendicular to the floor. For a forehand grip, where should the point of the V made by the thumb and index finger be positioned?
    *a. on the center of the top of the grip
    b. 1/4 inch forward from the center of the top of the grip
    c. 1/4 inch backward from the center of the top of the grip
    d. on the center of the back of the grip

65. For a forehand grip, what should be the position of the index finger?
    *a. comfortable against the second finger
    b. spread 1 inch from the second finger
    c. in a trigger-like position beneath the grip
    d. extended up the back of the grip

66. In the forehand grip, why should the handle be located in the fingers?
    a. for maximum power
    *b. for maximum control
    c. for minimum strain on the hand
    d. for safety

67. In hitting a forehand, what should be the position of your legs?
    a. straight
    *b. slightly bent
    c. bent at a right angle
    d. bent so that you are in a sitting position

68. In the backswing, how should your wrist be cocked to hit a forehand stroke?
    a. upward
    b. downward
    *c. to the right
    d. to the left

69. In the backswing, how should your elbow be positioned to hit a forehand stroke?
    a. straight
    b. slightly bent
    *c. bent at a right angle
    d. bent as much as possible

70. In the backswing, how should your elbow be positioned in relation to your body to hit a forehand stroke?
    a. tightly into the waist
    b. close to the waist
    c. slightly away from the body
    *d. away from your body

71. In the backswing of a forehand, how high should the racquet head be held?
    *a. head high
    b. shoulder high
    c. waist high
    d. hip high

72. You are hitting a forehand stroke. At the end of your backswing, what should be the position of your feet?

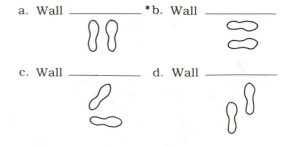

a. Wall _____   *b. Wall _____

c. Wall _____   d. Wall _____

73. In the backswing of a forehand, where should your weight be distributed?
    a. evenly over both feet
    *b. mostly over the back foot
    c. mostly over the front foot
    d. shifting from the back foot to the front foot

74. On a forehand shot, what does a player do in order to be able to take a full backswing?
    a. cock his or her wrist
    b. take a step backward with the right foot
    c. take a step foreward with the left foot
    *d. twist his or her body to the right

75. On the forward swing of a forehand shot, what part of the body leads the shot?
    *a. shoulder
    b. elbow
    c. wrist
    d. head

76. On the forward swing of a forehand shot, what is the position of the hand in relation to the elbow?
    a. even with the elbow
    b. ahead of the elbow
    *c. behind the elbow
    d. below the elbow

77. At contact on a forehand shot, what should be the position of the arm?
    *a. straight
    b. slightly bent
    c. bent at a right angle
    d. bent with the elbow close to the body

78. For a forehand shot, at what point should the ball be contacted by the racquet?
    a. out from the player's back foot
    b. out from the center of the player's body
    *c. out from the player's front foot
    d. slightly out in front of the player's front foot

79. Which statement best describes a good follow-through for a forehand stroke?
    a. Stop the racquet as soon as possible after contact.
    b. Stop the racquet when it points to the front wall.
    c. Stop the racquet when it points to the direction you intended to hit the ball.
    *d. Let the racquet swing freely through.

80. What happens if you extend your hitting arm as you begin to swing forward on a forehand shot?
    a. increase power
    *b. decrease power
    c. increase accuracy
    d. decrease accuracy

Backhand

81. How should the racquet be gripped to hit a backhand?
    a. with the same grip as the forehand
    b. with the hand more behind the racquet than a forehand
    *c. with the hand more over the top of the racquet than a forehand
    d. with the hand more under the racquet than the forehand

82. You are hitting a backhand stroke. At the end of your backswing, what should be the position of your feet?

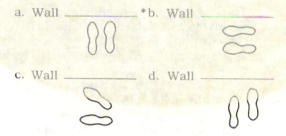

83. In the backswing of a backhand, where should your weight be distributed?
    a. evenly over both feet
    *b. mostly over the back foot
    c. mostly over the front foot
    d. shifting from the back foot to the front foot

84. In hitting a backhand, what should be the position of your legs?
    a. straight
    *b. slightly bent
    c. bent at a right angle
    d. bent so that you are in a sitting position

85. In the backswing, how should your wrist be cocked to hit a backhand stroke?
    *a. so that the racquet head is above the wrist
    b. so that the racquet head is below the wrist
    c. so that the racquet head is behind the wrist
    d. so that the racquet head is ahead of the wrist

86. In the backswing of a backhand stroke, how high should the racquet head be held?
    *a. slightly more than head high
    b. shoulder to head high
    c. waist to shoulder high
    d. hip to waist high

87. For a backhand shot, at what point should the ball be contacted by the racquet?
    a. out from the player's back foot
    b. out from the center of the player's body
    *c. out from the player's front foot
    d. slightly out in front of the player's front foot

88. Ideally, at what height should a backhand shot be contacted?
    *a. knee
    b. head
    c. neck
    d. chest

89. You are not getting as much power on your backhand as you think you should. What is the most probable cause?
    a. snapping your wrist before contact with the ball
    *b. snapping your wrist after contact with the ball
    c. taking too much follow-through
    d. taking too much backswing

90. Which statement best describes a good follow-through for a backhand stroke?
    a. Stop the racquet as soon as possible after contact.
    b. Stop the racquet when it points to the front wall.
    c. Stop the racquet when it points to the direction you intended to hit the ball.
    *d. Let the racquet swing freely through.

Around-the-Wall Ball

91. When is a shot an around-the-wall ball?
    a. when it hits all four walls
    b. when it hits high on a side wall, then rebounds to the opposite side wall and the front wall
    c. when it hits low on a side wall, then rebounds to the back wall and the opposite side wall
    *d. when it hits high on a side wall, then rebounds to the front wall and the opposite side wall

92. Where should the ball be aimed with hitting an around-the-wall shot?
    a. low on the side wall
    *b. high on the side wall
    c. low on the front wall
    d. high on the front wall

93. The path of what shot is shown in the diagram? The X is the player hitting the ball, and the "---" is the path of the ball. [Refer to Diagram 1.]
    *a. around-the-wall ball
    b. ceiling ball
    c. pinch ball
    d. Z ball

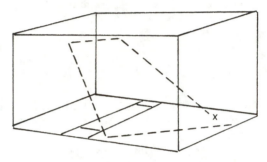

Diagram 1

Ceiling Shot

94. A ball strikes the ceiling, then rebounds to the floor and bounces deep into the court. What is this shot called?
    *a. ceiling shot
    b. deep shot
    c. change-of-pace shot
    d. lob shot

95. The path of what shot is shown in the diagram? The X is the player hitting the ball, and the "---" is the path of the ball. [Refer to Diagram 2.]
    a. around-the-wall ball
    *b. ceiling ball
    c. pinch ball
    d. Z ball

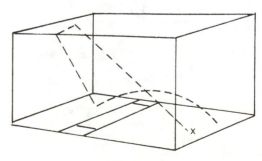

Diagram 2

96. Where should a ceiling shot be aimed?
    *a. at the ceiling 2 to 5 feet from the front wall
    b. at the ceiling 5 to 10 feet from the front wall
    c. at the front half of the ceiling
    d. at the ceiling above the service zone

97. A player hits a ceiling shot that strikes the ceiling above the service zone. What will probably happen?
    a. It will be a winner.
    *b. It will be a setup for a kill shot.
    c. It will rebound deep into the backcourt area.
    d. It will rebound very close to the front wall.

98. A player hits a ceiling shot that rebounds high off the back wall. What is the most probable cause of this?
    a. proper timing of the wrist snap
    b. ball hitting too close to the front wall
    c. player hitting ball at the top of his or her reach
    *d. player hitting ball with too much velocity

Forehand Ceiling Shot

99. How should the racquet be gripped to hit a forehand ceiling shot?
    *a. like a regular forehand shot
    b. slightly toward a backhand grip from a regular forehand grip
    c. more loosely than a regular forehand shot
    d. more tightly than a regular forehand shot

100. To hit a forehand ceiling shot, how should a player's feet be positioned in the backswing?

a. Wall _____   b. Wall _____

*c. Wall _____   d. Wall _____

101. In hitting a forehand ceiling shot, what forward path should the racquet take?
    a. directly over the player's head
    *b. directly over the player's right shoulder
    c. slightly to the right of the player's right shoulder
    d. a 45° angle from the player's shoulder

102. At what height should the ball be contacted in hitting a forehand ceiling shot?
    a. shoulder high
    b. head high
    c. an arm's length above the player's head
    *d. as high as the player can reach

103. In hitting a forehand ceiling shot, when should the ball be contacted?
    a. while it is in front of the player's body
    *b. while it is over the player's right shoulder
    c. not until it is behind the player's body
    d. as soon as the player can reach it

104. What is the action of the wrist in hitting a forehand ceiling shot?
    a. no wrist action
    b. a wrist snap just before contact
    *c. a wrist snap just after contact
    d. a wrist snap at contact

Backhand Ceiling Shot

105. To hit a backhand ceiling shot, how should a player's feet be positioned in the backswing?

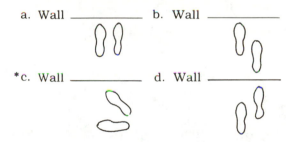

a. Wall _____   b. Wall _____

*c. Wall _____   d. Wall _____

106. In hitting a backhand ceiling shot, what forward path should the racquet take?
    a. directly over the player's head
    *b. directly over the player's right shoulder
    c. slightly to the right of the player's right shoulder
    d. a 45° angle from the player's right shoulder

107. In hitting a backhand ceiling shot, at what height should the ball be contacted?
    a. shoulder high
    b. head high
    c. slightly above head high
    *d. as high as the player can reach

108. You are attempting a backhand ceiling shot. Which should you do as you swing forward?
    a. Step backward.
    *b. Step forward.
    c. Keep your elbow in close to your body.
    d. Hit the ball when it is out from your back foot.

109. After contacting the ball for a backhand ceiling shot, which should the player do?
    a. Immediately stop the follow-through.
    *b. Take a full follow-through.
    c. Hold his or her position.
    d. Move up a few steps.

Drop Shot

110. What is the difference in hitting a drop shot and a regular forehand or backhand shot?
    *a. The shot is punched rather than stroked.
    b. The position of the body is more toward the front wall.
    c. The wrist is not cocked in the drop shot.
    d. The shot is hit close to the player's body.

Kill Shot

111. A shot is hit low on the front wall and is either impossible or nearly impossible to return. What is this shot called?
    a. drive shot
    *b. kill shot
    c. drop shot
    d. place shot

112. Which is the best kill shot?
    *a. one that results in a flat rollout
    b. one that rebounds off the back wall
    c. one that has blistering speed
    d. one that rebounds off the front and both side walls

113. Where should the body's center of gravity be in preparing to hit most types of kill shots?
    a. raised
    *b. lowered
    c. kept the same as for other shots
    d. shifted forward

Front Wall Kill Shot

114. You are attempting to hit a front wall kill shot. Which statement best describes the desired body position for this shot?
    a. Stand erect and bend your knees slightly.
    b. Bend your body slightly at your waist and bend your knees slightly.
    c. Bend your body slightly at your waist and bend your knees to get you as low as possible to the floor.
    *d. Bend your body and your knees to get you as low as possible to the floor.

115. At contact on a front wall kill shot, what should be the position of the arm?
    *a. straight and stretched out away from the body
    b. slightly bent and in close to the body
    c. bent at a right angle and out away from the body
    d. bent with the elbow close to the body

116. A player is attempting a front wall kill shot. At what height should the ball be contacted?
    a. above waist high
    b. hip to waist high
    c. knee to hip high
    *d. below knee high

Front Wall-Side Wall Kill

117. What shot takes the reverse path of a pinch shot?
    *a. front wall-side wall kill
    b. around-the-wall shot
    c. Z ball
    d. ceiling ball

Overhead Kill

118. At what height should the ball be contacted in hitting an overhand kill shot?
    a. shoulder high
    b. head high
    c. an arm's length above the player's head
    *d. as high as the player can reach

119. A player is attempting an overhead kill shot. Where should the ball be aimed?
    a. low on the front wall near a corner
    *b. low on a side wall near the front wall
    c. high on the front wall near a corner
    d. high on the side wall near the front wall

120. Generally, how hard should the ball be hit when attempting an overhead kill?
    a. very softly
    b. softly
    *c. moderately hard
    d. hard

Pass Shot

121. A player hits the ball parallel to a side wall and out of the opponent's reach. What is this called?
    a. pass shot
    b. crosscourt shot
    c. lob shot
    d. pinch shot

Down-the-Wall Pass Shot

122. A player is attempting a down-the-wall pass shot. Generally, how hard should the ball be hit?
     a. very softly
    *b. moderately hard
     c. hard
     d. very hard

123. A player is hitting a down-the-wall pass shot. When should the ball be contacted?
     a. before it is opposite the player's front foot
    *b. when it is opposite the player's front foot
     c. when it is opposite the center of the player's body
     d. when it is opposite the player's back foot

124. At contact on a down-the-wall pass shot, what should be the position of the player's arm?
    *a. straight and stretched out away from the body
     b. slightly bent and in close to the body
     c. bent at a right angle and out away from the body
     d. bent with the elbow close to the body

V Pass

125. A player is attempting a V pass. Generally, how hard should the ball be hit?
     a. softly
     b. moderately hard
    *c. hard
     d. very hard

Crosscourt Pass

126. Which passing shot hits the front wall and then the side wall before hitting the floor?
     a. down-the-wall pass
     b. V pass
    *c. wide angle pass
     d. pinch pass

127. A player is attempting a crosscourt pass. What should be the path of the player's racquet?
     a. an upward swing
     b. a downward swing
     c. a slightly upward swing
    *d. a level swing

Pinch Shot

128. A shot hits low on a side wall, then rebounds to the front wall and toward the opposite side wall. What is this shot called?
     a. side-front-side shot
     b. kill shot
     c. Z shot
    *d. pinch shot

129. The path of what shot is shown in the diagram? The X is the player hitting the ball and the "---" is the path of the ball. [Refer to Diagram 3.]
     a. around-the-wall ball
     b. front wall-side wall kill ball
    *c. pinch ball
     d. Z ball

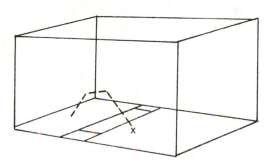

Diagram 3

130. How high on the side wall should a player aim a pinch shot?
    *a. floor to 1-1/2 feet above it
     b. floor to 3 feet above it
     c. ceiling to 3 feet below it
     d. center of wall

131. How close to the front wall should a player aim a pinch shot?
     a. front wall to 2 feet from it
    *b. 2 to 4 feet
     c. 4 to 8 feet
     d. no more than 4 feet

132. Generally, how hard should a player hit a pinch shot?
     a. very softly
     b. softly
    *c. moderately hard
     d. very hard

Reverse Pinch Shot

133. What is the difference in hitting a reverse pinch shot from hitting a pinch shot?
    a. The reverse pinch shot is hit with less velocity.
    *b. The reverse pinch shot is hit with more velocity.
    c. The reverse pinch shot is aimed higher on the wall.
    d. The reverse pinch shot is aimed lower on the wall.

Z Shot

134. A shot strikes the front wall, then a side wall, bounces, and then hits the opposite side wall. What is this shot called?
    a. pass shot
    b. wallpaper shot
    c. pinch shot
    *d. Z shot

135. The path of what shot is shown in the diagram? The X is the player hitting the ball and the "---" is the path of the ball. [Refer to Diagram 4.]
    a. around-the-wall ball
    b. ceiling ball
    c. pinch ball
    *d. Z ball

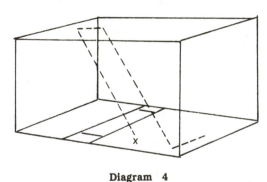

Diagram 4

Drive Shot

136. A shot is hit very hard and only strikes the front wall and the floor. What is this shot called?
    a. fly shot
    b. kill shot
    *c. drive shot
    d. photon

Lob Shot

137. A shot is hit high and softly on the front wall, rebounding high toward the back wall. What is this shot called?
    a. float shot
    b. fly shot
    *c. lob shot
    d. overhead shot

Serve

138. What is the method of putting the ball into play called?
    a. hitting
    b. striking
    *c. serving
    d. rallying

139. What is the best way for most players to improve their serving?
    a. learn the angles
    *b. learn to spot serve
    c. hit the ball harder
    d. use more wrist action

140. From what position should most serves be put into play?
    a. right side of the court
    b. left side of the court
    c. right or left side of the court
    *d. middle of the court

141. In the ready position for hitting a serve, what should be the position of the player's feet?

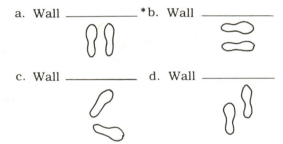

High Lob Serve

142. Which serve is shown in the diagram? The server is the X and the "---" is the path of the ball. [Refer to Diagram 5.]
    *a. high lob serve
    b. low lob serve
    c. high Z serve
    d. garfinkel serve

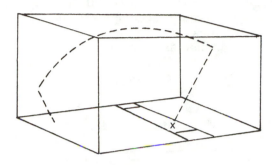

Diagram 5

143. A player is attempting an underhand high lob serve. What path should the racquet take?
    a. slightly upward
    *b. upward at a 45° angle
    c. upward at a 90° angle
    d. level

144. What should provide the velocity for the ball when a player hits a high lob serve?
    a. wrist action
    *b. arm action
    c. arm and wrist action
    d. arm, wrist and body action

145. At what height should an overhead high lob serve be contacted?
    *a. chest high or higher
    b. waist to chest high
    c. hip to waist high
    d. knee to hip high

146. A player hits a high lob serve. Where should it hit the side wall?
    a. front half of the court
    b. back half of the court
    c. front fifth of the court
    *d. back fifth of the court

Low Z Serve

147. Which serve is shown in the diagram? The server is the X, and the "---" is the path of the ball. [Refer to Diagram 6.]
    a. low drive serve
    *b. low Z serve
    c. garbage serve
    d. garfinkel serve

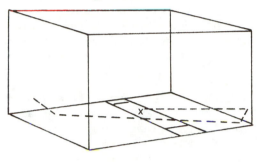

Diagram 6

148. Where should the low Z serve hit the second wall?
    *a. low and near the back corner
    b. high and near the back corner
    c. low and near the middle of the wall
    d. high and near the middle of the wall

149. How hard should a low Z serve be hit?
    a. softly
    b. moderately
    *c. hard
    d. very hard

Low Drive Serve

150. Which serve is shown in the diagram? The server is the X, and the "---" is the path of the ball. [Refer to Diagram 7.]
    *a. low drive serve
    b. low Z serve
    c. garbage serve
    d. garfinkel serve

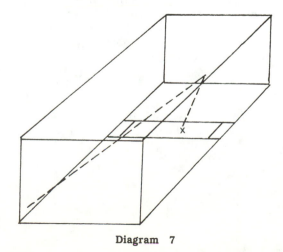

Diagram 7

151. A player is attempting a low drive serve. Where should the ball hit the front wall?
    a. floor to 6 inches above the floor
    *b. 6 to 12 inches above the floor
    c. 12 to 18 inches above the floor
    d. 18 inches to 3 feet above the floor

152. Where should a low drive serve hit after rebounding from the floor?
    a. low on the back wall
    *b. low on a side wall near a corner
    c. low on the middle of the back wall
    d. low on the middle of a side wall

High Z Serve

153. Which serve is shown in the diagram? The server is the X, and the "---" is the path of the ball. [Refer to Diagram 8.]
    a. high drive serve
    *b. high Z serve
    c. low lob serve
    d. lob serve

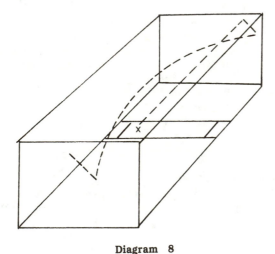

Diagram 8

154. You are attempting a high Z serve to the left back corner. Where should you stand to serve?
    a. the center of the service area
    b. one step to the left of the center of the service area
    c. 5 feet from the right wall
    *d. 5 feet from the left wall

155. How hard should a high Z serve be hit?
    a. very softly
    *b. softly
    c. hard
    d. very hard

156. You are attempting a high Z serve to the left back corner. Where should the ball hit the front wall?
    *a. high on the wall in the right corner
    b. high on the wall in the left corner
    c. midway up the wall on the right side
    d. midway up the wall on the left side

Low Lob Serve

157. Which serve is shown in the diagram? The server is the X, and the "---" is the path of the ball. [Refer to Diagram 9.]
    a. high drive serve
    b. high Z serve
    *c. low lob serve
    d. lob serve

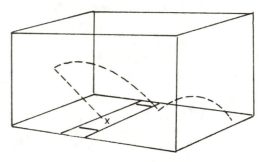

Diagram 9

158. A player is attempting a low lob serve. Where should the ball hit the front wall?
    a. within 5 feet of the ceiling
    b. about 8 feet from the ceiling
    c. about 5 feet from the floor
    *d. about 8 feet from the floor

159. Where should a low lob serve hit the floor?
    a. about 2 feet behind the short line
    *b. about 4 feet behind the short line
    c. about 10 feet from the back wall
    d. about 5 feet from the back wall

Strategy

160. What is the purpose of strategy?
    a. to win
    b. to take advantage of your opponent's weaknesses
    c. to take advantage of your strengths
    *d. to take advantage of your strengths and your opponent's weaknesses

161. What is generally the best strategy?
    a. hit the ball as hard as possible
    b. attempt a kill on every shot
    c. run your opponent
    *d. play the percentages

162. What type of player generally prefers playing in the front court?
    *a. a fast, aggressive player
    b. a slow, control player
    c. a lob player
    d. a patient player

163. You hit a shot. When should you move to prepare for your next shot?
    *a. as soon as you hit your shot
    b. as soon as your opponent's shot is hit
    c. as soon as you see what direction your opponent's shot is going
    d. as soon as you know what kind of shot your opponent is going to hit

Serve

164. Which factor is most important to consider in deciding on the type of serve to hit?
    a. what you serve best
    *b. what will create difficulty for your opponent
    c. what will keep your opponent guessing
    d. what will most likely result in an ace

165. How can you keep your opponent from anticipating the type of serve you will hit?
    a. Hit a different serve each time.
    b. Change to a different type of serve each time you start serving.
    *c. Mix up your serves.
    d. Change to a different type of serve after your opponent hits a winning return.

166. What is the major *disadvantage* of moving to the side of the court to serve?
    a. It tells your opponent the type of serve you will attempt.
    b. It tells your opponent where you are attempting to hit the serve.
    *c. It makes you vulnerable to a down-the-wall pass shot.
    d. It makes you vulnerable to a crosscourt pass shot.

167. What is the greatest advantage of the low drive serve?
    a. It is the easiest to learn.
    b. It causes your opponent the most amount of frustration.
    c. It is the hardest to return.
    *d. It forces your opponent to react quickly.

168. Where should a low Z serve aimed at a right-handed receiver's backhand hit the front wall?
    a. near the middle
    *b. near the right corner
    c. near the left corner
    d. near the ceiling

Return of Serve

169. What is the normal serve return position?
    a. four steps behind the short line in center court
    b. two steps off the back wall and near the left side wall
    c. two steps off the back wall and near the right side wall
    *d. two steps off the back wall and equidistant from both side walls

170. Generally, what is the safest return of serve?
    *a. ceiling ball
    b. around-the-wall ball
    c. pinch shot
    d. Z shot

171. The server moves toward the front court after making the serve. What is the best service return shot?
    a. pinch shot
    b. front wall kill shot
    c. front wall-side wall kill shot
    *d. crosscourt pass shot

172. Your opponent's serves are consistently landing and dying in the corner. What would be a good return of serve strategy?
    a. Move more quickly to the corner.
    b. Anticipate your opponent's serve better.
    *c. Move up and cut off the serve before it bounces.
    d. Move to the front court as soon as the ball is served.

173. When is the ceiling shot your most effective service return?
    a. when your opponent is using the low lob serve
    b. when your opponent is using the Z serve
    c. when your opponent is using the low drive serve
    *d. when your opponent is using a serve you cannot kill or pass

174. What is the greatest advantage of using the ceiling ball for a service return?
    a. It is an unexpected shot.
    *b. It allows the receiver to move to center court.
    c. It is the easiest shot to attempt.
    d. It requires the server to hit an overhead.

Singles

175. In singles, where should a player spend most of his or her time?
    a. front court
    *b. center court
    c. back court
    d. determined by the player's style of play

176. Generally, what is the best strategy in playing singles?
    a. Keep your opponent in front of you.
    b. Keep your opponent in the middle court.
    c. Keep your opponent in the back court.
    *d. Keep your opponent on the run.

177. You are playing singles and you serve to the left-hand corner. What is your best position for returning your opponent's shot?
    a. center of the back court, approximately four steps off the back wall
    b. center of the service area, within one step of the back service line
    *c. one step behind the back service line, slightly left of center
    d. one step behind the back service line, slightly right of center

178. In singles, what should shot selection in the front court be determined by?
    a. your best shots
    b. your opponent's weaknesses
    c. your position and your opponent's position
    d. your opponent's position

179. In singles, what is the best way to drive your opponent out of a front court position?
    a. a kill shot
    *b. a ceiling ball
    c. a side wall-front wall shot
    d. a back wall shot

180. You are playing singles. You have a backhand shot in the left front corner. Your opponent is in the middle of the service area. What is your best choice of shots?
    a. drop shot
    *b. down-the-wall pass shot
    c. crosscourt pass shot
    d. ceiling ball

181. You are playing singles. You are in the right front corner, and your opponent is behind the receiving line. What is your best choice of shots?
    a. ceiling ball
    b. down-the-wall pass shot
    c. crosscourt pass shot
    *d. pinch shot

182. In singles, you and your opponent are in the front court. What is your best choice of shots?
    *a. a pass shot
    b. a kill shot
    c. a drop shot
    d. a ceiling shot

183. In singles, generally, where should a player move after hitting each shot?
    a. to the front court
    b. to the service zone
    *c. to the center court
    d. to the back court

184. While playing singles, you are in the center court and your opponent is behind you. What is your best shot selection?
    a. down-the-wall pass shot
    b. crosscourt pass shot
    *c. pinch shot to the wall nearest your opponent
    d. pinch shot to the wall farthest from your opponent

185. You are playing singles. You are in the center court, and your opponent is in front of you. What is your best shot selection?
    *a. a pass shot
    b. a kill shot
    c. a pinch shot
    d. a Z ball

186. While playing singles, you want to run your opponent. What kind of shots should you hit?
    *a. pass shots
    b. kill shots
    c. ceiling balls
    d. Z balls

187. In singles, you are playing an opponent with little patience, and you want to keep him or her in the back court. What is your best choice of shots?
    a. pass shots
    b. kill shots
    *c. ceiling balls
    d. back wall shots

188. In singles, what is the most important shot for a back court player?
    a. passes
    b. kills
    *c. ceiling balls
    d. back wall shots

189. You are in the back court, and your opponent is in the front court. What should you *never* do in singles?
    a. Attempt a down-the-wall pass
    b. Attempt a crosscourt pass.
    c. Attempt a ceiling ball.
    *d. Attempt a kill shot.

190. In singles, you are in the middle court and your opponent is in the back court. Which is *not* a good choice of shots?
    a. pinch shot
    b. front wall-side wall kill shot
    *c. pass shot
    d. front wall kill shot

191. In singles, you are in the back court and your opponent is in the back court. Which is *not* a good choice of shots?
    *a. pass shot
    b. front wall kill shot
    c. pinch shot
    d. reverse pinch shot

192. In singles, generally, what is the best shot to use when your opponent is on the opposite side of the court?
    a. kill shot
    b. ceiling ball
    c. V pass
    *d. down-the-wall pass

193. In singles, when is forcing your opponent to hit a ball smashed right at him or her a good strategy?
    a. when your opponent is in the back court
    b. when your opponent is in front of you
    *c. when your opponent is backpedaling
    d. when your opponent is in back of you

194. In singles, when is a pinch shot used most successfully?
    a. when the opponent is in the center of the court
    b. when the opponent is in the front court
    *c. when the opponent is in the back court
    d. when the opponent is near a side wall

195. In singles, you are playing an opponent with exceptional quickness. What shots will best negate this advantage?
    a. kill shots
    b. pass shots
    *c. ceiling balls
    d. drop shots

Doubles

196. In doubles, what is the most frequently used kill shot?
    a. front wall kill
    b. front wall-side wall kill
    c. off-the-back wall kill
    *d. pinch shot

197. What is the most widely used method of playing doubles?
    *a. side by side
    b. I-formation
    c. center exchange
    d. limited position

198. A team is playing the side-by-side system of doubles. Both partners are right-handed. Who should cover the left side?
    a. the player with the better kill shot
    b. the more aggressive player
    c. the better all-around player
    *d. the player with the better backhand

199. A team is playing the side-by-side system of doubles. One player is right-handed, and the other player is left-handed. Which player should cover the left side of the court?
    a. the right-handed player
    *b. the left-handed player
    c. the player with the better overhead kill shot
    d. the better all-around player

200. A team is playing the side-by-side system of doubles. One player is right-handed, and the other player is left-handed. Which player should take the down-the-middle shots?
    a. the right-handed player
    b. the left-handed player
    c. the player with the better forehand
    *d. the player with the better backhand

201. A doubles team is using an I-formation system. What special skill(s) should the player covering the front court have?
    *a. be quick
    b. be a good shooter
    c. be a good ceiling ball player
    d. be patient

202. A doubles team is using an I-formation system. What special skill(s) should the player covering the back court have?
    a. be quick
    *b. be a good shooter and ceiling ball player
    c. be a good back wall ball player
    d. be aggressive

203. A doubles team is playing the center court exchange system. How is the court divided for coverage?
    *a. Each player covers one half of the court from front to back wall.
    b. One player covers the front court, and the other covers the middle and back court.
    c. One player covers about two thirds of the court from the front wall to the back wall, and the other covers the remaining third.
    d. One player covers the area on the right of an imaginary diagonal line drawn from the right back corner to the left front corner, and the other covers the area to the left of that line.

204. A doubles team is playing a center court exchange system. What abilities should both players have?
    a. be patient, control players
    b. be good shooters and ceiling ball players
    c. be good back wall ball and lob players
    *d. be quick and aggressive

205. A doubles team is playing a center court exchange system. When one partner is hitting the ball, what should the other partner do?
    a. Be sure to be out of the way.
    b. Move to the opposite side of the court.
    c. Prepare to cover the opposite end of the court.
    *d. Move to the middle of the court.

206. What is the advantage of playing a center court exchange system over playing a side-by-side system?
    a. Both players do not need to be as strong all-around players to be effective.
    b. It is confusing to the opponents.
    *c. The partner hitting the ball always knows where his or her partner is on the court.
    d. It gives a team more opportunities to shoot.

207. When should a doubles team choose to play a limited position system?
    a. when one player is especially strong in the front court
    b. when one player is especially strong in the back court
    c. when both players are of about equal ability
    *d. when one player is much stronger than the other

208. One member of a doubles team is extremely quick. The other is slower, but a good defensive player. What would be the most effective system of court coverage for this team?
    a. side by side
    *b. I-formation
    c. center court exchange
    d. limited position

209. You and your partner are playing a doubles team with one right-handed player and one left-handed player. They are playing a normal side-by-side system. Where is the best place to hit the serve?
    a. to the right back corner
    b. to the left back corner
    *c. to the center of the back court
    d. to the center of the middle court

210. In doubles, what is the biggest problem in serving hard drive serves to your partner's side of the court?
    a. Your partner may get hit by your serve.
    b. Your partner may get called for a hinder.
    c. Your partner may get called for an avoidable hinder.
    *d. Your partner may get hit in the back by the opponent's return.

211. In serving in doubles, you are hitting mostly hard drive and Z serves. You find you are having trouble getting into position before the return of serve is made. What should you do?
    a. Try for better angles.
    b. Try for more aces.
    c. Serve from a different position in the service zone.
    *d. Serve a slower type of serve.

212. To win, what area of the court must a doubles team control?
    a. the front court
    *b. the center court
    c. the back court
    d. the service zone area

213. After you serve in doubles, what should you do?
     *a. Move to center court and slightly toward the side where the ball is served.
     b. Move to center court and slightly away from the side where the ball is served.
     c. Move to the front court and slightly toward the side where the ball is served.
     d. Move to the front court and slightly away from the side where the ball is served.

214. In doubles, generally which shot is most effective in moving your opponents into the back court?
     a. kill shots
     b. pinch shots
     c. front wall-side wall shots
     *d. pass shots

Rules and Scoring

Scoring

215. In a tie breaker, how many points does a player have to score to win?
     a. 7
     *b. 11
     c. 15
     d. 21

216. To win a match, how many games must a player win?
     a. 1
     b. 2
     *c. 2 out of 3
     d. 3 out of 5

217. When is a tie breaker played?
     a. when each player or team has won 20 points
     b. when each player or team has won 14 points
     *c. when each player or team has won one game
     d. when each player or team has won two games

218. How much ahead does a player need to be to win a game?
     *a. 1 point
     b. 2 points
     c. must win a tie breaker if the score becomes tied at 14-14
     d. must win a tie breaker if the score becomes tied at 20-20

219. Where must a player stand to serve?
     a. behind the service line
     *b. in the service zone
     c. in the service box
     d. behind the short line

220. When there is no referee, whose responsibility is it to announce the score and when?
     *a. The server announces the score before every first serve.
     b. The server announces the score before each serve.
     c. The receiver announces the score before each first serve.
     d. Each player announces his or her own score between rallys.

Court

221. Which number in the diagram indicates the service line? [Refer to Diagram 10.]
     *a. 2
     b. 4
     c. 5
     d. 6

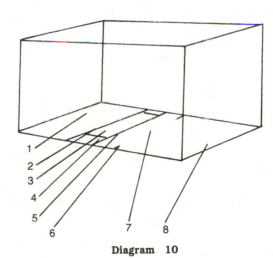

Diagram 10

222. Which number in the diagram indicates the short line? [Refer to Diagram 10, Question 221].
     a. 1
     b. 2
     *c. 5
     d. 6

223. Which number in the diagram indicates the service box? [Refer to Diagram 10, Question 221].
     a. 1
     b. 3
     *c. 4
     d. 7

224. Which number in the diagram indicates the service zone? [Refer to Diagram 10, Question 221.]
    a. 1
    *b. 3
    c. 4
    d. 8

225. Which number in the diagram indicates the receiving line? [Refer to Diagram 10, Question 221.]
    a. 2
    b. 4
    c. 5
    *d. 6

Serve

226. When does the serve change from one player to another?
    *a. when the server loses a rally
    b. after every point
    c. after every 5 points
    d. after a game is completed

227. A player is serving. The right foot is on the short line when the ball is contacted. What is the ruling?
    a. fault
    b. foot fault
    *c. legal play
    d. hand-out

228. When may the server leave the service zone?
    a. as soon as contact is made with the ball
    *b. as soon as the ball crosses the short line
    c. as soon as the ball hits the front wall
    d. as soon as the ball hits a side wall or the floor

229. A serve hits the front wall and then bounces in front of the service line. What is the ruling?
    a. long
    *b. short
    c. legal play
    d. out-of-bounds

230. On the serve, how many times must the ball bounce before it is contacted?
    a. zero
    b. zero or one
    *c. one
    d. one or two

231. A player serves the ball. What may it legally touch before hitting the front wall?
    a. a side wall
    b. the ceiling
    c. the intersection of the front wall and the floor
    *d. nothing

232. A player serves the ball. What may the ball legally touch after it hits the front wall and before it touches the floor?
    *a. a side wall
    b. the back wall
    c. the opponent's racquet
    d. the intersection of a side wall and the back wall

233. How many chances does a player have to make a good serve?
    a. one
    b. two
    *c. one or two, depending on the outcome of the first serve
    d. as many as it takes

234. In singles, a player serves two long serves. What is the situation?
    a. point
    b. fault
    *c. side-out
    d. dead ball serve

235. In singles, a first serve hits the server on the fly. What is the situation?
    a. hinder
    b. dead-ball serve
    c. legal play
    *d. sideout

236. In singles play, which serve always results in a sideout?
    a. short serve
    *b. out-of-order serve
    c. three-wall serve
    d. ceiling serve

237. After the server enters the service zone, how long does he or she have to make a good serve?
    a. 5 seconds
    *b. 10 seconds
    c. 15 seconds
    d. 30 seconds

238. In doubles, when may a team change its order of serving?
     a. after each time the opponents are "out"
     b. after every five points
     c. any time it begins a serve
    *d. at the beginning of a game

239. In doubles, when does only one player on a team get a turn to serve?
    *a. at the beginning of the game
     b. on each team's service turn
     c. when the score is tied at 20-20
     d. when a tiebreaker is being played

240. In doubles, where must the server's partner stand during the serve?
     a. in the service area
    *b. in the service box
     c. behind the service line
     d. out of the way

241. In doubles, how must the server's partner stand during the serve?
     a. both feet on the floor in the service box and one hand against the wall
     b. at least one foot on the floor in the service box and back against the wall
     c. at least one foot on the floor in the service box and one hand against the wall
    *d. both feet on the floor in the service box and back against the wall

242. When may the server's partner leave his or her position during the serve?
     a. after the ball is contacted
     b. after the ball hits the front wall
    *c. after the ball crosses the short line
     d. after an opponent hits the return

243. A served ball hits the server's partner on the fly while he or she is still in the service box. What is the situation?
     a. loss of serve
    *b. dead ball
     c. play continues
     d. point for server

244. In games without a referee, whose responsibility is it to make the calls involving serves?
     a. the server
    *b. the receiver
     c. the player with the best view of the ball
     d. the player closer to the ball

Return of Serve

245. In returning a serve, where must the player be?
     a. behind the service line
     b. behind the service zone
    *c. behind the receiving line
     d. in the back court

Play

246. How many times may the ball touch the floor on one shot and still be in play?
     a. zero
    *b. zero or one
     c. one
     d. zero, one or two

247. A player makes a shot. Which is a legal sequence of events?
     a. The ball hits the floor and front wall.
     b. The ball hits a side wall, the floor, and the front wall.
    *c. The ball hits the ceiling, the front wall, and the floor.
     d. The ball hits the ceiling, the floor, and the front wall.

248. During a rally, Player A, the server, hits the ball on the frame of the racquet. What is the situation?
     a. It is a dead ball.
     b. It is a point for the opponent.
    *c. The ball is still in play.
     d. Player A loses the serve.

249. Player A, the server, is rallying with Player B. Player B swings at the ball and misses it completely. What is the situation?
     a. It is a dead ball.
     b. It is a point for Player A.
    *c. The ball is still in play.
     d. It is a replay.

250. Player A, the server, is rallying with Player B. Player A hits the ball, and a broken ball occurs. What is the situation?
     a. Play continues until the rally is over.
    *b. Play is stopped and the point replayed.
     c. Player A wins the point.
     d. Player B serves.

251. Players A and B are rallying. Player A, the server, hits a ball that hits the knob on the door. What is the situation?
     a. Play continues.
    *b. Play is stopped and the point is replayed.
     c. Player A wins the point.
     d. Player B serves.

252. Players A and B are rallying. Player A, the server, hits a ball that hits Player B as it travels toward the front wall. If the ball had *not* hit Player B, it would have hit the front wall. What is the situation?
    a. Play continues.
    *b. Play is stopped and the point is replayed.
    c. Player A wins the point.
    d. Player B serves.

253. Players A and B are rallying. Player A, the server, hits a ball that hits Player B as it travels toward the front wall. The ball would *not* have hit the front wall even if it had *not* hit Player B. What is the situation?
    a. Play continues.
    *b. Play is stopped and the point is replayed.
    c. Player A wins the point.
    d. Player B serves.

254. Players A and B are rallying. Player A, the server, hits a shot and then fails to move so that Player B can hit a return. What is the situation?
    a. Player A wins the point.
    *b. Player B serves.
    c. Play continues.
    d. Dead ball is called.

255. Players A and B are rallying. Player A, the server, hits a shot and moves into a position to prevent Player B from having a clear shot at the front wall. What is the situation?
    a. Dead ball is called.
    b. Player A wins the point.
    *c. Player B serves.
    d. Play continues.

256. Players A and B are rallying. Player A, the server, hits a skip ball. What is the situation?
    a. Dead ball is called.
    b. Player A wins the point.
    *c. Player B serves.
    d. Play continues.

257. Two players are playing a game without an official. They disagree over a call made on the server. What should be the result?
    a. the server's point
    b. the receiver's point
    *c. point replayed
    d. call for an official

258. During a rally, you are sure the shot you are about to make will hit your opponent. What should you do?
    a. Hit your opponent.
    b. Forfeit the point.
    c. Stop and call an avoidable hinder.
    *d. Stop and call a safety hinder.

259. Which is a violation of the "unwritten rules" of racquetball?
    a. screening an opponent
    *b. making loud, unnecessary noises
    c. disagreeing with a call
    d. taking more than 10 seconds to serve

260. In a match without a referee, whose responsibility is it to make calls during a rally?
    *a. the hitter
    b. the hitter's opponent
    c. the player with the best view of the situation
    d. the player closest to the ball when the violation occurred

261. In a match without a referee, Players A and B are rallying. Player A hinders Player B from making a shot. Whose responsibility is it to make the hinder call and when should it be made?
    a. Player A before the shot is made
    b. Player A after the shot is made
    *c. Player B before the shot is made
    d. Player B after the shot is made

262. In a match without a referee, Players A and B are rallying. Player A realizes he or she has created an avoidable hinder. What should Player A do?
    a. nothing, as Player B should make the call
    b. say, "I'm sorry, please replay the point"
    c. accept winning the rally
    *d. award the rally to Player B

Acknowledgments

Colleagues and students who contributed suggestions and ideas for the Racquetball test questions are: D. James, G. Kerbaugh, and B. Petrakis.

Suggested Readings

Allsen, P.E. (1981). *Racquetball*. Dubuque, IA: Wm. C. Brown.

NAGWS. (1984). *Badminton/squash/racquetball guide 1984-86*. Reston, VA: American Alliance for Health, Physical Education, Recreation and Dance.

Sauser, J., & Shay, A. (1981). *Beginning racquetball drills*. Chicago, IL: Contemporary Books.

Stafford, R. (1984). *Racquetball: The sport for everyone*. Memphis, TN: Stafford.

Turner, E.T., & Hogan, M. (1987). *The complete book of racquetball*. Champaign, IL: Human Kinetics.

Recreational Dance

Julia M. Hobby, Consultant

The questions on recreational dance forms are divided into four content areas:

- Dance Fundamentals
- Square Dancing
- Folk Dancing
- Social Dancing

In the Dance Fundamentals area are questions appropriate for at least two of the three types of dance covered in this chapter.

Some confusion may be evident in the terminology used, especially in describing directions, such as *in front of*, *to the side*, and so forth. Such wording may need to be revised to fit the terminology used during instruction.

Dances and dance steps included in the square and folk dance sections are only a few of the infinite number that different teachers use across the country. Some of the questions may need revision to fit the dances taught.

Dance Fundamentals

History	1 to 21
Terminology	22 to 32
Techniques	33 to 106

History

Origin

1. What is the origin of dance?
   - *a. originated in primitive times as part of religious and food gathering ceremonies
   - b. originated in ancient civilizations as part of religious and war ceremonies
   - c. originated in the Middle Ages as part of social activities of country people
   - d. originated in 17th and 18th century Europe as part of social activities of the French court

2. What is probably the most ancient of dance forms?
   - a. the processional
   - b. the chain
   - *c. the closed circle
   - d. the quadrille

3. Who were the first people to describe dance movements on paper?
   - a. Greeks
   - b. Romans
   - *c. Egyptians
   - d. French

4. Which people first considered dance as an essential part of education?
   - *a. Greeks
   - b. Romans
   - c. Egyptians
   - d. French

Julia M. Hobby is an assistant professor of health, physical education, and recreation at Delta State University, Cleveland, Mississippi.

5. After what were the dance forms of the Old South patterned?
   *a. the English court
   b. the French court
   c. the English country people
   d. the New England middle class

6. Which dance style originated in America?
   a. folk dance
   b. round dance
   c. waltz
   *d. fox-trot

7. Who introduced folk dance into physical education programs in the United States?
   a. Martha Graham
   *b. Elizabeth Burchenal
   c. Henry Ward Beecher
   d. Samuel Woodworth

People

8. Who developed the minuet as a ballroom dance?
   a. King Louis XIV
   *b. Louis Pecour
   c. Queen Elizabeth I
   d. John Playford

9. Which group is traditionally considered the protagonist of dance in America?
   a. Indians
   b. Virginia planters
   *c. Puritans
   d. city dwellers

Books

10. In what year was *The English Dancing Master* written?
    a. 1600
    *b. 1651
    c. 1776
    d. 1901

Dances

11. When and where did the minuet come into prominence as a dance form?
    a. around 1500 in England
    b. around 1650 in Virginia
    *c. around 1750 in France
    d. around 1800 in Italy

12. Which dance is known as the supreme dance of the 18th century?
    *a. minuet
    b. country dance
    c. cotillion
    d. waltz

13. What was the most popular form of the early English country dances?
    a. round
    b. square
    c. square-eight
    *d. longway

14. For what were the early English country dances named?
    a. towns in which they originated
    b. choreographers of the dances
    *c. tunes to which they were danced
    d. major steps in the dances

15. What dance form was used in the early French contredanses and cotillions?
    a. longway
    b. round
    c. processional
    *d. square

16. From what dance form did the French contredanses develop?
    *a. English country dance
    b. minuet
    c. square dance
    d. quadrille

17. From what dance form did the quadrille develop?
    a. minuet
    *b. contredanses
    c. waltz
    d. square dance

18. Where did the waltz first appear as a popular dance form?
    a. England
    b. Germany
    *c. Vienna
    d. Paris

19. What is thought to be the origin of the polka?
    a. Germany
    b. England
    c. France
    *d. Bohemia

20. Where did the polka first become a popular dance form?
    a. French court
    b. English court
    *c. fashionable salons of Paris
    d. German countryside

21. What types of movements are characteristic of dances from countries with cold climates?
    *a. types using vigorous movements
    b. types using flowing motions
    c. types using very small spaces
    d. types using great amounts of space

Terminology

Saint-Simonienne
22. What is Saint-Simonienne?
  - a. a famous religious dance ritual
  - b. a famous early contredanse
  - c. an early, popular form of the minuet
  - *d. a figure allowing a continuous change of partners

Waltz
23. What does the word *waltz* mean?
  - a. a small company of soldiers
  - *b. to turn
  - c. underpetticoat
  - d. little steps

Square Dance
24. What is the folk dance of the United States?
  - a. contra dance
  - b. quadrille
  - c. polka
  - *d. square dance

Social Dance
25. What is the meaning today of the term *social dance*?
  - *a. ballroom dance
  - b. traditional dance
  - c. group dance
  - d. formal dance

Folk Dance
26. What is the meaning of the term *folk dance*?
  - a. dance of country people
  - b. ballroom dance
  - *c. traditional dance of a people
  - d. group dance

Contra Dance
27. What is a *contra dance*?
  - a. a dance of many couples in a circle
  - b. a dance of four couples in a square
  - *c. a dance of many couples in a line facing another line
  - d. a dance of eight couples in a double circle

Quadrille
28. Which dance form is the quadrille most like?
  - *a. square dance
  - b. contra dance
  - c. round dance
  - d. social dance

Locomotion
29. What is movement through space called?
  - a. meters
  - b. measures
  - *c. locomotion
  - d. rhythm patterns

Clockwise
30. When the dancers are facing the center of the circle, which is the same as clockwise movement?
  - a. circle to the right
  - *b. circle to the left
  - c. circulate
  - d. line of direction

Counterclockwise
31. When the dancers are facing the center of the circle, in which direction do they move for counterclockwise?
  - *a. to the right
  - b. to the left
  - c. to the man's right
  - d. to the lady's right

Line of Direction
32. Which is the meaning of *line of direction*?
  - *a. circle to the right
  - b. circle to the left
  - c. circle direction designated by caller
  - d. face a designated direction by caller

Techniques

Musical Components
33. What is considered to be the magic power of dance?
  - a. form
  - b. movement
  - c. music
  - *d. rhythm

34. The beats in a rhythm pattern are all the same value. What is this called?
  - *a. even rhythm
  - b. rhythm pattern
  - c. syncopated rhythm
  - d. underlying beat

35. What is said to be "the twin sister of dance"?
  - a. art
  - b. movement
  - *c. music
  - d. religion

36. What is the basic unit that measures time in music?
  - a. accent
  - b. measure
  - *c. beat
  - d. rhythm

37. What is the stress placed upon a beat in music called?
    *a. accent
    b. rhythm
    c. meter
    d. tempo

38. The accent is placed on the off beat. What is this called in music?
    a. uneven rhythm
    b. broken rhythm
    *c. syncopated rhythm
    d. even rhythm

39. What is one group of beats between two adjacent bars on a musical staff called?
    a. meter
    *b. measure
    c. phrase
    d. rhythm pattern

40. What is the rate of speed at which music is played?
    a. rhythm
    b. beat
    *c. tempo
    d. beat

41. What factors are present in rhythm?
    a. measure and beat
    b. accent and time
    *c. time and force
    d. force and measure

42. Which movement is in 4/4 time?
    *a. run
    b. skip
    c. slide
    d. gallop

43. Which movement is in 2/4 time?
    a. walk
    b. run
    c. hop
    *d. skip

44. Which basic dance step is in 4/4 time?
    a. two-step
    b. polka
    *c. schottische
    d. waltz

45. Which basic dance step is in 3/4 time?
    a. polka
    b. schottische
    c. shuffle
    *d. waltz

46. A piece of music is in 2/4 time. What does the 2 mean?
    *a. two beats per measure
    b. two beats per meter
    c. the note value that receives one beat
    d. the note value that receives two beats

47. A piece of music is in 3/4 time. What does the 4 mean?
    a. four beats per measure
    b. four beats per meter
    *c. the note value that receives one beat
    d. the note value that receives three beats

48. What does a 3/4 time signature mean?
    a. four beats to a measure, each quarter note gets one beat
    b. four beats to a measure, each quarter note gets three beats
    *c. three beats to a measure, each quarter note gets one beat
    d. three beats to a measure, each quarter note gets four beats

49. Where is the primary accent usually placed in music?
    *a. the first beat
    b. the second beat
    c. the third beat
    d. the last beat

50. Which note in the diagram is a half note? [Refer to Diagram 1.]
    a. A
    b. B
    *c. C
    d. D

Diagram 1

51. Which note in the diagram is a whole note? [Refer to Diagram 1, Question 50.]
    a. A
    *b. B
    c. C
    d. E

52. Which note in the diagram is a 16th note? [Refer to Diagram 1, Question 50.]
    a. A
    b. C
    *c. D
    d. E

53. Which picture shows a group of notes played in the usual time of two similar notes? [Refer to Diagram 1, Question 50.]
    a. F
    *b. G
    c. H
    d. I

Movement

54. Which is *not* a component of movement?
    a. direction
    *b. rhythm
    c. style
    d. tempo

55. What are the patterns of movement by dancers?
    a. form
    b. movement
    c. music
    *d. rhythm

56. What is considered to be the medium of dance?
    a. form
    *b. movement
    c. music
    d. rhythm

Locomotor Movements

57. You step from one foot to the other, transferring your weight from your heel to your toe. What step is this?
    a. run
    *b. walk
    c. leap
    d. slide

58. What is the rhythm pattern for a walk?
    *a. even
    b. uneven
    c. broken
    d. syncopated

59. Which locomotor movement is a step and a hop on the same foot?
    a. hop
    b. jump
    c. gallop
    *d. skip

60. What is the rhythm pattern for a skip?
    a. even
    *b. uneven
    c. broken
    d. syncopated

61. Which movement in a slide step to the right takes place on the quick beat?
    a. initial step with the right foot
    b. close step with left foot
    c. weight transfer to right foot after initial step
    *d. weight transfer to left foot after close step

62. What is the rhythm pattern for a slide?
    a. even
    *b. uneven
    c. broken
    d. syncopated

63. Which statement best describes a run?
    a. The steps are from one foot to the other, transferring the weight from the heel to the toe.
    b. The steps are from one foot to the other, pushing off with a spring and landing on the ball of the foot.
    *c. The steps are from one foot to the other, carrying the weight on the balls of the feet.
    d. A step with one foot is followed by a quick step with the other foot.

64. What is the rhythm pattern for a run?
    *a. even
    b. uneven
    c. broken
    d. syncopated

65. In what locomotor movement do you spring from the ball of one foot and land on the ball of the same foot?
    a. leap
    b. gallop
    c. jump
    *d. hop

66. What is the rhythm pattern for a hop?
    *a. even
    b. uneven
    c. broken
    d. syncopated

67. What is the rhythm pattern for a jump?
    *a. even
    b. uneven
    c. broken
    d. syncopated

68. You spring from one or both feet and land on both feet. What is this movement called?
    a. hop
    *b. jump
    c. leap
    d. two-step

69. What is the rhythm pattern for a gallop?
    a. even
    *b. uneven
    c. broken
    d. syncopated

70. How can a gallop best be described?
    a. a sideward move in which a step is followed by a close step
    *b. a forward movement in which a step is followed by a quick close step
    c. a step followed by a hop on the same foot
    d. a springing step from one foot to the other foot

71. What is the rhythm pattern for a leap?
    *a. even
    b. uneven
    c. broken
    d. syncopated

72. How should the shock be absorbed in a leap?
    a. by landing on the ball of the foot
    b. by landing on the heel of the foot
    c. by giving at the ankle
    *d. by bending the knee

Dance Steps

73. In which dance step would you take a step forward with the left foot, a step to the side with the right foot, a close step left to right foot, and transfer your weight to the left foot?
    a. two-step
    b. polka
    *c. waltz
    d. shuffle

74. Which best describes a schottische?
    a. hop, step, close, step
    *b. step, step, step, hop
    c. step, close, step, close
    d. step, hop, step, hop

75. What is the rhythm pattern for a schottische?
    *a. even
    b. uneven
    c. broken
    d. syncopated

76. What is the rhythm pattern for a two-step?
    a. even
    *b. uneven
    c. broken
    d. syncopated

77. In which basic dance step is the rhythm quick, quick, slow?
    a. polka
    b. schottische
    *c. two-step
    d. mazurka

78. On which beat is the hop in the polka?
    a. first
    b. second
    *c. pickup
    d. last

79. Which basic dance step can be described as hop, step, close, step?
    a. two-step
    *b. polka
    c. schottische
    d. mazurka

80. What is the rhythm pattern for a polka?
    a. even
    *b. uneven
    c. broken
    d. syncopated

81. In which basic dance step is the accent on the second beat?
    a. polka
    b. two-step
    c. waltz
    *d. mazurka

82. Which is a mazurka step pattern?
    *a. step, close, hop-cut
    b. stamp, stamp, leap, step
    c. leap, stamp, step
    d. step, step, pivot, hop-cut

83. Which dance step starts with the same foot always leading?
    a. two-step
    b. polka
    c. schottische
    *d. mazurka

84. Which step can best be described as step, step, point?
    a. waltz
    *b. minuet
    c. two-step
    d. mazurka

85. Which step can best be described as three running steps and a hop?
    a. mazurka
    b. polka
    c. gavotte
    *d. schottische

86. Which step can be performed to 2/4, 4/4, and 6/8 time?
    a. mazurka
    b. gavotte
    c. polka
    *d. two-step

87. Which steps have the same time signature?
    a. minuet and gavotte
    b. schottische and tango
    *c. mazurka and minuet
    d. gavotte and waltz

88. Which best describes the grapevine step?
    a. cross behind, step left, cross in front, step left
    b. cross behind, step right, cross in front, step right
    c. step right, cross behind, step right, cross in front
    *d. step left, cross behind, step left, cross in front

89. Which pattern describes the buzz step?
    a. hop-swing
    b. jump-kick
    *c. step-close
    d. step-hop

Dance Turns

90. Which turn has the pattern step, step, step hop; step, step, step hop; step hop, step hop; step hop, step hop?
    a. two-step turn
    *b. schottische turn
    c. polka turn
    d. shuffle turn

91. How many full turns can a couple make in a four-measure schottische turn?
    a. one
    *b. one or two
    c. two
    d. two or four

92. In a two-step turn, how many turns are there on each measure?
    a. one quarter
    *b. one half
    c. one
    d. one or two

Dance Formations

93. Which formation is *not* a single circle? [Refer to Diagram 2.]
    *d.

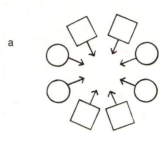

a

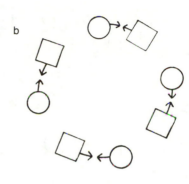

b

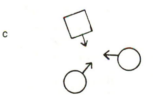

c

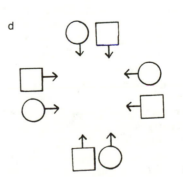

d

Diagram 2

94. In which formation are the couples in double
    file? [Refer to Diagram 3.]
    *a.

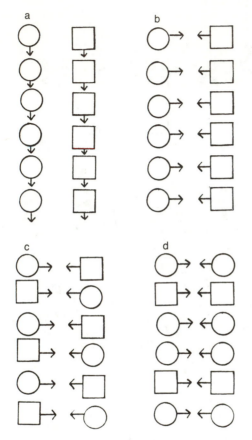

Diagram 3

95. In circle formations, what is the line of
    direction?
    a. facing the center of the circle
    b. backs to the center of the circle
    c. clockwise
    *d. counterclockwise

96. In a square, what position does the lady take?
    a. inside
    b. outside
    *c. right
    d. left

97. In this longway set, where is the head? [Refer
    to Diagram 4.]
    *d.

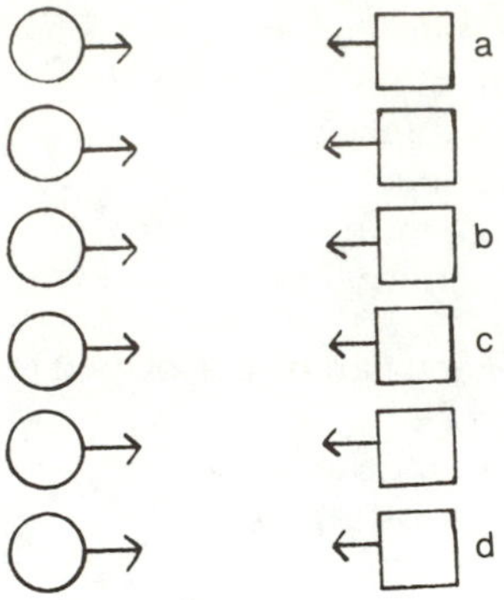

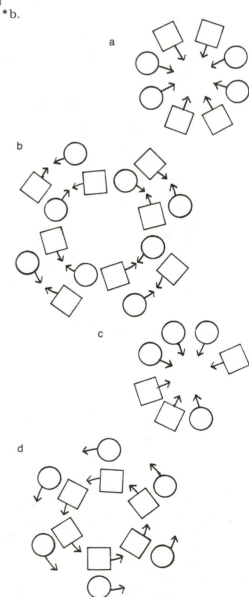

Diagram 4

98. Which is a Sicilian circle? [Refer to Diagram
    5.]
    *b.

Diagram 5

Dance Positions

99. Which diagram shows a back cross position? [Refer to Diagram 6.]
    *b.

Diagram 6

100. Which diagram shows a conversational position? [Refer to Diagram 7.]
    *a.

Diagram 7

101. Which diagram shows a promenade position? [Refer to Diagram 7, Question 100.]
    *d.

102. Which diagram shows an open position? [Refer to Diagram 7, Question 100.]
    *c.

103. Which diagram shows a closed position? [Refer to Diagram 8.]
    *a.

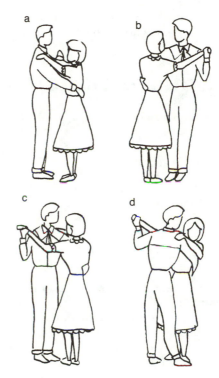

Diagram 8

104. What is the dance position for the minuet?
    *a. open couple position
    b. back cross position
    c. conversational position
    d. varsouvienne position

Dance Posture

105. What gives you that "light on your feet" feeling?
    a. keeping your weight on the balls of your feet
    *b. keeping your weight up
    c. bouncing as you move
    d. bending your knees

106. What kind of base of support should you have in dancing?
    a. wide with your feet shoulder width apart and your weight concentrated over the balls of your feet
    b. wide with your feet shoulder width apart and your weight concentrated over your whole foot
    *c. narrow with your feet close together and your weight concentrated over the balls of your feet
    d. narrow with your feet close together and your weight concentrated over your whole foot

Square Dancing

General Knowledge   107 to 119
Techniques   120 to 157

General Knowledge

107. In square dancing, how many dancers are in a square?
    a. 2
    b. 4
    *c. 8
    d. 12

108. Which characteristic is unique to square dancing?
    a. instrument involvement
    b. elaborate costumes
    *c. dance calls
    d. couple dances

109. On which side of the man does the lady stand in square dancing?
    *a. right
    b. left
    c. depends on dance
    d. does not matter

Terminology

110. Which couple in a square is designated number 1?
    a. the best dancers
    b. the couple forming the square
    *c. the couple with their backs to the music
    d. the couple facing the music

111. Which couple in a square is designated number 2?
    a. the second best dancers
    *b. the couple to the right of couple 1
    c. the couple to the left of couple 2
    d. the couple facing the music

112. Which couple or couples are the head?
    a. the couple with their backs to the music
    b. the couple facing the music
    c. Couples 1 and 2
    *d. Couples 1 and 3

113. What are Couples 2 and 4 called?
    a. the head couples
    *b. the side couples
    c. the active couples
    d. the lead-off couples

114. The caller says, "Swing your right-hand lady." Which lady will the man swing?
    a. his partner
    b. the lady in the couple to his left
    *c. the lady in the couple to his right
    d. the lady directly across from him

Rhythm

115. In which rhythm is most western square dance?
    *a. 2/4
    b. 3/4
    c. 4/4
    d. 6/8

116. In which rhythm are square dances *not* written?
    a. 2/4
    *b. 3/4
    c. 4/4
    d. 6/8

Courtesy

117. Several dancers in a square know the material being called. The others do *not* know the material. What should those knowing the material do?
    a. Explain the calls to the others.
    b. Repeat the calls in a slower tempo.
    c. Correct the mistakes of the others.
    *d. Keep silent.

118. What should the dancers do when an error is made in square dancing?
    a. Continue and try to pick up the call.
    b. Try to get those making the error back to the right place.
    *c. Go back to home places quickly and try to pick up the call.
    d. Stop and wait until that dance is over.

119. Which act is considered courteous in square dancing?
     a. dropping out of a square
     b. doing extra twirls and flourishes in the average square
     c. clapping the hands to the music
     *d. getting a substitute before leaving a square

Techniques

120. Which act is *unacceptable* when a couple is inactive?
     *a. standing still
     b. shifting weight from one foot to the other
     c. step hold, step hold
     d. forward two steps, backward two steps

121. What is the relationship of the calls to the figure being danced?
     a. The call is with the figure being danced.
     *b. The call is one ahead of the figure being danced.
     c. The call is two ahead of the figure being danced.
     d. The call is one or two ahead of the figure being danced.

122. What is the characteristic step for square dancing?
     a. skip
     b. run
     *c. shuffle
     d. walk

Composition

123. How many parts do most square dances have?
     a. two
     b. three
     *c. four
     d. six

124. Which part of a square dance is usually selected for a change of pace?
     a. an opener
     b. the main figure
     *c. a break
     d. a closer

Calls

125. Partners turn slightly to face each other. They shift their weight to their outside foot and point the inside foot toward their partner. What is this call?
     *a. honor your partner
     b. do-si-do
     c. forming the square
     d. do paso

126. Which best describes a do-si-do?
     a. Partners face, pass left shoulders, move back to back around each other, and return to position.
     *b. Partners face, pass right shoulders, move back to back around each other, and return to position.
     c. Partners face, pass left shoulders, move face to face around each other, and return to position.
     d. Partners face, pass right shoulders, move face to face around each other, and return to position.

127. What does "right to your partner" mean?
     *a. Partners join right hands.
     b. Partners join right hands and the lady turns clockwise under the man's right arm.
     c. Partners join right hands and the lady turns counterclockwise under the man's right arm.
     d. Partners join right hands and turn counterclockwise one time around.

128. What should a couple do when "promenade" is called?
     a. Join hands and turn counterclockwise one time around.
     b. Join hands and turn clockwise one time around.
     *c. Join hands and move counterclockwise around the square.
     d. Make a single file and move clockwise around the square.

129. When promenade is called, what lady does the man promenade?
     a. his partner
     b. the lady to his right
     c. the lady to his left
     *d. the lady with him when the call is made

130. How far do you promenade?
    a. around the square
    b. to your home position
    *c. all the way around if you are less than a quarter way around to your home position
    d. all the way around if you are less than halfway around to your home position

131. What step pattern do partners use in a waist swing?
    a. two-step
    b. schottische
    c. slide
    *d. shuffle

132. Corners take a left forearm grasp and turn each other once around and go back home. What has been called?
    a. do-si-do
    *b. allemande left
    c. forearm turn
    d. pass thru

133. A man and a lady are going around the outside of the square in different directions. What should happen when they meet?
    a. The person going clockwise goes on the outside.
    b. The person going counterclockwise goes on the outside.
    *c. The man goes on the outside.
    d. The lady goes on the outside.

134. When "swing your opposite ladies" is called, how do the men cross the square?
    a. 1 and 3 first
    b. 2 and 4 first
    c. man to the right passes by first
    *d. man to the left passes by first

135. In a grand right and left, with which hand do you begin and in what direction does the lady move?
    *a. right, clockwise
    b. right, counterclockwise
    c. left, clockwise
    d. left, counterclockwise

136. What does the lead-off couple do in "split the ring"?
    a. Each partner goes around the side couple nearest him or her and back home.
    b. Each partner goes between the side couple nearest him or her and back home.
    c. The couple goes around the couple opposite them.
    *d. The couple goes between the couple opposite them.

137. How do the dancers move in "pass thru"?
    a. Two couples are facing, and one couple goes between the other couple.
    b. Two couples are facing, and one couple splits, goes around the other couple, and comes back between the couple.
    *c. Two couples are facing, and each person passes by the opposite person with right shoulder to right shoulder.
    d. Two couples are facing, and each person passes by the opposite person with left shoulder to left shoulder.

138. The men go to the middle of the circle, touch hands with their fingers up, and move around the center of the circle. What movement is this?
    a. separate go around one
    *b. Texas star
    c. split the ring
    d. courtesy turn

139. At the end of a "ladies chain," who is the lady's partner?
    a. the same as before the ladies chain
    *b. the man opposite her before the ladies chain
    c. the man to her right before the ladies chain
    d. the man to her left before the ladies chain

140. What is the movement in the "right and left thru" for the two couples facing each other?
    *a. right hand to the opposite, courtesy turn
    b. right hand to the opposite, courtesy turn, right and left back
    c. right hand to the opposite, right back home
    d. right hand to the opposite, split the next two

141. Partners take a left forearm grasp and turn until facing their corner, then take a right forearm grasp until facing their partner, and make a courtesy turn. What movement is this?
    a. left and right thru
    b. grand left and right
    *c. do paso
    d. allemande left

142. How do you execute an allemande left?
    a. Give your left hand to your partner, turnabout, and give your right hand to the next person.
    b. Give your right hand to your partner and give your left hand to the next person.
    c. Pass the person across from you left shoulder to left shoulder.
    *d. Turn your back to your partner and give the next person your left hand, turnabout.

143. The buzz step is used in which call?
    a. promenade
    *b. swing
    c. allemande left
    d. do-si-do

144. To which step is sashay identical?
    *a. slide
    b. two-step
    c. shuffle
    d. buzz

145. What part of a call is, "All jump up and when you come down, swing your partner 'round and 'round"?
    *a. opener
    b. main figure
    c. break
    d. closer

146. What part of a call is, "Ladies to the center and back to the bar, gents to the center for a Texas star"?
    a. opener
    *b. main figure
    c. break
    d. closer

147. What part of a call is, "Allemande left with your left hand and right to your partner for a right and left grand"?
    a. opener
    b. main figure
    *c. break
    d. closer

Dances
148. Which skill is a basic movement in "Bend It Tight"?
    a. forearm turns
    *b. split the ring
    c. do-si-do
    d. promenade

149. Which skill is a basic movement in "Arkansas Traveler"?
    *a. forearm turns
    b. split the ring
    c. circle left
    d. pass thru

150. Which skill is a basic movement in "Four in the Middle"?
    a. star thru
    b. double pass thru
    *c. ladies chain
    d. wheel around

151. What skill is the basic movement in "Shoot the Owl"?
    a. ladies chain
    b. forearm turns
    c. dive thru
    *d. lead out to the right

152. In which dance is the basic movement forearm turns?
    *a. "Bird in the Cage"
    b. "Shoot the Owl"
    c. "Easy Bend the Line"
    d. "Inside Arch and Outside Under"

153. Which skill is used in "Take Me Home Country Roads"?
    a. ladies chain
    *b. do-si-do
    c. weave the ring
    d. grand right and left

154. What is the basic skill in "Hurry, Hurry, Hurry"?
    a. star thru
    b. allemande left
    c. promenade
    *d. ladies chain

155. Which dance is danced to a patter call?
    *a. "Arkansas Traveler"
    b. "Bad Bad Leroy Brown"
    c. "Four Leaf Clover"
    d. "Old-Fashioned Girl"

156. Which dance is performed to a singing call?
    a. "New Star Thru"
    *b. "King of the Road"
    c. "Duck Then Wheel Around"
    d. "A Long Way Over"

157. What is characteristic of the squares done to "Oh, Susanna," "Wabash Cannon Ball," and "Solomon Levi"?
    a. They are danced to calls.
    *b. The calls follow the tune of the song.
    c. The caller is a lady.
    d. They have no calls.

Folk Dancing

General Knowledge	**158 to 186**
Techniques	**187 to 230**

General Knowledge

158. Which dance would be particularly appropriate for getting acquainted or "mixing"?
    *a. "All American Promenade"
    b. "Take a Little Peek"
    c. "Virginia Reel"
    d. "Birdie in the Cage"

Purposes

159. Why did dance originate in Greece?
    a. to worship the gods
    b. to prepare for war
    c. to celebrate the harvest
    *d. to encourage physical fitness for men

160. What kind of dance is "Polster Tanc"?
    a. butcher's dance
    b. harvest dance
    c. soldier's dance
    *d. wedding dance

161. What discovery does the dance, "Mayim," celebrate?
    a. love
    b. gold
    c. friends
    *d. water

162. Which dance originated as a harvest dance?
    a. "Alunelu"
    *b. "Hora"
    c. "Korobushka"
    d. "Sevilla Se Bela Loza"

163. For what reason is the "Ländler" danced?
    a. harvest
    b. religion
    c. planting
    *d. courting

164. On what are Russian folk dances frequently based?
    a. agriculture production
    *b. occupations of the people
    c. past wars
    d. social customs

Courtesy

165. When your dancing partner makes a mistake, what should you do?
    a. stop, correct the mistake, then continue
    *b. try to cover up the mistake and continue
    c. stop, watch the others to learn how to correct the mistake
    d. stop, wait for another dance to begin

National Origin

166. What is the national dance of Sweden?
    a. polka
    b. waltz
    *c. polska
    d. quadrille

167. To what country is the tarantella native?
    a. Mexico
    *b. Italy
    c. Spain
    d. Austria

168. Which step was *not* given to American folk dance by the black people?
    *a. buzz step
    b. cake walk
    c. Charleston
    d. Suzie-cue

169. Which peoples did *not* influence American folk dance?
    a. blacks
    *b. Dutch
    c. English
    d. Mexicans

170. Kolas are native to which country?
    a. Greece
    b. Italy
    *c. Yugoslavia
    d. Switzerland

171. From what country does "Sevilla Se Bela Loza" come?
    a. Spain
    b. Italy
    *c. Yugoslavia
    d. Sweden

172. From what country does "Korobushka" come?
    *a. Russia
    b. Germany
    c. Austria
    d. Norway

173. What is the origin of "Road to the Isles"?
    a. English
    b. Irish
    *c. Scottish
    d. American

174. What is the origin of "Crested Hen"?
    a. American
    b. English
    c. Greek
    *d. Danish

175. What is the origin of the "Doudlebska Polka"?
    a. Danish
    *b. Czech
    c. Rumanian
    d. Hungarian

176. What is the origin of "Man in the Hay"?
    a. American
    b. English
    *c. German
    d. Russian

177. Which folk dance originated in America?
    a. "Man in the Hay"
    b. "Harmonica"
    c. "Road to the Isles"
    *d. "Jessie Polka"

178. What is the national dance of Greece?
    *a. "Kalamatianos"
    b. "Miserlou"
    c. "Syrtos"
    d. "Troika"

179. What is a well-known couple dance of Sweden?
    a. Morris
    b. gavotte
    c. circle waltz
    *d. hambo

180. What is a popular ancient dance of Romania?
    a. hambo
    *b. chain hora
    c. reel
    d. kola

181. In which country did the Morris dances originate?
    a. United States
    *b. England
    c. Germany
    d. Bulgaria

182. Which country is the home of the jig?
    *a. Ireland
    b. Israel
    c. Austria
    d. France

183. In which country did the gavotte originate?
    a. Holland
    b. Denmark
    c. Switzerland
    *d. France

Music

184. What is the difference in eastern and western folk music?
    a. Eastern is slower in tempo.
    *b. Eastern is in a minor key; western is in a major key.
    c. Eastern is happier.
    d. Eastern has abrupt mood changes; western maintains the same mood.

185. Which instrument is *not* used to accompany Mexican folk dances?
    a. guitars
    b. violins
    c. cornets
    *d. accordian

186. What accompaniment is frequently used with Israeli folk dances?
    a. clapping
    *b. singing
    c. slapping
    d. stamping

Techniques

Style

187. What determines the style of folk dances?
    a. past events
    b. preferences of the dancers
    c. national customs
    *d. regional traditions

188. What factor may cause a common step to look different in different dances?
    *a. style
    b. rhythm
    c. dress
    d. formation

Movements

189. What will help you turn faster when your elbows are hooked?
    a. keep your weight low
    *b. lean away from your partner
    c. lean toward your partner
    d. stay on the balls of your feet

190. What is the basic step in contra dances?
    *a. walk
    b. run
    c. grapevine
    d. polka

191. What is characteristic of the folk dances of Hungary?
    *a. extremes of melancholy and gaiety
    b. smooth, even rhythms
    c. hand clapping
    d. small, self-contained movements

192. In what country do dances allow great individual expression and spontaneous improvisation?
    a. France
    b. Germany
    c. Russia
    *d. Hungary

193. Which phrase describes the Polish Polonaise?
    a. a solo dance
    b. a circle dance with much clapping
    c. a spirited line dance
    *d. a couple dance of court origin

194. To what step in the "Harmonica" is the leap added for style?
    a. hopping step
    b. running step
    *c. grapevine step
    d. rocking step

195. Which statement describes a pas de basque?
    *a. Leap diagonally forward on left foot, step forward right in front of left, step back on left.
    b. Step forward left, step forward right, hop on right, hop on left.
    c. Hop left, step right, close left, and step out left with right.
    d. Leap diagonally forward left, hop left, step out left with right.

196. What are the basic steps in the "Alunelu"?
    a. brush, step, stop, brush
    b. step, slow, quick, quick
    *c. step, stamp
    d. walk, buzz step

197. What are the basic steps in the " Horo"?
    a. mazurka
    b. step, stamp
    c. brush, step, brush, step
    *d. step behind, step swing

198. What are the basic steps in the "Miserlou"?
    *a. grapevine, two-step
    b. walk, run
    c. walk, pivot turn
    d. schottische

199. Which is a possible figure in the "Grand March"?
    a. Texas star
    b. allemande left
    *c. Virginia reel
    d. grapevine

200. What are the basic steps in "Salty Dog Rag"?
    a. shuffle, two-step
    *b. grapevine schottische, step-hop
    c. heel-toe, slide
    d. walk, slide

201. What is the basic dance step in the "Troika"?
    a. walk
    *b. run
    c. mazurka
    d. bleking

202. What are the basic steps in "La Raspa"?
    a. walk, slide
    b. grapevine, two-step
    *c. bleking, run
    d. polka, run

203. What steps do you need to perform "Cotton-Eyed Joe"?
    *a. polka, two-step, and push step
    b. polka, push step, and pigeon step
    c. two-step, push step, and pigeon step
    d. polka, two-step, and pigeon step

204. Which folk dance involves clapping your hands at places in the dance?
    a. "Korobushka"
    b. "Cotton-Eyed Joe"
    c. "Road to the Isles"
    *d. "La Raspa"

205. In what country is it characteristic for dancers to brush and stamp their feet and tap their heels to create unique rhythms?
    a. Italy
    b. Rumania
    *c. Mexico
    d. Finland

206. What is characteristic of Italian folk dances?
    a. clapping
    *b. flirting
    c. singing
    d. stomping

207. Which step is characteristic of English country dances?
    a. walking
    b. jumping
    c. running
    *d. shuffling

208. For what are British dances noted?
   a. intricate steps and complex floor patterns
   *b. intricate steps and simple floor patterns
   c. simple steps and complex floor patterns
   d. simple steps and simple floor patterns

209. For what is Irish dance noted?
   a. dignity
   *b. exactness
   c. poise
   d. spirit

210. From which country are tremendous leaps, twisting, and jumping characteristic of the folk dances?
   a. Israel
   b. Romania
   *c. Russia
   d. Finland

211. Which step pattern is predominant in most Israeli folk dances?
   a. two-step
   *b. grapevine
   c. run
   d. walk

212. What are the main characteristics of American folk dance?
   a. complex floor patterns and movements
   b. complex floor patterns and simple movements
   *c. simple floor patterns and movements
   d. simple floor patterns and complex movements

213. In the folk dances of which country is moving from right to left characteristic?
   a. Greece
   *b. Israel
   c. Scotland
   d. Sweden

214. For what are Scottish folk dances noted?
   a. erectness of the body and carefree spirit
   b. heavy stomping and quick rhythm
   *c. exactness in timing and sharpness of the line
   d. shuffling steps and dignified spirit

215. In which country is it characteristic for folk dances to begin slowly and accelerate in tempo?
   a. Italy
   b. Mexico
   c. Israel
   *d. Romania

Formations

216. Which are the active couples in contra dances?
   a. the head and foot couples
   b. the even-numbered couples
   *c. the odd-numbered couples
   d. all the couples

217. What formation is used in contra dances?
   a. single circle
   b. double circle
   c. single file
   *d. double file

218. Which formation is most frequently used in Greek folk dances?
   a. square
   *b. broken circle
   c. double file
   d. Sicilian circle

219. What type of dance is "All the Way to Galway"?
   a. grand march
   *b. contra
   c. square
   d. round

220. Which formation might be used for a "Grand March"?
   a. single circle, facing center
   *b. double circle, facing line of direction
   c. double circle, facing center
   d. single file, facing line of direction

221. What type of dance is the "Grand Square Quadrille"?
   a. round dance
   b. grand march
   c. contra dance
   *d. square dance

222. What does the nine in the "Ninepin Reel" indicate?
   a. There are nine parts to the dance.
   b. Nine couples are needed for the dance.
   *c. A ninth person is added to a square formation.
   d. There are nine figures in the dance.

223. What formation is used in dancing "Turkey in the Straw"?
   *a. single circle, couple facing center
   b. single circle, couples facing line of direction
   c. double circle, couples facing each other
   d. double circle, couples facing line of direction

224. What formation is used in the "Kentucky Running Set"?
    a. double file, partners facing
    b. double file, partners facing head of line
  *c. single circle
    d. double circle

225. In which dance is it *not* necessary to have couples?
    a. "Virginia Reel"
  *b. "Hokey Pokey"
    c. "Alabama Gal"
    d. "Old Dan Tucker"

226. Which dance can be done effectively with fewer than three people?
    a. "Man in the Hay"
    b. "Mayim"
    c. "Troika"
  *d. "Salty Dog Rag"

227. In which country do men and women generally *not* dance together?
  *a. Greece
    b. Ireland
    c. Scotland
    d. Romania

228. Which dance formation is *not* used in American folk dance?
    a. circle
    b. contra
  *c. line
    d. square

229. Which formation is characteristic of Danish folk dances?
  *a. square
    b. circle
    c. double circle
    d. double file

Positions

230. Which positions are held in "Teton Mountain Stomp"?
  *a. closed
    b. promenade
    c. promenade, varsouvienne
    d. varsouvienne, bango

Social Dancing

General Knowledge   231 to 240
Techniques   241 to 291

General Knowledge

History

231. For whom or what is the fox-trot named?
    a. Redd Fox
  *b. Henry Fox
    c. Foxboro, a New England village
    d. a fox

232. When did the Charleston enjoy its greatest popularity?
  *a. 1920s
    b. 1930s
    c. 1940s
    d. 1950s

233. What caused the rise of the swing era?
    a. ragtime music
  *b. big band music
    c. World War II
    d. Vietnam War

234. Which was the first of the Latin dances popular in the United States?
  *a. tango
    b. rumba
    c. samba
    d. cha-cha

235. From what dance form did the rock-and-roll dances develop?
    a. Charleston
    b. Latin candes
  *c. lindy
    d. fox-trot

236. What influence did the black culture have on rock-and-roll dance?
    a. absence of dance patterns
    b. absence of partners
  *c. explosive movement of pelvic area
    d. more syncopated rhythm

National Origin

237. Which dance originated in the United States?
    a. cha-cha
  *b. fox-trot
    c. swing
    d. waltz

238. Which dance originated in Argentina?
    a. cha-cha
    b. swing
    c. waltz
  *d. tango

239. Which dance is Europe's main contribution to social dance?
    a. fox-trot
    b. swing
    *c. waltz
    d. polka

240. In which country did the cha-cha originate?
    *a. Cuba
    b. Argentina
    c. Brazil
    d. Mexico

Techniques

241. Which direction is the line of dance?
    a. clockwise
    b. varies
    *c. counterclockwise
    d. across the room the longest way

242. What are the main elements of social dancing?
    a. rhythm, style, animation, balance
    b. figures, appearance, partnership, expression
    *c. posture, footwork, animation, leading, following
    d. figures, rhythm, control, expression

243. Which factor contributes most to smooth social dancing?
    *a. flexed knees
    b. proper footwork
    c. diaphragm contraction
    d. proper timing

Style

244. Which factor has the *least* influence on style in social dancing?
    a. rhythmic qualities of the music
    b. culture of the country
    c. current style of movement
    *d. complexity of the steps

Music

245. In what dance time is most popular American dance music written?
    a. cha-cha
    *b. swing
    c. tango
    d. waltz

Posture

246. Which factor is most important in good dancing posture?
    a. weight on the heels
    b. knees relaxed
    c. shoulders down and relaxed
    *d. diaphragm in and upward

Footwork

247. Where should your weight be carried in social dancing?
    *a. balls of feet
    b. front of feet
    c. heels of feet
    d. entire surface of feet

248. In what position should the feet point in social dancing?
    a. both slightly out
    b. both slightly in
    *c. both straight ahead
    d. forward foot slightly outward, back foot straight ahead

249. Generally, when action begins, what is the position of the feet?
    *a. together
    b. right ahead of left
    c. left ahead of right
    d. depends on the dance

250. From where does the reach of the foot begin?
    a. ankle
    b. knee
    *c. hip
    d. waist

251. What happens to the size of steps as rhythm becomes faster?
    *a. shorter steps
    b. longer steps
    c. more reaching steps
    d. less reaching steps

252. In what direction should the man step in relation to the lady's foot?
    a. toward the inside of her foot
    b. toward the outside of her foot
    *c. toward her foot
    d. sideways of her foot

Positions

253. What is affected most by a poor dance position?
    a. style
    b. balance
    *c. leading and following
    d. footwork

254. Who should maintain the distance between partners?
    a. man's responsibility
    b. lady's responsibility
    *c. both partners' responsibility
    d. leader's responsibility

255. In a closed dance position, where should the man place his right hand?
    a. between his partner's shoulder blades
    *b. below his partner's shoulder blades
    c. at the center of the back at waist level
    d. on his partner's left shoulder

256. Where should the lady place her left hand in a closed dance position?
    a. behind her partner's neck
    *b. behind her partner's right shoulder
    c. behind her partner's shoulder joint
    d. behind her partner's upper arm

257. In the closed position, how high should the lady's right hand and man's left hand be held?
    a. man's head level
    b. just above the man's shoulder level
    *c. just above the lady's shoulder level
    d. between the level of the lady's shoulder and waist

258. Where is it best for the man to look when dancing in closed position?
    *a. at his partner
    b. over his partner's right shoulder
    c. over his partner's left shoulder
    d. at the other couples on the dance floor

259. In what dance position does a couple generally begin the waltz?
    a. swing position
    b. facing position
    c. open position
    *d. closed position

260. In what dance position do couples generally begin the fox-trot?
    a. right parallel position
    b. left parallel position
    c. reverse open position
    *d. closed position

Movements

261. In which situation would spotting be needed?
    *a. turns and pivots
    b. dangerous steps
    c. rhythm dances
    d. observation of other dancers

262. How are most dance steps started?
    *a. from a narrow base
    b. from a base of shoulder width
    c. from a base slightly less than shoulder width
    d. from a base slightly more than shoulder width

263. What is the most common fault in the backward walk?
    a. the lady leans away from her partner
    *b. the lady's step is taken from the knee
    c. the lady's heel touches the floor first
    d. the lady's step is too long

264. Which dance follows the rhythm pattern: slow, slow, quick, quick, slow?
    a. fox-trot
    b. rumba
    c. samba
    *d. tango

265. Which dance is characterized by the draw step?
    a. waltz
    b. cha-cha
    *c. tango
    d. lindy

266. What is characteristic of the rumba?
    a. smooth gliding steps
    *b. rolling motion
    c. swaying from side to side
    d. total body motion

267. What is the rhythm pattern of the samba?
    a. slow, slow, quick, quick
    b. slow, quick, quick, slow
    c. slow, quick, quick
    *d. slow, quick, slow

268. For the man, which dance follows the pattern: step left forward, right back in place, left in place next to right, right in place, left in place?
    a. rumba
    b. samba
    *c. cha-cha
    d. bossa nova

269. What part of the body leads the motion of the bossa nova?
    *a. shoulders
    b. waist
    c. hips
    d. arms

270. What is the rhythm pattern for a waltz?
    *a. even
    b. uneven
    c. broken
    d. syncopated

271. Which beat is accented in a waltz?
    *a. first
    b. second
    c. third
    d. fourth

272. For the man, what is the foot pattern for a fox-trot dance walk?
     *a. Step left forward, right forward, left forward, right forward.
     b. Step right forward, left forward, right forward, left forward.
     c. Step left forward, right forward, left backward, right backward.
     d. Step right backward, left backward, right backward, left backward.

273. What is the rhythm pattern for a fox-trot box step?
     a. even
     *b. uneven
     c. broken
     d. syncopated

274. What is the rhythm pattern for a fox-trot magic step?
     a. quick, quick, quick, quick
     b. quick, quick, slow, slow
     *c. slow, slow, quick, quick
     d. slow, quick, quick

275. Which choice does *not* indicate an error in the fox-trot?
     *a. leader's hand on follower's back
     b. bouncing
     c. long forward and backward steps
     d. pumping up and down of the arms

276. Which swing step follows the pattern: dig, step, dig, step, rock, step?
     a. single lindy
     *b. double lindy
     c. triple lindy
     d. roll

277. Which hands are joined for most of the swing steps?
     a. both hands
     *b. lady's right to man's left
     c. lady's left to man's right
     d. lady's right to man's right

278. Which best describes the position of the elbows of the hands joined together?
     a. always straight
     *b. never straight
     c. bent at a 90° angle
     d. bent at a 45° angle

279. Which choice does *not* indicate an error in the swing?
     a. jumping action
     b. straight arms
     *c. short rock step backward
     d. limp arms

280. Which swing step are you doing when the touch is on the first beat?
     a. single step
     *b. double step
     c. triple step
     d. shag

Leading

281. What is the man's most important point of contact in leading?
     a. left shoulder
     b. left hand
     c. right shoulder
     *d. right hand

282. Which factor has the most effect on the man's ability to lead?
     a. footwork
     *b. dance position hold
     c. knowing his partner
     d. rhythm of the dance

283. How should the man start each new step?
     a. with a right-foot lead
     *b. with a left-foot lead
     c. with the same lead as the previous step
     d. with the opposite lead from the previous step

284. What lead should the man give to make a forward move?
     *a. forward motion of the body
     b. pressure of the right hand
     c. sudden body tension
     d. pressure of the left hand

285. What lead should the man give to make a backward move?
     a. forward motion of the body
     *b. pull of the right hand
     c. sudden body tension
     d. pressure of the left hand

286. Dancing in a closed position, the man uses forward body action followed by right-hand pressure and right-elbow pull to the right. For what movement is this lead?
     a. an open position
     b. a right parallel position
     *c. a box step
     d. a box turn

287. Dancing in a closed position, the man holds the lady slightly closer with sudden body tension. For what movement is this lead?
     a. box turn
     b. right parallel position
     c. hesitation step
     *d. pivot turn

288. What lead is used for the chase in the cha-cha?
    a. The leader releases the right hand.
    b. The leader releases the left hand.
    c. The leader holds both hands.
  *d. The leader releases both hands.

289. What lead is used in the fox-trot when the man wants to step backward?
    a. the lift of the elbow
  *b. the pull with a flat hand
    c. the fingertip pressure
    d. the heel of the palm pressure

290. What lead is used in the waltz when the man wants to step backward?
    a. the lift of the elbow
  *b. the pull with a flat hand
    c. the fingertip pressure
    d. the heel of the palm pressure

291. How many leads are there in a full box step for the waltz?
    a. two
    b. three
    c. four
  *d. six

Acknowledgments

Colleagues and students who contributed suggestions and ideas for the Recreational Dance test questions are: E. Margolis, M. Priddy, and G. Sanders.

Suggested Readings

Ellfeldt, L. (1969). *Folk dance.* Dubuque, IA: Wm. C. Brown.

Ellfeldt, L., & Morton, V.L. (1974). *This is ballroom dance.* Palo Alto, CA: Mayfield.

Harris, J.A., Pittman, A.M., & Waller, M.S. (1978). *Dance a while* (5th ed.). Minneapolis: Burgess.

Heaton, A. (1976). *Social dance rhythms.* Provo, UT: Brigham Young University Press.

Phillips, P. (1969). *Contemporary square dance.* Dubuque, IA: Wm. C. Brown.

Pillich, W.F. (1967). *Social dance.* Dubuque, IA: Wm. C. Brown.

Soccer

Andreas Koth, Consultant

This collection of test questions on soccer is divided into six content areas:

- Technique
- Rules and Scoring
- History
- Terminology
- Equipment
- Strategy

Answers to the rules questions are based on 1986-87 rule books. Some answers, however, may need to be changed for the particular situation in which the test is used. Three factors should be considered before developing an answer key. Scholastic and collegiate rules differ somewhat; leagues and conferences sometimes play by their own rules; and rules change from year to year.

Soccer

Technique	1 to 108
Rules and Scoring	109 to 193
History	194 to 205
Terminology	206 to 219
Equipment	220 to 232
Strategy	233 to 285

Technique

1. What should a very skillful player be able to do?
    - a. pass the ball without gaining control
    - *b. move all over the field
    - c. play any position equally well
    - d. push an opponent before taking the ball away

Juggling

2. What is the most important kind of juggling?
    - a. with the head
    - b. with the chest
    - c. with the thigh
    - *d. with the feet

3. What is the most important principle of successful juggling?
    - a. Hit the ball softly.
    - *b. Keep the lifting surface parallel to the ground.
    - c. Hit the ball high to be able to get under it.
    - d. Stay relaxed.

Trapping

4. What is most important to remember in preparing to receive a ball?
    - a. Stop the ball before making the next move.
    - *b. Look around before the ball comes.
    - c. Look around after the ball is stopped.
    - d. Never stop the ball, but go right into the next move.

Andreas Koth is a certified soccer referee and the former soccer coach at Western Guilford High School, Greensboro, North Carolina, Augusta Preparatory School, Augusta, Georgia, and Georgia Southern College, Statesboro, Georgia.

5. Which action is *not* a basic technique in trapping the ball?
   a. giving with the ball at contact
   b. using the largest possible body surface to trap
   *c. keeping the body surface used to trap tense
   d. watching the oncoming ball as long as possible

6. A player has the option of trapping the ball with one of the body surfaces listed. Which part of the body is the best to use in most circumstances?
   a. chest
   b. thigh
   *c. inside of the foot
   d. sole of the foot

7. A player is preparing to trap the ball. What is most important for the player to be watching?
   a. the defender
   *b. the ball
   c. a teammate to receive a pass
   d. the direction the player wants to go after receiving the ball

8. Which description related to trapping is *incorrect*?
   a. Keep the eyes on the ball at all times.
   b. Maintain a relaxed body throughout the trap.
   c. Practice first on slow balls.
   *d. Block the ball with a stiff body.

9. A player needs speed in getting the ball underway in a dribble when receiving a pass. What is the best trap for the player to use?
   a. sole of the foot
   b. inside of the foot
   *c. deflecting foot
   d. inside of the leg

10. What is the best method of gaining control of a ball in low flight?
    a. chest trap
    *b. inside-of-the-thigh trap
    c. inside-of-the-leg trap
    d. sole-of-the-foot trap

11. A player is attempting to trap a low bouncing ball approaching from the side. What is the best trap to use?
    a. chest
    b. thigh
    *c. inside of the leg
    d. sole of the foot

12. What is a common error in trapping the ball with the foot?
    a. bending the knee of the trapping foot
    *b. lifting the foot too high
    c. keeping the foot along the ground
    d. attempting the trap too soon

13. A player is preparing to trap the ball with the sole of the foot. What direction should the player face?
    *a. the oncoming ball
    b. sideways to the oncoming ball
    c. the direction he or she intends to kick the ball
    d. the direction he or she intends to dribble the ball

14. What is the position of the player's foot when he or she is attempting a sole-of-the-foot trap?
    a. parallel to the ground and above the level of the ball
    b. oblique to the ground and above the level of the ball
    *c. oblique to the ground with the heel close to the ground
    d. perpendicular to the ground with the heel close to the ground

15. How is the ball trapped with the sole of the foot?
    a. by stepping on the oncoming ball
    b. by placing the foot on top of the ball
    c. by allowing the ball to rebound off the sole of the foot
    *d. by wedging the ball between the foot and the ground

16. A player is preparing to trap the ball with the inside of the foot. What direction should the player face?
    *a. the oncoming ball
    b. sideways to the oncoming ball
    c. the direction he or she intends to kick the ball
    d. the direction he or she intends to dribble the ball

17. A player is attempting to trap the ball with the inside of the foot. What should be the position of the player's leg and foot?
    a. leg straight and toe pointed outward
    b. leg straight and toe pointed inward
    *c. knee bent and toe pointed outward
    d. knee bent and toe pointed inward

18. Where should the ball be contacted on an inside-of-the-foot trap?
    *a. in front of the player's body
    b. to the side of the player's body
    c. below the player's body
    d. behind the player's body

19. A player is attempting an outside-of-the-foot trap. What direction should the player be facing?
    - a. the oncoming ball
    - *b. sideways to the oncoming ball
    - c. the direction he or she intends to kick the ball
    - d. the direction he or she intends to dribble the ball

20. A player is attempting an outside-of-the-foot trap. What should be the position of the player's leg and foot?
    - a. leg straight with toe pointed inward
    - b. leg straight with toe pointed outward
    - *c. knee bent and toe pointed inward
    - d. knee bent and toe pointed outward

21. A player is preparing to trap a ball in the air with an inside-of-the-foot trap. With what part of the foot should the ball make contact?
    - a. toe
    - *b. arch
    - c. front, next to the ball of the foot
    - d. back, below the ankle

22. What should be the position of the leg and foot when a player is attempting to trap a ball in the air with an inside-of-the-foot trap?
    - a. leg straight with the foot extended
    - b. leg straight and toe pointed outward
    - c. knee bent and foot extended
    - *d. knee bent and toe pointed outward

23. What is the most difficult foot trap to make successfully?
    - a. inside of foot on ground ball
    - b. outside of foot on ground ball
    - *c. instep on ball in air
    - d. outside of foot on ball in air

24. A player is preparing to make an instep trap on the ball. What direction should the player face?
    - a. facing the oncoming ball
    - *b. sideways to the oncoming ball
    - c. the direction he or she intends to kick the ball
    - d. the direction he or she intends to dribble the ball

25. What should be the position of the player's trapping leg when attempting an instep trap?
    - a. slightly bent at the hip and knee
    - *b. bent at right angles at the hip and knee
    - c. bent at the hip and straight at the knee
    - d. bent at the knee and straight at the hip

26. What should be the position of the player's trapping foot when attempting an instep trap?
    - *a. extended toward ball
    - b. sideways to the ball
    - c. bent at ankle, toe pointed inward
    - d. bent at ankle, toe pointed upward

27. Where should the ball make contact on an instep trap?
    - a. top of ankle
    - *b. all of shoelace area
    - c. inside of the foot at the arch
    - d. top of toes

28. A player is attempting an outside-of-the-foot trap on a ball in the air. What should be the position of the leg and foot?
    - a. leg straight and extended toward ball with toe pointed outward
    - b. leg straight and extended toward ball with toe pointed inward
    - *c. knee bent with foot more to the side than the knee and toe pointed inward
    - d. knee bent with knee more to the side than the foot and toe pointed inward

29. Where should the ball make contact on a thigh trap?
    - a. the upper part of the thigh
    - *b. the middle of the thigh
    - c. the lower part of the thigh
    - d. just above the knee

30. What position should the thigh be in in making a thigh trap?
    - a. perpendicular to the ground
    - *b. parallel with the ground
    - c. diagonal to the ground with the knee below hip level
    - d. diagonal to the ground with the knee above hip level

31. What stance should a player take to make a chest trap?

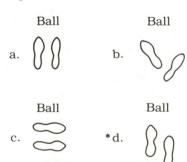

32. Where should the ball make contact on a chest trap?
    *a. upper chest
    b. middle of chest
    c. lower chest
    d. just above the waist

33. How should the trunk of the body be positioned to make a chest trap?
    a. straight up and down
    b. bent forward slightly at waist
    c. straight but bending at hips slightly toward the ground
    *d. arched back in upright position

34. A player wishes to use a chest trap to bring the ball dead at his or her feet. What must the player do as the ball is contacted?
    a. Bend forward and move into the ball.
    b. Stand erect and jump to kill the spin.
    *c. Bend forward over the ball.
    d. Arch slightly and move forward.

Dribbling

35. What should a player be able to see when dribbling?
    a. the ball
    b. the opponents
    c. the teammates
    *d. the ball and other players

36. What is the *least* important aspect of dribbling?
    a. change of speed
    b. change of direction
    c. use of different parts of the foot
    *d. surveying the field

37. Generally, where should the ball be in relation to a player's feet when dribbling?
    *a. close to the feet
    b. 3 to 5 feet ahead of the player's feet
    c. 5 to 8 feet ahead of the player's feet
    d. 7 to 10 feet ahead of the player's feet

38. How should the ball be dribbled?
    a. with the player's preferred foot
    b. with one foot only
    *c. with either foot depending on the situation
    d. alternately, one foot and then the other

39. How should a player's weight be distributed in dribbling the ball?
    a. evenly over both feet
    b. primarily on the dribbling foot
    c. slightly more on the nondribbling foot
    *d. totally on the nondribbling foot

40. What kind of footwork should a player generally use while dribbling?
    a. long, graceful strides
    b. long, stretching strides
    *c. short, quick strides
    d. short, slow strides

41. How should a player dribble the ball when being closely marked by an opponent?
    a. with the foot the player dribbles with best
    b. with both feet alternately
    c. with the insides of the feet
    *d. with the foot farther from the opponent

42. A player is dribbling the ball while being closely marked. How should the player shield the ball from the opponent?
    *a. by keeping his or her body between the ball and the opponent
    b. by bending over the ball
    c. by holding his or her arms out away from the body with the elbows bent
    d. by extending his or her arms out away from the body

43. A player is dribbling the ball while being closely marked by an opponent. The player decides to change directions. How is this best accomplished?
    a. by pulling the ball back with the sole of the foot closer to the opponent and quickly turning
    *b. by pulling the ball back with the sole of the foot farther from the opponent and quickly turning
    c. by contacting the ball with the inside of the foot closer to the opponent and quickly turning
    d. by contacting the ball with the outside of the foot farther from the opponent and quickly turning

44. A player must continuously look down at the ball when dribbling. What should this player do in a game situation?
    *a. dribble only as fast as he or she can to maintain control
    b. dribble next to the touchline
    c. dribble a lot during the game for practice
    d. dribble only with the dominant foot

45. A player dribbling the ball is approaching an opponent. The player attempts a step-over feint to elude the opponent. How is this best accomplished?
    a. Feint a dribble with the inside of one foot and push it with the inside of the other foot.
    b. Feint an inside-of-the-foot dribble and dribble with the outside of the foot.
    c. Feint an outside-of-the-foot dribble and dribble with the inside of the foot.
    *d. Feint an outside-of-the-foot dribble, step over the ball, and push it in the other direction with the other foot.

Kicking

46. Which is a basic rule for a successful kick?
    a. Keep the ankle joint loose.
    b. Look in the direction the kick is to be made.
    *c. Keep the eyes on the ball.
    d. Place the nonkicking foot behind the ball.

47. What should a player do to kick the ball a long distance?
    a. Use the inside of the foot.
    b. Use the outside of the foot.
    c. Dribble before kicking.
    *d. Run into the kick.

48. When kicking for power, height and distance, what is the best technique?
    a. head down, lean over ball, point toe down
    b. head up, use toe of shoe, lean forward
    *c. head tilted up, lean back, scoop ball up with instep
    d. head tilted slightly downward, knee over ball, kick with instep

49. A player drops the ball and kicks it just as it rebounds from the ground. Which kick is this?
    a. volley
    b. punt
    *c. drop kick
    d. half volley

50. The goalie drops the ball and kicks it before it touches the ground. What is this kick called?
    a. drop kick
    b. place kick
    c. free kick
    *d. punt

Passing

51. A player is attempting to pass the ball to a teammate. What is the best procedure to use?
    a. Pass behind him or her.
    *b. Pass in front of him or her.
    c. Pass straight to him or her.
    d. Pass to an open area.

52. A player wishes to pass the ball along the ground. Where should the ball be contacted? [Refer to Diagram 1.]
    *c.

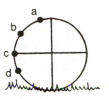

Diagram 1

53. A player wishes to lift a ground ball into the air with a pass. Where should the ball be contacted? [Refer to Diagram 1, Question 52.]
    *d.

54. A player is dribbling on the left side of the field. A teammate in the center of the field is open for a shot at goal. How should the dribbler pass the ball?
    a. with the outside of the right foot
    b. with the outside of the left foot
    c. with the inside of the right foot
    *d. with the inside of the left foot

55. A player is passing the ball with an inside of the foot kick. Where should the nonkicking foot be?
    *a. to the side of the ball
    b. to the side of the ball and 6 inches behind it
    c. to the side of the ball and 12 inches behind it
    d. to the side of the ball and 6 inches in front of it

56. What is the position of a player's body when contacting the ball with an inside-of-the-foot pass?
    a. vertical over the ball
    b. leaning forward over the ball
    *c. leaning slightly backward away from the ball
    d. sideways to the ball

57. What is the position of a player's kicking leg when contacting the ball with an inside-of-the-foot pass?
    a. straight leg with foot turned outward from the ankle
    b. straight leg with foot turned outward from the hip
    c. bent at knee with foot turned outward from the ankle
    *d. bent at knee with foot turned outward from the hip

58. What part of the foot contacts the ball on a heel pass?
    a. the inside of the heel
    b. the outside of the heel
    *c. the center of the heel
    d. the bottom of the heel

59. Where is the nonkicking foot when a player is attempting a heel pass?
    *a. to the side of the ball
    b. to the side of the ball and 6 inches behind it
    c. to the side of the ball and 6 inches ahead of it
    d. to the side of the ball and 12 inches behind it

60. Which statement applies to an instep kick?
    a. best used for short passes
    b. executed while the ball is in the air
    *c. used when both power and accuracy are needed
    d. more effective when the ball is bouncing

61. A player is performing a right-footed instep kick with the toe turned in. What will happen to the ball?
    *a. curve to the kicker's left
    b. curve to the kicker's right
    c. travel high and short
    d. develop topspin and ground quickly

62. A player is attempting an instep pass. How should the ball be approached in relation to the direction the pass will take?
    a. straight on
    *b. from no more than a 45° angle
    c. from about a 45° angle
    d. from at least a 45° angle

63. What is the position of the nonkicking foot when a player is making a low instep pass?
    *a. to the side of the ball
    b. to the side and 6 inches behind the ball
    c. to the side and 6 inches ahead of the ball
    d. to the side and 12 inches behind the ball

64. What is the difference in making a low instep pass and lofted instep pass?
    a. more bend in knee in making lofted pass
    *b. nonkicking foot closer to ball in making low pass
    c. more follow-through in low pass
    d. more body bend in lofted pass

65. Where is the ball contacted on an instep pass?
    a. at the center of instep
    *b. at the inside of instep
    c. at the outside of instep
    d. at the top of instep

66. What is the position of the foot in making an instep pass?
    a. extended with toes turned slightly out
    *b. extended with toes turned slightly in
    c. extended with toes pointing straight ahead
    d. bent at ankle with toes pointing straight ahead

67. How should a player follow through in performing an instep pass?
    a. with no follow-through
    b. with a short swing
    c. with an easy swing
    *d. with a maximum swing

68. Which statement best describes the movement needed to chip a ball?
    *a. Jab the foot under the ball.
    b. Scoop the ball up with the toe.
    c. Follow through higher than usual.
    d. Hit the ball softly.

69. Which kicking action is used to make a full volley pass?
    a. inside of the foot
    b. outside of the foot
    *c. instep
    d. heel

70. When should the ball be contacted for a full volley pass?
    a. waist high
    b. hip high
    *c. knee high
    d. ankle high

71. Which kicking action is used to make a half volley pass?
    a. inside of the foot
    b. outside of the foot
    *c. instep
    d. heel

72. When should the ball be contacted for a half volley pass?
    a. waist high
    b. hip high
    c. knee high
    *d. just after it hits the ground

73. When should the ball be contacted for an outside-of-the-heel volley?
    a. waist high
    b. hip high
    *c. thigh high
    d. knee high

74. How does a player "bend" the ball in passing?
    a. kicking with maximum power
    *b. kicking diagonally across the ball
    c. kicking through the ball
    d. kicking under the ball

75. A player is kicking with the right foot and wishes to swerve the ball to the left. How should the ball be contacted?
    a. Contact the right side of the ball with the inside of the foot.
    *b. Contact the right side of the ball with the instep.
    c. Contact the left side of the ball with the inside of the foot.
    d. Contact the left side of the ball with the instep.

Heading

76. What is the most important use of heading?
    a. shooting for goal
    *b. redirecting fly balls
    c. passing to teammates
    d. clearing the goal

77. When a player is heading the ball, what should the player be watching?
    a. the defensive players
    b. his or her teammates
    *c. the ball and other players
    d. the direction he or she intends to send the ball

78. How are a player's feet positioned in preparing to head the ball?
    a. squarely toward the ball with the weight evenly distributed
    b. one ahead of the other with the weight on the front foot
    *c. one ahead of the other with the weight on the back foot
    d. one ahead of the other with the weight evenly distributed

79. How should a player be positioned when heading the ball?
    *a. arched back
    b. upright stance
    c. bending upper body forward at the waist
    d. bending head forward at the shoulders

80. How should the ball be contacted when it is headed?
    a. Give with the ball at contact.
    b. Allow the ball to rebound off the head at contact.
    *c. Snap forward into the ball at contact.
    d. Push the ball.

81. Where is the ball contacted when it is headed?
    a. top of the head
    b. front portion of the top of the head
    c. hairline
    *d. forehead

82. Where is the ball contacted when it is back-headed?
    a. top of the head
    b. front portion of the top of the head
    *c. hairline
    d. forehead

Tackling

83. When is the best time to attempt a tackle?
    a. as the dribbler contacts the ball
    b. just before the dribbler would contact the ball
    c. as the dribbler brings his or her foot back to contact the ball
    *d. as the dribbler is receiving a pass

84. What position should a player take to play defense?
    a. Squarely face the opponent with the weight evenly distributed on both feet.
    *b. Turn at an angle to the opponent with the weight evenly distributed on both feet.
    c. Turn at an angle to the opponent with the weight mostly on the back foot.
    d. Turn at an angle to the opponent with the weight mostly on the front foot.

85. What should a player watch when defending against an opponent who has the ball?
    a. the opponent's eyes
    b. the opponent's waist
    c. the opponent's feet
    *d. the ball

86. Player A is dribbling the ball. Which defensive player is in position to make a sliding tackle on A?
    a. 1
    b. 2
    *c. 3
    d. 4

A—Ball   1

2

          4

3

87. How should a sliding tackle be made?
    a. Slide on the lower leg nearer the dribbler, and contact the ball with the foot away from the dribbler.
    *b. Slide on the lower leg farther from the dribbler, and contact the ball with the foot nearer the dribbler.
    c. Slide on the side of the body nearer the dribbler, and contact the ball with the foot away from the dribbler.
    d. Slide on the side of the body farther from the dribbler, and contact the ball with the foot nearer the dribbler.

88. Player A is dribbling the ball. Which defensive player is in position to make a block tackle?
    *a. 1
    b. 2
    c. 3
    d. 4

A—Ball   1

2

          4

3

89. What is the first objective in block tackling?
    a. to lift the ball over opponent's foot
    b. to send the ball between the opponent's legs
    *c. to stop the ball
    d. to take possession of the ball

90. Which tackle is most often used when the player is approaching the dribbler from the side?
    a. one-leg tackle
    b. pivot tackle
    *c. slide tackle
    d. two-leg tackle

91. Where should the ball be contacted when block tackling?
    a. on top with the sole of the tackler's foot
    b. slightly above the midpoint with the sole of the tackler's foot
    c. at the midpoint with the instep of the tackler's foot
    *d. slightly below the midpoint with the inside of the tackler's foot

Throw-In

92. What stance is recommended when the throw-in is made from a stationary position?

    *a. Touchline ____   b. Touchline ____

    c. Touchline ____   d. Touchline ____

93. How should the ball be held for a throw-in?
    a. both hands on the sides of the ball with the fingers spread
    *b. both hands to the side and slightly behind the ball with the fingers spread
    c. one hand on the side and one hand behind the ball with the fingers spread
    d. one hand behind the ball palming it

94. How far should the ball be brought back to begin the throw-in?
    *a. directly behind the head
    b. behind but above the level of the head
    c. over the head
    d. over the shoulder of the throwing arm

95. When should the ball be released on the throw-in?
    a. when it is behind the player's head
    b. when it is above the player's head
    *c. when it is in front of the player's head
    d. when it is in front of the shoulder of the throwing arm

96. What is the difference in making a stationary and a running throw-in?
    a. the grip on the ball
    b. the upper body position
    c. the follow-through
    *d. the stance

97. What error is most frequently made by players attempting a running throw-in?
    a. running too fast
    b. *not* getting the ball back far enough behind the head
    c. throwing the ball too soon
    *d. lifting the back foot before releasing the ball

Goalkeeping

98. Which procedure concerning goalkeeping skills is *incorrect?*
    a. Place the body directly in front of the ball.
    b. Keep the eyes on the ball at all times.
    c. Use two hands when catching the ball, with fingers spread apart.
    *d. After collecting the ball, move to the center of the goal area to clear it.

99. What stance should the goalkeeper take in preparing to defend the goal?

    *a. Goal line _____   b. Goal line _____

    c. Goal line _____   d. Goal line _____

100. Which statement describes the ready position for a goalkeeper?
    a. arms bent and out to the side, body upright, weight on the balls of the feet
    *b. arms bent and out to the side, upper body bending forward, weight on the balls of the feet
    c. arms straight and out in front, body upright, weight on the back foot
    d. arms straight and out in front, upper body bending forward, weight on the forward foot

101. How should the goalkeeper stand to catch a ground ball?
    a. square stance with feet shoulder width apart
    *b. square stance with feet together
    c. stride stance with weight on back foot
    d. stride stance with weight on front foot

102. How should the goalkeeper kneel to catch a ground ball?
    a. Face the ball and kneel on both knees so they are about shoulder width apart.
    b. Face the ball and kneel on both knees so they are close together.
    c. Face the ball and kneel on one knee so that the supporting knee and foot are shoulder width apart.
    *d. Face the ball and kneel on one knee, placing the knee next to the heel of the other foot.

103. What should the goalkeeper do in catching an air ball to keep from dropping it?
    *a. Bring it into the chest with the elbows close together.
    b. Get a firm grip on the ball with the palms of the hands.
    c. Catch the ball with the elbows away from the sides of the body.
    d. Wrap both arms around the ball.

104. How should the goalkeeper make contact with a high ball that he or she wishes to punch instead of catch?
    a. Tip it with the fingers of both hands.
    *b. Hit it with the flat part of the fists.
    c. Tip it with the fingers on one hand.
    d. Hit it with the heel of one hand.

105. What should the goalkeeper be careful *not* to do in making a lateral dive for the ball?
    a. Keep the arms bent until the last minute.
    b. Have the front of the body facing the playing field.
    c. Catch the ball with the fingers.
    *d. Hit the elbows on the ground.

106. What is the position of the goalkeeper's arm in making a sling throw?
    a. The arm is straight and moves forward parallel to the ground.
    *b. The arm is straight and moves forward diagonal to the ground from low to high.
    c. The arm is bent at the elbow and follows an overhand throwing motion.
    d. The arm is bent at the elbow and follows an underhand throwing motion.

107. Where should the ball be held for a punt?
    a. extended in front of the body, shoulder high
    *b. extended in front of the body, waist high
    c. extended in front of the body, knee high
    d. extended in front of the body, ankle high

108. What part of the foot should contact the ball on the punt?
    a. the toe
    b. the inside
    c. the outside
    *d. the top

Rules and Scoring

109. How is the game begun?
    a. with a drop ball
    *b. with a kickoff
    c. with a face-off
    d. with a goal kick

110. How many players from one team can play in a game at the same time?
    a. 6
    b. 9
    *c. 11
    d. 15

111. When do teams change ends of the field?
    *a. at halftime
    b. after second quarter
    c. after first and third quarters
    d. after a goal is scored

112. When may a trainer or coach enter the field of play?
    a. when an injury occurs
    b. during a time-out
    *c. when approved by the referee
    d. when a substitution is made

113. How is the goalkeeper distinguishable from the other players on a team?
    a. goalkeeper padding and equipment
    *b. different uniform
    c. stays in the goal area
    d. stays in the penalty area

114. What is the regulation time for intercollegiate soccer games?
    *a. two 45-minute halves
    b. two 40-minute halves
    c. four 20-minute quarters
    d. four 10-minute quarters

115. What is the regulation time for high school soccer games?
    a. two 45-minute halves
    *b. two 40-minute halves
    c. four 20-minute quarters
    d. four 10-minute quarters

116. How much time is there between halves?
    a. 2 minutes
    b. 5 minutes
    *c. 10 minutes
    d. 20 minutes

117. When does the clock *not* stop during a game?
    a. for a penalty kick
    *b. for a free kick
    c. after a goal is scored
    d. for a caution

Field

118. How long is a soccer field?
    a. 90 to 110 yards
    b. 90 to 120 yards
    *c. 100 to 120 yards
    d. 100 to 130 yards

119. What are the recommended dimensions for a high school soccer field?
    a. 50 yards by 100 yards
    b. 55 yards by 100 yards
    c. 60 yards by 110 yards
    *d. 65 yards by 110 yards

120. What are the recommended dimensions for a junior high school soccer field?
    a. 50 yards by 100 yards
    *b. 55 yards by 100 yards
    c. 60 yards by 110 yards
    d. 65 yards by 110 yards

121. There are two rectangles marked off on the field in front of the goal. What is the smaller one?
    a. the goal
    *b. the goal area
    c. the penalty area
    d. the goalkeeper's area

122. There are two rectangles marked off on the field in front of the goal. What is the larger one?
    a. the goal
    b. the goal area
    *c. the penalty area
    d. the goalkeeper's area

123. There is a short line parallel to and 12 yards in front of the center of the goal. For what is this used?
    *a. penalty kicks
    b. free kicks
    c. goal kicks
    d. drop balls

124. Part of a circle is drawn on the field in front of each penalty area. For what is this used?
    a. ball placement for taking penalty kicks
    b. ball placement for taking direct free kicks
    c. restraining line for shooting at the goal
    *d. restraining line for taking penalty kicks

Out-of-Bounds
125. A ball rolls on the touchline. What is the situation?
    *a. in bounds, play continues
    b. in bounds, drop ball between the two teams
    c. out-of-bounds, defensive team awarded a throw-in
    d. out-of-bounds, offensive team awarded a throw-in

126. When is the ball out-of-bounds?
    a. when it touches a line
    *b. when it completely crosses a line
    c. when it hits the goal post
    d. when it touches a referee

127. Two opposing players simultaneously contact the ball, and it goes out-of-bounds. What is the procedure?
    a. indirect free kick 5 yards inside the boundary line for the last team having clear possession
    *b. drop ball 5 yards inside the boundary line
    c. direct free kick in the center circle for the team last having clear possession
    d. drop ball in the center circle

Substitutions
128. What is the procedure for entering a substitute in the game?
    *a. The substitute reports to the scorers.
    b. The substitute can exchange places with a player on the field anytime his or her team has control of the ball.
    c. The coach signals the referee.
    d. The captain signals the referee.

129. In which situation may players *not* be substituted?
    a. when a goal has been scored
    b. when a throw-in occurs
    c. on corner kicks
    *d. on penalty kicks

130. In which situation may only the team having possession of the ball substitute a player?
    a. when a goal has been scored
    *b. when a throw-in occurs
    c. on indirect kicks
    d. on penalty kicks

131. When may a team *not* replace a player?
    a. when that player has been cautioned
    *b. when that player has been disqualified
    c. when that player has been substituted earlier
    d. when that player has been injured

132. When may a player on the field change places with the goalkeeper?
    a. anytime play is stopped so long as the referee is notified
    b. anytime during play or when play is stopped
    *c. only at the times when regular substitutions can be made
    d. only at the end of periods

133. A player is removed from the game for illegal equipment. What is the substitution situation?
    a. A player may substitute for this player immediately.
    *b. A player *cannot* substitute until the next opportunity to substitute.
    c. A substitution may *not* be made for this player.
    d. This player may *not* reenter the game.

134. Team A is taking a throw-in. A fullback and the goalie on this team change positions without notifying the referee. What happens?
    a. Team A takes the throw-in.
    b. Team B is awarded a penalty kick.
    *c. Team B is awarded an indirect free kick.
    d. Team B is awarded a direct free kick.

Equipment
135. Which statement describes the standard for soccer cleats?
    a. Plastic cleats are illegal.
    b. Detachable cleats or studs are illegal.
    c. Metal cleats are legal.
    *d. Rubber cleats are legal.

136. Which equipment is legal?
    a. casts
    b. face or glasses guards
    c. helmets
    *d. soft knee pads

Kickoff

137. When does the clock start on a kickoff?
    a. when the referee blows the whistle
    b. when the ball is contacted
    *c. when the ball has rolled its circumference into the opposing team's field of play
    d. when a second player contacts the ball

138. When does a kickoff occur?
    a. at the beginning of the game
    b. at the beginning of each period
    c. after a goal is scored
    *d. at the beginning of each half and after a goal is scored

139. Where must the players be on the kickoff?
    a. all players on their half of the field
    b. all players on their half of the field and the defending team 10 yards from the halfway line
    c. all players on the kicking team on their half of the field and the defending team 10 yards from the ball
    *d. all players on their half of the field and the defending team 10 yards from the ball

140. What are the requirements for a legal kickoff?
    a. The ball must be contacted by a forward.
    b. The ball must roll its circumference.
    *c. The ball rolls its circumference into the opposing team's field of play.
    d. The ball must clear the 10-yard center circle.

141. Who may play the ball after it is in play on a kickoff?
    *a. any player except the player who kicked off
    b. any player on the kicking team
    c. any player on the opposing team
    d. any player on the field

142. What choices does the winner of the toss have at the beginning of the game?
    a. kick off and defend
    *b. kick off or end of the field
    c. kick off or defend or end of the field
    d. kick off and end of the field

143. Which team kicks off in the second period?
    a. the same as the first period
    *b. the opposite team from the first period
    c. the team ahead in scoring
    d. the team behind in scoring

144. When may players cross over the halfway line on a kickoff?
    a. when the referee blows the whistle
    b. when the ball is contacted
    *c. when the ball is in play
    d. when the ball has cleared the center circle

145. On the kickoff the ball is kicked backward into the kicking team's field of play. What happens now?
    a. Play continues.
    *b. Kicking team rekicks.
    c. Opposing team is awarded the kickoff.
    d. Opposing team is awarded a penalty kick.

146. On the kickoff the ball rolls forward 2 inches and stops. What happens now?
    a. Play continues.
    *b. Kicking team rekicks.
    c. Opposing team is awarded the kickoff.
    d. Opposing team is awarded an indirect free kick.

147. On the kickoff the ball is contacted on the second hit by the same player who kicked off. What happens now?
    a. Play continues.
    b. Kicking team rekicks.
    *c. Opposing team is awarded an indirect free kick.
    d. Opposing team is awarded a penalty kick.

Goals

148. How many points does a goal count?
    *a. one
    b. two
    c. three
    d. five

149. How many points does a penalty kick count?
    *a. one
    b. two
    c. three
    d. five

150. When may a goal *not* be scored directly?
    a. from a drop ball
    b. from a penalty kick
    c. from a corner kick
    *d. from a kickoff

151. When may a goal be scored directly?
     a. from a throw-in
     b. from a kickoff
     *c. from a corner kick
     d. from an indirect free kick

152. When is a goal *not* scored?
     a. when the goalie standing outside the goal catches the ball and falls back into the goal
     *b. when the goalie stops the ball on the goal line
     c. when the ball rebounds off the crossbar into the goal
     d. when the ball rebounds off a defensive player into the goal

153. In a high school game, the score is tied at 2-2 at the end of regulation time. What is the situation?
     a. The game is over and the tie score recorded.
     b. An overtime period is played until a team scores.
     c. A 5-minute overtime period is played, and the score at the end of that period, tied or not, is recorded.
     *d. Two 10-minute overtime periods are played, and the score at the end of the second period, tied or not, is recorded.

154. On an indirect free kick in the penalty area, the fullback attempts to kick the ball to his or her goalie. The goalie falls and the ball goes into the net untouched. What is the decision?
     a. Award the opponents a goal.
     *b. Retake the kick.
     c. Award the opponents a corner kick.
     d. Award the opponents an indirect free kick.

Offside
155. When is a player offside?
     a. when the player crosses the halfway line before the ball is contacted by the kicker on the kickoff
     b. when an opposing player is closer than 10 yards to the ball on an indirect free kick
     c. when an opposing player other than the goalie is in the goal area during a penalty kick
     *d. when a player is nearer the opposing team's goal line than the ball at the moment the ball is played

156. A player is nearer the opposing team's goal line than the ball when it was played. When is the player offside?
     a. when in his or her team's own half of the field
     b. when there are two opposing players between the player and the opposing team's goal line
     c. when the ball was last touched by an opponent
     *d. when the ball was last touched by a teammate

157. An opposing team player, x_1, and the goalie are between Player A and the goal when a teammate, B, passes the ball behind x_1. Player A runs behind the defender, receives the ball, and kicks it into the goal. What happens now? [Refer to Diagram 2.]
     *a. The goal is good.
     b. The defending team is awarded an indirect free kick.
     c. The defending team is awarded a penalty kick.
     d. A drop ball is called.

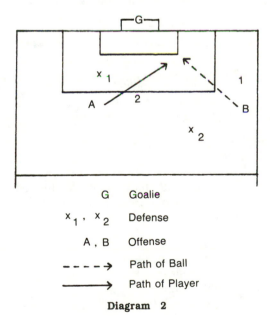

G	Goalie
x_1, x_2	Defense
A, B	Offense
- - - →	Path of Ball
——→	Path of Player

Diagram 2

158. When should a player be called offside?
     a. any time the player is in an offside position
     *b. when a player in an offside position tries to get involved in the play
     c. when a player in an offside position receives the ball from a throw-in
     d. when a player in an offside position receives the ball from a goal kick

Fouls

159. Which action is *not* an illegal play?
    a. charging into the goalkeeper
  *b. shielding the ball
    c. pushing off on an opponent
    d. calling "my ball"

160. What is the penalty for tripping an opponent outside the penalty area?
  *a. direct free kick
    b. indirect free kick
    c. penalty kick
    d. disqualification

161. What is the penalty for intentionally handling the ball outside the penalty area?
  *a. direct free kick
    b. indirect free kick
    c. penalty kick
    d. disqualification

162. What is the penalty when an offensive player has a "hand ball" in the penalty area?
    a. indirect free kick
    b. place kick
    c. penalty shot
  *d. direct kick from where hand ball occurred

163. What is the penalty for pushing an opponent in order to reach the ball?
    a. no penalty
  *b. direct free kick
    c. indirect free kick
    d. penalty kick

164. Which condition is *not* necessary for a fair charge?
    a. shoulder to shoulder contact
    b. arms and elbows close to the body
  *c. at least one foot on the ground
    d. outside the penalty area

165. What is the penalty for intentionally charging the goalkeeper in the penalty area?
    a. indirect free kick
    b. drop ball
    c. penalty kick
  *d. disqualification

166. An attacking player kicks the ball out of the goalie's hands after the goalie has control of the ball and kicks the ball into the net. What is the decision? ·
    a. allow the goal to count
    b. award a penalty kick to the defending team
  *c. award an indirect free kick to the defending team
    d. award a direct free kick to the defending team

167. A player charges an opponent when neither is in playing distance of the ball. What is the situation?
    a. continue play
    b. direct free kick
    c. penalty kick
  *d. indirect free kick

168. Which action is *not* a privilege of the goalkeeper?
    a. picking up the ball
    b. punting the ball
    c. combining bounces with a punt or throw
  *d. taking unlimited steps with the ball

169. How many steps may the goalkeeper take while holding the ball?
    a. one
    b. two
    c. three
  *d. four

170. If the goalkeeper takes too many steps before releasing the ball, what is the penalty?
    a. direct free kick
  *b. indirect free kick
    c. penalty kick
    d. drop ball

171. Where must the goalie be to handle the ball?
    a. in the goal
    b. in the goal area
  *c. in the penalty area
    d. anywhere in the playing field

172. How many yellow cards can a player receive in a game before being ejected?
  *a. one
    b. two
    c. three
    d. four

Kick

173. A forward shoots the ball and the goalie deflects it over the net. What is the ruling?
    a. throw-in
    b. goal kick
  *c. corner kick
    d. indirect free kick

Free Kick

174. A kick is awarded on a personal foul that can be kicked for a goal. What is this called?
    a. free kick
  *b. direct free kick
    c. indirect free kick
    d. drop kick

175. Generally, from where is a free kick taken?
    a. the center circle
    b. the halfway line
    c. the penalty area line
    *d. the spot of the foul

176. Where must opposing players be in relation to the ball on a free kick?
    a. outside the circle
    b. 10 yards from the line
    c. 5 yards from the ball
    *d. 10 yards from the ball

177. In which situation is a direct free kick awarded the opponents?
    a. offside
    b. illegal substitution
    *c. deliberately handling the ball
    d. leaving the field without permission

178. What type of kick is given for misconduct or unsportsmanlike conduct?
    a. penalty kick
    b. direct free kick
    *c. indirect free kick
    d. drop ball

Penalty Kick

179. When is a penalty kick awarded?
    a. when the offensive team commits a hand ball in the penalty area
    *b. when the defensive team commits a trip in the penalty area
    c. when the offensive team commits a push in the penalty area
    d. when the defensive team commits an obstruction in the penalty area

180. From where is a penalty kick taken?
    a. the spot of the foul
    b. either corner of the penalty area
    *c. the penalty kick line
    d. the circular line drawn from the penalty area

181. Who may be in the penalty area during a penalty kick?
    a. the kicker
    *b. the kicker and the goalie
    c. the kicker and the offensive team
    d. the kicker and the defensive team

182. Where must the goalie be for a penalty kick?
    a. standing in the goal
    *b. standing on the goal line between the goalposts
    c. standing in the goal area
    d. standing in the penalty area

Goal Kick

183. When is a goal kick taken?
    a. when a player has an open shot at the goal
    b. when an offensive player commits a foul in the goal area
    c. when a defensive player sends the ball over the goal line
    *d. when an offensive player sends the ball over the goal line

184. From where is a goal kick taken?
    a. the center of the goal line
    *b. the half of the goal area nearest to where the ball left the playing field
    c. the half of the penalty area nearest to where the ball left the playing field
    d. the restraining line in front of the penalty area

185. When may a goal kick be played by the defense?
    a. as soon as the ball is contacted
    b. as soon as the ball has traveled its circumference
    c. as soon as the ball has cleared the goal area
    *d. as soon as the ball has cleared the penalty area

Corner Kick

186. When is a corner kick taken?
    a. when a player has an open shot from the corner
    b. when an offensive player commits a foul in the goal area
    *c. when a defensive player sends the ball over the end line
    d. when an offensive player sends the ball over the end line

187. From where is a corner kick taken?
    a. the point on the goal line where the ball left the playing field
    *b. the quarter circle nearer where the ball left the playing field
    c. the intersection of the touchline and goal line
    d. either quarter circle

188. Where must the defending team stand during a corner kick?
    a. on the goal line
    b. outside the penalty area
    *c. at least 10 yards from the ball
    d. outside the goal area

189. A player taking a corner kick dribbles the ball. What happens?
    a. continue play
    b. rekick
    c. direct free kick for the opponents
    *d. indirect free kick for the opponents

Throw-In

190. When is a throw-in awarded?
    *a. when one team sends the ball over the touchline
    b. when the offensive team sends the ball over the goal line
    c. when the defensive team sends the ball over the goal line
    d. when the ball contacts the touchline

191. From where is a throw-in taken?
    *a. from where the ball crossed over the touchline
    b. from where the ball crossed over any boundary line
    c. from the intersection of the touchline and goal line
    d. from the intersection of the goal line and penalty line

192. What is *not* a specification for the player taking a throw-in?
    a. both of player's feet on the ground
    b. both hands with equal force on the ball
    c. ball delivered from back of the player's head
    *d. square stance facing the field

193. What is not allowed during a throw-in?
    a. The ball is sent into the field from behind the touchline where it left the field of play.
    b. The ball is thrown with a two-handed overhead throw.
    *c. An opponent jumps up and down in front of the thrower.
    d. The player making the throw-in has both feet on the ground when the throw-in is made.

History

Origin

194. Which country is considered the homeland of soccer?
    a. France
    b. Australia
    *c. England
    d. Brazil

195. In 13th and 15th century England, soccer was considered primarily a game for which group of people?
    a. monarchs and royalty
    b. knights
    *c. common people
    d. university students

196. When were the first rules used that are very similar to those used today?
    a. 1425
    b. 1863
    *c. 1871
    d. 1934

197. What was the game of soccer called prior to its present name?
    *a. football
    b. rugby
    c. speedball
    d. kickball

198. What was the original size of the field in many soccer matches?
    *a. the distance from village to neighboring village
    b. up to 1 mile in length
    c. 100 yards long
    d. 50 yards long and 50 yards wide

199. Who banned the playing of soccer and imposed severe prison sentences on those who played?
    a. King Louis XIV
    *b. King Edward III
    c. President Herbert Hoover
    d. Colonial legislatures in the U.S.

Organizations

200. What is the name of the organization that is in major control of soccer in the United States?
    a. United States Soccer League
    *b. United States Soccer Federation
    c. North American Soccer League
    d. Association of American Soccer

201. What is the name of the world-governing body of soccer?
    a. World Soccer Association
    *b. Fédération Internationale de Football Association
    c. The Association of World Soccer
    d. International World Football Association

Competition

202. What is the name of the competition held every 4 years for the world soccer championship?
     a. Soccer Cup
     *b. World Cup
     c. International Championship of Soccer
     d. World Championship of Football

203. What is the name of the professional soccer league in the United States?
     a. North American Professional Soccer League
     b. United States Soccer League
     *c. Major Indoor Soccer League
     d. American Pro Indoor Soccer League

Popularity

204. What is the status of soccer in the United States today in terms of popularity?
     a. remaining the same
     b. decreasing rapidly
     c. decreasing slowly
     *d. increasing rapidly

205. Why is soccer becoming so popular in school and community programs?
     *a. because it is inexpensive
     b. because of the growth and influence of the NASL
     c. because it can be played by men and women
     d. because skill is *not* considered important

Terminology

Defensive

206. What is the team trying to gain possession of the ball called?
     *a. defensive team
     b. offensive team
     c. attacking team
     d. opposing team

Trapping

207. What is it called when a player stops the ball?
     a. dribbling
     *b. trapping
     c. tackling
     d. catching

Attacking

208. What is the team that has possession of the ball called?
     *a. attacking team
     b. defending team
     c. ball control team
     d. shooting team

Tackling

209. What is *tackling*?
     a. knocking an opponent down
     *b. attempting to gain possession of the ball
     c. stopping a ball in the air
     d. stopping a ball on the ground

Dribbling

210. A player moves the ball by making a series of short taps with the feet. What is this called?
     *a. dribbling
     b. trapping
     c. tapping
     d. tackling

Stalemate

211. What does the term *stalemate* mean?
     a. a tie game
     b. a dead ball, when the goalie falls on the ball
     c. two opposing players waiting for each other to make a move
     *d. successfully stopping an offensive play

Cross

212. What does *to cross* mean?
     *a. to kick the ball from one side of the field to the other
     b. to have wing forwards exchange sides of the field
     c. to outman an opponent
     d. to go over the touchline

Halfback

213. What are halfbacks sometimes called?
     *a. midfielders
     b. stoppers
     c. fullbacks
     d. linemen

Volley

214. What is it called when a player strikes the ball before it bounces?
     a. full gainer
     b. full kick
     *c. volley
     d. punch

Juggling

215. A player is practicing by controlling the ball with various parts of the body. What is this called?
     a. passing
     b. trapping
     c. dribbling
     *d. juggling

Mark

216. What does *to mark* mean?
    a. to place the ball in the correct place after a foul
    b. to hit an opponent with the ball
    *c. to guard an opposing player
    d. to center the ball for an attempt at goal

Clearing

217. What does "clearing" mean?
    *a. to move the ball out of scoring range
    b. to get away from a defensive player
    c. to kick the ball to a teammate
    d. to kick the ball legally on the kickoff

Save

218. What is a save?
    a. a player keeping the ball from going over the touchline
    b. a player keeping the ball from going in the goal
    *c. the goalie keeping the ball from going in the goal
    d. a player intercepting the ball when the attacking team is fast breaking

Red Card

219. What is a red card?
    a. the emblem a player wears to indicate he or she is the goalie
    b. the emblem a player wears to indicate he or she is the team captain
    c. the signal the scorekeeper gives the referee to indicate an illegal substitution
    *d. the signal the referee uses to indicate the disqualification of a player

Equipment

Ball

220. What size ball is appropriate for players 13 years old and over?
    a. 2
    b. 3
    c. 4
    *d. 5

221. What size ball is appropriate for players 10 to 12 years old?
    a. 2
    b. 3
    *c. 4
    d. 5

222. What determines how long a soccer ball will last?
    a. weather conditions
    b. field conditions
    c. age of the players
    *d. air pressure of the ball

223. How can you determine whether a ball has the right air pressure without a gauge?
    a. using your full body weight, the thumbs should make no indention
    *b. using your full body weight, the thumbs should make a slight indention
    c. using only hand pressure, the thumbs should easily make an indention
    d. using only hand pressure, the thumbs should make a slight indention

Shoes

224. What is the appropriate footwear for soccer?
    a. street shoes
    b. tennis shoes
    *c. molded sole shoes
    d. jogging shoes

225. What is the most important consideration in selecting shoes?
    *a. suppleness
    b. stiffness
    c. weight
    d. tongue

226. Where should the bow knot be in tying the laces on a pair of soccer shoes?
    a. at the top of the instep
    b. at the bottom of the instep
    *c. on the outside side of the shoe
    d. on the inside side of the shoe

227. How do the professionals break in a new pair of soccer shoes?
    a. play in them short periods of time until comfortable
    b. soak them in cold water for about an hour
    c. jog in them until comfortable
    *d. tie them on their bare feet and soak in warm water for 20 minutes

228. When should a player wear removable cleated shoes?
    a. when the ground is dry
    b. when the ground is hard
    *c. when the ground is muddy
    d. when the field is artifical turf

Protective Equipment

229. What piece of protective equipment is recommended for all players?
     *a. shin guards
     b. knee guards
     c. hip pads
     d. helmets

230. What kind of headgear can goalies legally wear?
     a. hockey helmets with a face guard
     b. one color cap with a bill
     *c. one color, soft material head band
     d. baseball helmets

231. When is a player allowed to wear a knee brace?
     a. when the player has a legitimate knee problem as indicated by a physician
     *b. when the brace is wrapped and approved by the referee
     c. never
     d. anytime, no problem

232. By high school rules, when may a player compete in a cast?
     a. when the player has a legitimate problem as indicated by a physician
     b. when the cast is wrapped and approved by the referee
     c. anytime, no problem
     *d. never

Strategy

233. Why is it a good technique to pass instead of dribble?
     a. because it is important to involve teammates as much as possible
     b. because dribbling the ball further than 10 yards is against the rules
     *c. because it is quicker to pass the ball than to dribble it
     d. because a player is always a better passer than dribbler

234. Which system is *not* a commonly played strategy?
     a. 4-2-4
     b. 3-3-4
     c. WM system
     *d. 1-2-3-4

235. Which players form the M in the WM formation?
     *a. three fullbacks and the wing halfbacks
     b. insides, wingers, and center forward
     c. the forwards
     d. the backs

236. How are teams positioned to add depth on both offense and defense?
     a. in three lines across the field—forwards, halfbacks, and fullbacks
     *b. in interlocking triangles
     c. in interlocking diamonds
     d. in pairs so that each player has a backup

237. What system is Team B using? [Refer to Diagram 3.]
     a. 4-2-4
     b. 3-3-4
     *c. 4-3-3
     d. 1-3-3-4

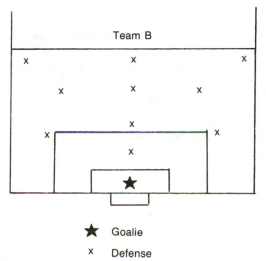

Diagram 3

238. Which position probably requires the most endurance?
     a. goalie
     b. wing
     *c. midfielder
     d. center forward

239. Which players generally need the most skill at dribbling?
     a. backs
     b. midfielders
     c. defenders
     *d. forwards

240. Why should the forwards *not* attack in a straight line across the field?
     *a. limits passing possibilities
     b. limits dribbling possibilities
     c. easy to be offside
     d. players too far apart

Team Position

241. What is a *striker?*
  a. a player who marks the opposing team's sweeper
  b. a player who kicks the ball extremely hard
  c. a highly skilled player
  *d. a player whose main purpose is to score goals

242. What is a *sweeper?*
  a. a player who takes corner kicks
  b. a player who backs up the goalie
  *c. a player who controls the defense
  d. a player who controls the offense

243. What is a *wing?*
  *a. a forward who generally plays near the side boundaries
  b. the player who takes a corner kick
  c. the player who takes a throw-in
  d. the fullback who helps the goalie defend the goal

244. Which player in the diagram is the left half-back? [Refer to Diagram 4.]
  *a. D
  b. F
  c. G
  d. I

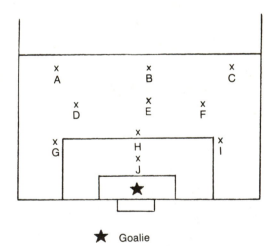

★ Goalie

Diagram 4

245. Which player in the diagram is the right full-back? [Refer to Diagram 4, Question 244.]
  a. D
  b. F
  c. G
  *d. I

Offense

246. Which is *not* a principle of offense?
  a. depth
  b. mobility
  c. width
  *d. delay

247. Generally, how many teammates should be within about 15 yards of the player who has the ball?
  a. only one
  *b. two to three
  c. three to five
  d. at least five

248. How much of the field's width should an attacking team try to use?
  a. the middle only
  b. the middle half of the field
  c. the middle two thirds of the field
  *d. the whole width

249. Should attacking players interchange positions?
  a. No, they should maintain their positions so their teammates know where they are.
  b. No, they should maintain their positions so they are spread out evenly across the field.
  *c. Yes, they can better maneuver and confuse the defense.
  d. Yes, they should, but only when the defense is playing man-to-man.

250. You have an open field with only the goalie between you and the goal. What is the best move to make?
  a. Take a direct kick.
  *b. Advance the ball, fake, and shoot at goal.
  c. Advance the ball and take a direct kick.
  d. Trap the ball and wait for your teammates.

251. A player is attempting to pass to a teammate who is closely guarded. What should the passer do?
  a. Wait to pass the ball until the opponent stops guarding him or her.
  *b. Wait to pass the ball until the teammate makes a feint that gets him or her open.
  c. Pass to the teammate and hope he or she can lose the opponent.
  d. Pass to the teammate to make him or her lose the opponent.

252. What is the best move for Player A to make? [Refer to Diagram 5.]
 - a. Shoot at the goal.
 - b. Pass to B.
 - c. Pass to D.
 - *d. Dribble toward the goal.

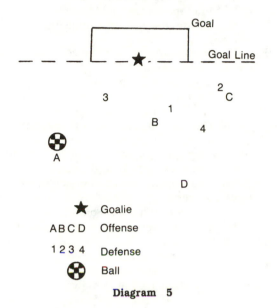

★ Goalie

A B C D   Offense

1 2 3 4   Defense

⊕ Ball

Diagram 5

253. What is the best move for Player D to make? (Refer to Diagram 5, Question 252.]
 - *a. Remain back as a safety.
 - b. Cut to the right wing.
 - c. Cut toward goal for a pass.
 - d. Remain stationary.

254. An opponent attacks you from the left while you are dribbling down the field. You do *not* want to lose control of the ball. What should you do?
 - a. Dribble toward the left side of the field.
 - *b. Dribble toward the right side of the field.
 - c. Dribble toward midfield.
 - d. Dribble toward your attacking opponent.

255. What should Player A do? [Refer to Diagram 6.]
 - a. Pass to B.
 - *b. Loft the ball to C for a head-in.
 - c. Dribble towards goal for a shot.
 - d. Remain stationary until B gets open.

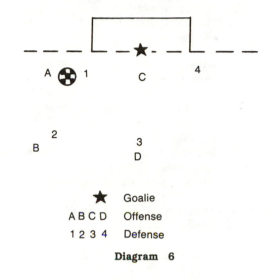

★ Goalie

A B C D   Offense

1 2 3 4   Defense

Diagram 6

256. What is the main function of the striker?
 - a. to mark the opposing team's sweeper
 - b. to lay the ball off to wing forwards
 - *c. to score goals
 - d. to create space by making runs

257. Who is responsible for most of the scoring by the offensive team?
 - a. halfbacks
 - *b. forwards
 - c. fullbacks
 - d. goalies

258. A player likes to do a lot of running and traveling with the ball. What might be the best position for this player?
 - a. wing fullback
 - b. sweeper
 - c. striker
 - *d. midfielder

259. What kick is most commonly used for penalty kicks?
 - a. drop kick
 - b. inside-of-foot kick
 - c. toe kick
 - *d. instep kick

260. Which shot is most frequently used by halfbacks in shooting on the goal?
 - *a. long, low power shots
 - b. headed shots
 - c. high, short corner shots
 - d. low, short deflection shots

261. On the kickoff, what is the usual position of the offensive wing forwards?
     *a. just behind the center line, near the touchlines
     b. on-side at the intersection of the center line and circle
     c. inside the circle on either side of the center forward
     d. about 10 yards downfield to receive the kick

262. What is the best way to attack the defense?
     a. Bunch the attacking players to one side.
     b. Do most of the shooting from outside the penalty area.
     c. Play the center halfback even with the five forwards on a straight line across the field.
     *d. Keep the attack spread out.

263. Which move is *not* an offensive tactic?
     a. finish
     b. mobility
     *c. delay
     d. support

264. What should an attacking player do when an opponent is about to take the ball away?
     a. Spin around the ball and continue with it.
     b. Take the ball to a free space.
     c. Pass to an open teammate.
     *d. all of the above

265. What is the best place for the goalie to throw or kick the ball?
     a. short and straight up the middle
     b. short and to the outside
     *c. long and to the outside
     d. long and straight up the middle

Defense

266. Which factor is *not* a basic principle of defense?
     a. depth
     b. balance
     c. delay
     *d. width

267. Your team has just lost possession of the ball. What is the best tactic?
     *a. Delay your opponent's attack.
     b. Try to retake possession.
     c. Concentrate the defense in front of the goal.
     d. Pressure the attacking player.

268. The ball is on the attacker's right wing. The left back is marking the player with the ball. What should the other backs do?
     a. Move in front of the goal to help the goalie.
     b. Maintain their positions.
     c. Move into positions that will form a line across the field.
     *d. Drop back in a diagonal line.

269. When the ball approaches the goal area, what should the defense do?
     *a. Go man-to-man.
     b. Play a zone.
     c. Pressure the attacking player.
     d. Concentrate in front of the goal.

270. An attacking player with the ball is coming toward the goal from the right side of the field. What area should the goalkeeper be sure to have covered?
     a. the middle of the goal
     *b. the area between him- or herself and the near post
     c. the area between him- or herself and the far post
     d. the right half of the goal

271. An attacking player with the ball is coming toward the goal from the left side of the field. What can the goalie do to reduce the area the player has to shoot for a goal?
     *a. Move into the goal area toward the player.
     b. Move into the goal area in front of the center of the goal.
     c. Move back even with the goal line in the center of the goal.
     d. Move back even with the goal line on the side toward the attacking player.

272. What is the best move for Player 3 to make? [Refer to Diagram 5, Question 252.]
     a. Help goalie defend goal.
     b. Play B man-to-man and have Player 1 play A.
     *c. Play A man-to-man.
     d. Remain stationary.

273. What should the goalie do? [Refer to Diagram 6, Question 255.]
     a. Call for Players 2 and 3 to help.
     b. Go out to stop shot from A.
     c. Mark C.
     *d. Stay at goal.

274. An opponent has the ball in his or her half of the field and is dribbling upfield. What should the defender do?
    a. let his or her goalie stop the dribbler
    b. run alongside of the dribbler
   *c. get in front of the dribbler
    d. tackle the dribbler from behind

275. An opponent has just received a pass. What is the first move the defender should make?
   *a. slowly attack the opponent so he or she *cannot* fake the defender out
    b. wait until the opponent passes the ball, then try to intercept it
    c. call for help
    d. run toward the opponent quickly to distract him or her

276. Your opponent has scored three goals in the first half. What should you do to try to prevent this player from scoring any more goals?
    a. Double-team him or her.
   *b. Try to prevent this player from receiving the ball.
    c. Try to defend this player more closely.
    d. Give this player more room so he or she does not beat you to the goal.

277. What is the primary job of the *stopper*?
   *a. to mark the opposing team's center forward
    b. to mark any free opposing forward
    c. to mark the overlapping halfback
    d. to stop the opposing center halfback from distributing the ball

278. The referee has called a tripping foul against the defense. The ball is placed 18 yards from the goal and the offense is awarded a direct kick. What is the best setup for the defense? [Refer to Diagram 7.]
   *b.

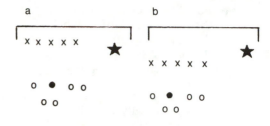

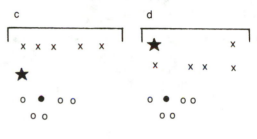

★ Goalie
x Defense
o Offense
● Ball

Diagram 7

279. What is not a duty of the goalkeeper?
   *a. heading
    b. directing teammates
    c. punting
    d. using his or her hands

280. What is the primary responsibility of the goalkeeper?
    a. to control the defense by directing traffic
    b. to set up the defensive wall on a kick
   *c. to keep the ball from crossing the goal line
    d. to stop penalty kicks

281. Which player does the left wing fullback usually mark?
    a. the opposing left halfback
    b. the opposing inside forward
   *c. the opposing right wing
    d. the opposing left wing fullback

282. In the standard man-to-man defense, which players do the fullbacks cover?
    *a. wing forwards
    b. wing halfbacks
    c. center forward and center halfback
    d. inside forwards

283. In the standard man-to-man defense, which player does the left wing cover?
    *a. the opposing right fullback
    b. the opposing left fullback
    c. the opposing right halfback
    d. the opposing left halfback

284. When using a 4-2-4 system, what are the defensive four usually called?
    a. fearsome foursome
    b. enforcers
    c. fearless fullbacks
    *d. diamond defense

285. Which move is *not* a defensive tactic?
    a. immediate chase
    b. fall back and delay
    *c. running to open space
    d. concentration

Acknowledgments

Colleagues and students who contributed suggestions and ideas for the Soccer test questions are: M. Cawley, N. Clay, D. Mitchell, D. Shadle, M. Thornton, G. Wallwork, and L. Wilkerson.

Suggested Readings

Harris, Jr., P.E., & Harris, L.R. (1983). *Fair or foul: The complete guide to soccer officiating in America.* Manhatten Beach, CA: Soccer for Americans.

Laitin, K., & Laitin, S. (1979). *The world's #1 best selling soccer book.* Manhatten Beach, CA: Soccer for Americans.

Maher, A.E. (1983). *Complete soccer handbook.* West Nyack, NY: Parker.

Nelson, R.L. (1980). *Soccer.* Dubuque, IA: Wm. C. Brown.

Trimby, R. (1977). *Soccer techniques and tactics.* New York: Arco.

NAGWS. (1984). *Soccer guide April 1984-April 1986.* Reston, VA: AAHPERD.

1985/1986 Official high school soccer rules. (1985). Kansas City, MO: National Federation of State High School Associations.

Softball

Sandra K. Johnson, Consultant

This collection of test questions on softball is divided into four content areas:

- **General Knowledge**
- **Techniques**
- **Strategy**
- **Rules**

These questions are appropriate for either men or women players. Many of these questions can be used for units in slow pitch softball; however, the instructor may need to add or revise some questions to accommodate the different features of the slow pitch game.

The instructor can make appropriate selections from a sizeable pool of questions, adding to, revising, and updating the collection as changes in techniques and rules occur.

General Knowledge

History	1 to 9
Terminology	10 to 24
Safety and Equipment	25 to 29

History

Origins

1. Where was softball invented?
   - a. Great Britain
   - *b. America
   - c. Austria
   - d. South Africa

2. In what city did softball originate?
   - a. Detroit, Michigan
   - b. Springfield, Massachusetts
   - *c. Chicago, Illinois
   - d. Cleveland, Ohio

3. Who was the person to first call the game softball?
   - a. George W. Hancock
   - *b. Walter A. Hakanson
   - c. Abner Doubleday
   - d. Lewis Rober

4. What was an original name given to softball?
   - a. fat ball
   - *b. kittenball
   - c. slow pitch
   - d. bat ball

5. Who proposed the first set of rules for softball?
   - *a. George W. Hancock
   - b. Jordan V. Hamrick
   - c. Gerald Y. Hendrick
   - d. James V. Haverford

6. In what year was softball begun?
   - a. 1870
   - b. 1880
   - *c. 1887
   - d. 1895

7. When was the name *softball* adopted for general use?
   - a. around 1910-1915
   - b. around 1920-1925
   - *c. around 1926-1930
   - d. around 1940-1945

Sandra K. Johnson is a former softball player, teacher, and coach and is currently at La Grange College, La Grange, Georgia.

Today

8. Where is the Softball Hall of Fame located?
    a. Houston, Texas
    b. Las Vegas, Nevada
    *c. Oklahoma City, Oklahoma
    d. Topeka, Kansas

9. What organization publishes the official softball rules?
    a. National Softball Association of America
    b. United States Softball-Baseball Association
    c. National Recreation Association
    *d. Amateur Softball Association

Terminology

Battery

10. What does the term *battery* mean?
    a. the batter's box
    b. the batter and catcher
    *c. the pitcher and catcher
    d. the batter, catcher, and umpire

Batting Average

11. What is the batting average of a player who has eight hits out of 40 trips to the plate?
    a. .160
    *b. .200
    c. .320
    d. .500

Texas Leaguer

12. What is a *Texas Leaguer*?
    a. a softball player from Texas
    b. a line drive down the foul line
    *c. a hit that drops between the infielder and the outfield
    d. another term for a line drive home run

Keystone Sack

13. What is another name for second base?
    a. hot corner
    *b. keystone sack
    c. initial sack
    d. middle sack

Hot Corner

14. Which base is referred to as the *hot corner*?
    a. home plate
    b. first base
    c. second base
    *d. third base

In the Hole

15. What does *in the hole* mean?
    a. being caught between two bases
    *b. having an unfavorable count when batting, like two strikes and no balls
    c. using an outside advantage, like the ground, to stop the ball
    d. the space between the batter's armpits and the top of the knees

Assist

16. What is an *assist*?
    a. scoring a runner with a fair fly ball that is caught
    b. electing to retire a base runner or the batter
    *c. throwing a batted ball, which results in a putout
    d. requesting a decision

Fielder's Choice

17. What is a *fielder's choice*?
    *a. deciding to retire either a base runner or a batter
    b. deciding to put a batter on base
    c. deciding which position to play
    d. deciding which outfielder should catch a fly ball

Cleanup

18. To what does the term *cleanup* usually refer?
    a. the ground around the bases that is smoothed after each game
    b. the home plate when it is swept off by the umpire
    *c. the fourth position in the batting order
    d. an extremely one-sided game score

Line Drive

19. What is a *line drive*?
    a. a ball hit down the first or third baseline
    b. a hit allowing two base runners to advance safely
    c. a home run hit with the bases loaded
    *d. a ball hit sharply in the air and directly into the playing field

Full Count

20. What is a *full count*?
    a. game score of 5 to 4
    b. team roster of 25 players
    *c. three balls and two strikes on the batter
    d. earned run average of the pitcher

Southpaw

21. What is a *southpaw*?
    - a. special kind of mitt for the catcher
    - *b. left-handed pitcher
    - c. left-handed batter
    - d. a knuckleball pitcher

Balk

22. What is a *balk*?
    - a. four balls
    - *b. a motion to pitch without delivering the ball
    - c. a batted ball that goes directly to the catcher and is caught
    - d. standing too close to the plate

Cut Off

23. What does to *cut off* mean?
    - a. to shorten the game because of the weather conditions
    - b. to confuse a defensive player making a play
    - c. to run down a base runner caught off base
    - *d. to intercept an outfielder's throw to a base in order to pick off another runner

Backing Up

24. To what does the term *backing up* refer?
    - a. having all of the outfielders move away from the infield
    - b. the pitcher stepping backward after delivering the ball
    - *c. being behind a player in case that player misses the ball
    - d. moving back deep within the batter's box

Safety and Equipment

Safety

25. What equipment is worn by the catcher for safety?
    - *a. mask and body protector
    - b. glove and uniform
    - c. mask and mitt
    - d. cleats and mask

26. What is the best procedure for preventing collisions between fielders?
    - a. waving other fielders off the ball
    - *b. calling the balls
    - c. staying within designated boundaries
    - d. wearing sun shades

Equipment

27. What is the size of most softballs used currently?
    - a. 10 inches
    - *b. 12 inches
    - c. 14 inches
    - d. 16 inches

28. What equipment is considered least essential to play a softball game?
    - a. bats
    - b. balls
    - *c. cleats
    - d. gloves

29. What is the minimum equipment needed to play a game of softball?
    - *a. bat and ball
    - b. ball, bat, and gloves
    - c. ball, bat, and four bases
    - d. ball and glove

Techniques

General Offensive Techniques	30
Batting	31 to 62
Bunting	63 to 65
Baserunning	66 to 73
Sliding	74 to 75
Pitching	76 to 82
Fielding	83 to 106
Throwing	107 to 115
Tagging	116 to 122
Player Characteristics	123 to 125

General Offensive Techniques

30. What are the major offensive skills?
    - a. throwing and catching
    - b. catching and batting
    - *c. batting and baserunning
    - d. baserunning and sliding

Batting

31. What is the most important skill involved in softball?
    - a. throwing
    - b. fielding
    - *c. batting
    - d. running

32. Which skill gives the most advantage to an offensive player?
    - a. power hitting
    - *b. place hitting
    - c. running speed
    - d. sliding ability

Selecting Bat

33. Which point is *least* important to consider when selecting a bat?
    a. size of the bat
    b. balance of the bat
    *c. position in the lineup
    d. size of the grip

34. What is the most important factor to consider when selecting a bat?
    a. to choose the same bat that the most powerful hitter on the team uses
    b. to choose a bat that is very light so the swing can be harder
    c. to choose a bat that is about the same length as the batter's arms
    *d. to choose a bat heavy enough to add force but still permit wrist action

Grip

35. Which grip should be used if the batter wants to hit a long ball?
    a. hands together about 3 inches from the bottom of the bat
    b. hands together about 1 inch from the bottom of the bat
    c. hands spread about 2 inches
    *d. hands together at the bottom of the bat

36. Which grip should be used when trying to punch the ball?
    a. medium grip
    b. long grip
    c. overlap grip
    *d. choke grip

37. Why is the long grip used?
    *a. for power
    b. for placement
    c. for correcting a swing that is too fast
    d. for hitting breaking pitches

38. Which grip should a batter use to increase leverage and add force to the hit?
    a. choke grip
    b. medium grip
    *c. long grip
    d. continental grip

39. The only bat available is too long for you. How should you hold the bat?
    a. at the end of the handle
    b. cross-handed
    *c. a few inches up the handle
    d. with the hands apart

Stance

40. What would be the desirable stance for a right-handed batter trying to hit the ball to right field?
    *a. front foot closer to the plate than the rear foot
    b. feet parallel and far away from the plate
    c. front foot farther from the plate than the rear foot
    d. feet parallel and close to the plate

41. Which diagram shows the stance of a right-handed batter adjusted to place hit into left field? [Refer to Diagram 1.]
    *b.

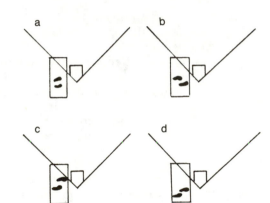

Diagram 1

42. Which batting stance is the best for a beginning softball player?
    a. closed
    b. open
    *c. square
    d. forward

43. What is your first concern once you enter the batter's box?
    a. Check the positions of the infielders.
    b. Look at the third base coach.
    *c. Take a comfortable stance.
    d. Check the base runners.

Weight Shift

44. What is the first thing the batter should do as the ball leaves the pitcher's hand?
    a. Drop the elbows to the waist.
    *b. Shift the weight to the rear foot.
    c. Rest the bat on the shoulder.
    d. Take a step forward on the front foot.

Contact

45. Where would the batter need to contact the ball to hit it to left field? [Refer to Diagram 2.]
    *a. a
    b. b
    c. c
    d. between b and c

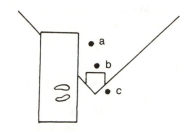

Diagram 2

Swing

46. What is the best action to use when swinging at the ball?
    a. Swing on top of the ball regardless of the pitch.
    b. Swing hard with a lunging action.
    c. Swing hard with no wrist action.
    *d. Swing smoothly with fast wrist action.

Power

47. Where is the major source of hitting power?
    *a. hip rotation
    b. shoulder momentum
    c. wrist action
    d. leg position

Power and Control

48. Which sequence of body movements will provide the hitter with the most power and control when hitting a line drive?
    1. extend the arms
    2. rotate the hips
    3. shift the weight forward
    4. contact the ball
    5. snap the wrists in line with the swing
       a. 1, 2, 3, 4, 5
       *b. 2, 1, 3, 5, 4
       c. 3, 1, 2, 5, 4
       d. 2, 3, 1, 4, 5

Lack of Control

49. What causes a lack of control when batting?
    *a. incorrect stance
    b. late swing
    c. wrong grip
    d. cocked wrists

Striking Out

50. What action should be taken to correct a tendency to strike out?
    *a. Shorten the grip and watch the ball closely.
    b. Shorten the grip and adjust the stride.
    c. Lengthen the grip and swing faster.
    d. Lengthen the grip and adjust the stride.

Hitting Foul

51. A right-handed batter consistently fouls the ball off to the right. What probably is the cause?
    *a. swinging too late
    b. swinging at an inside pitch
    c. swinging too early
    d. swinging at pitches that are too high

Hit Placement

52. What action should a right-handed batter take to place hit the ball to left field?
    a. Contact the ball opposite the body and follow through naturally.
    b. Contact the ball a little past the center of the body and follow through toward right field.
    c. Contact the ball anywhere over the plate and swing fast with a full follow-through.
    *d. Contact the ball in front of the body, snap the wrists sharply to cause a forceful follow-through.

53. A right-handed batter brings the left foot toward the plate while stepping into the swing. Where would you expect the ball to be hit?
    a. close to third base
    *b. between first and second
    c. over second base
    d. along the third baseline

54. Where is the *least* expected place for a left-handed batter to hit?
    a. over second base
    b. to right field
    c. to left field
    *d. down the third baseline

55. Where is the *least* expected place for a right-handed batter to hit?
    a. down the third baseline
    b. over second base
    *c. down the first baseline
    d. right center field

56. What should a right-handed batter do to hit to the opposite field?
    a. Contact the ball out front.
    *b. Contact the ball late.
    c. Follow through well behind the opposite shoulder.
    d. Use an open stance.

57. As a right-handed batter, your coach wants you to hit to right field. What is the most effective way to do this?
    *a. Wait on the pitch and swing late.
    b. Be ready for the pitch and swing early.
    c. Stand with your left foot ahead of your right foot.
    d. Stand with your right foot ahead of your left foot.

Pulled Ball

58. What should a right-handed batter do to pull the ball down the third baseline?
    a. Choke up on the bat.
    b. Move up in the box.
    c. Close the stance.
    *d. Contact the ball early.

59. Which diagram demonstrates a pulled ball? [Refer to Diagram 3.]
    *c.

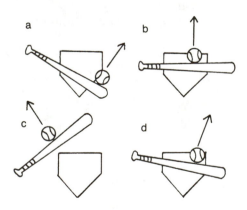

Diagram 3

Advance Runners

60. What is one basic rule all hitters should remember when trying to advance a runner from first with less than two outs?
    a. Keep the ball on the ground.
    *b. Hit behind the runner.
    c. Place the ball between first and second.
    d. Aim for the infielders' feet.

Base Hit

61. What is the best method of assuring a base hit?
    a. hitting a line drive that will drop behind the infielders
    *b. hitting a line drive between two players
    c. hitting a ground ball directly at an infielder
    d. hitting a ground ball between two infielders

Grounder

62. How should the batter swing to hit the ball on the ground?
    *a. down on the ball
    b. straight onto the ball
    c. up at the ball
    d. high

Bunting

Position

63. Which diagram shows the best position for bunting? [Refer to Diagram 4.]
    *a.

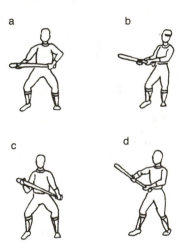

Diagram 4

64. What guides the angle of the bat when a right-handed batter is bunting?
    a. flexing the knees
    b. moving the left hand
    *c. moving the right hand
    d. pivoting the feet

Push Bunt

65. When should the ball be contacted on a push bunt?
    a. after the ball reaches the plate
    b. after the batter pivots toward first base
    c. after the bat has been squared to the pitcher
    *d. as the batter steps toward first base

Baserunning

66. Which diagram shows the correct method for running around the bases? [Refer to Diagram 5.]
    *a.

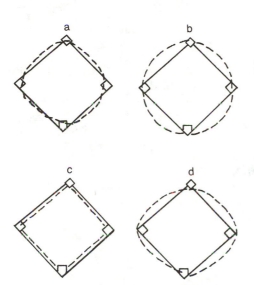

Diagram 5

67. What is the best thing for the batter to do when the ball is hit?
    a. Run slowly without watching the ball.
    b. Run slowly while watching the ball.
    *c. Run fast without watching the ball.
    d. Run fast while watching the ball.

Efficiency

68. What is the most efficient way to run the bases?
    *a. Tag the inside of the bag with either foot.
    b. Tag the outside of the bag with the right foot.
    c. Run directly toward the base.
    d. Tag the outside of the bag with the left foot.

69. Where should a base runner touch the bases to save the most time?
    *a. inside corner of the base
    b. outside corner of the base
    c. middle of the base
    d. It doesn't make any difference.

Strength

70. Which factor is *least* important in baserunning?
    a. speed
    b. alertness
    *c. strength
    d. strategy

Lead Foot

71. Which foot of a right-handed batter leads on the run toward first base and why?
    *a. right foot because it is free of body weight
    b. right foot because it is closest to first base
    c. left foot because it is free of body weight
    d. left foot because it is closest to first base

Stance at First Base

72. You are on first base waiting to run to second. Which diagram shows the proper stance? [Refer to Diagram 6.]
    *b.

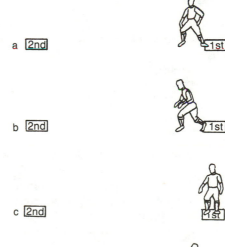

Diagram 6

Fly Ball

73. What should the base runner on third do when a deep fly ball is hit with less than two outs?
    *a. Tag up and wait to see if the ball is caught.
    b. Go halfway and advance if the ball is missed.
    c. Take three steps and wait for the coach's signal.
    d. Take two or three steps, tag, and go halfway.

Sliding

Advantage

74. What is an advantage of sliding?
    a. It is a faster way for a slow runner to reach base.
    b. It decreases the speed of the run.
    *c. It creates a smaller target for infielders to touch on a tag play.
    d. It helps avoid a force out.

Hook

75. What would be the best slide to use when trying to avoid an infielder's tag?
    a. headfirst
    *b. hook
    c. fade-away
    d. straight in

Pitching

Control

76. What is the most important thing for a pitcher to learn?
    a. pacing
    b. speed
    *c. control
    d. deception

Windup

77. Which technique would be most effective in helping the pitcher fool batters?
    a. a fast windup on a slow pitch
    b. a slow windup on a fast pitch
    c. no windup on some pitches
    *d. the same windup on all pitches

Stance

78. What should the pitcher do after releasing the ball?
    a. Face the batter.
    *b. Take an infielder's stance.
    c. Watch the pitch.
    d. Keep one foot on the rubber.

Slingshot Pitch

79. What type of pitch does the diagram show? [Refer to Diagram 7.]
    a. drop pitch
    b. windmill pitch
    c. rise pitch
    *d. slingshot pitch

Diagram 7

80. What is the difference between the slingshot and windmill deliveries?
    a. the path the ball travels to the plate
    b. the direction the ball curves or drops
    *c. the windup for release
    d. the preliminary stance

Knuckleball

81. Which diagram shows the proper grip to throw a knuckleball? [Refer to Diagram 8.]
    *c.

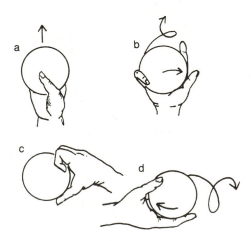

Diagram 8

Incurve

82. What technique is used to pitch an incurve?
    a. rotate wrist upward
    b. rotate wrist downward
    c. rotate wrist to the left
    *d. rotate wrist to the right

Fielding

General

83. What is the ready position for infielders?
    a. relaxed, crouched, weight on the heels, glove down near the ground
    *b. alert, knees and hips flexed, weight on the toes, arms relaxed
    c. alert, knees and hips flexed, feet together, arms relaxed at sides
    d. relaxed, knees slightly bent, feet spread

84. What is the major concept in catching a ball?
    *a. to absorb the force of the ball
    b. to get behind the ball
    c. to use two hands
    d. to keep the body away from the ball

Above the Waist

85. What is the most important thing to remember when catching a ball above the waist?
    a. to catch with the gloved hand only
    *b. to keep the thumbs together and fingers pointed up
    c. to wait for the ball to drop to waist level
    d. to hold the hands out in front of the body

Line Drive

86. How should the hands be held to catch a line drive at shoulder level?
    a. thumbs near each other and fingers pointing forward
    *b. thumbs near each other and fingers pointing upward
    c. hands held with palms forward and fingers pointing forward
    d. heels of hands together and fingers pointing forward

Low Throw

87. A throw is coming to you at knee level. What is the easiest way to make the catch?
    a. Fall to your knees and point your glove down.
    b. Fall to your knees and point your glove up.
    c. Step to your right and reach for the ball with your glove.
    *d. Bend your knees a little and open up your glove with the fingers pointed down.

Reading Hitter

88. Where should a fielder look to get the best hint of where the batter is trying to hit the ball?
    a. the catcher's signals
    *b. the batter's stance
    c. the coach at third base
    d. the position the batter is holding the bat

When to Move

89. When should a defensive player move on a hit ball?
    *a. as soon as the ball and bat make contact
    b. when the batter completes the swing
    c. after the ball's line of flight is established
    d. immediately before the batter swings

Force-Out

90. What procedure should the fielder follow in making a force-out?
    a. Touch the base, catch the ball, and move out of the way.
    b. Catch the ball, then stand on the base blocking the runner.
    c. Stand in front of the base and catch the ball.
    *d. Catch the ball, touch the base, and move out of the way.

Shortstop

91. What should the shortstop do if *not* in control of the ball?
    a. Throw it to first base anyway.
    b. Kick the ball to the second baseman.
    *c. Gain control of the ball, check the runners, and call time-out.
    d. Leave the ball alone and let another infielder pick it up.

Ground Ball

92. What is the most important consideration for an infielder when fielding a ground ball?
    a. getting in front of the ball
    *b. getting the glove down immediately
    c. charging the ball
    d. keeping the weight on the balls of the feet

93. What is the first thing an infielder should learn to field a ground ball successfully?
    a. to get in front of the ball
    b. to get in a ready position
    c. to play the ball
    *d. to keep the glove close to the ground

94. What is the correct method for fielding ground balls?
    a. Wait for the ball to roll to you.
    *b. Run to meet the ball and try to field it as early as possible.
    c. Wait until the ball has slowed down and then run to meet it.
    d. Creep up on the ball slowly.

95. A bouncing grounder is hit deep to your right. What is the quickest way to get to the ball?
    a. Stand up and run to the ball.
    b. Dive to your right and stab the ball.
    *c. Stay low and slide step to get behind the ball.
    d. Stay low and use a crossover step to get behind the ball.

96. What position is best for fielding a ground ball?
    *a. forward stride, knees bent and hips lowered, glove touching the ground
    b. forward stride, one knee on the ground, glove waist high
    c. side stride, one knee on the ground, glove waist high
    d. side stride, knees bent and hips lowered, glove touching the ground

97. How should the left fielder handle a hard hit ground ball?
    *a. Get down on one knee to block the ball.
    b. Charge the ball and scoop it up.
    c. Get in an infielder's stance to play the ball.
    d. Get down on two knees to block the ball.

98. Which factor would *decrease* a player's ability to catch a low bouncing ground ball?
    a. placing the body in line with the ball
    *b. placing the feet close together in the fielding stance
    c. giving slightly with the elbows as the ball contacts the hands
    d. bringing the throwing hand over the ball quickly after it contacts the glove

99. What is the best way for a right-handed person to field a ground ball?
    *a. Left foot forward, bend knees and hips.
    b. Feet parallel, bend from the waist.
    c. Right foot forward, bend knees and hips.
    d. Feet parallel, bend knees and hips.

Fly Ball

100. What principle must an outfielder know about the flight of the ball in order to judge a fly ball?
    a. The speed of the ball as it comes off the bat determines the distance the ball will go.
    *b. The angle of descent of the ball equals the angle of ascent.
    c. The height of the ball will determine the distance it will travel.
    d. The weight of the batter is proportional to the length of the hit.

101. Where should a fly ball be caught?
    a. at the waist
    b. at the shoulders
    *c. about head high
    d. below the waist

102. How should a fly ball be caught?
    a. with the bare hand and the glove covering it
    b. with the glove
    *c. with the glove and the hand covering it
    d. between the glove and the stomach

103. Which factors should be considered when judging a fly ball?
    1. sound
    2. speed
    3. wind
    4. direction
    5. height
    a. 2, 4
    b. 2, 3, 4
    c. 1, 2, 3, 4
    *d. 2, 3, 4, 5

104. You are the left fielder and see that the ball is going over your head on the right side. What should you do?
    a. Backpedal as fast as possible watching the ball at all times.
    *b. Turn and run, looking over the left shoulder.
    c. Turn and run, looking over the right shoulder.
    d. Turn and run, stopping when in line with the ball.

Factors

105. What factors determine the best position for fielding the ball?
    1. the height of the ball
    2. the position of other fielders
    3. the speed of the ball
    4. the throw the fielder must make
    a. 1, 2
    b. 2, 3
    c. 1, 2, 3
    *d. 1, 3, 4

Cut-Off Play

106. What should the infielder do who is designated as the cut-off player for a throw from the outfield?
    *a. Take a position in line with the throw approximately 20 to 30 feet in front of the base to which the throw is being made.
    b. Cut-off the ball regardless of the positions of the base runners.
    c. Take a position near second base because that allows the cut-off player to throw quickly to any base.
    d. Cut-off the ball only if the pitcher yells, "Cut."

Throwing

Sidearm

107. When is the sidearm throw used most often?
    *a. when the infielders need to make a quick throw
    b. when the pitcher is pitching
    c. when the catcher is attempting to throw out a runner stealing second base
    d. when the right fielder is attempting to throw out a base runner at first base

Flight From Outfield

108. Which flight of the ball is best when an outfielder is throwing the ball quickly to a base?
    a. high, lobbing ball that reaches the base before it bounces
    *b. low ball that reaches the base on one bounce
    c. low ball that reaches the base before it bounces
    d. medium high ball that reaches the base at chest level

Overhand

109. What is the correct procedure for a right-handed person to use on an overhand throw?
    a. Face the target, step ahead on the left foot.
    b. Left shoulder toward target, step ahead on the right foot.
    c. Face the target, step ahead on the right foot.
    *d. Left shoulder toward target, step ahead on the left foot.

110. What type of throw should the third baseman use when throwing to first base?
    *a. overhand
    b. sidearm
    c. snap with the wrist
    d. underhand

111. Which type of throw will be most effective for an outfielder trying to achieve distance?
    a. sidearm
    b. overhead
    c. bouncer
    *d. overhand

112. What is the advantage of the overhand throw?
    *a. its speed and power
    b. its accuracy
    c. its quickness
    d. its use by the pitcher

113. You must throw the ball from deep right field to home plate. What should you do to throw the ball that far?
    a. Run as fast as you can until you get close to first base, then fire in a sidearm throw.
    b. Run five steps, then heave the ball underhanded.
    c. Catch the ball and use an overhand throw immediately.
    *d. Catch the ball, take a hop-step, and throw overhanded immediately.

Outfield to Home

114. What is the best procedure for an outfielder to use when throwing the ball home?
    a. Throw the ball so that it reaches the catcher in the air.
    *b. Throw the ball so that it reaches the catcher on one bounce.
    c. Throw the ball so that it rolls into the catcher.
    d. Throw the ball so it will bounce at the catcher's feet.

Double Play

115. Where should the throw to the shortstop be to begin a successful double play?
    *a. about shoulder level, two steps behind second base on the outfield side of the bag
    b. about shoulder level, one step behind second base on the outfield side of the bag
    c. about waist level, two steps behind second base on the infield side of the bag
    d. about waist level, one step behind second base on the infield side of the bag

Tagging

Position

116. What is the correct position of an infielder getting ready to make a tag play?
    a. standing on top of the base
    b. standing to the right of the base
    c. standing slightly behind the base
    *d. straddling the base

117. What is the best body position for a tag play?
    a. Stay on one side of the bag.
    *b. Straddle the bag.
    c. Brace one foot behind the base.
    d. Block the base with the left foot.

118. How should a fielder tag a runner who is sliding into a base?
    a. Stand beside the base and place the glove hand on top of the base.
    b. Stand behind the base and place the glove hand in front of the base.
    *c. Straddle the base and place the glove hand in front of the base.
    d. Stand in front of the base and block the base.

Ball Placement

119. Where should the ball reach the baseman who is attempting to make a tag play?
    a. at waist level
    b. away from the runner's head
    c. at shoulder height
    *d. a few inches above the ground

Catcher

120. What is the best position for the catcher to be in when guarding home plate from a runner?
    a. in squat position with both knees on the ground
    *b. in squat position with one knee on the ground
    c. knees slightly bent and bent at the waist
    d. standing erect

Place to Tag

121. Where is the best place to tag a hook-sliding runner?
    a. on the player's waist or chest
    b. on the player's shoulder or arm
    *c. on the player's foot or ankle
    d. on the player's hip or thigh

122. Where is the best place to tag a base runner?
    *a. below the knees
    b. below the waist
    c. at the knees
    d. at the waist

Player Characteristics

Center Fielder

123. Which player is the fastest and most aggressive player in the outfield?
    a. left fielder
    *b. center fielder
    c. right fielder
    d. They should be equally fast and aggressive.

Shortstop

124. Which defensive position requires agility, speed, and a good throwing arm?
    *a. shortstop
    b. catcher
    c. pitcher
    d. left fielder

First Baseman

125. Which specific skill is most important for a first baseman?
    a. fast fielding ability
    *b. consistent catching ability
    c. accurate throwing ability
    d. quick moving ability

Strategy

Batting

126. What is the main offensive skill?
   *a. batting
   b. throwing
   c. baserunning
   d. pitching

Place Hitting

127. What is the most valuable offensive strategy?
   a. the hit-and-run play
   *b. place hitting
   c. fake bunting
   d. base stealing

First Batter

128. Which quality should the first batter in the lineup have?
   a. power hitter
   b. slow base runner
   *c. usually gets on base
   d. uses a big bat

129. What is the best trait for the lead-off batter to have?
   a. to be a strong hitter
   *b. to have a good eye for balls and strikes
   c. to be able to get the greatest number of bases from a hit
   d. to be a very fast runner

Weakest Hitter

130. Which batter is usually the weakest hitter?
   a. first batter
   b. fifth batter
   c. seventh batter
   *d. eighth batter

Best Hitter

131. Which batter is usually the best hitter?
   a. first batter
   b. second batter
   c. third batter
   *d. fourth batter

Strongest and Longest Hitter

132. What position in the batting order should the strongest and longest hitter occupy?
   a. second
   *b. fourth
   c. fifth
   d. seventh

Order

133. What is the general strategy concerning batting order?
   a. first, weak hitter; second, consistent hitter; third, fair hitter and bunter; fourth, longest and strongest hitter
   b. first, consistent hitter; second, fair hitter and bunter; third, weak hitter; fourth, longest and strongest hitter
   *c. first, one who can get on base; second, a fair hitter and bunter; third, a consistent hitter; and fourth, the strongest and longest hitter
   d. first, one who can get on base; second, a consistent hitter; third, a fair hitter and bunter; and fourth, the longest and strongest hitter

To Right Field

134. Where would be the best place to hit the ball if a runner is in scoring position at third base?
   *a. to right field
   b. to left field
   c. to second base
   d. through the pitcher's mound

135. You are the batter. You have teammates on second and third with no outs. What would you try to do?
   *a. Hit toward right field.
   b. Hit a home run.
   c. Hit through the pitcher.
   d. Hit through the second and third basemen.

Sacrifice Hit

136. What is the purpose of a sacrifice hit?
   a. to make an out when time is running out
   *b. to advance runners
   c. to make an out so a better batter can bat
   d. to check the ability of the outfield

Hit-and-Run Play

When to Use

137. In which situation can the hit-and-run play best be used?
   a. runner on first, two outs, behind by two runs
   b. runners on first and second, one out, score tied
   c. runner on second, no outs, behind by one run
   *d. runner on first, one out, score tied

138. When is the hit-and-run play used most?
   *a. There is a runner on first base.
   b. There is one out with the bases loaded.
   c. There is a base runner on third base.
   d. The next batter is a weak hitter and not likely to advance the runner.

Hit Placement

139. To which areas indicated on the diagram should a ball be hit when the hit-and-run play is on? [Refer to Diagram 9.]
   *a. Area a only
   b. Areas b and c
   c. Area b only
   d. Area c only

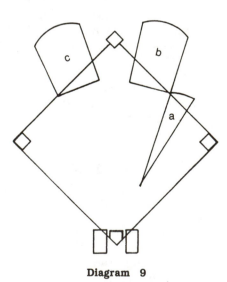

Diagram 9

140. What should the batter attempt to do on the hit-and-run play with a runner on first?
   a. Hit a fly ball.
   b. Hit a ground ball ahead of the runner.
   c. Swing at the ball but miss it to confuse the catcher.
   *d. Hit a ground ball behind the runner.

Bunt

When to Use

141. Which situation is best for bunting?
   *a. no outs, runner on first
   b. no outs, runner on third
   c. one out, runner on second
   d. one out, runner on third

142. When should a bunt be used?
   a. to catch the defensive team off guard
   *b. to advance a runner by bringing in the infield
   c. to bring in a runner from third base
   d. to draw the infield out of position

143. In which situation can a bunt best be used?
   a. runner on first, two outs, behind by two runs
   b. runners on first and second, one out, score tied
   *c. runner on first, no outs, behind by one run
   d. runners on first and third, one out, score tied

Squeeze Play

144. What is a squeeze play?
   a. a close play on a runner sliding into base
   *b. a play in which a runner on third base attempts to score on a bunt
   c. a play in which a runner is tagged out while sliding back into a base previously held
   d. a play in which the infielders pull in and cut off the runner at home plate

Base Runner

145. Which factor would be considered the *least* by a base runner who is on third base when a fly ball is hit?
   a. the number of outs
   *b. the number of base runners
   c. the throwing ability of the fielder
   d. the distance of the hit

Steal

146. When should a player attempt a steal?
   1. The catcher has a weak throwing arm.
   2. The ball is overthrown at a base.
   3. The infielders cover bases too slowly.
   4. The ball is played to another base.
   a. 1, 2
   *b. 1, 3
   c. 1, 3, 4
   d. 1, 2, 3, 4

Delayed

147. When is a delayed steal most effective?
    a. with base runners on first and second
    b. with a base runner on second
  *c. with base runners on first and third
    d. with bases full

Slide

148. A base runner is on third. The batter hits a drag bunt. Which slide is best for the base runner to attempt at home plate?
    a. headfirst slide
    b. straight slide
  *c. hook slide
    d. pop-up slide

Offensive Situations

Third Base Coach

149. The batting team is one run behind, with a runner on third and one out. The batter hits to the shortstop. A weak batter is up next. What is the best decision for the third base coach?
    a. Hold the runner on third and play it safe.
    b. Send the runner home and take a chance on a bad throw.
  *c. Hold the runner and pinch hit for the next batter.
    d. Send the runner home and pinch hit for the next batter.

Runner on Third

150. With a runner on third base, the batter hits a fly ball to center field. What should the runner on third base do?
  *a. Stay on base and attempt to score after the ball is caught.
    b. Stay on base to play it safe.
    c. Take a leadoff and run if the ball is missed.
    d. Take a leadoff and return to base if the ball is caught.

Ground Ball/Bases Loaded

151. What should the runner(s) do when a ground ball is hit with the bases loaded?
    a. Watch the base coach for a signal.
    b. Wait to see if the ball is foul.
  *c. Run to the next base.
    d. Check to see if the ball is caught.

General Defensive Strategy

Planning

152. What is the most valuable defensive strategy?
  *a. Rehearse what to do in different situations.
    b. Perfect the cut-off play.
    c. Establish a good batting order.
    d. Use a fast pitcher.

Batter's Position at Plate

153. What is the best gauge to determine the distance between the batter and the plate?
    a. the batter's hitting average
    b. the batter's stride
    c. the batter's height
  *d. the batter's reach

Left-Handed Batter

154. What defensive strategy should be used against a left-handed batter?
    a. Fielders shift to their right.
  *b. Fielders shift to their left.
    c. Fielders assume their normal positions.
    d. Fielders assume a closer position.

Defensive Adjustments

155. A right-handed batter has assumed a stance at the plate with the left foot drawn back from the inside line of the batter's box. What is the best adjustment the defense can make?
    a. Right fielder moves closer to foul line.
    b. Second baseman moves behind the base.
    c. Center fielder moves in toward the plate.
  *d. Shortstop moves toward third base.

Positions

Field Director

156. Which player is in the best position to direct defensive team play?
    a. pitcher
    b. shortstop
    c. center fielder
  *d. catcher

First Baseman

157. Although not necessarily fielding the ball, which player is involved in most ground ball plays to the infield?
  *a. first baseman
    b. second baseman
    c. third baseman
    d. shortstop

Second Baseman

158. As shown in the diagram, what is the best position for the second baseman when no one is on base? [Refer to Diagram 10.]
     *d.

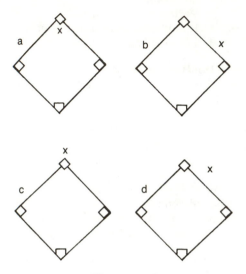

Diagram 10

Third Baseman/Bunt

159. What is the best position for the third baseman when expecting a bunt?
     a. even with the third baseline
     *b. approximately 5 to 7 feet in front of the bag toward home plate
     c. on the baseline 1 to 2 feet in front of the base
     d. one step away from the base and two steps in toward home plate

Shortstop

160. Which role is *not* the responsibility of the shortstop?
     a. to cover third base on slowly batted balls hit to the third baseman
     b. to assist on relays from left field
     *c. to field bunts along the third baseline
     d. to cover second base in double play situations when the ball is hit to the right side of the infield

Infield

161. What are the best positions for the infielders with two outs and the bases loaded?
     a. deep positions
     *b. medium positions
     c. close-in positions
     d. bunt positions

162. Where should the infield play when the bases are loaded and there are no outs?
     a. Remain at normal playing position.
     *b. Pull in front of the baseline.
     c. Move back 2 or 3 feet from normal position.
     d. Shift to the left.

163. Which infield depth is most appropriate when a runner is on third and the run is critical to the outcome of the game?
     a. regular infield depth
     b. deep infield depth
     c. double play infield depth
     *d. close-in infield depth

164. Which position is assumed by the infield when there is a runner on first with less than two outs?
     a. deep position
     *b. medium position
     c. close-in position
     d. bunt position

Fielders

165. The game is tied in the bottom of the seventh inning, and there are no outs with the bases loaded. How should the infield and outfield be positioned?
     a. infield deep, outfield in close
     b. infield in close, outfield deep
     *c. infield and outfield in close
     d. infield and outfield deep

Center Field

166. Who has priority to catch a ball hit into shallow center field?
     a. second baseman
     *b. center fielder
     c. right fielder
     d. shortstop

Outfield

167. Who is responsible for catching a fly ball falling between the infielders and outfielders?
     *a. outfielders
     b. infielders
     c. whoever calls it
     d. the fastest runner

Backup

First Baseman

168. When should the catcher back up the first baseman?
     a. when the ball is bunted toward third base
     b. when a long fly ball is hit to center field
     c. when there is a runner on second and a grounder is hit to the shortstop
     *d. when there is a runner on first and a grounder is hit to the shortstop

169. Which base is usually *not* backed up by the pitcher?
     *a. first base
     b. second base
     c. third base
     d. home

Third Baseman

170. A long drive is hit to deep left field with no outs. Which player should back up the third baseman?
     a. shortstop
     *b. pitcher
     c. catcher
     d. first baseman

171. Who should back up third base on a throw from right field?
     a. catcher
     b. shortstop
     c. second baseman
     *d. pitcher

Outfielders

172. When not actually fielding a ball, what is the outfielder's primary responsibility?
     a. covering the nearest base
     *b. backing up the other outfielders
     c. relaying throws to the infield
     d. telling the other fielders where to throw the ball

Right Fielder

173. The batter hits a line drive to right field. Which player should back up the right fielder?
     a. second baseman
     b. left fielder
     c. shortstop
     *d. center fielder

Cover

Home

174. Who covers home plate on a wild pitch with runners on base?
     a. catcher
     *b. pitcher
     c. first baseman
     d. third baseman

175. Who covers home plate when the catcher is drawn away?
     *a. pitcher
     b. first baseman
     c. third baseman
     d. Home plate is not covered when the catcher is away.

First

176. A bunted ball is fielded by the first baseman. Who covers first?
     *a. second baseman
     b. catcher
     c. pitcher
     d. right fielder

Relay

177. The batter hits a long fly ball to left field that the left fielder drops. Who should be the relay player for the throw by the left fielder?
     a. second baseman
     *b. shortstop
     c. third baseman
     d. center fielder

178. Which infielder should be the relay player for the right fielder?
     a. first baseman
     *b. second baseman
     c. pitcher
     d. catcher

Double Play

179. The shortstop successfully fields a hard bounding ball. There is a runner on first with less than two outs. What should the shortstop do with the ball?
     a. Throw to first for the sure out.
     b. Hold the ball to make sure the runners do not advance past second.
     c. Throw back to the pitcher to stop play.
     *d. Throw to the second baseman who then throws to first.

180. You are a right-handed pitcher. The first batter you face hits a single. The next batter hits a sharp grounder to you. What should you do?
    a. Throw to first base.
    b. Let the ball go through to the second baseman.
    *c. Turn to your left and throw to second.
    d. Turn to your right and throw to second.

181. There is a runner on first with one out. The ball is hit to the first baseman. What should the first baseman do?
    a. Tag first base and throw the ball to the pitcher.
    b. Touch the runner coming to first and run and touch the runner going to second.
    c. Throw to the second baseman on second.
    *d. Throw to the shortstop covering second.

Rundown

182. It is the bottom of the fifth inning and the score is tied at 1-1 with one out. The base runner gets caught between second and third base. There are no other base runners. To which base should the infielders chase the runner?
    a. first base
    *b. second base
    c. third base
    d. home plate

Cut Off

183. Who becomes the cut-off person when the ball is hit to deep right field with a play at home?
    *a. first baseman
    b. shortstop
    c. second baseman
    d. pitcher

184. Which player is in the best position to cut off throws from left field and why?
    a. second baseman because of position in center of the field
    *b. third baseman because of closeness to home plate
    c. pitcher because of strong arm
    d. shortstop because of versatility in handling the ball

185. There are runners on first and third. A ball is hit to center field. There is no chance to get the lead runner at home. Where should the ball be thrown?
    a. to the plate to keep any other runs from coming in
    b. to first to try to get the batter out
    c. to the cut-off player between first and second
    *d. to the cut-off player between second and third

Pitching

186. What is the best pitch for a pitcher to give a left-handed cleanup batter?
    a. low and inside
    b. low and outside
    *c. high and inside
    d. high and outside

187. How should the pitcher pitch to a batter who stands forward in the box?
    a. inside
    b. outside
    *c. fast
    d. slow

188. How should a pitcher pitch to a batter who stands away from the plate?
    a. inside
    *b. outside
    c. fast
    d. slow

Defensive Situations

First Base

189. What should the first baseman do on a throw that is obviously out of reach?
    *a. Leave the bag and field the ball.
    b. Keep one foot on the base and stretch in the direction of the throw.
    c. Jump and attempt to catch the ball with both hands.
    d. Jump and try to knock the ball down and make a play.

190. The runner is on second base. The batter hits a slow roller to the pitcher. Where should the pitcher throw the ball?
    *a. first base
    b. second base
    c. third base
    d. home plate

191. There are no outs, and a runner is on second. Where should the shortstop play the ball just fielded?
    a. Throw immediately to first base.
    b. Throw immediately to second base for a double play.
    c. Throw immediately to third.
    *d. Throw to first after checking the runner.

Second Base

192. With no one on base, the batter hits a short line drive to the right fielder. There are two outs. Where should the right fielder throw the ball if the ball is *not* caught?
    a. first base
    *b. second base
    c. third base
    d. home plate

193. Runners are on second and third bases with no outs. The batter hits a line drive into right field. Where should the right fielder throw the ball?
    a. first base
    *b. second base
    c. third base
    d. home plate

Third Base

194. With a base runner on first base, the batter hits a grounder in the hole between the shortstop and third baseman. There is only one out. Where should the left fielder throw the ball?
    a. first base
    b. second base
    *c. third base
    d. home plate

195. With base runners on first and third bases, the batter hits a ground ball right over second base to the center fielder. There is one out and both runners are going. Where should the center fielder throw the ball?
    a. first base
    b. second base
    *c. third base
    d. home plate

196. There is a base runner on first. The hit is to left field and the base runner advances beyond second base. Where should the ball be returned?
    a. second baseman
    *b. third baseman
    c. shortstop
    d. catcher

197. With base runners on second and third bases, the cleanup hitter hits a long fly ball to left field. There are no outs, and both base runners will tag up when the fly ball is caught. Where should the left fielder throw the ball?
    a. first base
    b. second base
    *c. third base
    d. home plate

Home Plate

198. The runner is on third base, and there are no outs. A fly ball is hit to the right fielder who catches it. Where should the right fielder throw the ball?
    a. first base
    b. second base
    c. third base
    *d. home plate

199. The bases are loaded with one out. The batter hits a medium deep fly ball to left field. Where should the ball be thrown?
    a. first base
    b. second base
    c. third base
    *d. home plate

Infield to First

200. Assume you are an infielder and receive the ball on a hit. There are no outs, and runners on first and second base. Where would you throw the ball?
    a. first base
    b. Look the lead runner back, then throw to first.
    *c. second base
    d. third base

201. Assume you are an infielder and receive the ball on a hit. There are no outs, and runners are on second and third. Where would you throw the ball?
    a. first base
    *b. Look the lead runner back, then throw to first.
    c. second base
    d. third base

202. Assume you are an infielder and receive the ball on a hit. There are two outs, and runners are on second and third. Where would you throw the ball?
    *a. first base
    b. Look the lead runner back, then throw to first.
    c. second base
    d. third base

203. Assume you are an infielder and receive the ball on a hit. There is one out, and runners are on second and third. Where would you throw the ball?
    a. first base
    *b. Look the lead runner back, then throw to first.
    c. second base
    d. third base

204. Assume you are an infielder and receive the ball on a hit. There are no outs, and a runner is on third. Where would you throw the ball?
    a. first base
    *b. Look the lead runner back, then throw to first.
    c. second base
    d. third base

205. Assume you are an infielder and receive the ball on a hit. There is one out, and a runner is on second. Where would you throw the ball?
    a. first base
    *b. Look the lead runner back, then throw to first.
    c. second base
    d. third base

206. Assume you are an infielder and receive the ball on a hit. There are two outs with a runner on third. Where would you throw the ball?
    *a. first base
    b. Look the lead runner back, then throw to first.
    c. second base
    d. third base

Infield to Second

207. Assume you are an infielder and receive the ball on a hit. There is no one out, and a runner is on first. Where would you throw the ball?
    a. first base
    b. Look the lead runner back, then throw to first.
    *c. second base
    d. third base

208. Assume you are an infielder and receive the ball on a hit. There is one out and a runner on first. Where would you throw the ball?
    a. first base
    b. Look the lead runner back, then throw to first.
    *c. second base
    d. third base

Rules

Game

Minimum Innings

209. What is the minimum number of innings for an official game?
    a. seven
    b. six
    *c. five
    d. four

Players

Minimum Number

210. If a team needs nine players to begin an official game, what is the minimum number of players needed to continue a game?
    a. six
    b. seven
    c. eight
    *d. nine

Field Positions

211. What positions do the Xs represent in the diagram? [Refer to Diagram 11.]
    a. left fielder, third baseman, second baseman, pitcher
    b. center fielder, shortstop, left fielder, right fielder
    *c. right fielder, second baseman, shortstop, third baseman
    d. left fielder, center fielder, second baseman, pitcher

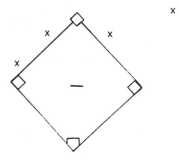

Diagram 11

Substitute

212. In which situation does a substitute officially become part of the game?
   a. if a runner, when advancing past the base where starting
   b. if a pitcher, after the umpire calls, "Play ball"
   *c. if a fielder, after taking the place of the replaced fielder
   d. if a batter, after the first pitch is made

Reenter Game

213. What right to reenter does a player have who has been removed from the game?
   a. Reenter only at the previous position.
   b. Reenter only as catcher.
   *c. Reenter only as coach.
   d. not to reenter except in emergency

Field and Equipment

Field

214. Which diagram shows the correct placement of the bases? [Refer to Diagram 12.]
   *c.

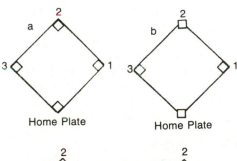

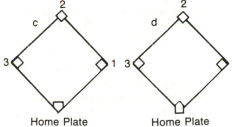

Diagram 12

Outfield

215. Which area is the outfield?
   *a. the fair territory beyond the infield
   b. the foul territory beyond the playing field
   c. the area provided for the spectators
   d. the area beyond the home run fence

Mitts

216. Which players may use a mitt?
   a. the catcher and the third baseman only
   b. the catcher only
   *c. the first baseman and the catcher only
   d. the pitcher and the third baseman only

Ball Size

217. What is the official size of a softball?
   a. 10 inches in diameter
   *b. 12 inches in diameter
   c. 14 inches in diameter
   d. 16 inches in diameter

Umpires

Calling Game—Rain

218. After four innings, it begins to rain. Who has the authority to terminate the game?
   a. the home team
   b. the visiting team
   c. the team with the most runs
   *d. the umpire

Illegal Turn

219. Which duty is the specific responsibility of the base umpire?
   a. determining whether a fly ball is caught legally
   b. deciding whether a batted ball is fair or foul
   *c. deciding whether a batter has made an illegal turn at first
   d. deciding whether the pitcher has made an illegal pitch

Pitching

Warm-Up Pitches

220. How many warm-up pitches is a pitcher allowed?
   *a. 1 minute or five warm-up pitches
   b. 2 minutes or six warm-up pitches
   c. 3 minutes or six warm-up pitches
   d. as many pitches as the pitcher and the umpire deem necessary

Number of Steps

221. How many steps may a pitcher take while releasing the ball?
   a. four
   b. three
   c. two
   *d. one

Pitching Distance

222. What are the pitching distances for men's and women's softball?
     - a. 40 feet for men, 40 feet for women
     - b. 42 feet for men, 38 feet for women
     - c. 46 feet for men, 46 feet for women
     - *d. 46 feet for men, 40 feet for women

Pitching Rubber

223. Which portion of the pitching rubber is it *not* permissible for the pitcher's foot to touch?
     - a. front
     - *b. side edge
     - c. middle
     - d. rear edge

Illegal Pitch

224. Which technique constitutes an illegal pitch?
     - a. one-step approach while delivering the ball
     - b. 1-second pause before delivering the ball
     - c. hand below the hip
     - *d. wrist farther from the body than the elbow

225. The pitcher throws an illegal pitch. What decision will the umpire make?
     - a. No pitch is called; the count remains the same.
     - b. A ball is called on the batter; the base runner may not advance.
     - c. An automatic walk occurs; the batter advances to first.
     - *d. A ball is called on the batter; base runners advance one base.

Legal Pitch

226. The batter is in the batter's box looking toward the third base coach for a signal. The pitch is delivered within the strike zone. What is the umpire's decision and why?
     - a. No pitch is called because the batter was not ready.
     - b. A ball is called because of an illegal pitch.
     - *c. A strike is called because time-out was not requested.
     - d. A ball is called because the batter was not ready.

No Pitch

227. Which situation constitutes a *no pitch*?
     - a. The catcher is in the catcher's box.
     - *b. The runner is called out for leaving the base too soon.
     - c. The pitcher delivers a pitch with excessive spin and the batter swings.
     - d. The pitcher's hand is taped.

Strike Zone

228. Where is the strike zone?
     - a. between the shoulders and ankles and over the plate
     - b. between the neck and the top of the knees and over the plate
     - *c. between the armpits and the top of the knees and over the plate
     - d. between the waist and the top of the knees and over the plate

Batting

Order

229. The batting order is A, B, C, D. Batter A hits a ground ball and runs to first base. Batter C is walked to first base by the pitcher. Batter D comes up to bat. Before the ball is pitched, the pitcher reminds the umpire that Batter B has *not* been up to bat. Which batter is out?
     - a. A
     - *b. B
     - c. C
     - d. D

Innings at Bat

230. The score going into the bottom of the seventh inning is 5 for Team A and 3 for Team B. Team A is the home team. How many times at bat will each team have during this game?
     - a. Team A, seven; Team B, seven
     - b. Team A, seven; Team B, six
     - *c. Team A, six; Team B, seven
     - d. Not enough information is given to determine the answer.

Stepping on Plate

231. The batter steps on the plate while contacting the ball. The ball is hit foul. What is the call by the umpire and why?
     - a. strike because the ball went foul
     - b. ball because the hit went foul
     - *c. The batter is out for contacting the ball while out of the batter's box.
     - d. The batter is out for hitting too many foul balls.

Missing Third Strike

232. The bases are loaded with no outs. The batter swings and misses a third strike. How is the batter put out?
     - a. The catcher must hold the ball to put the batter out.
     - b. The catcher must tag the batter to make the out.
     - c. The catcher must throw to first to put the batter out.
     - *d. The batter is automatically out.

Fair Ball

233. Which ball is a fair ball?
     *a. settles in fair territory in the infield
     b. touches fair territory and rolls foul in the infield
     c. rolls outside third base into the outfield
     d. hits foul territory in the outfield and bounces fair

Foul Ball

234. Which ball is considered a foul ball?
     a. ball that falls on fair ground beyond first or third base
     b. ball that touches first, second, or third base
     *c. ball that, after being hit, touches the batter in the batter's box
     d. ball on or over fair ground when bounding past the infield

235. Which hit is considered a foul ball?
     a. The ball hits third base and rolls out-of-bounds.
     *b. The ball lands on the line and rolls out-of-bounds in front of first base.
     c. The ball lands 3 feet in front of home plate.
     d. The ball settles on home plate.

Batter Not Out

236. In which situation is the batter *not* out?
     *a. A batter with one strike is hit by the batted ball.
     b. A batter's third strike is caught by the catcher.
     c. A batter with two strikes bunts foul.
     d. A batter's foul ball is caught by the catcher.

Foul Tip

237. On the first pitch, the batter hits a foul ball that goes shoulder high and is caught by the catcher. What is the ruling?
     a. The batter is out automatically.
     *b. A strike is called.
     c. The catcher may tag the runner out.
     d. The batter may try to beat the catcher's throw to first.

238. When does a foul tip become an out?
     *a. when it occurs on the third strike
     b. when it goes above the batter's head
     c. when it occurs on the second strike
     d. when it occurs on the first strike

239. The batter hits a foul tip on the second strike. The base runner on first base goes safely to second base. What is the ruling?
     a. The base runner must return to first base.
     b. The base runner may advance to third base without liability of being put out.
     c. The base runner is automatically out.
     *d. The base runner is allowed to remain at second base.

Ball Lodged in Fence

240. A batted ball rolls under the outfield fence. What is the ruling?
     a. Base runners may advance at their own risk.
     b. Ground rule triple is in effect.
     c. The batter must hit again.
     *d. The batter must stop at second base.

Base Hit

241. When is a batted ball scored as a hit?
     a. when a runner is forced out by a batted ball or would have been forced out, except for a fielding error
     b. when a player fielding a batted ball retires a preceding runner with ordinary effort
     c. when a fielder fails in an attempt to retire a preceding runner and in the scorer's judgment, the batter-base runner could have been retired at first base
     *d. when the batter-base runner reaches first base safely

Third-Strike Rule

242. What does the third-strike rule state?
     a. The batter receives a strike if the bat is dropped in the batter's box.
     *b. The batter may run to first base if the catcher drops the third strike and first base is not occupied with less than two outs.
     c. The pitcher may drop the ball after the batter has the third strike.
     d. The batter may run to first base if the catcher drops the third strike and the bases are loaded with less than two out.

Infield Fly Rule

243. There are runners on first and second. The batter hits an infield fly with one out. What is the decision of the umpire?
    a. The batter may advance to first in case ball is dropped; runners must advance.
    b. The batter is automatically out; runners may advance without risk of being put out.
    *c. The batter is automatically out; runners may advance at their own risk.
    d. The batter is out; runners are automatically out.

244. There are runners on first and second bases with one out. The batter hits a fly ball to the third baseman who drops it intentionally. What is the decision?
    *a. The batter is out; runners may advance at their own risk.
    b. The batter is out; runners may not advance.
    c. The batter becomes a base runner; runners advance one base without risk of being put out.
    d. The batter becomes a base runner; runners may advance at will without risk of being put out.

245. When is the infield fly rule in effect?
    *a. when the batter hits an infield fly with less than two outs and runners on first and second
    b. when the batter hits an infield fly with one out and a runner on first
    c. when the batter hits an infield fly with two outs and runners on first and second
    d. when the batter hits an infield fly with one out and runners on first and third

246. In which situation is the ball still in play?
    a. after a foul ball is dropped
    *b. after the infield fly rule is called
    c. after a batter is hit by a pitched ball
    d. after a ball has been blocked

Base Runner

Hit by Ball

247. A base runner, attempting to advance on a hit, is struck by the batted ball while off base and before the ball passes an infielder. What is the ruling?
    a. The ball is in play; the batter and base runner may advance at their own risk.
    *b. The ball is dead, the runner is out; the batter is awarded first base.
    c. The ball is dead; the batter and base runner are out.
    d. The ball is dead; base runner is awarded an extra base; batter is out.

248. A throw from the outfield to the catcher hits the base runner. What is the ruling?
    a. The runner is out; other base runners may not advance.
    b. The runner must go back to previously held base.
    *c. The runner is not out; other baserunners may advance.
    d. The runner is out; other base runners may advance.

Fly Ball

249. When may a base runner advance to another base when a fly ball is hit?
    *a. as soon as the ball is caught
    b. as soon as the ball is hit
    c. as soon as the ball leaves the pitcher's hand
    d. The base runner may not advance to another base on a fly ball.

Advance Due to Walk

250. When may a runner on first base advance without liability to be put out?
    a. when the batter hits a fly ball that is caught
    *b. when the base runner is forced to vacate the base because the batter is walked
    c. when the batter hits a foul ball that is dropped
    d. when the catcher misses a pitched ball on the third strike

Runs Into Baseman

251. Runners are on first and third bases. The base runner from third runs into the third baseman, who is attempting to field a bunt. What is the decision concerning the batter and runner on first?
    - a. They may advance to first and second bases with liability of being put out.
    - b. They may advance to second and third bases with liability to be put out.
    - *c. They may advance to first and second bases without liability to be put out.
    - d. They may advance to second and third bases without liability to be put out.

Advance Without Liability

252. In which situation is the runner allowed to advance without liability to be put out?
    - a. when the ball leaves the pitcher's hands on a pitch
    - *b. when a pitched ball goes over the backstop
    - c. when the ball is overthrown into foul territory and is not blocked
    - d. when the ball falls from the pitcher's hand during the windup

Legal to Leave Base

253. When is the earliest that it is legal for a base runner to leave the base?
    - a. when the pitcher's pivot foot crosses the front edge of the pitcher's plate as the step is taken toward home plate
    - b. when the catcher catches the ball
    - c. when the batter hits the ball
    - *d. when the pitcher's nonpivot foot crosses the front edge of the pitcher's plate as the step is taken toward home plate

Return to Base

254. In which situation may a base runner return to a base without liability of being put out?
    - a. when colliding with the shortstop who is fielding the ball on the baseline
    - b. when being struck by a batted ball between second and third base
    - c. when overrunning second base after touching it and not attempting to continue to third base
    - *d. when dislodging a base and *not* attempting to advance to the next base

Overthrow

255. The batter hits a grounder to the shortstop. On the throw to first, the ball is overthrown and goes under the player's bench. What will the runner be allowed to do?
    - *a. to advance at least to second without liability to be put out
    - b. to remain safe at first base
    - c. to advance around the bases with liability to be put out
    - d. to advance to any base without liability to be put out until the ball reaches the mound

Interference

256. The bases are loaded and the on-deck batter interferes with the defensive player's opportunity to make a play on the runner. Who is called out?
    - a. the batter
    - b. the runner on first
    - c. the runner on second
    - *d. the runner on third

Appeal Play

257. At what point in the ball game should an appeal play be made?
    - *a. before the next pitch
    - b. after the next pitch
    - c. after the inning is complete
    - d. at the end of the ball game

258. Which situation is an appeal play?
    - a. An infielder throws the batter out at first.
    - *b. A base runner leaves the base before a fly ball is touched by the fielder.
    - c. A batter strikes out.
    - d. A base runner is called out after being tagged by a fielder who juggles the ball.

259. Which play is *not* an appeal play?
    - a. The base runner fails to touch a base.
    - *b. The base runner leaves the base before the ball is pitched.
    - c. The base runner leaves the base before a caught fly ball is touched by a fielder.
    - d. The batter bats out of order.

Scoring

260. What determines the winner of a game?
    - *a. the team that scores the most runs in a regulation game
    - b. the team that has the most hits in a regulation game
    - c. the team that scores five runs first
    - d. the team that makes the fewest errors

Third-Out Run

261. In which third-out situation is a run scored?
    *a. The batter overruns first and is tagged out before reaching second base.
    b. The base runner leaves base before the pitcher releases the ball.
    c. The base runner is forced out by the batter becoming a base runner.
    d. The batter grounds to the first baseman who steps on the base.

Foul Tip

262. Which situation can *not* possibly help score a run?
    a. line drive
    b. sacrifice fly
    *c. foul tip
    d. foul ball

Recording Score

263. With runners on first and third, the batter hits a deep fly ball to right field that is caught by the right fielder. The runner on third base scores. How would this be scored?
    a. L-9
    b. F-9
    c. G-9
    *d. SAC-9

264. How is a strikeout recorded?
    a. SO
    *b. K
    c. BB
    d. SP

Reading Scorecard

265. What does the 3 under Column A indicate about Johnson? [Refer to Diagram 13.]
    a. batting average
    b. attempts to steal
    *c. assists
    d. position assignment

PLAYER	P	AB	R	H	PO	A	E	RBI
Johnson	6	3	1	2	2	3	0	1
Long	3	3	0	0	1	2	1	0
Burns	8	3	1	2	1	1	0	0

Box Score

Diagram 13

266. What is Burns' batting average for the game, and how is it decided? [Refer to Diagram 13, Question 265.]
    *a. .667; by dividing the number of hits by the number of times at bat
    b. .500; by dividing the number of runs by the number of hits
    c. .300; by dividing the number of times at bat by the number of runs
    d. .150; by dividing the number of times at bat by the number of hits

267. What does the 3 under column P indicate about Long? [Refer to Diagram 13, Question 265.]
    a. Long is the third batter.
    b. Long is the third baseman.
    *c. Long is the first baseman.
    d. Long is the pitcher.

Reading Scoring Block

268. What has occurred in the scoring block shown in the diagram? [Refer to Diagram 14.]
    a. hit to right field, double, error on throw to third
    b. hit to right field, single, to second on error by right fielder
    c. hit to right field, double, second out
    *d. hit to right field, double, out trying for third

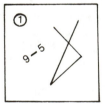

Diagram 14

269. What has occurred in the scoring block shown in the diagram? [Refer to Diagram 15.]
     a. hit to left field, error on third baseman advancing runner to second; second out in trying for third
     *b. hit to left field, runner advances to second on error by first baseman; runner is retired at third base on a play from the catcher to the shortstop for the second out
     c. hit to left field, runner advances to second on error by third baseman; runner is retired at third base on a play from the pitcher to the third baseman for the second out
     d. hit to left field; error on second baseman advancing runner to home for second run

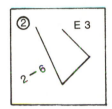

Diagram 15

Foul Tip

270. In which situation would a putout *not* be credited to the catcher?
     a. when the batter interferes with the catcher
     *b. when the batter hits a foul tip
     c. when the batter bats out of order
     d. when the batter hits a foul ball caught by the catcher

Fielder

271. In which situation would a putout *not* be credited to a fielder?
     a. when the fielder catches a line drive
     b. when the fielder catches a thrown ball that retires the batter
     c. when the fielder touches a base runner with the ball while the base runner is off base
     *d. when the runner leaves the base too soon

Sacrifice Fly

272. How is "turn at bat" scored for a player who hits a sacrifice fly?
     a. as a pass
     b. as a hit
     c. as one turn at bat
     *d. as no turn at bat

Acknowledgments

Colleagues and students who contributed suggestions and ideas for the Softball test questions are: D. Andrews, Y. Andrews, L. Bauguss, P. Bonner, C. Brown, C. Cooper, A. Davis, C. Edwards, W. Howlett, D. Layden, L. Lowden, G. Madren, L. McKinney, K. Millar, S. Morris, L. Nelson, K. Rogers, K. Setliff, J. Shelton, C. Speagle, and C. Wally.

Suggested Readings

Coaching manual level II—Technical. (1979). Vaniere, Ontario: Canadian Amateur Softball Association.

Dobson, M. J., & Sisley, B. L. (1980). *Softball for girls.* Huntington, NY: Robert E. Krieger.

Drysdale, S. J., & Harris, K. S. (1982). *Complete handbook of winning softball.* Rockleigh, NY: Allyn and Bacon.

Jones, B.J., & Murray, M.J. (1980). *Softball concepts for teachers and coaches.* Dubuque, IA: Wm. C. Brown.

Official guide and rule book. (1986). Oklahoma City, OK: Amateur Softball Association of America.

Sisley, B. L. (1980). *Success in softball: Drill cards for teachers and coaches.* Eugene, OR: Author.

Whiddon, N. S., & Hall, L. T. (1980). *Teaching softball.* Minneapolis: Burgess.

Swimming and Diving

Lynne P. Gaskin, Consultant

This collection of test questions on swimming and diving is divided into ten content areas:

- Principles
- General Techniques
- Safety
- Front Crawl and Back Crawl
- Sidestroke and Overarm Sidestroke
- Breaststroke, Inverted Breaststroke, and Butterfly
- Elementary Backstroke
- Trudgen, Trudgen Crawl, and Double Trudgen
- Identification and Comparison
- Diving and Jumping

When terms such as *top* and *bottom*, *upper* and *lower*, and *above* and *below* are used, it should be clear that these directional terms are used in relation to either the water or the swimmer. Some questions may need to be revised to make terminology consistent with that used in class.

Similar questions were included to provide more selection opportunities and to accommodate the different levels of technicality used by the instructor.

Principles

Newton's three laws of motion (inertia, acceleration, and action and reaction) and Archimedes's law of water displacement and buoyancy are stressed in this category. Included in this section are items on relaxation, leverage, speed, force, endurance, and gravity.

Resistance	1 to 7
Force	8 to 13
Efficiency	14 to 20
Buoyancy	21 to 25

Resistance

1. Why is streamlining of strokes important?
    *a. reduces the resistance of the water to motion
    b. increases the beauty of the stroke
    c. aids in the relaxation of the swimmer
    d. provides a more buoyant feeling

2. Why is it important to keep the body as level and streamlined as possible?
    a. to slow down the body movement
    b. to make the stroke more forceful
    c. to allow for change of direction
    *d. to lessen water resistance

Lynne P. Gaskin is a swimming and diving instructor and former swimming coach. She is currently at the University of North Carolina at Greensboro.

3. Why does a swimmer want to extend the body when swimming?
   - a. to feel good
   - b. to glide
   - *c. to reduce resistance
   - d. to rest

4. Why does a swimmer want to keep the arms close to the body during the recovery phase of a stroke?
   - a. It looks nice.
   - b. It balances the body.
   - *c. It causes less resistance.
   - d. It rests the arms.

5. What should a swimmer do to maximize the hand efficiency of a stroke?
   - a. Decrease hand resistance during both the recovery and propulsive phases of the stroke.
   - *b. Decrease hand resistance during the recovery phase and increase it during the propulsive phase.
   - c. Increase hand resistance during both the recovery and propulsive phases.
   - d. Increase hand resistance during the recovery phase and decrease it during the propulsive phase.

6. What is the best body position for reducing resistance?
   - *a. one that gives the smallest possible surface against the direction of travel
   - b. one in which the body is horizontal in the water
   - c. one in which the arms are close to the body
   - d. one that gives the largest possible surface against the direction of travel

7. The resistance that water furnishes can be used to the swimmer's advantage. In which situation is the resistance a *disadvantage*?
   - a. when the swimmer pushes with as broad a surface as possible
   - b. when the swimmer pushes in the direction opposite from the one the swimmer wants to go
   - *c. when the swimmer has enough motion to make a glide possible
   - d. when the swimmer pulls with as broad a surface as possible

Force

8. In which direction should the force be directed when stroking?
   - a. toward the bottom
   - b. sideward
   - c. upward
   - *d. toward the feet

9. In which direction is force applied in any swimming stroke?
   - a. in the direction in which the swimmer is moving
   - b. at right angles to the direction in which the swimmer is moving
   - *c. opposite to the direction in which the swimmer is moving
   - d. toward the bottom of the pool

10. Which action of any stroke causes the person to move through the water?
    - a. glide
    - b. negative
    - *c. positive
    - d. slice

11. Which type of pressure gives maximum force to any stroke?
    - a. pressure in the intended direction of travel
    - *b. pressure opposite to the intended direction of travel
    - c. pressure toward the surface of the water
    - d. pressure toward the bottom of the pool

12. Why should the feet stay under water when kicking?
    - a. to give maximum buoyancy
    - b. to give maximum speed
    - c. to give maximum strength
    - *d. to give maximum force

13. Which diagram illustrates Newton's third law of action and reaction? [Refer to Diagram 1.]
    *a.

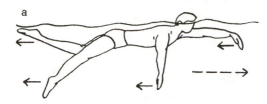

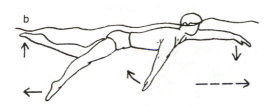

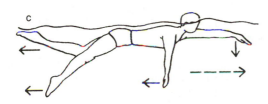

- - - - → Direction of Swimmer

———→ Direction of Force

Diagram 1

Efficiency

14. What is swimming efficiency?
    a. ability to swim a variety of strokes
    *b. ability to swim with a minimum of effort
    c. ability to swim with speed
    d. ability to swim with as few breaths as possible

15. What are the requirements for a swimmer who wishes to swim long distances?
    a. to be able to do strokes rapidly
    *b. to be able to swim with a minimum of effort
    c. to be able to swim a wide variety of strokes
    d. to be able to swim with full body tension

16. What is meant by muscular efficiency in swimming?
    *a. The muscles not contributing to the movement are relaxed.
    b. As many muscles as possible are being used.
    c. All muscles are relaxed when moving.
    d. All muscles are tensed when moving.

17. Why should one learn a variety of strokes?
    a. to become a good swimmer
    b. to become a distance swimmer
    c. to be able to swim a variety of strokes
    *d. to be able to swim both fast and restful strokes

18. What is the importance of timing in a swimming stroke?
    a. enables one to swim faster
    b. enables one to increase the number of times to breathe
    c. enables one to alternate resting and working phases of the stroke
    *d. enables one to coordinate arms, legs, and breathing efficiently

19. What is the best way to do a stroke?
    a. exactly as described in books
    *b. slightly modified for each individual
    c. quickly to build up speed
    d. slowly to build up endurance

20. Beginners usually progress faster when which condition is achieved?
    *a. relaxation in the water
    b. water temperature at 78°
    c. slow progression of skills
    d. pleasant instructor

Buoyancy

21. A body submerged in water is lifted by a force equal to the weight of the liquid it displaces. What principle does this define?
    a. inertia
    *b. buoyancy
    c. action and reaction
    d. leverage

22. To what does Archimedes's law refer?
    a. action and reaction
    *b. buoyancy
    c. submersion
    d. acceleration

23. Which fact *least* affects the buoyancy of an individual?
    a. body build
    b. amount of fat tissue
    *c. depth of the water
    d. relaxation

24. Which person will float most easily?
    a. the person who is muscular
    *b. the person who has some excess weight
    c. the person who has a large skeletal frame
    d. the person who is big boned and heavyset

25. Where is the center of buoyancy usually located?
    a. head
    *b. chest
    c. hips
    d. legs

General Techniques

Breathing	**26 to 27**
Bobbing	**28 to 29**
Floating	**30 to 38**
Gliding	**39 to 41**
Finning	**42 to 43**
Sculling	**44 to 47**
Treading	**48 to 52**
Turning	**53 to 55**
Surface Diving	**56 to 62**
Underwater Swimming	**63 to 67**
Resting Stroke	**68 to 71**
Position	**72 to 77**
Timing	**78 to 79**
Miscellaneous	**80 to 84**

Breathing

26. What is the proper breathing technique for any swimming stroke?
    *a. Air is inhaled through the mouth then exhaled through the nose and mouth.
    b. Air is inhaled through the nose and mouth then exhaled through the nose and mouth.
    c. Air is inhaled through the nose and exhaled through the nose.
    d. Air is inhaled through the mouth and exhaled through the mouth.

27. Which statement is *not* characteristic of proper breathing?
    a. Inhale quickly.
    b. Breathe at regular intervals.
    c. Breathe with little interference with stroke mechanics.
    *d. Inhale only through mouth, exhale only through nose.

Bobbing

28. What is the primary purpose of bobbing?
    a. to clear the head of water
    b. to overcome fear of the water
    c. to find out how deep the water is
    *d. to develop rhythmic breathing

29. Why is bobbing used?
    a. to increase arm strength
    *b. to increase breath control
    c. to increase submerging ability
    d. to decrease fear of going under water

Floating

30. Which type of float provides the most buoyant position for the body?
    a. back float
    b. prone float
    *c. jellyfish float
    d. side float

31. Which type of individual will most likely float best?
    *a. an individual with considerable fat tissue
    b. an individual who is short and muscular
    c. an individual with a muscular lower body
    d. an individual with a muscular upper body

32. What is the best position for the arms and hands when floating on the back?
    *a. in the water above the head
    b. in the water out to the sides
    c. above the water out to the sides
    d. on top of the water

33. What might contribute to one's ability to perform a back float?
    *a. extending the arms above the head
    b. exhaling
    c. attempting to keep the feet near the surface
    d. bending at the waist

34. What effect does a large volume of air in the lungs have on floating?
    a. makes it more difficult to float
    b. makes it impossible to float
    *c. makes it easier to float
    d. makes it impossible to sink

35. What is the most common error that beginners make when trying to float on the back?
    a. keeping the head in line with the body
    b. keeping the hips up
    c. dropping the legs below the level of the trunk
    *d. taking a sitting position in the water

36. What is the recommended sequence of body movements to recover to a standing position from a prone float?
    a. press arms, tuck knees
    b. press arms, lift body
    c. tuck knees, lift head, press arms
    *d. press arms, tuck knees, lift head

37. Which type of controlled breathing aids floating the most?
    a. long inhales, short exhales
    b. short inhales, long exhales
    *c. short inhales, short exhales
    d. long inhales, long exhales

38. Which diagram shows an *incorrect* way to float? [Refer to Diagram 2.]
    *c.

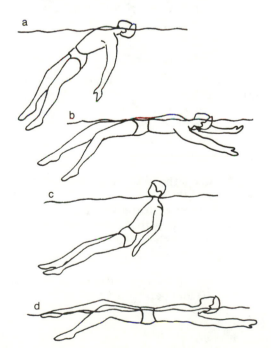

Diagram 2

Gliding

39. What is a prone glide?
    a. lying facedown with no push
    b. lying on the back with a slight push
    c. lying on the back with no push
    *d. lying facedown with a slight push

40. What is a glide?
    a. safety procedure
    b. power phase of the arms
    c. movement following each stroke
    *d. phase of a stroke following the power phase

41. What effect will a glide have upon a resting stroke?
    *a. increases efficiency
    b. decreases efficiency
    c. increases style
    d. decreases style

Finning

42. What is *finning*?
    a. swimming with fins
    b. smoothing the surface of the water
    *c. an arm action
    d. a water stunt

43. What should be done with the hands and lower arms when finning?
    a. Apply slight downward pressing movements against the water.
    b. Hold out of the water about shoulder height.
    c. Apply slight upward pressing movements.
    *d. Apply a series of thrusts toward the feet.

Sculling

44. What is *sculling*?
    a. another name for the dog paddle
    *b. a safety device
    c. the technical name for the crawl
    d. the technical name for treading water

45. Which skill requires a figure eight movement of the hands?
    a. finning
    b. floating
    c. treading
    *d. sculling

46. You are in a supine position moving in the direction of your head. What is the proper technique when the hands are sculling away from the body?
     *a. thumbs down and palms turned out
     b. thumbs up and palms turned in
     c. thumbs inside and palms turned down
     d. thumbs outside and palms turned up

47. What is the correct arm movement when sculling with the arms at the sides?
     a. lengthwise figure eight pattern
     b. lengthwise oval pattern
     *c. sideways figure eight pattern
     d. sideways oval pattern

Treading

48. Which kick is *least* effective for treading water?
     a. scissor kick
     b. breaststroke kick
     c. bicycle kick
     *d. flutter kick

49. What is the most efficient kick to use when treading water?
     *a. scissor kick
     b. flutter kick
     c. trudgen kick
     d. frog kick

50. What is the position of the body when treading?
     a. prone position
     *b. vertical position
     c. supine position
     d. horizontal position

51. How far out of the water should the body be when treading water?
     a. from the chest up
     b. from the waist up
     *c. from the chin up
     d. from the forehead up

52. What is the best way to keep the head above the surface of the water when in a vertical position?
     a. Reach up with the arms and move them vigorously.
     b. Work the hands rapidly with outward pressure on the water.
     c. Hold hands above the water and kick.
     *d. Move the hands back and forth with downward pressure on the water.

Turning

53. You want to change directions while swimming on the front. What is the first thing you should do?
     a. Pull harder with the arm closest to the direction of the turn.
     b. Push harder with the arm away from the direction of the turn.
     c. Tuck the body to make the turn sharper.
     *d. Turn your head in the direction you want to go.

54. What is the proper technique for a tank turn when swimming the front crawl?
     *a. The body turns away from the arm that first touches the side of the pool.
     b. The trailing arm is the first to make contact with the side of the pool.
     c. The body turns toward the arm that first touches the side of the pool.
     d. Both hands make contact simultaneously.

55. What is the proper technique for a tank turn when swimming on the back?
     a. The body turns away from the arm that first touches the side of the pool.
     b. The trailing arm is the first to make contact with the side of the pool.
     *c. The body turns toward the arm that first touches the side of the pool.
     d. Both hands make contact simultaneously.

Surface Diving

56. What is the most important factor in executing a surface dive?
     a. arm action
     b. pike of the body
     c. breath control
     *d. lift of the legs

57. What causes the body to go downward in a surface dive?
     a. pulling with the arms
     b. bending at the hips
     c. tucking the head
     *d. lifting the legs

58. How many underwater strokes are needed to reach a 10-foot depth on a good surface dive?
     *a. zero
     b. one
     c. two
     d. three

59. The surface dive requires the body to make two angles to get submerged. What are they?
    a. first a 45° angle and then a 180° angle
    *b. first a 90° angle and then a 90° angle
    c. first a 180° angle and then a 90° angle
    d. first a 180° angle and then a 45° angle

60. Which stunt is a lead-up to the surface dive?
    a. rolling over
    b. tub
    *c. handstand
    d. somersault

61. Which swimming skill leads most readily into a surface dive?
    a. front crawl
    b. sidestroke
    c. treading water
    *d. breaststroke

62. Which diagram shows the correct position of the body during the initial phase of the pike surface dive? [Refer to Diagram 3.]
    *b.

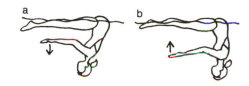

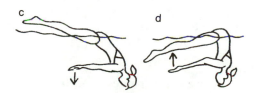

Arrows indicate the direction
the hands are facing

Diagram 3

Underwater Swimming

63. Which kick is most effective when swimming underwater?
    a. flutter kick
    b. scissor kick
    *c. breaststroke kick
    d. bicycle kick

64. Which skill is developed in underwater swimming?
    a. endurance
    *b. breath control
    c. speed swimming
    d. rhythmic breathing

65. In what way does underwater swimming help a swimmer?
    a. helps the swimmer level off the body
    b. helps the swimmer increase stroke speed
    c. helps the swimmer hold the breath longer
    *d. helps the swimmer reduce fear of the water

66. You are swimming underwater where the water is *not* very clear. What technique should you use?
    a. Swim rapidly so you can surface sooner.
    *b. Take very short strokes with hands reaching forward.
    c. Take very short strokes with hands out to the sides so not to interfere with your view.
    d. Shut your eyes to keep the dirt out.

67. Which stroke can be adapted most easily to underwater swimming?
    a. front crawl
    b. sidestroke
    *c. breaststroke
    d. trudgen

Resting Stroke

68. What is the function of a resting stroke?
    a. to let a swimmer catch a breath
    b. to protect against cramps and stitches
    *c. to provide a relaxing stroke for a tired swimmer
    d. to allow swimmers to talk to one another

69. What is characteristic of resting strokes?
    a. They are strenuous.
    b. They are hardly ever used.
    *c. They contain a glide.
    d. They are done on one's back.

70. What is the principal difference between a resting stroke and other strokes?
    a. body position
    *b. execution of a glide
    c. rhythm of stroke
    d. name of stroke

71. What is the main difference between a resting stroke and other strokes?
    a. the way it is taught
    b. the number of kicks used
    *c. the use of a glide
    d. the position of the head in the water

Position

72. What is meant by *leveling off*?
    a. swimming on the surface of the water
    b. having the head at hairline level in the water
    *c. assuming a prone position
    d. performing a surface dive

73. In what position is the body after leveling off?
    *a. horizontal
    b. vertical
    c. sideways
    d. lateral

74. What would you be most likely to see from a supine position?
    a. bottom of the pool
    b. gutters/sides of the pool
    c. racing lanes in the water
    *d. ceiling/sky

75. Which factor is the most important prerequisite to perfecting a stroke?
    *a. learning good body position
    b. learning rhythmical breathing
    c. adjusting to the water temperature
    d. bobbing at least 15 times consecutively

76. Of what importance is the position of the head?
    a. enables the swimmer to see where he or she is going
    *b. determines the body position
    c. causes a streamlined effect
    d. leads the rest of the body

77. Your body is riding too high in the water. How can this be changed?
    a. Put the head back and bring the legs up.
    b. Put the head back and lower the legs.
    *c. Bring the head up and lower the legs.
    d. Bring the head up and bring the legs up.

Timing

78. What is meant by timing in any swimming stroke?
    a. the alternation of the drive with the rest or glide
    b. the relationship between the recovery and the drive
    c. rhythmic breathing
    *d. coordination of the arms, legs, and breathing

79. Which factor is needed most to have an effective stroke?
    a. endurance
    b. strength
    *c. rhythm
    d. speed

Miscellaneous

Recovery

80. What is the part of a swimming stroke called in which the arms and legs are moving into a position to apply force?
    a. start
    *b. recovery
    c. approach
    d. drive

81. Which phase of the stroke calls for repositioning the arms and/or legs to create forward momentum?
    a. positive phase
    b. rest phase
    *c. recovery phase
    d. power phase

Eyes

82. Why do you keep your eyes open while swimming?
    *a. to know if you are going straight
    b. to know if you are getting to the edge
    c. to know if you are getting into deep water
    d. to know if your eyes are getting conditioned to water

Games

83. Why are water games especially effective?
    a. to help teach children to swim
    *b. to help adjust to the water
    c. to help motivate advanced swimmers
    d. to add variety to a lesson

Form

84. Which combination of factors is most essential when judging form of swimming strokes?
    a. rhythm, speed, style, power
    *b. rhythm, relaxation, power, form
    c. force, coordination, rate, time
    d. style, relaxation, coordination, time

Safety

Personal Safety

85. Which safety rule should be observed by all swimmers?
    a. Do not swim at night.
    *b. Do not swim alone.
    c. Do not swim in unknown water.
    d. Do not swim in water over 25 feet deep.

86. What should a swimmer do when frightened or fatigued?
    a. Call for help.
    b. Swim a fast crawl to shallow water.
    *c. Float or scull.
    d. Hold on to a swimming companion for support.

87. A poor swimmer stands up and unexpectedly finds the water is overhead in depth. How is the swimmer most likely to be successful in getting to shallow water?
    a. by trying to do a face float
    *b. by trying to do a back float
    c. by trying to start a sidestroke
    d. by keeping the arms high in the water to pull

88. What should poor swimmers do if they collide?
    a. The poorer swimmer should hold on to the stronger swimmer.
    *b. The swimmers should swim away from each other as quickly as possible.
    c. The swimmers should attempt to keep each other afloat.
    d. The swimmers should be courteous and assist each other in any way needed.

89. You are swimming in deep water and are grabbed by another swimmer who is in trouble. What should you do?
    a. Swim to shore, towing the other person.
    b. Hit the other person, hoping the grasp will be released.
    *c. Drop under water, push up on other person, and back away before coming up.
    d. Use your legs to push the other person away.

90. What is the best course to take when caught in a current?
    *a. Swim diagonally with the current.
    b. Swim diagonally across the current.
    c. Swim with the current.
    d. Swim against the current.

91. Which stroke is easiest to swim while clothed?
    a. front crawl
    b. elementary backstroke
    c. back crawl
    *d. sidestroke

Cramps

92. Which parts of the body most often get cramps when swimming?
    *a. the calf of the leg and foot
    b. the upper leg and knee
    c. the abdomen and chest
    d. the hand and arm

93. What is the most common cause of cramps in the fingers, toes, arms, or legs?
    a. swimming slowly
    *b. fatigue
    c. swimming in water that is too cold
    d. overeating

94. How can cramps be released, usually?
    a. by another person
    b. by getting out of the water
    *c. by stretching and rubbing
    d. by floating

95. What should be done to relieve a cramp?
    a. continue swimming to work it out
    b. swim to the edge and let the leg dangle
    c. get out of the water and massage the cramp
    *d. stretch the muscle

Survival Float

96. What should swimmers do if they must remain afloat for a long time?
    a. Tread water.
    *b. Use survival float.
    c. Swim front crawl.
    d. Swim a variety of strokes.

97. What is the proper breathing technique for the survival float?
    *a. Grab a breath above the surface of the water.
    b. Exhale gradually while under the water.
    c. Exhale forcefully while under water.
    d. Stay on top of the water and breathe normally.

98. You are doing the survival float and get water in your mouth. What should you do?
    a. Swallow it.
    b. Exhale the water with the air through your mouth.
    *c. Wait until your mouth gets above the surface and spit the water out.
    d. Hold your breath and swim to the nearest object.

99. How many breaths per minute would a swimmer take who is efficient in the survival float?
    *a. 3 to 4 breaths per minute
    b. 9 to 10 breaths per minute
    c. 12 to 15 breaths per minute
    d. 15 to 18 breaths per minute

100. You find yourself in the water with your street clothes on. When would it *not* be appropriate to disrobe and do the survival float until rescued?
    a. The water is deep.
    b. The water is murky.
    c. The water is rough.
    *d. The water is cold.

Flotation Device

101. What is a major problem with a weak swimmer using a flotation device?
    a. It gets in the way of learning a stroke.
    b. It is used to increase buoyancy.
    *c. It produces a dependence that would be unsafe.
    d. It holds the body in an unnatural position.

Diving and Jumping

102. Which diving procedure is necessary from a safety standpoint?
    a. Make entry a good distance from the board.
    b. Keep body completely extended.
    *c. Keep arms extended above the head until beginning the ascent to the surface.
    d. Keep the legs together, knees straight, and toes pointed.

103. Where is it safe to execute a back dive?
    *a. off a diving board
    b. off the side of the pool at the deep end
    c. Either of these places is safe.
    d. Neither place in a. and b. is safe.

104. In which situation would a jump be more suitable than a dive?
    a. The water is very deep.
    b. The water is very chilly.
    c. The water is just over your head.
    *d. The water is unknown.

105. What is the most important factor to check before diving?
    a. the presence of a buddy
    *b. the depth of the water
    c. the temperature of the water
    d. the spring of the board

Rescue

106. What is the first thing you should do if you see a swimmer struggling in the water?
    a. Go in the water after the person.
    *b. Look for a device with which to reach.
    c. Call for help.
    d. Try to calm the person by talking.

107. You are helping a person to shore who is within arm's reach. Where should you make contact with the person?
    a. hand
    *b. wrist
    c. hair
    d. neck

108. A swimmer is in trouble 2 to 3 feet from the side of the pool. You are on the deck near the swimmer. What should you do?
    a. Jump in and grab the person.
    b. Run to get the lifeguard.
    *c. Extend an arm or leg to the swimmer.
    d. Quickly find a towel or shirt to extend to the swimmer.

109. In what position should a person be to reach with an arm or a leg from the deck to rescue a swimmer?
    a. on hands and knees
    *b. on stomach
    c. on side
    d. on back

110. What would you do if someone were in trouble about 8 feet from the dock?
    a. extend an arm
    *b. extend a pole
    c. throw a ring buoy
    d. swim to person

111. In what position should a person be after extending a pole to a swimmer?
    *a. standing with legs bent and apart and with the weight back
    b. sitting on the side of the pool
    c. kneeling on one knee
    d. standing with weight on front leg to get greater reach

112. It is unsafe for a swimmer who is *not* trained in lifesaving to go into the water to make a rescue. Which situation would be an exception?
    a. to rescue an adult close to the side of the pool
    b. to rescue a child in deep water in the middle of the pool
    c. to rescue an adult in deep water in the middle of the pool
    *d. to rescue a child in the shallow water

113. A person is in trouble in the water 50 feet from shore. What can a swimmer of intermediate skill do?
    a. Swim out to help.
    b. Take a surfboard to the person.
    c. Throw a ring buoy.
    *d. Swim a rescue tube out to the person.

114. What would be the wisest thing for an advanced swimmer to do if someone were in trouble about a quarter of a mile from the dock?
    a. Float something out.
    b. Throw a ring buoy.
    c. Swim to the swimmer.
    *d. Row a boat to the person.

115. A lifeguard has just brought a swimmer to safety. The lifeguard is exhausted and asks you to help. The victim looks unconscious. What should you do first?
    a. Give the victim four quick breaths.
    b. Give the victim one breath every 5 seconds.
    *c. Find out if the victim is unconscious.
    d. Go for help.

Artificial Respiration

116. Which method of artificial respiration is recommended?
    a. back pressure, arm lift
    b. chest pressure, arm lift
    *c. mouth-to-mouth
    d. mouth-to-nose

117. An adult swimmer is rescued and *not* breathing. Which method of artificial respiration is most effective and simplest to do?
    a. nose-to-mouth
    b. arm lift, back pressure
    *c. mouth-to-mouth
    d. resusitator

118. What is the recommended number of breaths when giving an adult artificial respiration?
    *a. 10 to 12 per minute
    b. 13 to 15 per minute
    c. 16 to 18 per minute
    d. 19 to 21 per minute

119. You have given four quick breaths to a victim, repositioned the head, and tried giving another breath. You still feel air coming back at you. What do you suspect is wrong?
    *a. The victim has a foreign object in the airway.
    b. The victim's tongue is in the way.
    c. You did not blow enough air into the victim.
    d. You are blowing too fast.

120. What is the surest sign that air is *not* getting into the lungs?
    *a. Air is not coming out.
    b. The stomach is rising.
    c. The skin is not gaining color.
    d. The fingernails return to normal color.

Drowning

121. What is the ultimate cause of drowning?
    a. water in the stomach
    b. water in the lungs
    c. stomach cramps
    *d. suffocation

Swimming Areas

122. Which procedure would you follow to become familiar with a new swimming area?
    a. Make a series of bank dives and swim an underwater pattern.
    *b. Make a series of surface dives and swim an underwater pattern.
    c. Make no dives and swim only on top of water.
    d. Make no dives and only make jumping entries.

123. What are the most important conditions for swimming safely in a lake?
    a. There is clear and warm water.
    b. There are boats.
    c. There is an unobstructed beach area.
    *d. There is a lifeguard and a roped-off place to swim.

Boats and Canoes

124. You are in a boat that overturns. You are fully clothed. What should you do?
    *a. Stay with the boat.
    b. Swim to shore.
    c. Remove clothing.
    d. Call for help.

125. What rule should be followed when canoeing or boating?
    a. every passenger a good swimmer
    b. half the passengers good swimmers
    c. one passenger in the group a good swimmer
    *d. a life preserver on each nonswimmer

Front Crawl and Back Crawl

Front Crawl

Arms	126 to 135
Legs—Flutter Kick	136 to 142
Breathing	143 to 148
Head Position	149
Coordination and Body Position	150 to 153

Back Crawl

Arms	154 to 159
Legs (Inverted Flutter Kick)	160 to 163
Head Position	164
Coordination and Body Position	165 to 166

Front Crawl

Arms

126. How do the arms move in the front crawl?
    *a. They move continuously.
    b. They pause at the finish of each arm drive.
    c. They pause before entering the water.
    d. They work faster on the recovery than on the drive.

127. Which statement describes the power phase of the arm stroke in the front crawl?
    *a. alternating, pull with one arm followed by pull of other arm
    b. simultaneous, both arms press against the water at the same time
    c. as the arm enters the water, fingers first
    d. as the elbows are raised from the water

128. Where should each hand enter the water following the recovery in the front crawl?
    a. in front of the face
    b. in front of the opposite shoulder
    *c. in front of the same shoulder
    d. out to the side of the shoulder

129. In what position should the arms be when performing the front crawl?
    a. straight at all times
    *b. bent slightly when underwater
    c. along the side of the body while underwater
    d. bent 90° as they go underwater

130. Which part of the arm leads in the recovery phase of the front crawl?
    a. palm of hand
    b. forearm
    *c. elbow
    d. fingertips

131. Where do the arms recover when swimming the front crawl?
    *a. clearly out of the water
    b. on the surface of the water
    c. just under the surface of the water
    d. deep underwater

132. What is the correct recovery arm position for the front crawl?
    a. full extended
    b. fully flexed
    c. partially extended
    *d. partially flexed

133. Which statement is correct concerning the recovery phase of the front crawl arm stroke?
     *a. Elbow swings upward and forward with the hand trailing behind it.
     b. Elbow swings slightly upward and forward, and the hand swings forward before the elbow reaches the shoulder.
     c. Elbow swings forward in an extended position with the hand leading.
     d. Elbow swings upward and forward while the other hand and arm rest.

134. Which technique is an *error* in the recovery of the front crawl arm pull?
     a. wrist below elbow
     *b. wrist above elbow
     c. elbow out of water first
     d. fingers in the water first

135. Which part of the arm stroke for the front crawl is *incorrectly* stated?
     a. Fingers lead in entering the water in front of the shoulder.
     b. Hand presses backward near the centerline of the body as the elbow bends.
     c. Elbow draws close to the trunk and comes out of the water first.
     *d. Hands and arms reach forward in front of the head.

Legs—Flutter Kick
136. Where does the action of the flutter kick originate?
     a. the ankle joint
     *b. the hip joint
     c. the lower back
     d. the knee joint

137. Which statement describes the correct leg action for the front crawl?
     a. Knees are flexed and the lower leg supplies most of the power.
     *b. Legs are fairly straight and the power is supplied from the hips.
     c. Legs are fairly straight and the ankles flex to supply the power.
     d. Ankles, knees, and hips are flexed and all three supply power.

138. Which statement best describes the joint action of the flutter kick?
     a. flexibility at the ankle, knee, and hip joints
     b. flexibility at the ankles and knees but not at the hips
     *c. flexibility at the ankles and hips but not at the knees
     d. flexibility at the knees but not at the ankles and hips

139. What is the position of the legs for the thrust phase of the flutter kick?
     a. knees bent, ankles stiff
     b. knees stiff, ankles stiff
     *c. knees straight, ankles relaxed
     d. knees stiff, ankles bent

140. How high are the legs lifted in the flutter kick?
     a. The legs are lifted out of the water to the knees.
     *b. The heels only break the surface of the water.
     c. The feet are raised above the surface.
     d. The feet and legs stay several inches under the water.

141. What is the most important contribution the kick makes to the crawl stroke?
     a. aids in forward progress of the body
     *b. maintains balance and stability of the body
     c. increases the aesthetic quality of the stroke
     d. makes the stroke easier to perform

142. Why is the emphasis on the upbeat of the flutter kick?
     a. to keep the feet from going too far under the water
     b. to keep the knees from bending too much
     *c. to provide an efficient thrust for moving forward in the water
     d. to help keep the toes pointed, giving a better thrust

Breathing
143. Why is rhythmic breathing used in the front crawl?
     a. to limit oxygen debt
     b. to establish a beat
     c. to have a coordinated stroke
     *d. to have a more efficient stroke

144. When does the intake phase of breathing occur in the front crawl?
     a. as the arm on the breathing side just enters the water from the recovery
     b. as the arm on the breathing side leaves the water on the recovery
     *c. as the arm on the breathing side has just finished the pull in the water
     d. as the arm on the breathing side has just started the pull underwater

145. When does inhalation occur in the front crawl?
   a. as the arm on the breathing side enters the water
   b. as the arm opposite the breathing side recovers
   *c. as the arm on the breathing side leaves the water
   d. as the elbow opposite the breathing side leaves the water

146. What is the correct breathing movement in the front crawl?
   a. Lift the head and inhale, face to the front.
   b. Lift the head and inhale, face to the side.
   *c. Roll the head and inhale, face to the side.
   d. Roll the head to both sides and inhale on each side.

147. Which statement describes the position of the head during rhythmic breathing for the front crawl?
   a. Head is lifted out of the water.
   b. Head is kept forward.
   c. Head is submerged.
   *d. Head is turned to the side.

148. What is the proper head action to breathe when swimming the front crawl?
   a. Head lifts forward to get air.
   *b. Head turns to either side for a breath.
   c. Head and body turn to get breath.
   d. Head turns and lifts to get air.

Head Position

149. Which statement describes the proper head position for the front crawl?
   *a. Water level is just at the hairline.
   b. Water level is just at the nose level.
   c. Water level is above the head.
   d. Water level is just above the ears.

Coordination and Body Position

150. Which statement describes a front crawl?
   *a. Swimmer takes six flutter kicks for each cycle of the arms.
   b. Scissor kick is used twice for each cycle of the arms.
   c. Scissor and flutter kicks are combined for each cycle of the arms.
   d. Kick may vary but is done in coordination with the arm cycle.

151. You are swimming lengths of the front crawl and notice that you keep drifting to the left. What mistake are you most likely making?
   a. turning the right foot inward
   *b. pulling harder with the right arm than with the left arm
   c. bending the body at the waist
   d. pulling the arms too far beneath the body before recovering

152. Which statement best describes the relationship of the arm action to the kick for the total power of the front crawl?
   a. Power supplied by the arm action and the kick is nearly equal.
   b. Kick usually supplies more power than the arms.
   *c. Arm action usually provides about 70% of the total power.
   d. Kick supplies slightly less power than the arms.

153. What is another name for front crawl swimming?
   a. butterfly
   b. dolphin
   *c. freestyle
   d. breaststroke

Back Crawl

Arms

154. Which part of the arm enters the water first in the back crawl?
   a. wrist
   *b. little finger
   c. forearm
   d. elbow

155. When do the arms enter the water in the back crawl?
   a. together
   *b. one, then the other
   c. alternately, in uneven rhythm
   d. after the glide

156. In which direction should the hands and arms push and maintain force in the power phase of the back crawl?
   a. toward the head, close to the body
   *b. toward the feet, close to the body
   c. toward the head, directly under the body
   d. toward the feet, directly under the body

157. Where should the arms recover in the back crawl?
    a. directly under the body in the water
    b. close to the side of the body underwater
    *c. directly over the side of the body out of the water
    d. close to the body out of the water

158. A back crawl swimmer pulls with one arm while the other rests at the side. Is this good technique and why?
    a. No, the swimmer cannot bend the arm and push.
    *b. No, the swimmer sacrifices continuous power.
    c. Yes, the swimmer can relax the arm momentarily.
    d. Yes, the swimmer can give a more efficient push with the opposite arm.

159. What is a *fault* in the back crawl?
    a. allowing the arms to be slightly flexed
    b. rotating arms in opposition
    *c. letting the elbows enter before the hands
    d. reaching back with the small finger leading

Legs—Inverted Flutter Kick

160. Which kick is used in the back crawl?
    a. breaststroke kick
    b. dolphin kick
    c. inverted scissor kick
    *d. inverted flutter kick

161. When is most of the force applied in the back crawl kick?
    a. as the legs push downward
    *b. on the upward movement of the legs
    c. equally on the upward and downward movements of the legs
    d. alternately on the upward and downward movements of the legs

162. Which action is most important when executing the inverted flutter kick in the back crawl?
    a. Legs are kept straight.
    *b. Upbeat of the kick is emphasized.
    c. Ankles are flexed.
    d. Kick is from the knees.

163. What leg movement would most likely keep the swimmer from moving well when swimming the back crawl?
    *a. Legs are bicycling.
    b. Legs are moving from the knees only.
    c. Legs are moving too slowly.
    d. Legs are moving from the hips.

Head Position

164. What is the best head position for the back crawl?
    *a. head tilted slightly toward the chest
    b. head in normal line with the body
    c. head tilted back slightly
    d. head tilted back as far as possible

Coordination and Body Position

165. How many inverted flutter kicks are there in each back crawl stroke?
    a. three
    b. four
    c. five
    *d. six

166. Which diagram shows the correct position of the body in the water for the back crawl? [Refer to Diagram 4.]
    *c.

Diagram 4

Sidestroke and Overarm Sidestroke

Reference to the top arm means the arm at the surface of the water, over the hip; the bottom arm is the one closer to the bottom of the pool, extended above the head when the swimmer is in the glide position.

Sidestroke

Arms

167. What is the main use of the arms in the sidestroke?
    a. power
    b. speed
    *c. stability
    d. streamlining

168. In which direction should the arm that initiates the action pull when swimming the sidestroke?
    a. toward the bottom of the pool
    b. toward the top shoulder
    *c. toward the feet
    d. toward the neck

169. Which action is a *fault* in the arm pattern for the sidestroke?
    a. using force during the power phase of the arms
    b. keeping the top arm close to the body
    *c. letting the top arm push beyond the thigh line
    d. keeping both arms in the water

Legs—Scissor Kick

170. Which kick is most commonly used with the sidestroke?
    a. breaststroke kick
    b. inverted scissor kick
    c. flutter kick
    *d. scissor kick

171. What is the name of the kick used in the sidestroke?
    a. breaststroke kick
    *b. scissor kick
    c. flutter kick
    d. dolphin kick

172. Which part of the action provides the positive force in the scissor kick?
    a. bending of the knees
    b. outward separation of the legs
    *c. closing of the legs
    d. glide position of the legs

173. Which statement identifies the timing of the power phase of the sidestroke kick?
    a. as the knees are drawn up toward the body
    b. as the legs separate
    c. at the same time power is applied by both arms
    *d. at the same time the top arm pushes to the hip

174. Which leg goes forward in the scissor kick after the legs are brought up toward the hips?
    a. Bottom leg goes forward.
    *b. Top leg goes forward.
    c. Right leg goes forward.
    d. Left leg goes forward.

175. What is the proper position of the legs during the glide in the sidestroke?
    a. legs straight and together, toes drawn toward the knees
    b. legs straight and vertically separated
    c. legs straight and horizontally separated
    *d. legs straight and together, toes pointed

176. Which practice is a *fault* in the sidestroke kick?
    *a. moving the top leg toward the surface
    b. keeping the legs together at the end of the stroke
    c. keeping the legs together on the initial phase of the recovery
    d. letting the legs spread easily rather than forcibly

177. In which case would the swimmer be performing an inverted scissor kick?
    a. Top leg moves forward with the bottom leg.
    b. Top leg moves forward while the bottom leg moves backward.
    c. Top leg moves backward with the bottom leg.
    *d. Top leg moves backward while the bottom leg moves forward.

Head Position

178. What is the proper position for the head during the sidestroke?
    a. whole face in the water
    b. back of head in the water
    *c. cheek and ear in the water
    d. top of head in the water

179. Which factor is of greatest help in keeping the body from rolling when performing the sidestroke?
    a. position of the arm resting on the thigh
    b. position of the leading arm
    *c. position of the head
    d. position of the legs on the recovery phase

Breathing

180. Which statement best describes the recommended technique for exhaling in the sidestroke?
    a. Swimmer should exhale as the lower arm and the upper arm bend.
    b. Swimmer should exhale as the upper arm is in an extended position at the thigh.
    *c. Swimmer should exhale as the lower arm and the legs are going through their positive action.
    d. Swimmer should exhale as the upper arm and the legs are going through their positive action.

Coordination and Body Position

181. What is the body position on the sidestroke?
    a. vertical
    b. prone
    c. supine
    *d. side horizontal

182. At what stage in the sidestroke is the main power given?
    a. as knees are drawn up toward the body
    b. as legs separate, top leg moving forward
    c. as power is applied by both arms
    *d. as legs are brought together

183. Which other part of the sidestroke is in the recovery stage at the same time the top arm is recovering?
    a. bottom arm
    *b. legs
    c. inhalation
    d. glide

184. What is the relationship of the top arm to the legs in the sidestroke?
    *a. As the top arm pushes, the legs are brought together.
    b. As the top arm pushes, the legs are in a glide position.
    c. As the top arm pushes, the other arm pulls.
    d. As the top arm pushes, the legs are flutter kicking.

185. The sidestroke is described below. Is it listed in the correct sequence?
    1. Bottom arm starts and goes through the positive action while the top arm and legs recover.
    2. Body is in a side horizontal position with the back flat and the legs and arms extended.
    3. Top arm and legs go through their positive actions.
    4. A moderate glide follows.
    a. Yes, the order is correct.
    *b. No, switch 1. and 2.
    c. No, switch 2. and 3.
    d. No, switch 1. and 4.

Overarm Sidestroke

Arms

186. Where does the top arm enter the water in the overarm sidestroke?
    *a. in front of the face
    b. in front of the stomach
    c. in front of the shoulder
    d. above the head

187. Which occurrence is a *fault* in the overarm sidestroke?
    a. keeping the top arm in the air on the recovery
    *b. allowing the bottom arm to drop
    c. staying on the side
    d. pushing the top arm forcibly

Legs—Scissor Kick

188. What kick is used in the overarm sidestroke?
    a. breaststroke kick
    b. inverted breaststroke kick
    c. inverted scissor kick
    *d. scissor kick

Coordination

189. Which movement initiates the action at the beginning of the overarm sidestroke?
    *a. The arm under the head begins to pull.
    b. The trailing arm is lifted out of the water.
    c. The legs begin their recovery phase.
    d. All actions start simultaneously following the glide.

Comparisons

190. How does the inverted scissor kick differ from the standard scissor kick?
    a. The inverted kick is performed on the other side of the body.
    b. A longer glide is used with the inverted scissor kick.
    c. The two kicks do not differ appreciably.
    *d. The bottom leg goes forward on the inverted kick.

191. What makes the overarm sidestroke arm action more efficient than the regular sidestroke arm action?
    a. Bottom arm is recovered out of the water, which cuts down on the resistance of the negative action of the arm.
    *b. Top arm is recovered out of the water, which cuts down on the resistance of the negative action of the arm.
    c. Overarm sidestroke and the regular sidestroke have equally efficient arm actions.
    d. Sidestroke has a stronger arm action than the overarm sidestroke.

Breaststroke, Inverted Breaststroke, and Butterfly

Breaststroke

Arms	192 to 195
Legs	196 to 200
Coordination	201 to 206
Miscellaneous	207 to 209

Inverted Breaststroke

Arms	210 to 211
Legs	212 to 213
Coordination	214 to 215

Butterfly

Arms	216
Legs	217
Coordination	218
Use	219

Breaststroke

Arms

192. Various stages of the coordination of the breaststroke are listed. Which one is the power phase for the arms?
    *a. Palms are pulled diagonally back to just outside the shoulder line.
    b. Legs are together and extended; the arms are extended over the head with the hands together, palms down.
    c. Legs start to recover as the arms are pressing through the last part of their positive stage; the swimmer takes a breath.
    d. Legs kick as the arms are recovered to their extended position.

193. Why is it *inadvisable* to pull beyond the shoulders on the breaststroke?
    a. Such a pull becomes more tiring.
    b. Such a pull lifts the body out of the water.
    c. Such a pull takes longer for the arms to recover.
    *d. Such a pull diverts the forward motion to a different direction.

194. Where are the arms during the breaststroke glide?
    a. straight down at the sides
    b. straight overhead, directly in front of the shoulders
    *c. straight overhead with hands side-by-side
    d. straight overhead with palms together

195. What mistake in the breaststroke could cause a swimmer to bob up and down?
    *a. Arms are pulling down more than back toward the feet.
    b. Back is arched.
    c. Knees are bending up to the waist.
    d. Legs are doing a scissor kick.

Legs

196. Which kick exerts positive pressure against the insides of the legs and the insteps of the feet?
    a. dolphin kick
    *b. breaststroke kick
    c. flutter kick
    d. scissor kick

197. What pattern do the heels make when executing the breaststroke kick?
    *a. circles in an outward direction
    b. triangles in an inward direction
    c. circles in an inward direction
    d. triangles in an outward direction

198. When is the most force applied in the breast-stroke kick?
    a. when dropping the knees
    *b. during thrust of the legs
    c. when rotating ankles outward
    d. during beginning of leg recovery

199. Which parts of the legs and feet are used to create the push in the breaststroke kick?
    *a. inside of the legs below the knees and the heels of the feet
    b. outside of the legs below the knees and the top of the feet
    c. outside of the legs above the knees and the outside of the feet
    d. inside of the legs below the knees and the top of the feet

200. Which statement identifies one power phase of the breaststroke?
    a. arms, after they reach the shoulders
    b. arms, as they extend overhead
    c. legs, once they start to move following the glide
    *d. legs, as they return to the starting position

Coordination

201. Which statement describes the correct relationship of the arms and legs in the power phase of the breaststroke?
    a. Arms remain still as the legs kick.
    b. Arms and legs perform simultaneously.
    *c. Legs remain still as the arms pull.
    d. Arms and legs remain still at the same time.

202. Which statement about the coordination of the breaststroke is true?
    *a. Arms pull before the legs kick.
    b. Legs kick before the arms pull.
    c. Arms and legs work together.
    d. Inhalation is done with the kick.

203. Which action starts the breaststroke?
    a. Arms extend forward, beyond the head.
    b. Arms pull to the side of the body.
    c. Arms come out of the water.
    *d. Arms pull back in the water.

204. What should govern the length of the glide in the breaststroke?
    a. strength of the swimmer
    *b. duration of the forward movement
    c. length of time the breath can be held
    d. coordination of the arm and leg movements

205. Various stages of the coordination of the breaststroke are listed. Is the listing in the correct order for swimming the breaststroke?
    1. Palms are pulled diagonally back.
    2. Arms are extended in front of the head.
    3. Legs start to recover.
    4. Legs kick.
    5. A moderate glide follows.
    a. Yes, the listing is in the correct order.
    *b. No, switch 1. and 2.
    c. No, switch 2. and 3.
    d. No, switch 1. and 5.

206. Which error is likely to confuse most seriously the coordination of the breaststroke?
    *a. arm stroke too long
    b. failure to glide
    c. breathing too late
    d. use of a scissor kick

Miscellaneous

207. What is the correct position of the head in the breaststroke?
    *a. water at hairline
    b. water halfway covering the head
    c. water at eyebrows
    d. water below eyes

208. What is a legal turn for the breaststroke?
    a. touching the wall with one hand
    *b. touching the wall with two hands
    c. touching the wall with one foot
    d. touching the wall with both feet

209. When should the swimmer inhale on the breaststroke?
    *a. at the beginning of the arm drive
    b. at the end of the arm drive
    c. during the arm drive
    d. during the glide

Inverted Breaststroke

Arms

210. Which statement gives a true description of the inverted breaststroke?
    *a. Glide with both arms extended overhead.
    b. Arms and legs pull at same time.
    c. a scissor kick with four flutter kicks
    d. prone position

211. Where are the hands when recovering from the power phase of the inverted breaststroke?
    a. above the face
    b. by the sides of the head
    *c. under the ears
    d. out and down from the shoulders

Legs

212. When does the positive leg action occur in the inverted breaststroke?
    a. during the arm pull
    b. when the arms are near the end of their positive action
    c. during the glide
    *d. when the arms are being extended past the head

213. What happens after the swimmer completes the power phase of the legs in the inverted breaststroke?
    a. Power phase of the arms begins.
    *b. Swimmer glides.
    c. Negative phase of the leg stroke begins.
    d. Swimmer begins the next stroke.

Coordination

214. What is the coordination pattern of the inverted breaststroke?
    a. inhale, pull, kick, glide
    b. inhale and glide, pull, kick
    *c. pull, inhale, kick, glide
    d. pull, kick, breathe, glide

215. Which statement describes the glide position for the inverted breaststroke?
    a. arms at side, legs extended
    b. arms overhead, knees apart and feet cocked
    c. arms at side, feet dropped and cocked
    *d. arms overhead, legs extended

Butterfly

Arms

216. What is the arm pattern of the butterfly power phase?
    a. The arms pull straight back directly under the body.
    b. The arms pull in a circular pattern finishing near the chest.
    *c. The arms press diagonally downward and outward with the hands on the horizontal plane.
    d. The arms pull laterally and backward toward the feet finishing at the hips.

Legs

217. Which kick is used with the butterfly stroke?
    a. breaststroke kick
    b. scissor kick
    c. flutter kick
    *d. dolphin kick

Coordination

218. Which coordination is correct for the butterfly stroke?
    *a. two kicks: one kick cycle during arm pull and one during arm recovery
    b. two kick cycles at the end of the arm pull
    c. two kicks: the first upon entry of the hands, the second during the arm pull
    d. one to three kick cycles during the arm pull

Use

219. When is the butterfly stroke used most?
    *a. competitive swimming
    b. synchronized swimming
    c. recreational swimming
    d. lifesaving

Elementary Backstroke

Arms	220 to 222
Legs	223 to 226
Coordination	227 to 231
Miscellaneous	232 to 233

Arms

220. How far should the arms move up the body before extending out for the power phase of the elementary backstroke?
    a. Arms are extended when they reach the head.
    b. Arms are extended diagonally above the head.
    *c. Arms are extended laterally at shoulder level.
    d. Arms are extended diagonally below shoulder level.

221. Which statement correctly describes the recovery of the arms on the elementary backstroke?
    a. out of the water, close to the body
    *b. underwater, close to the body
    c. underwater, underneath the body
    d. out of the water, above the body

222. Why is it *incorrect* technique for a swimmer to keep the arms straight during the power phase of the elementary backstroke?
    a. Swimmer is forced to reach too far.
    *b. Swimmer pushes the water at an angle contrary to the desired direction.
    c. Swimmer cannot coordinate the arms with the legs as easily.
    d. Swimmer creates more resistance during the recovery.

Legs

223. Which kick is used with the elementary back-stroke?
     a. inverted scissor kick
     *b. inverted breaststroke kick
     c. back flutter kick
     d. dolphin kick

224. Which action of the legs is most important when executing the recovery of the elementary backstroke kick and why?
     a. Whipping action of the legs is most important because it provides the forward momentum.
     *b. Slow, easy action of the legs is most important because it lessens the resistance.
     c. Propulsive action of the legs is most important because it lessens the resistance.
     d. Whipping action of the legs is most important because it provides the balance.

225. What action should *not* be taken when performing the elementary backstroke kick?
     a. Recover the feet outside the knees.
     *b. Draw the knees up toward the stomach.
     c. Start the drive with the ankles.
     d. Extend the ankles as the legs drive.

226. Which phrase describes the correct ankle position in the first phase of the elementary backstroke kick?
     *a. Ankles are flexed.
     b. Ankles are flexed with toes pointing inward.
     c. Ankles are extended with toes flexed.
     d. Ankles and toes are extended.

Coordination

227. Which statement identifies the correct starting position for the elementary backstroke?
     a. legs extended and together, hands overhead
     b. knees a comfortable distance apart, feet turned out, hands to side
     *c. legs extended and together, hands at one's sides
     d. legs slightly apart, arms slightly away from sides of body

228. When does the kick on the elementary backstroke finish in relation to the arms?
     a. when arms start recovery
     b. when arms finish glide
     *c. when arms finish push
     d. when arms start push

229. A swimmer holds the glide until almost stopping while swimming the elementary backstroke. Is this good technique and why?
     *a. No, the swimmer uses more energy to begin movement on the next stroke.
     b. No, the swimmer gains efficiency and distance by gliding until stopping completely.
     c. Yes, the swimmer is able to rest longer.
     d. Yes, the swimmer creates less resistance by being more streamlined.

230. A swimmer sits in the water while swimming the elementary backstroke. What will most likely happen because of this body shape?
     a. Swimmer will sink.
     *b. Swimmer's head and shoulders will ride high in the water.
     c. Swimmer will do a scissor kick.
     d. Swimmer will get water in his or her face.

231. Why is it *not* good for a swimmer to be in a sitting position while doing the elementary backstroke?
     *a. There is more body area to push against the water.
     b. The swimmer cannot breathe as well.
     c. The swimmer stays in one place.
     d. The swimmer cannot move in a straight line.

Miscellaneous

232. Which part of the body is *not* under the water when swimming the elementary backstroke?
     a. arms
     *b. nose
     c. legs
     d. head

233. Which situation would most likely call for the use of the elementary backstroke?
     *a. long endurance swim
     b. competitive swim
     c. lifesaving rescue
     d. underwater swim

Trudgen, Trudgen Crawl, and Double Trudgen

Trudgen	234 to 236
Trudgen Crawl	237
Comparison	238
Double Trudgen	239

Trudgen

234. Which kind of kick is used with the trudgen stroke?
    a. flutter
    b. breaststroke
    *c. scissor
    d. dolphin

235. Which kick pattern describes the leg stroke for the trudgen?
    a. scissor kick and four flutter kicks
    b. inverted scissor kick and glide
    *c. scissor kick and glide
    d. scissor kick and inverted scissor kick

236. Which statement describes the coordination of the trudgen for a swimmer who breathes on the right side?
    *a. Power phase of the right leg and the right arm occurs simultaneously.
    b. Power phase of the right leg and the left arm occurs simultaneously.
    c. Power phase of the right leg precedes the power phase of the right arm.
    d. Power phase of the left leg precedes the power phase of the left arm.

Trudgen Crawl

237. Which description of the leg action for the trudgen crawl is correct?
    a. six flutter kicks
    *b. scissor kick and three flutter kicks
    c. scissor kick and glide
    d. inverted scissor kick and four flutter kicks

Comparison

238. What is the difference between the trudgen and the trudgen crawl?
    a. Trudgen uses both the scissor and the flutter kicks.
    *b. Trudgen crawl uses both the scissor and the flutter kicks.
    c. Trudgen uses only the flutter kick.
    d. Trudgen crawl uses only the scissor kick.

Double Trudgen

239. Which description of the leg stroke for the double trudgen is correct?
    a. scissor kick and glide
    *b. two scissor kicks
    c. scissor kick and inverted scissor kick
    d. scissor kick and four flutter kicks

Identification and Comparison

Identification

Beginner Stroke	240
Front Crawl	241 to 245
Sidestroke	246 to 247
Breaststroke	248 to 250
Elementary Backstroke	251 to 253
Back Crawl	254
Trudgen	255
Trudgen Crawl	256
Butterfly	257

Comparison

Front Crawl/Sidestroke	258
Front Crawl/Trudgen	259
Front Crawl/ Trudgen Crawl	260 to 262
Sidestroke/ Elementary Backstroke	263
Sidestroke/ Overarm Sidestroke	264
Back Crawl/ Overarm Sidestroke	265
Breaststroke/Sidestroke/ Elementary Backstroke	266
Breaststroke/ Inverted Breaststroke/ Elementary Backstroke	267

Identification

Beginner Stroke

240. Which stroke is essentially the crawl stroke with an underwater recovery of the arms?
    *a. beginner stroke
    b. elementary backstroke
    c. sidestroke
    d. trudgen

Front Crawl

241. With which skill is the flutter kick used?
    *a. front crawl
    b. sidestroke
    c. treading
    d. elementary backstroke

242. Which stroke is the fastest?
    a. butterfly
    b. trudgen
    *c. front crawl
    d. trudgen crawl

243. Which stroke is used most often?
    *a. front crawl
    b. back crawl
    c. butterfly
    d. breaststroke

244. Which stroke is *not* considered a resting stroke?
    a. sidestroke
    b. elementary backstroke
    c. breaststroke
    *d. front crawl

245. Which stroke is most effective for short-distance speed swimming?
    a. breaststroke
    *b. front crawl
    c. sidestroke
    d. elementary backstroke

Sidestroke

246. In which stroke do the legs provide most of the power?
    a. back crawl
    b. elementary backstroke
    *c. sidestroke
    d. trudgen

247. Which stroke is considered a resting stroke?
    a. butterfly
    b. front crawl
    c. back crawl
    *d. sidestroke

Breaststroke

248. Which stroke is the most restful?
    a. front crawl
    *b. breaststroke
    c. trudgen
    d. butterfly

249. Which stroke is the most difficult to coordinate?
    a. front crawl
    b. back crawl
    *c. breaststroke
    d. sidestroke

250. In which stroke does the swimmer exhale with the nose and mouth in the water?
    *a. breaststroke
    b. sidestroke
    c. elementary backstroke
    d. back crawl

Elementary Backstroke

251. Which stroke uses the same leg pattern as used for the breaststroke kick?
    a. front crawl
    b. combined stroke on the back
    c. sidestroke
    *d. elementary backstroke

252. Which stroke is considered more of a resting stroke?
    a. front crawl
    b. back crawl
    c. breaststroke
    *d. elementary backstroke

253. Which stroke has simultaneous arm and leg action during the force phase of both?
    *a. elementary backstroke
    b. breaststroke
    c. front crawl
    d. trudgen

Back Crawl

254. Which stroke uses an inverted kick?
    *a. back crawl
    b. overarm sidestroke
    c. trudgen
    d. butterfly

Trudgen

255. Which statement is characteristic of the trudgen stroke?
    *a. hybrid stroke
    b. racing stroke
    c. resting stroke
    d. safety stroke

Trudgen Crawl

256. The glide is *not* an element of which stroke?
    a. overarm sidestroke
    b. elementary backstroke
    c. inverted breaststroke
    *d. trudgen crawl

Butterfly

257. Which stroke is the most difficult to swim?
    a. front crawl
    b. back crawl
    c. breaststroke
    *d. butterfly

Comparison

Front Crawl/Sidestroke

258. In what respect are the front crawl and the sidestroke similar?
    a. speed value
    b. having continuous movement
    c. the movement of the legs
    *d. the use of continuous breathing

Front Crawl/Trudgen

259. Why is the trudgen considered more restful than the front crawl?
    a. glide on the arm stroke
    b. variety of kicks employed
    *c. glide on the leg stroke
    d. ease of breathing

Front Crawl/Trudgen Crawl

260. How does the kick for the trudgen crawl differ from the kick for the front crawl?
    a. Flutter kick is continuous.
    b. Scissor kick is continuous.
    *c. Flutter kick is mixed with a scissor kick.
    d. Flutter kick is mixed with a whip kick.

261. Why is the trudgen crawl easier to swim than the front crawl?
    a. because it is hard to coordinate the flutter kick with breathing
    b. because it is easier to do the scissor kick than the flutter kick
    c. because beginners are not coordinated well enough to do the front crawl
    *d. because the body turn to execute the scissor kick helps fit in the breathing

262. Which part of the front crawl stroke is identical to the trudgen crawl stroke?
    *a. arm pattern
    b. kick pattern
    c. breathe-kick pattern
    d. glide pattern

Sidestroke/Elementary Backstroke

263. In which pair of strokes is relaxation typical as compared to speed?
    a. butterfly and breaststroke
    b. trudgen and overarm sidestroke
    c. front crawl and back crawl
    *d. elementary backstroke and sidestroke

Sidestroke/Overarm Sidestroke

264. What advantage does the overarm sidestroke have over the sidestroke?
    a. less body roll
    b. better breathing position
    c. more force from arm stroke
    *d. less resistance on the arm recovery

Back Crawl/Overarm Sidestroke

265. Which strokes use an arm recovery above the water?
    a. elementary backstroke and inverted breaststroke
    b. sidestroke and front crawl
    *c. back crawl and overarm sidestroke
    d. breaststroke and front crawl

Breaststroke/Sidestroke/Elementary Backstroke

266. What element is common to the breaststroke, sidestroke, and elementary backstroke?
    a. kick
    b. arm pull
    *c. glide
    d. breathing style

Breaststroke/Inverted Breaststroke/Elementary Backstroke

267. Which kick is commonly used in the breaststroke, inverted breaststroke, and elementary backstroke?
    *a. whip kick
    b. scissor kick
    c. flutter kick
    d. dolphin kick

Diving and Jumping

Diving

Diving

Approach

268. Which part of springboard diving is *not* a part of the front approach?
    a. hurdle
    b. three steps
    c. initial stance
    *d. entry

269. Which approach is most commonly used in springboard diving?
    a. five steps and a hurdle
    b. four steps and a hurdle
    *c. three steps and a hurdle
    d. one step and a hurdle

270. How long are the approach steps in a running front dive from a springboard?
    a. Each step is about shoulder width long.
    b. Each step is a normal walking step.
    c. Each step is longer than a normal walking step.
    *d. Each step is longer than the preceding one.

Flight

271. Which factor in diving is the most important in controlling the direction the body will take in the air?
    *a. position of the head
    b. position of the feet
    c. length of the hurdle
    d. downward movement of the arms

Entry

272. What is the proper position of the body when entering the water in a headfirst dive?
    a. entire body arched
    b. back slightly arched
    *c. back and hips straight
    d. back straight, hips bent

273. What is the correct angle of entry for forward springboard dives?
    a. 35° to 45°
    b. 65° to 75°
    *c. 80° to 90°
    d. 110° to 125°

274. How close to the deck should the entry be on a front dive?
    a. 1 foot away
    b. 2 feet away
    *c. 3 feet away
    d. 4 feet away

275. What distance from the diving board should the entry be?
    *a. 2 to 4 feet
    b. 4 to 6 feet
    c. 6 to 8 feet
    d. It varies with the individual.

276. Which diagram shows the correct entry angle for a dive? [Refer to Diagram 5.]
    *d.

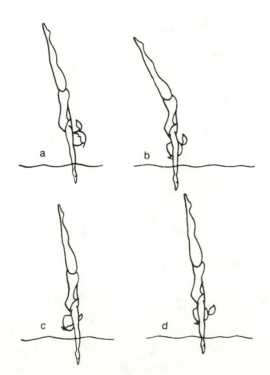

Diagram 5

Focus

277. Where should the eyes be focused during the approach of a dive?
    a. straight ahead
    b. about a foot beyond each step
    *c. at the end of the board
    d. on the water

278. Where do the eyes focus when approaching the water in a dive?
    a. on the chest
    *b. on the water
    c. on the top of the hands
    d. The eyes are closed.

Body Parts

279. What is the main factor controlling the body position in a dive?
    a. arm position
    *b. head position
    c. angle of the takeoff
    d. action of the legs

280. What is the best position for the head when taking off in a standing dive?
    a. head forward, chin pulled in
    *b. head easily erect, eyes looking straight ahead
    c. head slightly forward, eyes looking down to the water
    d. head back

281. Why is the position of the hands on entry important for the headfirst dive?
    a. direction
    *b. safety
    c. depth
    d. glide

282. What portion of the body is most important in achieving the desired entry in diving?
    a. arms
    b. trunk
    *c. hips
    d. legs

283. What are the two most important form aspects of successful deck diving?
    a. feet together, arms at sides
    b. eyes ahead, arms at sides
    c. head down, arms over head
    *d. head down, hips up

Learning

284. Which action should be the first step in learning to dive?
     - a. falling into the water from a standing position
     - b. falling into the water from a kneeling position
     - c. entering the water from a small spring
     - *d. falling into the water from a crouched position

285. Which factor is most important to a skilled diver?
     - *a. kinesthetic awareness
     - b. strength
     - c. weight
     - d. body structure

Errors

286. What causes the belly flop dive?
     - a. too much height
     - b. too much spring off the board
     - *c. lifting the head too soon
     - d. tucking the chin too far

287. Which error will cause an overthrow of the legs?
     - a. hurdling too high
     - *b. tucking the head too soon
     - c. springing out rather than up when leaving the deck
     - d. holding the head up too long

288. What causes the legs to flip over in a dive?
     - a. a forward spring
     - b. too high a hurdle
     - *c. head tucked too soon
     - d. pike of body

289. What is the most common fault in diving?
     - a. landing too close to the board
     - *b. leaning forward on the takeoff
     - c. pushing too hard from the toes
     - d. dropping the head after entry

Body Position

290. What is a piked body position?
     - a. Back is straight and the limbs are tucked.
     - *b. Back is straight and the hips are bent.
     - c. Back is flexed and the limbs are straight.
     - d. Back is flexed and the limbs are flexed.

291. What position is used in a jackknife?
     - a. layout
     - b. tuck
     - *c. pike
     - d. straddle

Judging

292. Which part of a dive is *not* important in evaluating the dive?
     - *a. depth
     - b. entry
     - c. height
     - d. approach

293. What is the best score possible on a judged dive?
     - a. 5 points
     - b. 8 points
     - *c. 10 points
     - d. 12 points

Jumping

294. Which statement describes a safe jump into shallow water?
     - a. The arms and legs fully extend.
     - b. The arms extend and the legs spread.
     - *c. The knees bend when the feet hit the bottom.
     - d. The arms, feet, and head tuck.

295. What should a swimmer remember to do when entering deep water from a jump?
     - a. Keep the arms to the sides.
     - *b. Spread the arms and legs.
     - c. Keep the legs together.
     - d. Begin moving the arms and legs.

Acknowledgments

Colleagues and students who contributed suggestions and ideas for the Swimming and Diving test questions are: A. Adams, M. Bartlett, S. Cline, J.M. Fog, L. Gaskin, A. Holland, M. Latta, J. Parrett, D. Preskitt, L. Robertson, K. Strickland, D. Walker, and C. Wiese.

Suggested Readings

American National Red Cross. (1981). *Swimming and aquatics safety*. Garden City, NY: Doubleday.

Armbruster, D.A., Allen, R.H., & Billingsley, H.S. (1973). *Swimming and diving* (6th ed.). St. Louis, MO: C. V. Mosby.

Counsilman, J.E. (1968). *The science of swimming*. Englewood Cliffs, NJ: Prentice-Hall.

Fairbanks, A.R. (1963). *Teaching springboard diving*. Englewood Cliffs, NJ: Prentice-Hall.

Vickers, B.J., & Vincent, W.J. (1984). *Swimming* (4th ed.). Dubuque, IA: Wm. C. Brown.

Tennis

Andrea Farrow, Consultant

This collection of test questions on tennis is divided into seven content areas:

- History
- Etiquette
- Equipment
- Terminology
- Rules and Scoring
- Technique
- Strategy

Some terminology may seem confusing, especially that describing body and racket positions in the Technique section. Such wording as *opposite of*, *diagonal to*, and so forth may be confusing if the instuctor used other descriptions. Some questions may need to be revised to make the terminology consistent with that used in class.

Many of the questions assume the player is right-handed. If these questions are used, it should be noted in the test directions, or a key should be made for left-handed players.

Tennis

History

Organizations

1. What organization makes the rules for tennis all over the world?
   - a. The World Tennis Organization
   - b. The International Lawn Tennis Organization
   - *c. The International Tennis Federation
   - d. The World Lawn Tennis Federation

2. What organization makes the rules for tennis in the United States?
   - *a. The United States Tennis Association
   - b. The United States Lawn Tennis Federation
   - c. The National Tennis Federation
   - d. The National Lawn Tennis Association

Andrea Farrow is a professor of health, physical education and recreation, and behavioral sciences at Delta State University, Cleveland, Mississippi. She has been a tournament player, professional teacher and coach for over 25 years, and has played in tournaments from the local to the national levels, taught at a number of private and public facilities, and coached in high school and college.

Tournaments

3. On what type of surface were the first great tournaments played?
   - a. hardwood floors
   - b. clay
   - c. concrete
   - *d. grass

4. What are the four tournaments in the grand slam?
   - *a. the U. S. Open, Wimbledon, the French Open, and the Australian Open
   - b. the U. S. Open, Wimbledon, the Italian Open, and the Grand Prix
   - c. the U. S. Open, Wimbledon, the All-Pro, and the Australian Open
   - d. the U. S. Open, the French Open, the Italian Open, and the Australian Open

5. What is the most famous tennis tournament?
   - a. The U.S. Open
   - b. The French Open
   - *c. Wimbledon
   - d. The Olympic

6. What is the name of the international team competition for men?
   - a. The Wightman Cup
   - b. The World Cup
   - *c. The Davis Cup
   - d. The Olympics

7. What is the Wightman Cup competition?
   - a. the international team competition for men
   - b. the international team competition for women
   - *c. the team competition for women between the U.S. and England
   - d. the team competition for men between the U.S. and Australia

Personalities

8. Who brought tennis to the United States?
   - a. Walter Wingfield
   - b. Jack Kramer
   - c. Bill Tilden
   - *d. Mary Outerbridge

9. Who is the only player to win the grand slam of tennis twice?
   - a. Don Budge
   - *b. Rod Laver
   - c. Maureen Connelly
   - d. Margaret Court

10. Who is the only American woman to win the grand slam of tennis?
    - *a. Maureen Connelly
    - b. Billie Jean King
    - c. Chris Evert-Lloyd
    - d. Althea Gibson

11. Who is the most outstanding black male tennis player of all time?
    - a. Chip Hooper
    - *b. Arthur Ashe
    - c. Lee Elder
    - d. Jackie Robinson

12. Who is the most outstanding black female tennis player of all time?
    - a. Maria Bueno
    - b. Maureen Connelly
    - *c. Althea Gibson
    - d. Chris Evert-Lloyd

Origin

13. Where did tennis originate?
    - a. U.S.
    - b. Southeast Asia
    - c. Greece
    - *d. France

14. From what social group did tennis originate?
    - a. peasants
    - *b. royalty
    - c. middle class
    - d. blue collar

Etiquette

Players

15. What should the receiver do if he or she is unable to determine whether a ball is good or out?
    - a. Call it out.
    - b. Ask the server to make the decision.
    - *c. Call it good.
    - d. Ask the server to play the point over.

16. What should a player do if he or she thinks the opponent made a bad call?
    - a. Overrule the call.
    - b. Question the opponent about the call.
    - c. Ask a spectator to make the call.
    - *d. Accept the call.

17. What is the first rule in tennis etiquette?
    - *a. "Do unto others as you would have them do unto you."
    - b. "If in doubt, call it out."
    - c. "Winning is everything."
    - d. "Good sportsmanship is for losers."

18. A ball is close to the line but out. The player returns the ball before making the call. What should the player do?
    a. Say nothing and play the ball good.
    *b. Immediately call the ball out.
    c. Wait until the ball is returned, catch it, and make the call.
    d. Ask to replay the point.

19. A ball rolls onto a neighboring court where play is in progress. When should the ball be recovered?
    a. It should be retrieved immediately so that it does not interfere with play on that court.
    *b. Its return should be requested from the players on that court at the end of the point in progress.
    c. It should be retrieved when the players on that court have finished a game.
    d. It should be retrieved when the players on that court have finished the point in progress.

20. The first serve of the player on Court 1 is a fault, and the ball rolls onto an adjacent court. What should the player on the adjacent court do?
    a. Return the ball immediately to the server on the other court.
    b. Leave the ball on his or her court until a player on the other court requests its return.
    c. Return the ball immediately to the other court.
    *d. Return the ball to a player on the other court at the end of the point.

21. Who should announce the score during a game? When?
    a. The server should announce the score as soon as a point is over.
    *b. The server should announce the score before serving the next point.
    c. The receiver should announce the score as soon as a point is over.
    d. The winner of the point should announce the score as soon as the point is over.

22. A match is in progress on Court 1. The players assigned to Court 2 must cross Court 1 in order to get to their court. When should they cross Court 1?
    a. during the point in progress
    *b. after the point in progress is finished
    c. *not* until the end of a game
    d. *not* until the players change sides of the court

23. What should a player try to do during the warm-up?
    *a. Hit the ball to the opponent so that maximum practice is possible.
    b. Hit the ball away from the opponent to tire him or her out.
    c. Hit the best shots possible to impress the opponent.
    d. Keep the opponent from practicing his or her shots as much as possible.

24. When should warm-up serves be taken?
    a. as each player gets his or her turn to serve the first time in the match
    b. as each player gets his or her turn to serve the first time in each set
    *c. at the end of the warm-up before any points are played
    d. whenever a player chooses to during the warm-up period

25. What should the server do before making the first serve?
    a. have at least two balls in his or her possession
    b. be sure the receiver is ready
    c. announce the score
    *d. all of the above

26. The server misses the first serve. Which procedure should be followed?
    *a. Receiver should clear the served ball from the court if it might interfere with play.
    b. Server should pick up another ball off the court and make the second serve.
    c. Receiver should chase the served ball and return it to the server.
    d. Receiver should chase the served ball and hit it to the server's side of the court.

Spectators

27. When should spectators applaud?
    *a. only after good shots resulting in winning points
    b. only after good shots made by the team they are rooting for
    c. only after good shots made by the team they are rooting for and errors made by the opponent
    d. only after points won by the team they are rooting for

28. When is it permissable for a spectator to ask a player for the score in the match?
    a. only at the end of the match
    b. anytime between points that will not interfere with play
    c. only when a set has ended
    *d. only when players are changing ends of the court

29. What should a spectator do if a player asks him or her to make a line call?
    a. Make the call.
    *b. Say that he or she cannot call it.
    c. Call it in favor of the player he or she is rooting for.
    d. Only call it if the correct call favors the player he or she is rooting for.

Equipment

Balls

30. How can a player determine if a can of balls is of acceptable quality?
    a. All pressurized balls are of acceptable quality.
    *b. "USTA Approved" is written on the can or box.
    c. All pressureless balls are of acceptable quality.
    d. "Tournament Quality" is written on the can or box.

31. What is the advantage in using pressureless balls over pressurized balls?
    a. They give players a smoother feeling hit.
    b. They are heavier and easier to control.
    *c. They do not go "dead."
    d. They are firmer and travel faster.

32. When should "Heavy Duty" balls be used?
    *a. when matches are played on abrasive hard court surfaces
    b. when matches are played on clay or grass
    c. when players want to use the balls for several matches
    d. when players are hard hitters

33. When should normal or regular felt balls be used?
    a. when matches are played on abrasive hard court surfaces
    *b. when matches are played on clay or grass
    c. when players are going to use the balls for only one match
    d. when players are practicing for a tournament

34. When do pressurized balls begin to go dead?
    a. as soon as they are hit the first time
    *b. as soon as the can is opened
    c. after they have been used for about three sets
    d. after the can has been open about a week

35. What weather condition greatly shortens the liveliness of pressurized balls?
    a. heat
    b. cold
    *c. wet
    d. dry

Rackets

36. Almost all wooden rackets can be used to measure the height of the net at its center. Why?
    a. The height of the net is the same as the length of the racket.
    b. The height of the net is one and one-half lengths of a racket.
    c. The height of the net is the length of a racket and the length of the grip on a racket.
    *d. The height of the net is the length of a racket and the width of the head of a racket.

37. What is the most notable innovation in tennis rackets?
    *a. the oversized racket head
    b. the increased length of rackets
    c. the variety of materials used in rackets
    d. the increased strength of materials used in rackets

38. What weight racket is appropriate for most women?
    a. extra light
    *b. light
    c. medium
    d. heavy

39. What weight racket is appropriate for most men?
    a. light
    *b. medium
    c. heavy
    d. extra heavy

40. A player holds the racket with a forehand grip. How can he or she determine if the grip is the correct size?
     a. If it feels comfortable, it is the correct size.
     b. The tip of the index finger should be even with the knuckle of the thumb.
     c. The tip of the second finger should be even with the knuckle of the thumb.
     *d. The tip of the thumb should be even with the knuckle of the second finger.

41. Of what material are the best racket grips made?
     a. rubber
     b. plastic
     c. imitation leather
     *d. leather

Strings

42. What is the advantage of having a racket strung with gut?
     a. The strings last longer.
     b. Gut is cheaper than nylon.
     *c. Gut has more snap when the ball is contacted.
     d. Gut is not susceptible to changes in humidity.

43. What is the advantage of having a racket strung with nylon?
     *a. The strings last longer.
     b. Nylon strings give a softer feeling hit.
     c. Nylon has more snap when the ball is contacted.
     d. Nylon can be strung to a higher tension than gut.

Terminology

Ace

44. What is an *ace*?
     a. a winning shot
     b. a smash untouched by the opponent
     *c. a serve untouched by the opponent
     d. a highly skilled player

Advantage

45. What is the next point after deuce called?
     a. game
     *b. advantage
     c. 40-all
     d. love

Alley

46. What is the lane between the singles and doubles sidelines called?
     *a. the alley
     b. crosscourt
     c. out-of-bounds
     d. no man's land

Baseline

47. What is the line at each end of the court called?
     a. back line
     b. center mark
     c. end line
     *d. baseline

Break

48. The receiver wins a game served by the opponent. What is this called?
     a. game point
     *b. service break
     c. advantage receiver
     d. match point

Center Mark

49. What is the *center mark*?
     *a. the line that divides the baseline into right and left
     b. the intersection of the center and service lines
     c. the position a player should take in the backcourt while waiting on a return
     d. the position a player should take at the net while waiting on a return

Crosscourt

50. A ball is hit from the back right corner of one court to the back right corner of the other. What is this called?
     a. drive
     *b. crosscourt shot
     c. down-the-line shot
     d. passing shot

Down-the-Line

51. A ball is hit across the net parallel with the sideline. What is this called?
     a. drive
     b. ace
     c. passing shot
     *d. down-the-line shot

Double Fault

52. A server hits both serves into the net. What is this called?
     a. fault
     *b. double fault
     c. advantage receiver
     d. service break

Foot Fault

53. The server is standing on the baseline while in the act of serving. What is this called?
    - a. fault
    - b. double fault
    - *c. foot fault
    - d. no service

Deuce

54. What score is considered deuce?
    - a. 0-0
    - b. 15-15
    - c. 30-30
    - *d. 40-40

Hold Service

55. What does it mean to *hold service*?
    - a. A player is receiving his or her turn to serve.
    - *b. A player wins his or her service game.
    - c. A player wins his or her opponent's service game.
    - d. A player is serving out of turn in doubles.

Let

56. What term refers to a point that must be replayed?
    - a. fault
    - b. replay
    - c. net
    - *d. let

Love

57. If a player has won no points, what is his or her score?
    - a. zero
    - *b. love
    - c. deuce
    - d. no score

Match Point

58. A player or team needs one more point to win a match. What is this called?
    - a. service break
    - b. holding service
    - *c. match point
    - d. break point

No Man's Land

59. Where is *no man's land*?
    - a. the forecourt near the net
    - *b. the midcourt area around the service line
    - c. the backcourt area near the baseline
    - d. the area behind the baseline

Poach

60. In doubles, a player at the net goes across the center line and intercepts a shot from the opponent. What is this called?
    - a. hogging the court
    - b. volleying
    - *c. poaching
    - d. hotdogging

Rally

61. Two players exchange a series of good shots. What is this called?
    - *a. rallying
    - b. volleying
    - c. driving
    - d. ground stroking

Rough and Smooth

62. With what are the terms *rough* and *smooth* generally associated?
    - a. the surface of the court
    - *b. the spinning of the racket
    - c. the covering of the ball
    - d. the strokes of a player

Match

63. What is a completed contest in tennis called?
    - a. game
    - b. set
    - *c. match
    - d. point

Dead Ball

64. What is a *dead ball*?
    - a. a ball hit into the net
    - b. the result of a shot that ends a point
    - c. the result of an error made by a player
    - *d. a ball that does not bounce as well as a normal ball

Right and Left Courts

65. Which sections are the right service courts in the diagram? [Refer to Diagram 1.]
    a. A and B
    b. C and D
    *c. A and D
    d. B and C

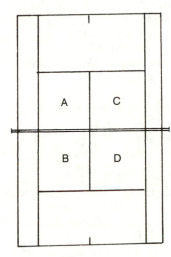

Diagram 1

Odd Courts

66. Which sections are the odd courts in the diagram? [Refer to Diagram 1, Question 65.]
    a. A and B
    b. C and D
    c. A and D
    *d. B and C

Sweet Spot

67. To what does the term *sweet spot* refer?
    *a. approximately the center of the racket face
    b. the best place on the court to hit the ball
    c. the correct position on the court to stand
    d. an undefended area of the court

Sudden Death

68. What is *sudden death*?
    a. losing a game point
    b. making an error at the net
    *c. playing a tiebreaker
    d. hitting a fault on the second serve

Tiebreaker

69. What is a tiebreaker?
    a. a third set played when each player has won one set
    *b. a scoring system that goes into effect at six games all
    c. a fifth set played when each player or team has won two sets
    d. the point played after deuce

Rules and Scoring

Spin for Serve

70. How do players usually decide who serves first?
    a. tossing a coin
    *b. spinning the racket
    c. rallying
    d. pinging

71. What choice can the winner of the toss make?
    a. serve first
    b. serve or receive first
    c. receive and side of court
    *d. serve or receive first or side of court

Scoring

72. When a player has won one point, what is his or her score?
    a. 1
    b. 5
    c. 10
    *d. 15

73. When a player has won three points, what is his or her score?
    a. 3
    b. 30
    *c. 40
    d. 45

74. When both players have won four points, what is the score?
    a. 40-all
    b. 50-all
    *c. deuce
    d. advantage-all

75. When the score is deuce and the server wins the next point, what is the score?
    a. game-server
    *b. advantage server
    c. advantage receiver
    d. game point

76. The score is advantage server and the receiver wins the next point. What is the score?
    a. game receiver
    b. advantage receiver
    c. advantage-advantage
  *d. deuce

77. When the score is advantage server and the server wins the next point, what is the score?
  *a. game
    b. deuce
    c. ad in
    d. advantage-advantage

78. The server has won three points. The receiver has won one point. What is the score?
    a. 3-1
  *b. 40-15
    c. 15-40
    d. game

79. The receiver has won three points. The server has *not* won a point. What is the score?
    a. game receiver
    b. 0-40
    c. 40-love
  *d. love-40

80. In which situation is the game completed?
  *a. One side has won four points and the other no more than two.
    b. One side has won four points and the other three points.
    c. A total of four points has been played.
    d. The score is 40-15.

81. A 12-point tiebreaker is being played. When is it completed?
    a. when one player has won 12 points
    b. when one player has won at least 12 points and is 2 ahead
  *c. when one player has won at least 7 points and is 2 ahead
    d. when one player has won 7 points

82. Which score is a completed set?
    a. 4-2
    b. 6-5
  *c. 7-5
    d. 2-1

83. What happens if the set score becomes 6-6?
  *a. A tiebreaker game is played.
    b. The player winning the next game wins.
    c. The player who won six games first won.
    d. The first player to be two games ahead wins.

84. How many sets are played by women for a match?
    a. one
  *b. two out of three
    c. three out of five
    d. two out of three or three out of five

85. How many sets are played by men for a match?
    a. one
    b. two out of three
    c. three out of five
  *d. two out of three or three out of five

Playing

86. If a ball hits a line, what is the decision?
  *a. good
    b. out
    c. replay
    d. let

87. How do the boundaries for doubles differ from those for singles?
  *a. In doubles, the alleys are added for play.
    b. In doubles, the alleys are added for serving and play.
    c. In doubles, the alleys are added for serving.
    d. There are no differences.

88. How many times can the ball be hit by players on one team before it crosses the net?
  *a. once
    b. once by each player
    c. twice so long as the ball does not bounce but once
    d. twice so long as the ball bounces between hits

89. During a match between Players A and B, the ball bounces twice on A's side of the court. What is the situation?
    a. continue play
    b. point for A
  *c. point for B
    d. replay

90. When do players change ends of the court?
    a. the end of even-numbered games
  *b. the end of odd-numbered games
    c. the end of each set
    d. the end of each game

91. During a match between players A and B, the ball hits the top of the net and goes over into A's court. What is the situation?
  *a. continue play
    b. point for A
    c. point for B
    d. replay

92. Players A and B are playing a point. Player A hits a ball that hits the net but does *not* go over. What is the situation?
    a. continue play
    b. point for A
    *c. point for B
    d. net ball

93. Players A and B are playing a point. Player A swings at a ball and misses it completely. The ball lands outside the court boundaries. What is the situation?
    *a. point for A
    b. point for B
    c. replay
    d. continue play

94. Teams A and B are playing a point. The net-man on Team A swings at a ball and misses it completely. His or her partner returns the ball to Team B's side of the court. What is the situation?
    *a. continue play
    b. point for Team A
    c. point for Team B
    d. interference

95. Players A and B are playing a point. Player A is standing outside the court boundaries. Player B hits a ball, which A catches before it bounces. What is the decision?
    a. point for A
    *b. point for B
    c. let
    d. reserve

96. Players A and B are playing a point. Player B hits a shot to A at the net. The ball hits A on the hand and rebounds into B's court. What is the situation?
    a. continue play
    b. point for A
    *c. point for B
    d. let

97. Teams A and B are playing a point. The ball is hit by a player on Team B. It brushes the shirt sleeve of his or her teammate before crossing the net to Team A's side. What is the situation?
    a. continue play
    *b. point for Team A
    c. point for Team B
    d. interference

98. Teams A and B are playing a point. The net-man on Team A tips the ball, but his or her partner manages to return it to Team B's side of the court. What is the situation?
    a. continue play
    b. point for Team A
    *c. point for Team B
    d. interference

99. Players A and B are playing a point. Player A hits a ball on the frame of his or her racket. The ball goes over the net into B's court. What is the situation?
    *a. continue play
    b. point for A
    c. point for B
    d. let

100. Players A and B are playing a point. The ball accidently hits A's racket twice before going over into B's court. What is the situation?
    *a. continue play
    b. point for A
    c. point for B
    d. let

101. Players A and B are playing a point. A ball from another court rolls onto the middle of B's side of the court. What is the situation?
    a. continue play
    b. interference
    c. reserve
    *d. let

102. Players A and B are playing a point. Player A is at the net. Player B hits a short lob. Player A hits an overhead that player B cannot possibly reach. As the ball bounces, a ball from another court rolls behind A on the court. What is the decision?
    a. interference
    *b. point for A
    c. let
    d. replay

103. Players A and B are playing a point. Player A is at the net and reaches over it to hit the ball. What is the situation?
    a. continue play
    b. point for A
    *c. point for B
    d. let

104. Players A and B are playing a point. Player A is at the net. When the ball comes, A hits it and follows through over the net. What is the situation?
    *a. continue play
    b. point for A
    c. point for B
    d. let

105. Players A and B are playing a point. Player A is at the net. After A hits a volley, he or she touches the net with the racket on the follow-through. What is the situation?
    a. continue play
    b. point for A
    *c. point for B
    d. interference

106. Players A and B are playing a point. Player B hits a drop shot. Player A rushes to the net to hit the return. After hitting the ball over, Player A runs into the net. What is the situation?
    a. continue play
    b. point for A
    *c. point for B
    d. interference

107. Which play is legal?
    a. reaching over the net to hit the ball
    *b. following through over the net after hitting the ball
    c. touching the net with the racket after hitting the ball
    d. touching the net with the player's body or clothing after hitting the ball

Serving

108. How many chances each point does a player get to make a good serve?
    a. one
    *b. two
    c. three
    d. four

109. The player is serving from X. Into which area must the ball be hit to be a good serve? [Refer to Diagram 2.]
    *d.

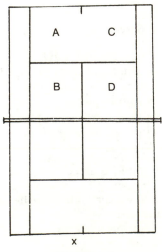

Diagram 2

110. Where should the service be made at the beginning of each game?
    a. from the court the server received in the previous game
    b. the opposite court from where the last serve was made in the previous game
    c. the left service court
    *d. the right service court

111. The score is 40-15. Where should the service be made?
    *a. the right court
    b. the left court
    c. It depends on in which court the game began.
    d. not enough information to determine the answer

112. On the first serve the ball hits the top of the net and lands in the alley on the receiver's side. What is the situation?
    a. The ball is in play.
    b. A let is called.
    c. A point is awarded to the receiver.
    *d. The server hits his or her second serve.

113. On the first serve the ball hits the top of the net and lands in the correct service court on the receiver's side. What is the procedure?
    a. The ball is in play.
    *b. A let is called.
    c. A point is awarded to the receiver.
    d. The server hits his or her second serve.

114. What is the limit on the number of times a let can be called?
    a. 1
    b. 2
    c. 10
    *d. no limit

115. On the first serve the ball lands on the center line. What is the situation?
    *a. ball in play
    b. point for the server
    c. point for the receiver
    d. second serve

116. What is the decision if the server tosses the ball and catches it instead of striking at it?
    a. A fault is called.
    *b. The server may try again without penalty.
    c. The server may try again, but if the same action is repeated, a fault is called.
    d. Receiver wins the point.

117. How long does a player's turn to serve last?
    a. Each player serves one point and then the serve changes to another player.
    b. Each player serves two points before the serve changes to another player.
    *c. Each player serves an entire game before the serve changes to another player.
    d. Each player serves four points before the serve changes to another player.

118. When may the server stand on or over the baseline?
    a. at the beginning of the serve
    b. after the ball is tossed into the air
    c. after the serve crosses the net
    *d. after the ball is contacted

119. Player A serves to Player B. Player B makes no attempt to return the serve and claims he or she was not ready. What is the decision?
    a. point for A
    b. point for B
    c. ace
    *d. let

120. Player A serves to Player B. Player B returns the serve in the net and claims he or she was not ready. What is the decision?
    *a. point for A
    b. point for B
    c. let
    d. second serve

121. In singles, when the serve is from the right side, where must the server stand?
    *a. behind the baseline and between the center mark and right singles sideline
    b. behind the baseline and on or between the center mark and right singles sideline
    c. on the baseline and between the center mark and right singles sideline
    d. on the baseline and on or between the center mark and right singles sideline

122. In singles, who serves first in the second set?
    a. the winner of the first set
    b. the loser of the first set
    c. the player who received first in the first set
    *d. the player who received in the last regular game of the first set

123. After the first game in a set of doubles, who must serve the second game?
    a. the player who received in the right court in the first game
    b. the player who received in the left court in the first game
    c. the player with the stronger serve
    *d. either player who received in the first game

124. After the second game in a set of doubles, who must serve the third game?
    a. either player on the receiving team in the second game
    b. the player who served the first game
    *c. the partner of the player who served the first game
    d. the partner of the player who served the second game

125. Four games have been played in a set of doubles. Who must serve the fifth game?
    a. either player on the team that served the first game
    b. either player on the team that served the second game
    c. the player who served the second game
    *d. the player who served the first game

126. When may a doubles team change its serving order?
    a. after every four games have been played
    *b. at the end of a set
    c. at the end of a match
    d. after each player has had a turn to serve

127. In doubles, who serves the first game of the second set?
    a. a player on the team that won the first set
    b. a player on the team that lost the first set
    c. a player on the team that received first in the first set
    *d. a player on the team that received in the last regular game of the first set

128. Player X receives service in the first game of the set in the court indicated. Where does he or she receive in the third game of the set? [Refer to Diagram 3.]
    *c.

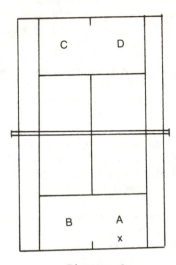

Diagram 3

129. When may players in a doubles match change sides of the court to receive?
    a. after every point
    b. each time the serving team begins a new game
    c. each time teams change sides of the net
    *d. at the end of a set

Technique

130. What most frequently causes a player to miss the ball completely?
    a. swinging too soon
    b. swinging too late
    *c. not watching the ball
    d. gripping the racket incorrectly

131. What is the first and most basic rule of tennis?
    a. Bend the knees.
    b. Stay on the toes.
    *c. Keep the eyes on the ball.
    d. Follow through on all strokes.

132. What causes most errors on shots?
    a. no follow-through
    b. poor footwork
    c. trying to hit the ball too hard
    *d. not watching the ball

133. On what should a player concentrate when playing a point?
    a. the other player(s)
    *b. the ball
    c. the lines on his or her side of the court
    d. the lines on both sides of the court

134. What is the best pace to hit the ball?
    *a. firmly and under control
    b. as hard as possible
    c. softly and barely over the net
    d. softly and to the backcourt

135. Where is the best place on the racket face to hit the ball?
    *a. in the center of the strings
    b. above the center of the strings
    c. below the center of the strings
    d. toward the handle from the center of the strings

136. What is the main factor in hitting a ball harder while maintaining control?
    a. increasing the snap of the wrist
    b. increasing the rotation of the shoulders
    c. transferring the weight forward sooner
    *d. improving the timing of the stroke

137. A player uses the same grip for a forehand and backhand. The V made by the thumb and index fingers is on the center of the top left bevel of the handle. Which grip is this?
    a. Australian
    *b. Continental
    c. Eastern
    d. Western

138. What is a major *disadvantage* of using the Continental grip?
    a. The ball cannot be hit as hard.
    b. It gives away the direction the ball will be hit.
    *c. It is more difficult to hit low balls.
    d. There is less ball control.

139. Which sentence best describes the waiting position?
    a. The player stands with his or her left side toward the net and with most of the weight on the right foot.
    b. The player stands with his or her left side toward the net and with the weight evenly distributed on both feet.
    c. The player stands squarely facing the net with the weight evenly distributed on both feet.
    *d. The player stands squarely facing the net with the weight on the balls of the feet.

140. How far apart should a player's feet be in the ready position?
     *a. about shoulder width
     b. more than shoulder width
     c. less than shoulder width
     d. about 6 inches

141. Where should the racket be held in the ready position?
     a. downward on the player's right side
     b. toward the net from the player's right shoulder
     c. diagonally in front of the player's body and toward the left net post
     *d. toward the net from the center of the player's body

142. What is the first action taken when moving to the right to hit a ball?
     *a. Pivot on the right foot.
     b. Pivot on the left foot.
     c. Take a sliding step to the right.
     d. Take a running step with the right foot

143. What is the first action taken when moving backward to hit a ball on the forehand side?
     a. Pivot on the right foot.
     *b. Pivot on the left foot.
     c. Take a backward running step with the right foot.
     d. Take a backward running step with the left foot.

144. A player is moving far to his or her left to hit a ball. What footwork pattern should be used?
     *a. run
     b. slide
     c. walk
     d. slide and run

145. A player is moving three or four steps backward to hit a ball. What footwork pattern should be used?
     a. run backward
     *b. slide
     c. walk
     d. turn and run

146. You take a stance to hit the ball. How should last second adjustments to the distance of the ball from your body be made?
     a. by reaching more or less with the arm
     b. by bending more or less at the waist
     *c. by moving the front foot
     d. by moving the back foot

147. A player moves to the right side line to hit a ground stroke. What footwork pattern should be used to get back to the home base position?
     a. pivot and walk
     b. pivot and run
     c. run
     *d. slide

148. What is the position of the wrist when stroking the ball?
     a. relaxed
     *b. firm
     c. ahead of the racket head
     d. behind the racket head

149. A player is hitting the ball with great velocity but little control. What is the most probable reason?
     *a. excessive wrist action
     b. swinging too hard
     c. taking the racket back too far
     d. not enough follow-through

Drives

150. Which statement describes the type of drive a player should try to hit most of the time?
     a. The ball clears the net by no more than 1 foot and lands close to the baseline.
     b. The ball clears the net by no more than 1 foot and lands between the service line and net.
     *c. The ball clears the net by at least 3 feet and lands between the service line and baseline.
     d. The ball clears the net by at least 3 feet and lands on the baseline.

151. In hitting a drive, where should the player's weight be at the moment of impact?
     *a. on the forward foot
     b. on the back foot
     c. evenly distributed over both feet
     d. in front of the forward foot

152. What stance should a player take to hit a drive?
     *a. sideways to the net with the feet shoulder width apart
     b. sideways to the net with the feet 6 inches apart
     c. facing the net with the feet shoulder width apart
     d. diagonal to the net with the feet 6 inches apart

153. In hitting a drive, what direction should the forward foot point?
     a. directly toward the sideline
     *b. diagonal to the net and sideline
     c. diagonal to the sideline and baseline
     d. directly toward the net

154. When should a player start the backswing for a drive?
    a. as soon as the ball crosses to his or her side of the net
    b. as soon as the ball bounces on his or her side of the net
    c. as soon as the ball begins to rise from the bounce on his or her side of the net
    *d. as soon as the ball leaves the opponent's racket face

155. At what height should the racket meet the tennis ball for the drive?
    a. between the waist and shoulders
    b. waist high or above
    *c. between the knees and waist
    d. between the ankles and hips

156. Which factor is most important in determining the direction the ball is hit?
    a. the grip
    b. the stance
    c. the backswing
    *d. the follow-through

157. What should be emphasized more than usual when hitting a low bouncing ball?
    a. The backswing is longer.
    b. The follow-through is longer.
    *c. The knees are bent more.
    d. The ball is hit sooner.

Forehand Drive

158. A player is holding the racket in a forehand grip. The point of the V made by his or her thumb and index finger is in the center of the top plate of the racket. Which grip is this?
    a. Continental
    *b. Eastern
    c. Western
    d. Australian

159. What is the advantage of using the Eastern forehand grip over any other forehand grip?
    *a. The wrist is not rotated in the stroke.
    b. The ball can be hit harder.
    c. It does not give away the direction the ball will be hit.
    d. It takes less strength to make a good stroke.

160. What is the position of the player s wrist when hitting a forehand drive?
    a. cocked in the backswing and uncocked at ball contact
    b. cocked in the backswing and uncocked as the forward swing begins
    *c. straight throughout the swing
    d. straight until ball contact and then rolled over the ball in the follow-through

161. What is the position of the player's elbow when hitting a forehand drive?
    *a. straight, but relaxed, and a comfortable distance from the player's body
    b. straight, stiff, and a comfortable distance from the player's body
    c. bent at a right angle and next to the player's waist
    d. bent at a right angle and a comfortable distance from the player's body

162. When is the player's weight shifted from the back to the front foot when hitting a forehand drive?
    a. in the backswing
    b. at the beginning of the forward swing of the racket
    *c. just before the racket contacts the ball
    d. in the follow-through

163. How far should a player take the racket back to hit a forehand drive?
    a. as far as he or she can possibly reach
    *b. until it points to the fence or wall behind him or her
    c. until it is opposite the player's right foot
    d. until it is opposite the center of the player's body

164. A player wants to hit a flat forehand drive. How high should the racket head be in the backswing?
    a. head high
    b. shoulder high
    *c. hip high
    d. ankle high

165. At what point should the ball be contacted when hitting a forehand drive?
    a. before the ball gets to the player's forward foot
    *b. opposite the player's forward foot
    c. opposite the center of the player's body
    d. opposite the player's back foot

166. Where should the racket head be at the end of the follow-through on a forehand drive?
    a. just a few inches in front of the contact point
    *b. head high and slightly to the left of the intended flight of the ball
    c. ankle high next to the left leg
    d. waist high and toward the left side line

167. The player is hitting a forehand drive. His or her wrist is cocked at contact. Where will the ball go?
    a. probably to the left of the intended target
    *b. probably to the right of the intended target
    c. probably into the net
    d. straight over the net

168. Where will a forehand hit off the player's back foot tend to go?
    *a. to the right of the intended target
    b. to the left of the intended target
    c. straight across the net
    d. into the net

169. A player consistently sends forehand drives too far to the left. What is the most probable cause?
    a. The player takes too little backswing.
    b. The forward swing is made too early.
    *c. The player is facing the net.
    d. The racket head is dragging behind the wrist.

Backhand Drive

170. What is the major advantage of a one-handed over a two-handed backhand?
    a. The ball can be hit harder.
    b. The ball can be controlled better.
    *c. The player has more reach.
    d. A greater variety of shots can be hit.

171. What is the major advantage of a two-handed over a one-handed backhand?
    a. The ball can be hit harder.
    *b. The racket has more support at ball contact.
    c. The player has more reach.
    d. A greater variety of shots can be hit.

172. A player is holding the racket in a backhand grip. His or her thumb is diagonally across the back of the grip. Which grip is this?
    a. Australian
    b. Continental
    *c. Eastern
    d. Western

173. What is the advantage of using the Eastern backhand grip over any other backhand grip?
    a. The wrist is not rotated in the stroke.
    b. The ball can be hit harder.
    c. It does not give away the direction the ball will be hit.
    *d. There is better support for the racket at ball contact.

174. How should the grip be changed from a forehand to a one-handed backhand?
    *a. The left thumb rolls the racket head clockwise while the right hand adjusts on the grip.
    b. The left hand rolls the racket head counterclockwise while the right hand adjusts on the grip.
    c. The left hand holds the racket head steady while the right hand adjusts on the grip.
    d. Both hands release their grips on the racket and the right hand adjusts.

175. A player is hitting a one-handed backhand. What is the position of the left arm and hand in the backswing?
    a. The arm and hand are at the player's left side.
    b. The arm and hand are held out of the way of the racket.
    *c. The arm is straight and the hand lightly holds the throat of the racket.
    d. The arm is bent and the hand lightly holds the throat of the racket.

176. How far should the racket be taken back in the backswing for a backhand drive?
    a. as far as the player can possibly reach
    b. until it is opposite the player's left foot
    c. until it is opposite the center of the player's body
    *d. until it points to the back fence or wall

177. A player is hitting a one-handed backhand. How high should the racket head be in the backswing?
    a. head high
    b. shoulder high
    *c. hip high
    d. knee high

178. A player is hitting a one-handed backhand. Where should ball contact be made?
    a. close to and a little to the rear of the player's body
    b. with a full arm extension and opposite the forward foot
    *c. with a full arm extension and a little in front of the forward foot
    d. close to the body and a little in front of the forward foot

179. At what height should the ball be contacted in hitting the backhand drive?
    a. shoulder high
    b. knee high
    *c. between the knees and waist
    d. between the waist and shoulders

180. Where should the body weight be during the follow-through of a backhand drive?
    *a. over the right foot
    b. over the left foot
    c. evenly distributed over both feet
    d. shifting from the left to right foot

181. Where should the follow-through end on a backhand drive?
    a. a few inches in front of the contact point
    *b. head high and slightly to the right of the intended flight of the ball
    c. waist high and toward the right side line
    d. ankle high by the player's right side

182. Which is *not* a common error in hitting backhand drives?
    a. leading the stroke with the elbow
    b. hitting the ball too close to the body
    c. having the racket head ear high in the backswing
    *d. dropping the racket head too low in the backswing

183. A player consistently has difficulty clearing the net with his or her backhand drive. What is the most probable cause?
    a. contacting the ball on the rise from the bounce
    b. contacting the ball as it drops from the height of the bounce
    *c. stroking so that the backswing is higher than the follow-through
    d. starting the backswing so late that the stroke is hurried

184. A player consistently sends balls too far to the left when hitting backhand drives. What is the most probable cause?
    a. too little backswing
    b. body facing the net
    *c. forward swing too late
    d. insufficient amount of force

185. How is the racket gripped for a two-handed backhand?
    a. Both hands are placed on the racket in Eastern forehand grips.
    b. The right hand uses an Eastern forehand and the left an Eastern backhand.
    *c. The right hand uses an Eastern backhand and the left an Eastern forehand.
    d. Both hands are placed on the racket in Continental grips.

186. What is the relationship between the position of the hands on the grip for a two-handed backhand?
    a. The index finger of the right hand overlaps the little finger of the left hand.
    b. The index finger of the right hand interlocks between the third and little fingers of the left hand.
    *c. The hands are as close together as possible without overlapping or interlocking.
    d. There is a space of about 1 inch between the right and left hands.

187. A player is hitting a two-handed backhand. Where should the racket head be in the backswing?
    a. shoulder high
    b. waist high
    *c. hip high
    d. ankle high

188. A player is hitting a two-handed backhand. How are the arms positioned in the backswing?
    *a. Both are straight.
    b. Both are bent at the elbows.
    c. The right is bent at a right angle and the left is straight.
    d. The left is bent at a right angle and the right is straight.

189. A player is hitting a two-handed backhand. How are the arms positioned at contact?
    *a. Both are straight.
    b. Both are bent at the elbows.
    c. The right is bent and the left is straight.
    d. The left is bent and the right is straight.

190. A player is hitting a two-handed backhand. Where should contact be made?
    a. slightly in front of the player's forward foot
    *b. opposite the player's forward foot
    c. opposite the center of the player's body
    d. opposite the player's back foot

Volley

191. Which statement applies to the volley?
    a. It requires a long, vigorous forward swing.
    b. It is used primarily from the backcourt.
    *c. It requires a punching action.
    d. It is most frequently hit with a backhand.

192. A player is using a different grip to hit a backhand volley from the one he or she is using to hit a forehand volley. What grip is he or she probably using?
    *a. Eastern
    b. Continental
    c. Western
    d. Semiwestern

193. A player is using the same grip to hit both forehand and backhand volleys. What grip is recommended for a player doing this?
    a. Eastern
    *b. Continental
    c. Western
    d. Australian

194. A player has the option to stand still or move in a direction to hit the volley. What is his or her best choice?
    a. stand still
    *b. move forward
    c. move sideways
    d. move backward

195. What is the difference in the ready position for playing at the net from playing in the backcourt?
    *a. The racket head is held higher.
    b. The racket head is held lower.
    c. The player's left side faces the net.
    d. The player takes a wider stance.

196. What wrist action is used in volleying?
    *a. None, the wrist is locked.
    b. The wrist is snapped at contact on the forehand but not the backhand.
    c. The wrist is snapped at contact on the backhand but not the forehand.
    d. The wrist is snapped at contact on the forehand and backhand.

197. How can the backswing of the volley best be described?
    a. long
    *b. short
    c. quick
    d. slow

198. When should the ball be contacted in hitting a volley?
    a. when it is below the level of the net
    b. when it is above the level of the net
    *c. as soon as possible after it crosses the net
    d. as late as possible

199. What are the movements when hitting a volley?
    *a. short backswing, contact in front of the body with a short punching motion
    b. long backswing, contact even with the center of the body with a short punching motion
    c. short backswing, contact slightly behind the body with a short punching motion
    d. backswing varies, contact in front of the body with a short punching motion

200. A ball is below the level of the net. What should the player change from hitting the normal volley?
    a. Open the face of the racket more.
    b. Close the face of the racket more.
    *c. Open the racket face and bend the knees more.
    d. Close the racket face and bend at the waist more.

201. What is the position of the racket face if the player is hitting the volley above the level of the net?
    a. open
    *b. closed
    c. flat
    d. diagonal-open

202. How long should the follow-through be for a volley?
    a. no follow-through
    b. 5 to 6 feet
    c. 3 to 5 feet
    *d. 1 to 2 feet

203. A player is going to hit a volley on his or her forehand side. What footwork should be used?
    *a. The left foot steps toward the ball.
    b. The right foot steps toward the ball.
    c. The right foot steps away from the ball.
    d. The right foot steps to the right.

204. A player is going to hit a volley on his or her backhand side. What footwork should be used?
    *a. The right foot steps toward the ball.
    b. The left foot steps to the left.
    c. The left foot steps away from the ball.
    d. The left foot steps toward the ball.

Lob

205. What are the differences in hitting a drive and lob?
     a. The backswing and follow-through are shorter for the lob.
     b. Getting into position to hit the ball is *not* as important in hitting a lob.
     *c. The racket face is more open and the low-to-high path of the swing is more exaggerated in hitting a lob.
     d. The knees are bent less and the swing is softer in hitting a lob.

206. Which statement describes the follow-through for a lob?
     a. There is no follow-through.
     b. It is the same as for a drive.
     c. It is shorter than for a drive.
     *d. It follows the desired trajectory of the ball.

207. What is the difference in an offensive and defensive lob?
     *a. its height
     b. its depth
     c. the amount of spin
     d. its pace

Overhead

208. What grip is used to hit an overhead?
     a. the forehand
     b. the backhand
     *c. the service
     d. the volley

209. What stance is used to hit an overhead?

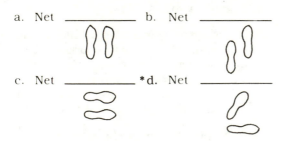

210. What footwork is used to move back to hit an overhead?
     *a. Step back with the right foot and slide.
     b. Pivot on the right foot, turn, and run.
     c. Move backward using running steps.
     d. Step across with the left foot, turn, and run.

211. Where should the player's body be in relation to the ball to hit an overhead?
     a. directly under the ball
     b. directly behind the ball
     *c. behind the ball and slightly to the left
     d. under the ball and slightly to the left

212. When should a player begin the backswing for an overhead?
     a. as soon as he or she gets into position to hit
     *b. as he or she turns to get into position
     c. while moving to get into position
     d. as the ball begins its descent

213. From where should the forward swing of the racket begin for an overhead?
     *a. between the shoulder blades
     b. behind the head
     c. above the head
     d. above the right shoulder

214. Where should the ball be contacted for an overhead?
     *a. about 1 foot in front of the right shoulder and as high as the player can reach
     b. about 2 feet in front of the right shoulder and just above head level
     c. about 1 foot in front of the player's head and as high as the player can reach
     d. above the player's right shoulder and as high as the player can reach

215. What should vary according to the distance the player is from the net in hitting an overhead?
     a. the backswing
     b. the follow-through
     c. the wrist snap
     *d. the racket face angle

Drop Shot

216. Should a drop shot be hit with spin?
     a. No, it is hit flat.
     *b. Yes, it is hit with underspin.
     c. Yes, it is hit with topspin.
     d. It only has spin when it is hit from the backcourt area.

217. Which statement describes the swing when hitting a drop shot?
     a. The path is the same as for a drive.
     b. The swing is from low to high.
     *c. The swing is from high to low.
     d. The swing is parallel with the court surface.

218. When is the racket face opened to give the drop shot spin?
     a. as the racket is taken back in the backswing
     b. at the end of the backswing
     c. at the beginning of the forward swing
     *d. just before the ball is contacted

Drop Volley

219. What is the difference in hitting a normal volley and a drop volley?
    *a. The racket face is opened and the wrist is relaxed in a drop volley.
    b. The racket face is opened and the ball is hit later in a drop volley.
    c. The racket face is closed and the wrist is relaxed in a drop volley.
    d. The racket face is closed and the ball is hit later in a drop volley.

Half Volley

220. What provides the velocity for the ball hit with a half volley?
    a. the backswing of the racket
    b. the forward swing of the racket
    *c. the speed of the rebound from the court
    d. the wrist snap

221. How should a half volley be hit?
    a. The racket should swing forward to hit the ball well in front of the player.
    b. The racket should swing forward to hit the ball out to the side of the player.
    c. The racket should be placed behind the ball out to the side of the player.
    *d. The racket should be placed behind the ball well in front of the player.

Spin

222. The racket head starts from a position behind and below the ball and moves upward and forward through the ball, finishing with a high follow-through. What kind of spin will be put on the ball?
    a. slice
    b. underspin
    *c. top spin
    d. side spin

223. What type of spin will be put on a ball if the racket face is open at contact?
    *a. slice
    b. top spin
    c. overspin
    d. side spin

Serve

224. Why is it desirable to put spin on the ball when serving?
    a. It gives it more velocity.
    b. It makes the ball bounce deeper in the court.
    *c. It permits a wider margin of error as the ball crosses the net.
    d. It is easier to hit a spin serve.

225. What is the key to a good serve?
    a. the stance
    b. the grip
    c. the swing
    *d. the ball toss

226. How high should the ball be tossed for the serve?
    a. 6 inches higher than the top of the head
    b. 2 feet higher than the top of the head
    *c. 6 inches higher than the player can reach with the racket
    d. 2 feet higher than the player can reach with the racket

227. What would be the best ball toss for the serve of those shown in the diagram? [Refer to Diagram 4.]
    *d.

Diagram 4

228. The player is holding one ball. How should the ball be held to make the toss for the serve?
    a. between the thumb and index finger with the palm up
    *b. between the thumb, index, and second finger with the palm up
    c. in the palm of the hand with the palm up
    d. in the palm of the hand with the palm to the side

229. What will be the result if the service toss is too low?
    *a. The swing will be hurried and cramped.
    b. The ball will be hit out-of-bounds.
    c. The ball will be hit into the net.
    d. The ball will hit on the frame of the racket.

230. A player is practicing the toss for the flat serve and allowing the ball to bounce after the toss. Where should a properly tossed ball bounce in relation to the player's feet? [Refer to Diagram 5.]
    *b.

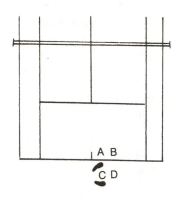

Diagram 5

231. What serving grip is recommended for beginners?
    a. Australian
    b. Continental
    *c. Eastern
    d. Western

232. What grip is used on the serve by most advanced players?
    a. Australian
    *b. Continental
    c. Eastern
    d. Western

233. Which diagram shows the correct stance for the serve?

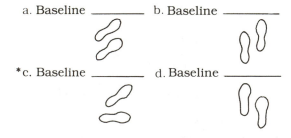

234. How is the timing of the ball toss and swing related?
    *a. The movement of the ball tossing hand and racket swinging arm is down together and up together.
    b. As the racket begins its backward movement, the ball is tossed.
    c. As the ball reaches its height in the toss, the racket swing begins.
    d. The ball is tossed when the racket movement pauses between the backswing and forward swing.

235. From what position should the forward motion of the swing begin for the serve? [Refer to Diagram 6.]
    *d.

Diagram 6

236. What is the position of the right elbow at the end of the backswing for the serve?
    *a. bent and slightly above the level of the right shoulder
    b. bent and slightly below the level of the right shoulder
    c. bent and tucked in close to the right side
    d. straight and the arm is extended upward

237. Where is the point of contact for the serve?
    a. directly over the player's head
    b. in front of the player and slightly to the left of the player's head
    *c. in front of the player and slightly to the right of the player's head
    d. in back of the player and slightly to the left of the player's head

238. On the serve, at what point in the ball's flight should it be contacted?
    a. as it goes up
    b. as it reaches its peak
    *c. as it begins to come down
    d. as soon as it can be reached

239. What is the proper follow-through after contacting the ball in serving?
    *a. down across the left side of the body
    b. straight down in front of the body
    c. down and to the right side of the body
    d. stopped as soon as possible after contact

240. What is the difference in hitting a flat and slice serve?
    a. the ball toss
    b. the stance
    *c. the contact point on the ball
    d. the racket grip

241. What is the same when hitting a flat and top-spin serve?
    a. the ball toss
    b. the wrist action
    c. the forward swing
    *d. the stance

Receiving Serve

242. What stance should a player take to receive a serve?
    *a. the same stance used in the ready position for drives
    b. the same stance used in the ready position at the net
    c. a stance facing the right sideline with his or her feet shoulder width apart
    d. a stance facing the side he or she anticipates the serve will be hit

243. A player is expecting an unusually fast serve. What should he or she change from receiving a normal serve?
    a. Be more alert.
    b. Try to anticipate the direction and begin moving before the ball is served.
    *c. Move a step or two farther from the net and take a shorter backswing.
    d. Move up a step and take a shorter follow-through.

Strategy

244. What causes most points to be scored?
    a. accurate placement shots
    b. powerful serves
    c. overpowering ground strokes
    *d. errors

245. Which is the best strategy for beginners?
    *a. Keep the ball in play.
    b. Hit all balls to the opponent's backhand.
    c. Hit the ball to the deep corners of the court.
    d. Use a second serve that is sure to be good.

246. What is the best tennis strategy?
    a. Drive all balls to the opponent's backhand.
    *b. Force the opponent out of position.
    c. Put spin on all shots.
    d. Alternate hitting drop shots and drives.

247. The opponent is standing in the center of the court just behind the service line. Where is the best place to hit the ball?
    a. over his or her head
    b. just over the net with a drop shot
    *c. at his or her feet
    d. down the middle with a hard hit drive

248. In most cases, which stroke should a player force his or her opponent to use to produce the most errors?
    a. serve
    b. volley
    c. forehand
    *d. backhand

249. On what should a player concentrate during the warm-up?
    *a. finding the opponent's weaknesses
    b. hiding his or her weaknesses
    c. getting a good feel for hitting the ball
    d. running the opponent with his or her best shots

250. Which type opponent will help most in improving a player's game?
    a. one that is easy to beat
    b. one that can barely be beaten
    *c. one that is more skillful
    d. one that has equal ability

251. Which stroke is considered to be the weapon of attack?
    a. the forehand
    *b. the serve
    c. the volley
    d. the overhead

252. What is a good shot to use to defend against a power player?
    a. a hard hit forehand
    b. a powerful serve
    *c. a lob
    d. a forcing volley

253. Your opponent has hit a shot that pulls you out of the court and has you in trouble. What is the best return?
    *a. defensive lob
    b. drive down the line
    c. drop shot down the line
    d. offensive lob

254. A player has moved to the right of his or her doubles sideline at the baseline to hit a shot. What return will give him or her the *least* distance to move in order to be ready for the opponent's next shot?
    a. a deep down-the-line forehand drive
    *b. a deep crosscourt forehand drive
    c. a short crosscourt forehand drive
    d. a deep lob to the middle of the court

255. Generally speaking, what is the best shot?
    a. one that bounces in the forecourt
    b. one that bounces near the service line
    c. one that bounces between the service and baselines
    *d. one that bounces inside and near the baseline

256. A player is consistently hitting the ball too short. What should he or she change to make it go deeper?
    a. Hit it harder.
    *b. Hit it higher over the net.
    c. Use more wrist action.
    d. Use more follow-through.

257. A player knows that his or her opponent is slow in getting to the net. What shot should he or she use frequently?
    a. forehand crosscourt
    b. backhand down-the-line
    c. short serve
    *d. drop shot

258. When is the best time for a player to go to the net?
    a. after a hard hit down-the-line forehand
    b. after a hard hit crosscourt forehand
    c. after a shot to the opponent's backhand
    *d. after a ball played from inside the baseline

259. Which shot is considered to be the highest percentage shot?
    a. a down-the-line drive
    *b. a crosscourt drive
    c. the second serve
    d. an overhead

260. Why is it *not* advisable for a player to "run around" a particular stroke?
    *a. It pulls the player out of position.
    b. It tells the opponent about the player's weakness.
    c. The player does not get practice on that stroke to improve it.
    d. It interferes with the total game plan.

261. Two players are rallying during a game. How deep in the court should they be standing to wait for their opponent's return?
    a. on the service line
    b. halfway between the service and baselines
    c. in front of the baseline
    *d. behind the baseline

262. What should a player do after hitting each stroke?
    a. See if the shot is in or out.
    *b. Return to the center of the angle of the possible return.
    c. Admire his or her shot.
    d. Return to the center of the court.

263. Which points are considered the "critical points" in a game?
    a. first and sixth
    b. second and fourth
    *c. first, third, and sixth
    d. second, fourth, and sixth

264. What should a player do on critical points?
    a. go all out
    b. try to hit a winner on the serve or return of serve
    c. get to the net before the opponent
    *d. play "percentage tennis"

265. Which game is considered the most critical in a set?
    a. first
    b. fourth
    *c. seventh
    d. tenth

266. A player hits an approach shot and comes toward the net. When should he or she stop to make the next shot?
    a. when reaching the service line
    b. after two more steps
    c. when the ball crosses to his or her side of the net
    *d. as the opponent begins his or her forward swing

Singles

267. Where is the best ready position for rallying in singles? [Refer to Diagram 7.]

   *c.

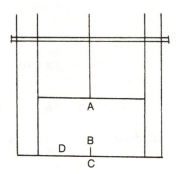

Diagram 7

268. A singles player hits the ball and charges the net. What options does the opponent have?
   a. hit the ball at him or her
   *b. hit a passing shot or lob
   c. hit the ball at him or her or lob
   d. hit the ball at him or her or a passing shot

269. A singles player hits an approach shot and comes to the net. Where should the approach shot be directed most frequently?
   *a. to the opponent's backhand corner
   b. to the opponent's forehand corner
   c. crosscourt to the service line
   d. down the middle to the baseline

270. A singles player hits an approach shot to the opponent's backhand corner and comes to the net. What position should he or she take at the net?
   a. center of the net
   *b. slightly to the right of the center of the net
   c. slightly to the left of the center of the net
   d. halfway between the right side line and center line

Doubles

271. In doubles, what pattern of play should most beginners use?
   *a. one up and one back
   b. both up at the net
   c. both back at the baseline
   d. both at the service line

272. In doubles, what pattern of play is recommended for advanced players?
   a. one up and one back
   *b. both up or both back
   c. both at the net
   d. both at the baseline

273. In doubles, which player should play the left court?
   a. the one with the best net game
   b. the one with the best backhand
   c. the quicker player
   *d. the better player

274. Both Teams A and B are in up-and-back positions. Team A lobs over the net person's head on Team B. What should the net person on Team B do?
   a. Turn and run back to try to hit the ball after it bounces.
   b. Stay in the same place and duck.
   *c. Move to the other side of the court, staying at the net.
   d. Run back to the baseline on the other side of the court.

275. What is the net person's first responsibility in doubles?
   *a. to protect the alley
   b. to go for the kill
   c. to return short shots
   d. to hit any ball that comes down the middle

276. Both players on a doubles team are at the net. The ball comes down the center of the court. Generally, who should take it?
   a. the player on the right
   *b. the player on the left
   c. the player with the better forehand volley
   d. the better player

277. A doubles team is playing up and back. The back player hits a ball crosscourt that lands short and near the sideline. What should the net player do?
   a. move to the center of the court to intercept the crosscourt return
   b. stay in the center of his or her half of the court
   c. move back and toward the center to cover more court
   *d. move toward the sideline to cover the alley

278. In doubles, where should the net player stand when the ball is in the position shown on the diagram? (Refer to Diagram 8.)
    *a.

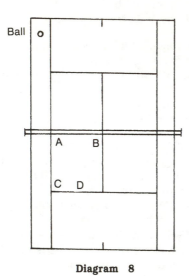

Diagram 8

279. A doubles team is playing up and back. The back player hits a lob down the line. What should his or her net player do?
    *a. Move to the center of the court to intercept the crosscourt return.
    b. Stay in the center of his or her half of the court.
    c. Move back to the baseline to cover the anticipated lob return.
    d. Move toward the sideline to cover the alley.

280. Team A is playing up and back. The back player hits a good lob down the line over the head of the opposing net person. What should Team A do?
    a. The players stay up and back.
    b. The up player moves back and the back player moves up.
    c. The up player moves to the baseline with his or her partner.
    *d. The back player moves to the net with his or her partner.

281. Both players on Team A are at the net. Team B hits a lob over the Team A player on the right side. What should the players on Team A do?
    a. The player on the right runs back to hit the ball, and his or her partner stays at the net.
    b. The player on the left side runs back to hit the ball, and his or her partner moves to the other side at the net.
    *c. The player on the left side runs back to hit the ball, and his or her partner runs back to the left side of the baseline.
    d. The player on the right side runs back to hit the ball, and his or her partner runs back to the left side of the baseline.

282. Team A is playing up and back. Team B hits a short ball to the player in the back. The back player hits an approach shot and comes to the net. What should the up player do?
    a. move in closer to the net
    *b. move several steps back but stay at the net
    c. run to the baseline to cover a possible lob
    d. move back to the middle of his or her half of the court

Serving

283. What kinds of first and second serves should a player try to hit?
    a. The player should try for an ace on the first serve and dink on the second.
    b. The player should try for an ace on the first serve and hit a medium paced deep second serve.
    *c. The player should hit a first serve with 50% or better accuracy and a slightly less paced ball on the second serve.
    d. The player should hit a first serve with 80% or better accuracy and more spin on the second serve.

284. Where should the player stand to serve from the right court in singles? [Refer to Diagram 9.]

    *a

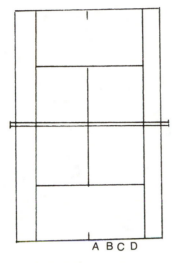

A B C D

Diagram 9

285. In singles, where should the server try to place the ball?
    *a. deep to either corner of the service court
    b. deep to the center of the service court
    c. to the middle of the service court
    d. short to the sideline corner of the service court

286. In singles, what is the primary purpose of serving a ball to the right court near the center line?
    a. to surprise the receiver
    *b. to force the receiver to make a backhand return
    c. to cut down the possible angle of return
    d. to draw the receiver out of position

287. The player is serving in doubles from the right-hand court. Where should he or she stand? [Refer to Diagram 10.]

    *c.

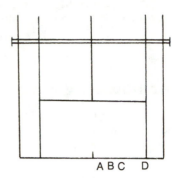

A B C   D

Diagram 10

288. In doubles, where should the server's partner stand during the serve? [Refer to Diagram 11.]

    *b.

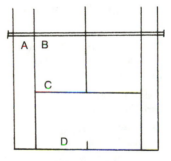

Diagram 11

Receiving Serve

289. A server moves to the right several steps from his or her normal serving position. What should the receiver do?
    *a. The receiver should move to the right.
    b. The receiver should move to the left.
    c. The receiver should move toward the net a step.
    d. The receiver should stay in the same place.

290. For the doubles serve, what is the highest percentage return shot?
    *a. crosscourt to the server
    b. down the line past the net person
    c. lob over the net person
    d. drive at the net person

291. In doubles, the server is coming to net in back of his or her serve. What is the best return?
    a. a hard crosscourt drive to the back court
    *b. a soft shot to the server's feet
    c. a lob over down the middle of the court
    d. a down-the-line passing shot

Acknowledgments

Colleagues and students who contributed suggestions and ideas for the Tennis test questions are: E. Bailey, J. Edington, W. Ozbirn, and J. Rogers.

Suggested Readings

Barton, J.R., & Grice, W.A. (1978). *Tennis.* College Station, TX: Unlimited Products.

Johnson, J.D., & Xanthos, P.J. (1980). *Tennis* (4th ed.). Dubuque, IA: Wm. C. Brown.

Johnson, M.L., & Hill, D.L. (1980). *Tennis.* Topeka, KS: Josten.

Payne, G. (1982). *A tennis manual for beginning and intermediate players* (3rd ed.). Dubuque, IA: Kendall/Hunt.

Pelton, B.C. (1980). *Tennis* (3rd ed.). Glenview, IL: Scott Foresman.

Stahr, T., Smith, T., & Moss, J. *A friend at court.* New York: CBS.

Talbert, W.F., & Olds, K.D. (1983). *Tennis tactics: Singles and doubles.* New York: Harper & Row.

Track and Field

Le Roy T. Walker, Consultant

Questions for track and field are presented within the following categories:

- General knowledge
- Conditioning and training
- Sprints
- Middle- and long-distance running
- Hurdles
- Relays
- Discus
- Shot put
- Javelin
- Standing and running long jumps
- High jump
- Rules

The questions for the various events cover topics such as principles, techniques, and rules. The rules, current with 1986 regulations, are related to the type and level of competition so answers to rules questions will be affected by these factors.

Questions for the pole vault and hammer throw are not included because these events are not usually covered in high school instructional programs.

General Knowledge

History	1 to 8
Terminology	9 to 23
Safety	24 to 25
Mechanical Principles	26 to 27
Miscellaneous	28 to 31

History

1. Who was the "Queen of the Olympics" in 1960, winning three gold medals in running events?
   - *a. Wilma Rudolph
   - b. Olga Connoly
   - c. Madeline Manning
   - d. Barbara Ferrell

2. Who was the first person to go under 3:50 in the mile?
   - a. Jim Ryun
   - *b. John Walker
   - c. Tony Waldrop
   - d. Roger Bannister

3. Who ran the first sub-4-minute mile?
   - a. Wes Santee
   - b. John Landy
   - c. Gunder Hagg
   - *d. Roger Bannister

4. Where did track originate?
   - a. Rome
   - b. Atlantis
   - *c. Greece
   - d. Italy

Le Roy T. Walker was Head Coach of the United States Olympic Track and Field Team in 1976.

5. How far back do formal records of the Olympic Games date?
   a. 400 B.C.
   *b. 776 B.C.
   c. 960 B.C.
   d. 1896 A.D.

6. When were women first allowed to compete in the Modern Olympics?
   a. 1924
   *b. 1928
   c. 1932
   d. 1936

7. Where did track and field athletics, as known today, originate?
   a. Sweden
   *b. British Isles
   c. West Germany
   d. Canada

8. Women were not allowed to participate in the first Olympics but they had a festival on a smaller scale. What was this festival called?
   a. Pythian
   b. Ismthian
   c. Nemean
   *d. Herea

Terminology

9. What is a *scratch*?
   *a. touching the ground beyond the take-off board
   b. marking the area where the shot fell
   c. dropping out of an event
   d. skipping a trial

10. What is the 60° sector?
    a. the exchange zone
    b. the first section of a race
    *c. the area where the discus must be released
    d. the approach to the high jump

11. What are flats?
    a. runways for the long jump
    b. tracks
    *c. track shoes without spikes
    d. instruments used for measuring

12. What does *boxed* mean?
    a. stopping quickly and then deciding to start again on another approach
    b. exchanging the positions of the feet after releasing the shot
    c. getting hit by a runner
    *d. having a competitor in front and on the side

13. To what does the curb refer?
    a. the takeoff board for the long jump
    *b. the inside border of the track
    c. the circle for the discus thrower
    d. the takeoff line

14. To what does *kick* refer?
    a. the exchange of feet after a release
    b. the distance one member of a relay team must run
    c. the trail leg in hurdling
    *d. the increased speed at the end of the race

15. What is a medley relay?
    *a. a relay race in which members of a relay team run different distances
    b. a relay race in which the team is coed
    c. a novelty track event
    d. a relay race in which members of the team participate in several events

16. What is a *break*?
    a. changing the rhythm of the run
    b. skipping a trial
    *c. leaving the starting blocks before the starter fires the gun
    d. time when runners are called back after a false start

17. What is a flat race?
    *a. a race run without hurdles
    b. a short distance race
    c. a preliminary race
    d. the last section of a race

18. What is meant by *snapdown*?
    *a. dropping the lead leg after hurdle clearance
    b. slowing the approach in the running long jump
    c. crossing in front of another runner
    d. thrusting the arms downward after clearing the high jump bar

19. What does *breaking for the pole* mean?
    a. approaching the high bar
    b. planting the pole for the vault
    *c. cutting over to the inside of the track
    d. kicking while in flight on the long jump

20. What is an *anchor*?
    a. a nickname for the shot
    *b. the final leg of a relay
    c. the placement of the foot for the takeoff on the pole vault
    d. the spot where the contestant leaves the ground

21. What is a flight?
    a. preliminary round of a race
    *b. round of trials for field events
    c. position of body going over the hurdles
    d. approach to the pole vault

22. What is a heat?
    *a. preliminary round of a race
    b. round of trials for field events
    c. warm-up activity
    d. false start

23. What does AAU stand for?
    *a. Amateur Athletic Union
    b. American Athletic Union
    c. Association of Amateur Unions
    d. Athletic Association Union

Safety

24. Which situation provides the safest conditions?
    *a. The shot put has just been measured and the official in the field rolls the shot back to the circle for the next competitor.
    b. The javelin thrower is wearing tennis shoes with rubber grips on the soles.
    c. The javelin throw, in wet weather, is executed from the middle area of the runway for the best traction.
    d. The discus thrower takes position in the circle as a warning to others of a throw.

25. Which event would involve the greatest safety concern for spectators?
    a. shot put
    b. 50-yard dash
    c. running long jump
    *d. javelin throw

Mechanical Principles

26. What are the main factors in determining momentum?
    a. speed and flexibility
    b. mass and power
    *c. mass and speed
    d. power and endurance

27. Which factor explains why it is difficult to stop suddenly while running?
    *a. Inertia is acting on the body.
    b. Acceleration is too great.
    c. Momentum is too great.
    d. A counterforce cannot be developed quickly enough.

Miscellaneous

28. Which event is *not* included in the pentathlon?
    a. sprint
    b. high jump
    *c. discus
    d. long jump

29. Which factor is most influential in determining how one performs in track and field events?
    a. body build
    b. condition
    c. mental attitude
    *d. training

30. Which event is *not* classified as a field event?
    a. shot put
    b. high jump
    *c. hurdles
    d. javelin

31. What strategy for placement should one use if there are so many competitors that flights are used in the field events?
    a. The competitor should finish in a flight below his or her capacity to get a better chance of advancement.
    *b. The competitor should strive to finish in the highest position flight of the event.
    c. The competitor should not strive too hard to conserve energy for the finals.
    d. The competitor should not strive too hard to distract competitors from his or her good points.

Conditioning and Training

Systems

Circuit

32. Which form of conditioning involves exercises, stations, and work rates?
    *a. circuit
    b. Fartlek
    c. interval
    d. overload

33. What is the method used in circuit training?
    a. The performer moves from one station to another completing certain tasks at each.
    b. The performer runs around the track alternating running and walking.
    *c. The performer runs an up- and down-hill course.
    d. The performer runs around the track alternating sprinting and jogging.

Interval

34. What is the value of interval training to the coach?
    a. It may be used to train participants in all events.
    b. It is easy to supervise a large number of people at once.
    *c. It may be individualized to suit individual needs.
    d. It may be used competitively to stimulate interest in practice.

35. Which statement is true of interval training?
    a. 15 to 20 repetitions are optimal.
    b. Rest intervals should be equal to run intervals.
    c. Repetitions should be 3 to 4 seconds slower than racing pace.
    *d. Time required is less than other workouts.

36. What are the variable situations in interval training?
    a. length of distance, pace
    b. recovery interval, repetitions
    c. length of distance, pace, repetitions
    *d. length of distance, pace, recovery interval, repetitions

Fartlek

37. What statement is true of Fartlek training?
    *a. Aerobic and anaerobic endurance is increased.
    b. Variety provided is minimal.
    c. Progress is measured easily.
    d. Inexperienced runners benefit the most.

Weights

38. Which training program is recommended *least* for improving strength, flexibility, endurance, and agility?
    a. circuit
    b. Fartlek
    *c. heavy weights
    d. interval

Fast Running

39. Which statement is true of continuous, fast running training?
    a. Heart rate should exceed 120 beats/minute.
    b. Recovery time is shorter than interval training.
    c. Hill training phase is important.
    *d. Aggregate repetitions exceed racing distance.

Factors

Strength

40. What is meant by *overload* with reference to strength conditioning?
    a. building strength by exercising more than one muscle group at a time
    b. building strength in a specific muscle by exercising other muscles in the same group as well
    *c. building strength by gradually increasing the weight load of the exercise or the number of repetitions
    d. building strength by lifting weights in a prescibed weight-training program

Endurace

41. How is anaerobic endurance training accomplished?
    a. working continuously for long periods of time
    b. performing long bouts of easy exercise with no rest periods between bouts
    *c. performing short bouts of maximal effort with brief rest periods between bouts
    d. working for short periods of time at any easy level

Flexibility

42. Why is flexibility a major objective in conditioning?
    a. It aids in increasing endurance.
    *b. It aids in preventing muscle injury.
    c. It improves muscle explosiveness.
    d. It contributes to strength development.

Stretching

43. Stretching exercises are most beneficial in conditioning for which event?
    a. discus
    b. relay
    c. sprint
    *d. hurdles

44. How is an overall beneficial stretch performed?
    *a. in a slow, relaxed manner
    b. with fast movements
    c. with tension
    d. with jerky movements

45. What does the triangle exercise stretch?
    a. hips
    b. abdomen
    c. hamstrings
    *d. quadriceps

Warm-Up

46. What is the purpose of warming up?
    a. to improve skill
    b. to build endurance
    c. to enlarge the muscles
    *d. to reduce chance of injury

47. Why are warm-ups considered important?
    a. They use specific skill exercises to stretch muscles.
    b. They concentrate on exercising one specific area of the body.
    *c. They concentrate on flexibility exercises to stretch muscles.
    d. They develop strength and endurance.

Miscellaneous

48. The conditioning activities preceding a track and field unit/season should be aimed at increasing which factors?
    a. skill, flexibility, and form
    b. skill, speed, and endurance
    c. strength, speed, and form
    *d. strength, endurance, and flexibility

49. Why is it important for a physical exam and general conditioning to precede more specific and intensive training?
    a. so that participants will have a wider range of strength to build on
    b. so that participants will have a head start in developing the needed coordination
    c. so that participants who need more help can be spotted early
    *d. so that participants will be generally healthy and less likely to be injured

50. A runner has just finished a race in warm weather and is tired and perspiring. What procedure should be followed?
    a. The runner should find a shady area to sit down.
    b. The runner should take a cold shower and put on light clothing.
    c. The runner should put on sweat clothes immediately to absorb the perspiration.
    *d. The runner should slowly reduce activity.

51. What is a by-product of exercise that eventually will result in the runner's legs stiffening up?
    a. oxygen debt
    *b. lactic acid
    c. triglycerides
    d. aerobic

52. What should a runner do about shin splints?
    a. Run on sand.
    b. Run on the toes.
    *c. Run on surfaces with good traction.
    d. Run flat-footed.

53. What should a competitor eat before competing?
    a. The competitor should refrain from eating until after competing.
    b. The competitor should eat high protein foods such as steak.
    c. The competitor should drink plenty of juices.
    *d. The competitor should eat a meal high in carbohydrates such as a baked potato.

Sprints

Note. Questions cover events under the 800-meter distance.

General	**54 to 55**
Mechanical Principles	**56**
Techniques	**57 to 82**
Strategy	**83 to 87**
Conditioning	**88 to 89**
Rules	**90 to 102**

General

54. Why is sprinting considered the most basic track event?
    * *a. Good sprinting and running form is essential to all track events.
    b. Sprinting is the easiest event for beginners to learn.
    c. Sprinting is best for developing good coordination and agility.
    d. Sprinting is the most efficient method of conditioning for beginners.

55. Which event requires the most endurance?
    * *a. 200-meter dash
    b. 400-meter pursuit relay
    c. 50-yard dash
    d. 80-meter hurdles

Mechanical Principles

56. What event is related to this principle: A body is said to be balanced when the center of gravity falls within the base of support?
    a. discus
    b. long jump
    * *c. sprint start
    d. high jump

Techniques

Start

57. Which statement is correct about the start?
    a. The front foot initiates the drive.
    b. The eyes should be focused toward the finish line.
    c. The blocks should be spaced to crowd the line.
    * *d. The feet should have even pressure on the blocks.

58. Which foot is usually placed to the rear in the starting blocks?
    a. foot of the right leg
    b. foot of the weakest leg
    * *c. foot of the strongest leg
    d. foot of the left leg

59. Where should the sprinter's entire concentration be focused while in the blocks?
    a. the competition
    b. the first move
    * *c. the sound of the pistol
    d. the lean needed at the finish line

60. What is the effect of the bridge in sprint starts?
    * *a. to place the shoulders as high as possible
    b. to place the hips as high as possible
    c. to place the arms at a better angle
    d. to place the legs in a direct line

61. What is the correct hip elevation for a crouch start?
    a. hips slightly above shoulders so the weight is shifted slightly beyond the center of gravity
    b. hips level with the shoulders so the runner is balanced
    * *c. hips slightly above shoulders in order for the legs to be in position to deliver optimum power
    d. hips level with shoulders in order for the legs to be in position to deliver optimum power

62. Which sprint start would put the runner into stride the fastest and most effectively?
    a. bunch start
    * *b. medium start
    c. elongated start
    d. crouch start

63. Which sprint start has proven to be the most effective?
    a. bunch
    b. elongated
    c. medium
    * *d. None, because of different body builds

64. Which statement is the best description of sprinters when "on the mark"?
    a. Head and neck are relaxed, and the rear knee is off the ground.
    * *b. Head and neck are relaxed, and the rear knee is on the ground.
    c. Head and neck are raised, and the rear knee is off the ground.
    d. Head and neck are raised and the rear knee is on the ground.

65. Which statement best describes the "set" phase of the start?
    a. hips even with shoulders, weight over hands, head in line with trunk
    * *b. hips slightly above trunk, weight slightly ahead of hands, head in line with trunk
    c. hips even with shoulders, weight ahead of hands, eyes focused 10 to 30 feet down the track
    d. hips slightly above shoulders, weight over hands, eyes focused 1 to 3 feet down the track

66. What does the sprinter do on the "set" command?
    a. takes the back leg off the block
    b. straightens the elbows
  *c. raises the hips to just above shoulder level
    d. raises the head to look down the lane

67. Where should the runner look when hearing the command, "Set"?
    a. at the starter
    b. at the finish tape
  *c. directly down to the ground
    d. at the ground a few feet ahead

68. Where should the runner focus when coming out of the blocks in a sprint?
    a. on the nearest opponent
    b. on the finish line
  *c. on the ground a few meters forward
    d. on the ground at the feet

69. What is the most important concern in the initial phase of the start?
    a. keeping hands and feet behind the line
  *b. reaching top speed quickly
    c. listening for the starter's commands
    d. remaining relaxed and at ease

Starting blocks

70. When should sprinters adjust their blocks?
  *a. when first arriving at the starting line
    b. after stretching
    c. just before the start of the race
    d. when told to set them

71. What is the purpose of the starting blocks for sprint starts?
    a. power
  *b. thrust
    c. overcoming inertia
    d. speed

72. What should the runner do coming out of the starting blocks?
    a. Raise the head and look down the track.
  *b. Take shorter steps than full running strides.
    c. Raise whole body to normal upright position.
    d. Take long running strides.

Running

73. Which technique is the same for both sprinting and long-distance running?
    a. method of starting
    b. amount of arm-pumping action
    c. amount of upper body lean
  *d. part of foot used in push off

74. How far out of the blocks have most sprinters come to a fully upright position?
    a. 5 to 10 meters
  *b. 10 to 12 meters
    c. 15 to 20 meters
    d. 25 to 30 meters

75. What is the best way to run a curve?
    a. Lean forward.
    b. Lean into the curve.
    c. Lean away from the curve.
  *d. Maintain the same body posture.

76. What does extraneous arm movement cause in running?
    a. unnecessary tiring of arm muscles
  *b. increase in total energy output
    c. takes away from the beauty of running
    d. helps increase running speed

77. What may be the result of running with the fists clenched tightly?
  *a. increased tenseness and reduced rhythmical flow
    b. reduced tenseness and increased rhythmical flow
    c. increased forward momentum
    d. decreased chance of falling

78. What are the characteristics of a good sprinter at full speed?
  *a. a long stride, high knee lift in front, piston-like arm action, with the rear leg kick as high as the knee
    b. a long stride, high knee lift in front, very vigorous arm action, with the rear leg kick a little higher than the knee
    c. a long stride, high knee lift in front, piston-like arm action, with the rear leg kick as low as possible
    d. a long stride, very vigorous arm action, with the rear leg kick as low as possible

79. Which technique produces an efficient run and why?
    a. running on the balls of the feet because this allows greater push and results in greater speed
    *b. running with high knee action because this action frees the lower leg and allows the stride to be increased without lowering the center of gravity
    c. pulling forward with the arms because this increases the momentum and gives greater speed
    d. running with a gallop because the runner hits the track harder and is able to push off faster

80. What are the characteristics of effective running?
    *a. optimum stride, rhythm, balance, and opposition of arms and legs
    b. optimum stride, rhythm, head back, and opposition of arms and legs
    c. optimum stride, head forward, minimum movement of arms
    d. optimum stride, rhythm, balance, and knees low

81. Which sequence gives the best phasing of sprint or dash events?
    a. start, running form, acceleration, finish
    b. start, pace, running form, finish
    c. start, running form, pace, finish
    *d. start, acceleration, running form, finish

Finish

82. The runner approaching the finish line looks back over the right shoulder to see how near the opponent is. Is this a good procedure and why?
    a. Yes, this allows the head runner to adjust the finish kick if the opponent is near.
    b. Yes, this allows the lead runner to see the location of the opposing runners.
    c. No, the lead runner may trip and fall.
    *d. No, the lead runner loses time and cuts speed when turning.

Strategy

83. What strategy should the sprinter use concerning speed?
    *a. Come out of the blocks with tremendous explosive power.
    b. Gradually build speed and explode at the finish.
    c. Maintain easy, long strides with no explosion of power.
    d. Pace to the opponents and then decide whether an explosion is needed.

84. What is a good race plan for the 200?
    a. Reach full speed for first 40 meters, maintain a fast pace next 120 meters, and run the fastest the last 40 meters.
    *b. Reach full speed for first 50 meters, maintain a fast pace next 100 meters, and run the next 50 meters efficiently to minimize deceleration.
    c. Maintain a fast pace but put out all in the last leg of the race.
    d. Try to stay in the first or second position then sprint the last 20 meters.

85. What is the best position to be in when a runner is preparing to start the kick for the finish line?
    a. on the inside shoulder of the runner immediately in front
    b. in the farthest lane from the inside lane
    *c. on the outside shoulder of the runner immediately in front
    d. in the lane directly to the left of the runner immediately in front

86. What would be best to do if a strong head wind is blowing during a race?
    a. Tuck your head to decrease resistance.
    b. Shorten your stride to conserve energy.
    c. Drop out of the race and wait for better weather.
    *d. Get behind another runner and let that runner act as a windbreak.

87. What procedure should the runner follow toward the end of the race?
    a. Slow down about 2 or 3 meters before the finish line.
    b. Slow down at the finish line.
    *c. Run at full speed to a point 5 to 10 meters beyond the finish line.
    d. Speed up during the last 5 meters and slow down crossing the line.

Conditioning

88. What should conditioning for sprints include?
    * *a. strength, flexibility, and coordination exercises
    b. endurance, arm and back strengthening exercises
    c. endurance exercises only
    d. strength exercises only

89. What is a good warm-up for sprinters before a race?
    a. Do 20 push-ups.
    b. Run a fast 3 miles after appropriate warm-up.
    c. Jog 6 miles at an easy pace.
    * *d. Do acceleration runs after appropriate warm-up.

Rules

Start

90. Which procedure is legal when starting a race?
    a. placing fingers on the starting line
    * *b. placing fingers behind the starting line
    c. placing fingers beyond the starting line
    d. placing thumbs only on the starting line

91. Why are staggered starts used?
    a. to restrict fast runners
    b. to give slower runners a head start
    * *c. to equalize distance when races are run on curves
    d. to help the starter see false starts more easily

92. After the starter says "Set," one of the competitors rolls forward just before the gun is fired. What should the starter do?
    a. Warn the competitor of the infraction; no false start is charged.
    b. Let the race continue; no false start occurred.
    c. Call them back; charge one with a false start.
    * *d. False start; have all runners stand and restart the race.

Finish

93. How is the winner of a race determined?
    * *a. the runner who first reaches the finish line with any part of the torso
    b. the runner whose foot first touches the finish line
    c. the runner whose arm first reaches the finish line
    d. the runner whose chest first reaches the finish line

94. What part of the athlete's body must be first to cross the finish line?
    a. hand
    * *b. torso
    c. leg
    d. elbow

Timing

95. At what moment should the timekeeper stop the watch?
    a. when the entire body of the runner has crossed the finish line
    b. when the runner has stepped on or over the finish line
    * *c. when any part of the runner's torso reaches the nearest edge of the finish line
    d. when any part of the runner's trunk or neck reaches the nearest edge of the finish line

96. The watches for the third-place timers read 22.2, 20.9, and 20.5. What is the official time for third place?
    a. 20.5
    * *b. 20.9
    c. 21.2
    d. 22.2

97. The first-place timers read times of 21.0, 20.8, and 20.4. What is the official time for first place?
    a. 20.4
    b. 20.7
    * *c. 20.8
    d. 21.0

Impeding

98. A runner continues to veer to the right, forcing the challenger to run wider and wider in an attempt to pass. What is the runner on the inside doing?
    * *a. impeding the progress of the challenger
    b. running a longer route
    c. jostling the other runner
    d. disqualifying both runners

99. How soon may a runner cross in front of another runner when racing on a curved track?
    a. when one stride ahead of the runner
    * *b. when two strides ahead of the runner
    c. when three strides ahead of the runner
    d. whenever the runner wishes

Disqualification

100. The runner in Lane 3 is 10 meters ahead of the next runner and accidentally steps out of the lane while running the 55-meter dash. Should the runner be disqualified?
    a. No, there has been no interference with another runner.
    b. Yes, progress of another runner has been impeded.
    *c. Yes, a foul has been committed.
    d. No, the other runner has ample time to change lanes.

101. What will disqualify a runner from a race?
    *a. delaying the start of the race more than once
    b. running out of one's lane
    c. passing to take the pole position
    d. reaching for the tape

102. How is a runner disqualified in the 55-meter dash?
    a. having three false starts
    b. crossing the finish with arms outstretched
    c. using a standing start
    *d. running in another runner's lane

Middle- and Long-Distance Running

Middle Distance	**103 to 111**
Long Distance	**112 to 121**
Cross Country	**122 to 124**

Middle Distance

Strategy

103. What is the purpose of a *rabbit* in middle-distance running?
    a. to set psychological strategy
    b. to set up a box situation
    c. to serve as a rear runner
    *d. to serve as a pace setter

104. Which factor is it *not* essential for a runner to know about the opponent in middle distances?
    a. how far the opponent sprints at the start or finish
    b. if the opponent is a front runner or a follower
    c. what point the opponent responds to a challenger
    *d. what type of training method the opponent uses

105. Generally, when does the runner sprint in middle-distance running?
    a. the first quarter and the last quarter of the race
    *b. the last quarter of the race
    c. the last half of the race
    d. the last three quarters of the race

106. What is good strategy in middle-distance running?
    a. Develop an arhythmical cadence to prevent passing.
    *b. Run at the right shoulder and slightly behind the lead runner.
    c. Pass the lead runner even if it means losing rhythm.
    d. Match strides with the closest opponent.

107. What are two important factors in middle-distance running?
    *a. pacing and endurance
    b. explosive start and endurance
    c. long strides and sprinting
    d. explosive start and sprinting

108. What are the essential elements of middle-distance running?
    a. form, endurance, and short stride
    b. form, flow, and time
    c. speed, concentration, and force
    *d. speed, endurance, and pace judgment

109. Which strategy is *not* correct for a middle-distance race?
    *a. Your opponent has great speed but less strength. You should set the pace and when you are side-by-side, sprint to pass.
    b. Your opponent is trying to pass. You should run wide on the curves to keep the opponent from sneaking around you.
    c. Your opponent may box you in unless you run at the opponent's right shoulder.
    d. Your opponent has great strength but little speed. Let the opponent set the pace and outsprint the opponent at the end.

Training

110. What are the training needs of the 800-meter run?
    *a. 50% anerobic, 50% aerobic
    b. 70% anerobic, 30% aerobic
    c. 30% anerobic, 70% aerobic
    d. 20% anerobic, 80% aerobic

Terminology

111. What is the purpose of the *float*?
    a. to maintain a steady pace through small deceleration
    b. to change speeds after the start phase
   *c. to reduce tension and maintain form
    d. to get equal splits from equal exertion

Long Distance

Technique

112. What should be true of a long-distance runner approaching the halfway mark?
    a. The arm action is relaxed, the front knee action is approaching the high lift typical of a sprinter, the trunk is leaning forward, and the rear leg kick is just higher than the knee.
    b. The arm action is a pumping motion, the front knee action is approaching the high lift typical of a sprinter, the trunk is upright, and the rear leg is rather high.
   *c. The arm action is relaxed, the front knee action is low, the trunk is upright, and the rear leg kick is low.
    d. The arm action is a pumping motion; the front knee action is low, the trunk is upright, and the rear leg kick is just higher than the knee.

113. Which statement is *not* correct about distance running?
    a. The body lean should be slight.
    b. The arm action is small.
    c. The mouth and nose are used for breathing.
   *d. The foot action is toe-to-heel.

114. Which characteristic is of *least* importance when choosing a distance runner?
    a. determination
   *b. body build
    c. endurance
    d. emotional stability

Conditioning

115. What should a distance runner do at the conclusion of a workout?
    a. Sit down and rest.
    b. Do four pick-up runs.
    c. Stand and relax.
   *d. Do easy jogging or walking.

116. What is a *disadvantage* of the Lydiard system of distance training?
   *a. It requires a long time period.
    b. It provides little variety.
    c. It does not have enough speed work.
    d. It could cause an early peak.

117. Which diet would be best for a distance runner?
   *a. 700 grams of carbohydrates, 150 grams of fat, 100 grams of protein
    b. 500 grams of carbohydrates, 150 grams of fat, 250 grams of protein
    c. 500 grams of carbohydrates, 200 grams of fat, 100 grams of protein
    d. 400 grams of carbohydrates, 200 grams of fat, 200 grams of protein

Strategy

118. What caution must the front runner take in long-distance races?
   *a. *not* setting too fast a pace
    b. watching the runner behind
    c. knowing the time of the run
    d. knowing how close behind everyone is

119. What strategy will produce the best results in distance races?
    a. Run a slow first half of the race and then sprint to the finish.
   *b. Run at an even, relaxed pace throughout the race.
    c. Run a sprint the first half of the race and then coast to the finish.
    d. Run slowly in the beginning of the race, sprint the middle, and then run slow to the finish

120. Which tactic is *not* good strategy in distance running?
    a. Move quickly and with surprise when passing an opponent.
    b. Increase speed gradually near the finish.
   *c. Keep up with a fast leader.
    d. Pass an opponent on straightaways to conserve energy.

Terminology

121. What is a runner called who starts off very fast in a long-distance race?
    a. flash
    b. fast runner
    c. speed-o
   *d. rabbit

Cross Country

Technique

122. What should the cross country runner do to compensate for a steep uphill terrain?
    a. Maintain an erect body position.
    b. Keep the weight back slightly.
   *c. Keep the weight forward.
    d. Keep the weight far back.

Strategy

123. What finish would likely assure a win for a cross country team?
    a. a runner places first in the race
    b. a runner beats the course time
    c. runners take first and second in the race
    *d. runners finish within 15-25 seconds of each other

Training

124. Which type of training is recommended for cross country?
    a. Fartlek
    *b. interval
    c. weight
    d. circuit

Hurdles

General	125
Technique	126 to 143
Rules	144 to 147

General

125. Which event is *not* a field event?
    a. high jump
    b. discus
    c. shot put
    *d. hurdles

Technique

126. What can be expected when the hurdler's takeoff is relatively close to the hurdle?
    a. The hurdler has the ability to get over the hurdle quicker than if the takeoff had been farther away from the hurdle.
    *b. The hurdler has to jump the hurdle in order to clear the hurdle.
    c. The hurdler is better able to maintain sprinting speed and form.
    d. The hurdler will be able to take the lead leg directly across the top of the hurdle.

127. What is the most appropriate solution if the hurdler consistently arrives at the takeoff point of the first hurdle on the wrong foot?
    a. Take smaller steps.
    b. Change takeoff point.
    c. Learn to use other leg as the lead leg.
    *d. Reverse the position of the feet at the start.

128. Which running stride action is most important to the hurdler?
    *a. The hurdler can raise the lead leg straight up and over the hurdle and straight down on the other side.
    b. The hurdler has a quick snapdown of the lead leg and a long first step.
    c. The hurdler brings the trail leg through and places it almost directly in front of the landing leg.
    d. The hurdler has balance on takeoff and over the hurdle.

129. Which hint would be helpful to the hurdler?
    a. Overstride between the hurdles to cover more distance quicker.
    b. Thrust both arms forward going over the hurdle for more power.
    *c. Skim over the hurdle as close as possible.
    d. Keep the shoulders diagonal to the top of the hurdle.

130. What is the correct relationship of the torso to the leading leg when going over the hurdle?
    *a. leaning toward the leg to allow for a good shift of weight for the next stride and to keep motion going forward as much as possible
    b. leaning toward the leg in order to use leverage for bringing the trailing leg over the hurdle in good position
    c. upright in relation to the leg to help assure that the snapdown of the lead leg does not come too far from the hurdle
    d. upright in relation to the leg to be certain of enough height to clear the hurdle and to be in a more natural position for running

131. What does hip flexibility enable the hurdler to do?
    a. to push off the lead leg
    *b. to rotate the trail leg
    c. to land well coming off the hurdle
    d. to straighten the takeoff leg

132. What is the position of the arm on the same side as the lead leg when hurdling?
    a. placed as far away as possible from the side of the body
    *b. maintained close to the side of the body
    c. held diagonally across the body
    d. extended forward of the knee

133. How can the hurdler get over the hurdle as low as possible without breaking stride too much?
    *a. Clear the bar with the leading leg extended and the trailing leg tucked or bent.
    b. Take off from both feet simultaneously.
    c. Clear the bar with the leading leg tucked and the trailing leg extended.
    d. Take off with the leading leg.

134. What will likely happen if the performer increases stride length while hurdling?
    a. will clear the hurdles with more height
    *b. will knock down more hurdles
    c. will take off closer to the hurdles
    d. will take off farther from the hurdles

135. What action is essential to speed in getting over the hurdle?
    a. floating over the hurdle
    *b. using a quick leg snap over the hurdle
    c. sitting back over the hurdle
    d. swinging the arms forward

136. How many running strides should be taken between high hurdles?
    a. two
    *b. three
    c. four
    d. five

137. What step pattern should the hurdler develop?
    *a. consistent three steps between hurdles
    b. three steps through the entire race
    c. three steps from start to first hurdle
    d. three steps from last hurdle to finish

138. What is the most important aspect of the sprint in hurdle racing?
    a. The arm action should be especially powerful at the end of the race.
    b. The focus should be on the ground a few feet ahead.
    c. The leg kick in back should be very high to aid in clearing the hurdle.
    *d. The hurdler should try to increase stride frequency.

139. Where should the lead leg land on the first stride off the hurdle?
    a. about 30 inches in front of the hurdle and slightly behind the center of gravity
    b. about 12 inches in front of the hurdle and beneath the center of gravity
    c. about 12 inches in front of the hurdle and slightly in front of the center of gravity
    *d. about 30 inches in front of the hurdle and beneath the center of gravity

140. A hurdler is having trouble with strides in between the hurdles. What is probably the cause?
    a. clearing the hurdle too high
    b. starting the jump too close to the hurdle
    c. failing to buck with the body to get maximum distance
    *d. failing to take a full first stride with the trail leg

141. What is the major advantage of being consistent with the number of strides between hurdles?
    a. allows takeoff on the same foot each time
    *b. allows runner to reduce running time
    c. prevents runner from breaking stride
    d. enables runner to develop strength in takeoff leg

142. Which step with the trailing leg is the key to achieving three strides rather than five between hurdles?
    *a. first
    b. second
    c. third
    d. Each is equally important.

143. Which key words describe hurdling?
    *a. lift, kick, snap
    b. kick, lift, snap
    c. impact, stretch, rotate
    d. rotate, impact, stretch

Rules

144. The runner knocks a hurdle down carrying the legs up and over. What is the judge's decision?
    a. The competitor is disqualified from competition.
    b. The competitor must run in the next heat.
    *c. The competitor is eligible for a win and a record.
    d. The competitor can win but is ineligible for a record.

145. How many hurdles are in the 110-meter high hurdle race?
    a. 9
    *b. 10
    c. 11
    d. 12

146. Which foul will disqualify a runner in the hurdles?
    a. knocking down one of the hurdles
    *b. carrying the rear leg below hurdle frame extended
    c. extending an arm into the next lane
    d. hitting the hurdle then falling down after clearing it

147. How high are the hurdles used in women's races that are equivalent to the low hurdles used by men?
    a. 2 feet
    *b. 2 feet 6 inches
    c. 3 feet
    d. 3 feet 6 inches

Relays

Techniques	**148 to 160**
Strategy	**161 to 164**
Rules	**165 to 171**
Terminology	**172 to 173**

Techniques

148. Which technique is *not* used in the thumbs-down method of baton exchange?
    a. The receiving hand is lower than the hip.
    b. The receiving palm is facing down.
    c. The receiving fingers are pointed back.
    *d. The receiving elbow is pointed upward.

149. What is the recommended exchange for relays in which each leg is 200 meters or more?
    a. nonvisual
    b. basket pass
    *c. visual
    d. two looks

150. How is the baton passed in the pursuit relay?
    a. right hand to left hand, sight exchange
    b. left hand to right hand, sight exchange
    c. right hand to left hand, blind exchange
    *d. left hand to right hand, blind exchange

151. The moment of baton exchange is completed in how many strides?
    *a. one
    b. two
    c. three
    d. four

152. What is a common method used for nonvisual exchanges in relay events?
    a. right-to-left underhand exchange
    b. left-to-right underhand exchange
    c. alternate underhand exchange
    *d. right-to-left and left-to-right overhand exchange

153. What is the correct way to pass the baton in the first and third legs?
    a. The incoming runner carries the baton in the left hand and passes to the right hand of the outgoing runner.
    *b. The incoming runner carries the baton in the right hand and passes to the left hand of the outgoing runner.
    c. The incoming runner carries the baton in the left hand and passes to the left hand of the outgoing runner.
    d. The incoming runner carries the baton in the right hand and passes to the right hand of the outgoing runner.

154. Why is the visual exchange better when the passer has run 400 meters or more in a relay?
    a. The passer may fool the receiver with the drive near the end of that leg.
    b. The passing zone is shorter so more accuracy is essential.
    c. The receiver may otherwise tend to overanticipate and not grasp the baton.
    *d. The passer is likely to be somewhat fatigued so extra caution is needed.

155. Which baton exchange style is most frequently used for both visual and nonvisual exchanges?
    a. the basket pass
    b. the underarm extension—palm up pass
    c. the overarm extension—palm up pass
    *d. the underarm extension—palm down pass

156. In which area of the exchange zone should the exchange take place to maintain the momentum of both runners?
    *a. in the last 5 meters
    b. in the middle 5 meters
    c. in the first 5 meters
    d. it depends on the runners

157. The baton is dropped by a runner outside of the passing zone. Who should pick it up?
    a. It does not matter.
    b. The runner who passed it.
    *c. The runner who dropped it.
    d. The runner nearest to it.

158. What should the receiver do when the incoming runner hits the "set" line?
    a. Begin the sprint.
    b. Yell "go."
    c. Have already run through the passing zone.
    *d. Prepare for the sprint.

159. What should the runner receiving the baton do?
    a. Stand still until receiving it.
    b. Watch the incoming runner hand the baton.
    *c. Approach top speed before the exchange is made.
    d. Jog along until receiving the baton.

160. A left-to-right exchange is about to be made. On which side of the lane should the receiver start running to leave room for both runners on the lane?
    a. on the right side
    *b. on the left side
    c. Runners should decide beforehand.
    d. Start running in the middle and then quickly shift to the right side.

Strategy

161. Which runner is *not* strategically placed in a 4 × 100 meter relay race?
    a. first runner: good starter, maintains speed, good passer
    b. second runner: accelerates less on a straightaway, good receiver and passer
    *c. third runner: accelerates less on a straightaway, good receiver and passer
    d. fourth runner: able to catch and hold off opponents, covers least distance well

162. Which statement is true about the order of runners in the 400-meter relay?
    a. The slowest runner runs last.
    b. The worst curve runner runs third.
    *c. The fastest runner out of the blocks runs first.
    d. The best curve runner runs second.

163. What leg of a relay does the fastest runner usually run?
    a. first
    b. second
    c. third
    *d. fourth

164. Who should be the first runner in the 400-meter relay?
    *a. best starter who is also a good curve runner
    b. fastest runner
    c. second fastest runner
    d. best curve runner

Rules

165. One member of the relay team does not switch the baton to the opposite hand from which it was received before passing it off. What is the ruling?
    a. foul, counts as an attempt
    b. false start
    c. disqualification
    *d. acceptable

166. Which diagram shows the space where the baton is passed in the 4 × 400? [Refer to Diagram 1.]
    *c.

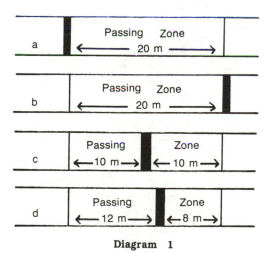

Diagram 1

167. Why would a relay team for the 800 be disqualified?
    a. picking up the baton by the runner who dropped it outside the passing zone
    b. using a blind pass and dropping the baton
    c. picking up the baton by the passer inside the passing zone
    *d. picking up the baton by the passer outside the passing zone

168. In what order do the runners in the 800-meter medley relay usually run the race?
    - a. 200-200-200-200
    - b. 100-100-200-400
    - *c. 200-100-100-400
    - d. 400-200-100-100

169. What is the length of the passing zone?
    - a. 11 meters
    - *b. 20 meters
    - c. 22 meters
    - d. 24 meters

170. Why is a staggered start used during the pursuit relay?
    - a. to avoid crowding
    - b. to view the baton exchanges better
    - c. to make use of the outside lanes
    - *d. to equalize the distance

171. After a preliminary heat, a relay team discovers one of the runners is too ill to compete. Another runner fills in. What is the ruling?
    - *a. legal if illness is certified by meet physician
    - b. illegal, team is disqualified
    - c. legal if the coach says the competitor is too ill
    - d. legal, you are allowed one substitution

Terminology

172. What is the area 10 meters in front of the relay passing zone?
    - a. the pick-up zone
    - *b. the international zone
    - c. the hand-off zone
    - d. the exchange zone

173. What is a medley relay?
    - a. a race where alternate runners run back and forth over the same course
    - b. a race in which the members of the relay team run the same distances
    - *c. a race in which the members of the relay team run different distances
    - d. a race in which only two people are on a team

Discus

Note. Some questions in the Discus category are also appropriate for the Shot Put category.

Technique	**174 to 188**
Mechanical Principles	**189 to 192**
Rules	**193 to 198**

Technique

General

174. Which statements describe the best technique of throwing the discus?
    - a. strong, slow twist; strong arms and shoulders, use of law of centrifugal force; release at chest level at about 30° angle
    - b. fast, controlled twist; general body strength; use of law of inertia; release at shoulder level about 45° angle
    - c. strong, slow twist; strong arms and shoulders; use of law of inertia; release at shoulder level at about 30° angle
    - *d. fast, controlled twist; general body strength, use of law of centrifugal force; release at shoulder level at about 45° angle

175. Which actions describe the discus throw?
    - *a. a twist and a whip
    - b a spin and a jump
    - c. a lift and a release
    - d. a curl and a stretch

Starting Position

176. In which direction should the body be directed when starting to throw the discus?
    - a. right side of body facing direction of throw
    - *b. left side of body facing direction of throw
    - c. both shoulders parallel to direction of throw with right foot forward
    - d. both shoulders parallel to direction of throw with left foot forward

177. What body plane is facing the front of the circle in the discus stance?
    - *a. back
    - b. front
    - c. right
    - d. left

Grip

178. What is the proper position of the fingers when gripping the discus?
    - a. The second joint of each finger is over the edge, relaxed, and spread.
    - b. The first joint of each finger is over the edge and closed for a tighter grip.
    - *c. The first joint of each finger is over the edge, relaxed, and spread.
    - d. The second joint of each finger is over the edge and closed to add force.

179. Which is the correct way to hold the discus?
    a. with the thumb and first two fingers
    *b. with the thumb and first joint of each finger
    c. with the thumb and second joint of each finger
    d. with the thumb and second joint of the first, second, and third fingers

Turns

180. How many turns does the discus thrower take before releasing the discus?
    a. one
    *b. one and one half
    c. one and three fourths
    d. two

181. What is the advantage of the one-and-one-half turn in the discus throw?
    *a. The thrower maintains longer contact with the ground.
    b. The thrower places the feet closer together at the start.
    c. The thrower's right leg is extended and the hip and trunk are driven to the front.
    d. The thrower can add distance to the attempt.

182. What is the purpose of the turning process when throwing the discus?
    a. to develop leverage
    b. to develop linear movement
    *c. to develop momentum
    d. to develop centrifugal force

Release

183. Which release is considered good in the discus?
    *a. The discus spins off the index finger in a clockwise rotation.
    b. The discus spins off the index finger in a counterclockwise rotation.
    c. The discus spins off all four fingers in a clockwise rotation.
    d. The discus spins off all four fingers in a counterclockwise rotation.

184. How is the discus released?
    a. off the second finger in a clockwise motion
    b. off the second finger in a counterclockwise motion
    *c. off the index finger in a clockwise motion
    d. off the index finger in a counterclockwise motion

185. At which angle is the release for the discus?
    a. 30° angle
    b. 40° angle
    *c. 45° angle
    d. 60° angle

186. What would be the probable cause of the discus wobbling in flight?
    a. allowing eyes to focus on the ground
    b. permitting the discus to release early
    *c. permitting too much pressure by the thumb
    d. permitting the discus to lead the trunk during the turn

Reverse

187. Which statement best describes the purpose of the reverse in throwing and putting events?
    a. It keeps the participant from fouling.
    *b. It allows the participant to use a maximum amount of the allotted space for forward momentum.
    c. It is the most efficient way to stop forward momentum.
    d. It aids the participant in maintaining balance.

188. What is the purpose of the reverse in the discus?
    *a. to regain balance
    b. to get more momentum
    c. to add more force
    d. to get more height

Mechanical Principles

189. What principle best explains why a small person may be able to throw the discus as far as a much larger person?
    a. law of inertia
    b. Newton's second law
    *c. momentum = mass × velocity
    d. transfer of momentum

190. To which event does this principle apply: Summation of forces takes place in a given direction if forces are applied successively at the point of greatest velocity of the previous force?
    *a. discus
    b. long jump
    c. sprint
    d. high jump

191. To which event does this principle apply: To efficiently control momentum, an individual follows through by widening the base of support and lowering the center of gravity?
   *a. discus
   b. long jump
   c. sprint
   d. high jump

192. To which event does this principle apply: An object turns less rapidly when acted upon by a force if the mass is distributed at a distance from the center of rotation?
   *a. discus
   b. long jump
   c. sprint
   d. high jump

Rules

193. Which occurrence does *not* constitute a foul in the discus throw?
   a. A competitor touches the ground on or outside the circle before the throw is marked.
   *b. A competitor leaves from the rear half of the circle.
   c. A competitor lets the discus go in making an attempt.
   d. A competitor stoops down inside the circle after the throw.

194. How is the measurement of the discus throw taken?
   a. from the center of the circle to the nearest edge of the first mark made by the discus
   *b. from the nearest edge of the first mark made by the discus to the outside edge of the circle
   c. from the nearest edge of the first mark made by the discus to the inside edge of the circle
   d. from the inside edge of the circle to the point where the discus stops rolling

195. What is the rank of Thrower C, as shown in the diagram? [Refer to Diagram 2.]
   a. first
   b. third
   c. fifth
   *d. eighth

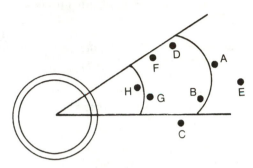

Diagram 2

196. When may the discus thrower leave the throwing circle?
   a. as soon as the discus is released
   b. as soon as the discus touches the ground
   *c. as soon as the throw is marked
   d. as soon as the official gives the signal

197. How many throws does each competitor usually take in the finals of the discus throw?
   a. one
   *b. three
   c. four
   d. five

198. Sector lines for the shot and discus closely resemble which diagram? [Refer to Diagram 3.]
   *c.

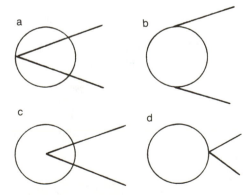

Diagram 3

Shot Put

General

199. Which event best illustrates the principle of summation of forces?
    *a. shot put
    b. sprint
    c. running long jump
    d. high jump

Techniques

200. The body goes through which sequence of actions in the shot put?
    a. uncoiling of trunk, the glide and thrust of the leg, release
    b. hop with a thrust, shift, reverse, release
    c. thrust with nonsupporting leg, glide, uncoiling of the trunk, release
    *d. glide with thrust of nonsupporting leg, transfer of weight, uncoiling movement of the trunk, release

201. Where should the shot rest in the preparatory phase of the shot put?
    a. palm of the hand
    *b. base of the fingers
    c. between the first and second joints of the fingers
    d. at the tip of the fingers

202. Which grip is recommended for the shot put?
    a. held flat in palm of hand on the shoulder close to the jawbone
    b. held flat in palm of hand just above shoulder and close to jawbone
    *c. held by first three fingers with thumb and little finger curled around side of shot, on shoulder and close to jawbone
    d. held by first three fingers with thumb and little finger curled around side of shot, just above shoulder and close to jawbone

203. For what reason is the shot put held outside of the rear of the circle in the initial stages of the glide?
    *a. The distance that force can be applied is increased.
    b. The rules specify for this to be done.
    c. The position balances the raised leg.
    d. The position held leads into a correct release.

204. Which word best describes a shot-putter's movement across the circle?
    *a. shift
    b. hop
    c. slide
    d. stretch

205. What is the purpose of the shift in putting the shot?
    a. to gather the muscles and begin the forward momentum across the circle
    *b. to gain momentum and place the body in the best position to impart force to the shot
    c. to place most of the weight on the side of the body supporting the shot and to steady the shot
    d. to stop forward momentum after the release and to maintain balance

206. What is the purpose of the movement across the circle in the shot put?
    a. to produce a smoother put
    *b. to gain momentum
    c. to give better balance
    d. to produce better form

207. What is the correct position of the arm, wrist, and fingers as the shot leaves the hand?
    a. arm extended, wrist extended, fingers extended
    b. arm flexed, wrist flexed, fingers extended
    *c. arm extended, wrist flexed, fingers flexed
    d. arm flexed, wrist extended, fingers flexed

208. Which action has the *least* effect on the distance the shot is put?
    *a. form of the follow-through
    b. speed across the circle
    c. lifting of chest and head
    d. sustained push action on the shot

209. Which factor is *not* a key influence on the longest possible distance achieved when shot putting?
    a. height of release
    b. angle of release
    *c. body size
    d. velocity

210. Which part of the body is last to exert force to the shot?
    *a. arms
    b. legs
    c. trunk
    d. shoulders

211. Which action in the put is most critical to the release of the shot?
    a. reverse
    b. release
    *c. glide
    d. follow-through

Rules

212. Which put is valid?
    a. The shot falls outside the sector lines.
    b. The shot is released below shoulder level.
    *c. The contestant falls within the circle.
    d. The contestant touches the top of the stopboard.

213. In which case is a shot delivery valid?
    a. The shot is put from behind, but not below, the shoulder and falls within the sector lines.
    b. The shot is put from in front of but below the shoulder and falls within the sector lines.
    *c. The shot is put from in front of the shoulders and falls within the sector lines.
    d. The shot is put from in front of and above the shoulder and falls within 3 feet of the sector line.

214. Attempting the second put in the shot put competition, a contestant steps on, but not over, the toeboard. The put falls within the sector lines. What is the decision?
    a. The put counts, and the contestant is permitted a third put.
    b. The put is measured, and if longer than the previous put, it is counted.
    *c. The put is not measured, and the contestant is allowed a third attempt.
    d. The put is not measured, and the contestant is not allowed a third attempt.

215. Which action is *not* a foul in the shot put?
    *a. leaving the circle from the rear half after the put
    b. leaving the circle before the distance of the put has been marked
    c. allowing the shot to come below the shoulder during the put
    d. allowing the hand to touch the top of the toeboard after the put

216. Where should you enter and leave the shot put circle?
    *a. rear
    b. left side
    c. front
    d. right side

Terminology

217. What is the name of the curved piece of wood used as the foul line for the shot put circle?
    a. scratch board
    *b. toeboard
    c. marker board
    d. fault board

218. What is a reverse?
    *a. change in foot position
    b. short step
    c. backward reach
    d. backward head turn

Javelin

Principle	219
Technique	220 to 232
Rules	233 to 234
Conduct	235 to 236

Principle

219. What primary principle is involved in the javelin throw?
    *a. transfer to momentum
    b. law of inertia
    c. Acceleration is proportional to the force and inversely proportional to the mass.
    d. angle of release

Technique

220. What is the most important consideration in the javelin throw?
    a. that the javelin be thrown on the run
    *b. that the momentum of the body be maintained throughout the approach and release
    c. that the run be a relaxed, easy run
    d. that the approach take approximately 15 to 17 strides

221. Which attribute seems most important for the successful javelin thrower?
    *a. good speed and coordination
    b. good overall strength
    c. good power
    d. good leg strength

222. Which term is associated with the javelin?
    a. heave
    b. fling
    *c. pull
    d. thrust

223. Where does the javelin rest when the throwing arm is fully extended to the back?
    *a. in the palm and on the inner portion of the forearm
    b. in the palm alone
    c. in the fingers and thumb and on the inner portion of the forearm
    d. in the fingers and thumb only

224. What event uses crossover steps?
    a. pole vault
    *b. javelin
    c. high jump
    d. shot put

225. Why does the athlete execute a front crossover step from the run when throwing the javelin?
    a. to curtail the build up of momentum
    b. to avoid the toeboard
    *c. to turn the trunk into throwing position
    d. to balk without being penalized

226. What kind of modification of the run is used at the end of the approach in throwing the javelin?
    *a. a series of crossover steps
    b. a two-step accompanied by a slight reduction in speed
    c. a hop on the same foot as the throwing arm
    d. a skip just before release

227. How does the body weight shift during the release of the javelin?
    a. from the right to the left foot
    b. from the left to the right foot
    c. from the forward to the rear foot
    *d. from the rear to the forward foot

228. Which order indicates the proper sequence of the final steps and release of the javelin? [Refer to Diagram 4.]
    a. 1, 2, 3, 4, 5
    b. 1, 2, 4, 3, 5
    *c. 4, 1, 2, 3, 5
    d. 2, 1, 4, 3, 5

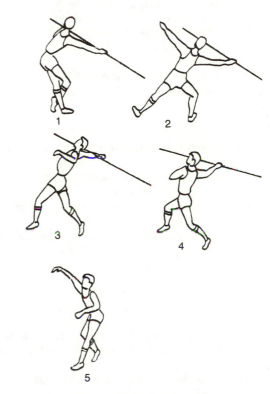

Diagram 4

229. What should the trajectory of the javelin be at release?
    a. 25°
    *b. 35°
    c. 47°
    d. 52°

230. What is the importance of a correct follow-through in throwing events?
    a. It ensures the effectiveness of the final impetus.
    b. It improves the total efficiency of the throw.
    c. It helps the performer regain balance.
    *d. It demonstrates the correctness of the actions preceding it.

231. Why is an approach used in field events?
 a. It improves the form or style of the performance.
 b. It allows the performer to relax before the event.
 c. It improves the accuracy of a throw or direction of a jump.
 *d. It increases the momentum to propel the body or object.

232. What does the amount of reverse indicate?
 a. degree of skill
 b. speed of action before the reverse
 c. area of competition
 *d. momentum used

Rules

233. What constitutes a disqualification in the javelin throw?
 a. turning one's back to the throwing area after the release
 *b. throwing the javelin with an underhand motion
 c. throwing the javelin over the shoulder
 d. holding the javelin with two hands in the competition area

234. Which throw would be legal in the javelin?
 a. The shaft strikes the ground at the same time as the apex.
 b. The javelin is thrown with both hands.
 c. The thrower touches a runway line in the approach.
 *d. The thrower takes an approach of 100 feet.

Conduct

235. When is the best time to retrieve the javelin?
 a. after the next person has thrown
 *b. when the official signals everyone to retrieve
 c. immediately after the throw
 d. when everyone has thrown

236. Which reason would be the most important for trying to make the first trial in a jumping or throwing event?
 a. Success on the first attempt will relieve some of the pressure of the next attempt.
 b. Success on the first attempt will conserve one's energy for other events.
 *c. Success on the first attempt may be so high that second and third trials can be passed.
 d. Success on the first trial will help develop confidence in the form being used.

Standing and Running Long Jumps

Standing Long Jump	237 to 240
Running Long Jump	241 to 266
Triple Jump	267 to 268

Standing Long Jump

Technique

237. What is the purpose of the rocking motion prior to the standing long jump?
 *a. to help the jumper gain momentum for the thrust from the board
 b. to give the jumper an opportunity for concentration and mental practice
 c. to give the jumper the kinesthetic feel of moving through space
 d. to prepare the jumper's leg muscles for the thrust by alternately tensing and relaxing them

238. Should the jumper swing the arms back and forth preparing for the takeoff in the standing long jump and why?
 a. Yes, this gives better balance.
 *b. Yes, this gives added momentum.
 c. No, this creates poor balance.
 d. No, this causes the body to jerk.

239. How are the arms used to keep the body balance forward on the standing long jump?
 a. held at the sides
 b. swung upward
 *c. swung forward
 d. held forward

Rule

240. Which technique is *not* a foul in the standing long jump?
 *a. curling the toes over the end of the board
 b. lifting the left foot before lifting the right foot
 c. touching the ground in front of the board while jumping
 d. taking two springs during the jump

Running Long Jump

Principle

241. Which part of the body serves as the fulcrum in the running long jump?
 *a. hips
 b. arms
 c. torse
 d. legs

242. What is the activity related to this principle: An individual unsupported in the air is unable to raise or lower the center of gravity moving through space?
    a. discus
    *b. long jump
    c. sprint
    d. high jump

Sequence
243. Which arrangement gives the recommended sequence for performing the elements of the running long jump?
    a. high jump, landing, fast run, and flight
    *b. fast run, high jump, flight, landing
    c. fast run, landing, high jump, flight
    d. fast run, flight, high jump, landing

Approach
244. Which statement is accurate about the approach in the running long jump?
    a. All strides are of equal length.
    b. The speed of the run is not of great importance.
    c. The head has to be lowered to hit the takeoff board.
    *d. The run is made with knees high.

245. Where is the best place to put a check mark for the running long jump?
    a. near the end of the approach
    *b. at the beginning of the approach
    c. near the middle of the approach
    d. nowhere because it may be confusing

246. What is the purpose of the check mark in the running long jump?
    a. to help the competitor know how many more steps to take before reaching the takeoff board
    *b. to aid the competitor in beginning the same distance from the takeoff board each time
    c. to train the competitor to take the same number of steps before every jump
    d. to assist the competitor warmup before jumping

247. Which technique is *not* recommended in the running long jump?
    a. increased speed on the approach
    *b. long final stride
    c. balance while in the air
    d. a forward motion on landing

Takeoff
248. What should the performer be thinking about during the takeoff in the running long jump?
    a. jumping long
    *b. jumping high
    c. not scratching
    d. no concentration is required if the training has been adequate

249. What would *not* be a probable cause of a poor takeoff in the running long jump?
    a. failure to use check marks
    b. failure to plant feet correctly
    c. failure to lift legs enough
    *d. failure to pull arms down

250. What is the most important factor in determining lift at the takeoff for the long jump?
    *a. last three strides
    b. approach distance
    c. approach speed
    d. takeoff foot

251. What should the long jumper do to get higher vertical lift in the takeoff?
    a. Increase the length of the approach.
    b. Increase the speed.
    c. Swing extended arms forcefully forward and upward.
    *d. Carry head, shoulders, and chest high during the takeoff.

252. Which statement best describes the correct procedure for long jumping?
    a. The approach should be as short as possible to allow for better spring.
    *b. The takeoff foot should be at the front edge of the takeoff board.
    c. The angle of takeoff should be about 25°
    d. There should be a long reaching stride when placing the foot on the takeoff board.

253. What correction should be made if the jumper consistently arrives beyond the takeoff board?
    a. Shorten all strides in the approach to the takeoff board.
    b. Shorten the last two strides before hitting the takeoff board.
    *c. Move one check mark back the distance over the takeoff board.
    d. Move both check marks back the distance over the takeoff board.

Flight

254. What action takes place with the legs in a hitch kick?
    - a. a whiplike action
    - *b. a running action
    - c. a bend-and-tuck action
    - d. a hurdlelike action

255. Which style of the running long jump emphasizes completion of one step in the air?
    - a. the sail
    - b. the hang
    - *c. the hitch kick
    - d. the pike

256. In which event is the hang style used?
    - a. high jump
    - *b. long jump
    - c. pole vault
    - d. discus

257. What should the runner who is performing the running long jump do to increase distance while in the air?
    - a. Reach forward with both hands.
    - b. Run while in the air.
    - c. Force the hips forward.
    - *d. Nothing can be done.

258. What is one technique used in the long jump to delay the landing?
    - a. tuck
    - *b. sail
    - c. layout
    - d. bunch

Landing

259. What is the best way to keep from falling backward when landing in the long jump?
    - a. Thrust arms up and forward.
    - b. Swing both legs forward and extend just before landing.
    - *c. Move head and shoulders forward and put chin on chest.
    - d. Lower both arms and then swing forward.

260. A long jumper is continually falling on hands and knees. What error is probably causing this to occur?
    - a. approach is too long
    - b. approach is too short
    - c. last stride is too long
    - *d. last stride is too short

261. Where should the legs be in relation to the body at landing on the running long jump?
    - a. bent underneath the body
    - b. bent behind the body
    - c. straight underneath the body
    - *d. extended forward of the body

262. Why do running long jumpers try to fall forward when landing?
    - a. to avoid fouling
    - b. to lessen the possibility of injury
    - *c. to score a better jump
    - d. to keep from sliding

Safety

263. What gives the long jumper the best protection against knee injury?
    - a. wearing knee supports
    - *b. bending the knees upon landing
    - c. taping the knees
    - d. straightening the knees upon landing

Rules

264. What is the length of the runway for the running long jump?
    - *a. 130 feet
    - b. 100 feet
    - c. varies for individuals, but is limited to 20 to 30 meters
    - d. unlimited and varies for individuals

265. Which statement is *not* true of the long jump?
    - a. The runway length is unlimited.
    - b. The pit elevation is equal to the takeoff board.
    - *c. The jumper is allowed 1 minute to jump.
    - d. A jump outside the pit is a foul.

266. Which diagram shows the correct procedure for measuring this running long jump? The two short lines indicate marks made by the hands and the longer line indicates the mark made by the feet. [Refer to Diagram 5.]
    - *a.

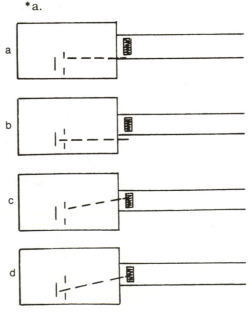

Diagram 5

Triple Jump

267. Which statement is accurate about the triple jump?
      a. The strides of the approach should be of equal length.
      b. The approach is longer than in the long jump.
      c. The hop portion should attain maximal height.
     *d. The step portion should attain minimal height.

268. Which statement is correct about the triple jump?
     *a. The hop and jump portions should be nearly equal.
      b. The hop and step portions should be equal.
      c. The step and jump portions should be equal.
      d. The hop, step, and jump portions should be equal.

High Jump

Principles	269 to 270
Techniques	271 to 292
Rules	293 to 300

Principles

269. What event is related to this principle: Rotary motion can be produced by transferring angular momentum from one part of the body to the entire body?
      a. discus
      b. long jump
      c. sprint
     *d. high jump

270. What event is related to this principle: A force can be lessened if distributed over a larger area for a greater length of time?
      a. discus
      b. long jump
      c. sprint
     *d. high jump

Techniques

Approach

271. What suggestion might one make to help correct the error of not converting momentum to a vertical push in high jumping?
      a. Lengthen approach to get more speed.
      b. Get closer to the bar before planting takeoff foot.
     *c. Lower hips in next to last stride for takeoff.
      d. Slow down approach to control momentum.

272. The approach in a high jump is taken at what angle?
      a. less than a 45° angle
      b. greater than a 45° angle
      c. at the angle most comfortable to the competitor
     *d. at approximately a 45° angle

273. What is the approach of the high jump?
     *a. a curved path
      b. a straightaway
      c. a zigzag path
      d. a downhill path

Takeoff

274. What is the most important aspect of the high jump?
     *a. approach run and takeoff
      b. lift
      c. bar clearance
      d. landing

275. Should the angle of takeoff in high jumping be nearly vertical?
      a. Yes, because an angled takeoff may cause a foul.
     *b. Yes, because the purpose is to raise the center of gravity.
      c. No, because a lower angled jump is more efficient.
      d. No, because it is harder to get a good thrust this way.

276. What is true of the takeoff foot in high jumping?
     *a. It should be firmly planted and usually perpendicular to the bar.
      b. It should touch the ground about 2 feet from the bar.
      c. It should be parallel to the bar.
      d. It should touch the ground first with the ball of the foot.

277. In the Western roll, what usually happens if a high jumper takes off too close to the bar?
     a. strikes the bar with trailing foot
     *b. strikes the bar with thigh of trailing leg
     c. comes down on top of the bar
     d. strikes the bar on the way up

278. What feature of the high jump is most important to consider?
     a. the jumping style
     b. the kick and upward swing
     *c. the run-up and takeoff spot
     d. the layout over the bar

279. Where do most faults occur in high jumping?
     a. in bar clearance
     *b. in the takeoff
     c. in the approach
     d. in the air

280. Where should the jumper's concentration be focused during the approach?
     a. on the cross bar
     b. on a point in the approach run
     c. on the angle of approach
     *d. on the vertical lift takeoff

Clear

281. What advantage in effectiveness does the Fosbury Flop have over other high jumping styles?
     a. The jump is made with the outside leg.
     *b. The speed of the approach can be used.
     c. The jumper clears with the back to the bar.
     d. The approach is at a 35° angle to the bar.

282. What is the key to changing horizontal to vertical momentum in the Western roll?
     a. arm and shoulder action
     b. last three approach strides longer
     *c. rocker action on last approach stride
     d. action of the lead leg

283. What should be done in the Fosbury Flop to bring the legs up after the hips clear the bar?
     a. Whip arms up and back.
     b. Pull arms into chest.
     *c. Bring head to chest.
     d. Arch back and hips.

284. What can the jumper do in the straddle roll to get the hips up while crossing the bar?
     a. Throw arms up.
     b. Tuck legs.
     c. Extend legs.
     *d. Drop head.

285. What is the main difference between the Western roll and the straddle roll?
     a. approach
     b. takeoff
     *c. clearance
     d. landing

286. Which is the easiest but least effective method of high jumping?
     *a. scissors
     b. Fosbury Flop
     c. Western roll
     d. Straddle

287. Why does the straddle roll seem to offer the greatest potential of developing the highest jumpers?
     a. because the arm close to the bar swings upward on the takeoff creating upward momentum
     b. because the center of gravity is raised with this layout position
     c. because the arms are kept close to the body during the roll to prevent them from hitting the bar
     *d. because the layout position reduces the height the body must be lifted over the bar

288. Which form of high jumping seems to be the best mechanically?
     *a. Fosbury Flop
     b. Western
     c. straddle
     d. scissor

289. Where do differences in the form of the Western and straddle rolls occur?
     *a. in bar clearance and landing
     b. in approach and takeoff
     c. in pacing and approach
     d. in takeoff and leg lift

290. What is characteristic of a good high jump?
     a. There is an early lean toward the bar.
     b. The arms stay by the sides during the kick-up.
     *c. The kick-up leg is thrust upward forcefully.
     d. Maximum height is reached before crossing the bar.

291. Where should the bar be placed for the beginning high jumper?
     a. at a medium height to standardize for all jumpers
     b. high to give challenge
     *c. low to give confidence through achievement
     d. at varying heights to teach adjustments

Landing

292. What is one of the most important things to remember when landing from a high jump, pole vault, or running long jump?
    a. Roll.
    b. Make a firm landing.
    c. Get up quickly.
    *d. Relax.

Rules

Scoring

293. Who is awarded first place in this tie in the high jump? [Refer to Diagram 6.]
    *d.

4 ft. 0 in.	4 ft. 1 in.	4 ft. 2 in.	4 ft. 3 in.	4 ft. 4 in.	4 ft. 5 in.	4 ft. 6 in.
a •••	X√	√	X√	•••	XX√	XXX
b √	√	√	X•••	X√	XX√	XXX
c √	√	X•••	√	XX√	XX√	XXX
d √	•••	•••	XX√	XX√	X√	XXX

••• Passed
X Failure
√ Cleared

Diagram 6

294. The last two competitors in the high jump failed with three attempts at a height of 4 feet 6 inches but were successful on the first attempt at 4 feet 5 inches. Who will win the first-place award?
    a. one with the lowest number of trials at winning height
    b. one with fewest attempts throughout competition
    *c. one with fewest misses throughout competition
    d. Both are awarded first place.

295. How is a tie in the high jump resolved?
    a. Award the higher place to the jumper with the lowest number of total misses.
    *b. Give the higher place to the jumper with the lowest number of trials at the height of the tie.
    c. Award both jumpers the same place and divide the points between them.
    d. Give both jumpers three more trials at the height at which the tie occurred.

Miscellaneous

296. What is the high jump competitor *not* allowed to do?
    a. to begin jumping at any height
    *b. to take off from 2 feet
    c. to pass a jump at a certain height
    d. to leave the event to compete in another

297. When is a high jump competitor eliminated, assuming there has been no pass at a missed height?
    a. places markers in runway to assist in run-up and takeoff
    b. has two consecutive failures at the same height
    *c. has three consecutive failures, each at a different height
    d. touches the ground beyond the plane of uprights twice at one height

298. While competing at the high jump, a contestant leaves to run the 100-yard dash. On returning, the bar is 4 inches above the scheduled height. What is the decision of the officials?
    a. The bar is lowered to the previous height, and the competitor is permitted three attempts.
    b. The bar is lowered 2 inches, and the competitor is permitted three attempts.
    c. The bar is lowered 2 inches, and the competitor is permitted only one attempt at that height.
    *d. The bar remains at its present height, and all previous heights are considered passes.

299. The high jump bar vibrates and falls after the jumper is out of the pit. What is the result?
    a. The jump is good because the jumper was already out of the pit.
    *b. The jump is considered a miss.
    c. The jump must be made again because the wind may have blown the bar down.
    d. There is no ruling.

300. Which occurrence is legal for a high jumper?
    a. running under the bar but not attempting a jump
    b. clearing the bar jumping off two feet
    *c. passing a jump at a certain height
    d. missing at one height and then attempting at a lower height

Rules

Throwing Events

301. Which occurrence is a foul in all throwing events?
   a. leaving the circle from the back half after the throw has been marked
   b. bringing the foot in the air over the outside of the circle
   *c. touching any area or surface outside the circle or on the scratch line before the throw is marked
   d. passing up one of the final throws

Track Events

302. When are staggered starts used?
   a. with three or more competitors
   b. with hurdle races
   *c. for races run around curves
   d. for 55- and 100-meter sprints

303. You have 30 contestants entered in a 100-meter dash. How many preliminary heats must you run on a track with six lanes?
   a. five
   *b. seven
   c. eight
   d. nine

304. How many shots are fired for a false start?
   *a. one
   b. two
   c. three
   d. four

305. In which direction are track events run?
   a. clockwise
   *b. counterclockwise
   c. both directions
   d. either direction

306. What is the second voiced signal in a starter's call?
   a. "Ready"
   b. "Runners, take your mark"
   *c. "Set"
   d. "Go"

307. How many false starts disqualify a runner under federation rules?
   a. one
   *b. two
   c. three
   d. four

308. A runner collapses at the finish line. Under which condition is the runner considered a finisher?
   a. The upper part of the body crossed the line.
   b. Any part of the body crossed the line.
   c. At least three quarters of the body crossed the line.
   *d. The entire body crossed the line.

Officials

309. Which duty is *not* the responsibility of the starter?
   *a. Check to see if judges and timers are ready to begin.
   b. Recall runners in case of a false start.
   c. Issue instructions and conduct of the race to competitors.
   d. Fire the gun after the set position when all competitors are motionless.

310. Who is responsible for procuring the track and getting the necessary officials?
   a. marshall
   b. surveyor
   c. clerk of course
   *d. meet director

311. Which official has the final decision in the declaration of fouls or questions of contest?
   a. the games committee
   b. the clerk of the course
   *c. the track referee
   d. the head judge

Scoring

312. Northwest High School is competing with four other schools in a conference meet. So far, Northwest has won first place in the discus, first place in the shot put, second place in the 55-meter dash, and third place in the 100-meter dash. What is their score thus far in the meet?
   a. 10 points
   b. 12 points
   *c. 14 points
   d. 16 points

Records

313. Which condition is *not* a qualification for acceptance of a performance as a national record?
    a. state of the weather
    b. condition of the track or field
    c. force and direction of the wind
    *d. number of teams in competition

Acknowledgments

Colleagues and students who contributed suggestions and ideas for the Track and Field test questions are: J. Adams, B. Berry, C. Broad, K. Bryant, W. Butler, B. A. Byerly, L. Crowell, K. Ferguson, B. Fern, F. Fortner, E. Green, D. Hall, C. Jarman, S. Lilly, B. Little, J. Pafford, B. Pope, and A. Wynns.

Suggested Readings

Cretzmeyer, F.X., Alley, L.E., & Tipton, C.M. (1974). *Track and field athletics* (8th ed.). St. Louis: C.V. Mosby.

Diagram Group. (1979). *Enjoying track and field sports*. New York: Paddington Press.

Doherty, J.K. (1976). *Track and field omnibook* (2nd ed.). Los Altos, CA: Track and Field News.

Ecker, T. (1976). *Track and field: Technique through dynamics*. Los Altos, CA: Track and Field News.

Gambretta, V. (1981). *Track and field coaching manual: Coaching techniques and guidelines formulated by the Athletics Congress Olympic Development Committee*. Champaign, IL: Leisure Press.

Jacoby, E. (1983). *Applied techniques in track and field*. Champaign, IL: Leisure Press.

Mitchell, J., & Simmons, M. (Eds.). (1986). *NCAA men's and women's cross country and track and field rules*. Mission, KS: National Collegiate Athletic Association.

Paish, W.H.C. (1976). *Track and field athletes*. London: Lepus Books.

Randolph, J. (Ed.). (1982). *Championship track and field*. Champaign, IL: Leisure Press.

Wakefield, F., & Harkins, D. (1977). *Track and field fundamentals for girls and women* (4th ed.). St. Louis: C.V. Mosby.

Walker, L.T. (1983). *Track and field for boys and girls*. Chicago: Athletic Institute.

Volleyball

Samye Johnson, Consultant

This collection of volleyball test questions is divided into five content areas:

- Technique
- General Knowledge
- Terminology
- Rules and Scoring
- Strategy

Users of these test questions should be aware that men's and women's rules vary somewhat as do high school and collegiate rules. Leagues and conferences may adapt some rules to fit their special needs, and a few rules may change each year in volleyball. Consequently, some questions or answers may need to be adapted to a particular group of students or changed to be consistent with current rules.

Volleyball

Technique	1 to 153
General Knowledge	154 to 172
Terminology	173 to 208
Rules and Scoring	209 to 300
Strategy	301 to 386

Technique

1. What are the most important physical assets involved in receiving the serve, digging, and setting?
   - a. size and quickness
   - b. coordination and strength
   - c. footwork and quickness
   - *d. coordination and quickness

2. Which skill should *not* be executed with one hand?
   - a. spike
   - b. dig
   - *c. setup
   - d. serve

3. What should a player watch while playing?
   - a. opponent
   - *b. ball
   - c. lines
   - d. coach

4. What is the most accurate method of directing the ball to a specific place on the court?
   - a. forearm pass
   - *b. set
   - c. spike
   - d. dig

5. What is the advantage in using a slide step to move laterally?
   - a. to get out of the way of teammates
   - *b. to keep the head and body facing the net
   - c. to save time to get the arms together
   - d. to get the feet parallel to the net

Samye Johnson was Outstanding College Athlete in America in 1969 and 1970 and also holds the overall volleyball college coaching record of 226 wins and 134 losses. She is assistant professor of health, physical education, and recreation, and is the volleyball coach at Mississippi University for Women, Columbia, Mississippi.

Pass

6. What is the optimum path, or trajectory, of a pass?
    a. The ball falls directly over the setter's head so he or she does *not* have to shift position.
    *b. The ball is moderately high so the receiver has time to shift position.
    c. The ball is very high so the setter has sufficient time to shift position and look for spikers.
    d. The ball goes directly to the spiker so the opponents do *not* have time to set up the block.

Forearm Pass

7. What is the most important reason to hit the forearm pass?
    *a. to hit a ball at waist level or lower
    b. to substitute for an overhead pass
    c. to set the ball
    d. to allow time for players to get into position

8. For which is the forearm pass *least* likely to be used?
    a. receive a serve
    *b. set for a spike
    c. return low balls
    d. receive a spike

9. Why are few balls illegally hit from a forearm pass?
    a. Contact with the forearms can be made quickly.
    b. The forearms do not give at contact.
    *c. The forearms present a solid surface from which the ball rebounds.
    d. The forearm pass is used mostly to return hard hit balls.

10. What will *not* occur when the forearm pass is executed properly?
    a. The ball will be directed toward the center front position.
    *b. The ball will have a height of 5 to 8 feet.
    c. The ball will be placed in front of the setter.
    d. The ball will have adequate height to give the setter time to get into position.

11. Which technique should *not* be used in a forearm pass?
    a. straightening and rotating the elbows inward
    *b. contacting the ball on the heels of the hands and wrists
    c. pointing the thumbs downward
    d. connecting the hands in some manner

12. How should the player's body be positioned in preparing to hit a forearm pass?
    a. The player's right shoulder and arm should be in line with the approaching ball.
    b. The player's right shoulder and arm should be in line with the intended target.
    c. The midline of the player's body should be in line with the intended target.
    *d. The midline of the player's body should be in line with the approaching ball.

13. A player is preparing to hit a forearm pass. How should the player's feet be positioned?
    a. in a side stride position, shoulder width apart
    b. in a side stride position, more than shoulder width apart
    *c. in a front-back stride position, foot opposite intended direction of the pass slightly in front
    d. in a front-back stride position, foot opposite intended direction of the pass slightly in back

14. A player is preparing to hit a forearm pass. How are the player's arms positioned?
    *a. away from the body at a 45° angle to the floor
    b. away from the body and parallel to the floor
    c. close to the body at a 45° angle to the floor
    d. close to the body and pointing to the floor

15. In hitting the forearm pass, what is the reason for hitting the ball on the inner part of the forearms?
    a. so the pass will be legal
    b. so the speed of the oncoming ball can be absorbed
    c. so the ball can be hit below the waist
    *d. so there is a flat surface for rebounding the ball

16. How are the elbows positioned in hitting a forearm pass?
    *a. straight or extended
    b. slightly bent or flexed
    c. bent at a 45° angle
    d. bent at a 90° angle

17. How are the hands held in hitting a forearm pass?
    a. The back of one hand is placed diagonally across the palm of the other, and both palms are open.
    b. Each hand is made into a fist, and then the hands are brought together with the thumbs side by side and palms facing each other.
    c. Each hand is made into a fist, and then the hands are brought together with the little fingers side by side and the palms facing upward.
    *d. The hands are together with the fatty part of the base of the thumbs side by side.

18. What is the angle of the wrists in hitting a forearm pass?
    a. extended
    *b. hyperextended
    c. flexed slightly
    d. flexed greatly

19. On what part of the body should the ball make contact in a forearm pass?
    a. the knuckles of the thumbs
    b. the wrists
    c. above the thumbs on the boney sides of the forearms
    *d. the inside surfaces of the forearms

20. Which movement(s) should occur in contacting the ball with a forearm pass?
    a. Arms swing from the elbows.
    b. Arms swing from the elbows and shoulders.
    c. Knees extend.
    *d. Knees and hips extend.

21. Where should the body weight be centered in hitting a forearm pass?
    *a. shifting forward as the legs extend
    b. on the front foot throughout the hit
    c. on the back foot throughout the hit
    d. evenly distributed over both feet throughout the hit

22. What provides the force in hitting the ball with a forearm pass?
    a. swinging the arms from the elbows
    b. swinging the arms from the shoulders
    *c. extending the legs
    d. uncocking the wrists

23. A player is hitting a forearm pass. Where should the hands be at the end of the follow-through?
    a. no higher than the waist
    *b. no higher than the shoulders
    c. head high
    d. directly above the head

24. A player is hitting a forearm pass. When should the hands be unclasped?
    a. as soon as the ball is contacted
    b. as the follow-through begins
    *c. at the end of the follow-through
    d. as the hands reach chest height

25. A player is anticipating returning a hard spike with a forearm pass. What adjustments should be made from the normal forearm pass position?
    *a. a wider stride and deeper knee flexion
    b. greater knee and elbow flexion
    c. more leg extension at contact
    d. more arm swing at contact

26. A player is hitting a forearm pass. What is the relationship between the amount of stride a player should take and the distance the pass must travel?
    *a. the greater the distance, the more stride
    b. the greater the distance, the less stride
    c. The stride is the same for all distances.
    d. The stride varies with direction, not distance.

27. A player is hitting a forearm pass. He or she must change the direction of the ball's path with the hit. How should this be accomplished?
    a. Squarely face the approaching ball and swing the arms in the direction of the target.
    b. Squarely face the approaching ball and swing the body and arms in the direction of the target.
    *c. Squarely face the target and follow through in the direction of the target.
    d. Squarely face the target and swing the arms from the direction of the approaching ball toward the target.

28. What most frequently causes the ball to be hit illegally on a forearm pass?
    a. hitting the ball too low on the forearms
    b. hitting the ball on the wrists
    c. hitting the ball with the elbows bent
    *d. hitting the ball with the forearms uneven

29. The player in the diagram is hitting a forearm pass. What common error is the player making? [Refer to Diagram 1.]
    *a. reaching to the side for the ball
    b. flexing at the knees and hips
    c. taking a front-back stride position
    d. keeping the elbows extended and the hands together

Diagram 1

30. The player is hitting a forearm pass and contacts the ball on the thumbs. What will probably happen?
    a. The hit will be illegal.
    b. The ball will be hit in the intended direction.
    c. The ball will travel farther than intended.
    *d. The control of the ball will be lost.

31. A player is hitting a forearm pass. The ball is too close to his or her body to make a good hit. What will probably result?
    a. The ball will be hit too horizontally.
    b. The hit will be illegal.
    *c. The ball will be hit straight up or over the player's head.
    d. The ball will be hit with too much power.

Back Forearm Pass

32. What change is made in technique(s) to hit a back forearm pass instead of a forearm pass?
    *a. The ball is hit closer to the player's body and contacted at a point higher than the player's shoulders.
    b. The ball is hit closer to the player's hands and more arm swing is used.
    c. The knees and hips are flexed less.
    d. The stance is a side stride position.

33. A player is hitting a back forearm pass. How should the player's body be positioned?
    a. directly facing the approaching ball
    *b. back of the shoulders and hips square to the target
    c. right side square to the target
    d. facing halfway between the direction of the approaching ball and intended target

Overhand Pass

34. What is the most important factor to remember in setting?
    a. to move quickly to get the ball
    b. to push the ball out and up
    c. to position oneself under the ball
    *d. to place the ball in the proper spiking zone

35. What is the most frequent use of the overhand pass?
    a. to pass a low ball to the front line
    *b. to set the ball for a spike
    c. to receive a serve
    d. to change the direction of an approaching ball

36. Which skill utilizes primarily the legs to increase the distance the ball travels?
    a. serve
    b. dive
    *c. set
    d. dig

37. Why is learning the overhand pass valuable in volleyball?
    a. to assist the weak server
    b. to enable more players to participate in the game
    c. to return the ball quickly to the other side
    *d. to maneuver into position for effective attack play

38. What best describes the abilities needed by a setter?
    a. cool head, steady hands, and good eyesight
    b. fast feet, anticipation, and good eyesight
    *c. superior speed, mobility, and anticipation
    d. steady hands, mobility, and fast feet

39. Setters want to be able to take advantage of their spikers' strengths and the blockers' weaknesses. In order to do this, what combination of abilities would be most important?
    a. superior reactions and ball-handling skills
    *b. mental alertness, control, and spiker's preferences
    c. superior speed, flexibility, and agility
    d. quick movements, mobility, and competitive spirit

40. What characteristics are most advantageous for the setter?
    a. strong fingers
    b. flexible shoulders
    *c. flexible wrists
    d. good eyes

41. Which quality should be of *least* concern in choosing a setter?
    a. competitive spirit
    b. mental alertness
    *c. size
    d. speed

42. The ball is being set up for a spike. Which of the two passes is generally better and why? [Refer to Diagram 2.]
    *a. A, because the spiker has a better choice of attack plays
    b. A, because the spiker can jump higher to spike
    c. B, because it will be easier to time the spike
    d. B, because the spiker need not jump as high

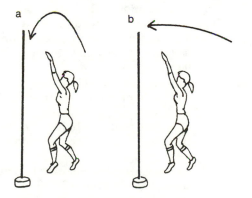

Diagram 2

43. How should the player's body be positioned in relation to the ball in hitting an overhand pass?
    a. The approaching ball should be in line with the arm and shoulder of the player's dominant side.
    b. The approaching ball should be in line with the arm and shoulder of the player's right side.
    *c. The approaching ball should be in line with the midline of the player's body.
    d. The approaching ball should be in line with the arm and shoulder opposite the intended flight of the ball.

44. How should the feet be positioned in hitting an overhand pass?
    a. side stride position facing the approaching ball
    b. side stride position facing the intended direction of the hit
    c. front-back stride position facing the approaching ball
    *d. front-back stride position facing the intended direction of the hit

45. A player is getting ready to hit an overhand pass. Which statement best describes the ready position for the feet and legs?
    *a. The knees are flexed, and the weight is evenly distributed over both feet.
    b. The knees are flexed, and the weight is primarily over the back foot.
    c. The knees are extended, and the weight is primarily over the front foot.
    d. The knees are extended, and the weight is evenly distributed over both feet.

46. The player is preparing to hit an overhand pass. How should the wrists be held?
    a. relaxed
    *b. hyperextended
    c. flexed
    d. extended

47. The player is preparing to hit an overhand pass. How should the fingers be positioned?
    *a. relaxed and pointing diagonally upward
    b. relaxed and pointing straight upward
    c. slightly flexed, tense, and pointing diagonally upward
    d. slightly flexed, tense, and pointing straight upward

48. What parts of the hands should contact the ball in hitting the overhand pass?
    a. the heels of the hands, finger pads, and thumbs
    *b. the finger pads and thumbs
    c. the palms of the hands, finger pads, and thumbs
    d. the thumbs and finger pads of the first two fingers

49. Which parts of the hands supply the primary force in hitting an overhand pass?
    a. the heels of the hands, finger pads, and thumbs
    b. the finger pads and thumbs
    c. the finger pads of the last three fingers
    *d. the thumbs and finger pads of the first two fingers

50. What is the position of the hands when executing the overhand pass?
    *a. The thumbs and index fingers form a triangle.
    b. The thumbs and index fingers form a U.
    c. The thumbs and index fingers form a diamond.
    d. The thumbs and index fingers form a W.

51. What is the position of the elbows at the beginning of an overhand pass?
    a. in close to the body at the waist
    *b. in close to the body at the chest
    c. away from the body at the waist level
    d. away from the body at the shoulder level

52. What is the reason for compensating for the impact of the ball on the overhand pass?
    *a. to have a better controlled pass
    b. to prevent injuries to the fingers
    c. to have time to face the direction of the intended ball flight
    d. to change the level of the ball's flight

53. Where should contact with the ball be made in hitting an overhand pass?
    a. 6 inches to a foot directly above the head
    *b. 6 to 8 inches off the forehead
    c. 6 to 8 inches out from the nose
    d. 6 inches to a foot out from the chest

54. A player is hitting an overhand pass to the setter. Which angle at contact will provide the best trajectory for the pass? [Refer to Diagram 3.]
    *b.

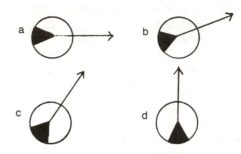

Diagram 3

55. What provides the force in hitting an overhand pass?
    a. extension of the legs
    b. flexion of the wrists
    c. flexion of the wrists and arms
    *d. extension of the wrists, arms, and legs

56. What is the position of the hands in the follow-through in hitting an overhand pass?
    a. The hands stop as soon as the ball is contacted.
    b. The hands are pulled back away from the ball on contact.
    *c. The hands follow the ball until the arms are completely extended.
    d. The hands move upward and then out away from the midline of the player's body.

57. What is the position of the legs and feet in the follow-through in hitting an overhand pass?
    a. The legs completely extend, and the weight is evenly distributed over both feet.
    *b. The legs completely extend, and the weight is primarily centered over the front foot.
    c. The legs remain slightly flexed, and the weight is evenly distributed over both feet.
    d. The legs remain slightly flexed, and the weight is primarily centered over the front foot.

58. What causes the most illegal hits on the overhand pass?
    *a. one hand following through ahead of the other
    b. slapping the ball
    c. passing on the run
    d. hitting the ball too soon

59. The player is hitting an overhand pass. The arms are extended before the ball is contacted. What will result?
    a. loss of ball control
    *b. loss of power
    c. over hitting
    d. excessively high trajectory

60. The player is hitting an overhand pass. The player's legs are *not* bent. What will result?
    a. a good hit
    b. loss of ball control
    *c. loss of power
    d. over hitting

61. The player is hitting an overhand pass. The ball is contacted at the level of the player's chin. What will result?
    a. a good pass
    *b. a flat pass
    c. a straight up pass
    d. a weak pass

62. The player is hitting an overhand pass. The ball is hit with the ends of the player's fingers. What will result?
    a. a good pass
    b. a flat pass
    c. a pass straight up
    *d. a weak pass

63. A player consistently hits the ball over the net in attempting a set. What is probably causing this?
    a. The player is still getting into position while hitting the ball.
    b. The player is contacting the ball too low.
    *c. The player is *not* sideways to the net when hitting the ball.
    d. The player is using a side stride position.

64. What is the major difference in hitting a forward overhand pass and a backward overhand pass?
    a. the player's body position
    b. the contact point
    c. the extension of the legs
    *d. the follow-through of the arms and hands

65. A player is hitting a back overhand pass. The ball is hit at a position above and slightly behind the player's head. What will result?
    a. a flat pass
    b. a pass straight up
    c. an overhit
    *d. a good pass

66. Which set in the diagram would be considered a regular set? [Refer to Diagram 4.]
    a. 1
    b. 2
    c. 4
    *d. 5

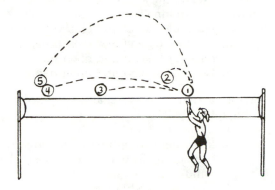

Diagram 4

67. Which set in the diagram would be considered a Japanese set? [Refer to Diagram 4, Question 66.]
    *a. 1
    b. 2
    c. 3
    d. 5

68. Which set in the diagram would be considered a shoot set? [Refer to Diagram 4, Question 66.]
    a. 2
    b. 3
    *c. 4
    d. 5

Spike

69. Which factor is most critical when spiking?
    *a. making sure the hit is in front of the body
    b. making sure the set is good
    c. making sure the arm is cocked with the elbow leading
    d. making sure the hand contacts the ball above the center of gravity

70. What is the most important factor to consider when spiking?
    a. jumping as high as possible
    *b. timing the moving ball accurately
    c. hitting the ball as hard as possible
    d. placing the ball to an open area

71. What is the spiker's first responsibility?
    a. spiking the ball as hard as possible
    b. hitting the ball into an open area
    *c. getting the ball over the net
    d. keeping the ball inside the boundary lines

72. Which techniques are recommended for successful spiking?
    a. one-foot takeoff and closed hand
    b. two-foot takeoff and closed hand
    c. one-foot takeoff and open hand
    *d. two-foot takeoff and open hand

73. Which action is most crucial to the placement of a spiked ball?
    a. hitting on-hand
    *b. following through with the fingers
    c. contacting the ball with the heel of the hand
    d. rotating the shoulders

74. Which angle is the *least* acceptable for a spike?
    a. down the line
    b. power angle
    c. crosscourt
    *d. end line

75. Which spike is generally the easiest to hit?
    a. down the line
    *b. crosscourt to the middle
    c. crosscourt to the sideline
    d. dink

76. Many beginning spikers try to get all their power from which movement?
    *a. arm swing
    b. shoulder rotation
    c. forward momentum of run
    d. wrist action

77. Which movements contribute to the power in hitting a spike?
    a. wrist and arm extension, upper body rotation, and jump
    b. wrist and arm extension, approach, and jump
    *c. wrist and arm extension, upper body rotation, and approach
    d. upper body rotation, jump, and approach

78. The spike can be hit most effectively from which position?
    a. the off-hand position
    *b. the on-hand position
    c. the center front position
    d. the right front position

79. How far should a spiker be from the net at the beginning of the approach?
    a. two steps
    b. three steps
    c. 3 to 5 feet
    *d. 8 to 10 feet

80. From where on the court should a spiker begin his or her approach?
    *a. 1 to 2 feet outside the sideline
    b. the sideline
    c. 1 to 2 feet inside the sideline
    d. 3 to 5 feet inside the sideline

81. Why is an approach desirable in hitting a spike?
    a. It increases the accuracy of the hit.
    *b. It increases the height of the jump.
    c. It gives the spiker more control in jumping.
    d. It gives the spiker more time to judge the set.

82. How can a player convert his or her forward momentum into a straight vertical jump on an approach to a spike?
    a. by landing simultaneously on the soles of the feet before jumping
    b. by landing simultaneously on the balls of the feet and rocking to the toes before jumping
    c. by landing simultaneously on the balls of the feet before takeoff for the spike
    *d. by landing simultaneously on the heels and rolling to the balls of the feet and toes before jumping

83. What movements contribute to the height of the jump in hitting a spike?
    a. leg extension
    b. upward movement of the arms
    c. arching of the back
    *d. leg extension and upward movement of the arms

84. How high should a player jump to hit a spike?
    *a. as high as possible
    b. 3 feet off the floor
    c. until the spiking hand is above the net
    d. 3 feet above the net

85. What is the position of the spiker's hand at the beginning of the forward swing to hit the ball?
    a. over the spiker's right shoulder
    b. out to the side of the spiker's shoulder
    c. over the spiker's head
    *d. above and slightly behind the spiker's head

86. Right before the ball is spiked, what is the position of the spiker's body?
    a. square to the net
    *b. rotated in the direction of the spiking arm
    c. side to the net
    d. rotated in the direction of the non-hitting arm

87. How should contact be made with the ball on the spike?
    a. The player contacts the ball with the hand made into a fist.
    b. The player contacts the ball with the fingers.
    *c. The player contacts the ball with the heel of the hand and then the rest of the hand.
    d. The player contacts the ball with the four knuckles on the hitting hand.

88. When should the approaching ball be hit on the spike?
    *a. The ball is hit before it crosses in front of the body.
    b. The ball travels across the body before it is hit.
    c. The ball is hit when it is in the center of the body.
    d. The ball is hit when it is over the player's head.

89. How should the ball be hit on the spike?
    a. with backspin
    *b. with topspin
    c. with sidespin
    d. flat

90. How can the force of landing after a spike best be absorbed?
    *a. by landing on the toes of both feet and bending at the ankles and knees
    b. by landing on the total area of the feet with the legs bending at the ankles and knees
    c. by landing in a side stride position with the legs bending at the ankles and knees
    d. by landing in a side stride position with a rebound bounce

91. The spiker hits the net as he or she executes the spike. What might have caused the spiker to do this?
    *a. The takeoff was made from one foot.
    b. The approach was made too soon.
    c. The ball was hit too late.
    d. The spiker's arm was *not* extended at contact.

92. A player consistently spikes the ball into the net. What might correct this error?
    a. hitting the ball later
    b. taking a longer approach
    *c. hitting the ball sooner
    d. decreasing the arm action

Off-Hand Spike

93. When should the approaching ball be hit on an off-hand spike?
    a. The ball is hit before it crosses in front of the body.
    *b. The ball travels across the body before it is hit.
    c. The ball is hit when it is in the center of the body.
    d. The ball is hit when it is over the player's head.

Dink

94. What is the difference in hitting a spike and a dink?
    a. the height of the jump
    b. the position of the arm at the beginning of the forward swing
    *c. the amount of wrist action
    d. the amount of shoulder rotation before the hit

95. What is a common error on the dink?
    a. hitting the ball into the net
    b. flexing the wrist to give the ball direction
    *c. carrying the ball with the fingers and palm
    d. using it too often

Half-Speed Spike

96. What is the difference in hitting a power angle and a half-speed spike?
    a. the speed of the approach
    b. the height of the jump
    c. the amount of shoulder rotation
    *d. the speed of the arm swing

Block

97. In which skill should the hands be kept parallel and the fingers rigid?
    a. spike
    b. overhand pass
    *c. block
    d. forearm pass

98. A player is preparing to block a spike. How should the player's feet be positioned?
    *a. side stride position, shoulder width apart
    b. side stride position, very close together
    c. front-back stride position, shoulder width apart
    d. front-back stride position, more than shoulder width apart

99. A player is in the ready position before jumping to block a spike. How should the arms be positioned?
    a. Arms are at player's side ready to make upward swing.
    *b. Arms are bent so that player's hands are out in front and slightly to the outside of his or her shoulders.
    c. Arms are extended upward and slightly in front of the player's body.
    d. Arms are extended straight upward over the player's shoulders.

100. What direction should a player face when preparing to jump to block a spike?
    *a. squarely facing the net
    b. sideways to the net
    c. facing the opposing team's setter
    d. facing the line of the spiker's approach

101. What footwork pattern is used to move into position to make a single block?
    a. crossover steps
    *b. slide steps
    c. running steps
    d. pivot turns

102. In blocking, what footwork pattern is used by the middle blocker moving to the right or left to get into position to block?
    a. slide steps
    b. crossover steps
    *c. slide, crossover, and pivot
    d. crossover, slide, and pivot

103. When should the blocker extend his or her arms upward for the block?
    a. as he or she moves into position to jump for the block
    *b. as he or she jumps upward to block the ball
    c. just before reaching the peak of the jump
    d. as the spiker begins the forward motion for the spike

104. What is the best footwork for a player to use in blocking a spike?
    a. Take one step forward and a one-foot takeoff.
    b. Take two steps forward and a one-foot takeoff.
    c. Take one step forward and a two-foot takeoff.
    *d. Take no steps and a two-foot takeoff.

105. How close should a blocker's hands be to the plane of the net at the height of his or her jump?
    *a. in the plane
    b. just to the blocker's side of the net
    c. 6 inches from the net on the blocker's side
    d. 1 foot from the net on the blocker's side

106. On a regular set, when should the player jump to block a spike?
    a. as the spiker jumps
    b. just before the spiker jumps
    *c. just after the spiker jumps
    d. as the spiker begins the forward arm motion to hit the spike

107. The opposing team has set the ball only a foot or two above the net. What should the defender do to block the spike?
    a. Extend the arms in front of the body to meet the ball sooner.
    b. Move closer to the net to block sooner.
    *c. Jump with the spiker before the ball is set.
    d. Turn the hands upward to make a soft block.

108. How are the player's hands positioned for a block?
    a. open, fingers rigid and close together
    b. open, fingers relaxed and close together
    *c. open, fingers rigid and spread apart
    d. open, fingers relaxed and spread apart

109. A player is blocking a spike. How far apart should the player's thumbs be?
    a. touching each other
    *b. 1 to 2 inches
    c. 6 inches apart
    d. slightly less than the width of the ball apart

110. What part of the player's body should contact the ball on the block?
 a. fingers
 b. wrist
 *c. palm
 d. whole hand

111. What should a player be watching when getting ready to block?
 a. the ball
 b. the setter
 *c. the spiker
 d. the net

112. A player has blocked a spike. Which statement best describes the desired follow-through?
 a. Hands follow through in the direction of the intended flight of the ball.
 b. Hands follow through straight ahead.
 c. There is no follow-through.
 *d. Hands are drawn back away from the net.

113. You are a blocker and extend your arms up in line with your ears to prevent a spike. Is this a good technique?
 a. Yes, the ball cannot be hit between your hands.
 b. Yes, this prevents the blocker from touching the net.
 c. No, the blocker cannot adjust to the direction of the ball.
 *d. No, the blocker cannot block aggressively.

114. Why should a short blocker use a soft block?
 *a. to cover a greater area above the net
 b. to deflect the ball to a teammate
 c. to control the blocked ball better
 d. to slow up the spike

115. What is the position of the blocker's hands in hitting a soft block?
 a. relaxed and ready to draw back from the ball
 b. relaxed to absorb the force of the contact
 *c. parallel to the net or tilted slightly upward
 d. parallel to the net or tilted slightly downward

Serve

116. What is the easiest serve to learn but offers the opposition very little difficulty in playing it?
 a. the sidearm serve
 *b. the underhand serve
 c. the overhand floater serve
 d. the overhand topspin serve

117. What is the server's primary responsibility?
 a. to direct the ball to the back corners of the opponent's court
 b. to direct the ball to the weakest player on the receiving team
 *c. to get the ball over the net and within the court
 d. to hit a serve that has great velocity

118. Which serve is used by more U.S. volleyball players participating in power volleyball today?
 a. underhand serve
 b. overhand topspin serve
 *c. overhand floater serve
 d. roundhouse serve

119. What is the most important aspect of the serve?
 *a. the placement of the ball
 b. the speed of the ball
 c. the spin on the ball
 d. the height of the ball

120. What type of serve moves in unpredictable directions making it difficult for the receiver to pass the ball?
 a. topspin serve
 *b. floater serve
 c. sidearm serve
 d. roundhouse serve

121. What type of serve drops very fast after it crosses the net?
 *a. topspin serve
 b. floater serve
 c. sidearm serve
 d. underhand serve

122. What is the most common serving error made by beginnings?
 a. point of contact
 b. closed hand
 *c. ball toss
 d. follow-through

Underhand Serve

123. What is the basic reason for using the underhand serve?
 a. It does not take as much strength to hit it.
 b. It is the most deceptive to receive.
 c. It is the most difficult to receive.
 *d. It is the easiest to learn.

124. What serving action will increase the accuracy of the underhand serve?
    a. increasing the length of the backswing
    b. flattening the arc of the arm swing
    c. contacting the ball with the wrists or forearm
   *d. following through in the direction of the ball's intended flight

125. What should a player do to increase the speed of an underhand serve?
   *a. Increase the length of the backswing and follow through.
    b. Contact the ball with the fist.
    c. Flatten the arc of the arm swing.
    d. Hold the ball closer to the body.

126. How should a player stand to hit an underhand serve?

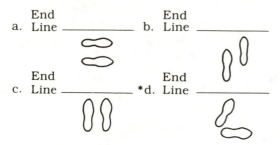

127. Where is the ball held by the server to hit an underhand serve?
   *a. diagonally in front of the server with the arm extended
    b. directly toward the net with the arm extended
    c. directly toward the right side line with the arm slightly bent
    d. toward the right net post with the elbow in close to the player's waist

128. How should a server make contact with the ball on an underhand serve?
    a. with a closed fist, using the thumb and index finger as the hitting surface
    b. with a closed fist, using the heel of the hand and fingers as the hitting surface
   *c. with the hand open, using the heel of the hand as the hitting surface
    d. with the hand open, using the wrist as the hitting surface

129. Which describes the path of the arm swing in hitting an underhand serve?
    a. diagonal to the net, left to right
    b. diagonal to the net, right to left
   *c. perpendicular to the net
    d. semicircular, parallel to the court surface

Overhand Serve

130. What is the most important factor in hitting an overhand serve?
    a. an open striking hand
    b. the transfer of weight
   *c. a correctly tossed ball
    d. the timing of the striking hand

131. How should a player stand to hit an overhand serve?

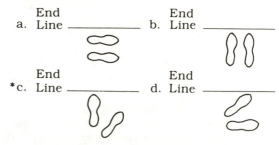

132. Where is the ball held when the server is going to hit an overhand serve?
   *a. chest high, toward the net and in line with the right shoulder
    b. chest high, toward the net and in line with the left shoulder
    c. waist high, diagonal to the right side line
    d. waist high, directly toward the right side line

133. How high should the ball be tossed from the player's hand to hit an overhand serve?
    a. 1 foot
   *b. 2 to 3 feet
    c. 3 to 4 feet
    d. 5 to 6 feet

134. A player is hitting an overhand serve. What should be the position of the player's body at the end of the backswing?
    a. shoulders and hips square to the net
    b. shoulders and hips diagonal to the net
   *c. left shoulder pointing to the net
    d. left shoulder pointing to the right net post

135. A player is hitting an overhand serve. What is the position of the player's arm at the end of the backswing?
    a. elbow bent, pointing down and slightly away from the player's waist
    b. elbow bent, pointing to sideline and level with the shoulder
   *c. elbow bent, pointing opposite direction from the net and level with the shoulder
    d. elbow slightly bent, hand pointing upward above the right shoulder

136. What surface makes contact with the ball when a player is hitting a floater overhand serve?
     a. heel and fingers of a closed fist
     *b. heel of the hand
     c. heel and fingers of an open hand
     d. palm of the hand

137. What surface makes contact with the ball when a player is hitting a topspin overhand serve?
     a. heel and fingers of a closed fist
     b. heel of the hand
     *c. heel and fingers of an open hand
     d. palm of the hand

138. What wrist action should take place in hitting a floater overhand serve?
     *a. The wrist stays in hyperextension throughout the swing.
     b. The wrist stays straight throughout the swing.
     c. The wrist is snapped forward from hyperextension as the ball is contacted.
     d. The wrist is snapped forward from a straight position as the ball is contacted.

139. What wrist action should take place in hitting a topspin overhand serve?
     a. The wrist stays in hyperextension throughout the swing.
     b. The wrist stays straight throughout the swing.
     *c. The wrist is snapped forward from hyperextension as the ball is contacted.
     d. The wrist is snapped forward from a straight position as the ball is contacted.

Receiving the Serve

140. Which skill is most often used to receive a serve?
     a. set
     *b. forearm pass
     c. dig
     d. dive

141. Which is a common error in receiving the serve?
     a. absorbing too much of the force of the serve
     b. moving directly behind the ball to hit it
     *c. swinging the arms upward at contact
     d. standing in a front-back stride position

Defense

142. A player on the opposing team is going up to hit a spike. What is the basic ready position for the back row defensive players?
     a. standing relaxed in a side stride position
     b. standing relaxed in a front-back stride position
     c. semisquatting in a side stride position
     *d. semisquatting in a front-back stride position

Dig

143. A defensive player hits a dig off of a spike. How should the ball be played?
     a. with forward arm motion to give the pass height
     *b. with backward arm motion to absorb the force of the hit
     c. with no arm motion to control the flight of the ball
     d. with arm motion toward the target to increase accuracy

144. From what height should a ball be played on a dig?
     a. between the chest and waist
     b. between the waist and hips
     c. between the hips and knees
     *d. between the knees and ankles

145. A player is off balance after hitting a dig. What should the player do?
     a. Fall on both knees.
     b. Fall on one knee.
     c. Catch his or her weight with the hands.
     *d. Do a shoulder roll.

146. When should a two-handed dig be attempted?
     a. only when the player is in a balanced position
     b. only when the player's body is directly behind the ball
     *c. only when the ball is in line with or inside the player's lead knee
     d. only when the player can comfortably reach the ball

Shoulder Roll

147. What is the first movement a player should make to execute a shoulder roll?
     *a. a backward pivot on the foot of the leading leg
     b. a backward pivot on the foot of the trailing leg
     c. tuck both knees
     d. roll diagonally across the back

Dive

148. A defensive player is going to have to dive to get a ball. Which phrase best describes the height from which the dive should begin?
    a. a standing position
    b. a semisquat position
    c. a crouching position
    *d. a very low body position

149. What is the angle of the arms in hitting a ball from a dive?
    a. parallel with the court surface
    b. perpendicular with the court surface
    *c. a 45° angle with the court surface
    d. a 75° angle with the court surface

150. On what part(s) of the body should a player try to land when hitting a ball from a dive?
    a. the side of one hip and thigh
    b. the hips
    c. the back
    *d. the chest and stomach

Net Recovery

151. What is the key to successfully recovering the ball from the net?
    *a. taking the ball as low to the floor as possible
    b. facing the net
    c. judging where the ball will drop
    d. not catching the ball

152. A player is attempting to recover a ball hit into the net. What direction should the player face?

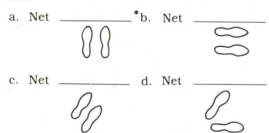

153. Which net ball will rebound farthest from the net?
    a. a hard hit ball to the top of the net
    b. a hard hit ball to the bottom of the net
    c. a soft hit ball to the bottom of the net
    *d. a hard hit ball to the middle of the net

General Knowledge

Origin

154. Who developed the game of volleyball?
    *a. William Morgan
    b. James Naismith
    c. Dr. George Fisher
    d. Frances Schaafsma

155. When was the game of volleyball invented?
    a. 1850
    *b. 1895
    c. 1945
    d. 1962

156. Where did the game of volleyball originate?
    a. Japan
    b. China
    *c. United States
    d. Brazil

Purpose

157. What was the purpose of developing the game of volleyball?
    a. to be a sport in the Olympics
    b. to give women a fall team sport
    c. to have a sport that could be played on the beach
    *d. to be a recreational indoor sport

Name

158. What was volleyball first called?
    a. miniball
    *b. mintonette
    c. mininet
    d. net volley

Organizations

159. What is the governing body of volleyball in the United States?
    a. American Volleyball Association
    *b. United States Volleyball Association
    c. YMCA
    d. National Association for Girls and Women in Sport

Competition

160. What Olympics first included volleyball for both men and women?
    a. 1948
    b. 1956
    *c. 1964
    d. 1976

161. Who won the gold medal for men in the 1984 Olympics?
    *a. United States
    b. China
    c. Japan
    d. Brazil

Etiquette

162. A player hits the net while the ball is in play, but the whistle does not sound. What should the player do?
    a. Continue playing because it is the official's responsibility to call violations.
    b. Call the violation to the official's attention, stopping play.
    *c. Call the violation to the official's attention as soon as the ball is dead.
    d. Tell his or her coach as soon as the ball is dead.

163. When is a player expected to make an "honor call"?
    a. any time he or she touches the net, and it is *not* called by the official
    *b. any time he or she commits a foul, and it is *not* called by the official
    c. any time he or she illegally hits the ball, and it is *not* called by the official
    d. any time he or she commits a foot fault, and it is *not* called by the linesman

164. How should a player return the ball to the opponents on a point or side-out?
    a. Throw the ball to an official who will return it to the opponents.
    b. Throw the ball over the net to the other side.
    *c. Roll the ball under the net to the appropriate player.
    d. Throw the ball over the net to the appropriate player.

Equipment and Safety

165. In which of the following cases may the court be declared unfit for play?
    a. Snow or rain has made the court soft or slippery.
    b. Play can be dangerous due to any hazardous condition of the court surface or equipment.
    c. Fog or darkness makes it impossible to officiate properly.
    *d. All of the above.

166. Which ball is considered suitable equipment?
    a. a brown ball for indoor play
    b. a leather ball for outdoor play
    c. a rubber ball for indoor play
    *d. a white ball for indoor play

167. Why are knee pads worn by most inexperienced players?
    a. to allow them to use their knees more
    *b. to prevent injury when digging and diving
    c. to slide under low balls
    d. to show that they are aggressive defensive players

168. Which warm-up routine is most suitable for volleyball players?
    a. running a mile before the game
    b. lifting weights before the game
    c. running 100-yard sprints before the game
    *d. doing stretching and resisting exercises before the game

169. What is the most important purpose of the warm-up period before a game?
    a. to practice fancy shots to psych out the opponents
    *b. to rehearse the activities to be performed
    c. to talk over the strategy to be used
    d. to learn special skills needed for the game

170. Which condition would be a safety hazard during a match?
    a. bleachers 8 feet from the sidelines
    b. referee stand on the sideline facing the scorer
    c. mercury lights in the gym
    *d. weight training equipment 5 feet behind the end lines

171. Where should extra balls be kept during a game?
    a. on the floor next to the referee stand
    b. on the floor next to the serving position
    *c. well away from the playing area
    d. outside the court

172. What does *not* contribute to safety on the court?
    *a. participating in every sequence of plays
    b. playing designated positions
    c. maintaining awareness of teammates
    d. calling for the ball

Terminology

Dink

173. What is a *dink*?
     - a. a powerful smash into the opponents' court
     - b. an attempt to recover a hard spiked ball
     - c. a service that lands in the court for a point
     - *d. a soft shot hit with the fingers

Off-Hand Spike

174. Which hitter is executing an off-hand spike?
     - a. a right-handed hitter at the left front
     - *b. a right-handed hitter at the right front
     - c. a left-handed hitter at the center front
     - d. a left-handed hitter at the right front

Off-Side Hitter

175. What is the player hitting from the right front position called?
     - a. the strong hitter
     - b. the power hitter
     - *c. the off-side hitter
     - d. the on-side hitter

Set

176. What is the technique used to put the ball into position for a player to attack?
     - a. serve
     - b. volley
     - *c. set
     - d. forearm pass

Multiple Block

177. Two or more players at the same time attempt to block a spike. What is this called?
     - *a. a multiple block
     - b. an attack block
     - c. a simultaneous block
     - d. a team block

Spike

178. A ball is hit downward with great force into the opponents' court. What is this called?
     - a. dink
     - b. serve
     - c. block
     - *d. spike

Overhand Floater Serve

179. A player hits a serve that has no spin and an erratic path as it approaches the receiver. What is this serve called?
     - *a. an overhand floater
     - b. an overhand topspin
     - c. a roundhouse
     - d. a slice

Side-Out

180. What is the term used when the serving team loses the serve?
     - a. service over
     - *b. side-out
     - c. lost serve
     - d. switching

Block

181. A defensive player is attempting to intercept a spike close to the net. What is this called?
     - a. set
     - b. net recovery
     - c. dink
     - *d. block

Serve

182. What technique is used to put the ball in play?
     - *a. serve
     - b. forearm pass
     - c. overhand pass
     - d. spike

Dig

183. What is it called when a player makes a play on a hard hit low ball?
     - a. drive
     - *b. dig
     - c. set
     - d. pass

Switching

184. What is *switching*?
     - a. serve changing from one team to the other
     - b. players going in and out of the game
     - *c. players changing positions after the serve
     - d. players changing positions in the lineup

Angle Spike

185. What is an *angle spike*?
     - a. a spike hit sharply downward
     - b. a spike hit down the line
     - *c. a spike hit crosscourt
     - d. a spike hit from behind the attack area

Foul

186. What is an infraction of the rules called?
     - a. violation
     - *b. foul
     - c. illegal play
     - d. error

Dive

187. A player makes a do-or-die attempt to keep a low ball in play. What is this called?
    *a. dive
    b. dig
    c. forearm pass
    d. set

Ace

188. What is it called when a point is scored as the direct result of a serve?
    a. a fake
    *b. an ace
    c. a dink
    d. a save

Referee

189. What is the official in charge of the game called?
    a. head official
    b. umpire
    *c. first referee
    d. head referee

Screening

190. The serving team moves to conceal the actions of the server as the serve is made. What is this called?
    a. hiding
    b. concealing
    c. covering
    *d. screening

Time-Out

191. What is the temporary suspension of play called?
    *a. time-out
    b. rest period
    c. halftime
    d. free time

Free Ball

192. A ball is hit over the net with upward flight. No attempt is made to spike on the third hit. What is this called?
    a. forearm pass
    b. overhand pass
    *c. free ball
    d. defensive hit

Back Set

193. A set is made over the head and back of the setter. What is this called?
    a. an overhand pass
    b. an overhead pass
    *c. a back set
    d. a setup

Covering

194. An offensive player gets into position to field any ball rebounding from a block. What is this called?
    a. a save
    b. a dive
    c. positioning
    *d. covering

Attack Block

195. A defensive player attempts to intercept the ball before it crosses the net. What is this called?
    a. net foul
    *b. attack block
    c. offensive block
    d. soft block

Auxiliary Setter

196. Which player is an *auxiliary setter*?
    a. a setter from the back row
    b. the second best setter on the team
    *c. a player designated to set the ball when the setter makes the first contact on that side
    d. the second string setter

Defense

197. When is a team on defense?
    *a. when the ball is controlled by the opponents
    b. when a team serves
    c. when a team receives the serve
    d. when a team with the ball *cannot* set up a spike play

Double Hit

198. What is the term used when a player hits the ball two or more times in a row?
    a. double fault
    *b. double hit
    c. two hits
    d. violation

Forearm Pass

199. A player hits the ball underhanded off the lower arms. What is this called?
    a. underhand pass
    b. bump
    *c. forearm pass
    d. serve

Middle-Back Defense

200. A team uses the middle back player to dig deep spikes. What is this defense called?
    a. an M formation
    b. a 5-1 formation
    *c. a middle-back defense
    d. a W defense

Middle-Up Defense

201. A team uses the middle back player to dig short dink shots. What is this defense called?
   - a. a dink defense
   - *b. a middle-up defense
   - c. a W formation
   - d. an M formation

M Formation

202. A team's setter is in the middle front position. What is this offense called?
   - a. a middle-up offense
   - b. a 5-1 attack
   - *c. an M formation
   - d. a W formation

4-2 Attack

203. A team is using two setters and four spikers. What is this offense called?
   - a. a 2-4 attack
   - *b. a 4-2 attack
   - c. a setter switch
   - d. a four-hitter attack

5-1 Attack

204. A team is using only one setter. What is this called?
   - *a. a 5-1 attack
   - b. a one-setter attack
   - c. a setter switch
   - d. an M formation

Multiple Offense

205. What is a *multiple offense*?
   - a. a team with more than one offensive play
   - b. a situation in which two players are eligible to spike
   - *c. a situation in which the setter is a back row player
   - d. a team with many complicated plays

Net Recovery

206. A player attempts to play a ball that has been hit into the net. What is this called?
   - a. net ball
   - *b. net recovery
   - c. dig
   - d. save

No-Block Defense

207. What is a *no-block defense*?
   - a. a situation in which no attempt is made to block a hard hit spike
   - b. a situation in which the attempt to block a spike is missed
   - c. a situation in which the attempt to block a spike sends the ball up and back into the blocking team's court
   - *d. a situation in which the defensive positions are taken because the opponents *cannot* aggressively spike the ball

On-Hand Spike

208. What is an *on-hand spike*?
   - a. one in which the spiker hits the ball with the open hand
   - b. one in which the spiker hits the ball with the fist
   - *c. one in which the right-handed spiker hits a ball coming from the right
   - d. one in which the right-handed spiker hits a ball coming from the left

Rules and Scoring

209. After the serve, how long should the ball be played?
   - a. until the coach calls time-out
   - *b. until the referee blows the whistle
   - c. until an illegal hit is made
   - d. until a net foul occurs

Playing Area

210. What is the approximate size of a volleyball court?
   - a. 30 by 30 feet
   - *b. 30 by 60 feet
   - c. 60 by 60 feet
   - d. 60 by 90 feet

211. How much clear area should there be around an indoor court?
   - a. 2-1/2 feet
   - b. 4 feet
   - *c. 6-1/2 feet
   - d. 10 feet

212. A playing area does *not* have the required clearance above the court. A serve hits the ceiling. What is the ruling?
   - a. play continues
   - b. reserve
   - c. second serve
   - *d. side-out

213. A playing area does *not* have the required clearance above the court. A ball hit by the receiving team touches the ceiling and rebounds into the serving team's court. What is the ruling?
    a. play continues
    b. replay
    c. side-out
    *d. point

214. A playing area does *not* have the required clearance above the court. When the serve is received, the ball hits an object above the court and rebounds into the receiving team's court. What is the ruling?
    *a. play continues
    b. replay
    c. side-out
    d. point

215. For men's play, what is the net height measured from the center of the court?
    a. 7 feet, 4-1/8 inches
    b. 7 feet, 6 inches
    *c. 7 feet, 11-5/8 inches
    d. 8 feet

216. For women's play, what is the net height measured from the center of the court?
    *a. 7 feet, 4-1/8 inches
    b. 7 feet, 6 inches
    c. 7 feet, 11-5/8 inches
    d. 8 feet

217. A ball hit by the receiving team hits an antenna and goes over into the serving team's court. What is the ruling?
    a. play continues
    b. replay
    *c. point
    d. side-out

Ball

218. A three-ball system is being used during a match. Who may give the ball to the server?
    a. the first referee
    b. the second referee
    c. any player
    *d. the ball retriever nearest the serving area

Team Representation

219. Who may address the first referee for purposes other than requesting time-out or substitution?
    *a. the captain
    b. the coach
    c. any player
    d. the captain or coach

220. Who may address the referees for the purpose of requesting time-out or substitution?
    a. the captain
    b. the coach
    c. any player
    *d. the captain or coach

Time-Out

221. When can a team request a time-out?
    *a. anytime the ball is dead
    b. when the ball is dead and they are serving
    c. when the ball is dead and they are receiving
    d. anytime they are controlling the ball

222. How many time-outs is a team allowed in a game?
    a. one
    *b. two
    c. three
    d. four

223. How long is the designated time-out period in intercollegiate play?
    a. 10 seconds
    b. 15 seconds
    *c. 30 seconds
    d. 45 seconds

224. How long is the time-out period in high school play?
    a. 15 seconds
    b. 30 seconds
    c. 45 seconds
    *d. 60 seconds

225. A high school team has had its allowed time-outs for a game. It inadvertently requests another time-out. What happens?
    a. It is awarded, and they are penalized loss of service or loss of point.
    b. It is awarded and subtracted from the next game.
    c. It is disallowed, and they are penalized loss of service or opponents are awarded a point.
    *d. It is disallowed, and they are given a warning.

226. A team has had its allowed time-outs for a game. It requests another one as an attempt to gain an advantage over the opponents. What happens?
   a. It is awarded, and they are penalized loss of service or loss of a point.
   b. It is awarded and subtracted from the next game.
   *c. It is disallowed, and they are penalized loss of service or opponents are awarded a point.
   d. It is disallowed, and they are given a warning.

227. What can the players do during a time-out?
   a. Sit down on the team bleacher.
   b. Go to the dressing room.
   c. Get a drink of water from the water fountain.
   *d. Speak or listen to the coach without leaving the court.

Sanctions

228. Which act will *not* result in a team or player receiving a warning?
   *a. The team captain addresses the first referee while the ball is dead.
   b. A player talks to an opponent to distract him or her.
   c. A player unintentionally delays the game.
   d. A player leaves the court during an interruption in play without permission.

229. Which act will result in a penalty?
   a. insulting an opponent
   *b. a second minor offense
   c. physical aggression toward an official
   d. disruptive coaching by a player on the bench

230. A player is disqualified for aggressive behavior toward an opponent. How long does the disqualification last?
   a. for a game
   *b. for the match
   c. for the tournament
   d. for the season

Teams

231. How many players are on a volleyball team?
   *a. 6
   b. 8
   c. 9
   d. 12

232. How many players may be on a team including substitutes?
   a. 8
   b. 10
   *c. 12
   d. 15

Substitutions

233. How many substitutions is a team allowed each game in international competition?
   a. 4
   *b. 6
   c. 10
   d. 12

234. What must a substitute do before entering a game?
   a. report to the scorer
   b. report to the first referee
   *c. report to the second referee
   d. report to the official's table

235. How many substitutes may enter a game at one time?
   a. only one
   b. one or two
   c. one to three
   *d. as many as the team wishes

236. How many times may a player who starts the game enter the game as a substitute?
   a. once
   *b. twice
   c. three times
   d. four times

237. How many players may enter the game in each position of the service order?
   a. one
   b. two
   c. three
   *d. any number

238. A player reenters the game. What position in the serving order may he or she take?
   *a. his or her original position
   b. the serving position
   c. the left front position
   d. any position

239. What occurs when an illegal substitution is requested?
    a. It is allowed, and the team is penalized loss of serve or a point is awarded the opponents.
    b. It is *not* allowed, and the team is penalized loss of serve or a point is awarded the opponents.
    *c. It is *not* allowed, and the team is charged with a time-out.
    d. It is not allowed, and the team is penalized loss of serve or a point is awarded the opponents.

240. Where must a substitute stand when waiting to enter the game?
    a. next to the first referee
    b. next to the second referee
    c. next to the scorer's table
    *d. in the designated substitution zone

241. What must players do that are entering or leaving a game?
    a. Change places as soon as the time-out for substitution is called.
    b. Raise one hand before changing places.
    *c. Raise one hand and touch the raised hands as they change places.
    d. Raise both hands and touch hands as they change places.

Injured Player

242. A player is injured, but the team wants to keep the player in the game. How long may the team take before having to replace the player or take a charged time-out?
    *a. 15 seconds
    b. 30 seconds
    c. 1 minute
    d. 3 minutes

Wrong Position Entry

243. A player on the receiving team entered the game in the wrong position in the service order. His or her team is now serving and has scored two points since the player entered the game. What happens?
    a. player removed, points kept, and side-out called
    *b. player removed, points lost, and side-out called
    c. player's position corrected, points kept, and side-out called
    d. player's position corrected, points lost, and serve kept

244. A player on the receiving team has entered the game in the wrong position in the serving order. The serving team has scored two points just prior to the discovery of the error. What happens?
    a. player removed, points kept, and serve kept
    b. player removed, points lost, and serve kept
    *c. player's position corrected, points kept, and serve kept
    d. player's position corrected, points lost, and serve kept

Number of Games

245. How many games make up a match in most noninternational play?
    a. one
    b. two
    *c. best two out of three
    d. best three out of five

246. How many games must be played to make a match in international play?
    a. two
    b. best two out of three
    *c. best three out of five
    d. best four out of seven

Coin Toss

247. When is a coin tossed to see which team will serve?
    a. before the first game
    b. before the first and third games
    *c. before the first and deciding games
    d. before every game

248. What choices does the winner of the coin toss have?
    *a. first serve or team area in that game
    b. first serve in the first or second game
    c. first serve and team area in that game
    d. first serve in the first and second game

Change of Playing Areas

249. When do teams change playing areas?
    a. after each game
    b. after each eight points
    c. after one team reaches eight points in every game
    *d. after each game and after one team reaches eight points in a deciding game

Time Between Games

250. In collegiate play, how long is the time be-
     tween games in a match consisting of the best
     two out of three games?
     a. 1 minute
     *b. 2 minutes
     c. 5 minutes
     d. 10 minutes

251. In high school play, how long is the time be-
     tween games in a match consisting of the best
     two out of three games?
     a. 1 minute
     b. 2 minutes
     *c. 3 minutes
     d. 5 minutes

Timed Game

252. How long is a timed game?
     a. 8 minutes of continuous time
     *b. 8 minutes of ball in play time or 15
        points, whichever occurs first
     c. 15 minutes of continuous time or 15
        points, whichever occurs first
     d. 15 minutes of ball in play time

Serving Position

253. What position does the server play?
     *a. right back
     b. right front
     c. left back
     d. left front

254. Which is *not* a violation of the foot fault rule
     while serving?
     a. stepping on the end line as the ball is
        contacted
     b. stepping on or over the end line as the
        ball is contacted
     c. stepping on the end line before the ball
        is contacted
     *d. stepping over the end line before the
        ball crosses the net

255. In high school play, where must the server
     stand to contact the ball?
     a. anywhere behind the end line
     *b. behind the end line and within 10 feet
        of the extended right sideline
     c. behind the end line and within 10 feet
        of the extended left sideline
     d. behind the end line and anywhere to
        the right of the middle of the court

256. In collegiate play, where must the server
     stand to contact the ball?
     a. anywhere behind the end line
     *b. behind the end line and within 9 feet,
        10 inches of the extended right sideline
     c. behind the end line and within 9 feet,
        10 inches of the extended left sideline
     d. behind the end line and anywhere to
        the right of the middle of the court

257. When the ball is served, where must the right
     front be in relation to his or her teammates?
     *a. toward the right sideline from the
        middle front and toward the net from
        the right back
     b. closer to the right sideline than any of
        the other players except the right back
     c. closer to the net than any of the backs
     d. anywhere in his or her sixth of the
        playing area

Serving Readiness

258. How long does the server have to put the
     ball in play after the first referee's readiness
     whistle?
     a. 2 seconds
     b. 3 seconds
     *c. 5 seconds
     d. 10 seconds

259. A player serves before the first referee blows
     the readiness whistle. What happens?
     a. play continues
     b. side-out
     *c. reserve
     d. delay of game penalty

Serving Faults

260. Which event is *not* a service fault?
     a. the serve touching the net
     b. the serve touching an antenna
     c. a player helping the serve over the net
     *d. the server bouncing the ball before
        serving

261. The serve hits the top of the net and goes over
     into the opponents' court. What is the ruling?
     a. play continues
     *b. side-out
     c. reserve
     d. second serve

262. What happens when a service fault occurs?
     *a. side-out
     b. point
     c. reserve
     d. second serve

Serving Order

263. How long does a player continue to serve?
    a. one serve for each player
    b. until he or she has served five times
    *c. until his or her team commits a fault
    d. until he or she makes a bad serve

264. A player serves out of order. While the player is serving, the error is discovered. What happens?
    a. The order is corrected, the points scored are lost, and the correct player serves.
    b. The order is corrected, the points scored are kept, and the correct player serves.
    *c. The order is corrected, the points scored are lost, and side-out is called.
    d. The order is retained, the points scored are kept, and side-out is called.

265. Who serves first in the second game?
    *a. the team that received first in the first game
    b. the team that served first in the first game
    c. the team that won the first game
    d. the team that lost the first game

266. When does a team rotate?
    a. when the team loses the serve
    *b. when the team gains the serve
    c. when the team loses a point
    d. when the team makes a point

267. Which describes the proper method of rotation?
    a. one position to the right
    b. one position to the left
    *c. one position clockwise
    d. one position counterclockwise

268. A player is the third server on a team. In what position did that player begin the game?
    a. right middle
    b. right front
    *c. middle front
    d. left back

Screening

269. A player on the serving team is trying to keep the receiving team from watching the server hit the ball. What happens?
    a. legal play
    b. replay
    c. warning
    *d. side-out

Number of Contacts

270. If a ball is *not* hit on a block, how many times may a team contact the ball before it must go over the net into the opponent's court?
    a. one
    b. two
    *c. three
    d. four

271. If a ball is touched by a blocker, how many times may a team contact the ball before it must go over the net into the opponent's court?
    a. one
    b. two
    *c. three
    d. four

Contact With the Body

272. With what parts of the body may a player legally contact the ball?
    a. hands and forearms
    b. hands and arms
    *c. any part of the body on or above the waist
    d. any part of the body

Successive Contacts

273. A player on the receiving team hits a ball straight up in the air and then hits it again, passing it to a teammate. What is the ruling?
    a. Play continues, and it is counted as one hit.
    b. Play continues, and it is counted as two hits.
    c. A double foul is called and a point awarded.
    *d. A double hit is called and a point awarded.

274. When may a player hit the ball twice in a row?
    a. never
    *b. when the first hit was an attempted block
    c. when the hits are made with different body parts
    d. when the first hit was a ball recovered from the net

Simultaneous Contacts

275. Two players on the same team contact the ball at the same time in attempting to receive a serve. What is the ruling?
    a. A point is awarded to the serving team.
    b. Play continues, and it counts as one hit.
    *c. Play continues, and it counts as two hits.
    d. A double hit is called.

276. Two players on the same team hit the ball at the same time. In what situation is one of these players allowed to make the next hit on the ball?
    a. no situation
    b. after any simultaneous hit
    c. when the simultaneous hit was the first hit after the ball came over the net
    *d. when the simultaneous hit was an attempt to make a block

277. Two players on opposing teams simultaneously contact the ball. The ball falls to the serving team's side of the net. What happens?
    *a. Play continues, and the serving team has three hits.
    b. Play continues, and the serving team has two hits.
    c. A double foul is called, and the ball reserved.
    d. Side-out is called.

Held Ball

278. A ball comes to rest momentarily in the hands of two opposing players. What happens?
    a. play continues
    b. double hit
    *c. held ball
    d. double fault

279. A player is hitting an overhand pass. The ball comes to rest in the palms of the player's hands. What happens?
    a. legal play
    *b. held ball
    c. double hit
    d. palming

Blocking

280. Who may block a spike?
    a. any player on the defensive team
    b. only the player opposite the spiker
    c. only the two players closest to the spiker
    *d. only the front row players

281. When may a ball be blocked by the defensive team?
    a. not until the ball has crossed the net into their court
    b. not until the ball is above the net
    *c. not until the ball has been hit by the spiker
    d. not until the ball is in a downward path

Attacking

282. A back row player on the serving team returns the ball to the opponent's court while in front of the attack line. When contact with the ball was made, it was below the level of the net. What is the decision?
    *a. legal play
    b. point
    c. side-out
    d. replay

283. A back row player on the serving team spikes the ball into the opponent's court. The spiker was behind the attack line when jumping to make the spike. What was the decision?
    *a. legal play
    b. point
    c. side-out
    d. replay

284. A back row player on the serving team spikes the ball into the opponent's court. The spiker was at the net when the hit was made. What is the decision?
    a. legal play
    b. point
    *c. side-out
    d. replay

Net

285. Which event is *not* a fault related to the net?
    a. player touching the net accidentally
    b. player touching the net while spiking
    c. player's clothing touching the net
    *d. net touching player due to hard-hit ball

Center Line

286. Which event is a center line violation?
    *a. touching the opponents' playing area with the hands
    b. stepping on the center line
    c. stepping on center line and opponents' playing area
    d. having one or both feet on or above the center line

Double Fault

287. A player on one team holds the ball at the same time that a player on the other team falls into the net. What is the decision?
    a. play continues
    b. double hit
    c. double foul
    *d. double fault

Scoring

288. What score indicates a completed game?
   a. 10-5
   b. 15-14
   *c. 18-16
   d. 21-17

289. When has a team won a game?
   a. when it reaches 15 points first
   *b. when it reaches 15 points and is two points ahead
   c. when it is ahead and time runs out
   d. when a total of 15 points have been played and it is at least two points ahead

290. What is the score of a defaulted game?
   a. 1-0
   b. 2-0
   *c. 15-0
   d. 21-0

Coed Rules

291. In coed volleyball, how high is the net?
   a. 7 feet, 4-1/8 inches
   b. 7 feet, 6 inches
   *c. 7 feet, 11-5/8 inches
   d. 8 feet

292. What is the rule about playing positions in coed volleyball?
   a. At least three females must be on the playing team at all times.
   b. Three males and three females must be on the playing team at all times.
   c. No more than four males may be on the playing team at one time.
   *d. Male and female players must alternate in the serving order.

293. What is the rule about playing the ball in coed volleyball?
   a. A female must be the setter.
   *b. If the ball is hit more than once by a team, one hit must be by a female.
   c. If the ball is hit more than once by a team, one hit must be by a male.
   d. The hits by one team must alternate male and female.

Reverse Coed Rules

294. What is the rule about playing positions in reverse coed volleyball?
   a. At least three females must be on the playing team at all times.
   b. Three males and three females must be on the playing team at all times.
   c. No more than four males may be on the playing team at one time.
   *d. Male and female players must alternate in the serving order.

295. What is the rule about playing the ball in reverse coed volleyball?
   a. A male must be the setter.
   b. If the ball is hit more than once by a team, one hit must be by a female.
   *c. If the ball is hit more than once by a team, one hit must be by a male.
   d. The hits by one team must alternate male and female.

296. What is a restriction on male players in reverse coed volleyball?
   a. Male players may not set the ball.
   *b. Male players may not spike from in front of the attack line.
   c. Male players may not serve first in a game.
   d. The ball may not be hit consecutively by male players.

Beach Rules

297. What is the difference in beach volleyball playing rules and regular rules?
   a. smaller playing area
   b. nine instead of six players
   c. two hits per team instead of three
   *d. changing playing areas after each five points are scored

298. What are the lines made of in beach volleyball?
   *a. ropes
   b. lime
   c. indentations in the sand
   d. metal wires

Doubles Rules

299. What is *not* a difference in the rules of doubles and regulation volleyball?
   a. The court is shorter in doubles.
   b. There are no substitutes in doubles.
   c. The serve can be made from anywhere behind the end line in doubles.
   *d. No spiking is allowed in doubles.

300. In doubles play, how may points must be won to win a game?
   a. 5
   *b. 11
   c. 15
   d. 21

Strategy

General Offense

301. What is the basic attack pattern of play?
    *a. pass-set-spike
    b. pass-pass-set
    c. set-spike-block
    d. serve-set-spike

302. Who is the "quarterback" of the team?
    a. the captain
    b. the coach
    c. the left front
    *d. the setter

303. What do the numbers in offensive systems mean?
    a. number of spikers and number of blockers
    b. number of attackers and number of nonattackers
    *c. number of spikers and number of setters
    d. number of front row players and number of back row players

Setting

304. Generally, where should the ball be set?
    a. near the center of the net
    *b. 1 to 2 feet inside the sidelines
    c. 3 to 5 feet inside the sidelines
    d. 8 to 10 feet inside the sidelines

305. Generally, how high should the ball be hit for a set?
    a. 1 foot above the top of the net
    b. 2 to 3 feet above the top of the net
    *c. 6 to 8 feet above the top of the net
    d. 15 to 20 feet above the top of the net

306. Which set is considered to be the highest percentage set?
    *a. regular set
    b. Japanese set
    c. two-set
    d. shoot set

307. What is the purpose of the Japanese set?
    a. to give the spiker plenty of time to judge the ball
    b. to create a one-on-one blocking situation
    c. to attack the space between the outside and middle blocker
    *d. to beat the blockers with quickness of execution

308. What is the purpose of the two-set?
    a. to give the spiker plenty of time to judge the ball
    *b. to create a one-on-one blocking situation
    c. to attack the space between the outside and middle blocker
    d. to beat the blockers with quickness of execution

309. What is the purpose of the three-set?
    a. to give the spiker plenty of time to judge the ball
    b. to create a one-on-one blocking situation
    *c. to attack the space between the outside and middle blocker
    d. to beat the blockers with quickness of execution

310. What is the purpose of the shoot set?
    a. to give the spiker plenty of time to judge the ball
    b. to create a one-on-one blocking situation
    *c. to attack the space between the outside and middle blocker
    d. to beat the blockers with quickness of execution

311. When should the setter send the ball wider than usual on a regular set?
    a. when setting to the on-hand spiker
    *b. when setting to the off-hand spiker
    c. when the pass to the setter is inaccurate
    d. when the spiker is left-handed

312. All the spikers have about the same ability. Which spiker should the setter send the ball to most often?
    a. the left front
    b. the center front
    *c. the on-hand spiker
    d. the off-hand spiker

313. When should a setter attempt a back set?
    *a. only on a good pass
    b. only when in trouble
    c. only when the right front is left-handed
    d. only when setting from the left front position

314. What should be changed about the regular set if the spiker is short?
    a. Set the ball higher.
    b. Set the ball lower.
    c. Set the ball closer to the net.
    *d. Set the ball further from the net.

Spiking

315. What is the easiest spike to hit?
  *a. on-hand crosscourt
  b. on-hand down-the-line
  c. off-hand crosscourt
  d. off-hand down-the-line

316. What is the most difficult spike to hit successfully?
  a. on-hand crosscourt
  b. on-hand down-the-line
  c. off-hand crosscourt
  *d. off-hand down-the-line

317. A spiker is not sure where the block is or how the defense is aligned. Where should the ball be hit?
  a. down-the-line
  *b. crosscourt
  c. down-the-middle
  d. dink

318. The ball is set too close to the net. What should the spiker do?
  a. Hit as hard as possible.
  b. Aim between the two blockers.
  *c. Dink the ball.
  d. Let the blockers hit the ball.

319. The spiker is against a one-player block. What is generally the best spike to attempt?
  a. down-the-line
  *b. crosscourt
  c. down-the-middle
  d. dink

320. What is the main reason for the side set?
  a. easiest for the spiker to hit
  b. easiest for setter to set
  *c. provides longest spiking angle on the court
  d. most difficult to block

Blocking

321. What is the purpose of the attack block?
  a. to make it easy for teammates to hit the pass
  b. to hit the ball before the spiker can
  *c. to hit the ball before it crosses the net
  d. to hit the spiker with the blocked ball

322. Which is the best time for a player to use a soft block?
  a. when the ball is set close to the net
  *b. when the ball is set off the net
  c. when the spiker hits the ball very hard
  d. when the spiker is very short

323. What adjustment should the outside blocker make from the usual blocking position?
  *a. Turn the hand nearest the side line toward the middle of the opponents' court.
  b. Turn his or her body toward the middle of the opponents' court.
  c. Tilt both hands toward the nearest sideline.
  d. Jump about 6 inches lower than usual.

Serving

324. Which serve is the best offensive weapon?
  a. underhand
  b. sidearm
  c. roundhouse
  *d. overhand

325. Which serve will generally cause the receiving team the greatest difficulty?
  a. a serve to the front half of the court
  b. a serve to the back half of the court
  *c. a serve to the back corners of the court
  d. a serve to the middle of the court

326. Which is *not* a good serving strategy?
  a. Hit away from the best spiker.
  b. Hit to a known weak passer.
  c. Serve to a substitute.
  *d. Attempt mostly difficult short or corner serves.

327. The receiving team is playing a multiple offense. Where should serves be sent more frequently than with other offenses?
  a. crosscourt
  *b. down-the-line
  c. short
  d. deep

328. The receiving team is playing a multiple offense. Where should the ball be served to take advantage of a potential weakness in this system?
  *a. in the path of the setter
  b. to the right back position
  c. to the left front position
  d. barely over the net

4-2 Offense

329. What is the advantage of the 4-2 offense?
  *a. simple and easy
  b. provides for multiple offense
  c. deceptive to opponents
  d. has a backup setter

330. What is the disadvantage of the 4-2 offense?
  a. hard to learn
  b. requires highly skilled players
  *c. does not provide for multiple offense
  d. requires exceptional setting ability

331. In what positions do the setters generally begin with a 4-2 offense?
    *a. center front and center back
    b. right front and left back
    c. right back and center front
    d. left front and right back

332. Where do the strongest two spikers generally begin in a game with a 4-2 offense?
    *a. left front and right back
    b. center front and center back
    c. left front and right front
    d. left front and center back

333. A team playing a 4-2 offense is receiving the serve. Where should the front row setter be if he or she is the center front?
    a. at the net in the center of the court
    *b. at the net and slightly to the right of the center
    c. at the net and slightly to the left of center
    d. at the attack line in the center of the court

334. A team playing a 4-2 offense is receiving the serve. Where should the front row setter be if he or she is the right front?
    a. at the net in the center of the court
    b. at the net and in the right third of the court
    *c. at the net and next to the right sideline
    d. at the attack line and in the right third of the court

335. A team playing a 4-2 offense is receiving the serve. Where should the front row setter be if he or she is the left front?
    a. at the net in the center of the court
    b. at the net and in the left third of the court
    *c. at the net and next to the left sideline
    d. at the attack line and in the left third of the court

336. A team playing a 4-2 offense is receiving the serve. Which phrase describes the positions of the five receivers?
    *a. offset to the left and in the middle area of the court
    b. offset to the right and in the middle area of the court
    c. in a U formation, the top of which points to the net
    d. in a W formation and in the middle area of the court

337. A team playing a 4-2 offense is receiving the serve. Which players are in position to receive the deep serves?
    a. left back, center back, and right back
    b. left back and center back
    c. right back and center back
    *d. left back and right back

338. A team playing a 4-2 offense is receiving the serve. The front row setter is in the center front position. Which players are in position to receive the short to medium depth serves on the right side?
    *a. right front
    b. center front
    c. right back
    d. center back

339. A team playing a 4-2 offense is receiving the serve. The front row setter is in the right front position. Which players are in position to receive the short to medium depth serves on the right side?
    a. right front
    *b. center front
    c. right back
    d. center back

340. A team playing a 4-2 offense is receiving the serve. The front row setter is in the left front position. Which players are in position to receive the short to medium depth serves on the left side?
    a. left front
    *b. center front
    c. left back
    d. center back

341. A team playing a 4-2 offense is receiving the serve. Which diagram shows the target area for the pass? [Refer to Diagram 5.]
     *a.

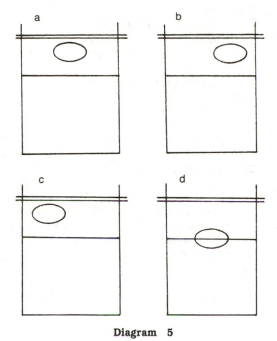

Diagram 5

342. A team is playing a 4-2 offense. All spikers are of about equal ability. Where should most of the set be placed?
    a. center front
    b. right front
    *c. left front
    d. center or left front

343. An advanced level team is playing a 4-2 offense. What should be the setter's first consideration in deciding where to set the ball?
    a. ability of the spikers
    b. on- or off-handedness of spikers
    c. preferred hand of spikers
    *d. blocking capabilities of the opponents

344. A team is playing a 4-2 offense. The pass is mishandled, and a front court spiker must set the ball. Where should the ball be set?
    a. to the center of the net
    *b. to the front court spiker on other side
    c. almost straight up
    d. to a spiker behind the attack line

345. A team is playing a 4-2 offense. The pass is mishandled and is hit to the middle of the court between a front and back row player. Who should take the ball and where should it be set?
    a. front row player setting to the left front position
    b. front row player setting to the right front position
    *c. back row player setting to the left front position
    d. back row player setting to the right front position

346. A team is playing a 4-2 offense. The pass is mishandled and is hit to the left sideline between a front and back row player. Who should take the ball and where should it be set?
    a. front row player setting to the left front position
    b. front row player setting to the right front position
    c. back row player setting to the left front position
    *d. back row player setting to the right front position

5-1 Offense

347. What is the major advantage of the 5-1 offense?
    a. simple and easy
    *b. provides for multiple offense
    c. deceptive to opponents
    d. has a backup setter

348. Why should beginning teams *not* use a 5-1 offense?
    a. too hard to learn positions
    b. no provision for a multiple offense
    *c. requires highly skilled setter and spikers
    d. has no backup setter

349. In what position does the setter generally begin with a 5-1 offense?
    a. center front
    b. right front
    *c. right back
    d. left back

350. A team playing a 5-1 offense is receiving the serve. Where should the front row setter be if he or she is the center front?
    a. at the net in the center of the court
    *b. at the net and slightly to the right of the center
    c. at the net and slightly to the left of center
    d. at the attack line in the center of the court

351. A team playing a 5-1 offense is receiving the serve. Where should the front row setter be if he or she is the right front?
    a. at the net in the center of the court
    b. at the net and in the right third of the court
    *c. at the net and next to the right side line
    d. at the attack line and in the right third of the court

352. A team playing a 5-1 offense is receiving the serve. Where should the front row setter be if he or she is the left front?
    a. at the net in the center of the court
    b. at the net and in the left third of the court
    *c. at the net and next to the left side line
    d. at the attack line and in the left third of the court

353. A team playing a 5-1 offense is receiving the serve. The setter is in the right back position. Where should he or she be on the court?
    *a. immediately behind and slightly to the right of the right front
    b. immediately behind the right front
    c. immediately behind and slightly to the right of the center front
    d. anywhere in the right back sixth of the court

354. A team playing a 5-1 offense is receiving the serve. The setter is in the center back position. Where should he or she be on the court?
    a. immediately behind and slightly to the left of the right front
    b. immediately behind the center front
    *c. immediately behind and slightly to the right of the center front
    d. immediately behind and slightly to the left of the center front

355. A team playing a 5-1 offense is receiving the serve. The setter is in the left back position. Where should he or she be on the court?
    *a. immediately behind and slightly to the left of the left front
    b. immediately behind the left front
    c. immediately behind and slightly to the left of the center front
    d. anywhere in the left back sixth of the court

356. A team playing a 5-1 offense is receiving the serve. What is the most difficult position for the setter to play?
    a. left front
    *b. left back
    c. center back
    d. right back

357. A team playing a 5-1 offense is receiving the serve. The setter is in the left back position and is having trouble reaching the passing area to make the set from the usual receiving pattern. What is an alternative pattern the team might play?
    a. Pass the ball higher.
    b. Designate an auxiliary setter.
    c. Move the passing area to the center front.
    *d. Use a four-player serve reception.

358. A team playing a 5-1 offense is receiving the serve. The setter is in the right back or center back position. Which diagram shows the target area for the pass? [Refer to Diagram 5, Question 341.]
    *b.

359. A team is playing a 5-1 offense. The setter is forced to make the first hit on the ball. A technique player has been designated to make the set. Which player is in the best position to be technique player?
    a. right front
    *b. right back
    c. center front
    d. left back

6-0 Offense

360. Which player is the setter in a 6-0 offense?
    a. right front
    b. center front
    *c. right back
    d. center back

361. Why do few teams use a 6-0 offense?
    *a. requires six exceptional setters, spikers, and passers
    b. does not allow for a multiple offense
    c. is not deceptive to opponents
    d. provides poor service reception coverage

6-2 Offense

362. What is the advantage of a 6-2 offense over a 6-0 offense?
    a. is not as hard to learn
    b. is more deceptive to opponents
    *c. Only two players must be good setters.
    d. Only four players must be good spikers.

363. A team is playing a 6-2 offense. When receiving serve, what problems does this offense have?
    a. the same as a 4-2 offense
    *b. the same as a 5-1 offense
    c. the same as a 6-0 offense
    d. the same as a middle-up offense

Covering the Spiker

364. A team is attempting to cover a spiker. In all systems what pattern is the same?
    a. Each player covers his or her sixth of the court.
    b. The center players cover the middle of the court.
    *c. The three players nearest the spiker form a semicircle around the spiker.
    d. The five players form a semicircle around the spiker.

365. A team is playing a 4-2 offense. The set is to the left front position. Which player moves to the deep back position to cover the spiker?
    a. left back
    b. center back
    *c. right back
    d. center front

366. A team is playing a multiple offense. The set is to the center front position. Which players move to the deep back position to cover the spiker?
    a. left back and right back
    b. center back and right back
    c. right back and center back
    *d. left back and right front

General Defense

367. What is the basic objective in positioning the defense?
    a. to put a player in each sixth of the court
    b. to put the best defenders on the back row
    *c. to put the players in the area of the court where the ball will come the highest percentage of the time
    d. to put a good defender between two weaker defenders throughout the lineup

368. The set is made to the left front on the opposing team. In a double block, which players should be the blockers?
    a. left and center fronts
    *b. right and center fronts
    c. left front and left back
    d. right front and right back

369. The opponents' set is made to the center front position. What players usually attempt the double block in this situation?
    a. center and left fronts
    *b. center and right fronts
    c. left and right fronts
    d. center front and center back

370. What is the blocker's first responsibility in all center hit situations?
    a. to take away the angle hits
    b. to take away the crosscourt hit
    *c. to take away the straight ahead hit
    d. to take away the dink

371. Which spike will probably be angled more sharply downward?
    a. one set away from the net
    *b. one set close to the net
    c. one set to the on-hand spiker
    d. one set to the off-hand spiker

372. A spiker's shoulders and hips are perpendicular to the net as he or she prepares to hit the ball. What direction is the spike *least* likely to go?
    *a. down-the-line
    b. crosscourt
    c. dink
    d. power angle

Middle-Up Defense

373. What is the strength of the middle-up defense?
    *a. good coverage of dinks and balls off the blockers
    b. good coverage of the entire court area
    c. good coverage of the back court area
    d. good coverage of crosscourt spikes

374. What is the disadvantage of the middle-up defense?
    a. hard to make transition to offense
    b. hard to learn
    c. All players must be strong defenders.
    *d. Middle back of court may be open.

375. Which diagram shows the base positions for a middle-up defense? [Refer to Diagram 6.]
    *a.

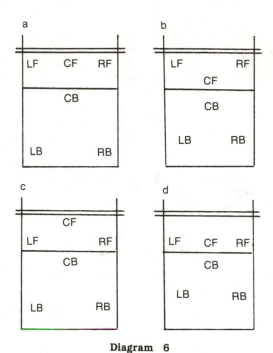

Diagram 6

376. How is an anticipated spike down the line covered in a middle-up defense?
    a. The side blocker moves to the sideline and puts his or her outside hand in line with the ball.
    *b. The side blocker moves to a position so that both hands are in line with the down the line path of the ball.
    c. The two blockers move to a position so that the center of the block is in the down the line path of the ball.
    d. The side blocker moves slightly toward the sideline, and the back on that side moves up and to the sideline.

377. A team is playing a middle-up defense. What should the front row nonblocking player do on the block?
    a. Move behind the blockers to cover the dink.
    b. Move back diagonally toward the middle of the court to the attack line.
    *c. Move straight back to the attack line.
    d. Move several steps away from the net and toward the blockers.

378. What is a common error made by the back-court players in the middle-up defense?
    a. playing too deep
    *b. playing too close to the net
    c. playing too close to the side line
    d. playing too close to the middle of the court

Middle-Back Defense

379. What is the advantage of the middle-back defense?
    a. easy to learn
    b. easy to make a transition to offense
    c. good coverage of the whole court
    *d. good coverage of the deep court area

380. What is the major disadvantage of the middle-back defense?
    a. hard to learn
    b. hard to make transition to offense
    c. opens sideline areas to power spikes
    *d. opens court to dinks and half-speed spikes

381. Which diagram shows the base positions for the middle-back defense? [Refer to Diagram 7.]
    *c.

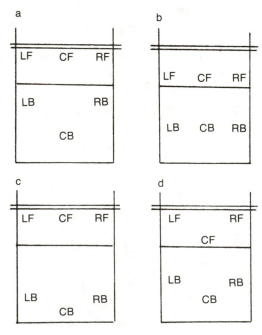

Diagram 7

382. Where should the center back play on the block in the middle-back defense?
      a. in the center back of the court near the end line
      *b. near the end line and between the two blockers and in line with the ball
      c. in the middle of the back half of the court
      d. halfway between the other two backs

No-Block Defense

383. On the no-block defense, what is the responsibility of the setter if the team is playing a multiple offense?
      *a. to play defense first
      b. to get into position for the set
      c. to keep from having to make the pass
      d. to hide behind another defender

Free Ball

384. What positions does a team take in a free ball situation?
      a. usual defensive positions
      *b. usual serve reception positions
      c. usual no-block positions
      d. special free-ball defensive positions

Transition

385. What is the major problem in moving from offense to defense in a 5-1 offense?
      a. getting the spiker into position
      b. getting the center back into position
      *c. getting the setter to a back row position
      d. getting the center front into position

386. What defensive position does the setter usually take when a team is playing a 5-1 offense?
      a. center front
      b. right front
      c. center back
      *d. right back

Acknowledgments

Colleagues and students who contributed suggestions and ideas for the Volleyball test questions are: B. Anderson, D. Conder, N. Frank, M. Herring, A. Jeffreys, C. Littlejohn, M. Reams, E. Redding, J. Rogers, J. Vandiver, C. Vaughn, and C. Weinmann.

Suggested Readings

Bertucci, B. (Ed.). (1982). *Championship volleyball: By the experts* (2nd ed.). Champaign, IL: Leisure Press.

Beutelstahl, D. (1978). *Volleyball—Playing to win*. New York: Arco.

Campbell, M.J. (1983). *Volleyball*. Topeka, KS: Jostens.

Gozansky, S. (1983). *Championship volleyball techniques and drills*. West Nyack, NY: Parke.

N.A.G.W.S. volleyball guide June 1986-June 1987. (1984). Reston, VA: AAHPERD.

1986/87 official high school volleyball rules. (1986). Kansas City, MO: National Federation of State High School Associations.

Schaafsma, F., Heck, A., & Sarver, C.T. (1985). *Volleyball for coaches and teachers* (2nd ed.). Dubuque, IA: Wm. C. Brown.

Weight Training

George T. White, Consultant

This collection of test questions on weight training is divided into seven content areas:

- History
- Terminology
- Equipment
- Principles
- Techniques
- Strategy
- Rules of Competition

The emphasis is on the scientific principles involved in weight lifting, techniques used in the various lifts, and training strategies.

Most of the facts and concepts presented in this chapter relate to free weights. However, some questions pertain to various machines, including Nautilus equipment.

In most questions where muscle action is a part of the question or responses, the scientific name for the muscle is given along with the layperson's terminology. The test user may choose to use either or both, depending on the level of knowledge of the students taking the test. In the body positions described, anatomical position is assumed unless otherwise stated.

The questions listed under the topics "Muscle Action" in the Principles area, and "Lifts" and "Muscles Exercised" in the Techniques area are organized so that they move sequentially from the upper body to the lower body.

Weight Training

History

Origin

1. Who was Milo of Crotona?
    *a. one of the first to practice progressive weight training
    b. the inventor of dumbbells
    c. the first Olympic weight lifting champion
    d. a weight lifting champion of the ancient Olympics

George T. White is an assistant professor of health, physical education, and recreation at Delta State University, Cleveland, Mississippi. He is a former high school coach and athletic trainer.

2. According to recorded history, what were the earliest weight training objects?
   a. German gymnastics bells
   b. Roman dumbbells
   c. Chinese barbells
   *d. Greek halteres

3. Of what were the earliest dumbbells made?
   *a. ax handle and bells
   b. broom handles and large boulders
   c. axle rods and rims of wheels
   d. thick tree limbs and large boulders

4. From what country does the term dumbbell come?
   a. United States
   *b. England
   c. Germany
   d. Greece

People

5. Who is known for developing the use of dumb-bells as a training aid?
   a. Soo Wong Lee
   b. Frederick Jahn
   *c. John Paugh
   d. George Hackensmidt

6. Who brought weight training to the United States?
   a. Chinese immigrants
   *b. German immigrants
   c. English circus performers
   d. Irish circus performers

Competition

7. When did weight lifting first appear as an Olympic event?
   *a. 1896
   b. 1916
   c. 1932
   d. 1928

Values

8. For many years, coaches tried to keep their athletes from lifting weights. Why?
   a. considered it too tiring
   *b. feared it would make them muscle-bound
   c. feared it would take their concentration away from the sport
   d. considered it too dangerous

Terminology

Elastic Rebound

9. A muscle flexes and immediately extends. What is this called?
   a. hyperextension
   *b. elastic rebound
   c. hypertrophy
   d. negative exercise

Flexion

10. Two body parts connected by a joint are brought closer together. What is this called?
   *a. flexion
   b. extension
   c. abduction
   d. adduction

Abduction

11. What is moving away from the centerline of the body called?
   a. flexion
   b. extension
   *c. abduction
   d. adduction

Adduction

12. What is moving toward the centerline of the body called?
   a. flexion
   b. extension
   c. abduction
   *d. adduction

Extension

13. The angle between two body parts becomes greater. What is this called?
   a. flexion
   *b. extension
   c. abduction
   d. adduction

Prone

14. An exerciser is lying on the front of the body facing downward. What is this called?
   a. horizontal
   b. vertical
   *c. prone
   d. supine

Supine

15. An exerciser is lying on the back of the body facing upward. What is this called?
   a. horizontal
   b. vertical
   c. prone
   *d. supine

Load

16. What is *load*?
    * *a. actual amount of weight lifted in completing a movement
    * b. amount of weight lifted per pound of body weight of the lifter
    * c. amount of weight lifted by a specific class of weight lifter
    * d. amount of body weight carried by the lifter

Reps

17. What are *reps*?
    * *a. a complete cycle of movements
    * b. a number of different exercises
    * c. a complete round in circuit training
    * d. a designated number of sets

Sticking Point

18. What is the *sticking point*?
    * a. the place at which a weight lifting movement is completed
    * b. the place at which a weight must be held for a specified amount of time in competition
    * *c. the place at which the greatest resistance occurs in a movement
    * d. the balance point of a weight training apparatus

Overloading

19. A lifter is able to do the desired number of repetitions during the first set. The lifter then increases the weight or resistance by about 5%. What is this called?
    * a. muscular endurance
    * b. hypertrophy
    * *c. overloading
    * d. hyperextending

Isokinetic

20. In which form of exercise is muscle tension kept at a maximum through the full range of movement?
    * *a. isokinetic
    * b. isometric
    * c. isotonic
    * d. negative

Isometric

21. In which form of exercise does the joint angle and muscle length remain constant?
    * a. isokinetic
    * b. isotonic
    * *c. isometric
    * d. negative

Isotonic

22. In which form of exercise is there a concentric muscle contraction which shortens the muscle and moves a load?
    * a. isokinetic
    * *b. isotonic
    * c. isometric
    * d. negative

Negative Exercise

23. In which form of exercise is movement limited by eccentric contractions while increasing the length of the muscle?
    * a. isokinetic
    * b. isotonic
    * c. isometric
    * *d. negative

Negative Accentuated Exercise

24. What is the exercise called in which the weight is lifted by two limbs and slowly lowered by one?
    * a. negative exercise
    * b. negative emphasized exercise
    * *c. negative accentuated exercise
    * d. negative only exercise

Blitz

25. A lifter trains 5 days a week but only exercises one group of muscles each day. What is this called?
    * a. superset
    * *b. blitz
    * c. overloading
    * d. negative exercises

Superset

26. What is it called when a lifter fatigues one group of muscles and then immediately follows with a set for the antagonists?
    * a. burn
    * *b. superset
    * c. blitz
    * d. preexhaustion

Hypertrophy

27. What is the enlarging of a muscle called?
    * a. hyperextension
    * b. atrophy
    * *c. hypertrophy
    * d. overloading

Power

28. What is the combination of speed and strength called?
    a. negative exercise
    b. endurance
    c. dead lifts
    *d. power

Cuts

29. What are *cuts*?
    *a. muscular definitions showing separations between muscle fiber groups
    b. way of determining classes of weight lifters
    c. way of determining classes of body builders
    d. way of eliminating lifters from competition

Deltoid

30. Which muscle group in the diagram is the deltoid? [Refer to Diagram 1.]
    *a.

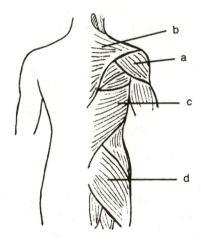

Back of Body

Diagram 1

Latissimus Dorsi

31. Which muscle group in the diagram is the latissimus dorsi? [Refer to Diagram 1, Question 30.]
    *c.

Gluteus Maximus

32. Which muscle group in the diagram is the gluteus maximus? [Refer to Diagram 1, Question 30.]
    *d.

Quadriceps

33. Which muscle group in the diagram is the quadriceps? [Refer to Diagram 2.]
    *d.

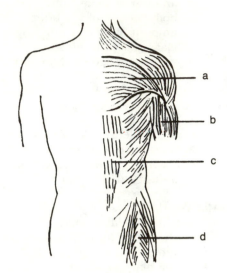

Front of Body

Diagram 2

Pectoralis Major

34. Which muscle group in the diagram is the pectoralis major? [Refer to Diagram 2, Question 33.]
    *a.

Biceps

35. Which muscle group in the diagram is the biceps? [Refer to Diagram 2, Question 33.]
    *b.

Power Lifters

36. Which weight training group uses extremely heavy weights, many sets, and few repetitions?
    *a. power lifters
    b. weight lifters
    c. athletes
    d. bodybuilders

Weight Lifters

37. Which weight training group lifts close to maximum weight and does about three repetitions at one given time?
    a. power lifters
    *b. weight lifters
    c. athletes
    d. bodybuilders

Bodybuilders

38. Which weight training group concentrates on repeated sets with high numbers of repetitions in each set?
    a. power lifters
    b. weight lifters
    c. athletes
    *d. bodybuilders

Bench Press

39. An exerciser takes a supine position on a bench and lifts a weight from the chest to a straight-arm position. What is this called?
    *a. bench press
    b. clean and jerk
    c. dead lift
    d. snatch

Dead Lift

40. An exerciser crouches with the head up and moves to a standing position with the bar resting across the thighs. What is this called?
    a. clean and jerk
    *b. dead lift
    c. snatch
    d. squat

Power Clean

41. What is the lift called in which the weight is moved from knee level to shoulder level in one movement?
    a. clean and jerk
    b. dead lift
    *c. power clean
    d. snatch

Snatch

42. What is the lift called in which there is a single continuous movement that pulls the barbell from the floor to an overhead position with the arms fully straightened?
    a. clean and jerk
    b. dead lift
    c. power clean
    *d. snatch

Clean and Jerk

43. An exerciser lifts a weight to the chest in one move and over the head in the second move. What is this called?
    a. bench press
    *b. clean and jerk
    c. dead lift
    d. snatch

Squat

44. A barbell is placed across the back of a lifter's neck and shoulders. The lifter sinks into a crouch and then straightens to an upright standing position. What is this called?
    a. dead lift
    b. power clean
    *c. squat
    d. snatch

Equipment

Board

45. A lifter is doing calf raises with a dumbbell. How thick should the board be?
    a. 1 inch
    *b. 2 inches
    c. 3 inches
    d. 6 inches

Bench

46. What special piece of equipment is needed to do a preacher curl?
    a. chair
    b. squat rack
    c. T bar
    *d. bench

E-Z Curl Bar

47. What is the difference in a regular barbell and an E-Z curl bar?
    a. length of the bar
    b. amount of weight that can be put on the bar
    *c. shape of the bar
    d. balance point of the bar

Incline Bench

48. With which exercise would an incline bench be most useful?
    a. French curl
    b. toe raises
    *c. deltoid extension
    d. squat lifts

Barbells/Dumbbells

49. What is the advantage of buying barbells over dumbbells?
    a. Barbells have better balance.
    b. Barbells require the lifter to use equal effort with both arms.
    *c. The amount of weight can be changed on barbells.
    d. Barbells are cheaper.

50. What is the advantage of buying dumbbells over barbells?
    a. Dumbbells have better balance.
    *b. Dumbbells require the lifter to use equal effort with both arms.
    c. The amount of weight can be changed on dumbbells.
    d. Dumbbells are cheaper.

Set of Weights

51. Generally, how much should a beginning set of weights weigh?
    a. 40 to 50 pounds
    b. 50 to 100 pounds
    *c. 100 to 150 pounds
    d. 150 to 200 pounds

Collar

52. What is a *collar*?
    a. a definition line separating muscle fiber groups
    b. the apparatus lifters use for neck support
    c. successfully moving from a squat position to a standing position with the barbell on the shoulders and back of the neck
    *d. the metal devices that slip over the bar and lock the weights in place

Machines

53. What is the major advantage of using a variable resistance weight machine instead of free weights?
    a. wider variety of exercises
    b. adaptable to a greater ranger of weights
    *c. same effort of muscles throughout the exercise
    d. increased range of motion

54. Which machine is used to help develop explosive power, flexibility, speed, and quickness?
    a. the incline bench
    b. the leg machines
    c. the lat machine
    *d. the leaper

55. What is the advantage of using a circuit training machine over free weights?
    *a. weight can be changed quickly
    b. wider variety of lifts possible
    c. balance is truer
    d. wider range of weights possible

56. What is the lightest weight available on a Nautilus machine?
    a. 10 pounds
    *b. 20 pounds
    c. 25 pounds
    d. 40 pounds

Principles

Physiology

57. How much blood does the heart pump through the body at rest per minute?
    a. 1 to 2 liters
    *b. 4 to 6 liters
    c. 15 to 20 liters
    d. 20 to 30 liters

58. How much blood does the heart pump through the body during strenuous exercise, such as running, per minute?
    a. 1 to 2 liters
    b. 4 to 6 liters
    c. 15 to 20 liters
    *d. 20 to 30 liters

59. Which body system carries oxygen to the cells?
    a. respiratory
    *b. circulatory
    c. muscular
    d. digestive

60. What body system brings oxygen to the blood?
    a. circulatory
    *b. respiratory
    c. digestive
    d. nervous

61. What is a *burn*?
    *a. result of forcing extra blood into the muscle
    b. result of overworking a muscle with two heavy a weight
    c. result of overworking a muscle with too many repetitions
    d. result of a weight rubbing or resting against skin

62. What is the major physiological effect of weight training at the active muscle site?
    a. increases in hemoglobin
    b. increases in muscle cells
    c. increases in red blood cells
    *d. increases in capillarization

63. When energy is used in the cells, what is this process called?
    a. respiration
    b. circulation
    *c. metabolism
    d. digestion

64. What energy production cycle is utilized without the presence of oxygen?
    *a. anaerobic
    b. aerobic
    c. oxygen debt
    d. metabolism

65. What happens when a muscle contracts?
    a. Energy is expended.
    b. Number of muscle cells increase.
    c. Oxygen level in muscle is increased.
    *d. Energy is expended and heat is produced.

66. Which is the most accurate description of how muscular contraction takes place?
    a. Muscle fibers shorten.
    b. Muscles shorten.
    c. Muscle fibers move toward the center of the muscle.
    *d. Filaments of the myofibrils slide toward each other.

67. How many muscles are there in the body?
    a. about 100
    b. about 400
    *c. about 600
    d. about 1,000

68. Which is the smallest unit in a muscle?
    a. bundle
    b. muscle fiber
    c. sarcolemma
    *d. myofibril

69. What type of muscle tissue moves the bones?
    a. antagonistic
    *b. skeletal
    c. smooth
    d. concentric

70. How much weight is one muscle fiber able to support?
    a. 10 times its own weight
    b. 100 times its own weight
    c. 500 times its own weight
    *d. 1,000 times its own weight

71. What percentage of the body weight is normally skeletal muscle?
    a. 20 to 25%
    *b. 40 to 45%
    c. 75 to 80%
    d. 80 to 90%

72. What increases as muscles get stronger?
    a. number of muscles
    b. number of muscle bundles
    c. number of muscle fibers
    *d. number of myofibrils

73. What happens to muscles when an exerciser stops lifting weights for a period of time?
    a. Muscle turns to fat.
    b. Muscle stays the same.
    c. Number of muscle fibers will decrease.
    *d. Percentage of body muscle and body fat may change.

74. Under ideal conditions, how much of a muscle's strength will the muscle regain in the first 30 seconds after fatigue?
    a. 25%
    b. 40%
    *c. 70%
    d. 90%

75. If a muscle is fully fatigued, how long does it take to make a complete recovery?
    a. 5 minutes
    b. 15 minutes
    c. 30 minutes
    *d. 45 minutes

76. A person's potential for strength development is *not* determined by which factor?
    a. genetic inheritance
    b. muscle size
    c. leverage
    *d. height

77. Which activity is *not* a good way to develop aerobic fitness?
    a. cycling
    b. swimming
    *c. weight training
    d. cross-country skiing

78. What is the ability of the muscles to continue to contract or do work over a long time period?
    *a. muscular endurance
    b. load
    c. hypertrophy
    d. overloading

79. Which statement is true concerning the effects of exercise on aging?
    a. Exercise helps keep the brain healthy.
    b. Exercise helps keep bones stronger.
    c. Exercise improves skin quality.
    *d. All of the above are true.

80. Which techniques are ways of overloading a muscle?
    a. increasing amount of weight lifted
    b. increasing amount of weight lifted or number of repetitions
    *c. increasing amount of weight lifted or number of repetitions or number of sets
    d. increasing amount of weight lifted or number of repetitions or number of sets or number of days per week of exercise

Biomechanics

81. What type of lever is the most common in the human body?
    a. first class
    b. second class
    *c. third class
    d. fourth class

82. In which type of lever is the force between the axis and the resistance?
    a. first class
    b. second class
    *c. third class
    d. fourth class

83. What is the force in the lever system when a person is lifting weights?
    *a. muscles
    b. bones
    c. joints
    d. weights

Muscle Action

84. Which is the easiest way to identify the muscle groups involved in an exercise?
    *a. They are generally above the joint moved and toward the center of the body.
    b. They are generally below the joint moved.
    c. They are generally away from the center of the body from the joint moved.
    d. They cross the joint moved.

85. Which muscle groups move the arm downward?
    a. deltoids and latissimus dorsi
    b. deltoids and trapezius
    *c. latissimus dorsi and pectoralis major
    d. pectoralis major and trapezius

86. Which muscle group moves the arm upward?
    *a. deltoids
    b. latissimus dorsi
    c. pectoralis major
    d. trapezius

87. Which muscle group is on the front of the upper arm?
    *a. biceps
    b. triceps
    c. quadriceps
    d. soleus

88. Which muscle group flexes the elbow joint?
    *a. biceps
    b. triceps
    c. quadriceps
    d. soleus

89. Which muscle group extends the elbow joint?
    a. biceps
    *b. triceps
    c. quadriceps
    d. soleus

90. Which muscle group is primarily involved in flexing the trunk?
    a. hamstrings
    b. quadriceps
    *c. rectus abdominis
    d. gastrocnemius

91. What does the contraction of the erector spinae muscle cause?
    a. trunk flexion
    *b. trunk extension
    c. hip extension
    d. hip adduction

92. What is the primary muscle group of the buttocks?
    a. hamstrings
    b. triceps
    c. quadriceps
    *d. gluteus maximus

93. What is the movement caused by the gluteus maximus?
    *a. hip extension
    b. hip flexion
    c. trunk extension
    d. trunk flexion

94. Which muscle group causes the thigh to be raised forward?
    a. hamstrings
    b. triceps
    *c. quadriceps
    d. gluteus maximus

95. Which muscle helps in hip extension and knee flexion?
    *a. hamstrings
    b. quadriceps
    c. gluteus maximus
    d. gastrocnemius

96. Which muscle group is primarily involved in moving the top of the feet away from the front of the legs?
    a. hamstrings
    b. quadriceps
    c. rectus abdominis
    *d. gastrocnemius

Nutrition
97. How long should an exerciser wait after eating a meal before working out?
    a. no wait necessary
    b. 30 minutes
    c. 1 hour
    *d. 2 hours

98. How long should an exerciser wait after working out before eating a big meal?
    a. no wait necessary
    b. 30 minutes
    *c. 1 hour
    d. 2 hours

99. When should weight trainers eat special diets?
    a. on training days
    *b. when balanced meals are *not* available
    c. several days before competitions
    d. on the day of competition

100. What is *not* found in a well-balanced diet?
    *a. five or more servings of breads and cereals
    b. four or more servings of vegetables and fruits
    c. two or more servings of meat, fish, and eggs
    d. two or more servings of milk and milk products

101. What is the major ingredient in the diet of serious weight lifters?
    *a. carbohydrates
    b. fats
    c. proteins
    d. vitamins

102. What effect does taking protein supplements have on general body functioning?
    *a. may cause dehydration
    b. increases energy level
    c. improves strength
    d. improves endurance

103. What effect does taking extra vitamins have on improving strength?
    a. faster increases in strength
    b. greater strength developed
    c. slows strength development
    *d. none

104. What are the synthetic hormones used to stimulate growth of protein tissue?
    a. amphetamines
    *b. steroids
    c. estrogens
    d. testosterones

105. When an exerciser works hard, what percent of the calories comsumed are lost as body heat?
    a. 25%
    b. 50%
    *c. 75%
    d. 90%

Sex Differences
106. At about what age does the difference in oxygen uptake between males and females become evident?
    a. 1 year old
    b. 2 years old
    c. 6 to 8 years old
    *d. 12 to 13 years old

107. At about what age does there become a marked difference in the strength of males and females?
    a. 2 years old
    b. 6 years old
    *c. 11 to 13 years old
    d. 16 years old

108. Generally, how does the strength of a woman compare to that of a man?
    a. 25% of a man's strength
    *b. 50 to 60% of a man's strength
    c. 50 to 75% of a man's strength
    d. 75% of a man's strength

109. Why do women *not* gain muscle bulk as men do through weight training?
    a. have fewer muscle fibers
    *b. differences in male and female hormones
    c. have less muscle tissue
    d. have fewer muscles

110. Why do women have a lower strength-weight ratio than men?
    a. fewer muscles
    b. fewer muscle fibers
    *c. more body fat
    d. lower center of gravity

111. Which item is *not* a factor in male strength superiority?
    a. anatomical structure
    b. hormonal factors
    c. less fatty tissue
    *d. more red blood cells

112. Which item is *not* a factor in men generally having more endurance than women?
    a. men having more hemoglobin and red blood cells per unit of blood
    b. men having larger hearts and lungs
    *c. men having higher heart rates
    d. men having less body fat

113. On which characteristic do men generally score *less* than women?
    a. endurance
    b. strength
    *c. manual dexterity
    d. speed

114. On which characteristic do women generally score better than men?
    a. endurance
    *b. agility
    c. strength
    d. speed

Techniques

Measurements

115. When should body measurements be taken?
    *a. before exercise
    b. immediately after exercise
    c. 30 minutes after exercise
    d. 1 hour after exercise

116. How should the neck be measured?
    a. head up, neck muscles relaxed, tape at largest circumference
    b. head up, neck muscles fully contracted, tape at largest circumference
    *c. head up, neck muscles relaxed, tape at smallest circumference
    d. head up, neck muscles fully contracted, tape at smallest circumference

117. How should biceps be measured?
    a. at greatest girth with arm relaxed
    *b. at greatest girth with muscles fully contracted
    c. 6 inches above the elbow with arm relaxed
    d. 6 inches above the elbow with muscles fully contracted

118. How should the forearm be measured?
    a. at greatest girth with arm relaxed
    *b. at greatest girth with muscles fully contracted
    c. halfway between the wrist and elbow with arm relaxed
    d. halfway between the wrist and elbow with muscles fully contracted

119. How should the shoulder girdle be measured?
    a. tape straight around the body, slightly above the nipples, with the muscles relaxed
    b. tape straight around the body, slightly below the nipples, with the muscles relaxed
    *c. tape 1 inch below the tip of the shoulders, including the shoulders
    d. tape 6 inches below the tip of the shoulders, including the shoulders

120. How should the normal chest be measured?
    *a. head up, normal breathing, latissimus dorsi relaxed, tape straight around the body slightly above the nipples
    b. head up, normal breathing, latissimus dorsi fully contracted, tape straight around the body slightly above the nipples
    c. head up, normal breathing, latissimus dorsi relaxed, tape straight around the body 6 inches below the shoulders
    d. head up, normal breathing, latissimus dorsi fully contracted, tape straight around the body 6 inches below the shoulders

121. How should the expanded chest be measured?
    a. head up, normal breathing, latissimus dorsi relaxed, tape straight around the body slightly below the nipples
    b. head up, normal breathing, latissimus dorsi fully contracted, tape straight around the body slightly below the nipples
    *c. head up, breath deeply inhaled, latissimus dorsi relaxed, tape straight around the body slightly above the nipples
    d. head up, breath deeply inhaled, latissimus dorsi fully contracted, tape straight around the body slightly above the nipples

122. Which statement indicates that the expanded chest measurement probably needs to be retaken?
    a. Expanded chest is less than 2 to 3 inches larger than normal chest.
    b. Expanded chest is less than 5 to 6 inches larger than normal chest.
    c. Expanded chest is more than 1 to 2 inches larger than normal chest.
    *d. Expanded chest is more than 2 to 3 inches larger than normal chest.

123. How should the waist be measured?
    a. body erect and relaxed, breath fully inhaled, tape around body slightly above the navel
    b. body erect and tense, breath fully inhaled, tape around the body about 6 inches above the navel
    *c. body erect and relaxed, breathing normally, tape around body slightly above the navel
    d. body erect and tense, breathing normally, tape around the body about 6 inches above the navel

124. How should the thigh be measured?
    a. feet shoulder width apart, muscles fully contracted, tape midway between knee and buttocks
    b. feet 6 inches apart, muscles relaxed, tape midway between knee and buttocks
    c. feet shoulder width apart, muscles fully contracted, tape around largest girth
    *d. feet 6 inches apart, muscles relaxed, tape around largest girth

125. How should the calf be measured?
    *a. with weight evenly distributed over both feet, tape around greatest girth
    b. with weight evenly distributed over both feet, tape around smallest girth
    c. with weight on toes, tape around greatest girth
    d. with weight on toes, tape around smallest girth

126. What is a simple way to determine if a person is losing fat?
    a. Measure the wrist regularly.
    b. Measure the waist regularly.
    *c. Measure the upper arm or thigh regularly.
    d. Measure the neck regularly.

Lifts

127. Which exercise is *not* one of the eight basic lifts with free weights?
    a. barbell curl
    b. bent-over rowing
    *c. snatch
    d. calf raises

128. What is the starting position for a clean?
    *a. knees bent, feet under the bar, and back straight
    b. knees bent, feet just back of the bar, and back straight
    c. knees straight, feet under the bar, and back curved
    d. knees straight, feet just back of the bar, and back curved

129. How is the bar gripped for a clean?
    a. hands shoulder width apart in an underhand grip
    *b. hands shoulder width apart in an overhand grip
    c. hands 8 inches wider than shoulder width in an underhand grip
    d. hands 8 inches wider than shoulder width in an overhand grip

130. How is the bar lifted to shoulder level in the clean?
    a. The bar is lifted straight up to shoulder level using the arm and shoulder muscles.
    b. With the knees bent the bar is lifted to shoulder level, and then the exerciser stands up.
    *c. When the bar approaches the shoulders, the exerciser makes a slight dip with the knees and moves the elbows under the bar.
    d. As the bar approaches the hips, the exerciser leans backward and moves the elbows quickly under the bar.

131. What is the primary reason for using a wrist curl?
    a. to develop the front of the upper arms
    *b. to develop the front of the forearms
    c. to develop the wrists
    d. to develop the hands

132. A lifter is using a lateral wrist curl. How is this exercise done to develop the muscles on the outside of the forearms?
    a. by placing a weight only on end of dumbbell behind the hand
    *b. by placing a weight only on end of dumbbell in front of the hand
    c. by gripping the dumbbell next to the weight behind the hand
    d. by gripping the dumbbell next to the weight in front of the hand

133. What is considered a set for the wrist roller?
    a. raising the weight 5 times
    *b. raising and lowering the weight 5 times
    c. raising the weight 10 times
    d. raising and lowering the weight 10 times

134. With which exercise would a short barbell be most useful?
    *a. wrist work
    b. pectorals work
    c. close-grip bench press
    d. heavy weight squats

135. What is the difference in a barbell curl and a reverse curl?
    a. direction bar is lifted
    b. starting position of the bar
    *c. grip on the bar
    d. type of bar used

136. How should the bar be gripped for a lying triceps curl?
    a. hands next to each other
    *b. hands 8 to 10 inches apart
    c. hands shoulder width apart
    d. hands slightly more than shoulder width apart

137. How should the bar be gripped for a triceps pulldown?
    a. hands next to each other
    *b. hands 8 to 10 inches apart
    c. hands shoulder width apart
    d. hands slightly wider than shoulder width apart

138. What is the beginning position for a standing triceps curl?
    *a. hands 8 to 10 inches apart, bar straight overhead
    b. hands shoulder width apart, bar straight overhead
    c. hands 8 to 10 inches apart, bar behind neck
    d. hands shoulder width apart, bar behind neck

139. In bent-over rowing, what is the position of the exerciser's body?
    a. back parallel to the floor and slightly bent, legs straight
    b. back parallel to the floor and slightly bent, knees slightly bent
    c. back parallel to the floor and straight, legs straight
    *d. back parallel to the floor and straight, knees slightly bent

140. How is the barbell gripped in bent-over rowing?
    a. shoulder width apart with an overhand grip
    *b. 8 inches wider than shoulder width with an overhand grip
    c. shoulder width apart with an underhand grip
    d. 8 inches wider than shoulder width with an underhand grip

141. What is the difference in bent-over rowing and bent-over rowing with dumbbells?
    a. grip for the lift
    b. position of the back
    c. muscles exercised
    *d. arms exercised separately

142. What is the beginning arm and hand position for a bent-over triceps curl?
    a. arm flexed at a 90° angle, palm facing backward
    *b. arm flexed at a 90° angle, palm facing inward
    c. arm parallel to floor, palm facing upward
    d. arm parallel to floor, palm facing downward

143. How should the bar be held for upright rowing?
    a. hands shoulder width apart and with an underhand grip
    b. hands 6 inches apart and with an underhand grip
    c. hands shoulder width apart and with an overhand grip
    *d. hands 6 inches apart and with an overhand grip

144. You are using the upright rowing lift. Where should the elbows be at the top of the lift?
    *a. above the bar
    b. even with the bar
    c. slightly below the bar
    d. under the bar

145. What is the difference in upright rowing and upright rowing with dumbbells?
    a. grip for the lift
    b. position of the elbows
    *c. equipment used
    d. muscles exercised

146. Where is the bar held at the beginning of the overhead press?
    a. in front of the thighs
    *b. at shoulder level in front of the body
    c. at shoulder level behind the head
    d. directly over head

147. How is the bar gripped for the overhead press?
    a. hands 1 foot apart with palms facing inward
    b. hands shoulder width apart with palms facing outward
    c. hands shoulder width apart with palms facing inward
    *d. hands wider than shoulder width apart with palms facing outward

148. As the bar goes up in an overhead press, how should the lifter stand?
    a. Lean slightly backward.
    b. Lean slightly forward.
    *c. Take care *not* to lean backward.
    d. Take care *not* to lean forward.

149. How are the dumbbells gripped in an alternate dumbbell press?
    a. palms facing forward
    b. palms facing backward
    *c. palms facing inward
    d. palms facing outward

150. For a barbell curl, how should the bar be held?
    *a. hands shoulder width apart and with an underhand grip
    b. hands 8 inches wider than shoulder width apart and with an underhand grip
    c. hands shoulder width apart and with an overhand grip
    d. hands 8 inches wider than shoulder width apart and with an overhand grip

151. What is the position of the lifter's back in doing a barbell curl?
    *a. straight
    b. leaning slightly backward
    c. leaning slightly forward
    d. parallel to the floor

152. How should the bar be held for a bench press?
    a. hands shoulder width apart with palms facing away from the head
    b. hands far enough apart so that elbows are at a 45° angle and palms facing the head
    *c. hands far enough apart so that elbows are at a 90° angle and palms facing away from the head
    d. hands far enough apart so that elbows are more than a 90° angle and palms facing the head

153. A lifter is using the bench press and wants to emphasis development of his or her chest. How can the basic lift be changed to do this?
    *a. Use a wider grip.
    b. Use a narrower grip.
    c. Lift more repetitions.
    d. Lift more sets.

154. You are doing parallel bar dips. How far should you dip?
    a. until the elbows reach a 90° angle
    b. until the upper arms are parallel with the floor
    *c. until the upper arms break parallel with the floor
    d. as far as possible

155. You are doing a straight-arm pullover. With what should you be especially careful?
    *a. doing a proper warm-up
    b. not lifting too much weight
    c. using a wide enough grip
    d. having the feet secured

156. A lifter is using a lat pulldown. What is the position of the lifter's body?
    a. standing with back straight
    b. standing with back slightly curled
    *c. kneeling with back straight
    d. kneeling with back slightly curled

157. How should the bar be gripped for a lat pulldown?
    a. hands shoulder width apart with palms facing forward
    b. hands shoulder width apart with palms facing backward
    *c. hands about 4 feet apart with palms facing forward
    d. hands about 4 feet apart with palms facing backward

158. How many repetitions should be done on a trunk twist?
    a. 10
    b. at least 25
    *c. at least 50
    d. no more than 50

159. How are the feet positioned in a dead lift?
    a. close together and under the bar
    b. close together and back of the bar
    *c. spread apart and under the bar
    d. spread apart and back of the bar

Sit-Ups
160. What is the position for the arms in a sit-up?
    a. arms extended forward
    *b. hands clasped behind the head
    c. arms extended over the head
    d. arms by your sides

161. How should the legs be positioned for a sit-up?
    a. bent at a 45° angle with feet held down
    *b. bent at a 90° angle with feet held down
    c. slightly bent without feet being held down
    d. straight without feet being held down

162. If you *cannot* do sit-ups with your hands clasped behind your head, what should you do?
    *a. Extend your arms forward as you are coming up.
    b. Place your hands on your knees.
    c. Extend your arms over your head.
    d. Hold your arms by your sides.

163. Which arm position requires the greatest abdominal strength on a sit-up?
    a. arms extended forward
    *b. hands clasped behind the head
    c. arms folded across the chest
    d. arms by the sides

164. How should sit-ups be done so as *not* to develop a large rectus abdominal muscle?
    *a. Do high repetitions.
    b. Do three sets of 10 each.
    c. Use weights for more overload.
    d. Do straight leg sit-ups.

165. In doing a sit-up, how can the muscles on the sides of the abdominals (obliques) be better exercised?
    a. by doing more repetitions
    b. by doing more sets
    c. by folding the arms across the chest
    *d. by touching an elbow to the opposite knee

166. What is the danger in performing sit-ups with straight legs?
    a. straining the abdominal muscles
    b. straining the hip flexors
    c. hyperextending the knees
    *d. hyperextending the lower back

167. In order to prevent possible damage, how should sit-ups be performed?
    a. with straight legs and feet secured
    b. with straight legs and feet movable
    c. with knees bent and feet secured
    *d. with knees bent and feet movable

Standing Toe Touches
168. In order to prevent possible damage, how should standing toe touches be performed?
    *a. slowly
    b. quickly
    c. Lunge to touch toes and relax.
    d. only to a comfortable distance

Squats
169. When the bar is on the squat rack, how high should the bar be?
    a. about 1 foot above the lifter's shoulders
    b. even with the lifter's shoulders
    *c. several inches below the lifter's shoulders
    d. about 1 foot below the lifter's shoulders

170. Where is the bar at the beginning of the squat?
    a. behind the lifter's head
    b. over the lifter's head
    c. in front of the lifter's chest
    *d. behind the lifter's neck

171. In the squat, how much should the knees be flexed at the lowest point in the exercise?
     a. only slightly
     *b. until the thighs are parallel with the floor
     c. until the knees are at a 90° angle
     d. as much as possible

172. How should the feet be positioned in performing a squat?
     a. a comfortable distance apart with toes pointed straight ahead
     *b. a comfortable distance apart with toes pointed outward
     c. shoulder width apart with toes pointed straight ahead
     d. shoulder width apart with toes pointed outward

173. In order to prevent possible knee damage, how should deep knee bends be performed?
     a. very slowly
     b. very quickly
     *c. only to a 90° half squat
     d. only with the feet shoulder width apart

174. How many repetitions should be performed doing calf raises with a dumbbell?
     a. 10 with the toes pointing straight ahead
     b. 10 with toes pointing outward and 10 with toes pointing straight ahead
     c. 10 with toes pointing inward and 10 with toes pointing straight ahead
     *d. 10 with toes pointing outward, 10 with toes pointing straight ahead, and 10 with toes pointing inward

Muscles Exercised

175. Which muscles are developed by using the neck flexion exercise?
     a. front of neck
     b. sides of neck
     *c. front and sides of neck
     d. back of neck

176. What muscle is developed by doing shoulder shrugs?
     a. shoulders (deltoids)
     b. chest (pectoralis)
     *c. upper back (trapezius)
     d. back of neck (splenius)

177. Which exercise is best for developing the upper back (trapezius)?
     a. curls
     *b. shrugs
     c. bench presses
     d. inclined bench presses

178. What is the primary reason to use the bent-arm pullover?
     a. to develop the shoulders (deltoids)
     b. to develop the upper arms (biceps and triceps)
     c. to develop the upper back (trapezius and rhomboids)
     *d. to develop the chest (pectoralis) and muscles under the armpits (latissimus dorsi)

179. What is the primary reason for doing bent-over lateral raises?
     a. to develop the upper arms (biceps and triceps)
     *b. to develop the upper back (trapezius) and back of shoulders (posterior deltoids)
     c. to develop the chest (pectoralis)
     d. to develop the front of the forearms (brachioradialis)

180. Which exercise is best for developing the top of the shoulders (middle deltoids)?
     a. bench presses
     b. shrugs
     *c. lateral raises
     d. curls

181. What is the primary reason for using the press behind the neck?
     a. to develop the back of the neck muscles (splenius)
     b. to develop the back muscles (erector spinae)
     c. to develop the middle and back of the shoulders (middle and posterior deltoids)
     *d. to develop the front of the shoulders (anterior deltoids) and back of the upper arms (triceps)

182. What is the primary purpose for doing lateral raises?
     a. to develop the muscles under the armpits (latissimus dorsi)
     b. to develop the chest (pectoralis)
     *c. to develop the middle of the shoulders (middle deltoid) and upper back (trapezius)
     d. to develop the upper arms (biceps and triceps)

183. Which muscles are exercised by using upright rowing?
     a. back (erector spinae)
     b. back of the arms (triceps)
     c. below the shoulders (latissimus dorsi)
     *d. front and middle of the shoulders (front and middle deltoids)

184. What is the primary purpose of doing forward raises?
    a. to develop the chest (pectoralis)
    b. to develop the upper back (trapezius)
    c. to develop the upper arms (biceps and triceps)
    *d. to develop the front of the shoulders (anterior deltoids)

185. A lifter is using a swingbell curl. On what muscle can more tension be placed by keeping the elbows stationary?
    a. shoulder (deltoids)
    b. chest (pectoralis)
    *c. front of upper arm (biceps)
    d. back of upper arm (triceps)

186. What muscles are being exercised in an inclined dumbbell curl?
    a. shoulder (deltoids)
    b. chest (pectoralis)
    *c. front of upper arm (biceps)
    d. back of upper arm (triceps)

187. What is the primary reason to use the alternate dumbbell curl?
    a. to develop the shoulder (deltoids)
    b. to develop the upper back (trapezius)
    c. to develop the chest (pectoralis)
    *d. to develop the front of the upper arm (biceps)

188. Which muscles are developed by using the one-arm dumbbell curl?
    *a. front of the upper arm
    b. back of the upper arm
    c. front of the lower arm
    d. wrists

189. Which exercise is best for developing the front of the upper arms (biceps)?
    *a. curls
    b. military presses
    c. French curls
    d. lat pulls

190. What muscles are developed by using the barbell curl?
    a. back part of the arms (triceps)
    *b. front part of the arms (biceps)
    c. front of the shoulders (front deltoids)
    d. chest (pectoralis)

191. Which exercise is best for developing the back of the upper arms (triceps)?
    a. curls
    b. military presses
    *c. French curls
    d. lat pulls

192. Which muscles are *not* primarily involved in the bent-over rowing lift?
    a. front of upper arm (biceps)
    *b. back of upper arm (triceps)
    c. upper back (trapezius)
    d. back of shoulders (posterior deltoid)

193. Primarily, what muscles does the bench press develop?
    *a. chest (pectoralis) and front part of the shoulders (anterior deltoids)
    b. chest (pectoralis) and all of shoulders (deltoids)
    c. upper back (trapezius) and front of upper arms (biceps)
    d. upper back (trapezius) and back of upper arms (triceps)

194. Which exercise is best for developing the chest (pectoralis major)?
    *a. bench presses
    b. shrugs
    c. lateral raises
    d. curls

195. What is the advantage of using dumbbells over a barbell in the inclined press?
    *a. to increase development of the chest (pectoralis)
    b. to increase development of the front of the upper arms (biceps)
    c. to increase development of the back of the upper arms (triceps)
    d. to increse development of the shoulders (deltoids)

196. What muscles are developed by doing lateral raises while lying down?
    a. upper arms (biceps and triceps)
    b. upper back (trapezius)
    *c. chest (pectoralis) and front of the shoulders (anterior deltoid)
    d. front of upper arm (biceps) and chest (pectoralis)

197. What muscles are developed by doing flies?
    a. upper arms (biceps and triceps)
    b. upper back (trapezius)
    c. shoulders (deltoids)
    *d. chest (pectoralis)

198. What is the primary purpose of doing push-ups?
    a. to develop the front of the upper arms (biceps)
    *b. to develop the back of the upper arms (triceps), chest (pectoralis), and front of shoulders (anterior deltoid)
    c. to develop the upper arms (biceps and triceps) and upper back (trapezius)
    d. to develop the upper arms (biceps and triceps) and shoulders (deltoids)

199. What is the primary reason for using T-bar rowing?
    a. to develop the chest (pectoralis)
    b. to develop the front of the upper arms (biceps)
    *c. to develop the muscles under the armpits (latissimus dorsi)
    d. to develop the shoulders (deltoids)

200. What is the primary purpose of doing a chin behind the neck?
    a. to develop the front of the upper arms (biceps)
    b. to develop the shoulders (deltoids)
    c. to develop the upper back (trapezius)
    *d. to develop the muscles under the armpits (latissimus dorsi)

201. Which exercise is best for developing the muscles below the armpits (latissimus dorsi)?
    a. curls
    b. military presses
    c. French curls
    *d. lat pulls

202. What muscle group does the lat machine especially work?
    a. abdominal
    b. deltoids
    c. pectorals
    *d. latissimus dorsi

203. Which exercise is best for developing the stomach muscles (rectus abdominus)?
    *a. leg lifts
    b. push-ups
    c. curls
    d. bench presses

204. What muscles are exercised in a bent-leg sit-up?
    a. upper back (trapezius)
    b. back (erector spinae)
    c. front of thighs (quadriceps)
    *d. abdominal (rectus abdominis)

205. Which muscles are being exercised in leg raises?
    *a. abdominal (rectus abdominus) and part of thigh (rectus femoris)
    b. hips (gluteus maximus) and thighs (quadriceps and hamstrings)
    c. abdominal (rectus abdominus) and hips (gluteus maximus)
    d. back (erector spinae) and abdominal (rectus abdominus)

206. Which muscles are exercised in the side bend lift?
    a. shoulders (deltoids)
    *b. sides of the waist (obliques)
    c. upper arms (biceps and triceps)
    d. chest (pectoralis)

207. Which muscles are primarily involved in side hip raises?
    a. arms
    b. shoulders (deltoids)
    c. back (erector spinae)
    *d. side of hips (obliques)

208. Which muscles do most leg press machines exercise *least*?
    a. lower back
    b. buttocks
    c. upper legs
    *d. abdominal

209. What is the primary purpose of doing the dead lift?
    a to develop the arms (biceps, triceps, brachioradialis)
    b. to develop the shoulders (deltoids)
    c. to develop the shoulders (deltoids) and upper back (trapezius)
    *d. to develop the back (erector spinae), hips (gluteus maximus), and thighs (quadriceps femoris and hamstrings)

210. What is the primary reason to do the leg press?
    *a. to develop the hips (gluteus maximus) and upper legs (quadriceps and hamstrings)
    b. to develop the legs (quadriceps, hamstrings, and gastrocnemius)
    c. to develop the abdomen (rectus abdominus) and thighs (quadriceps and hamstrings)
    d. to develop the back (erector spinae) and thighs (quadriceps and hamstrings)

211. Which muscles are primarily being exercised in hip raises?
    a. arms and legs
    b. back (erector spinae)
    *c. abdominal (rectus abdominus)
    d. shoulders (deltoids)

212. Which exercise is best for developing the hips (gluteus maximus)?
    a. leg curls
    *b. leg presses
    c. toe raises
    d. leg extensions

213. Which exercise is best for developing the front of the thighs (quadriceps)?
    a. toe raises
    b. leg curls
    *c. leg extensions
    d. leg presses

214. Which muscles are developed by the knee extension lift?
    a. foot
    b. back of lower leg (gastrocnemius)
    *c. front of thigh (quadriceps)
    d. back of thigh (hamstrings)

215. Which muscles are developed by the squat?
    a. shoulders (deltoids)
    b. upper back (trapezius)
    *c. front of thighs (quadriceps) and hips (gluteus maximus and hamstrings)
    d. abdominals (rectus abdominis) and front of thighs (quadriceps)

216. What is the primary purpose of doing the back hyperextension lift?
    a. to develop the upper back (trapezius)
    *b. to develop the hips (gluteus maximus) and back (erector spinae)
    c. to develop the back of the thighs (hamstrings)
    d. to develop the front of the thighs (quadriceps)

217. Which muscles are developed by the leg curl lift?
    a. foot
    b. back of lower leg (gastrocnemius)
    c. front of thigh (quadriceps)
    *d. back of thigh (hamstrings)

218. Which exercise is best for developing the back of the thighs (hamstrings)?
    *a. leg curls
    b. toe raises
    c. leg extensions
    d. leg presses

Strategy

219. Which factor is *not* considered in deciding whether a person should have a physical examination before beginning a weight training program?
    a. smoking cigarettes
    b. overweight
    *c. over 21
    d. family history of diabetes

220. An exerciser is using a training plan consisting of lifting one set with a light weight and one with a heavy weight. What percentage of the exerciser's maximum lift should be lifted on each set?
    a. 20% and 80%
    b. 25% and 75%
    c. 50% and 80%
    *d. 60% and 70%

221. How can restricting flexibility through weight lifting be prevented?
    a. by increasing repetitions
    b. by decreasing weight being lifted
    *c. by using a full range of motion in lifting
    d. by using a variety of exercises and lifts

222. For what purpose can special inflatable belts and rubberized airtight clothing be used effectively?
    a. to spot reduce
    b. to increase weight loss
    c. to decrease fat tissue
    *d. none

223. What safety factor must be considered any time one is working with free weights?
    *a. competent spotter
    b. lift at the same time of day
    c. lift the same weight in all repetitions
    d. at least a 15-minute warm-up

224. For most weight lifters, how much time should be taken off between training sessions?
    a. 8 hours
    b. 12 hours
    *c. 1 day
    d. 2 days

225. How many times a week should a weight training program be used?
    a. once
    *b. three or four
    c. five or six
    d. seven

226. How many times a week must an exerciser train to maintain strength?
    *a. one
    b. two
    c. three
    d. four

227. An exerciser goes on a weight training program for 4 weeks and then quits. How long will it takes to lose the gains made?
    a. 1 week
    *b. 2 weeks
    c. 4 weeks
    d. 6 weeks

228. When a Universal machine is being used, how long should it take to raise and lower a weight?
    a. same amount of time to raise as to lower a weight
    b. twice as long to raise a weight as to lower one
    *c. twice as long to lower a weight as to raise one
    d. three times as long to raise a weight as to lower one

Beginning Training

229. In your first session of weight training, you determined how much weight you should lift for each exercise. Now you are into your second session. How many repetitions and how much weight should you use in your second set?
    a. 10 repetitions, 50% of weight
    *b. 10 repetitions, 70% of weight
    c. 8 repetitions, 90% of weight
    d. 8 repetitions, 100% of weight

230. What kind of set plan is recommended for beginners using free weights?
    *a. one set with a light weight and one with a heavy weight
    b. two sets with a medium weight
    c. one set with a light weight and two with a heavy weight
    d. three sets with a medium weight

231. To plan a weight training program using free weights, what must a beginner find out?
    a. how many repetitions he or she can do with a 50-pound weight
    *b. how much weight is heavy to lift for one time
    c. how much weight is heavy to lift using 10 repetitions
    d. how many repetitions he or she can do with a 10-pound weight

232. What determines how much weight is needed for training?
    a. weight of the person
    b. general physical condition of the person
    c. the arm strength of the person
    *d. the leg strength of the person

233. You are a beginner in using free weights. How should you determine how much weight you can lift for one time?
    *a. Progressively increase the amount of weight you are lifting by 10 to 15 pounds until you feel you are lifting about 90% of your maximum.
    b. Progressively increase the amount of weight you are lifting by 10 pounds until you reach your maximum.
    c. Start with the heaviest weight you think you can lift and move up or down 10 pounds from there until you find your maximum.
    d. Start with the heaviest weight you think you can lift and move up or down from there until you feel you are lifting about 90% of your maximum.

234. You are a beginner in using free weights and are trying to find out how much weight you can lift for one time. How much rest should you take between lifting each weight?
    a. none
    b. 30 seconds
    *c. 1 to 2 minutes
    d. 5 minutes

235. When you plan a weight program, which muscles should you develop?
    *a. the largest muscles
    b. all the muscles
    c. the upper body muscles
    d. the arm and leg muscles

236. You are getting started in estimating how much you should be able to lift on a bench press. With what percentage of your body weight is it recommended that you begin your trials?
    a. 40%
    b. 50%
    *c. 60%
    d. 75%

237. You are getting started in estimating how much you should be able to lift on a barbell curl. With what percentage of your body weight is it recommended that you begin your trials?
    *a. 40%
    b. 50%
    c. 60%
    d. 75%

238. You are getting started in estimating how much you should be able to lift in upright rowing. With what percentage of your body weight is it recommended that you begin your trials?
    a. 40%
    *b. 45%
    c. 60%
    d. 75%

239. You are getting started in estimating how much you should be able to lift in bent-over rowing. With what percentage of your body weight is it recommended that you begin your trials?
    a. 45%
    *b. 50%
    c. 60%
    d. 75%

240. You are getting started in estimating how much you should be able to lift in bent-over rowing. With what percentage of your body weight is it recommended that you begin your trials?
    a. 45%
    *b. 50%
    c. 60%
    d. 75%

241. You are getting started in estimating how much you should be able to lift on a squat. With what percentage of your body weight is it recommended that you begin your trials?
    a. 40%
    b. 50%
    c. 60%
    *d. 75%

242. You are getting started in estimating how much you should be able to lift in calf raises with a dumbbell. With what percentage of your body weight is it recommended that you begin your trials?
    *a. 40%
    b. 50%
    c. 60%
    d. 75%

243. In your first session of weight training, you determined how much weight you should lift for each exercise. Now you are ready for your second session. How many repetitions and how much weight should you use in your first set?
    a. 10 repetitions, 50% of weight
    *b. 10 repetitions, 60% of weight
    c. 8 repetitions, 75% of weight
    d. 8 repetitions, 100% of weight

244. You are beginning a weight training program. How long should you do the eight basic lifts before adding more lifts or sets?
    a. about 6 weeks
    b. about 3 months
    *c. about 6 months
    d. about 1 year

245. You are a beginner in using free weights and are trying to find out how much weight to lift at the beginning of your program. What is the first thing you should do?
    a. See how many repetitions you can do with a 50-pound weight.
    b. Select the heaviest weight you think you can lift and try to lift it.
    *c. Select a fairly light weight and lift it 10 to 15 times for a warm-up.
    d. Select a weight you think is about 90% of your maximum and try to lift it.

Increasing Strength

246. The heaviest weight that an exerciser is lifting in a set is 70 pounds. How many repetitions should the exerciser be able to do with that weight before increasing the amount of weight being lifted?
    a. 5
    *b. 10
    c. 15
    d. 20

247. You are ready to increase the amount of weight you are lifting. How much should you increase it?
    a. 5 pounds
    b. 10 pounds
    *c. 5% of what you are lifting
    d. 10% of what you are lifting

248. An exerciser has been using a two-set routine. He or she decides to add a third set. What plan should be used?
    a. two light and one heavy
    b. one light, one medium, and one heavy
    c. three medium
    *d. one light and two heavy

249. What is the purpose of the preexhaustion principle?
    a. to prevent soreness in the muscles
    *b. work a muscle beyond its fatigue point
    c. to increase blood flow to the muscles before heavy work
    d. to increase oxygen content of muscle fibers

Training Effects

250. How much does strength usually increase in 12 weeks if the lifter is training for one or two sets, three times a week?
    a. 10%
    *b. 25%
    c. 40%
    d. 50%

251. How much additional strength can a lifter expect to gain by using three instead of two sets when training?
    a. none
    *b. less in proportion to the increase in work
    c. more in proportion to the increase in work
    d. at least 50% more

252. Your muscles feel tired and ache a little as you begin a workout. What does this indicate?
    a. You are not getting enough sleep.
    b. You are lifting too heavy weights.
    c. You are doing too many repetitions.
    *d. You are overtraining.

253. If you do *not* recover from a training session within 2 or 3 days, what is probably happening?
    *a. You are overtraining.
    b. You need to take more vitamins.
    c. You need to add more carbohydrates to your diet.
    d. You have an inflamed joint or torn muscle.

254. How much may the amount of air received by the lungs each minute increase during exercise?
    a. over 5 times
    b. over 10 times
    *c. over 25 times
    d. over 50 times

255. An exerciser wishes to develop muscular endurance rather than strength. What is the best procedure?
    a. Increase the weight and decrease the repetitions.
    *b. Decrease the weight and increase the repetitions.
    c. Keep the weight the same and decrease the repetitions.
    d. Decrease the weight and keep the repetitions the same.

256. An exerciser is interested in developing muscle bulk as well as strength. What is the best procedure?
    *a. Increase the weight and decrease the repetitions.
    b. Decrease the weight and increase the repetitions.
    c. Keep the weight the same and decrease the repetitions.
    d. Decrease the weight and keep the repetitions the same.

257. A person wants to use weight training to help gain weight. What procedure should be used?
    *a. high resistance and low repetitions
    b. high resistance and high repetitions
    c. low resistance and high repetitions
    d. low resistance and low repetitions

258. You want to use your weight training program to help develop cardiovascular fitness. How is this best accomplished?
    *a. Cut out rest periods.
    b. Increase repetitions.
    c. Increase sets.
    d. Increase number of exercises.

259. What can a lifter do to get more pump in the muscles?
    a. more repetitions
    b. more weight
    c. more sets
    *d. shorter rest periods

Breathing

260. What breathing pattern should be followed in lifting weights?
    a. Take a deep breath before lifting and hold it throughout the lift.
    b. Take a deep breath and exhale before lifting.
    c. Take a deep breath as you are lifting and exhale as you let the weight down.
    *d. Take a deep breath before lifting and exhale as you lift.

261. What should a person *not* do in breathing while exercising?
    a. Breathe normally.
    b. Take deep breaths.
    c. Exhale while lifting a weight.
    *d. Hold the breath.

262. What may cause a person to black out during weight lifting?
    a. improper diet
    b. lifting too much weight
    c. too many repetitions
    *d. holding the breath during lifting

Nautilus

263. According to Nautilus concepts, on what is muscular growth dependent?
    a. slow repetitions and nutrition
    b. stimulation and intensity
    *c. stimulation, rest, and nutrition
    d. slow repetitions, intensity, and rest

264. How can an individual release the greatest energy to an isolated muscle according to the Nautilus concepts?
    a. by taking adequate rest between exercises
    b. by using heavy weights
    c. by exhaling while lifting
    *d. by relaxing other body parts

265. What part of an exercise should be emphasized in Nautilus training?
    a. the beginning
    b. the positive
    *c. the negative
    d. the ending

266. You are beginning a Nautilus training program. How many times should you train the first week?
    a. two times with a day in between
    b. three times with a day between each
    c. 4 days in a row
    *d. 5 days in a row

267. Generally, how many times a week should a lifter train according to Nautilus?
    a. two
    *b. three
    c. five
    d. seven

268. How many exercises per workout are recommended by Nautilus?
    a. no more than 10
    *b. no more than 12
    c. at least 12
    d. at least 15

269. How many exercises for the upper body per workout are recommended by Nautilus?
    *a. four to six
    b. five
    c. six to eight
    d. seven

270. How many exercises for the lower body per workout are recommended by Nautilus?
    a. four to six
    b. five
    *c. six to eight
    d. eight

271. According to Nautilus concepts, how long should an exercise last?
    a. 15 to 35 seconds
    *b. 30 to 70 seconds
    c. 1 minute
    d. 1½ to 2 minutes

272. How many repetitions per exercise are recommended by Nautilus?
    a. four to six
    b. six to eight
    *c. eight to twelve
    d. ten to fifteen

273. In the Nautilus concept, how long should a repetition last?
    a. 2 seconds
    b. 4 seconds
    *c. 6 seconds
    d. 10 seconds

274. A lifter is using a Nautilus program. How long should it take to raise and lower the weight?
    a. three times as long to lower as to raise the weight
    *b. two times as long to lower as to raise the weight
    c. two times as long to raise as to lower the weight
    d. the same time to raise and to lower the weight

Rules of Competition

Power Lifting

275. Which lift is *not* used in competitive power lifting?
    *a. snatch
    b. bench press
    c. squat
    d. dead lift

276. How many attempts can be taken on each lift in competitive power lifting?
    a. one
    b. two
    *c. three
    d. five

277. On the bench press in power lifting, how long must the bar be held stationary at the chest before pressing the weight?
    a. until it is steady
    b. 2 seconds
    c. 5 seconds
    *d. until the judge signals

278. On the squat in power lifting, how low must the lifter squat?
    a. until the thighs are parallel with the floor
    *b. until the thighs break parallel with the floor
    c. until the knees are at a 90° angle
    d. until the knees are at a 45° angle

279. What is the maximum weight for a lifter in the lightest weight class in power lifting?
    a. 100 pounds
    *b. 114 pounds
    c. 123 pounds
    d. 132 pounds

Olympic Weight Lifting

280. How many events are there in Olympic weight lifting?
    a. one
    *b. two
    c. three
    d. four

281. What events are included in Olympic weight lifting?
    a. bench press and squat
    b. dead lift and squat
    *c. snatch and clean and jerk
    d. snatch and dead lift

Novice

282. How much should a person be able to snatch to enter novice competitions?
    *a. 10 to 20 pounds less than body weight
    b. pounds equal to body weight
    c. 10 to 20 pounds more than body weight
    d. 25 to 50 pounds more than body weight

283. How much should a person be able to clean-and-jerk to enter novice competitions?
    a. 10 to 20 pounds less than body weight
    b. pounds equal to body weight
    *c. 10 to 30 pounds over body weight
    d. 50 to 75 pounds over body weight

Suggested Readings

Berger, R.A. (1984). *Introduction to weight training*. Englewood Cliffs, NJ: Prentice-Hall.

Hesson, J. (1985). *Weight lifting for life*. Englewood, CO: Morton.

Rasch, P.J. (1982). *Weight training* (4th ed.). Dubuque, IA: Wm. C. Brown.

Reynolds, B. (1976). *Complete weight training book*. Mountain View, CA: Anderson World Books.

Tuten, R., Moore, C., & Knight, V. (1983). *Weight training for everyone*. Winston-Salem, NC: Hunter Textbooks.

Appendix

Computer Program for Calculating Kuder-Richardson Formula 21

This program is for the Apple II series of computers using DOS 3.3.

```
1    HOME
5    VTAB 3: PRINT "KUDER RICHARDSO
     N #21": PRINT : PRINT : PRINT
10   PRINT "TYPE NUMBER OF QUESTIO
     NS ON THE TEST"
15   INPUT "AND PRESS RETURN: ";K:
     PRINT
20   INPUT "TYPE NUMBER OF SCORES
     AND PRESS RETURN: ";N: PRINT
25   PRINT "TYPE IN EACH SCORE AND
     AFTER EACH"
30   PRINT "PRESS RETURN: ": PRINT
35   DIM A(N) ,B(N) ,C(N)
40   FOR X = 1 TO N
45   PRINT "SCORE #";X;: INPUT "?
     ";A(X): PRINT
50   NEXT X
55   HOME
60   FOR X = 1 TO N
65   AV = AV + A(X)
70   NEXT X
75   M = AV / N
80   FOR X = 1 TO N
85   B(X) = A(X) − M
90   C(X) = B(X) * B(X)
95   T = T + C(X)
100  NEXT X
105  SD = SQR (T / N)
110  KR = (K/(K − 1)) * ((1) − (M * (K − M)) /
     (K * (SD * SD)))
115  VTAB 5
120  PRINT "MEAN = ";M: PRINT
125  PRINT "STANDARD DEVIATION =
     ";SD: PRINT
130  PRINT "KUDER RICHARDSON #21
     = ";KR
```

Below is a practice run of the program for a 50-question test. Ten students took the test with resulting scores of 15, 20, 25, 30, 35, 40, 22, 23, 27, and 28.

KUDER RICHARDSON #21

TYPE NUMBER OF QUESTIONS ON THE TEST AND PRESS RETURN: 50

TYPE NUMBER OF SCORES AND PRESS RETURN: 10

TYPE IN EACH SCORE AND AFTER EACH PRESS RETURN:

SCORE #1? 15

SCORE #2? 20

SCORE #3? 25

SCORE #4? 30

SCORE #5? 35

SCORE #6? 40

SCORE #7? 22

SCORE #8? 23

SCORE #9? 27

SCORE #10? 28

MEAN = 26.5

STANDARD DEVIATION = 6.91736944

KUDER RICHARDSON #21 = .754803489

Index

This index is arranged alphabetically by activity. Entries concerning test development are listed under the heading "Test Development and Analysis."

SWIMMING AND DIVING

TRACK AND FIELD